Rifle Cartridge Databook

By

John E. Parnell

ISBN 978-1625129987

© **2013 Tutor Turtle Press, LLC**

Tutor Turtle Press, LLC

1027 S. Pendleton St., Suite B-10, Easley, SC 29642

info@TutorTurtlePress.com

(864) 553 - 1533

SMOKELESS POWDER PROPERTIES AND STORAGE

S A A M I

SPORTING ARMS AND AMMUNITION MANUFACTURERS' INSTITUTE, INC. 555 DANBURY RD.
WILTON, CT 06897

Ammunition handloading has become increasingly popular in recent years. This article discusses properties of smokeless powder and offers recommendations for its storage.

This article is intended to increase the knowledge of all concerned individuals and groups regarding smokeless powder. The statements and recommendations made are not intended to supersede local, state or Federal regulations. Proper authorities should be consulted on regulations for storage and use of smokeless powder in each specific community. A second leaflet entitled *"SPORTING AMMUNITION PRIMERS: PROPERTIES, HANDLING & STORAGE FOR HANDLOADING"* supplements this leaflet on smokeless powder.

PROPERTIES OF SMOKELESS POWDER

Smokeless powders, or propellants, are essentially mixtures of chemicals designed to burn under controlled conditions at the proper rate to propel a projectile from a gun. Smokeless powders are made in three forms:

1. Thin, circular flakes or wafers

2. Small cylinders

3. Small spheres

Single-base smokeless powders derive their main source of energy from nitrocellulose. The energy released from double-base smokeless powders is derived from both nitrocellulose and nitroglycerin.

All smokeless powders are extremely flammable; by design, they are intended to burn rapidly and vigorously when ignited.

Oxygen from the air is not necessary for the combustion of smokeless powders since they contain sufficient built-in oxygen to burn completely, even in an enclosed space such as the chamber of a firearm.

In effect, ignition occurs when the powder granules are heated above their ignition temperature. This can occur by exposing powder to:

1. A flame such as a match or primer flash.

2. An electrical spark or the sparks from welding, grinding, etc.

3. Heat from an electric hot plate or a fire directed against or near a closed container even if the powder itself is not exposed to the flame. When smokeless powder burns, a great deal of gas at high temperature is formed. If the powder is confined, this gas will create pressure in the surrounding structure. The rate of gas generation is such, however, that the pressure can be kept at a low level if sufficient space is available, or if the gas can escape.

In this respect smokeless powder differs from blasting agents or high explosives such as dynamite or blasting gelatin, although smokeless powder may contain chemical ingredients common to some of these products.

High explosives such as dynamite are made to detonate, that is, to change from solid state to gaseous state with evolution of intense heat at such a rapid rate that shock waves are propagated through any medium in contact with them. Such shock waves exert pressure on anything they contact, and, as a matter of practical consideration, it is almost impossible to satisfactorily vent away the effects of a detonation involving any appreciable quantity of dynamite.

Smokeless powder differs considerably in its burning characteristics from common "black powder."

Black powder burns essentially at the same rate out in the open (unconfined) as when in a gun. When ignited in an unconfined state, smokeless powder burns inefficiently with an orange-colored flame. It produces a considerable amount of light brown noxious smelling smoke. It leaves a residue of ash and partially burned powder. The flame is hot enough to cause severe burns.

The opposite is true when it burns under pressure as in a cartridge fired in a gun. Then it produces very little smoke, a small glow, and leaves very little or no residue. The burning rate of smokeless powder increases with increased pressure.

If burning smokeless powder is confined, gas pressure will rise and eventually can cause the container to burst. Under such circumstances, the bursting of a strong container creates effects similar to an explosion.

For this reason, the Department of Transportation (formerly Interstate Commerce Commission) sets specifications for shipping containers for propellants and requires tests of loaded containers - under actual fire conditions - before approving them for use. When smokeless powder in D.O.T.-approved containers is ignited during such tests, container seams split open or lids pop off - to release gases and powder from confinement at low pressure.

HOW TO CHECK SMOKELESS POWDER FOR DETERIORATION

Although modern smokeless powders are basically free from deterioration under proper storage conditions, safe practices require a recognition of the signs of deterioration and its possible effects.

Powder deterioration can be checked by opening the cap on the container and smelling the contents. Powder undergoing deterioration has an irritating acidic odor. (Don't confuse this with common solvent odors such as alcohol, ether and acetone.)

Check to make certain that powder is not exposed to extreme heat as this may cause deterioration. Such exposure produces an acidity which accelerates further reaction and has been known, because of the heat generated by the reaction, to cause spontaneous combustion. Never salvage powder from old cartridges and do not attempt to blend salvaged powder with new powder. Don't accumulate old powder stocks.

The best way to dispose of deteriorated smokeless powder is to burn it out in the open at an isolated location in small shallow piles (not over 1" deep). The quantity burned in any one pile should never exceed one pound. Use an ignition train of slow burning combustible material so that the person may retreat to a safe distance before powder is ignited.

CONSIDERATIONS FOR STORAGE OF SMOKELESS POWDER

Smokeless powder is intended to function by burning, so it must be protected against accidental exposure to flame, sparks or high temperatures.

For these reasons, it is desirable that storage enclosures be made of insulating materials to protect the powder from external heat sources.

Once smokeless powder begins to burn, it will normally continue to burn (and generate gas pressure) until it is consumed.

D.O.T.-approved containers are constructed to open up at low internal pressures to avoid the effects normally produced by the rupture or bursting of a strong container.

Storage enclosures for smokeless powder should be constructed in a similar manner:

1. Of fire-resistant and heat-insulating materials to protect contents from external heat.

2. Sufficiently large to satisfactorily vent the gaseous products of combustion which would result if the quantity of smokeless powder within the enclosure accidentally ignited.

If a small, tightly enclosed storage enclosure is loaded to capacity with containers of smokeless powder, the walls of the enclosure will expand to move outwards to release the gas pressure - if the powder in storage is accidentally ignited. Under such conditions, the effects of the release of gas pressure are similar or identical to the effects produced by an explosion. Hence, only the smallest practical quantities of smokeless powder should be kept in storage, and then in strict compliance with all applicable regulations and recommendations of the National Fire Protection Association (reprinted at end of article).

RECOMMENDATIONS FOR STORAGE OF SMOKELESS POWDER

STORE IN A COOL, DRY PLACE. Be sure the storage area selected is free from any possible sources of excess heat and is isolated from open flame, furnaces, hot water heaters, etc. Do not store smokeless powder where it will be exposed to the sun's rays. Avoid storage in areas where mechanical or electrical equipment is in operation. Restrict from the storage areas heat or sparks which may result from improper, defective or overloaded electrical circuits.

DO NOT STORE SMOKELESS POWDER IN THE SAME AREA WITH SOLVENTS, FLAMMABLE GASES OR HIGHLY COMBUSTIBLE MATERIALS.

STORE ONLY IN DEPARTMENT OF TRANSPORTATION APPROVED CONTAINERS. Do not transfer the powder from an approved container into one which is not approved.

DO NOT SMOKE IN AREAS WHERE POWDER IS STORED OR USED. Place appropriate "No Smoking" signs in these areas.

DO NOT SUBJECT THE STORAGE CABINETS TO CLOSE CONFINEMENT.

STORAGE CABINETS SHOULD BE CONSTRUCTED OF INSULATING MATERIALS AND WITH A WEAK WALL, SEAMS OR JOINTS TO PROVIDE AN EASY MEANS OF SELF-VENTING.

DO NOT KEEP OLD OR SALVAGED POWDERS. Check old powders for deterioration regularly. Destroy deteriorated powders immediately.

OBEY ALL REGULATIONS REGARDING QUANTITY AND METHODS OF STORING. Do not store all your powders in one place. If you can, maintain separate storage locations. Many small containers are safer than one or more large containers.

KEEP YOUR STORAGE AND USE AREA CLEAN. Clean up spilled powder promptly. Make sure the surrounding area is free of trash or other readily combustible materials.

KNOWING THE FOLLOWING RECOMMENDATIONS ON STORAGE AND HANDLING ISSUED BY THE NATIONAL FIRE PROTECTION ASSOCIATION

BATTERY MARCH PARK QUINCY, MA 02269 AND REPRINTED WITH THEIR PERMISSION:

NFPA 495 Code for the Manufacture, Transportation , Storage and Use of Explosive Materials 1985 Edition

This edition of NFPA 495, Code for the Manufacture, Transportation, Storage, and Use of Explosive Materials, was prepared by the Technical Committee on Explosives, released by the Correlating Committee on Chemicals and Explosives, and acted on by the National Fire Protection Association, Inc. at its Annual Meeting held May 13-17, 1985, in Chicago, Illinois. It was issued by the Standards Council on June 6, 1985, with an effective date of June 26, 1985, and supersedes all previous editions.

The 1985 edition of this standard has been approved by the American National Standards Institute.

Changes other than editorial are indicated by a vertical rule in the margin of the pages on which they appear. These lines are included as an aid to the user in identifying changes from the previous edition.

Origin and Development of NFPA 495

This Code, originally developed by the Committee on Hazardous Chemicals and Explosives, was first adopted by the NFPA in 1959. Following reorganization of the Committee in 1960, NFPA 495 was assigned to the Technical Committee on Explosives. Amendments were adopted in 1963, 1965, 1967, 1968, 1969, and 1970. A complete revision was adopted in 1972, and this complete revision was amended in 1973.

In 1976, the Technical Committee on Explosives began a detailed review of the 1973 edition, primarily to amend its requirements so that there were no conflicts with the regulations promulgated by the various federal agencies concerned with explosive materials (U.S. Bureau of Alcohol, Tobacco, and Firearms, U.S. Mine Safety and Health Administration, U.S. Department of Transportation, etc.) This review, plus editorial and minor technical amendments, resulted in this 1982 edition of NFPA 495.

Chapter 10. Small Arms Ammunition and Primers, Smokeless Propellants, and Black Powder Propellants

10-1   Basic Requirements.

    10-1.1 In addition to all other applicable requirements of this Code, intrastate transportation of small arms ammunition, small arms primers, smokeless propellants, and black powder shall comply with U.S. Department of Transportation Hazardous Materials Regulations.

    10-1.2 This chapter applies to channels of distribution of and to the users of small arms ammunition, small arms primers, smokeless propellants, and black powder.

    10-1.3 This chapter does not apply to in-process storage and intra-plant transportation during manufacture.

    10-1.4 This chapter applies to the transportation and storage of small arms ammunition and components.

    10-1.5 This chapter does not apply to safety procedures in the use of small arms ammunition and components.

10-3   Smokeless Propellants

    10-3.1 Quantities of smokeless propellants not exceeding 25 lb. (11.3 kg), in shipping containers approved by the U.S. Department of Transportation, may be transported in a private vehicle.

10-3.2 Quantities of smokeless propellants exceeding 25 lb (11.3 kg) but not exceeding 50 lb. (22.5 kg), transported in a private vehicle, shall be transported in a portable magazine having wood walls of at least 1-in. (25.4 mm) nominal thickness.

10-3.3 Transportation of more than 50 lb. (22.7 kg) of smokeless propellants in a private vehicle is prohibited.

10-3.4 Commercial shipments of smokeless propellants in quantities not exceeding 100 lb. (45.4 kg) are classified for transportation purposes as flammable solids when packaged according to U.S. Department of Transportation Hazardous Materials Regulations (Title 49, Code of Federal Regulations, Part 173.197a) and shall be transported accordingly.

10-3.5 Commercial shipments of smokeless propellants exceeding 100 lb. (45.4 kg) or not packaged in accordance with the regulations cited in 10-3.4 shall be transported according to U.S. Department of Transportation regulations for Class B propellant explosives.

10-3.6 Smokeless propellants shall be stored in shipping containers specified by U.S. Department of Transportation Hazardous Materials Regulations.

10-3.7 Smokeless propellants intended for personal use in quantities not exceeding 20 lb. (9.1 kg) may be stored in original containers in residences. Quantities exceeding 20 lb. (9.1 kg), but not exceeding 50 lb. (22.7 kg), may be stored in residences if kept in a wooden box or cabinet having walls of at least 1-in. (25.4 mm) nominal thickness.

10-3.8 Not more than 20 lb. (9.1 kg) of smokeless propellants, in containers of 1-lb. (0.45 kg) maximum capacity, shall be displayed in commercial establishments.

10-3.9 Commercial stocks of smokeless propellants shall be stored as follows:

(a) Quantities exceeding 20 lb. (9.1 kg), but not exceeding 100 lb. (45.4 kg), shall be stored in potable wooden boxes having walls of at least 1-in. (25.4 mm) thickness.

(b) Quantities exceeding 100 lb (45.4 kg), but not exceeding 900 lb. (363 kg), shall be stored in nonportable storage cabinets having walls of at least 1-in. (25.4 mm) thickness. Not more than 400 lb. (181 kg) may be stored in any one cabinet and cabinets shall be separated by a distance of at least 25 ft. (7.63 m) or by a fire partition having a fire endurance of at least 1 hour.

(c) Quantities exceeding 800 lb. (363 kg), but not exceeding 5,000 lb. (2268 kg), may be stored in a building if the following requirements are met:

1. The warehouse or storage room shall not be accessible to unauthorized personnel.

2. Smokeless propellant shall be stored in nonportable storage cabinets having wood walls at least 1 in. (25.4 mm) thick and having shelves with no less than 3 ft. (0.92 m) separation between shelves.

3. No more than 400 lb. (181 kg) shall be stored in any one cabinet.

4. Cabinets shall be located against walls of the storage room or warehouse with at least 40 ft. (12.2 m) between cabinets.

5. Separation between cabinets may be reduced to 20 ft. (6.1 m) if barricades twice the height of the cabinets are attached to the wall, midway between each cabinet. The barricades shall extend at least 10 ft. (3 m) outward, shall be firmly attached to the wall, and shall be constructed of 1/2 in. (6.4 mm) boiler plate, 2-in. (55 mm) thick wood, brick or concrete block.

6. Smokeless propellant shall be separated from materials classified by the US Department of Transportation as flammable liquids, flammable solids, and oxidizing materials by a distance of 25 ft. (7.63 m) or by a fire partition having a fire endurance of at least 1 hour.

7. The building shall be protected by an automatic sprinkler system installed according to NFPA 13, Standard for the Installation of Sprinkler Systems.

(d) Smokeless propellants not stored according to (a), (b) and (c) above shall be stored in a Type 4 magazine constructed and located according to Chapter 6. Reprinted with permission from MFPA 495-1985, Code for the Manufacture, Transportation, Storage and Use of Explosive Materials, Copyright © 1985, National Fire Protection Association, Quincy, MA 02269. This reprinted material is not the complete and official position of the NFPA on the referenced subject which is represented only by the standard in its entirety.

x

WARNING

The information contained in this manual, including ballistic data, was derived from tightly controlled laboratory conditions. This information and data may vary considerably depending on many factors, including the components used, component assembly, the type of firearm used, reloading techniques, safety precautions practiced, etc.

Never mix any two powders regardless of type, brand, or source. Never substitute any smokeless powder for Black Powder or its substitute.

Tutor Turtle Press LLC and the Author expressly disclaims any and all warranties with respect to any and all products sold or distributed by it, the safety or suitability thereof, or the results obtained including, without limitation, any implied warranty of merchantability or fitness for a particular purpose and/or any other warranty. Buyers and users of this databook assume all risk, responsibility and liability whatsoever for any and all injuries (including death), losses or damages to persons or property (including consequential damages), arising from the use of any product or data, whether or not occasioned by seller's negligence or based on strict liability or principles of indemnity or contribution. Tutor Turtle Press LLC and the Author neither assumes nor authorizes any person to assume for it any liability in connection with the use of any product or data.

The individual accessing this databook assumes the risk of safe loading practices. Failure to do so could result in severe personal injury (or death) and/or property damage.

REDUCE RIFLE AND HANDGUN CHARGE WEIGHTS BY 10% TO ESTABLISH A STARTING LOAD.

DO NOT EXCEED THE LOADS LISTED IN THIS DATABOOK.

Table of Contents

There are four books in the Reloading Series:

Reloading Logbook .... (ISBN 978-1625124395) $9.95
Handgun Cartridge Databook .... (ISBN 978-1625129970) $9.95
Rifle Cartridge Databook .... (ISBN 978-1625129987) $14.95
Shot Shell Databook .... (ISBN 978-1625129994) $19.95

The books are available from your favorite online or brick-and-mortar bookstore, your favorite gun shop, or directly from the publisher:

Tutor Turtle Press, LLC
1027 S. Pendleton St., Suite B-10
Easley, SC 29642

www.TutorTurtlePress.com

Cartridge: 17 Ackley Hornet — Load Type: Rifle

Bullet Weight (Gr.)	Manufacturer	Powder	Bullet Diam.	C.O.L.	Starting Loads Grs.	Vel. (ft/s)	Pressure	Maximum Loads Grs.	Vel. (ft/s)	Pressure
20 GR. HDY V-MAX	Hodgdon	H4198	.172"	1.800"	11.5	3246	32,700 CUP	12.5C	3515	44,400 CUP
20 GR. HDY V-MAX	Hodgdon	H4227	.172"	1.800"	8.5	3080	41,200 CUP	9.2	3238	45,700 CUP
20 GR. HDY V-MAX	Hodgdon	Lil'Gun	.172"	1.800"	9.4	3369	40,600 CUP	10.0	3509	45,300 CUP
25 GR. HDY HP	Hodgdon	H335	.172"	1.760"	12.5	2898	35,500 CUP	13.3	3046	45,400 CUP
25 GR. HDY HP	Hodgdon	H322	.172"	1.760"	12.0	2894	42,500 CUP	13.0C	3153	45,400 CUP
25 GR. HDY HP	Hodgdon	H4198	.172"	1.760"	10.9	3015	38,800 CUP	11.6	3176	45,900 CUP
30 GR. BER HP	Hodgdon	BL-C(2)	.172"	1.800"	13.0	2795	36,900 CUP	13.5	2922	43,200 CUP
30 GR. BER HP	Hodgdon	H335	.172"	1.800"	11.7	2752	38,500 CUP	12.5	2894	44,500 CUP
30 GR. BER HP	Hodgdon	Benchmark	.172"	1.800"	12.2	2900	43,200 CUP	13.0C	2975	44,800 CUP
30 GR. BER HP	Hodgdon	H322	.172"	1.800"	11.5	2745	36,100 CUP	12.2	2984	45,700 CUP
30 GR. BER HP	Hodgdon	H4198	.172"	1.800"	10.0	2711	33,400 CUP	10.7	2923	45,600 CUP

Cartridge: 17 Hornet — Load Type: Rifle

Bullet Weight (Gr.)	Manufacturer	Powder	Bullet Diam.	C.O.L.	Starting Loads Grs.	Vel. (ft/s)	Pressure	Maximum Loads Grs.	Vel. (ft/s)	Pressure
20 GR. HDY V-MAX	Hodgdon	H4198	.172"	1.715"	11.0	3226	32,200 PSI	11.8C	3463	39,300 PSI
20 GR. HDY V-MAX	IMR	IMR 4227	.172"	1.715"	9.3	3204	40,700 PSI	10.1	3356	45,400 PSI
20 GR. HDY V-MAX	Winchester	296	.172"	1.715"	8.0	3173	40,900 PSI	8.7	3301	45,100 PSI
20 GR. HDY V-MAX	Hodgdon	H110	.172"	1.715"	8.0	3173	40,900 PSI	8.7	3301	45,100 PSI
20 GR. HDY V-MAX	Hodgdon	Lil'Gun	.172"	1.715"	9.7	3538	44,600 PSI	10.0	3629	48,200 PSI
25 GR. HDY V-MAX	Hodgdon	H335	.172"	1.715"	12.4	2984	39,200 PSI	13.2C	3145	45,900 PSI
25 GR. HDY V-MAX	Hodgdon	H322	.172"	1.715"	12.0	3091	30,600 PSI	12.8C	3283	36,200 PSI
25 GR. HDY V-MAX	Hodgdon	H4198	.172"	1.715"	10.3	2983	34,900 PSI	11.1C	3187	42,500 PSI
25 GR. HDY V-MAX	IMR	IMR 4227	.172"	1.715"	8.5	2856	40,900 PSI	9.3	3032	45,700 PSI
25 GR. HDY V-MAX	Hodgdon	Lil'Gun	.172"	1.715"	8.6	3125	45,000 PSI	8.9	3195	48,000 PSI
30 GR. BER HP	Hodgdon	H335	.172"	1.715"	11.8	2718	36,700 PSI	12.5C	2866	44,000 PSI
30 GR. BER HP	Hodgdon	H322	.172"	1.715"	11.7	2853	40,500 PSI	12.5C	3020	48,000 PSI
30 GR. BER HP	Hodgdon	H4198	.172"	1.715"	10.0	2815	38,700 PSI	10.8C	3024	47,300 PSI

Cartridge: 17 Ackley Bee — Load Type: Rifle

Bullet Weight (Gr.)	Manufacturer	Powder	Bullet Diam.	C.O.L.	Starting Loads Grs.	Vel. (ft/s)	Pressure	Maximum Loads Grs.	Vel. (ft/s)	Pressure
25 GR. HDY HP	Hodgdon	BL-C(2)	.172"	1.650"	16.0	3100	33,000 CUP	17.0	3294	39,300 CUP
25 GR. HDY HP	Hodgdon	H335	.172"	1.650"	16.0	3080	32,400 CUP	17.0	3288	39,600 CUP
25 GR. HDY HP	Hodgdon	H4198	.172"	1.650"	12.5	2976	32,400 CUP	13.5	3365	45,300 CUP
25 GR. HDY HP	Hodgdon	H4227	.172"	1.650"	10.0	2910	36,500 CUP	11.0	3131	45,300 CUP

Cartridge: 17 Mach IV Load Type: Rifle					Starting Loads			Maximum Loads		
Bullet Weight (Gr.)	Manufacturer	Powder	Bullet Diam.	C.O.L.	Grs.	Vel. (ft/s)	Pressure	Grs.	Vel. (ft/s)	Pressure
25 GR. HDY HP	Hodgdon	BL-C(2)	.172"	1.770"	19.0	3372	38,700 CUP	20.0	3674	48,000 CUP
25 GR. HDY HP	Hodgdon	H335	.172"	1.770"	19.0	3360	38,000 CUP	20.0	3680	48,800 CUP
25 GR. HDY HP	Hodgdon	H4198	.172"	1.770"	15.0	3237	36,500 CUP	16.0	3576	49,800 CUP

Cartridge: 17 Remington Fireball Load Type: Rifle					Starting Loads			Maximum Loads		
Bullet Weight (Gr.)	Manufacturer	Powder	Bullet Diam.	C.O.L.	Grs.	Vel. (ft/s)	Pressure	Grs.	Vel. (ft/s)	Pressure
20 GR. HDY V-MAX	Hodgdon	H335	.172"	1.830"	18.5	3704	40,600 CUP	20.5	4027	50,000 CUP
20 GR. HDY V-MAX	IMR	IMR 8208 XBR	.172"	1.830"	18.0	3636	33,900 CUP	20.2C	4038	44,700 CUP
20 GR. HDY V-MAX	Hodgdon	Benchmark	.172"	1.830"	18.5	3758	40,300 CUP	20.0C	4013	49,100 CUP
20 GR. HDY V-MAX	Hodgdon	H322	.172"	1.830"	18.0	3652	37,500 CUP	19.5C	4019	49,200 CUP
20 GR. HDY V-MAX	IMR	IMR 4198	.172"	1.830"	15.3	3636	37,700 CUP	16.7	4017	50,600 CUP
20 GR. HDY V-MAX	Hodgdon	H4198	.172"	1.830"	16.0	3811	39,200 CUP	17.3	4037	47,800 CUP
25 GR. HDY HP	Hodgdon	H335	.172"	1.800"	17.7	3510	41,700 CUP	19.4	3744	50,400 CUP
25 GR. HDY HP	IMR	IMR 8208 XBR	.172"	1.800"	17.0	3453	34,900 CUP	19.2	3854	48,900 CUP
25 GR. HDY HP	Hodgdon	Benchmark	.172"	1.800"	17.5	3550	41,900 CUP	19.0	3745	48,500 CUP
25 GR. HDY HP	Hodgdon	H322	.172"	1.800"	17.0	3504	38,500 CUP	18.3	3704	48,900 CUP
25 GR. HDY HP	IMR	IMR 4198	.172"	1.800"	15.0	3463	40,500 CUP	16.2	3692	50,000 CUP
25 GR. HDY HP	Hodgdon	H4198	.172"	1.800"	15.4	3549	40,500 CUP	17.0	3789	49,900 CUP
30 GR. BER HP	Hodgdon	H335	.172"	1.800"	17.8	3366	39,500 CUP	18.8	3512	49,000 CUP
30 GR. BER HP	IMR	IMR 8208 XBR	.172"	1.800"	16.5	3316	38,400 CUP	18.6	3634	50,200 CUP
30 GR. BER HP	Hodgdon	Benchmark	.172"	1.800"	17.0	3307	39,700 CUP	18.7C	3569	49,400 CUP
30 GR. BER HP	Hodgdon	H322	.172"	1.800"	16.5	3295	38,500 CUP	18.0	3533	49,300 CUP
30 GR. BER HP	IMR	IMR 4198	.172"	1.800"	14.8	3277	40,600 CUP	15.8	3456	49,000 CUP
30 GR. BER HP	Hodgdon	H4198	.172"	1.800"	14.9	3299	42,400 CUP	15.9	3481	50,400 CUP

Cartridge: 17-222 Load Type: Rifle					Starting Loads			Maximum Loads		
Bullet Weight (Gr.)	Manufacturer	Powder	Bullet Diam.	C.O.L.	Grs.	Vel. (ft/s)	Pressure	Grs.	Vel. (ft/s)	Pressure
25 GR. HDY HP	Hodgdon	H380	.172"	2.070"	22.0	3476	40,900 CUP	23.5	3655	46,400 CUP
25 GR. HDY HP	Hodgdon	BL-C(2)	.172"	2.070"	20.0	3521	40,400 CUP	21.3	3755	49,400 CUP
25 GR. HDY HP	Hodgdon	H335	.172"	2.070"	20.0	3509	39,600 CUP	21.0	3740	49,400 CUP
25 GR. HDY HP	Hodgdon	H4895	.172"	2.070"	19.5	3439	39,800 CUP	20.5	3646	48,000 CUP
25 GR. HDY HP	Hodgdon	H4198	.172"	2.070"	16.2	3448	42,500 CUP	17.2	3601	49,800 CUP

Cartridge:17-223 Load Type:Rifle					Starting Loads			Maximum Loads		
Bullet Weight (Gr.)	Manufacturer	Powder	Bullet Diam.	C.O.L.	Grs.	Vel. (ft/s)	Pressure	Grs.	Vel. (ft/s)	Pressure
25 GR. HDY HP	Hodgdon	H414	.172"	2.130"	24.5	3766		26.5	3989	
25 GR. HDY HP	Hodgdon	H380	.172"	2.130"	24.0	3779		26.0	3946	
25 GR. HDY HP	Hodgdon	BL-C(2)	.172"	2.130"	21.5	3635		23.5	3940	
25 GR. HDY HP	Hodgdon	H335	.172"	2.130"	21.0	3618		23.0	3929	
25 GR. HDY HP	Hodgdon	H4895	.172"	2.130"	21.0	3681		23.0	3960	

Cartridge:17 Remington Load Type:Rifle					Starting Loads			Maximum Loads		
Bullet Weight (Gr.)	Manufacturer	Powder	Bullet Diam.	C.O.L.	Grs.	Vel. (ft/s)	Pressure	Grs.	Vel. (ft/s)	Pressure
20 GR. HDY V-MAX	Hodgdon	CFE 223	.172"	2.170"	25.8	4201	42,200 CUP	27.4	4466	48,100 CUP
20 GR. HDY V-MAX	Hodgdon	Varget	.172"	2.170"	23.5	3936	37,800 CUP	25.5C	4208	45,200 CUP
20 GR. HDY V-MAX	Hodgdon	BL-C(2)	.172"	2.170"	23.5	4049	39,400 CUP	25.0	4213	43,700 CUP
20 GR. HDY V-MAX	Hodgdon	H335	.172"	2.170"	21.0	4132	44,100 CUP	23.5	4290	47,700 CUP
20 GR. HDY V-MAX	Hodgdon	H4895	.172"	2.170"	23.0	4037	37,000 CUP	25.5C	4436	47,500 CUP
20 GR. HDY V-MAX	IMR	IMR 8208 XBR	.172"	2.170"	24.0	4138	40,500 CUP	25.5	4378	48,500 CUP
20 GR. HDY V-MAX	Hodgdon	Benchmark	.172"	2.170"	22.0	3985	38,000 CUP	24.5	4342	50,500 CUP
20 GR. HDY V-MAX	Hodgdon	H322	.172"	2.170"	21.0	3963	37,500 CUP	23.2	4292	49,500 CUP
25 GR. HDY HP	Hodgdon	H414	.172"	2.150"	25.0	3748	39,300 CUP	27.0	3989	48,300 CUP
25 GR. HDY HP	Winchester	760	.172"	2.150"	25.0	3748	39,300 CUP	27.0	3989	48,300 CUP
25 GR. HDY HP	Hodgdon	H380	.172"	2.150"	24.5	3756	41,900 CUP	26.0	3950	46,100 CUP
25 GR. HDY HP	Hodgdon	CFE 223	.172"	2.150"	24.4	3882	43,000 CUP	26.0	4109	51,100 CUP
25 GR. HDY HP	Hodgdon	Varget	.172"	2.150"	22.0	3759	39,600 CUP	24.5	4123	50,800 CUP
25 GR. HDY HP	IMR	IMR 4064	.172"	2.150"				24.0C	4005	50,700 CUP
25 GR. HDY HP	Hodgdon	BL-C(2)	.172"	2.150"	22.5	3872	44,000 CUP	24.0	4051	49,000 CUP
25 GR. HDY HP	IMR	IMR 4895	.172"	2.150"				23.5	3995	51,400 CUP
25 GR. HDY HP	Hodgdon	H335	.172"	2.150"	19.5	3811	45,700 CUP	21.0	3963	51,300 CUP
25 GR. HDY HP	Hodgdon	H4895	.172"	2.150"	21.0	3760	40,500 CUP	23.0	4033	48,500 CUP
25 GR. HDY HP	IMR	IMR 8208 XBR	.172"	2.150"	22.7	3882	42,800 CUP	24.2	4072	48,500 CUP
25 GR. HDY HP	IMR	IMR 3031	.172"	2.150"				22.5	4015	51,700 CUP
25 GR. HDY HP	Hodgdon	Benchmark	.172"	2.150"	21.5	3791	43,000 CUP	23.3	4038	50,600 CUP
25 GR. HDY HP	Hodgdon	H322	.172"	2.150"	19.5	3656	40,500 CUP	21.8	3921	49,700 CUP
30 GR. BER HP	Hodgdon	H414	.172"	2.150"	24.0	3487	39,600 CUP	27.0	3839	50,300 CUP
30 GR. BER HP	Winchester	760	.172"	2.150"	24.0	3487	39,600 CUP	27.0	3839	50,300 CUP
30 GR. BER HP	IMR	IMR 4007 SSC	.172"	2.150"	24.4	3589	46,700 CUP	26.0C	3807	51,300 CUP
30 GR. BER HP	Hodgdon	H380	.172"	2.150"	22.0	3378	43,300 CUP	24.5	3648	50,500 CUP
30 GR. BER HP	Hodgdon	CFE 223	.172"	2.150"	22.8	3522	42,700 CUP	24.3	3746	51,700 CUP

3

Bullet Weight (Gr.)	Manufacturer	Powder	Bullet Diam.	C.O.L.	Grs.	Vel. (ft/s)	Pressure	Grs.	Vel. (ft/s)	Pressure
30 GR. BER HP	Hodgdon	Varget	.172"	2.150"	20.0	3405	39,700 CUP	22.5	3742	49,700 CUP
30 GR. BER HP	Hodgdon	H4895	.172"	2.150"	20.0	3495	44,000 CUP	22.0	3696	49,900 CUP
30 GR. BER HP	IMR	IMR 8208 XBR	.172"	2.150"	21.2	3527	42,900 CUP	22.6	3700	48,800 CUP
30 GR. BER HP	Hodgdon	Benchmark	.172"	2.150"	20.0	3444	43,200 CUP	22.0	3709	50,500 CUP
30 GR. BER HP	Hodgdon	H322	.172"	2.150"	18.0	3311	38,700 CUP	20.0	3594	49,800 CUP

Cartridge:20 Tactical
Load Type:Rifle

Bullet Weight (Gr.)	Manufacturer	Powder	Bullet Diam.	C.O.L.	Grs.	Vel. (ft/s)	Pressure	Grs.	Vel. (ft/s)	Pressure
33 GR. HDY V-MAX	Hodgdon	Varget	.204"	2.245"	25.0	3344	37,900 PSI	27.0C	3659	49,600 PSI
33 GR. HDY V-MAX	Hodgdon	BL-C(2)	.204"	2.245"	25.0	3478	39,000 PSI	28.0	3775	49,000 PSI
33 GR. HDY V-MAX	Hodgdon	H335	.204"	2.245"	24.5	3643	44,700 PSI	26.7	3917	54,600 PSI
33 GR. HDY V-MAX	Hodgdon	H4895	.204"	2.245"	25.0	3573	42,700 PSI	27.0C	3800	50,600 PSI
33 GR. HDY V-MAX	Hodgdon	Benchmark	.204"	2.245"	23.0	3506	41,900 PSI	25.5	3844	54,500 PSI
33 GR. HDY V-MAX	Hodgdon	H322	.204"	2.245"	23.0	3529	42,900 PSI	25.5	3852	54,900 PSI
33 GR. HDY V-MAX	Hodgdon	H4198	.204"	2.245"	20.0	3434	40,500 PSI	22.5	3844	55,100 PSI
36 GR. BER HP	Hodgdon	Varget	.204"	2.200"	25.0	3456	45,200 PSI	27.0C	3681	54,300 PSI
36 GR. BER HP	Hodgdon	BL-C(2)	.204"	2.200"	25.0	3353	38,900 PSI	28.0	3771	53,700 PSI
36 GR. BER HP	Hodgdon	H335	.204"	2.200"	23.5	3518	45,900 PSI	25.5	3751	54,700 PSI
36 GR. BER HP	Hodgdon	H4895	.204"	2.200"	24.0	3453	42,900 PSI	26.5C	3746	54,900 PSI
36 GR. BER HP	Hodgdon	Benchmark	.204"	2.200"	22.0	3358	42,000 PSI	24.5	3678	54,400 PSI
36 GR. BER HP	Hodgdon	H322	.204"	2.200"	22.0	3434	44,900 PSI	24.2	3686	54,500 PSI
36 GR. BER HP	Hodgdon	H4198	.204"	2.200"	20.0	3434	45,000 PSI	22.0	3675	55,000 PSI

Cartridge:204 Ruger
Load Type:Rifle

Bullet Weight (Gr.)	Manufacturer	Powder	Bullet Diam.	C.O.L.	Grs.	Vel. (ft/s)	Pressure	Grs.	Vel. (ft/s)	Pressure
24 GR. HDY NTX	Hodgdon	H335	.204"	2.290"	27.4	4184	47,100 PSI	29.5	4456	55,200 PSI
24 GR. HDY NTX	Hodgdon	H4895	.204"	2.290"	27.0	4061	43,400 PSI	29.5C	4423	54,900 PSI
24 GR. HDY NTX	IMR	IMR 8208 XBR	.204"	2.290"	27.0	3997	40,600 PSI	30.0C	4447	56,000 PSI
24 GR. HDY NTX	Hodgdon	Benchmark	.204"	2.290"	27.3	4109	45,500 PSI	29.0	4373	54,500 PSI
24 GR. HDY NTX	Hodgdon	H322	.204"	2.290"	26.3	4143	48,700 PSI	28.0	4358	56,000 PSI
24 GR. HDY NTX	IMR	IMR 4198	.204"	2.290"	23.0	4166	48,200 PSI	24.5	4383	54,900 PSI
24 GR. HDY NTX	Hodgdon	H4198	.204"	2.290"	22.6	4294	54,100 PSI	24.0	4400	56,600 PSI
26 GR. BAR VG FB	Hodgdon	CFE 223	.204"	2.250"	29.5	4067	46,300 PSI	31.5	4282	52,600 PSI
26 GR. BAR VG FB	Hodgdon	Varget	.204"	2.250"	27.5	3962	47,500 PSI	30.0C	4110	51,000 PSI
26 GR. BAR VG FB	Hodgdon	BL-C(2)	.204"	2.250"	28.9	4004	47,200 PSI	30.7	4173	52,700 PSI
26 GR. BAR VG FB	IMR	IMR 4895	.204"	2.250"	27.7	3934	47,100 PSI	29.5C	4169	54,700 PSI
26 GR. BAR VG FB	Hodgdon	H335	.204"	2.250"	26.8	4149	52,200 PSI	28.5	4278	54,900 PSI
26 GR. BAR VG FB	Hodgdon	H4895	.204"	2.250"	28.2	4067	48,900 PSI	30.0C	4302	57,300 PSI

26 GR. BAR VG FB	IMR	IMR 8208 XBR	.204"	2.250"	27.7	4132	48,400 PSI	29.5C	4309	54,900 PSI
26 GR. BAR VG FB	Hodgdon	Benchmark	.204"	2.250"	27.0	4036	47,600 PSI	28.7	4279	56,700 PSI
26 GR. BAR VG FB	Hodgdon	H322	.204"	2.250"	25.9	4055	52,200 PSI	27.5	4229	57,100 PSI
26 GR. BAR VG FB	IMR	IMR 4198	.204"	2.250"	22.7	4015	49,400 PSI	24.2	4257	56,700 PSI
26 GR. BAR VG FB	Hodgdon	H4198	.204"	2.250"	23.0	4124	54,100 PSI	24.5	4258	57,300 PSI
30 GR. BER FB VAR	Hodgdon	CFE 223	.204"	2.235"	28.7	3761	40,700 PSI	31.3	4202	57,000 PSI
30 GR. BER FB VAR	Hodgdon	Varget	.204"	2.235"	27.1	3640	41,300 PSI	29.5C	4028	55,200 PSI
30 GR. BER FB VAR	Hodgdon	BL-C(2)	.204"	2.235"	28.5	3748	43,300 PSI	30.7	4073	55,200 PSI
30 GR. BER FB VAR	IMR	IMR 4895	.204"	2.235"	27.4	3687	44,500 PSI	29.5C	4024	56,600 PSI
30 GR. BER FB VAR	Hodgdon	H335	.204"	2.235"	26.1	3814	48,200 PSI	28.1	4054	57,300 PSI
30 GR. BER FB VAR	Hodgdon	H4895	.204"	2.235"	26.2	3800	44,500 PSI	28.5	4124	56,800 PSI
30 GR. BER FB VAR	IMR	IMR 8208 XBR	.204"	2.235"	26.7	3798	44,500 PSI	28.8	4118	56,400 PSI
30 GR. BER FB VAR	Hodgdon	Benchmark	.204"	2.235"	25.7	3754	44,500 PSI	28.0	4076	56,800 PSI
30 GR. BER FB VAR	Hodgdon	H322	.204"	2.235"	24.5	3740	44,500 PSI	26.6	4054	56,700 PSI
30 GR. BER FB VAR	IMR	IMR 4198	.204"	2.235"	21.9	3695	45,900 PSI	23.9	3979	56,600 PSI
30 GR. BER FB VAR	Hodgdon	H4198	.204"	2.235"	22.2	3789	45,100 PSI	24.2	4073	56,300 PSI
32 GR. HDY V-MAX	Hodgdon	CFE 223	.204"	2.250"	29.0	3826	45,400 PSI	30.9	4091	55,000 PSI
32 GR. HDY V-MAX	Hodgdon	Varget	.204"	2.250"	27.0	3557	38,300 PSI	29.0C	3798	47,400 PSI
32 GR. HDY V-MAX	Hodgdon	BL-C(2)	.204"	2.250"	28.5	3772	43,000 PSI	30.7	4081	55,500 PSI
32 GR. HDY V-MAX	IMR	IMR 4895	.204"	2.250"	27.0	3627	40,500 PSI	29.0C	3949	51,900 PSI
32 GR. HDY V-MAX	Hodgdon	H335	.204"	2.250"	26.0	3703	40,600 PSI	28.3	4044	54,800 PSI
32 GR. HDY V-MAX	Hodgdon	H4895	.204"	2.250"	27.0	3669	40,500 PSI	29.0C	3980	51,100 PSI
32 GR. HDY V-MAX	IMR	IMR 8208 XBR	.204"	2.250"	27.5	3917	47,500 PSI	29.0	4130	56,500 PSI
32 GR. HDY V-MAX	Hodgdon	Benchmark	.204"	2.250"	26.0	3770	45,500 PSI	28.0	4047	57,100 PSI
32 GR. HDY V-MAX	Hodgdon	H322	.204"	2.250"	25.5	3826	48,300 PSI	27.5	4030	56,400 PSI
32 GR. HDY V-MAX	IMR	IMR 4198	.204"	2.250"	22.0	3725	42,700 PSI	23.5	4006	55,400 PSI
35 GR. BER HP	Hodgdon	CFE 223	.204"	2.240"	28.8	3695	44,500 PSI	30.6	3991	55,600 PSI
35 GR. BER HP	Hodgdon	Varget	.204"	2.240"	28.0	3705	48,300 PSI	29.0C	3812	53,100 PSI
35 GR. BER HP	IMR	IMR 4064	.204"	2.240"	26.0	3444	40,000 PSI	27.5C	3728	51,000 PSI
35 GR. BER HP	Hodgdon	BL-C(2)	.204"	2.240"	28.5	3734	47,200 PSI	30.7	3937	54,900 PSI
35 GR. BER HP	IMR	IMR 4895	.204"	2.240"	26.5	3550	43,300 PSI	28.3C	3864	55,500 PSI
35 GR. BER HP	Hodgdon	H335	.204"	2.240"	25.5	3665	45,400 PSI	27.5	3915	56,600 PSI
35 GR. BER HP	Hodgdon	H4895	.204"	2.240"	26.0	3576	42,200 PSI	28.2C	3910	55,700 PSI
35 GR. BER HP	IMR	IMR 8208 XBR	.204"	2.240"	27.0	3830	50,700 PSI	28.2	3961	56,300 PSI
35 GR. BER HP	IMR	IMR 3031	.204"	2.240"	25.0	3602	44,400 PSI	26.1C	3793	52,800 PSI
35 GR. BER HP	Hodgdon	Benchmark	.204"	2.240"	25.0	3590	44,100 PSI	26.6	3863	56,600 PSI
35 GR. BER HP	Hodgdon	H322	.204"	2.240"	24.0	3586	45,600 PSI	26.3	3828	55,400 PSI
40 GR. HDY V-MAX	Hodgdon	CFE 223	.204"	2.250"	27.3	3518	46,500 PSI	29.0	3769	56,700 PSI
40 GR. HDY V-MAX	Hodgdon	Varget	.204"	2.250"	26.0	3395	44,100 PSI	28.1C	3647	55,100 PSI

Bullet Weight	Manufacturer	Powder	Bullet Diam.	C.O.L.	Grs.	Vel. (ft/s)	Pressure	Grs.	Vel. (ft/s)	Pressure
40 GR. HDY V-MAX	IMR	IMR 4064	.204"	2.250"	25.5	3379	43,600 PSI	27.5C	3616	52,000 PSI
40 GR. HDY V-MAX	Hodgdon	BL-C(2)	.204"	2.250"	28.0	3569	47,300 PSI	30.0	3774	56,200 PSI
40 GR. HDY V-MAX	IMR	IMR 4895	.204"	2.250"	26.0	3415	44,700 PSI	27.8C	3695	56,000 PSI
40 GR. HDY V-MAX	Hodgdon	H335	.204"	2.250"	25.0	3508	47,300 PSI	26.8	3738	56,700 PSI
40 GR. HDY V-MAX	Hodgdon	H4895	.204"	2.250"	26.0	3500	45,500 PSI	27.7C	3741	56,000 PSI
40 GR. HDY V-MAX	IMR	IMR 8208 XBR	.204"	2.250"	26.0	3586	48,300 PSI	27.3	3754	56,300 PSI
40 GR. HDY V-MAX	IMR	IMR 3031	.204"	2.250"	24.0	3456	46,300 PSI	25.6C	3694	56,600 PSI
40 GR. HDY V-MAX	Hodgdon	Benchmark	.204"	2.250"	24.0	3419	45,200 PSI	25.7	3646	55,400 PSI
40 GR. HDY V-MAX	Hodgdon	H322	.204"	2.250"	23.0	3319	41,500 PSI	25.1	3639	55,900 PSI
50 GR. BER HPBT	IMR	IMR 4007 SSC	.204"	2.300"	26.0	3035	44,600 PSI	29.0C	3312	55,600 PSI
50 GR. BER HPBT	Hodgdon	CFE 223	.204"	2.300"	25.2	3279	54,400 PSI	26.8	3370	55,700 PSI
50 GR. BER HPBT	Hodgdon	Varget	.204"	2.300"	24.0	3071	44,900 PSI	26.0	3287	55,200 PSI
50 GR. BER HPBT	IMR	IMR 4064	.204"	2.300"	24.0	3079	44,900 PSI	25.8C	3330	55,800 PSI
50 GR. BER HPBT	Hodgdon	BL-C(2)	.204"	2.300"	25.0	3089	42,900 PSI	27.0	3334	54,500 PSI
50 GR. BER HPBT	IMR	IMR 4895	.204"	2.300"	24.0	3092	45,400 PSI	26.2C	3344	56,000 PSI
50 GR. BER HPBT	Hodgdon	H335	.204"	2.300"	22.5	3039	43,700 PSI	24.3	3268	54,700 PSI
50 GR. BER HPBT	Hodgdon	H4895	.204"	2.300"	24.0	3167	46,900 PSI	25.7	3352	56,000 PSI
50 GR. BER HPBT	IMR	IMR 8208 XBR	.204"	2.300"	23.0	3129	47,800 PSI	24.9	3327	56,100 PSI
50 GR. BER HPBT	IMR	IMR 3031	.204"	2.300"	22.0	3046	44,500 PSI	24.0	3284	55,100 PSI
50 GR. BER HPBT	Hodgdon	Benchmark	.204"	2.300"	22.5	3110	47,800 PSI	24.0	3256	54,300 PSI
50 GR. BER HPBT	Hodgdon	H322	.204"	2.300"	22.0	3105	48,300 PSI	23.5	3252	55,100 PSI

Cartridge: 22 Hornet Load Type: Rifle					Starting Loads			Maximum Loads		
Bullet Weight (Gr.)	Manufacturer	Powder	Bullet Diam.	C.O.L.	Grs.	Vel. (ft/s)	Pressure	Grs.	Vel. (ft/s)	Pressure
30 GR. BAR VG FB	IMR	IMR 4227	.224"	1.750"	10.0	2321	37,300 CUP	11.7C	2703	37,600 CUP
30 GR. BAR VG FB	Winchester	296	.224"	1.750"	11.1	2807	33,000 CUP	12.3	3150	41,500 CUP
30 GR. BAR VG FB	Hodgdon	H110	.224"	1.750"	11.1	2807	33,000 CUP	12.3	3150	41,500 CUP
30 GR. BAR VG FB	Hodgdon	Lil'Gun	.224"	1.750"	11.7	2863	26,300 CUP	13.0	3055	29,700 CUP
35 GR. HDY V-MAX	Hodgdon	H4198	.224"	1.725"	10.5	2223	23,100 CUP	11.5C	2420	26,300 CUP
35 GR. HDY V-MAX	Hodgdon	H4227	.224"	1.725"	10.5	2630	35,600 CUP	11.6C	2896	42,500 CUP
35 GR. HDY V-MAX	Hodgdon	H110	.224"	1.725"	11.0	2805	32,700 CUP	12.3	3060	41,400 CUP
35 GR. HDY V-MAX	Hodgdon	Lil'Gun	.224"	1.725"	12.0	2694	22,000 CUP	13.0	2842	24,000 CUP
40 GR. SPR SP	Hodgdon	H4198	.224"	1.725"	10.5	2253	26,100 CUP	11.5C	2488	32,800 CUP
40 GR. SPR SP	Hodgdon	H4227	.224"	1.725"	9.0	2421	39,900 CUP	10.2	2567	43,000 CUP
40 GR. SPR SP	Hodgdon	H110	.224"	1.725"	10.0	2569	32,400 CUP	11.2	2795	41,800 CUP
40 GR. SPR SP	Hodgdon	Lil'Gun	.224"	1.725"	12.0	2667	24,900 CUP	13.0	2826	28,400 CUP
45 GR. BAR XBT	Hodgdon	H4198	.224"	1.850"	10.5	2217	31,500 CUP	11.5C	2390	36,900 CUP
45 GR. BAR XBT	Hodgdon	H4227	.224"	1.850"	8.5	2198	37,000 CUP	9.8	2346	42,700 CUP
45 GR. BAR XBT	Hodgdon	H110	.224"	1.850"	9.0	2323	35,200 CUP	9.9	2503	40,400 CUP

Bullet Weight (Gr.)	Manufacturer	Powder	Bullet Diam.	C.O.L.	Grs.	Vel. (ft/s)	Pressure	Grs.	Vel. (ft/s)	Pressure
45 GR. BAR XBT	Hodgdon	Lil'Gun	.224"	1.850"	12.0	2641	35,700 CUP	13.0	2770	38,500 CUP
45 GR. HDY SP	IMR	IMR 4198	.224"	1.750"				10.5C	2010	20,100 CUP
45 GR. HDY SP	Hodgdon	H4198	.224"	1.750"	10.5	2239	28,000 CUP	11.5C	2400	32,000 CUP
45 GR. HDY SP	IMR	IMR 4227	.224"	1.750"	8.5	2312	39,900 CUP	9.8	2484	42,000 CUP
45 GR. HDY SP	IMR	SR 4759	.224"	1.750"				8.0C	2000	24,700 CUP
45 GR. HDY SP	Hodgdon	H110	.224"	1.750"	9.0	2342	33,500 CUP	10.4	2574	43,000 CUP
45 GR. HDY SP	Hodgdon	Lil'Gun	.224"	1.750"	12.0	2622	26,500 CUP	13.0	2787	31,600 CUP
50 GR. SIE SP	Hodgdon	H4198	.224"	1.850"	10.5	2102	28,200 CUP	11.5C	2296	34,100 CUP
50 GR. SIE SP	Hodgdon	H4227	.224"	1.850"	8.4	2131	39,700 CUP	9.4	2256	41,800 CUP
50 GR. SIE SP	Hodgdon	H110	.224"	1.850"	9.0	2249	37,500 CUP	10.0	2422	42,300 CUP
50 GR. SIE SP	Hodgdon	Lil'Gun	.224"	1.850"	12.0	2556	31,600 CUP	13.0	2713	35,300 CUP
53 GR. BAR XFB	Hodgdon	H4198	.224"	1.850"	10.0	2025	31,600 CUP	11.0C	2165	40,600 CUP
53 GR. BAR XFB	Hodgdon	H4227	.224"	1.850"	8.0	1887	37,600 CUP	8.7	2062	43,000 CUP
53 GR. BAR XFB	Hodgdon	H110	.224"	1.850"	8.0	1997	38,300 CUP	9.0	2159	41,000 CUP
53 GR. BAR XFB	Hodgdon	Lil'Gun	.224"	1.850"	11.0	2310	32,800 CUP	12.0	2509	39,000 CUP
55 GR. HDY SP	Hodgdon	H4198	.224"	1.850"	10.0	1955	30,000 CUP	11.5C	2273	41,000 CUP
55 GR. HDY SP	Hodgdon	H4227	.224"	1.850"	8.0	1915	41,800 CUP	9.0	2095	43,000 CUP
55 GR. HDY SP	Hodgdon	Lil'Gun	.224"	1.850"	12.0	2551	39,400 CUP	13.0	2652	42,900 CUP

| Cartridge: 22 K Hornet | | | | | Starting Loads | | | Maximum Loads | | |
Load Type: Rifle										
Bullet Weight (Gr.)	Manufacturer	Powder	Bullet Diam.	C.O.L.	Grs.	Vel. (ft/s)	Pressure	Grs.	Vel. (ft/s)	Pressure
30 GR. BAR VG FB	IMR	IMR 4227	.224"	1.750"	10.8	2241	27,300 CUP	12.0C	2569	30,600 CUP
30 GR. BAR VG FB	Winchester	296	.224"	1.750"	11.0	2996	40,200 CUP	11.7	3108	43,100 CUP
30 GR. BAR VG FB	Hodgdon	H110	.224"	1.750"	11.0	2996	40,200 CUP	11.7	3108	43,100 CUP
30 GR. BAR VG FB	Hodgdon	Lil'Gun	.224"	1.750"	12.7	3150	35,200 CUP	13.5	3332	43,000 CUP
35 GR. HDY V-MAX	Hodgdon	H4227	.224"	1.725"	11.0	2809	39,500 CUP	12.3	3023	46,000 CUP
35 GR. HDY V-MAX	Hodgdon	H110	.224"	1.725"	11.5	2901	35,100 CUP	12.8	3137	45,500 CUP
35 GR. HDY V-MAX	Hodgdon	Lil'Gun	.224"	1.725"	12.5	2980	29,900 CUP	13.5	3122	35,300 CUP
40 GR. NOS BT	Hodgdon	H4227	.224"	1.900"	11.0	2684	37,500 CUP	12.2C	2871	45,500 CUP
40 GR. NOS BT	Hodgdon	H110	.224"	1.900"	11.5	2779	33,100 CUP	12.9	3045	45,600 CUP
40 GR. NOS BT	Hodgdon	Lil'Gun	.224"	1.900"	12.5	2891	29,400 CUP	13.5	3001	33,800 CUP
45 GR. BAR XBT	Hodgdon	H4227	.224"	1.850"	10.5	2524	40,900 CUP	11.3	2633	45,300 CUP
45 GR. BAR XBT	Hodgdon	H110	.224"	1.850"	10.5	2578	38,700 CUP	11.2	2686	45,300 CUP
45 GR. BAR XBT	Hodgdon	Lil'Gun	.224"	1.850"	12.0	2773	36,700 CUP	13.0	2896	40,200 CUP
45 GR. SPR SP	Hodgdon	H4227	.224"	1.750"	10.7	2574	40,700 CUP	11.7	2747	45,500 CUP
45 GR. SPR SP	Hodgdon	H110	.224"	1.750"	11.5	2684	37,000 CUP	12.4	2841	45,500 CUP
45 GR. SPR SP	Hodgdon	Lil'Gun	.224"	1.750"	12.0	2716	28,100 CUP	13.2	2893	35,800 CUP
50 GR. SIE BK	Hodgdon	H4198	.224"	1.900"	11.5	2246	30,100 CUP	12.5C	2460	38,700 CUP

50 GR. SIE BK	Hodgdon	H4227	.224"	1.900"	10.0	2398	40,200 CUP	11.0	2538	45,700 CUP
50 GR. SIE BK	Hodgdon	H110	.224"	1.900"	10.4	2491	37,900 CUP	11.1	2619	45,800 CUP
50 GR. SIE BK	Hodgdon	Lil'Gun	.224"	1.900"	12.0	2675	34,300 CUP	13.0	2826	40,700 CUP
53 GR. BAR XFB	Hodgdon	H4198	.224"	1.850"	11.2	2195	30,200 CUP	12.5C	2386	42,600 CUP
53 GR. BAR XFB	Hodgdon	H4227	.224"	1.850"	9.5	2208	39,000 CUP	10.5	2366	45,900 CUP
53 GR. BAR XFB	Hodgdon	H110	.224"	1.850"	9.5	2274	40,300 CUP	10.2	2379	46,100 CUP
53 GR. BAR XFB	Hodgdon	Lil'Gun	.224"	1.850"	11.5	2552	38,700 CUP	12.3	2695	45,700 CUP
55 GR. HDY SP	Hodgdon	H4198	.224"	1.850"	11.5	2223	31,100 CUP	12.5C	2388	39,400 CUP
55 GR. HDY SP	Hodgdon	H4227	.224"	1.850"	10.0	2315	43,400 CUP	11.0	2445	46,100 CUP

Cartridge: 218 Bee Load Type: Rifle					Starting Loads			Maximum Loads		
Bullet Weight (Gr.)	Manufacturer	Powder	Bullet Diam.	C.O.L.	Grs.	Vel. (ft/s)	Pressure	Grs.	Vel. (ft/s)	Pressure
35 GR. HDY V-MAX	Hodgdon	H4227	.224"	1.650"	11.0	2656	30,400 CUP	13.3	3035	38,300 CUP
35 GR. HDY V-MAX	Hodgdon	H110	.224"	1.650"	12.5	2974	33,900 CUP	13.2	3066	37,400 CUP
35 GR. HDY V-MAX	Hodgdon	Lil'Gun	.224"	1.650"	12.0	2868	25,400 CUP	14.0	3205	37,100 CUP
40 GR. SIE BK	Hodgdon	H4227	.224"	1.820"	11.0	2608	33,800 CUP	12.8	2865	38,700 CUP
40 GR. SIE BK	Hodgdon	H110	.224"	1.820"	12.5	2866	33,000 CUP	13.3	2981	38,200 CUP
40 GR. SIE BK	Hodgdon	Lil'Gun	.224"	1.820"	12.5	2846	26,500 CUP	14.0	3130	37,400 CUP
46 GR. SPR JFP	Hodgdon	H4198	.224"	1.670"	13.5	2417	26,700 CUP	15.0C	2708	37,200 CUP
46 GR. SPR JFP	Hodgdon	H4227	.224"	1.670"	9.0	2143	23,300 CUP	10.7	2424	38,200 CUP
46 GR. SPR JFP	Hodgdon	H110	.224"	1.670"	8.0	2127	25,400 CUP	9.0	2331	36,400 CUP
46 GR. SPR JFP	Hodgdon	Lil'Gun	.224"	1.670"	9.0	2385	29,900 CUP	10.2	2586	37,300 CUP
50 GR. NOS BT	Hodgdon	H4198	.224"	1.900"	13.5	2420	29,500 CUP	14.9C	2654	38,500 CUP
50 GR. NOS BT	Hodgdon	H4227	.224"	1.900"	9.5	2195	29,500 CUP	10.8	2421	38,400 CUP
50 GR. NOS BT	Hodgdon	H110	.224"	1.900"	8.5	2174	30,000 CUP	9.4	2332	38,600 CUP
50 GR. NOS BT	Hodgdon	Lil'Gun	.224"	1.900"	9.0	2320	31,500 CUP	10.2	2503	36,400 CUP

Cartridge: 221 Fireball Load Type: Rifle					Starting Loads			Maximum Loads		
Bullet Weight (Gr.)	Manufacturer	Powder	Bullet Diam.	C.O.L.	Grs.	Vel. (ft/s)	Pressure	Grs.	Vel. (ft/s)	Pressure
35 GR. HDY V-MAX	Hodgdon	H4198	.224"	1.745"	18.0	3056	31,900 CUP	20.0C	3423	44,700 CUP
35 GR. HDY V-MAX	Hodgdon	H4227	.224"	1.745"	14.8	3110	37,500 CUP	16.5	3403	50,600 CUP
35 GR. HDY V-MAX	Hodgdon	Lil'Gun	.224"	1.745"	14.0	3354	47,200 CUP	16.0	3535	49,900 CUP
36 GR. BAR VG FB	Hodgdon	H4198	.224"	1.830"	18.0	3177	35,000 CUP	19.0C	3361	41,500 CUP
36 GR. BAR VG FB	IMR	IMR 4227	.224"	1.830"	15.5	3081	41,300 CUP	16.7	3264	49,100 CUP
36 GR. BAR VG FB	IMR	SR 4759	.224"	1.830"	13.0	3017	38,100 CUP	15.0	3262	49,200 CUP
36 GR. BAR VG FB	Hodgdon	Lil'Gun	.224"	1.830"	14.5	3297	41,500 CUP	15.7	3500	48,800 CUP
40 GR. NOS BT	Hodgdon	H335	.224"	1.830"	20.0	2782	31,500 CUP	22.0	3048	41,200 CUP
40 GR. NOS BT	Hodgdon	H322	.224"	1.830"	19.7	2883	33,200 CUP	21.0C	3087	39,100 CUP

Bullet Weight (Gr.)	Manufacturer	Powder	Bullet Diam.	C.O.L.	Grs.	Vel. (ft/s)	Pressure	Grs.	Vel. (ft/s)	Pressure
40 GR. NOS BT	Hodgdon	H4198	.224"	1.830"	17.0	2851	30,000 CUP	19.0C	3195	40,300 CUP
40 GR. NOS BT	Hodgdon	H4227	.224"	1.830"	14.5	3042	43,100 CUP	16.0	3251	50,200 CUP
40 GR. NOS BT	Hodgdon	Lil'Gun	.224"	1.830"	14.5	3172	42,100 CUP	16.0	3384	48,900 CUP
45 GR. BAR X	Hodgdon	H335	.224"	1.830"	19.8	2783	36,300 CUP	22.0	3077	50,000 CUP
45 GR. BAR X	Hodgdon	H322	.224"	1.830"	19.0	2762	31,600 CUP	20.5C	2978	39,900 CUP
45 GR. BAR X	Hodgdon	H4198	.224"	1.830"	17.6	2934	37,200 CUP	19.5C	3184	46,500 CUP
45 GR. BAR X	Hodgdon	H4227	.224"	1.830"	13.8	2848	43,500 CUP	15.3	3015	48,600 CUP
45 GR. BAR X	Hodgdon	Lil'Gun	.224"	1.830"	13.4	2944	41,400 CUP	14.9	3155	49,400 CUP
45 GR. SIE SPT	Hodgdon	H335	.224"	1.800"	20.0	2740	32,600 CUP	22.0	3030	44,300 CUP
45 GR. SIE SPT	Hodgdon	H322	.224"	1.800"	19.0	2767	31,400 CUP	20.5C	2955	37,000 CUP
45 GR. SIE SPT	Hodgdon	H4198	.224"	1.800"	17.5	2851	31,700 CUP	19.5C	3178	43,700 CUP
45 GR. SIE SPT	Hodgdon	H4227	.224"	1.800"	14.0	2872	40,900 CUP	15.7	3078	49,100 CUP
45 GR. SIE SPT	Hodgdon	Lil'Gun	.224"	1.800"	13.8	2964	39,300 CUP	15.3	3202	49,000 CUP
50 GR. SPR TNT HP	Hodgdon	H335	.224"	1.830"	19.8	2674	33,100 CUP	22.0	3041	48,600 CUP
50 GR. SPR TNT HP	Hodgdon	H322	.224"	1.830"	19.0	2703	31,600 CUP	21.0C	2968	40,100 CUP
50 GR. SPR TNT HP	Hodgdon	H4198	.224"	1.830"	16.5	2661	27,800 CUP	18.5C	2996	40,800 CUP
50 GR. SPR TNT HP	Hodgdon	H4227	.224"	1.830"	13.0	2629	36,500 CUP	14.8	2901	51,200 CUP
50 GR. SPR TNT HP	Hodgdon	Lil'Gun	.224"	1.830"	13.0	2835	43,400 CUP	14.6	2994	48,200 CUP
52 GR. SIE HPBT	Hodgdon	H335	.224"	1.830"	19.6	2662	35,500 CUP	21.8	2958	48,200 CUP
52 GR. SIE HPBT	Hodgdon	H322	.224"	1.830"	18.9	2693	35,100 CUP	21.0C	2987	46,800 CUP
52 GR. SIE HPBT	Hodgdon	H4198	.224"	1.830"	16.7	2692	33,700 CUP	18.5C	2967	45,300 CUP
52 GR. SIE HPBT	Hodgdon	H4227	.224"	1.830"	13.0	2612	40,900 CUP	14.5	2798	48,100 CUP
52 GR. SIE HPBT	Hodgdon	Lil'Gun	.224"	1.830"	13.0	2768	43,200 CUP	14.5	2951	48,800 CUP
55 GR. HDY SPSX	Hodgdon	H335	.224"	1.830"	19.3	2602	36,700 CUP	21.5	2891	49,400 CUP
55 GR. HDY SPSX	Hodgdon	H322	.224"	1.830"	18.9	2681	36,000 CUP	21.0C	2944	48,200 CUP
55 GR. HDY SPSX	Hodgdon	H4198	.224"	1.830"	16.7	2655	34,100 CUP	18.5	2922	46,800 CUP
55 GR. HDY SPSX	Hodgdon	H4227	.224"	1.830"	13.5	2643	48,100 CUP	14.5	2742	49,300 CUP
55 GR. HDY SPSX	Hodgdon	Lil'Gun	.224"	1.830"	13.0	2714	45,200 CUP	14.5	2877	49,800 CUP

Cartridge: 222 Remington Load Type: Rifle						Starting Loads			Maximum Loads	
Bullet Weight (Gr.)	Manufacturer	Powder	Bullet Diam.	C.O.L.	Grs.	Vel. (ft/s)	Pressure	Grs.	Vel. (ft/s)	Pressure
35 GR. HDY V-MAX	IMR	IMR 8208 XBR	.224"	2.025"	23.0	3181	32,000 PSI	25.0C	3464	40,500 PSI
35 GR. HDY V-MAX	Hodgdon	Benchmark	.224"	2.025"	23.5	3138	33,700 CUP	25.0C	3368	40,900 CUP
35 GR. HDY V-MAX	Hodgdon	H322	.224"	2.025"	23.5	3316	36,500 CUP	25.2C	3591	45,600 CUP
35 GR. HDY V-MAX	IMR	IMR 4198	.224"	2.025"	18.7	3252	34,300 PSI	20.8	3659	47,500 PSI
35 GR. HDY V-MAX	Hodgdon	H4198	.224"	2.025"	20.5	3366	36,500 CUP	22.0	3591	43,300 CUP
35 GR. HDY V-MAX	IMR	IMR 4227	.224"	2.025"	15.0	3195	38,500 PSI	17.4	3500	46,500 PSI
35 GR. HDY V-MAX	Hodgdon	H4227	.224"	2.025"	15.0	3095	38,100 CUP	17.2	3342	43,000 CUP

35 GR. NOS BT LF	IMR	IMR 8208 XBR	.224"	2.130"	22.1	3096	32,500 PSI	24.5C	3516	42,200 PSI
35 GR. NOS BT LF	Hodgdon	Benchmark	.224"	2.130"	22.5	3316	34,600 PSI	25.0C	3665	48,600 PSI
35 GR. NOS BT LF	Hodgdon	H322	.224"	2.130"	21.6	3290	39,700 PSI	23.2	3527	47,600 PSI
35 GR. NOS BT LF	IMR	IMR 4198	.224"	2.130"	18.5	3220	36,800 PSI	19.9	3539	47,800 PSI
35 GR. NOS BT LF	Hodgdon	H4198	.224"	2.130"	19.3	3472	44,800 PSI	20.5	3612	47,300 PSI
36 GR. BAR VG FB	Hodgdon	H335	.224"	2.150"	23.0	3293	43,000 PSI	24.5	3472	48,700 PSI
36 GR. BAR VG FB	IMR	IMR 8208 XBR	.224"	2.150"	22.0	3144	36,700 PSI	25.0C	3582	40,400 PSI
36 GR. BAR VG FB	IMR	IMR 3031	.224"	2.150"	21.1	3147	40,700 PSI	22.4C	3356	47,000 PSI
36 GR. BAR VG FB	Hodgdon	Benchmark	.224"	2.150"	22.0	3178	38,500 PSI	24.0C	3471	48,300 PSI
36 GR. BAR VG FB	Hodgdon	H322	.224"	2.150"	22.3	3331	41,400 PSI	23.7	3535	47,500 PSI
36 GR. BAR VG FB	IMR	IMR 4198	.224"	2.150"	18.3	3199	40,000 PSI	19.5	3433	48,100 PSI
36 GR. BAR VG FB	Hodgdon	H4198	.224"	2.150"	19.3	3277	40,500 PSI	20.5	3470	46,700 PSI
40 GR. SIE HP	Hodgdon	H335	.224"	2.125"	22.5	3125	38,400 CUP	25.0	3371	44,600 CUP
40 GR. SIE HP	Hodgdon	H4895	.224"	2.125"	20.0	2572	23,300 CUP	24.0C	3133	34,200 CUP
40 GR. SIE HP	IMR	IMR 8208 XBR	.224"	2.125"	22.5	3049	30,400 PSI	25.0C	3452	42,800 PSI
40 GR. SIE HP	Hodgdon	Benchmark	.224"	2.125"	23.5	3110	34,800 CUP	25.0	3303	40,700 CUP
40 GR. SIE HP	Hodgdon	H322	.224"	2.125"	20.7	2966	31,700 CUP	23.0	3313	44,000 CUP
40 GR. SIE HP	IMR	IMR 4198	.224"	2.125"	19.0	3226	36,300 PSI	21.2C	3583	48,700 PSI
40 GR. SIE HP	Hodgdon	H4198	.224"	2.125"	19.5	3201	35,200 CUP	21.4	3480	45,700 CUP
40 GR. SIE HP	IMR	IMR 4227	.224"	2.125"	14.0	2984	38,100 PSI	16.0	3240	45,200 PSI
45 GR. SPR SP	Winchester	748	.224"	2.130"				25.5	3210	41,000 CUP
45 GR. SPR SP	Hodgdon	BL-C(2)	.224"	2.130"	23.0	2774	28,100 CUP	25.5	3100	37,400 CUP
45 GR. SPR SP	IMR	IMR 4895	.224"	2.130"	22.0	2829	33,100 PSI	24.0C	3134	42,800 PSI
45 GR. SPR SP	Hodgdon	H335	.224"	2.130"	21.5	2962	36,500 CUP	24.0	3252	46,200 CUP
45 GR. SPR SP	Hodgdon	H4895	.224"	2.130"	20.0	2510	25,000 CUP	23.8C	3080	35,900 CUP
45 GR. SPR SP	IMR	IMR 8208 XBR	.224"	2.130"	22.2	3121	38,700 PSI	23.6	3327	47,200 PSI
45 GR. SPR SP	IMR	IMR 3031	.224"	2.130"	20.0	2806	31,000 PSI	22.5C	3226	45,800 PSI
45 GR. SPR SP	Hodgdon	Benchmark	.224"	2.130"	23.0	3092	39,700 CUP	24.5	3290	44,900 CUP
45 GR. SPR SP	Hodgdon	H322	.224"	2.130"	20.5	2914	34,600 CUP	22.5	3173	43,600 CUP
45 GR. SPR SP	IMR	IMR 4198	.224"	2.130"	17.8	3083	40,600 PSI	19.8	3311	47,600 PSI
45 GR. SPR SP	Hodgdon	H4198	.224"	2.130"	18.9	3011	33,400 CUP	21.0	3315	44,800 CUP
45 GR. SPR SP	Hodgdon	H4227	.224"	2.130"	11.0	2259	24,300 CUP	14.5	2863	46,100 CUP
50 GR. HDY SP	Hodgdon	CFE 223	.224"	2.130"	24.1	2970	35,200 PSI	26.2	3268	47,600 PSI
50 GR. HDY SP	Hodgdon	Varget	.224"	2.130"	23.0	2884	33,600 CUP	25.0C	3114	40,600 CUP
50 GR. HDY SP	IMR	IMR 4320	.224"	2.130"	22.5	2802	36,900 PSI	25.0C	3100	47,600 PSI
50 GR. HDY SP	IMR	IMR 4064	.224"	2.130"	21.0	2711	33,500 PSI	23.5C	3065	46,200 PSI
50 GR. HDY SP	Winchester	748	.224"	2.130"				24.0	2980	38,000 CUP
50 GR. HDY SP	Hodgdon	BL-C(2)	.224"	2.130"	22.5	2693	25,500 CUP	25.0	3000	38,600 CUP
50 GR. HDY SP	IMR	IMR 4895	.224"	2.130"	22.0	2845	37,800 PSI	24.0C	3106	47,400 PSI
50 GR. HDY SP	Hodgdon	H335	.224"	2.130"	21.3	2861	37,100 CUP	23.6	3120	45,700 CUP

Bullet	Mfr	Powder	Dia	OAL						
50 GR. HDY SP	Hodgdon	H4895	.224"	2.130"	20.0	2466	23,900 CUP	23.8C	3022	36,500 CUP
50 GR. HDY SP	IMR	IMR 8208 XBR	.224"	2.130"	21.9	3006	39,200 PSI	23.3	3201	47,100 PSI
50 GR. HDY SP	IMR	IMR 3031	.224"	2.130"	20.0	2740	32,000 PSI	22.4C	3156	47,800 PSI
50 GR. HDY SP	Hodgdon	Benchmark	.224"	2.130"	22.5	2994	39,200 CUP	24.0	3168	45,800 CUP
50 GR. HDY SP	Hodgdon	H322	.224"	2.130"	20.2	2810	33,300 CUP	22.2	3079	43,200 CUP
50 GR. HDY SP	IMR	IMR 4198	.224"	2.130"	17.0	2850	37,100 PSI	19.3	3152	49,000 PSI
50 GR. HDY SP	Hodgdon	H4198	.224"	2.130"	18.5	2890	34,000 CUP	20.5	3160	44,200 CUP
53 GR. HDY HP	Hodgdon	CFE 223	.224"	2.140"	23.7	2904	35,700 PSI	25.8	3211	48,800 PSI
53 GR. HDY HP	Hodgdon	Varget	.224"	2.140"	23.0	2863	33,500 CUP	25.0C	3097	42,700 CUP
53 GR. HDY HP	IMR	IMR 4320	.224"	2.140"	21.5	2670	34,600 PSI	24.1	3033	48,600 PSI
53 GR. HDY HP	IMR	IMR 4064	.224"	2.140"	20.5	2662	33,300 PSI	23.0C	3024	47,400 PSI
53 GR. HDY HP	Winchester	748	.224"	2.140"				22.9	2855	36,000 CUP
53 GR. HDY HP	Hodgdon	BL-C(2)	.224"	2.140"	22.0	2639	29,300 CUP	24.5	2967	42,100 CUP
53 GR. HDY HP	IMR	IMR 4895	.224"	2.140"	21.0	2684	34,400 PSI	23.5C	3051	48,200 PSI
53 GR. HDY HP	Hodgdon	H335	.224"	2.140"	20.5	2748	35,900 CUP	23.0	3006	46,000 CUP
53 GR. HDY HP	Hodgdon	H4895	.224"	2.140"	20.0	2585	27,800 CUP	23.5C	3043	41,600 CUP
53 GR. HDY HP	IMR	IMR 8208 XBR	.224"	2.140"	21.4	2844	36,100 PSI	22.8	3117	48,200 PSI
53 GR. HDY HP	IMR	IMR 3031	.224"	2.140"	19.5	2693	33,200 PSI	21.7C	3064	47,600 PSI
53 GR. HDY HP	Hodgdon	Benchmark	.224"	2.140"	21.5	2852	38,800 CUP	23.0	3063	45,500 CUP
53 GR. HDY HP	Hodgdon	H322	.224"	2.140"	19.3	2724	34,900 CUP	21.5	3005	46,000 CUP
53 GR. HDY HP	IMR	IMR 4198	.224"	2.140"	16.5	2742	36,500 PSI	18.7	3025	47,900 PSI
53 GR. HDY HP	Hodgdon	H4198	.224"	2.140"	17.5	2800	35,300 CUP	19.5	3038	45,500 CUP
55 GR. SPR SP	Hodgdon	CFE 223	.224"	2.130"	23.9	2894	35,000 PSI	25.9	3174	47,600 PSI
55 GR. SPR SP	Hodgdon	Varget	.224"	2.130"	23.0	2860	34,500 CUP	25.0C	3095	43,000 CUP
55 GR. SPR SP	IMR	IMR 4320	.224"	2.130"	21.5	2647	34,500 PSI	24.0C	2961	46,000 PSI
55 GR. SPR SP	IMR	IMR 4064	.224"	2.130"	21.5	2739	36,500 PSI	23.0C	2954	44,400 PSI
55 GR. SPR SP	Winchester	748	.224"	2.130"				24.0	2900	38,000 CUP
55 GR. SPR SP	Hodgdon	BL-C(2)	.224"	2.130"	22.0	2625	28,200 CUP	24.2	2876	35,400 CUP
55 GR. SPR SP	IMR	IMR 4895	.224"	2.130"	21.0	2632	32,700 PSI	23.5C	3017	47,300 PSI
55 GR. SPR SP	Hodgdon	H335	.224"	2.130"	20.5	2776	35,300 CUP	23.0	3037	45,600 CUP
55 GR. SPR SP	Hodgdon	H4895	.224"	2.130"	20.0	2569	28,900 CUP	23.5C	3023	39,900 CUP
55 GR. SPR SP	IMR	IMR 8208 XBR	.224"	2.130"	21.8	2905	38,400 PSI	23.2C	3120	48,500 PSI
55 GR. SPR SP	IMR	IMR 3031	.224"	2.130"	19.5	2687	33,500 PSI	21.6C	3004	46,300 PSI
55 GR. SPR SP	Hodgdon	Benchmark	.224"	2.130	21.5	2843	38,100 CUP	23.2	3052	45,100 CUP
55 GR. SPR SP	Hodgdon	H322	.224"	2.130"	19.0	2654	31,600 CUP	21.2	2953	45,100 CUP
55 GR. SPR SP	IMR	IMR 4198	.224"	2.130"	16.5	2722	35,900 PSI	18.7	3017	47,700 PSI
55 GR. SPR SP	Hodgdon	H4198	.224"	2.130"	17.5	2733	33,400 CUP	19.5	3017	45,300 CUP
60 GR. HDY V-MAX	Hodgdon	CFE 223	.224"	2.160"	22.3	2652	33,300 PSI	24.3	2972	47,900 PSI
60 GR. HDY V-MAX	Hodgdon	Varget	.224"	2.160"	22.0	2734	36,600 CUP	23.5C	2906	42,800 CUP

Bullet Weight	Manufacturer	Powder	Bullet Diam.	C.O.L.	Grs.	Vel. (ft/s)	Pressure	Grs.	Vel. (ft/s)	Pressure
60 GR. HDY V-MAX	IMR	IMR 4320	.224"	2.160"	20.0	2408	32,400 PSI	23.0C	2805	47,800 PSI
60 GR. HDY V-MAX	IMR	IMR 4064	.224"	2.160"	20.0	2530	34,500 PSI`	22.3C	2862	47,800 PSI
60 GR. HDY V-MAX	Hodgdon	BL-C(2)	.224"	2.160"	22.0	2590	33,200 CUP	23.5	2803	44,000 CUP
60 GR. HDY V-MAX	IMR	IMR 4895	.224"	2.160"	20.0	2573	36,200 PSI	22.4C	2907	49,100 PSI
60 GR. HDY V-MAX	Hodgdon	H335	.224"	2.160"	20.0	2602	34,400 CUP	21.3	2759	42,900 CUP
60 GR. HDY V-MAX	Hodgdon	H4895	.224"	2.160"	21.7	2802	38,500 CUP	23.1C	2937	43,500 CUP
60 GR. HDY V-MAX	IMR	IMR 8208 XBR	.224"	2.160"	20.5	2737	39,200 PSI	21.8	2920	48,200 PSI
60 GR. HDY V-MAX	IMR	IMR 3031	.224"	2.160"	18.5	2476	32,900 PSI	20.6C	2838	48,700 PSI
60 GR. HDY V-MAX	Hodgdon	Benchmark	.224"	2.160"	19.7	2627	35,900 CUP	21.0	2805	42,800 CUP
60 GR. HDY V-MAX	Hodgdon	H322	.224"	2.160"	19.0	2592	34,800 CUP	20.7	2818	42,900 CUP
60 GR. HDY V-MAX	IMR	IMR 4198	.224"	2.160"	15.5	2552	37,100 PSI	17.6	2832	48,400 PSI
60 GR. HDY V-MAX	Hodgdon	H4198	.224"	2.160"	16.9	2633	36,100 CUP	18.0	2771	42,400 CUP
63 GR. SIE SP	Hodgdon	CFE 223	.224"	2.125"	22.8	2724	36,500 PSI	24.8	2986	48,900 PSI
63 GR. SIE SP	Hodgdon	Varget	.224"	2.125"	22.0	2718	34,500 CUP	24.0C	2935	43,800 CUP
63 GR. SIE SP	IMR	IMR 4320	.224"	2.125"	20.5	2450	34,900 PSI	23.0C	2774	48,400 PSI
63 GR. SIE SP	IMR	IMR 4064	.224"	2.125"	20.0	2490	34,400 PSI	22.4C	2812	47,700 PSI
63 GR. SIE SP	Hodgdon	BL-C(2)	.224"	2.125"	22.0	2626	32,600 CUP	24.2	2864	43,200 CUP
63 GR. SIE SP	IMR	IMR 4895	.224"	2.125"	20.5	2485	35,400 PSI	23.0C	2827	49,200 PSI
63 GR. SIE SP	Hodgdon	H335	.224"	2.125"	19.8	2672	37,800 CUP	22.0	2830	45,700 CUP
63 GR. SIE SP	Hodgdon	H4895	.224"	2.125"	20.0	2537	30,300 CUP	23.5C	2965	45,500 CUP
63 GR. SIE SP	IMR	IMR 8208 XBR	.224"	2.125"	20.2	2681	39,300 PSI	21.5	2865	48,400 PSI
63 GR. SIE SP	IMR	IMR 3031	.224"	2.125"	19.0	2527	35,400 PSI	20.9C	2809	48,400 PSI
63 GR. SIE SP	Hodgdon	Benchmark	.224"	2.125	21.0	2732	39,000 CUP	22.5	2903	45,700 CUP
63 GR. SIE SP	Hodgdon	H322	.224"	2.125"	18.6	2531	33,600 CUP	20.7	2780	44,400 CUP
63 GR. SIE SP	IMR	IMR 4198	.224"	2.125"	16.0	2519	37,600 PSI	18.0	2759	48,500 PSI
63 GR. SIE SP	Hodgdon	H4198	.224"	2.125"	16.9	2597	36,200 CUP	18.8	2793	43,800 CUP

Cartridge: 223 Remington
Load Type: Rifle

					Starting Loads			Maximum Loads		
Bullet Weight (Gr.)	Manufacturer	Powder	Bullet Diam.	C.O.L.	Grs.	Vel. (ft/s)	Pressure	Grs.	Vel. (ft/s)	Pressure
35 GR. NOS BT LF	Hodgdon	Varget	.224"	2.280"	25.2	3424	38,500 PSI	28.0C	3751	49,300 PSI
35 GR. NOS BT LF	IMR	IMR 4320	.224"	2.280"	25.5	3313	39,500 PSI	28.0C	3620	49,800 PSI
35 GR. NOS BT LF	Hodgdon	BL-C(2)	.224"	2.280"	26.6	3430	39,900 PSI	29.5	3740	50,100 PSI
35 GR. NOS BT LF	IMR	IMR 4895	.224"	2.280"	24.3	3263	36,400 PSI	27.0C	3620	47,700 PSI
35 GR. NOS BT LF	Hodgdon	H335	.224"	2.280"	25.7	3647	44,600 PSI	27.9	3885	53,200 PSI
35 GR. NOS BT LF	Hodgdon	H4895	.224"	2.280"	24.3	3522	39,600 PSI	27.0C	3891	53,000 PSI
35 GR. NOS BT LF	IMR	IMR 8208 XBR	.224"	2.280"	25.2	3560	41,100 PSI	28.0C	3891	53,400 PSI
35 GR. NOS BT LF	IMR	IMR 3031	.224"	2.280"	23.4	3423	40,000 PSI	26.0C	3771	51,600 PSI
35 GR. NOS BT LF	Hodgdon	Benchmark	.224"	2.280"	24.5	3555	42,700 PSI	27.2C	3851	52,900 PSI
35 GR. NOS BT LF	Hodgdon	H322	.224"	2.280"	24.3	3610	43,800 PSI	25.8	3771	50,600 PSI

35 GR. NOS BT LF	IMR	IMR 4198	.224"	2.280"	20.4	3651	47,600 PSI	21.7	3804	52,100 PSI
35 GR. NOS BT LF	Hodgdon	H4198	.224"	2.280"	20.4	3599	45,100 PSI	21.7	3780	52,000 PSI
36 GR. BAR VG FB	Hodgdon	Varget	.224"	2.200"	24.8	3278	37,000 PSI	27.5C	3593	47,300 PSI
36 GR. BAR VG FB	IMR	IMR 4320	.224"	2.200"	25.2	3289	39,700 PSI	28.0C	3653	52,200 PSI
36 GR. BAR VG FB	Hodgdon	BL-C(2)	.224"	2.200"	26.8	3345	40,400 PSI	28.5	3500	46,000 PSI
36 GR. BAR VG FB	IMR	IMR 4895	.224"	2.200"	24.8	3289	39,700 PSI	27.0C	3606	50,100 PSI
36 GR. BAR VG FB	Hodgdon	H335	.224"	2.200"	26.0	3647	48,300 PSI	27.7	3790	53,200 PSI
36 GR. BAR VG FB	Hodgdon	H4895	.224"	2.200"	25.5	3487	36,500 PSI	27.3C	3755	49,200 PSI
36 GR. BAR VG FB	IMR	IMR 8208 XBR	.224"	2.200"	25.4	3548	44,500 PSI	27.0C	3728	50,600 PSI
36 GR. BAR VG FB	IMR	IMR 3031	.224"	2.200"	23.3	3398	41,600 PSI	24.8C	3600	48,200 PSI
36 GR. BAR VG FB	Hodgdon	Benchmark	.224"	2.200"	24.4	3508	44,100 PSI	26.0	3702	50,800 PSI
36 GR. BAR VG FB	Hodgdon	H322	.224"	2.200"	24.2	3523	44,300 PSI	25.7	3721	52,700 PSI
36 GR. BAR VG FB	IMR	IMR 4198	.224"	2.200"	21.2	3579	43,500 PSI	22.5	3834	52,500 PSI
36 GR. BAR VG FB	Hodgdon	H4198	.224"	2.200"	21.1	3511	36,800 PSI	22.5	3723	51,800 PSI
40 GR. NOS BT	Hodgdon	CFE 223	.224"	2.280"	27.5	3457	40,600 PSI	29.0	3667	48,200 PSI
40 GR. NOS BT	Hodgdon	Varget	.224"	2.280"	25.0	3310	34,400 CUP	28.0C	3674	47,200 CUP
40 GR. NOS BT	IMR	IMR 4320	.224"	2.280"	26.0	3267	43,500 PSI	27.7C	3456	48,900 PSI
40 GR. NOS BT	Hodgdon	BL-C(2)	.224"	2.280"	26.5	3368	35,400 CUP	28.5	3612	45,400 CUP
40 GR. NOS BT	IMR	IMR 4895	.224"	2.280"	24.9	3164	35,200 PSI	26.5C	3390	44,200 PSI
40 GR. NOS BT	Hodgdon	H335	.224"	2.280"	26.0	3299	34,400 CUP	28.0	3572	44,600 CUP
40 GR. NOS BT	Hodgdon	H4895	.224"	2.280"	25.0	3204	32,100 CUP	27.5C	3573	44,500 CUP
40 GR. NOS BT	IMR	IMR 8208 XBR	.224"	2.280"	25.0	3433	41,500 PSI	26.7C	3659	50,400 PSI
40 GR. NOS BT	IMR	IMR 3031	.224"	2.280"	23.5	3291	42,600 PSI	25.2C	3498	46,200 PSI
40 GR. NOS BT	Hodgdon	Benchmark	.224"	2.280"	25.3	3404	39,600 CUP	27.3	3666	51,000 CUP
40 GR. NOS BT	Hodgdon	H322	.224"	2.280"	23.5	3376	34,600 CUP	25.5	3574	48,000 CUP
40 GR. NOS BT	IMR	IMR 4198	.224"	2.280"	19.5	3269	42,500 PSI	22.2	3652	53,400 PSI
40 GR. NOS BT	Hodgdon	H4198	.224"	2.280"	20.5	3147	29,400 CUP	22.5	3601	49,600 CUP
45 GR. SFIRE	Hodgdon	H335	.224"	2.220"	23.0	3172	42,000 PSI	25.3	3428	50,700 PSI
45 GR. SFIRE	IMR	IMR 8208 XBR	.224"	2.220"	23.0	3124	38,800 PSI	26.0C	3491	52,100 PSI
45 GR. SFIRE	IMR	IMR 3031	.224"	2.220"	21.0	2981	37,000 PSI	24.0C	3400	52,300 PSI
45 GR. SFIRE	Hodgdon	Benchmark	.224"	2.220"	22.5	3130	39,600 PSI	25.0	3410	51,000 PSI
45 GR. SFIRE	Hodgdon	H322	.224"	2.220"	22.0	3088	38,900 PSI	24.6C	3399	50,800 PSI
45 GR. SFIRE	IMR	IMR 4198	.224"	2.220"	19.0	3108	41,000 PSI	21.0	3395	52,400 PSI
45 GR. SFIRE	Hodgdon	H4198	.224"	2.220"	19.0	3097	40,200 PSI	21.8	3414	51,400 PSI
45 GR. SIE SP	Hodgdon	CFE 223	.224"	2.240"	27.5	3358	40,800 PSI	29.0	3536	47,200 PSI
45 GR. SIE SP	Hodgdon	Varget	.224"	2.240"	25.0	3071	30,200 CUP	28.0C	3477	43,700 CUP
45 GR. SIE SP	IMR	IMR 4320	.224"	2.240"	25.5	3158	40,300 PSI	27.8C	3342	46,300 PSI
45 GR. SIE SP	Hodgdon	BL-C(2)	.224"	2.240"	26.5	3266	36,000 CUP	28.5	3559	48,000 CUP
45 GR. SIE SP	Hodgdon	H335	.224"	2.240"	24.0	3280	41,500 CUP	26.2	3456	51,000 CUP

Bullet	Mfr	Powder	Dia	COL						
45 GR. SIE SP	Hodgdon	H4895	.224"	2.240"	25.0	3211	33,800 CUP	27.5C	3454	43,400 CUP
45 GR. SIE SP	IMR	IMR 8208 XBR	.224"	2.240"	24.5	3287	41,700 PSI	26.8	3550	52,000 PSI
45 GR. SIE SP	IMR	IMR 3031	.224"	2.240"	22.7	3065	37,700 PSI	25.2C	3374	45,800 PSI
45 GR. SIE SP	Hodgdon	Benchmark	.224"	2.240"	25.3	3327	41,100 CUP	27.3	3554	51,100 CUP
45 GR. SIE SP	Hodgdon	H322	.224"	2.240"	23.0	3164	36,000 CUP	25.0	3424	47,400 CUP
45 GR. SIE SP	IMR	IMR 4198	.224"	2.240"	19.5	3205	44,600 PSI	22.1	3495	52,000 PSI
45 GR. SIE SP	Hodgdon	H4198	.224"	2.240"	20.0	3009	28,800 CUP	22.0	3472	49,100 CUP
50 GR. SPR SP	Hodgdon	CFE 223	.224"	2.210"	27.0	3241	41,500 PSI	28.5	3505	53,600 PSI
50 GR. SPR SP	Hodgdon	Varget	.224"	2.210"	26.5	3242	40,800 CUP	27.5C	3383	44,800 CUP
50 GR. SPR SP	IMR	IMR 4320	.224"	2.210"	24.8	3006	39,400 PSI	27.5C	3270	48,900 PSI
50 GR. SPR SP	Winchester	748	.224"	2.210"				26.0	3200	40,000 CUP
50 GR. SPR SP	Hodgdon	BL-C(2)	.224"	2.210"	26.0	3187	34,200 CUP	28.0	3428	47,100 CUP
50 GR. SPR SP	IMR	IMR 4895	.224"	2.210"	25.2	3118	43,300 PSI	26.7C	3211	45,200 PSI
50 GR. SPR SP	Hodgdon	H335	.224"	2.210"	24.0	3166	43,000 CUP	26.0	3393	51,700 CUP
50 GR. SPR SP	Hodgdon	H4895	.224"	2.210"	25.0	3200	38,300 CUP	27.5C	3468	51,300 CUP
50 GR. SPR SP	IMR	IMR 8208 XBR	.224"	2.210"	23.5	3111	40,500 PSI	25.8	3407	53,300 PSI
50 GR. SPR SP	IMR	IMR 3031	.224"	2.210"	23.5	3169	44,600 PSI	25.0	3268	46,900 PSI
50 GR. SPR SP	Hodgdon	Benchmark	.224"	2.210"	24.0	3139	38,600 CUP	26.5	3396	50,400 CUP
50 GR. SPR SP	Hodgdon	H322	.224"	2.210"	22.0	3018	36,500 CUP	24.0	3301	49,300 CUP
50 GR. SPR SP	IMR	IMR 4198	.224"	2.210"	19.8	3094	42,800 PSI	21.9	3352	52,100 PSI
50 GR. SPR SP	Hodgdon	H4198	.224"	2.210"	19.5	3023	32,400 CUP	21.5	3223	45,900 CUP
53 GR. SIE HP	Hodgdon	CFE 223	.224"	2.200"	27.0	3245	45,900 PSI	28.5	3415	52,900 PSI
53 GR. SIE HP	Hodgdon	Varget	.224"	2.200"	24.0	3026	38,400 CUP	27.0C	3389	47,900 CUP
53 GR. SIE HP	IMR	IMR 4320	.224"	2.200"	24.0	2929	40,400 PSI	27.5C	3273	52,300 PSI
53 GR. SIE HP	IMR	IMR 4064	.224"	2.200"	24.0	2964	41,600 PSI	25.7C	3178	45,600 PSI
53 GR. SIE HP	Winchester	748	.224"	2.200"				26.0	3200	43,500 CUP
53 GR. SIE HP	Hodgdon	BL-C(2)	.224"	2.200"	26.0	3090	36,600 CUP	28.0	3328	47,600 CUP
53 GR. SIE HP	IMR	IMR 4895	.224"	2.200"	24.5	3012	43,900 PSI	26.4C	3238	52,300 PSI
53 GR. SIE HP	Hodgdon	H335	.224"	2.200"	24.0	3060	44,100 CUP	26.0	3300	52,000 CUP
53 GR. SIE HP	Hodgdon	H4895	.224"	2.200"	25.0	3166	37,400 CUP	27.0C	3383	48,600 CUP
53 GR. SIE HP	IMR	IMR 8208 XBR	.224"	2.200"	23.0	3032	41,400 PSI	25.4	3310	53,400 PSI
53 GR. SIE HP	IMR	IMR 3031	.224"	2.200"	22.0	2959	40,700 PSI	24.5C	3260	53,300 PSI
53 GR. SIE HP	Hodgdon	Benchmark	.224"	2.200"	24.0	3102	39,900 CUP	26.0	3308	49,800 CUP
53 GR. SIE HP	Hodgdon	H322	.224"	2.200"	21.5	2912	39,200 CUP	23.5	3183	48,900 CUP
53 GR. SIE HP	IMR	IMR 4198	.224"	2.200"	19.0	2972	43,800 PSI	21.4	3268	48,200 PSI
53 GR. SIE HP	Hodgdon	H4198	.224"	2.200"	19.5	2986	34,200 CUP	21.5	3188	46,700 CUP
55 GR. BAR TSX FB	Hodgdon	CFE 223	.224"	2.180"	24.7	3065	44,600 PSI	27.4	3317	54,000 PSI
55 GR. BAR TSX FB	Hodgdon	Varget	.224"	2.180"	22.8	2996	47,600 PSI	24.0C	3134	53,300 PSI
55 GR. BAR TSX FB	IMR	IMR 4320	.224"	2.180"	22.1	2805	41,900 PSI	24.6	3078	52,100 PSI
55 GR. BAR TSX FB	IMR	IMR 4064	.224"	2.180"	21.2	2871	43,900 PSI	23.5C	3116	52,500 PSI

55 GR. BAR TSX FB	Winchester	748	.224"	2.180"	22.5	2862	39,200 PSI	25.0	3104	48,500 PSI
55 GR. BAR TSX FB	Hodgdon	BL-C(2)	.224"	2.180"	23.4	2888	41,900 PSI	26.0	3135	50,300 PSI
55 GR. BAR TSX FB	IMR	IMR 4895	.224"	2.180"	21.5	2837	43,000 PSI	23.9C	3107	52,300 PSI
55 GR. BAR TSX FB	Hodgdon	H335	.224"	2.180"	21.3	2920	48,900 PSI	22.7	3063	53,000 PSI
55 GR. BAR TSX FB	Hodgdon	H4895	.224"	2.180"	21.0	2910	43,700 PSI	22.6	3110	51,500 PSI
55 GR. BAR TSX FB	IMR	IMR 8208 XBR	.224"	2.180"	21.5	2949	47,600 PSI	23.0	3105	52,900 PSI
55 GR. BAR TSX FB	IMR	IMR 3031	.224"	2.180"	20.0	2878	46,800 PSI	21.3	3024	52,200 PSI
55 GR. BAR TSX FB	Hodgdon	Benchmark	.224"	2.180"	20.0	2885	47,600 PSI	22.2	3066	52,200 PSI
55 GR. BAR TSX FB	Hodgdon	H322	.224"	2.180"	21.0	2953	48,600 PSI	22.4	3083	51,300 PSI
55 GR. HDY FMJ	IMR	Trail Boss	.224"	2.200"				4.0	1074	
55 GR. HDY FMJ	Hodgdon	Titegroup	.224"	2.200"				3.1	1064	4,000 CUP
55 GR. HDY FMJ	Hodgdon	Clays	.224"	2.200"				3.2	1060	3,700 CUP
55 GR. SFIRE	Hodgdon	Varget	.224"	2.220"	23.5	2990	45,200 PSI	25.1C	3149	51,700 PSI
55 GR. SFIRE	IMR	IMR 4320	.224"	2.220"	23.0	2796	39,300 PSI	25.5	3100	51,100 PSI
55 GR. SFIRE	IMR	IMR 4064	.224"	2.220"	21.0	2711	37,100 PSI	23.0C	2945	44,800 PSI
55 GR. SFIRE	Hodgdon	BL-C(2)	.224"	2.220"	24.0	2937	40,800 PSI	27.0	3220	51,500 PSI
55 GR. SFIRE	IMR	IMR 4895	.224"	2.220"	22.0	2827	40,500 PSI	24.6C	3106	50,700 PSI
55 GR. SFIRE	Hodgdon	H335	.224"	2.220"	21.4	2969	47,000 PSI	22.8	3099	51,800 PSI
55 GR. SFIRE	Hodgdon	H4895	.224"	2.220"	22.0	2941	40,600 PSI	24.6C	3226	53,500 PSI
55 GR. SFIRE	Hodgdon	Benchmark	.224"	2.220"	21.0	2903	42,600 PSI	23.4	3128	51,000 PSI
55 GR. SFIRE	Hodgdon	H322	.224"	2.220"	21.0	2894	42,800 PSI	23.1	3113	51,700 PSI
55 GR. SFIRE	Hodgdon	H4198	.224"	2.220"	18.0	2852	42,700 PSI	20.4	3084	51,400 PSI
55 GR. SPR SP	Hodgdon	CFE 223	.224"	2.200"	26.0	3133	43,300 PSI	27.8	3329	51,300 PSI
55 GR. SPR SP	Hodgdon	Varget	.224"	2.200"	25.5	3174	41,300 CUP	27.5C	3384	49,700 CUP
55 GR. SPR SP	IMR	IMR 4320	.224"	2.200"	23.5	2874	41,300 PSI	26.1C	3146	50,700 PSI
55 GR. SPR SP	IMR	IMR 4064	.224"	2.200"	23.0	2867	40,300 PSI	25.7C	3201	52,600 PSI
55 GR. SPR SP	Winchester	748	.224"	2.200"				26.3	3150	39,000 CUP
55 GR. SPR SP	Hodgdon	BL-C(2)	.224"	2.200"	25.5	3069	37,200 CUP	27.5	3313	48,500 CUP
55 GR. SPR SP	IMR	IMR 4895	.224"	2.200"	23.0	2843	39,500 PSI	26.2C	3219	53,200 PSI
55 GR. SPR SP	Hodgdon	H335	.224"	2.200"	23.0	3018	40,800 CUP	25.3	3203	49,300 CUP
55 GR. SPR SP	Hodgdon	H4895	.224"	2.200"	25.0	3176	39,700 CUP	26.0	3315	49,000 CUP
55 GR. SPR SP	IMR	IMR 8208 XBR	.224"	2.200"	23.0	3024	42,100 PSI	25.3	3268	53,100 PSI
55 GR. SPR SP	IMR	IMR 3031	.224"	2.200"	21.6	2907	41,100 PSI	24.6C	3233	52,500 PSI
55 GR. SPR SP	Hodgdon	Benchmark	.224"	2.200"	24.0	3113	42,600 CUP	25.6	3264	50,000 CUP
55 GR. SPR SP	Hodgdon	H322	.224"	2.200"	21.0	2841	38,600 CUP	23.0	3106	48,900 CUP
55 GR. SPR SP	IMR	IMR 4198	.224"	2.200"	18.8	2885	41,600 PSI	20.4	3122	53,600 PSI
55 GR. SPR SP	Hodgdon	H4198	.224"	2.200"	19.0	2841	34,800 CUP	21.0	3150	47,600 CUP
60 GR. HDY V-MAX	Hodgdon	CFE 223	.224"	2.250"	25.0	3007	46,000 PSI	26.7	3176	53,400 PSI
60 GR. HDY V-MAX	Hodgdon	Varget	.224"	2.250"	25.0	2924	40,400 CUP	27.0C	3159	51,900 CUP

15

60 GR. HDY V-MAX	IMR	IMR 4320	.224"	2.250"	23.7	2860	45,400 PSI	25.3C	3006	52,100 PSI
60 GR. HDY V-MAX	IMR	IMR 4064	.224"	2.250"	23.0	2837	42,500 PSI	24.7C	3055	52,600 PSI
60 GR. HDY V-MAX	Hodgdon	BL-C(2)	.224"	2.250"	25.0	2948	44,900 CUP	27.0	3137	51,900 CUP
60 GR. HDY V-MAX	IMR	IMR 4895	.224"	2.250"	23.7	2884	45,000 PSI	25.2C	3052	52,700 PSI
60 GR. HDY V-MAX	Hodgdon	H335	.224"	2.250"	22.5	2910	43,700 CUP	24.0	3075	50,600 CUP
60 GR. HDY V-MAX	Hodgdon	H4895	.224"	2.250"	24.0	2918	37,600 CUP	26.0C	3174	50,100 CUP
60 GR. HDY V-MAX	IMR	IMR 8208 XBR	.224"	2.250"	21.5	2857	43,500 PSI	23.6	3057	51,700 PSI
60 GR. HDY V-MAX	IMR	IMR 3031	.224"	2.250"	21.0	2815	42,500 PSI	22.5	3008	51,700 PSI
60 GR. HDY V-MAX	Hodgdon	Benchmark	.224"	2.250"	23.0	2913	42,500 CUP	24.6	3086	49,900 CUP
60 GR. HDY V-MAX	Hodgdon	H322	.224"	2.250"	22.0	2873	40,300 CUP	23.5	3063	49,800 CUP
60 GR. HDY V-MAX	IMR	IMR 4198	.224"	2.250"	18.3	2795	42,500 PSI	19.5	2945	52,000 PSI
60 GR. HDY V-MAX	Hodgdon	H4198	.224"	2.250"	18.0	2747	42,500 CUP	20.0	2953	47,600 CUP
62 GR. SFT SCIR	Hodgdon	CFE 223	.224"	2.260"	23.8	2884	44,100 PSI	25.9	3110	53,700 PSI
62 GR. SFT SCIR	Hodgdon	Varget	.224"	2.260"	22.1	2773	44,700 PSI	24.1	2974	52,600 PSI
62 GR. SFT SCIR	IMR	IMR 4320	.224"	2.260"	22.7	2729	45,200 PSI	24.4	2920	52,700 PSI
62 GR. SFT SCIR	IMR	IMR 4064	.224"	2.260"	21.9	2671	42,200 PSI	23.6	2928	53,200 PSI
62 GR. SFT SCIR	Winchester	748	.224"	2.260"	22.3	2779	44,600 PSI	24.0	2967	52,400 PSI
62 GR. SFT SCIR	Hodgdon	BL-C(2)	.224"	2.260"	22.5	2772	45,100 PSI	24.2	2949	52,500 PSI
62 GR. SFT SCIR	IMR	IMR 4895	.224"	2.260"	22.4	2782	46,900 PSI	24.1	2956	53,400 PSI
62 GR. SFT SCIR	Hodgdon	H335	.224"	2.260"	19.3	2678	47,500 PSI	21.4	2887	53,600 PSI
62 GR. SFT SCIR	Hodgdon	H4895	.224"	2.260"	21.0	2740	42,300 PSI	23.0	3004	53,000 PSI
62 GR. SFT SCIR	IMR	IMR 8208 XBR	.224"	2.260"	21.4	2787	43,400 PSI	23.2	2999	53,000 PSI
62 GR. SFT SCIR	IMR	IMR 3031	.224"	2.260"	20.3	2700	43,500 PSI	22.0	2940	53,100 PSI
62 GR. SFT SCIR	Hodgdon	Benchmark	.224"	2.260"	20.8	2755	45,400 PSI	22.7	2948	52,800 PSI
62 GR. SFT SCIR	Hodgdon	H322	.224"	2.260"	19.5	2717	45,400 PSI	21.2	2904	52,300 PSI
63 GR. SIE SP	Hodgdon	CFE 223	.224"	2.200"	25.0	2957	46,300 PSI	26.4	3113	53,500 PSI
63 GR. SIE SP	Hodgdon	Varget	.224"	2.200"	24.5	3000	42,400 CUP	26.4C	3199	50,700 CUP
63 GR. SIE SP	IMR	IMR 4320	.224"	2.200"	23.0	2733	42,500 PSI	25.5	2975	52,900 PSI
63 GR. SIE SP	IMR	IMR 4064	.224"	2.200"	22.5	2765	44,400 PSI	24.8C	3028	52,600 PSI
63 GR. SIE SP	Winchester	748	.224"	2.200"				25.0	2970	47,500 CUP
63 GR. SIE SP	Hodgdon	BL-C(2)	.224"	2.200"	24.0	2847	36,600 CUP	26.0	3054	46,300 CUP
63 GR. SIE SP	IMR	IMR 4895	.224"	2.200"	22.9	2758	42,700 PSI	25.3	3054	53,500 PSI
63 GR. SIE SP	Hodgdon	H335	.224"	2.200"	22.5	2820	41,000 CUP	25.0	3051	50,000 CUP
63 GR. SIE SP	Hodgdon	H4895	.224"	2.200"	23.5	2831	43,300 CUP	25.5	3078	50,000 CUP
63 GR. SIE SP	IMR	IMR 8208 XBR	.224"	2.200"	21.0	2783	43,000 PSI	23.1	2995	52,400 PSI
63 GR. SIE SP	IMR	IMR 3031	.224"	2.200"	21.0	2737	42,900 PSI	23.3	3018	53,000 PSI
63 GR. SIE SP	Hodgdon	Benchmark	.224"	2.200"	22.0	2845	41,800 CUP	24.2	3066	50,500 CUP
63 GR. SIE SP	Hodgdon	H322	.224"	2.200"	20.0	2672	38,100 CUP	22.0	2862	48,400 CUP
63 GR. SIE SP	IMR	IMR 4198	.224"	2.200"	18.5	2756	48,100 PSI	20.0	2946	53,500 PSI
63 GR. SIE SP	Hodgdon	H4198	.224"	2.200"	18.0	2680	33,600 CUP	20.0	2846	44,600 CUP

69 GR. SIE HPBT	Hodgdon	CFE 223	.224"	2.235"	23.5	2788	43,800 PSI	25.8	3029	54,600 PSI
69 GR. SIE HPBT	Hodgdon	Varget	.224"	2.235"	24.0	2784	39,200 CUP	26.0C	3010	50,200 CUP
69 GR. SIE HPBT	IMR	IMR 4320	.224"	2.235"	23.0	2673	43,500 PSI	24.8	2873	53,100 PSI
69 GR. SIE HPBT	IMR	IMR 4064	.224"	2.235"	22.5	2690	42,200 PSI	24.0C	2872	50,900 PSI
69 GR. SIE HPBT	Winchester	748	.224"	2.235"				24.5	2870	51,500 CUP
69 GR. SIE HPBT	Hodgdon	BL-C(2)	.224"	2.235"	24.5	2833	40,600 CUP	26.5	3029	50,100 CUP
69 GR. SIE HPBT	IMR	IMR 4895	.224"	2.235"	23.3	2783	44,600 PSI	24.8C	2953	53,600 PSI
69 GR. SIE HPBT	Hodgdon	H335	.224"	2.235"	22.0	2801	42,400 CUP	24.0	2960	49,500 CUP
69 GR. SIE HPBT	Hodgdon	H4895	.224"	2.235"	24.0	2870	41,100 CUP	26.0C	3069	49,700 CUP
69 GR. SIE HPBT	IMR	IMR 8208 XBR	.224"	2.235"	21.0	2696	42,200 PSI	23.8	2959	52,900 PSI
69 GR. SIE HPBT	IMR	IMR 3031	.224"	2.235"	21.0	2707	42,900 PSI	22.5	2906	52,800 PSI
69 GR. SIE HPBT	Hodgdon	Benchmark	.224"	2.235"	21.5	2770	39,700 CUP	23.5	2970	49,700 CUP
69 GR. SIE HPBT	Hodgdon	H322	.224"	2.235"	21.0	2746	40,500 CUP	23.0	2932	49,400 CUP
69 GR. SIE HPBT	IMR	IMR 4198	.224"	2.235"	18.3	2706	46,300 PSI	19.5	2818	52,300 PSI
70 GR. SPR SP	Hodgdon	CFE 223	.224"	2.140"	23.0	2719	45,600 PSI	24.7	2900	53,800 PSI
70 GR. SPR SP	Hodgdon	Varget	.224"	2.140"	23.5	2827	41,000 CUP	26.0C	3024	48,400 CUP
70 GR. SPR SP	IMR	IMR 4320	.224"	2.140"	20.3	2490	38,200 PSI	24.3	2799	52,900 PSI
70 GR. SPR SP	IMR	IMR 4064	.224"	2.140"	19.5	2485	42,000 PSI	23.5C	2831	53,300 PSI
70 GR. SPR SP	Hodgdon	BL-C(2)	.224"	2.140"	24.5	2774	41,700 CUP	26.5	2954	50,800 CUP
70 GR. SPR SP	IMR	IMR 4895	.224"	2.140"	20.2	2562	45,700 PSI	24.5C	2917	52,300 PSI
70 GR. SPR SP	Hodgdon	H335	.224"	2.140"	21.0	2520	34,500 CUP	23.5	2867	47,900 CUP
70 GR. SPR SP	Hodgdon	H4895	.224"	2.140"	23.0	2782	40,400 CUP	25.0	2997	50,500 CUP
70 GR. SPR SP	IMR	IMR 8208 XBR	.224"	2.140"	20.0	2621	44,100 PSI	21.8	2797	52,800 PSI
70 GR. SPR SP	IMR	IMR 3031	.224"	2.140"	19.0	2582	47,200 PSI	21.2	2729	50,900 PSI
70 GR. SPR SP	Hodgdon	Benchmark	.224"	2.140"	20.5	2665	45,200 CUP	22.8	2869	51,000 CUP
70 GR. SPR SP	Hodgdon	H322	.224"	2.140"	19.0	2515	37,500 CUP	23.0	2962	51,200 CUP
75 GR. JLK VLD	IMR	IMR 4007 SSC	.224"	2.250"	23.0	2463	39,400 PSI	26.0C	2780	52,300 PSI
75 GR. JLK VLD	Hodgdon	CFE 223	.224"	2.250"	23.0	2680	45,200 PSI	25.0	2876	54,400 PSI
75 GR. JLK VLD	Hodgdon	Varget	.224"	2.250"	22.5	2693	40,600 CUP	25.0C	2907	48,400 CUP
75 GR. JLK VLD	IMR	IMR 4320	.224"	2.250"	22.5	2554	39,700 PSI	24.2C	2766	53,200 PSI
75 GR. JLK VLD	IMR	IMR 4064	.224"	2.250"	21.0	2531	37,500 PSI	24.0C	2827	53,400 PSI
75 GR. JLK VLD	Hodgdon	BL-C(2)	.224"	2.250"	23.0	2646	39,800 CUP	26.0	2858	49,500 CUP
75 GR. JLK VLD	IMR	IMR 4895	.224"	2.250"	21.2	2506	41,200 PSI	23.8C	2786	51,800 PSI
75 GR. JLK VLD	Hodgdon	H335	.224"	2.250"	21.0	2624	41,300 CUP	23.0	2814	50,000 CUP
75 GR. JLK VLD	Hodgdon	H4895	.224"	2.250"	22.5	2696	39,900 CUP	24.5	2905	50,000 CUP
75 GR. JLK VLD	IMR	IMR 8208 XBR	.224"	2.250"	20.0	2538	40,800 PSI	22.7	2804	53,900 PSI
75 GR. JLK VLD	IMR	IMR 3031	.224"	2.250"	20.0	2543	40,000 PSI	21.8C	2740	53,500 PSI
75 GR. JLK VLD	Hodgdon	Benchmark	.224"	2.250"	21.5	2610	41,900 CUP	23.5	2829	49,400 CUP
75 GR. JLK VLD	Hodgdon	H322	.224"	2.250"	20.0	2594	40,700 CUP	22.0	2785	48,100 CUP

77 GR. SIE HPBT	IMR	IMR 4007 SSC	.224"	2.260"	22.0	2392	40,000 PSI	25.0C	2672	50,500 PSI
77 GR. SIE HPBT	Hodgdon	CFE 223	.224"	2.260"	22.5	2627	45,400 PSI	24.3	2811	53,500 PSI
77 GR. SIE HPBT	Hodgdon	Varget	.224"	2.260"	21.0	2528	42,700 CUP	23.7C	2737	50,700 CUP
77 GR. SIE HPBT	IMR	IMR 4320	.224"	2.260"	20.5	2347	42,000 PSI	23.1C	2654	50,300 PSI
77 GR. SIE HPBT	IMR	IMR 4064	.224"	2.260"	20.0	2397	42,200 PSI	22.7C	2698	53,000 PSI
77 GR. SIE HPBT	Hodgdon	BL-C(2)	.224"	2.260"	23.0	2640	42,500 CUP	24.9	2804	50,700 CUP
77 GR. SIE HPBT	IMR	IMR 4895	.224"	2.260"	20.0	2379	41,800 PSI	23.0C	2708	53,100 PSI
77 GR. SIE HPBT	Hodgdon	H335	.224"	2.260"	21.0	2582	44,400 CUP	22.6	2738	51,700 CUP
77 GR. SIE HPBT	Hodgdon	H4895	.224"	2.260"	20.0	2474	40,300 CUP	22.6C	2727	50,200 CUP
77 GR. SIE HPBT	IMR	IMR 8208 XBR	.224"	2.260"	20.5	2535	41,800 PSI	23.2	2792	55,000 PSI
77 GR. SIE HPBT	IMR	IMR 3031	.224"	2.260"	18.5	2365	42,200 PSI	21.3C	2692	53,700 PSI
77 GR. SIE HPBT	Hodgdon	Benchmark	.224"	2.260"	20.5	2523	27,400 CUP	22.8	2763	50,000 CUP
77 GR. SIE HPBT	Hodgdon	H322	.224"	2.260"	20.0	2578	44,900 CUP	21.8	2721	50,900 CUP
80 GR. SIE MK	IMR	IMR 4007 SSC	.224"	2.550"	22.0	2266	34,100 PSI	25.0C	2558	44,900 PSI
80 GR. SIE MK	Hodgdon	CFE 223	.224"	2.550"	23.0	2638	46,700 PSI	24.4	2785	53,600 PSI
80 GR. SIE MK	Hodgdon	Varget	.224"	2.550"	22.0	2547	40,300 CUP	25.0C	2869	51,500 CUP
80 GR. SIE MK	IMR	IMR 4320	.224"	2.550"	21.5	2484	42,600 PSI	23.1	2647	51,700 PSI
80 GR. SIE MK	IMR	IMR 4064	.224"	2.550"	20.0	2415	39,500 PSI	22.7C	2673	51,900 PSI
80 GR. SIE MK	Hodgdon	BL-C(2)	.224"	2.550"	23.0	2576	39,700 CUP	25.5	2768	49,400 CUP
80 GR. SIE MK	IMR	IMR 4895	.224"	2.550"	20.0	2346	41,300 PSI	23.0C	2708	53,900 PSI
80 GR. SIE MK	Hodgdon	H335	.224"	2.550"	20.0	2453	39,700 CUP	22.5	2744	50,000 CUP
80 GR. SIE MK	Hodgdon	H4895	.224"	2.550"	21.5	2578	40,100 CUP	24.0	2825	50,000 CUP
80 GR. SIE MK	IMR	IMR 8208 XBR	.224"	2.550"	19.0	2456	44,400 PSI	21.0	2628	52,900 PSI
80 GR. SIE MK	IMR	IMR 3031	.224"	2.550"	18.5	2336	42,600 PSI	21.0	2632	51,500 PSI
80 GR. SIE MK	Hodgdon	Benchmark	.224"	2.550"	20.5	2525	43,900 CUP	22.5	2700	49,600 CUP
80 GR. SIE MK	Hodgdon	H322	.224"	2.550"	20.0	2546	40,700 CUP	22.0	2744	49,000 CUP
82 GR. BER BT TARG	Hodgdon	H414	.224"	2.375"	23.2	2478	44,700 PSI	25.0	2667	53,700 PSI
82 GR. BER BT TARG	Winchester	760	.224"	2.375"	23.2	2478	44,700 PSI	25.0	2667	53,700 PSI
82 GR. BER BT TARG	Hodgdon	CFE 223	.224"	2.375"	21.7	2518	44,000 PSI	23.5	2724	53,300 PSI
82 GR. BER BT TARG	Hodgdon	Varget	.224"	2.375"	20.0	2417	44,000 PSI	21.5	2590	52,800 PSI
82 GR. BER BT TARG	IMR	IMR 4320	.224"	2.375"	20.5	2398	45,000 PSI	22.2	2582	53,300 PSI
82 GR. BER BT TARG	Hodgdon	BL-C(2)	.224"	2.375"	21.1	2429	43,300 PSI	22.9	2617	52,200 PSI
82 GR. BER BT TARG	IMR	IMR 4895	.224"	2.375"	20.0	2380	43,100 PSI	21.7	2590	52,700 PSI
82 GR. BER BT TARG	Hodgdon	H4895	.223"	2.375"	18.9	2448	46,500 PSI	20.4	2585	52,700 PSI
82 GR. BER BT TARG	IMR	IMR 8208 XBR	.224"	2.375"	18.4	2392	44,440 PSI	19.9	2554	52,100 PSI
90 GR. SIE HPBT	Hodgdon	H414	.224"	2.380"	22.5	2332	41,700 PSI	24.0	2482	52,100 PSI
90 GR. SIE HPBT	Winchester	760	.224"	2.380"	22.5	2332	41,700 PSI	24.0	2482	52,100 PSI
90 GR. SIE HPBT	Hodgdon	CFE 223	.224"	2.380"	21.0	2391	45,900 PSI	22.8	2554	53,500 PSI
90 GR. SIE HPBT	Hodgdon	Varget	.224"	2.380"	21.0	2332	46,700 PSI	22.3C	2447	52,100 PSI
90 GR. SIE HPBT	IMR	IMR 4320	.224"	2.380"	21.0	2338	47,800 PSI	22.5C	2476	53,800 PSI

90 GR. SIE HPBT	Hodgdon	BL-C(2)	.224"	2.380"	21.0	2291	41,400 PSI	22.5	2491	52,300 PSI
90 GR. SIE HPBT	IMR	IMR 4895	.224"	2.380"	21.0	2356	46,200 PSI	22.5C	2527	53,000 PSI
90 GR. SIE HPBT	Hodgdon	H4895	.224"	2.380"	20.0	2352	47,500 PSI	21.5	2481	53,500 PSI
90 GR. SIE HPBT	IMR	IMR 8208 XBR	.224"	2.380"	18.0	2270	45,600 PSI	19.6	2419	52,800 PSI

| Cartridge: 222 Remington Magnum | | | | | Starting Loads | | | Maximum Loads | | |
| Load Type: Rifle | | | | | | | | | | |
Bullet Weight (Gr.)	Manufacturer	Powder	Bullet Diam.	C.O.L.	Grs.	Vel. (ft/s)	Pressure	Grs.	Vel. (ft/s)	Pressure
40 GR. SIE SP	Hodgdon	BL-C(2)	.224"	2.145"	27.5	3513	37,800 CUP	30.0	3818	49,200 CUP
40 GR. SIE SP	Hodgdon	H335	.224"	2.145"	27.5	3532	39,000 CUP	30.0	3803	47,800 CUP
40 GR. SIE SP	Hodgdon	H4895	.224"	2.145"	26.5	3363	34,800 CUP	29.0	3490	45,400 CUP
40 GR. SIE SP	Hodgdon	H322	.224"	2.145"	25.0	3318	35,300 CUP	27.0	3622	48,400 CUP
40 GR. SIE SP	Hodgdon	H4198	.224"	2.145"	23.0	3592	45,400 CUP	24.5	3760	49,100 CUP
40 GR. SIE SP	Hodgdon	H4227	.224"	2.145"	15.5	2714	29,400 CUP	17.0	3062	36,600 CUP
45 GR. SPR SP	IMR	IMR 4320	.224"	2.220"				28.0	3340	50,000 CUP
45 GR. SPR SP	IMR	IMR 4064	.224"	2.220"				27.0C	3245	49,000 CUP
45 GR. SPR SP	Hodgdon	BL-C(2)	.224"	2.220"	26.0	3302	36,600 CUP	28.0	3664	50,100 CUP
45 GR. SPR SP	IMR	IMR 4895	.224"	2.220"				28.0	3425	49,000 CUP
45 GR. SPR SP	Hodgdon	H335	.224"	2.220"	26.0	3343	37,800 CUP	28.0	3647	49,600 CUP
45 GR. SPR SP	Hodgdon	H4895	.224"	2.220"	26.5	3314	35,400 CUP	29.0	3442	49,700 CUP
45 GR. SPR SP	IMR	IMR 3031	.224"	2.220"				26.5	3425	49,000 CUP
45 GR. SPR SP	Hodgdon	H322	.224"	2.220"	24.5	3159	33,300 CUP	26.5	3532	50,300 CUP
45 GR. SPR SP	IMR	IMR 4198	.224'	2.220"				23.0	3420	50,000 CUP
45 GR. SPR SP	Hodgdon	H4198	.224"	2.220"	22.0	3392	42,400 CUP	24.0	3641	50,200 CUP
45 GR. SPR SP	IMR	SR 4759	.224"	2.220"				17.0	3010	49,200 CUP
50 GR. HDY SP	IMR	IMR 4320	.224"	2.305"				27.5	3260	49,700 CUP
50 GR. HDY SP	IMR	IMR 4064	.224"	2.305"				27.0C	3320	49,300 CUP
50 GR. HDY SP	Winchester	748	.224"	2.305"				27.2	3220	43,000 CUP
50 GR. HDY SP	Hodgdon	BL-C(2)	.224"	2.305"	25.0	3212	38,400 CUP	27.0	3433	47,300 CUP
50 GR. HDY SP	IMR	IMR 4895	.224"	2.305"				27.0	3310	49,500 CUP
50 GR. HDY SP	Hodgdon	H335	.224"	2.305"	25.0	3232	41,400 CUP	27.0	3476	48,200 CUP
50 GR. HDY SP	Hodgdon	H4895	.224"	2.305"	26.0	3166	41,400 CUP	28.5	3306	45,900 CUP
50 GR. HDY SP	IMR	IMR 3031	.224"	2.305"				26.0C	3350	49,000 CUP
50 GR. HDY SP	Hodgdon	H322	.224"	2.305"	24.0	3128	38,100 CUP	26.0	3385	49,300 CUP
50 GR. HDY SP	IMR	IMR 4198	.224"	2.305"				21.5	3255	49,500 CUP
50 GR. HDY SP	Hodgdon	H4198	.224"	2.305"	21.5	3147	39,600 CUP	23.5	3379	45,400 CUP
50 GR. HDY SP	IMR	SR 4759	.224"	2.305"				17.0	2935	49,700 CUP
53 GR. SIE HP	Winchester	748	.224"	2.275"				27.2	3270	45,500 CUP
53 GR. SIE HP	Hodgdon	BL-C(2)	.224"	2.275"	25.0	3074	39,000 CUP	27.0	3313	47,800 CUP

Bullet Weight (Gr.)	Manufacturer	Powder	Bullet Diam.	C.O.L.	Grs.	Vel. (ft/s)	Pressure	Grs.	Vel. (ft/s)	Pressure
53 GR. SIE HP	Hodgdon	H335	.224"	2.275"	25.0	3089	40,000 CUP	27.0	3340	47,600 CUP
53 GR. SIE HP	Hodgdon	H4895	.224"	2.275"	25.5	3137	40,800 CUP	28.0	3272	48,500 CUP
53 GR. SIE HP	Hodgdon	H322	.224"	2.275"	24.0	3014	39,200 CUP	25.0	3285	49,800 CUP
53 GR. SIE HP	Hodgdon	H4198	.224"	2.275"	21.0	3076	38,400 CUP	23.0	3282	45,900 CUP
55 GR. HDY SP	Hodgdon	H414	.224"	2.325"	28.5	2968	35,400 CUP	31.0	3209	44,600 CUP
55 GR. HDY SP	Hodgdon	H380	.224"	2.325"	28.5	2952	39,000 CUP	31.0	3136	44,900 CUP
55 GR. HDY SP	IMR	IMR 4320	.224"	2.325"				27.0	3095	50,200 CUP
55 GR. HDY SP	IMR	IMR 4064	.224"	2.325"				26.5C	3180	50,000 CUP
55 GR. HDY SP	Winchester	748	.224"	2.325"				27.2	3215	42,500 CUP
55 GR. HDY SP	Hodgdon	BL-C(2)	.224"	2.325"	24.5	3021	38,000 CUP	26.5	3240	46,800 CUP
55 GR. HDY SP	IMR	IMR 4895	.224"	2.325"				26.0	3115	49,600 CUP
55 GR. HDY SP	Hodgdon	H335	.224"	2.325"	24.0	3086	39,800 CUP	26.0	3294	48,100 CUP
55 GR. HDY SP	Hodgdon	H4895	.224"	2.325"	25.5	3121	39,000 CUP	28.0	3257	48,900 CUP
55 GR. HDY SP	IMR	IMR 3031	.224"	2.325"				25.5	3215	49,900 CUP
55 GR. HDY SP	Hodgdon	H322	.224"	2.325"	22.5	2867	36,500 CUP	24.5	3191	49,300 CUP
55 GR. HDY SP	IMR	IMR 4198	.224"	2.325"				20.5	3090	50,000 CUP
55 GR. HDY SP	Hodgdon	H4198	.224"	2.325"	21.0	3024	37,800 CUP	23.0	3222	46,300 CUP
55 GR. HDY SP	IMR	SR 4759	.224"	2.325"				16.0	2685	50,000 CUP
63 GR. SIE SP	Hodgdon	H414	.224"	2.280"	27.5	2786	34,200 CUP	30.0	3085	45,400 CUP
63 GR. SIE SP	Hodgdon	H380	.224"	2.280"	27.5	2839	39,000 CUP	30.0	2977	45,200 CUP
63 GR. SIE SP	Hodgdon	BL-C(2)	.224"	2.280"	24.0	2913	39,600 CUP	26.0	3078	49,600 CUP
63 GR. SIE SP	Hodgdon	H335	.224"	2.280"	23.5	2910	41,400 CUP	25.5	3057	49,100 CUP
63 GR. SIE SP	Hodgdon	H4895	.224"	2.280"	24.5	2869	37,800 CUP	26.5	3046	48,400 CUP
63 GR. SIE SP	Hodgdon	H322	.224"	2.280"	21.5	2763	38,100 CUP	23.5	2934	48,900 CUP
63 GR. SIE SP	Hodgdon	H4198	.224"	2.280"	18.5	2845	40,200 CUP	20.5	3019	47,800 CUP

Cartridge: 22 PPC
Load Type: Rifle

Bullet Weight (Gr.)	Manufacturer	Powder	Bullet Diam.	C.O.L.	Starting Loads			Maximum Loads		
					Grs.	Vel. (ft/s)	Pressure	Grs.	Vel. (ft/s)	Pressure
40 GR. NOS BT	Hodgdon	CFE 223	.224"	2.065"	30.0	3321	37,700 CUP	32.0	3545	45,000 CUP
40 GR. NOS BT	Hodgdon	Varget	.224"	2.065"	27.5	3314	36,000 CUP	29.5C	3560	45,700 CUP
40 GR. NOS BT	IMR	IMR 8208 XBR	.224"	2.065"	27.0	3366	38,400 CUP	29.3C	3684	47,000 CUP
40 GR. NOS BT	Hodgdon	Benchmark	.224"	2.065"	27.0	3349	37,500 CUP	30.0	3675	49,200 CUP
50 GR. SPR SP	Hodgdon	CFE 223	.224"	2.065"	30.0	3256	38,600 CUP	32.0	3463	47,900 CUP
50 GR. SPR SP	Hodgdon	Varget	.224"	2.065"	27.5	3205	37,100 CUP	29.5	3408	48,200 CUP
50 GR. SPR SP	Hodgdon	BL-C(2)	.224"	2.065"	29.0	3210	41,500 CUP	30.5	3316	47,000 CUP
50 GR. SPR SP	Hodgdon	H335	.224"	2.065"	26.0	3183	40,900 CUP	28.0	3418	50,000 CUP
50 GR. SPR SP	Hodgdon	H4895	.224"	2.065"	26.0	2989	37,100 CUP	28.0	3347	46,500 CUP
50 GR. SPR SP	IMR	IMR 8208 XBR	.224"	2.065"	26.0	3213	40,600 CUP	28.8C	3507	50,400 CUP
50 GR. SPR SP	Hodgdon	Benchmark	.224"	2.065"	27.0	3204	40,000 CUP	29.0	3430	49,600 CUP

Bullet Weight (Gr.)	Manufacturer	Powder	Bullet Diam.	C.O.L.	Grs.	Vel. (ft/s)	Pressure	Grs.	Vel. (ft/s)	Pressure
50 GR. SPR SP	Hodgdon	H322	.224"	2.065"	25.0	3204	42,000 CUP	26.0	3385	48,000 CUP
53 GR. HDY HP	Hodgdon	CFE 223	.224"	2.065"	30.0	3253	40,200 CUP	32.0	3478	50,200 CUP
53 GR. HDY HP	Hodgdon	Varget	.224"	2.065"	26.5	3179	39,100 CUP	28.5	3363	48,900 CUP
53 GR. HDY HP	Hodgdon	BL-C(2)	.224"	2.065"	29.0	3152	44,500 CUP	30.5	3288	48,000 CUP
53 GR. HDY HP	Hodgdon	H335	.224"	2.065"	25.5	3107	42,500 CUP	27.5	3344	49,000 CUP
53 GR. HDY HP	Hodgdon	H4895	.224"	2.065"	26.0	3079	41,500 CUP	28.0	3321	49,000 CUP
53 GR. HDY HP	IMR	IMR 8208 XBR	.224"	2.065"	25.5	3112	37,300 CUP	28.2	3418	48,700 CUP
53 GR. HDY HP	Hodgdon	Benchmark	.224"	2.065"	26.5	3141	40,200 CUP	28.5	3368	49,400 CUP
53 GR. HDY HP	Hodgdon	H322	.224"	2.065"	24.0	3046	39,800 CUP	26.0	3333	48,500 CUP
55 GR. SPR SP	Hodgdon	CFE 223	.224"	2.050"	30.0	3221	39,600 CUP	32.0	3417	48,600 CUP
55 GR. SPR SP	Hodgdon	Varget	.224"	2.050"	26.5	3147	43,600 CUP	28.5	3317	47,800 CUP
55 GR. SPR SP	Hodgdon	BL-C(2)	.224"	2.050"	28.5	3091	42,500 CUP	30.0	3285	50,000 CUP
55 GR. SPR SP	Hodgdon	H335	.224"	2.050"	24.5	2951	39,800 CUP	26.5	3216	47,500 CUP
55 GR. SPR SP	Hodgdon	H4895	.224"	2.050"	26.0	3047	42,000 CUP	28.0	3346	50,000 CUP
55 GR. SPR SP	IMR	IMR 8208 XBR	.224"	2.050"	25.0	3006	35,400 CUP	28.0	3362	48,600 CUP
55 GR. SPR SP	Hodgdon	Benchmark	.224"	2.050"	26.0	3080	39,900 CUP	28.2	3310	49,600 CUP
55 GR. SPR SP	Hodgdon	H322	.224"	2.050"	24.0	3052	41,400 CUP	26.0	3306	50,000 CUP

Cartridge: 22 BR Remington
Load Type: Rifle

Bullet Weight (Gr.)	Manufacturer	Powder	Bullet Diam.	C.O.L.	Starting Loads			Maximum Loads		
					Grs.	Vel. (ft/s)	Pressure	Grs.	Vel. (ft/s)	Pressure
40 GR. NOS BT	Hodgdon	Varget	.224"	2.090"	31.5	3558	36,500 CUP	33.5	3788	43,500 CUP
40 GR. NOS BT	Hodgdon	BL-C(2)	.224"	2.090"	32.5	3571	40,700 CUP	34.9	3814	48,700 CUP
40 GR. NOS BT	Hodgdon	H335	.224"	2.090"	29.5	3555	42,300 CUP	31.5	3744	49,200 CUP
40 GR. NOS BT	Hodgdon	H4895	.224"	2.090"	31.0	3594	38,300 CUP	32.8	3834	46,400 CUP
40 GR. NOS BT	Hodgdon	Benchmark	.224"	2.090"	30.0	3542	41,400 CUP	32.0	3816	49,200 CUP
40 GR. NOS BT	Hodgdon	H322	.224"	2.090"	28.0	3561	38,000 CUP	30.0	3795	49,000 CUP
40 GR. NOS BT	Hodgdon	H4198	.224"	2.090"	25.5	3645	43,200 CUP	27.6	3859	50,400 CUP
45 GR. SPR SP	Hodgdon	Varget	.224"	1.945"	31.5	3502	36,800 CUP	33.5	3693	43,600 CUP
45 GR. SPR SP	Hodgdon	BL-C(2)	.224"	1.945"	34.0	3369	40,400 CUP	36.0	3746	48,000 CUP
45 GR. SPR SP	Hodgdon	H335	.224"	1.945"	31.0	3441	41,200 CUP	33.0	3759	48,600 CUP
45 GR. SPR SP	Hodgdon	H4895	.224"	1.945"	30.0	3429	41,600 CUP	32.5	3768	49,000 CUP
45 GR. SPR SP	Hodgdon	Benchmark	.224"	1.945"	29.5	3486	41,100 CUP	31.6	3702	48,900 CUP
45 GR. SPR SP	Hodgdon	H322	.224"	1.945"	29.0	3409	41,000 CUP	31.5	3741	49,400 CUP
50 GR. SPR SP	Hodgdon	Varget	.224"	1.945"	31.5	3426	38,900 CUP	33.5	3624	44,600 CUP
50 GR. SPR SP	Hodgdon	BL-C(2)	.224"	1.945"	33.5	3440	41,400 CUP	35.5	3649	49,000 CUP
50 GR. SPR SP	Hodgdon	H335	.224"	1.945"	30.0	3419	40,600 CUP	32.0	3628	48,800 CUP
50 GR. SPR SP	Hodgdon	H4895	.224"	1.945"	29.5	3404	41,200 CUP	32.0	3606	48,000 CUP
50 GR. SPR SP	Hodgdon	Benchmark	.224"	1.945"	29.5	3398	40,400 CUP	31.5	3618	49,700 CUP

Bullet Weight	Manufacturer	Powder	Bullet Diam.	C.O.L.	Grs.	Vel. (ft/s)	Pressure	Grs.	Vel. (ft/s)	Pressure
50 GR. SPR SP	Hodgdon	H322	.224"	1.945"	28.0	3292	37,000 CUP	30.5	3637	50,000 CUP
53 GR. HDY HP	Hodgdon	Varget	.224"	2.065"	31.0	3425	43,400 CUP	33.0	3638	51,100 CUP
53 GR. HDY HP	Hodgdon	BL-C(2)	.224"	2.065"	32.5	3403	41,200 CUP	35.0	3592	48,800 CUP
53 GR. HDY HP	Hodgdon	H335	.224"	2.065"	29.5	3371	40,400 CUP	31.5	3587	49,200 CUP
53 GR. HDY HP	Hodgdon	H4895	.224"	2.065"	29.5	3377	41,900 CUP	31.5	3566	49,000 CUP
53 GR. HDY HP	Hodgdon	Benchmark	.224"	2.065"	28.5	3305	41,200 CUP	30.5	3523	49,200 CUP
53 GR. HDY HP	Hodgdon	H322	.224"	2.065"	28.0	3270	38,000 CUP	30.0	3544	48,400 CUP
55 GR. SPR SP	Hodgdon	Varget	.224"	2.050"	30.0	3308	41,600 CUP	32.5	3530	49,300 CUP
55 GR. SPR SP	Hodgdon	BL-C(2)	.224"	2.050"	32.5	3329	41,500 CUP	34.5	3531	48,200 CUP
55 GR. SPR SP	Hodgdon	H335	.224"	2.050"	29.5	3269	40,800 CUP	31.5	3489	49,800 CUP
55 GR. SPR SP	Hodgdon	H4895	.224"	2.050"	29.0	3212	37,100 CUP	31.0	3478	49,400 CUP
55 GR. SPR SP	Hodgdon	Benchmark	.224"	2.050"	28.5	3302	41,600 CUP	30.5	3470	49,600 CUP
55 GR. SPR SP	Hodgdon	H322	.224"	2.050"	28.0	3219	40,000 CUP	30.0	3439	48,800 CUP
63 GR. SIE SP	Hodgdon	Varget	.224"	2.015"	28.5	3134	44,500 CUP	30.5	3307	49,300 CUP
63 GR. SIE SP	Hodgdon	BL-C(2)	.224"	2.015"	31.0	3049	40,200 CUP	33.0	3298	48,400 CUP
63 GR. SIE SP	Hodgdon	H335	.224"	2.015"	26.5	3032	41,400 CUP	29.0	3290	49,900 CUP
63 GR. SIE SP	Hodgdon	H4895	.224"	2.015"	26.0	2994	41,600 CUP	28.0	3146	49,400 CUP
63 GR. SIE SP	Hodgdon	Benchmark	.224"	2.015"	27.0	3088	42,000 CUP	29.0	3270	49,300 CUP
63 GR. SIE SP	Hodgdon	H322	.224"	2.015"	24.0	2962	40,800 CUP	26.5	3120	48,800 CUP
70 GR. SPR SP	Hodgdon	Varget	.224"	1.900"	26.0	2858	43,000 CUP	28.0	3035	49,500 CUP
70 GR. SPR SP	Hodgdon	BL-C(2)	.224"	1.900"	26.5	2811	41,200 CUP	28.5	3009	49,500 CUP
70 GR. SPR SP	Hodgdon	H335	.224"	1.900"	24.0	2740	41,600 CUP	26.0	2959	49,900 CUP
70 GR. SPR SP	Hodgdon	H4895	.224"	1.900"	23.0	2707	41,400 CUP	24.5	2845	50,000 CUP
70 GR. SPR SP	Hodgdon	Benchmark	.224"	1.900"	26.0	2919	43,400 CUP	28.0	3095	49,700 CUP
70 GR. SPR SP	Hodgdon	H322	.224"	1.900"	22.0	2696	40,000 CUP	24.0	2889	49,900 CUP

Cartridge: 224 Weatherby Magnum
Load Type: Rifle

Bullet Weight (Gr.)	Manufacturer	Powder	Bullet Diam.	C.O.L.	Starting Loads			Maximum Loads		
					Grs.	Vel. (ft/s)	Pressure	Grs.	Vel. (ft/s)	Pressure
45 GR. SIE SP	Hodgdon	H414	.224"	2.375"	34.5	3420		36.5	3631	
45 GR. SIE SP	Hodgdon	H380	.224"	2.375"	32.0	3425		35.0	3731	
45 GR. SIE SP	Hodgdon	BL-C(2)	.224"	2.375"	29.5	3457		32.0	3808	
45 GR. SIE SP	Hodgdon	H335	.224"	2.375"	29.5	3447		32.0	3865	
45 GR. SIE SP	Hodgdon	H4895	.224"	2.375"	29.5	3419		32.0	3861	
50 GR. HDY SP	Hodgdon	H414	.224"	2.375"	34.0	3415		36.0	3602	
50 GR. HDY SP	Hodgdon	H380	.224"	2.375"	31.0	3232		34.0	3705	
50 GR. HDY SP	Hodgdon	BL-C(2)	.224"	2.375"	29.0	3427		31.5	3723	
50 GR. HDY SP	Hodgdon	H335	.224"	2.375"	28.5	3298		31.0	3607	
50 GR. HDY SP	Hodgdon	H4895	.224"	2.375"	28.5	3199		31.0	3648	
53 GR. SIE HP	Hodgdon	H414	.224"	2.310"	33.5	3352		35.5	3525	

Bullet Weight (Gr.)	Manufacturer	Powder	Bullet Diam.	C.O.L.	Grs.	Vel. (ft/s)	Pressure	Grs.	Vel. (ft/s)	Pressure
53 GR. SIE HP	Hodgdon	H380	.224"	2.310"	29.5	3111		32.0	3482	
53 GR. SIE HP	Hodgdon	BL-C(2)	.224"	2.310"	26.5	2945		29.0	3493	
53 GR. SIE HP	Hodgdon	H335	.224"	2.310"	26.0	2894		28.5	3462	
53 GR. SIE HP	Hodgdon	H4895	.224"	2.310"	27.5	3032		30.0	3522	
55 GR. HDY SP	Hodgdon	H4831	.224"	2.375"	31.5	2834		34.0	3200	
55 GR. HDY SP	Hodgdon	H4350	.224"	2.375"	32.0	2879		34.0	3240	
55 GR. HDY SP	Hodgdon	H414	.224"	2.375"	33.0	3242		35.0	3497	
55 GR. HDY SP	Hodgdon	H380	.224"	2.375"	29.5	3045		32.0	3461	
55 GR. HDY SP	Hodgdon	BL-C(2)	.224"	2.375"	26.5	2910		28.0	3341	
55 GR. HDY SP	Hodgdon	H335	.224"	2.375"	27.5	3033		29.0	3367	
55 GR. HDY SP	Hodgdon	H4895	.224"	2.375"	27.5	2971		30.0	3503	
60 GR. HDY SP	Hodgdon	H4831	.224"	2.375"	31.0	2781		33.5	3041	
60 GR. HDY SP	Hodgdon	H4350	.224"	2.375"	31.0	2832		34.0	3240	
60 GR. HDY SP	Hodgdon	H414	.224"	2.375"	31.0	2958		33.0	3245	
60 GR. HDY SP	Hodgdon	H380	.224"	2.375"	28.5	2931		31.0	3281	
60 GR. HDY SP	Hodgdon	BL-C(2)	.224"	2.375"	26.0	2894		28.0	3178	
60 GR. HDY SP	Hodgdon	H335	.224"	2.375"	26.0	2873		28.0	3147	
60 GR. HDY SP	Hodgdon	H4895	.224"	2.375"	26.0	2792		28.0	3205	
70 GR. SPR SP	Hodgdon	H4831	.224"	2.310"	30.0	2395		32.0	2486	
70 GR. SPR SP	Hodgdon	H4350	.224"	2.310"	30.0	2644		32.0	2777	
70 GR. SPR SP	Hodgdon	H414	.224"	2.310"	29.0	2847		31.0	2969	
70 GR. SPR SP	Hodgdon	H380	.224"	2.310"	27.0	2804		29.0	2914	

Cartridge: 219 Wasp — Load Type: Rifle					Starting Loads			Maximum Loads		
Bullet Weight (Gr.)	Manufacturer	Powder	Bullet Diam.	C.O.L.	Grs.	Vel. (ft/s)	Pressure	Grs.	Vel. (ft/s)	Pressure
40 GR. SIE SP	Hodgdon	H4895	.224"	2.130"				28.0	3312	
55 GR. HDY SP	Hodgdon	H4895	.224"	2.130"				28.0	3501	

Cartridge: 225 Winchester — Load Type: Rifle					Starting Loads			Maximum Loads		
Bullet Weight (Gr.)	Manufacturer	Powder	Bullet Diam.	C.O.L.	Grs.	Vel. (ft/s)	Pressure	Grs.	Vel. (ft/s)	Pressure
40 GR. SPR SP	Hodgdon	H414	.224"	2.370"	36.0	3404	32,400 CUP	39.0	3829	43,300 CUP
40 GR. SPR SP	Winchester	760	.224"	2.370"	36.0	3404	32,400 CUP	39.0	3829	43,300 CUP
40 GR. SPR SP	Hodgdon	BL-C(2)	.224"	2.370"	33.0	3772	46,400 CUP	36.0	4020	49,200 CUP
40 GR. SPR SP	Hodgdon	H4895	.224"	2.370"	31.5	3583	39,600 CUP	34.0	3811	48,200 CUP
40 GR. SPR SP	Hodgdon	H322	.224"	2.370"	28.0	3628	39,700 CUP	31.0	3896	49,800 CUP
45 GR. HDY SP	Hodgdon	H414	.224"	2.425"	35.5	3473	38,400 CUP	38.5	3696	45,400 CUP
45 GR. HDY SP	Winchester	760	.224"	2.425"	35.5	3473	38,400 CUP	38.5	3696	45,400 CUP
45 GR. HDY SP	Hodgdon	H380	.224"	2.425"	34.0	3451	43,200 CUP	37.0	3749	47,300 CUP

45 GR. HDY SP	Hodgdon	BL-C(2)	.224"	2.425"	32.0	3535	42,600 CUP	35.0	3890	47,300 CUP
45 GR. HDY SP	Hodgdon	H4895	.224"	2.425"	31.0	3504	39,600 CUP	33.5	3736	49,300 CUP
45 GR. HDY SP	Hodgdon	H322	.224"	2.425"	27.0	3303	36,500 CUP	30.0	3685	50,000 CUP
50 GR. SIE SP	Hodgdon	H414	.224"	2.400"	35.5	3389	40,400 CUP	38.5	3702	47,600 CUP
50 GR. SIE SP	Winchester	760	.224"	2.400"	35.5	3389	40,400 CUP	38.5	3702	47,600 CUP
50 GR. SIE SP	Hodgdon	H380	.224"	2.400"	33.0	3394	44,400 CUP	36.0	3659	47,300 CUP
50 GR. SIE SP	Hodgdon	BL-C(2)	.224"	2.400"	32.0	3342	43,200 CUP	35.0	3768	49,300 CUP
50 GR. SIE SP	Hodgdon	H335	.224"	2.400"	31.5	3337	43,000 CUP	34.5	3721	49,100 CUP
50 GR. SIE SP	Hodgdon	H4895	.224"	2.400"	31.0	3330	38,400 CUP	34.0	3722	48,400 CUP
50 GR. SIE SP	Hodgdon	H322	.224"	2.400"	26.0	3164	37,500 CUP	29.0	3401	48,900 CUP
52 GR. SPR SP	Hodgdon	H414	.224"	2.500"	35.5	3334	41,400 CUP	38.5	3662	49,600 CUP
52 GR. SPR SP	Winchester	760	.224"	2.500"	35.5	3334	41,400 CUP	38.5	3662	49,600 CUP
52 GR. SPR SP	Hodgdon	H380	.224"	2.500"	32.5	3316	42,600 CUP	35.0	3542	49,600 CUP
52 GR. SPR SP	Hodgdon	BL-C(2)	.224"	2.500"	31.5	3282	43,200 CUP	34.0	3656	50,100 CUP
52 GR. SPR SP	Hodgdon	H335	.224"	2.500"	31.5	3271	42,600 CUP	34.0	3662	50,000 CUP
52 GR. SPR SP	Hodgdon	H4895	.224"	2.500"	29.5	3239	37,200 CUP	32.0	3463	49,600 CUP
52 GR. SPR SP	Hodgdon	H322	.224"	2.500"	26.0	3128	39,200 CUP	28.5	3333	48,000 CUP
55 GR. HDY SP	Hodgdon	H4350	.224"	2.420"	35.0	2970	37,600 CUP	37.0	3189	46,000 CUP
55 GR. HDY SP	Hodgdon	H414	.224"	2.420"	35.0	3287	39,600 CUP	38.0	3596	47,600 CUP
55 GR. HDY SP	Winchester	760	.224"	2.420"	35.0	3287	39,600 CUP	38.0	3596	47,600 CUP
55 GR. HDY SP	Hodgdon	H380	.224"	2.420"	32.5	3196	43,200 CUP	35.0	3493	46,900 CUP
55 GR. HDY SP	Hodgdon	BL-C(2)	.224"	2.420"	31.5	3220	43,200 CUP	34.0	3643	49,400 CUP
55 GR. HDY SP	Hodgdon	H335	.224"	2.420"	31.0	3192	42,600 CUP	33.5	3601	48,700 CUP
55 GR. HDY SP	Hodgdon	H4895	.224"	2.420"	29.5	3159	36,000 CUP	32.0	3476	48,000 CUP
55 GR. HDY SP	Hodgdon	H322	.224"	2.420"	25.5	3052	38,600 CUP	28.0	3283	48,900 CUP
60 GR. HDY SP	Hodgdon	H4350	.224"	2.410"	34.0	2911	37,000 CUP	36.0	3120	44,400 CUP
60 GR. HDY SP	Hodgdon	H414	.224"	2.410"	34.0	3124	39,600 CUP	37.0	3408	49,100 CUP
60 GR. HDY SP	Winchester	760	.224"	2.410"	34.0	3124	39,600 CUP	37.0	3408	49,100 CUP
60 GR. HDY SP	Hodgdon	H380	.224"	2.410"	32.0	3133	45,000 CUP	35.0	3387	48,500 CUP
60 GR. HDY SP	Hodgdon	BL-C(2)	.224"	2.410"	30.5	3235	45,000 CUP	33.0	3428	48,700 CUP
60 GR. HDY SP	Hodgdon	H335	.224"	2.410"	30.0	3197	44,600 CUP	32.5	3404	48,000 CUP
60 GR. HDY SP	Hodgdon	H4895	.224"	2.410"	29.0	3125	43,200 CUP	32.0	3396	49,000 CUP
70 GR. SPR SP	Hodgdon	H4350	.224"	2.310"	32.0	2696	39,100 CUP	35.0	2949	47,800 CUP
70 GR. SPR SP	Hodgdon	H414	.224"	2.310"	31.5	2759	38,100 CUP	33.5	2940	47,200 CUP
70 GR. SPR SP	Winchester	760	.224"	2.310"	31.5	2759	38,100 CUP	33.5	2940	47,200 CUP

Cartridge: 22-250 Remington Load Type: Rifle						Starting Loads			Maximum Loads	
Bullet Weight (Gr.)	Manufacturer	Powder	Bullet Diam.	C.O.L.	Grs.	Vel. (ft/s)	Pressure	Grs.	Vel. (ft/s)	Pressure
35 GR. NOS LF	Hodgdon	Varget	.224"	2.350"	35.6	3929	42,900 PSI	39.5C	4421	61,000 PSI

35 GR. NOS LF	IMR	IMR 4320	.224"	2.350"	37.5	4084	50,600 PSI	39.9	4393	61,600 PSI
35 GR. NOS LF	IMR	IMR 4064	.224"	2.350"	34.7	3855	41,200 PSI	38.5C	4342	56,400 PSI
35 GR. NOS LF	IMR	IMR 4895	.224"	2.350"	36.8	4087	48,400 PSI	39.2	4396	59,900 PSI
35 GR. NOS LF	Hodgdon	H4895	.224"	2.350"	34.1	4120	47,200 PSI	37.5C	4432	58,200 PSI
35 GR. NOS LF	IMR	IMR 8208 XBR	.224"	2.350"	35.1	4096	46,900 PSI	39.0	4469	60,700 PSI
35 GR. NOS LF	IMR	IMR 3031	.224"	2.350"	32.9	4016	44,300 PSI	35.0	4306	55,600 PSI
35 GR. NOS LF	Hodgdon	Benchmark	.224"	2.350"	35.7	4170	48,700 PSI	38.0	4476	62,600 PSI
36 GR. BAR VG FB	Hodgdon	Varget	.224"	2.350"	37.8	4061	50,800 PSI	40.2C	4277	59,800 PSI
36 GR. BAR VG FB	IMR	IMR 4320	.224"	2.350"	37.1	3995	49,800 PSI	39.5	4254	59,600 PSI
36 GR. BAR VG FB	IMR	IMR 4064	.224"	2.350"	35.7	3976	48,300 PSI	38.0C	4202	55,700 PSI
36 GR. BAR VG FB	IMR	IMR 4895	.224"	2.350"	37.1	4063	50,900 PSI	40.0C	4367	63,100 PSI
36 GR. BAR VG FB	Hodgdon	H4895	.224"	2.350"	36.6	4130	50,700 PSI	39.0C	4376	61,400 PSI
36 GR. BAR VG FB	IMR	IMR 8208 XBR	.224"	2.350"	36.5	4137	50,700 PSI	38.8	4404	62,300 PSI
36 GR. BAR VG FB	IMR	IMR 3031	.224"	2.350"	33.7	3953	45,500 PSI	35.8	4333	61,500 PSI
36 GR. BAR VG FB	Hodgdon	Benchmark	.224"	2.350"	35.6	4108	51,700 PSI	37.8	4335	61,100 PSI
40 GR. NOS BT	Hodgdon	H414	.224"	2.350"	38.0	3644	39,600 CUP	41.0	3933	47,100 CUP
40 GR. NOS BT	Winchester	760	.224"	2.350"	38.0	3644	39,600 CUP	41.0	3933	47,100 CUP
40 GR. NOS BT	IMR	IMR 4007 SSC	.224"	2.350"	37.8	3649	41,100 PSI	40.2C	3973	50,900 PSI
40 GR. NOS BT	Hodgdon	H380	.224"	2.350"	38.0	3647	34,500 CUP	41.0	3855	39,200 CUP
40 GR. NOS BT	Hodgdon	CFE 223	.224"	2.350"	40.0	4036	47,600 PSI	43.0C	4328	58,300 PSI
40 GR. NOS BT	Hodgdon	Varget	.224"	2.350"	37.5	3936	43,400 CUP	39.5	4135	51,100 CUP
40 GR. NOS BT	IMR	IMR 4320	.224"	2.350"	37.0	3945	52,400 PSI	39.5	4201	62,600 PSI
40 GR. NOS BT	IMR	IMR 4064	.224"	2.350"	36.0	3877	47,700 PSI	38.5C	4187	60,500 PSI
40 GR. NOS BT	IMR	IMR 4895	.224"	2.350"	36.0	3807	45,500 PSI	39.0C	4189	60,200 PSI
40 GR. NOS BT	Hodgdon	H4895	.224"	2.350"	34.0	3750	43,800 CUP	37.0	4060	48,700 CUP
40 GR. NOS BT	IMR	IMR 8208 XBR	.224"	2.350"	35.0	3944	47,000 PSI	39.0	4336	63,500 PSI
40 GR. NOS BT	IMR	IMR 3031	.224"	2.350"	34.0	3941	50,200 PSI	36.3	4224	62,100 PSI
40 GR. NOS BT	Hodgdon	Benchmark	.224"	2.350"	34.0	3837	41,600 CUP	36.5	4114	50,100 CUP
45 GR. BAR XBT	Hodgdon	H414	.224"	2.340"	38.0	3537	40,200 CUP	41.0	3899	47,600 CUP
45 GR. BAR XBT	Winchester	760	.224"	2.350"	38.0	3537	40,200 CUP	41.0	3899	47,600 CUP
45 GR. BAR XBT	Hodgdon	H380	.224"	2.340"	38.0	3612	37,900 CUP	41.0	3839	43,500 CUP
45 GR. BAR XBT	Hodgdon	Varget	.224"	2.340"	35.0	3652	46,000 CUP	38.0	3921	49,200 CUP
45 GR. BAR XBT	IMR	IMR 4320	.224"	2.340"	36.0	3780	53,100 PSI	38.2	3990	62,500 PSI
45 GR. BAR XBT	IMR	IMR 4064	.224"	2.340"	35.0	3708	48,700 PSI	38.0C	4042	63,000 PSI
45 GR. BAR XBT	Hodgdon	BL-C(2)	.224"	2.340"	32.0	3612	42,600 CUP	35.0	3928	49,100 CUP
45 GR. BAR XBT	IMR	IMR 4895	.224"	2.340"	35.0	3666	47,400 PSI	38.0	4007	61,700 PSI
45 GR. BAR XBT	Hodgdon	H335	.224"	2.340"	31.5	3593	41,400 CUP	34.5	3908	48,500 CUP
45 GR. BAR XBT	Hodgdon	H4895	.224"	2.340"	34.0	3660	47,300 CUP	37.0	3918	49,100 CUP
45 GR. BAR XBT	IMR	IMR 3031	.224"	2.340"	33.0	3704	47,600 PSI	35.2	4015	62,300 PSI

45 GR. BAR XBT	Hodgdon	Benchmark	.224"	2.340"	33.5	3786	45,300 CUP	36.0	3979	51,000 CUP
45 GR. BAR XBT	Hodgdon	H322	.224"	2.340"	31.0	3490	44,600 CUP	32.5	3720	48,500 CUP
50 GR. SIE SP	Hodgdon	H4350	.224"	2.350"	39.0	3410	43,600 CUP	42.0	3579	48,900 CUP
50 GR. SIE SP	Hodgdon	H414	.224"	2.350"	37.0	3494	41,400 CUP	40.0	3765	48,600 CUP
50 GR. SIE SP	Winchester	760	.224"	2.350"	37.0	3494	41,400 CUP	40.0	3765	48,600 CUP
50 GR. SIE SP	IMR	IMR 4007 SSC	.224"	2.350"	37.8	3647	51,400 PSI	40.2C	3945	63,100 PSI
50 GR. SIE SP	Hodgdon	H380	.224"	2.350"	38.0	3562	41,700 CUP	41.0	3742	45,300 CUP
50 GR. SIE SP	Hodgdon	CFE 223	.224"	2.350"	37.0	3702	51,100 PSI	39.8	3968	62,600 PSI
50 GR. SIE SP	Hodgdon	Varget	.224"	2.350"	34.5	3596	43,600 CUP	37.5	3834	50,400 CUP
50 GR. SIE SP	IMR	IMR 4320	.224"	2.350"	35.0	3582	50,200 PSI	38.0	3864	62,800 PSI
50 GR. SIE SP	IMR	IMR 4064	.224"	2.350"	34.5	3560	47,900 PSI	37.0	3866	61,900 PSI
50 GR. SIE SP	Hodgdon	BL-C(2)	.224"	2.350"	31.5	3506	43,600 CUP	34.5	3740	48,400 CUP
50 GR. SIE SP	IMR	IMR 4895	.224"	2.350"	35.0	3587	49,100 PSI	37.6	3862	61,500 PSI
50 GR. SIE SP	Hodgdon	H335	.224"	2.350"	31.5	3519	44,400 CUP	34.5	3753	48,700 CUP
50 GR. SIE SP	Hodgdon	H4895	.224"	2.350"	33.5	3530	43,800 CUP	36.5	3827	50,200 CUP
50 GR. SIE SP	IMR	IMR 8208 XBR	.224"	2.350"	33.0	3728	55,200 PSI	36.0	3925	62,900 PSI
50 GR. SIE SP	IMR	IMR 3031	.224"	2.350"	33.0	3601	49,500 PSI	35.0	3862	62,600 PSI
50 GR. SIE SP	Hodgdon	Benchmark	.224"	2.350"	33.5	3718	45,900 CUP	36.0	3903	51,400 CUP
50 GR. SIE SP	Hodgdon	H322	.224"	2.350"	30.0	3441	46,200 CUP	32.0	3628	50,300 CUP
52 GR. HDY A-MAX	Hodgdon	H4350	.224"	2.350"	39.0	3402	43,800 CUP	41.0	3557	49,400 CUP
52 GR. HDY A-MAX	Hodgdon	H414	.224"	2.350"	37.0	3461	42,000 CUP	40.0	3692	48,900 CUP
52 GR. HDY A-MAX	Winchester	760	.224"	2.350"	37.0	3461	42,000 CUP	40.0	3692	48,900 CUP
52 GR. HDY A-MAX	IMR	IMR 4007 SSC	.224"	2.350"	36.0	3407	47,100 PSI	40.0C	3775	62,700 PSI
52 GR. HDY A-MAX	Hodgdon	H380	.224"	2.350"	38.0	3509	41,900 CUP	41.0	3717	46,600 CUP
52 GR. HDY A-MAX	Hodgdon	CFE 223	.224"	2.350"	36.0	3596	47,600 PSI	39.3	3932	63,100 PSI
52 GR. HDY A-MAX	Hodgdon	Varget	.224"	2.350"	34.0	3630	45,500 CUP	36.0	3784	50,000 CUP
52 GR. HDY A-MAX	IMR	IMR 4320	.224"	2.350"	35.0	3550	52,000 PSI	37.5	3789	62,400 PSI
52 GR. HDY A-MAX	IMR	IMR 4064	.224"	2.350"	34.5	3538	50,200 PSI	36.9C	3795	62,400 PSI
52 GR. HDY A-MAX	Hodgdon	BL-C(2)	.224"	2.350"	31.0	3461	44,600 CUP	34.0	3702	49,700 CUP
52 GR. HDY A-MAX	IMR	IMR 4895	.224"	2.350"	34.5	3509	48,200 PSI	37.0	3808	62,000 PSI
52 GR. HDY A-MAX	Hodgdon	H335	.224"	2.350"	31.0	3417	43,200 CUP	33.5	3657	49,200 CUP
52 GR. HDY A-MAX	Hodgdon	H4895	.224"	2.350"	32.5	3467	44,400 CUP	35.5	3729	49,600 CUP
52 GR. HDY A-MAX	IMR	IMR 8208 XBR	.224"	2.350"	32.5	3612	52,200 PSI	35.5	3837	60,100 PSI
52 GR. HDY A-MAX	IMR	IMR 3031	.224"	2.350"	32.0	3474	48,000 PSI	34.0	3768	62,500 PSI
52 GR. HDY A-MAX	Hodgdon	Benchmark	.224"	2.350"	32.5	3602	45,800 CUP	34.6	3755	49,800 CUP
52 GR. HDY A-MAX	Hodgdon	H322	.224"	2.350"	29.0	3379	45,500 CUP	31.0	3498	48,000 CUP
55 GR. SPR SP	Hodgdon	Hybrid 100V	.224"	2.350"	36.0	3254	43,500 PSI	39.0	3466	50,600 PSI
55 GR. SPR SP	Hodgdon	H4350	.224"	2.350"	37.0	3296	46,400 CUP	39.0	3490	47,800 CUP
55 GR. SPR SP	Hodgdon	H414	.224"	2.350"	36.0	3324	40,200 CUP	39.0	3582	46,700 CUP
55 GR. SPR SP	Winchester	760	.224"	2.350"	36.0	3324	40,200 CUP	39.0	3582	46,700 CUP

55 GR. SPR SP	IMR	IMR 4007 SSC	.224"	2.350"	37.8	3656	56,600 PSI	39.0	3786	62,300 PSI
55 GR. SPR SP	Hodgdon	H380	.224"	2.350"	38.0	3507	45,400 CUP	41.0	3713	50,700 CUP
55 GR. SPR SP	Hodgdon	CFE 223	.224"	2.350"	36.0	3557	49,300 PSI	39.2	3855	63,500 PSI
55 GR. SPR SP	Hodgdon	Varget	.224"	2.350"	34.0	3490	46,100 CUP	36.5	3664	50,400 CUP
55 GR. SPR SP	IMR	IMR 4320	.224"	2.350"	34.0	3480	52,900 PSI	36.5	3689	62,200 PSI
55 GR. SPR SP	IMR	IMR 4064	.224"	2.350"	34.0	3461	50,000 PSI	36.3	3713	62,000 PSI
55 GR. SPR SP	Hodgdon	BL-C(2)	.224"	2.350"	31.0	3410	43,800 CUP	34.0	3606	49,600 CUP
55 GR. SPR SP	IMR	IMR 4895	.224"	2.350"	34.0	3486	50,900 PSI	36.5	3725	62,400 PSI
55 GR. SPR SP	Hodgdon	H335	.224"	2.350"	30.5	3400	44,400 CUP	33.0	3589	51,100 CUP
55 GR. SPR SP	Hodgdon	H4895	.224"	2.350"	32.5	3446	45,000 CUP	35.5	3670	49,300 CUP
55 GR. SPR SP	IMR	IMR 8208 XBR	.224"	2.350"	32.0	3514	52,300 PSI	35.8	3768	62,700 PSI
55 GR. SPR SP	IMR	IMR 3031	.224"	2.350"	32.0	3474	51,300 PSI	34.1	3691	62,500 PSI
55 GR. SPR SP	Hodgdon	Benchmark	.224"	2.350"	31.6	3532	46,200 CUP	33.6	3674	50,200 CUP
55 GR. SPR SP	Hodgdon	H322	.224"	2.350"	28.0	3339	46,200 CUP	30.0	3480	49,800 CUP
55 GR. SPR SP	IMR	Trail Boss	.224"	2.350"	9.1	1664	17,200 PSI	13.0	1984	26,600 PSI
60 GR. HDY V-MAX	Hodgdon	Suprform	.224"	2.350"	39.0	3390	45,500 PSI	43.0C	3738	60,000 PSI
60 GR. HDY V-MAX	Hodgdon	Hybrid 100V	.224"	2.350"	35.0	3168	44,900 PSI	38.0C	3366	50,900 PSI
60 GR. HDY V-MAX	Hodgdon	H4350	.224"	2.350"	39.0	3374	51,600 PSI	41.5C	3570	60,500 PSI
60 GR. HDY V-MAX	Hodgdon	H414	.224"	2.350"	37.0	3273	47,600 PSI	40.0	3548	60,300 PSI
60 GR. HDY V-MAX	Winchester	760	.224"	2.350"	37.0	3273	47,600 PSI	40.0	3548	60,300 PSI
60 GR. HDY V-MAX	Hodgdon	H380	.224"	2.350"	37.5	3335	51,000 PSI	40.5	3580	62,000 PSI
60 GR. HDY V-MAX	Hodgdon	CFE 223	.224"	2.350"	35.0	3441	51,900 PSI	37.6	3688	63,800 PSI
60 GR. HDY V-MAX	Hodgdon	Varget	.224"	2.350"	33.0	3318	52,200 PSI	35.8	3503	60,400 PSI
60 GR. HDY V-MAX	Hodgdon	BL-C(2)	.224"	2.350"	34.0	3276	47,100 PSI	37.0	3560	61,000 PSI
60 GR. HDY V-MAX	Hodgdon	H335	.224"	2.350"	31.5	3272	50,800 PSI	34.0	3494	61,400 PSI
60 GR. HDY V-MAX	Hodgdon	H4895	.224"	2.350"	32.0	3340	51,700 PSI	35.0	3551	61,300 PSI
60 GR. HDY V-MAX	IMR	IMR 8208 XBR	.224"	2.350"	31.5	3412	55,600 PSI	34.0	3550	61,000 PSI
60 GR. HDY V-MAX	Hodgdon	Benchmark	.224"	2.350"	29.0	3183	49,000 PSI	32.0	3406	59,900 PSI
60 GR. HDY V-MAX	Hodgdon	H322	.224"	2.350"	29.0	3222	50,900 PSI	31.5	3434	62,000 PSI
62 GR. BAR TAC-X BT	Hodgdon	Suprform	.224"	2.385"	38.3	3240	38,900 PSI	42.5C	3628	54,900 PSI
62 GR. BAR TAC-X BT	Hodgdon	H414	.224"	2.385"	35.8	3247	45,400 PSI	38.9	3537	59,300 PSI
62 GR. BAR TAC-X BT	Winchester	760	.224"	2.385"	35.8	3247	45,400 PSI	38.9	3537	59,300 PSI
62 GR. BAR TAC-X BT	IMR	IMR 4007 SSC	.224"	2.385"	34.2	3136	44,500 PSI	38.0	3512	61,200 PSI
62 GR. BAR TAC-X BT	Hodgdon	CFE 223	.224"	2.385"	34.0	3284	49,200 PSI	37.0	3584	63,600 PSI
62 GR. BAR TAC-X BT	Hodgdon	Varget	.224"	2.385"	32.9	3354	54,200 PSI	35.0	3500	60,400 PSI
62 GR. BAR TAC-X BT	IMR	IMR 4064	.224"	2.385"	31.5	3239	47,300 PSI	35.0	3544	61,200 PSI
62 GR. BAR TAC-X BT	IMR	IMR 4895	.224"	2.385"	32.8	3312	51,000 PSI	35.6	3549	62,000 PSI
62 GR. BAR TAC-X BT	Hodgdon	H4895	.224"	2.385"	31.9	3467	57,800 PSI	34.0	3564	60,900 PSI
62 GR. BAR TAC-X BT	IMR	IMR 8208 XBR	.224"	2.385"	31.6	3367	52,400 PSI	34.0	3554	62,400 PSI

Bullet Weight (Gr.)	Manufacturer	Powder	Bullet Diam.	C.O.L.	Grs.	Vel. (ft/s)	Pressure	Grs.	Vel. (ft/s)	Pressure
62 GR. BAR TAC-X BT	IMR	IMR 3031	.224"	2.385"	31.1	3419	54,200 PSI	33.0	3613	62,200 PSI
63 GR. SIE SP	Hodgdon	Suprform	.224"	2.350"	38.0	3294	44,600 PSI	42.7C	3674	61,400 PSI
63 GR. SIE SP	Hodgdon	Hybrid 100V	.224"	2.350"	35.0	3146	44,700 PSI	38.0C	3382	53,900 PSI
63 GR. SIE SP	Hodgdon	H4350	.224"	2.350"	36.0	3210	45,400 CUP	38.0	3391	48,000 CUP
63 GR. SIE SP	Hodgdon	H414	.224"	2.350"	35.0	3262	43,200 CUP	38.0	3432	47,100 CUP
63 GR. SIE SP	IMR	IMR 4350	.224"	2.350"	38.0	3308	52,900 PSI	40.0C	3467	60,300 PSI
63 GR. SIE SP	Winchester	760	.224"	2.350"	35.0	3262	43,200 CUP	38.0	3432	47,100 CUP
63 GR. SIE SP	IMR	IMR 4007 SSC	.224"	2.350"	34.0	3121	46,000 PSI	38.0	3483	62,300 PSI
63 GR. SIE SP	Hodgdon	H380	.224"	2.350"	36.0	3266	46,600 CUP	38.5	3419	51,200 CUP
63 GR. SIE SP	Hodgdon	CFE 223	.224"	2.350"	35.0	3400	53,900 PSI	37.3	3597	64,000 PSI
63 GR. SIE SP	Hodgdon	Varget	.224"	2.350"	29.5	3039	39,500 CUP	34.0	3426	50,400 CUP
63 GR. SIE SP	IMR	IMR 4064	.224"	2.350"	33.0	3269	50,800 PSI	35.3	3499	62,900 PSI
63 GR. SIE SP	IMR	IMR 4895	.224"	2.350"	33.0	3287	51,500 PSI	35.5	3502	62,700 PSI
63 GR. SIE SP	Hodgdon	H4895	.224"	2.350"	31.5	3317	47,300 CUP	34.0	3486	50,400 CUP
63 GR. SIE SP	IMR	IMR 8208 XBR	.224"	2.350"	30.0	3256	52,400 PSI	33.0	3459	62,100 PSI
63 GR. SIE SP	IMR	IMR 3031	.224"	2.350"	31.0	3284	53,300 PSI	33.1	3457	62,700 PSI
70 GR. SPR SP	Hodgdon	H1000	.224"	2.330"	36.0	3042	41,100 CUP	38.0	3187	47,500 CUP
70 GR. SPR SP	Hodgdon	Suprform	.224"	2.330"	37.0	3206	50,500 PSI	40.8C	3499	63,700 PSI
70 GR. SPR SP	Hodgdon	H4831	.224"	2.330"	35.0	2976	42,000 CUP	38.0	3189	50,300 CUP
70 GR. SPR SP	Hodgdon	Hybrid 100V	.224"	2.330"	35.0	3091	49,000 PSI	38.0C	3322	58,500 PSI
70 GR. SPR SP	Hodgdon	H4350	.224"	2.330"	34.0	3007	44,800 CUP	36.0	3129	49,600 CUP
70 GR. SPR SP	Hodgdon	H414	.224"	2.330"	31.0	2860	42,000 CUP	34.0	3117	49,400 CUP
70 GR. SPR SP	IMR	IMR 4350	.224"	2.330"	36.0	3162	54,500 PSI	38.2C	3324	62,500 PSI
70 GR. SPR SP	Winchester	760	.224"	2.350"	31.0	2860	42,000 CUP	34.0	3117	49,400 CUP
70 GR. SPR SP	IMR	IMR 4007 SSC	.224"	2.330"	33.0	3024	49,400 PSI	36.5	3308	63,000 PSI
70 GR. SPR SP	Hodgdon	H380	.224"	2.330"	33.0	3006	45,200 CUP	35.0	3161	51,500 CUP
70 GR. SPR SP	Hodgdon	CFE 223	.224"	2.330"	33.0	3147	52,600 PSI	35.8	3373	63,200 PSI
70 GR. SPR SP	Hodgdon	Varget	.224"	2.330"	29.5	3006	44,700 CUP	32.0	3196	50,300 CUP
70 GR. SPR SP	IMR	IMR 4320	.224"	2.330"	31.0	3111	55,000 PSI	33.5	3282	62,600 PSI
70 GR. SPR SP	IMR	IMR 4064	.224"	2.330"	31.0	3106	53,200 PSI	33.5	3298	62,600 PSI
70 GR. SPR SP	IMR	IMR 4895	.224"	2.330"	31.0	3111	53,500 PSI	33.3	3278	62,300 PSI
70 GR. SPR SP	Hodgdon	H4895	.224"	2.330"	28.0	2933	43,000 CUP	31.5	3196	50,700 CUP
70 GR. SPR SP	IMR	IMR 8208 XBR	.224"	2.230"	28.0	3015	49,800 PSI	31.0	3246	61,600 PSI
70 GR. SPR SP	IMR	IMR 3031	.224"	2.330"	29.0	3068	53,600 PSI	31.5	3248	63,600 PSI

Cartridge: 220 Swift Load Type: Rifle					Starting Loads			Maximum Loads		
Bullet Weight (Gr.)	Manufacturer	Powder	Bullet Diam.	C.O.L.	Grs.	Vel. (ft/s)	Pressure	Grs.	Vel. (ft/s)	Pressure
35 GR. NOS LF	Hodgdon	H414	.224"	2.680"	41.4	4011	43,600 CUP	45.0	4304	51,800 CUP
35 GR. NOS LF	Winchester	760	.224"	2.680"	41.4	4011	43,600 CUP	45.0	4304	51,800 CUP

35 GR. NOS LF	IMR	IMR 4007 SSC	.224"	2.680"	40.5	3893	41,400 CUP	45.0C	4270	51,900 CUP
35 GR. NOS LF	Hodgdon	H380	.224"	2.680"	41.2	3988	41,200 CUP	44.8	4226	47,700 CUP
35 GR. NOS LF	Hodgdon	Varget	.224"	2.680"	38.5	4035	43,500 CUP	41.0	4251	51,100 CUP
35 GR. NOS LF	IMR	IMR 4064	.224"	2.680"	37.8	3955	42,800 CUP	40.2	4238	51,300 CUP
35 GR. NOS LF	IMR	IMR 4895	.224"	2.680"	38.3	3987	47,000 CUP	40.7	4222	52,100 CUP
35 GR. NOS LF	Hodgdon	H4895	.224"	2.680"	37.6	4171	47,400 CUP	40.0	4401	52,300 CUP
35 GR. NOS LF	IMR	IMR 3031	.224"	2.680"	36.2	4019	45,200 CUP	38.5	4248	51,300 CUP
36 GR. BAR VG FB	IMR	IMR 4007 SSC	.224"	2.635"	41.4	3873	40,000 CUP	45.0C	4232	50,500 CUP
36 GR. BAR VG FB	Hodgdon	Varget	.224"	2.635"	40.0	4076	44,600 CUP	42.5	4306	50,900 CUP
36 GR. BAR VG FB	IMR	IMR 4064	.224"	2.635"	38.3	3988	43,900 CUP	40.7	4248	51,300 CUP
36 GR. BAR VG FB	IMR	IMR 4895	.224"	2.635"	38.5	3985	44,300 CUP	41.0	4237	50,700 CUP
36 GR. BAR VG FB	Hodgdon	H4895	.224"	2.635"	37.6	4002	44,300 CUP	40.0	4251	50,800 CUP
36 GR. BAR VG FB	IMR	IMR 8208 XBR	.224"	2.635"	38.0	4078	46,800 CUP	40.0	4296	53,000 CUP
36 GR. BAR VG FB	IMR	IMR 3031	.224"	2.635"	36.0	3983	43,800 CUP	37.9	4252	50,600 CUP
40 GR. SIE HP	Hodgdon	H414	.224"	2.680"	42.5	3928	45,500 CUP	46.0	4213	51,600 CUP
40 GR. SIE HP	Winchester	760	.224"	2.680"	42.5	3928	45,500 CUP	46.0	4213	51,600 CUP
40 GR. SIE HP	IMR	IMR 4007 SSC	.224"	2.680"	41.0	3735	49,400 CUP	45.0C	4122	49,400 CUP
40 GR. SIE HP	Hodgdon	H380	.224"	2.680"	40.5	3867	44,400 CUP	44.0	4124	50,000 CUP
40 GR. SIE HP	Hodgdon	Varget	.224"	2.680"	38.0	4007	49,800 CUP	40.5	4113	49,800 CUP
40 GR. SIE HP	IMR	IMR 4064	.224"	2.680"	36.0	3777	44,700 CUP	40.0	4110	51,400 CUP
40 GR. SIE HP	IMR	IMR 4895	.224"	2.680"	36.0	3743	42,500 CUP	40.5	4093	51,300 CUP
40 GR. SIE HP	Hodgdon	H335	.224"	2.680"	37.0	3923	44,400 CUP	40.0	4158	53,100 CUP
40 GR. SIE HP	Hodgdon	H4895	.224"	2.680"	37.0	3768	41,400 CUP	40.0	4126	52,000 CUP
40 GR. SIE HP	IMR	IMR 3031	.224"	2.680"	35.0	3904	48,100 CUP	38.5	4189	52,000 CUP
45 GR. HDY SP	Hodgdon	H414	.224"	2.680"	41.5	3849	48,700 CUP	45.0	4100	51,700 CUP
45 GR. HDY SP	Winchester	760	.224"	2.680"	41.5	3849	48,700 CUP	45.0	4100	51,700 CUP
45 GR. HDY SP	IMR	IMR 4007 SSC	.224"	2.680"	39.0	3583	37,200 CUP	44.0C	4054	53,000 CUP
45 GR. HDY SP	Hodgdon	H380	.224"	2.680"	40.5	3784	42,000 CUP	44.0	4041	52,400 CUP
45 GR. HDY SP	Hodgdon	Varget	.224"	2.680"	36.0	3777	47,100 CUP	40.2	4002	52,100 CUP
45 GR. HDY SP	Hodgdon	H4895	.224"	2.680"	36.5	3676	38,400 CUP	39.5	3996	52,100 CUP
50 GR. HDY SP	Hodgdon	H414	.224"	2.680"	40.5	3663	45,900 CUP	44.0	3826	49,600 CUP
50 GR. HDY SP	Winchester	760	.224"	2.680"	40.5	3663	45,900 CUP	44.0	3826	49,600 CUP
50 GR. HDY SP	IMR	IMR 4007 SSC	.224"	2.680"	38.0	3430	36,100 CUP	43.0	3922	52,500 CUP
50 GR. HDY SP	Hodgdon	H380	.224"	2.680"	40.0	3668	41,400 CUP	43.5	3947	53,800 CUP
50 GR. HDY SP	Hodgdon	Varget	.224"	2.680"	34.5	3616	47,200 CUP	36.0	3770	50,200 CUP
50 GR. HDY SP	IMR	IMR 4064	.224"	2.680"	35.0	3640	46,900 CUP	38.4	3905	53,000 CUP
50 GR. HDY SP	Hodgdon	BL-C(2)	.224"	2.680"	35.0	3431	40,200 CUP	38.0	3888	51,000 CUP
50 GR. HDY SP	IMR	IMR 4895	.224"	2.680"	35.0	3661	48,700 CUP	38.7	3868	52,900 CUP
50 GR. HDY SP	Hodgdon	H4895	.224"	2.680"	35.0	3460	39,000 CUP	38.0	3840	51,200 CUP

50 GR. HDY SP	IMR	IMR 3031	.224"	2.680"	33.0	3861	48,600 CUP	36.5	3877	53,100 CUP
52 GR. SIE HPBT	Hodgdon	H414	.224"	2.680"	39.5	3596	43,100 CUP	42.0	3792	49,900 CUP
52 GR. SIE HPBT	Winchester	760	.224"	2.680"	39.5	3596	43,100 CUP	42.0	3792	49,900 CUP
52 GR. SIE HPBT	IMR	IMR 4007 SSC	.224"	2.680"	38.0	3451	40,500 CUP	42.0	3820	52,600 CUP
52 GR. SIE HPBT	Hodgdon	H380	.224"	2.680"	39.0	3632	47,100 CUP	41.5	3792	51,400 CUP
52 GR. SIE HPBT	Hodgdon	Varget	.224"	2.680"	34.0	3516	42,700 CUP	36.5	3687	50,300 CUP
52 GR. SIE HPBT	Hodgdon	BL-C(2)	.224"	2.680"	35.7	3546	44,200 CUP	38.0	3801	51,200 CUP
52 GR. SIE HPBT	Hodgdon	H4895	.224"	2.680"	33.8	3588	45,100 CUP	36.0	3736	50,000 CUP
55 GR. HDY SP	Hodgdon	H4831	.224"	2.680"	41.5	3194	36,600 CUP	46.0	3616	46,600 CUP
55 GR. HDY SP	Hodgdon	Hybrid 100V	.224"	2.680"	38.0	3358	44,700 CUP	42.0C	3627	52,600 CUP
55 GR. HDY SP	Hodgdon	H4350	.224"	2.680"	39.0	3225	42,000 CUP	42.0	3619	50,800 CUP
55 GR. HDY SP	Hodgdon	H414	.224"	2.680"	40.5	3536	47,300 CUP	44.0	3833	53,700 CUP
55 GR. HDY SP	Winchester	760	.224"	2.680"	40.5	3536	47,300 CUP	44.0	3833	53,700 CUP
55 GR. HDY SP	IMR	IMR 4007 SSC	.224"	2.680"	37.0	3286	37,900 CUP	42.0	3771	52,900 CUP
55 GR. HDY SP	Hodgdon	H380	.224"	2.680"	39.0	3580	45,900 CUP	42.5	3839	53,300 CUP
55 GR. HDY SP	Hodgdon	Varget	.224"	2.680"	34.0	3516	47,000 CUP	36.0	3645	51,900 CUP
55 GR. HDY SP	IMR	IMR 4064	.224"	2.680"	34.0	3498	46,100 CUP	37.5	3742	52,500 CUP
55 GR. HDY SP	Hodgdon	BL-C(2)	.224"	2.680"	34.0	3426	44,400 CUP	36.0	3682	49,900 CUP
55 GR. HDY SP	IMR	IMR 4895	.224"	2.680"	34.0	3546	48,500 CUP	38.0	3739	53,000 CUP
55 GR. HDY SP	Hodgdon	H4895	.224"	2.680"	34.0	3481	45,900 CUP	37.0	3698	52,000 CUP
55 GR. HDY SP	IMR	IMR 3031	.224"	2.680"	32.0	3490	47,300 CUP	35.2	3687	52,700 CUP
60 GR. NOS PART	Hodgdon	H4831	.224"	2.680"	41.5	3252	41,600 CUP	46.0C	3556	51,800 CUP
60 GR. NOS PART	Hodgdon	Hybrid 100V	.224"	2.680"	37.5	3287	44,800 CUP	41.0C	3550	50,900 CUP
60 GR. NOS PART	Hodgdon	H4350	.224"	2.680"	37.0	3230	39,800 CUP	41.0	3527	50,600 CUP
60 GR. NOS PART	Hodgdon	H414	.224"	2.680"	38.5	3425	43,900 CUP	41.7	3647	51,400 CUP
60 GR. NOS PART	Winchester	760	.224"	2.680"	38.5	3425	43,900 CUP	41.7	3647	51,400 CUP
60 GR. NOS PART	IMR	IMR 4007 SSC	.224"	2.680"	36.0	3193	42,200 CUP	40.5	3590	53,100 CUP
60 GR. NOS PART	Hodgdon	H380	.224"	2.680"	35.0	3188	44,400 CUP	38.0	3413	51,900 CUP
60 GR. NOS PART	Hodgdon	Varget	.224"	2.680"	33.0	3242	40,000 CUP	36.0	3473	49,000 CUP
60 GR. NOS PART	IMR	IMR 4064	.224"	2.680"	33.0	3322	46,600 CUP	36.0	3539	51,800 CUP
60 GR. NOS PART	IMR	IMR 4895	.224"	2.680"	33.0	3270	44,100 CUP	36.0	3520	53,100 CUP
60 GR. NOS PART	Hodgdon	H4895	.224"	2.680"	30.5	3165	39,200 CUP	33.5	3401	49,600 CUP
62 GR. BAR TAC-X BT	Hodgdon	Hybrid 100V	.224"	2.680"	37.8	3254	42,200 CUP	42.0	3539	51,800 CUP
62 GR. BAR TAC-X BT	Hodgdon	H4350	.224"	2.680"	37.2	3177	43,500 CUP	40.5C	3389	52,400 CUP
62 GR. BAR TAC-X BT	Hodgdon	H414	.224"	2.680"	37.2	3181	42,900 CUP	40.4	3394	51,200 CUP
62 GR. BAR TAC-X BT	Winchester	760	.224"	2.680"	37.2	3181	42,900 CUP	40.4	3394	51,200 CUP
62 GR. BAR TAC-X BT	IMR	IMR 4007 SSC	.224"	2.680"	36.2	3127	43,700 CUP	39.3	3357	51,900 CUP
62 GR. BAR TAC-X BT	Hodgdon	H380	.224"	2.680"	36.7	3160	45,900 CUP	39.0	3338	51,700 CUP
62 GR. BAR TAC-X BT	Hodgdon	Varget	.224"	2.680"	32.3	3161	44,100 CUP	34.3	3315	50,400 CUP
62 GR. BAR TAC-X BT	IMR	IMR 4064	.224"	2.680"	33.2	3236	45,300 CUP	35.3	3369	50,000 CUP

Bullet Weight	Manufacturer	Powder	Bullet Diam.	C.O.L.	Grs.	Vel. (ft/s)	Pressure	Grs.	Vel. (ft/s)	Pressure
62 GR. BAR TAC-X BT	IMR	IMR 4895	.224"	2.680"	33.4	3217	46,300 CUP	35.5	3360	50,600 CUP
62 GR. BAR TAC-X BT	Hodgdon	H4895	.224"	2.680"	31.7	3121	45,700 CUP	33.7	3364	51,400 CUP
63 GR. SIE SP	Hodgdon	H4831	.224"	2.680"	41.5	3180	37,200 CUP	46.0	3586	52,000 CUP
63 GR. SIE SP	Hodgdon	Hybrid 100V	.224"	2.680"	37.5	3269	42,700 CUP	41.0C	3517	51,200 CUP
63 GR. SIE SP	Hodgdon	H4350	.224"	2.680"	37.0	3181	46,000 CUP	39.0	3474	52,000 CUP
63 GR. SIE SP	Hodgdon	H414	.224"	2.680"	38.5	3339	44,400 CUP	42.0	3595	52,100 CUP
63 GR. SIE SP	Winchester	760	.224"	2.680"	38.5	3339	44,400 CUP	42.0	3595	52,100 CUP
63 GR. SIE SP	IMR	IMR 4007 SSC	.224"	2.680"	36.0	3226	43,800 CUP	39.5	3509	52,800 CUP
63 GR. SIE SP	Hodgdon	H380	.224"	2.680"	38.0	3405	45,900 CUP	41.0	3580	51,900 CUP
63 GR. SIE SP	Hodgdon	Varget	.224"	2.680"	32.0	3181	42,200 CUP	34.0	3407	49,300 CUP
63 GR. SIE SP	Hodgdon	H4895	.224"	2.680"	32.5	3218	40,800 CUP	35.5	3484	51,000 CUP
70 GR. SPR SP	Hodgdon	H1000	.224"	2.680"	42.0	3149	43,800 CUP	44.0	3317	50,200 CUP
70 GR. SPR SP	Hodgdon	H4831	.224"	2.680"	37.0	2991	45,800 CUP	42.0	3359	52,600 CUP
70 GR. SPR SP	Hodgdon	Hybrid 100V	.224"	2.680"	37.0	3188	44,800 CUP	40.0C	3397	51,800 CUP
70 GR. SPR SP	Hodgdon	H4350	.224"	2.680"	36.0	3027	45,200 CUP	38.0	3313	51,200 CUP
70 GR. SPR SP	Hodgdon	H414	.224"	2.680"	34.0	2955	44,200 CUP	37.0	3148	50,300 CUP
70 GR. SPR SP	Winchester	760	.224"	2.680"	34.0	2955	44,200 CUP	37.0	3148	50,300 CUP
70 GR. SPR SP	IMR	IMR 4007 SSC	.224"	2.680"	34.0	3066	46,600 CUP	37.8	3320	53,100 CUP
70 GR. SPR SP	Hodgdon	Varget	.224"	2.680"	31.0	3103	46,500 CUP	33.0	3247	49,900 CUP

Cartridge: 220 Jaybird
Load Type: Rifle

Bullet Weight (Gr.)	Manufacturer	Powder	Bullet Diam.	C.O.L.	Starting Loads Grs.	Vel. (ft/s)	Pressure	Maximum Loads Grs.	Vel. (ft/s)	Pressure
52 GR. HDY BTHP	Hodgdon	H4350	.224"	2.450"	43.0	3508		47.0	3992	
55 GR. SPR SP	Hodgdon	H4350	.224"	2.350"	43.0	3509		47.0	3981	
60 GR. HDY HP	Hodgdon	H4831	.224"	2.450"	43.0	3362		47.0	3772	
60 GR. HDY HP	Hodgdon	H4350	.224"	2.450"	41.0	3235		45.0	3763	
68 GR. HDY HP	Hodgdon	H414	.224"	2.450"	38.0	3294		41.0	3570	
69 GR. SIE HP	Hodgdon	H4831	.224"	2.450"	43.0	3318		47.0	3654	

Cartridge: 22 CHeetah Mark II
Load Type: Rifle

Bullet Weight (Gr.)	Manufacturer	Powder	Bullet Diam.	C.O.L.	Starting Loads Grs.	Vel. (ft/s)	Pressure	Maximum Loads Grs.	Vel. (ft/s)	Pressure
50 GR. HDY SP	Hodgdon	H4350	.224"	2.580"	46.0	3901		51.0	4069	
50 GR. HDY SP	Hodgdon	H380	.224"	2.580"	43.0	3801		47.0	4057	
55 GR. SIE SP	Hodgdon	H4350	.224"	2.580"	46.0	3776		51.0	4017	
55 GR. SIE SP	Hodgdon	H380	.224"	2.580"	41.0	3708		45.0	3972	

Cartridge:223 Winchester Super Short Magnum Load Type:Rifle					Starting Loads			Maximum Loads		
Bullet Weight (Gr.)	Manufacturer	Powder	Bullet Diam.	C.O.L.	Grs.	Vel. (ft/s)	Pressure	Grs.	Vel. (ft/s)	Pressure
35 GR. NOS LF	Hodgdon	H414	.224"	2.200"	47.0	4167	51,400 PSI	50.5	4430	60,700 PSI
35 GR. NOS LF	Winchester	760	.224"	2.200"	47.0	4167	51,400 PSI	50.5	4430	60,700 PSI
35 GR. NOS LF	IMR	IMR 4007 SSC	.224"	2.200"	44.0	4149	54,200 PSI	48.5C	4414	63,500 PSI
35 GR. NOS LF	Hodgdon	H380	.224"	2.200"	45.0	4084	52,500 PSI	49.0	4311	59,800 PSI
35 GR. NOS LF	Hodgdon	CFE 223	.224"	2.200"	44.5	4317	55,800 PSI	49.0	4520	62,900 PSI
35 GR. NOS LF	Hodgdon	Varget	.224"	2.200"	39.0	4027	50,000 PSI	43.5	4364	62,500 PSI
35 GR. NOS LF	IMR	IMR 4320	.224"	2.200"	41.0	4044	50,300 PSI	46.0	4416	63,100 PSI
35 GR. NOS LF	IMR	IMR 4064	.224"	2.200"	40.0	4057	49,400 PSI	44.7	4433	61,800 PSI
35 GR. NOS LF	Hodgdon	BL-C(2)	.224"	2.200"	43.0	4188	51,800 PSI	47.5	4488	61,800 PSI
35 GR. NOS LF	IMR	IMR 4895	.224"	2.200"	40.0	4021	49,200 PSI	45.0	4427	62,700 PSI
35 GR. NOS LF	Hodgdon	H4895	.224"	2.200"	38.0	4041	48,300 PSI	43.0	4438	62,000 PSI
35 GR. NOS LF	IMR	IMR 8208 XBR	.224"	2.200"	38.0	4051	49,400 PSI	42.7	4439	62,700 PSI
35 GR. NOS LF	IMR	IMR 3031	.224"	2.200"	38.0	4047	48,700 PSI	42.4	4458	62,700 PSI
36 GR. BAR VG FB	Hodgdon	H414	.224"	2.120"	47.5	4257	55,700 PSI	50.5	4415	62,200 PSI
36 GR. BAR VG FB	Winchester	760	.224"	2.120"	47.5	4257	55,700 PSI	50.5	4415	62,200 PSI
36 GR. BAR VG FB	IMR	IMR 4007 SSC	.224"	2.120"	43.0	4064	52,700 PSI	47.5C	4355	62,400 PSI
36 GR. BAR VG FB	Hodgdon	H380	.224"	2.120"	44.0	4045	49,300 PSI	49.0	4377	61,400 PSI
36 GR. BAR VG FB	Hodgdon	CFE 223	.224"	2.120"	45.5	4308	57,700 PSI	48.5	4473	63,500 PSI
36 GR. BAR VG FB	Hodgdon	Varget	.224"	2.120"	39.0	4086	51,300 PSI	43.2	4368	62,400 PSI
36 GR. BAR VG FB	IMR	IMR 4320	.224"	2.120"	40.0	4029	50,600 PSI	44.0	4373	63,500 PSI
36 GR. BAR VG FB	IMR	IMR 4064	.224"	2.120"	40.0	4065	50,700 PSI	44.0	4404	63,100 PSI
36 GR. BAR VG FB	Hodgdon	BL-C(2)	.224"	2.120"	42.0	4162	51,400 PSI	46.7	4468	62,300 PSI
36 GR. BAR VG FB	IMR	IMR 4895	.224"	2.120"	39.0	4078	50,100 PSI	43.5	4430	63,100 PSI
36 GR. BAR VG FB	Hodgdon	H4895	.224"	2.120"	37.0	4037	48,100 PSI	41.5	4417	62,600 PSI
36 GR. BAR VG FB	IMR	IMR 8208 XBR	.224"	2.120"	37.0	4014	48,300 PSI	41.5	4400	63,100 PSI
36 GR. BAR VG FB	IMR	IMR 3031	.224"	2.120"	37.0	4135	52,900 PSI	40.8	4420	62,800 PSI
40 GR. NOS BT	Hodgdon	H414	.224"	2.200"	47.5	4069	53,300 PSI	50.5	4301	62,400 PSI
40 GR. NOS BT	Winchester	760	.224"	2.200"	47.5	4069	53,300 PSI	50.5	4301	62,400 PSI
40 GR. NOS BT	IMR	IMR 4007 SSC	.224"	2.200"	43.0	3902	50,400 PSI	47.0	4183	62,600 PSI
40 GR. NOS BT	Hodgdon	H380	.224"	2.200"	46.3	4114	54,300 PSI	49.3	4292	62,300 PSI
40 GR. NOS BT	Hodgdon	CFE 223	.224"	2.200"	42.3	4092	54,800 PSI	45.0	4290	63,100 PSI
40 GR. NOS BT	Hodgdon	Varget	.224"	2.200"	41.0	4074	54,100 PSI	43.5	4278	63,800 PSI
40 GR. NOS BT	IMR	IMR 4320	.224"	2.200"	43.0	3979	48,700 PSI	46.8	4319	62,500 PSI
40 GR. NOS BT	IMR	IMR 4064	.224"	2.200"	41.0	3946	44,800 PSI	45.2	4362	62,500 PSI
40 GR. NOS BT	Hodgdon	BL-C(2)	.224"	2.200"	43.4	4190	56,400 PSI	46.2	4352	61,800 PSI
40 GR. NOS BT	IMR	IMR 4895	.224"	2.200"	42.0	4010	45,200 PSI	44.7	4289	60,600 PSI
40 GR. NOS BT	Hodgdon	H4895	.224"	2.200"	40.4	4121	54,300 PSI	43.0	4320	62,900 PSI

40 GR. NOS BT	IMR	IMR 8208 XBR	.224"	2.200"	40.0	4110	52,900 PSI	42.5	4307	62,600 PSI
40 GR. NOS BT	IMR	IMR 3031	.224"	2.200"	39.0	3992	42,200 PSI	42.5	4334	63,400 PSI
45 GR. BAR X	Hodgdon	H4350	.224"	2.100"	47.0	3887	54,100 PSI	50.0C	4131	63,000 PSI
45 GR. BAR X	Hodgdon	H414	.224"	2.100"	46.0	3887	53,100 PSI	49.0	4097	62,800 PSI
45 GR. BAR X	Winchester	760	.224"	2.100"	46.0	3887	53,100 PSI	49.0	4097	62,800 PSI
45 GR. BAR X	Hodgdon	H380	.224"	2.100"	46.0	3992	54,100 PSI	49.0	4199	63,400 PSI
45 GR. BAR X	Hodgdon	Varget	.224"	2.100"	40.7	3935	51,400 PSI	43.3	4136	61,800 PSI
45 GR. BAR X	IMR	IMR 4320	.224"	2.100"	41.5	3761	48,800 PSI	45.8	4165	62,800 PSI
45 GR. BAR X	IMR	IMR 4064	.224"	2.100"	41.0	3843	50,200 PSI	44.6	4210	63,700 PSI
45 GR. BAR X	Hodgdon	BL-C(2)	.224"	2.100"	43.0	4002	52,800 PSI	46.0	4208	63,100 PSI
45 GR. BAR X	IMR	IMR 4895	.224"	2.100"	41.0	3853	50,400 PSI	44.6	4194	62,500 PSI
45 GR. BAR X	Hodgdon	H4895	.224"	2.100"	40.0	3951	51,200 PSI	42.8	4153	61,900 PSI
45 GR. BAR X	IMR	IMR 3031	.224"	2.100"	39.0	3877	51,100 PSI	42.0	4164	62,100 PSI
50 GR. BAR XLC	Hodgdon	H4350	.224"	2.100"	47.0	3781	50,200 PSI	50.0C	4023	61,500 PSI
50 GR. BAR XLC	Hodgdon	H414	.224"	2.100"	46.0	3761	48,800 PSI	49.0	3993	59,600 PSI
50 GR. BAR XLC	Winchester	760	.224"	2.100"	46.0	3761	48,800 PSI	49.0	3993	59,600 PSI
50 GR. BAR XLC	IMR	IMR 4007 SSC	.224"	2.100"	43.0	3419	47,200 PSI	48.0C	3920	63,700 PSI
50 GR. BAR XLC	Hodgdon	H380	.224"	2.100"	45.0	3776	51,000 PSI	48.0	4002	62,000 PSI
50 GR. BAR XLC	Hodgdon	Varget	.224"	2.100"	41.0	3784	50,500 PSI	44.0	4015	61,800 PSI
50 GR. BAR XLC	IMR	IMR 4320	.224"	2.100"	42.0	3705	53,200 PSI	44.8	3967	63,100 PSI
50 GR. BAR XLC	IMR	IMR 4064	.224"	2.100"	41.0	3759	53,300 PSI	43.9	4024	63,100 PSI
50 GR. BAR XLC	Hodgdon	BL-C(2)	.224"	2.100"	43.0	3846	50,800 PSI	46.0	4058	62,100 PSI
50 GR. BAR XLC	IMR	IMR 4895	.224"	2.100"	41.4	3782	53,000 PSI	44.0	4003	62,300 PSI
50 GR. BAR XLC	Hodgdon	H4895	.224"	2.100"	40.0	3805	51,600 PSI	42.9	4021	62,700 PSI
50 GR. BAR XLC	IMR	IMR 3031	.224"	2.100"	38.0	3647	50,100 PSI	41.2	3964	62,200 PSI
52 GR. SPR HPBT	Hodgdon	Hybrid 100V	.224"	2.150"	43.2	3630	53,400 PSI	46.0C	3857	61,300 PSI
52 GR. SPR HPBT	Hodgdon	H4350	.224"	2.150"	46.0	3753	51,500 PSI	49.0C	3959	62,300 PSI
52 GR. SPR HPBT	Hodgdon	H414	.224"	2.150"	45.0	3765	54,700 PSI	48.0	3979	62,200 PSI
52 GR. SPR HPBT	Winchester	760	.224"	2.150"	45.0	3765	54,700 PSI	48.0	3979	62,200 PSI
52 GR. SPR HPBT	IMR	IMR 4007 SSC	.224"	2.150"	42.0	3373	45,200 PSI	47.0	3851	62,400 PSI
52 GR. SPR HPBT	Hodgdon	H380	.224"	2.150"	43.4	3702	52,500 PSI	46.2	3914	61,300 PSI
52 GR. SPR HPBT	Hodgdon	Varget	.224"	2.150"	40.0	3758	54,000 PSI	43.0	3948	63,600 PSI
52 GR. SPR HPBT	IMR	IMR 4320	.224"	2.150"	41.5	3698	49,900 PSI	44.3	3939	61,000 PSI
52 GR. SPR HPBT	IMR	IMR 4064	.224"	2.150"	40.7	3729	50,700 PSI	43.3	3970	61,300 PSI
52 GR. SPR HPBT	Hodgdon	BL-C(2)	.224"	2.150"	42.0	3873	59,800 PSI	44.7	4005	63,200 PSI
52 GR. SPR HPBT	IMR	IMR 4895	.224"	2.150"	41.0	3755	52,100 PSI	43.7	3958	61,400 PSI
52 GR. SPR HPBT	Hodgdon	H4895	.224"	2.150"	38.8	3805	54,400 PSI	41.3	3948	61,600 PSI
52 GR. SPR HPBT	IMR	IMR 8208 XBR	.224"	2.150"	37.8	3721	55,200 PSI	40.2	3894	62,500 PSI
52 GR. SPR HPBT	IMR	IMR 3031	.224"	2.150"	38.5	3704	51,200 PSI	41.0	3934	61,700 PSI

55 GR. HDY V-MAX	IMR	IMR 7828	.224"	2.200"	47.9	3497	52,100 PSI	51.0C*	3770	62,600 PSI
55 GR. HDY V-MAX	Hodgdon	H4831	.224"	2.200"	46.0	3579	53,000 PSI	49.0C	3743	62,600 PSI
55 GR. HDY V-MAX	Hodgdon	Hybrid 100V	.224"	2.200"	43.0	3408	49,100 PSI	47.0C	3682	58,100 PSI
55 GR. HDY V-MAX	IMR	IMR 4831	.224"	2.200"	45.6	3552	53,100 PSI	48.5C	3782	61,800 PSI
55 GR. HDY V-MAX	Hodgdon	H4350	.224"	2.200"	44.5	3713	55,900 PSI	47.5	3881	63,100 PSI
55 GR. HDY V-MAX	Hodgdon	H414	.224"	2.200"	44.0	3713	55,300 PSI	46.8	3886	63,000 PSI
55 GR. HDY V-MAX	IMR	IMR 4350	.224"	2.200"	44.9	3571	52,000 PSI	47.8C	3804	61,700 PSI
55 GR. HDY V-MAX	Winchester	760	.224"	2.200"	44.0	3713	55,300 PSI	46.8	3886	63,000 PSI
55 GR. HDY V-MAX	IMR	IMR 4007 SSC	.224"	2.200"	42.0	3410	50,400 PSI	46.0	3743	61,100 PSI
55 GR. HDY V-MAX	Hodgdon	H380	.224"	2.200"	41.8	3628	54,900 PSI	44.5	3787	62,600 PSI
55 GR. HDY V-MAX	Hodgdon	Varget	.224"	2.200"	38.0	3651	53,300 PSI	40.5	3836	62,100 PSI
55 GR. HDY V-MAX	IMR	IMR 4320	.224"	2.200"	40.0	3627	53,900 PSI	42.5	3807	61,900 PSI
55 GR. HDY V-MAX	IMR	IMR 4064	.224"	2.200"	39.3	3583	52,100 PSI	41.8	3826	62,300 PSI
55 GR. HDY V-MAX	Hodgdon	BL-C(2)	.224"	2.200"	39.0	3687	54,800 PSI	41.8	3841	62,800 PSI
55 GR. HDY V-MAX	IMR	IMR 4895	.224"	2.200"	39.0	3608	53,400 PSI	41.5	3783	61,600 PSI
55 GR. HDY V-MAX	Hodgdon	H4895	.224"	2.200"	36.5	3622	53,200 PSI	39.0	3798	62,100 PSI
55 GR. HDY V-MAX	IMR	IMR 8208 XBR	.224"	2.200"	35.3	3557	54,600 PSI	37.6	3715	62,000 PSI
55 GR. HDY V-MAX	IMR	IMR 3031	.224"	2.200"	36.5	3594	55,200 PSI	38.7	3772	63,500 PSI
60 GR. NOS PART	IMR	IMR 7828	.224"	2.150"	47.0	3446	50,300 PSI	50.2C*	3712	62,000 PSI
60 GR. NOS PART	Winchester	Supreme 780	.224"	2.150"	46.1	3411	54,500 PSI	49.0	3602	62,100 PSI
60 GR. NOS PART	Hodgdon	H4831	.224"	2.150"	43.5	3522	58,300 PSI	46.3C	3661	63,500 PSI
60 GR. NOS PART	Hodgdon	Hybrid 100V	.224"	2.150"	41.4	3528	57,800 PSI	44.0	3681	63,300 PSI
60 GR. NOS PART	IMR	IMR 4831	.224"	2.150"	45.0	3473	50,700 PSI	48.0C	3709	61,300 PSI
60 GR. NOS PART	Hodgdon	H4350	.224"	2.150"	41.0	3568	57,800 PSI	43.8	3723	63,400 PSI
60 GR. NOS PART	Hodgdon	H414	.224"	2.150"	41.0	3530	53,800 PSI	44.0	3707	61,000 PSI
60 GR. NOS PART	IMR	IMR 4350	.224"	2.150"	43.2	3430	49,700 PSI	46.0	3707	61,200 PSI
60 GR. NOS PART	Winchester	760	.224"	2.150"	41.0	3530	53,800 PSI	44.0	3707	61,000 PSI
60 GR. NOS PART	IMR	IMR 4007 SSC	.224"	2.150"	41.0	3334	51,200 PSI	45.5	3670	62,400 PSI
60 GR. NOS PART	Hodgdon	H380	.224"	2.150"	39.5	3503	57,900 PSI	42.0	3626	61,700 PSI
60 GR. NOS PART	Hodgdon	Varget	.224"	2.150"	36.0	3510	55,400 PSI	38.5	3656	61,400 PSI
60 GR. NOS PART	IMR	IMR 4320	.224"	2.150"	39.5	3511	54,200 PSI	42.0	3675	61,700 PSI
60 GR. NOS PART	IMR	IMR 4064	.224"	2.150"	38.9	3531	53,800 PSI	41.4	3733	63,400 PSI
60 GR. NOS PART	Hodgdon	BL-C(2)	.224"	2.150"	36.8	3483	54,000 PSI	39.2	3634	60,600 PSI
60 GR. NOS PART	IMR	IMR 4895	.224"	2.150"	38.5	3502	53,800 PSI	41.1	3720	62,400 PSI
60 GR. NOS PART	Hodgdon	H4895	.224"	2.150"	35.0	3479	53,700 PSI	37.3	3625	62,200 PSI
60 GR. NOS PART	IMR	IMR 8208 XBR	.224"	2.150"	32.9	3383	56,100 PSI	35.0	3524	62,100 PSI
60 GR. NOS PART	IMR	IMR 3031	.224"	2.150"	36.0	3476	54,200 PSI	38.5	3649	62,900 PSI
69 GR. SIE HPBT	Hodgdon	H1000	.224"	2.230"	46.8	3329	53,700 PSI	49.8C	3472	60,100 PSI
69 GR. SIE HPBT	IMR	IMR 7828	.224"	2.230"	45.0	3214	52,200 PSI	47.8C*	3464	62,300 PSI
69 GR. SIE HPBT	Winchester	Supreme 780	.224"	2.230"	44.7	3289	57,700 PSI	47.5	3464	63,400 PSI

69 GR. SIE HPBT	Hodgdon	H4831	.224"	2.230"	43.5	3312	54,700 PSI	46.5C	3489	63,200 PSI
69 GR. SIE HPBT	Hodgdon	Hybrid 100V	.224"	2.230"	40.0	3318	56,300 PSI	42.5	3470	63,500 PSI
69 GR. SIE HPBT	IMR	IMR 4831	.224"	2.230"	43.0	3283	53,300 PSI	45.6	3469	61,100 PSI
69 GR. SIE HPBT	Hodgdon	H4350	.224"	2.230"	40.0	3321	52,400 PSI	42.5	3505	63,300 PSI
69 GR. SIE HPBT	Hodgdon	H414	.224"	2.230"	39.5	3332	54,700 PSI	42.5	3481	61,700 PSI
69 GR. SIE HPBT	IMR	IMR 4350	.224"	2.230"	42.0	3290	53,400 PSI	45.0	3494	62,800 PSI
69 GR. SIE HPBT	Winchester	760	.224"	2.230"	39.5	3332	54,700 PSI	42.5	3481	61,700 PSI
69 GR. SIE HPBT	IMR	IMR 4007 SSC	.224"	2.230"	39.0	3125	49,700 PSI	43.0	3444	62,500 PSI
69 GR. SIE HPBT	Hodgdon	H380	.224"	2.230"	38.5	3290	57,300 PSI	41.2	3428	62,600 PSI
69 GR. SIE HPBT	Hodgdon	Varget	.224"	2.230"	36.0	3324	55,900 PSI	38.5	3492	62,900 PSI
69 GR. SIE HPBT	IMR	IMR 4320	.224"	2.230"	37.3	3290	54,500 PSI	39.7	3461	63,100 PSI
69 GR. SIE HPBT	IMR	IMR 4064	.224"	2.230"	36.7	3288	54,100 PSI	39.0	3450	62,100 PSI
69 GR. SIE HPBT	IMR	IMR 4895	.224"	2.230"	36.0	3251	54,500 PSI	38.2	3441	63,600 PSI
69 GR. SIE HPBT	Hodgdon	H4895	.224"	2.230"	34.5	3278	56,500 PSI	36.8	3426	61,800 PSI
69 GR. SIE HPBT	IMR	IMR 3031	.224"	2.230"	32.9	3158	56,900 PSI	35.0	3297	63,200 PSI
75 GR. HDY V-MAX	Hodgdon	H1000	.224"	2.360"	46.0	3250	55,900 PSI	49.0C	3378	62,400 PSI
75 GR. HDY V-MAX	IMR	IMR 7828	.224"	2.360"	44.2	3070	50,700 PSI	47.0	3293	61,900 PSI
75 GR. HDY V-MAX	Winchester	Supreme 780	.224"	2.360"	43.0	3183	56,600 PSI	45.7	3345	63,300 PSI
75 GR. HDY V-MAX	Hodgdon	H4831	.224"	2.360"	42.0	3201	56,500 PSI	45.1	3352	63,200 PSI
75 GR. HDY V-MAX	Hodgdon	Hybrid 100V	.224"	2.360"	38.5	3217	58,300 PSI	41.0	3351	63,500 PSI
75 GR. HDY V-MAX	IMR	IMR 4831	.224"	2.360"	42.3	3156	54,500 PSI	45.1	3370	63,000 PSI
75 GR. HDY V-MAX	Hodgdon	H4350	.224"	2.360"	39.0	3227	57,900 PSI	41.5	3376	63,700 PSI
75 GR. HDY V-MAX	Hodgdon	H414	.224"	2.360"	39.0	3249	58,500 PSI	41.5	3356	62,600 PSI
75 GR. HDY V-MAX	IMR	IMR 4350	.224"	2.360"	41.5	3150	53,700 PSI	44.2	3375	62,500 PSI
75 GR. HDY V-MAX	Winchester	760	.224"	2.360"	39.0	3249	58,500 PSI	41.5	3356	62,600 PSI
75 GR. HDY V-MAX	IMR	IMR 4007 SSC	.224"	2.360"	38.0	3071	51,800 PSI	42.2	3331	63,100 PSI
75 GR. HDY V-MAX	Hodgdon	Varget	.224"	2.360"	34.5	3174	55,200 PSI	36.8	3330	61,700 PSI
75 GR. HDY V-MAX	IMR	IMR 4320	.224"	2.360"	36.2	3138	53,700 PSI	38.5	3294	62,300 PSI
75 GR. HDY V-MAX	IMR	IMR 4064	.224"	2.360"	36.5	3228	57,200 PSI	38.8	3355	62,700 PSI
75 GR. HDY V-MAX	IMR	IMR 4895	.224"	2.360"	36.7	3180	55,900 PSI	39.0	3347	63,400 PSI
75 GR. HDY V-MAX	Hodgdon	H4895	.224"	2.360"	33.0	3119	56,200 PSI	35.2	3266	61,200 PSI
77 GR. SIE HPBT	Hodgdon	H1000	.224"	2.230"	44.5	3221	57,400 PSI	47.7C	3359	63,500 PSI
77 GR. SIE HPBT	IMR	IMR 7828	.224"	2.230"	43.7	3104	54,500 PSI	46.5	3296	62,900 PSI
77 GR. SIE HPBT	Winchester	Supreme 780	.224"	2.230"	41.4	3065	53,400 PSI	44.0	3218	60,900 PSI
77 GR. SIE HPBT	Hodgdon	H4831	.224"	2.230"	40.5	3159	57,600 PSI	43.3	3299	62,700 PSI
77 GR. SIE HPBT	Hodgdon	Hybrid 100V	.224"	2.230"	36.8	3130	57,900 PSI	39.2	3259	62,700 PSI
77 GR. SIE HPBT	IMR	IMR 4831	.224"	2.230"	42.1	3159	54,400 PSI	44.8	3360	62,500 PSI
77 GR. SIE HPBT	Hodgdon	H4350	.224"	2.230"	37.0	3135	54,600 PSI	39.5	3289	61,000 PSI
77 GR. SIE HPBT	Hodgdon	H414	.224"	2.230"	37.0	3120	55,100 PSI	39.5	3270	62,100 PSI

77 GR. SIE HPBT	IMR	IMR 4350	.224"	2.230"	41.0	3173	54,900 PSI	43.7	3360	63,200 PSI
77 GR. SIE HPBT	Winchester	760	.224"	2.230"	37.0	3120	55,100 PSI	39.5	3270	62,100 PSI
77 GR. SIE HPBT	IMR	IMR 4007 SSC	.224"	2.230"	37.0	2977	50,800 PSI	41.0	3229	62,300 PSI
77 GR. SIE HPBT	Hodgdon	Varget	.224"	2.230"	33.5	3099	59,100 PSI	35.8	3249	63,000 PSI
77 GR. SIE HPBT	IMR	IMR 4320	.224"	2.230"	36.4	3118	58,000 PSI	38.7	3301	62,400 PSI
77 GR. SIE HPBT	IMR	IMR 4064	.224"	2.230"	36.6	3168	54,900 PSI	38.9	3316	63,300 PSI
77 GR. SIE HPBT	IMR	IMR 4895	.224"	2.230"	36.8	3178	53,600 PSI	39.2	3327	63,100 PSI
77 GR. SIE HPBT	Hodgdon	H4895	.224"	2.230"	32.0	3048	58,100 PSI	34.2	3196	62,700 PSI

Cartridge: 6mm-222
Load Type: Rifle

Bullet Weight (Gr.)	Manufacturer	Powder	Bullet Diam.	C.O.L.	Starting Loads Grs.	Vel. (ft/s)	Pressure	Maximum Loads Grs.	Vel. (ft/s)	Pressure
60 GR. SIE HP	Hodgdon	BL-C(2)	.243"	2.200"	23.0	2903	37,800 CUP	25.0	3172	47,100 CUP
60 GR. SIE HP	Hodgdon	H4895	.243"	2.200"	21.5	2748	42,000 CUP	23.5	3043	50,200 CUP
60 GR. SIE HP	Hodgdon	H4198	.243"	2.200"	17.0	2792	37,800 CUP	19.0	3023	48,500 CUP
75 GR. HDY HP	Hodgdon	BL-C(2)	.243"	2.200"	22.0	2714	40,800 CUP	24.0	2915	49,100 CUP
75 GR. HDY HP	Hodgdon	H4895	.243"	2.200"	20.0	2443	39,600 CUP	22.0	2660	46,700 CUP
75 GR. HDY HP	Hodgdon	H4198	.243"	2.200"	16.0	2469	36,600 CUP	18.0	2718	47,600 CUP
85 GR. SPR SP	Hodgdon	BL-C(2)	.243"	2.260"	20.5	2554	42,000 CUP	22.5	2742	49,600 CUP
85 GR. SPR SP	Hodgdon	H4895	.243"	2.260"	19.5	2375	42,400 CUP	20.5	2505	49,600 CUP
85 GR. SPR SP	Hodgdon	H4198	.243"	2.260"	14.5	2292	37,800 CUP	16.5	2514	47,600 CUP
100 GR. HDY SP	Hodgdon	BL-C(2)	.243"	2.260"	19.0	2305	43,700 CUP	21.0	2469	47,600 CUP
100 GR. HDY SP	Hodgdon	H4895	.243"	2.260"	17.0	1998	36,000 CUP	19.0	2212	49,100 CUP
100 GR. HDY SP	Hodgdon	H4198	.243"	2.260"	13.0	1912	36,000 CUP	15.0	2090	46,300 CUP

Cartridge: 6 x 45mm (6mm-223)
Load Type: Rifle

Bullet Weight (Gr.)	Manufacturer	Powder	Bullet Diam.	C.O.L.	Starting Loads Grs.	Vel. (ft/s)	Pressure	Maximum Loads Grs.	Vel. (ft/s)	Pressure
60 GR. SIE HP	Hodgdon	BL-C(2)	.243"	2.260"	28.0	2925	41,500 CUP	30.0	3156	50,000 CUP
60 GR. SIE HP	Hodgdon	H335	.243"	2.260"	25.5	2958	44,500 CUP	27.5	3160	47,500 CUP
60 GR. SIE HP	Hodgdon	H4895	.243"	2.260"	25.5	2872	40,000 CUP	27.5C	3102	48,500 CUP
60 GR. SIE HP	Hodgdon	Benchmark	.243"	2.260"	24.0	2636	32,000 CUP	27.0C	3042	41,600 CUP
60 GR. SIE HP	Hodgdon	H322	.243"	2.260"	23.0	2849	39,500 CUP	25.0	3097	47,000 CUP
62 GR. BAR VG	IMR	IMR 8208 XBR	.243"	2.350"	24.0	2636	33,000 CUP	27.0C	3019	44,600 CUP
62 GR. BAR VG	Hodgdon	Benchmark	.243"	2.350"	24.0	2726	36,400 CUP	27.0C	3064	49,400 CUP
70 GR. HDY SP	Hodgdon	BL-C(2)	.243"	2.260"	27.5	2844	39,300 CUP	29.5	3038	48,500 CUP
70 GR. HDY SP	Hodgdon	H335	.243"	2.260"	25.5	2845	45,000 CUP	27.5	3066	50,000 CUP
70 GR. HDY SP	Hodgdon	H4895	.243"	2.260"	25.5	2809	44,000 CUP	27.5	3034	49,500 CUP
70 GR. HDY SP	IMR	IMR 8208 XBR	.243"	2.260"	24.0	2555	32,000 CUP	27.0C	2916	41,200 CUP
70 GR. HDY SP	Hodgdon	Benchmark	.243"	2.260"	24.0	2609	45,200 CUP	27.0C	2962	45,200 CUP

70 GR. HDY SP	Hodgdon	H322	.243"	2.260"	23.0	2758	39,800 CUP	25.0	2985	47,500 CUP
75 GR. HDY HP	Hodgdon	BL-C(2)	.243"	2.260"	27.0	2726	42,500 CUP	29.0	2832	47,000 CUP
75 GR. HDY HP	IMR	IMR 4895	.243"	2.260"	24.5	2453	34,400 CUP	26.5C	2710	41,900 CUP
75 GR. HDY HP	Hodgdon	H335	.243"	2.260"	24.0	2660	39,300 CUP	26.0	2860	48,500 CUP
75 GR. HDY HP	Hodgdon	H4895	.243"	2.260"	25.0	2704	39,300 CUP	27.0C	2952	48,000 CUP
75 GR. HDY HP	IMR	IMR 8208 XBR	.243"	2.260"	24.0	2513	31,400 CUP	27.0C	2882	44,500 CUP
75 GR. HDY HP	IMR	IMR 3031	.243"	2.260"	23.0	2487	33,000 CUP	25.0C	2766	42,900 CUP
75 GR. HDY HP	Hodgdon	Benchmark	.243"	2.260"	24.0	2587	34,200 CUP	27.0C	2923	47,200 CUP
75 GR. HDY HP	Hodgdon	H322	.243"	2.260"	23.0	2774	45,500 CUP	24.0	2860	47,500 CUP
80 GR. SPR SP	Hodgdon	BL-C(2)	.243"	2.350"	25.5	2649	41,400 CUP	27.5	2846	49,000 CUP
80 GR. SPR SP	IMR	IMR 4895	.243"	2.350"	24.5	2491	36,800 CUP	26.5C	2703	45,100 CUP
80 GR. SPR SP	Hodgdon	H335	.243"	2.350"	24.0	2656	42,000 CUP	26.0	2862	49,500 CUP
80 GR. SPR SP	Hodgdon	H4895	.243"	2.350"	25.0	2689	40,900 CUP	27.0C	2904	48,500 CUP
80 GR. SPR SP	IMR	IMR 8208 XBR	.243"	2.350"	24.0	2576	34,400 CUP	27.0C	2867	44,200 CUP
80 GR. SPR SP	IMR	IMR 3031	.243"	2.350"	23.0	2542	37,300 CUP	25.0C	2765	43,000 CUP
80 GR. SPR SP	Hodgdon	Benchmark	.243"	2.350"	24.0	2608	36,400 CUP	27.0C	2919	48,600 CUP
80 GR. SPR SP	Hodgdon	H322	.243"	2.350"	21.5	2503	37,600 CUP	23.5	2783	47,500 CUP
85 GR. SPR SP	Hodgdon	BL-C(2)	.243"	2.350"	25.5	2566	42,000 CUP	27.5	2811	49,500 CUP
85 GR. SPR SP	IMR	IMR 4895	.243"	2.350"	24.0	2452	36,700 CUP	26.0C	2697	47,100 CUP
85 GR. SPR SP	Hodgdon	H335	.243"	2.350"	23.5	2587	40,000 CUP	25.5	2818	49,500 CUP
85 GR. SPR SP	Hodgdon	H4895	.243"	2.350"	24.0	2559	39,300 CUP	26.0C	2786	49,000 CUP
85 GR. SPR SP	IMR	IMR 8208 XBR	.243"	2.350"	23.5	2525	34,800 CUP	26.5C	2842	48,000 CUP
85 GR. SPR SP	IMR	IMR 3031	.243"	2.350"	23.0	2536	38,900 CUP	24.9C	2743	48,000 CUP
85 GR. SPR SP	Hodgdon	Benchmark	.243"	2.350"	23.0	2518	35,800 CUP	26.2C	2829	49,300 CUP
85 GR. SPR SP	Hodgdon	H322	.243"	2.350"	21.5	2480	41,500 CUP	23.5	2695	49,000 CUP
90 GR. SPR SP	Hodgdon	BL-C(2)	.243"	2.350"	25.0	2523	41,000 CUP	27.0	2744	50,000 CUP
90 GR. SPR SP	IMR	IMR 4895	.243"	2.350"	24.0	2449	38,700 CUP	26.0C	2646	48,100 CUP
90 GR. SPR SP	Hodgdon	H335	.243"	2.350"	22.5	2442	40,900 CUP	25.0	2731	49,500 CUP
90 GR. SPR SP	Hodgdon	H4895	.243"	2.350"	23.5	2509	41,500 CUP	25.5	2721	50,000 CUP
90 GR. SPR SP	IMR	IMR 8208 XBR	.243"	2.350"	23.0	2438	35,600 CUP	26.0C	2729	46,300 CUP
90 GR. SPR SP	IMR	IMR 3031	.243"	2.350"	22.0	2438	38,700 CUP	24.5C	2660	48,800 CUP
90 GR. SPR SP	Hodgdon	Benchmark	.243"	2.350"	23.0	2453	36,600 CUP	26.0C	2739	48,900 CUP
90 GR. SPR SP	Hodgdon	H322	.243"	2.350"	20.5	2391	41,000 CUP	22.5	2531	49,500 CUP
100 GR. HDY SP	Hodgdon	H414	.243"	2.340"	26.0	2310	39,300 CUP	28.0	2484	43,500 CUP
100 GR. HDY SP	Hodgdon	H380	.243"	2.340"	26.0	2397	41,000 CUP	28.0	2506	47,000 CUP
100 GR. HDY SP	Hodgdon	BL-C(2)	.243"	2.340"	24.5	2404	43,000 CUP	26.5	2619	50,000 CUP
100 GR. HDY SP	IMR	IMR 4895	.243"	2.340"	23.5	2305	36,600 CUP	25.5C	2497	47,700 CUP
100 GR. HDY SP	Hodgdon	H335	.243"	2.340"	21.5	2305	44,000 CUP	23.0	2443	50,000 CUP
100 GR. HDY SP	Hodgdon	H4895	.243"	2.340"	22.0	2414	42,000 CUP	24.0C	2616	50,000 CUP

100 GR. HDY SP	IMR	IMR 8208 XBR	.243"	2.340"	23.0	2365	38,300 CUP	25.0C	2558	46,200 CUP
100 GR. HDY SP	IMR	IMR 3031	.243"	2.340"	22.0	2331	39,200 CUP	24.0C	2488	44,400 CUP
100 GR. HDY SP	Hodgdon	Benchmark	.243"	2.340"	23.5	2456	43,900 CUP	24.5C	2546	48,700 CUP

Cartridge:6 x 47mm Load Type:Rifle					Starting Loads			Maximum Loads		
Bullet Weight (Gr.)	Manufacturer	Powder	Bullet Diam.	C.O.L.	Grs.	Vel. (ft/s)	Pressure	Grs.	Vel. (ft/s)	Pressure
60 GR. SIE HP	Hodgdon	BL-C(2)	.243"	2.400"	28.5	2963	34,200 CUP	30.5	3233	45,300 CUP
60 GR. SIE HP	Hodgdon	H335	.243"	2.400"	28.0	2911	33,600 CUP	30.0	3202	45,100 CUP
60 GR. SIE HP	Hodgdon	H4895	.243"	2.400"	26.0	2919	35,600 CUP	28.5	3098	43,100 CUP
60 GR. SIE HP	Hodgdon	H322	.243"	2.400"	26.0	3040	38,100 CUP	28.0	3222	44,500 CUP
60 GR. SIE HP	Hodgdon	H4198	.243"	2.400"	22.0	2895	35,400 CUP	24.0	3170	49,800 CUP
70 GR. HDY SP	Hodgdon	BL-C(2)	.243"	2.445"	28.0	2902	39,300 CUP	30.0	3050	48,000 CUP
70 GR. HDY SP	Hodgdon	H335	.243"	2.445"	27.5	2884	37,900 CUP	29.5	3029	47,200 CUP
70 GR. HDY SP	Hodgdon	H4895	.243"	2.445"	26.0	2745	37,600 CUP	28.0	2915	44,700 CUP
70 GR. HDY SP	Hodgdon	H322	.243"	2.445"	26.0	2935	43,000 CUP	28.0	3116	49,800 CUP
70 GR. HDY SP	Hodgdon	H4198	.243"	2.445"	21.0	2726	39,300 CUP	23.0	2944	49,400 CUP
75 GR. SPR HP	Hodgdon	BL-C(2)	.243"	2.445"	27.5	2792	37,500 CUP	29.5	2997	47,400 CUP
75 GR. SPR HP	Hodgdon	H335	.243"	2.445"	27.0	2744	37,100 CUP	29.0	2953	46,900 CUP
75 GR. SPR HP	Hodgdon	H4895	.243"	2.445"	25.5	2709	38,200 CUP	27.5	2911	47,500 CUP
75 GR. SPR HP	Hodgdon	H322	.243"	2.445"	24.0	2698	40,300 CUP	26.0	2958	48,400 CUP
75 GR. SPR HP	Hodgdon	H4198	.243"	2.445"	20.5	2664	41,500 CUP	22.5	2852	48,900 CUP
80 GR. SPR SP	Hodgdon	BL-C(2)	.243"	2.440"	27.0	2725	40,400 CUP	29.0	2935	48,500 CUP
80 GR. SPR SP	Hodgdon	H335	.243"	2.440"	26.5	2696	39,900 CUP	28.5	2909	48,200 CUP
80 GR. SPR SP	Hodgdon	H4895	.243"	2.440"	25.0	2622	40,400 CUP	27.0	2860	49,800 CUP
80 GR. SPR SP	Hodgdon	H322	.243"	2.440"	23.5	2604	41,400 CUP	25.5	2808	48,000 CUP
80 GR. SPR SP	Hodgdon	H4198	.243"	2.440"	20.0	2527	39,800 CUP	22.0	2700	46,900 CUP
85 GR. SPR SP	Hodgdon	BL-C(2)	.243"	2.440"	26.0	2636	43,100 CUP	28.0	2847	50,300 CUP
85 GR. SPR SP	Hodgdon	H335	.243"	2.440"	25.5	2601	42,200 CUP	27.5	2797	48,900 CUP
85 GR. SPR SP	Hodgdon	H4895	.243"	2.440"	24.0	2483	39,800 CUP	26.0	2712	49,400 CUP
85 GR. SPR SP	Hodgdon	H322	.243"	2.440"	23.0	2514	40,800 CUP	25.0	2713	48,000 CUP
85 GR. SPR SP	Hodgdon	H4198	.243"	2.440"	19.5	2400	37,100 CUP	21.5	2571	46,900 CUP

Cartridge:6mm PPC Load Type:Rifle					Starting Loads			Maximum Loads		
Bullet Weight (Gr.)	Manufacturer	Powder	Bullet Diam.	C.O.L.	Grs.	Vel. (ft/s)	Pressure	Grs.	Vel. (ft/s)	Pressure
55 GR. NOS BT	Hodgdon	CFE 223	.243"	2.100"	31.0	3073	36,900 CUP	33.0	3324	44,100 CUP
55 GR. NOS BT	Hodgdon	BL-C(2)	.243"	2.100"	31.0	3138	42,600 CUP	33.0	3323	49,900 CUP
55 GR. NOS BT	Hodgdon	H335	.243"	2.100"	28.0	3096	40,100 CUP	30.2	3342	50,700 CUP
55 GR. NOS BT	Hodgdon	Benchmark	.243"	2.100"	28.0	3206	42,100 CUP	30.0	3405	50,000 CUP

55 GR. NOS BT	Hodgdon	H322	.243"	2.100"	27.5	3161	39,100 CUP	29.5	3390	49,600 CUP
55 GR. NOS BT	Hodgdon	H4198	.243"	2.100"	25.0	3281	42,300 CUP	26.7	3443	50,200 CUP
58 GR. HDY V-MAX	Hodgdon	CFE 223	.243"	2.075"	30.0	3019	35,900 CUP	32.0	3243	43,400 CUP
58 GR. HDY V-MAX	Hodgdon	BL-C(2)	.243"	2.075"	30.0	3061	42,500 CUP	32.0	3243	49,600 CUP
58 GR. HDY V-MAX	Hodgdon	H335	.243"	2.075"	27.0	2998	38,500 CUP	29.0	3215	49,200 CUP
58 GR. HDY V-MAX	IMR	IMR 8208 XBR	.243"	2.075"	27.5	3084	39,400 CUP	30.0C	3353	49,800 CUP
58 GR. HDY V-MAX	Hodgdon	Benchmark	.243"	2.075"	27.7	3118	39,800 CUP	29.5	3322	50,000 CUP
58 GR. HDY V-MAX	Hodgdon	H322	.243"	2.075"	27.0	3161	42,500 CUP	29.0	3355	50,600 CUP
58 GR. HDY V-MAX	Hodgdon	H4198	.243"	2.075"	24.0	3109	40,200 CUP	25.7	3349	49,300 CUP
60 GR. SIE HP	Hodgdon	CFE 223	.243"	2.080"	30.0	2997	38,600 CUP	32.0	3208	46,600 CUP
60 GR. SIE HP	Hodgdon	Varget	.243"	2.080"	27.0	2901	40,200 CUP	29.0	3076	44,100 CUP
60 GR. SIE HP	Hodgdon	BL-C(2)	.243"	2.080"	30.0	2959	44,000 CUP	31.5	3041	46,500 CUP
60 GR. SIE HP	Hodgdon	H335	.243"	2.080"	26.0	2891	45,200 CUP	28.0	3201	49,000 CUP
60 GR. SIE HP	Hodgdon	H4895	.243"	2.080"	27.0	2913	44,500 CUP	29.0	3218	48,500 CUP
60 GR. SIE HP	IMR	IMR 8208 XBR	.243"	2.080"	27.0	3053	40,000 CUP	30.0C	3334	51,100 CUP
60 GR. SIE HP	Hodgdon	Benchmark	.243"	2.080"	26.0	2909	36,100 CUP	29.0	3236	48,600 CUP
60 GR. SIE HP	Hodgdon	H322	.243"	2.080"	26.0	3090	45,000 CUP	27.0	3165	47,000 CUP
60 GR. SIE HP	Hodgdon	H4198	.243"	2.080"	21.0	2856	46,500 CUP	23.0	2973	49,500 CUP
65 GR. HDY V-MAX	Hodgdon	CFE 223	.243"	2.075"	30.0	2999	39,200 CUP	32.0	3200	46,000 CUP
65 GR. HDY V-MAX	Hodgdon	BL-C(2)	.243"	2.075"	29.0	2907	40,500 CUP	31.0	3121	49,300 CUP
65 GR. HDY V-MAX	Hodgdon	H335	.243"	2.075	26.7	2933	41,400 CUP	28.4	3111	49,500 CUP
65 GR. HDY V-MAX	IMR	IMR 8208 XBR	.243"	2.140"	27.0	3064	42,300 CUP	29.5C	3253	50,900 CUP
65 GR. HDY V-MAX	Hodgdon	Benchmark	.243"	2.075"	26.6	3003	42,700 CUP	28.3	3159	49,800 CUP
65 GR. HDY V-MAX	Hodgdon	H322	.243"	2.075"	26.3	2984	38,900 CUP	28.0	3178	49,400 CUP
65 GR. HDY V-MAX	Hodgdon	H4198	.243"	2.075"	23.5	3011	41,700 CUP	25.5	3218	50,500 CUP
70 GR. NOS BT	Hodgdon	Varget	.243"	2.100"	27.0	2845	39,800 CUP	29.0	3034	48,000 CUP
70 GR. NOS BT	Hodgdon	BL-C(2)	.243"	2.100"	29.0	2812	42,500 CUP	31.0	3012	47,500 CUP
70 GR. NOS BT	Hodgdon	H335	.243"	2.100"	25.0	2846	44,000 CUP	27.5	3033	48,500 CUP
70 GR. NOS BT	Hodgdon	H4895	.243"	2.100"	26.0	2714	42,000 CUP	28.0	3034	46,500 CUP
70 GR. NOS BT	IMR	IMR 8208 XBR	.243"	2.100"	27.0	2900	47,400 CUP	29.5C	3193	50,300 CUP
70 GR. NOS BT	Hodgdon	Benchmark	.243"	2.100"	26.0	2803	35,500 CUP	29.0	3149	50,500 CUP
70 GR. NOS BT	Hodgdon	H322	.243"	2.100"	25.0	2967	46,500 CUP	26.5	3068	50,000 CUP
70 GR. NOS BT	Hodgdon	H4198	.243"	2.100"	21.0	2745	47,000 CUP	22.0	2839	50,400 CUP
75 GR. SPR HP	Hodgdon	CFE 223	.243"	2.115"	29.0	2776	35,700 CUP	31.0	3050	46,000 CUP
75 GR. SPR HP	Hodgdon	Varget	.243"	2.115"	26.0	2737	40,000 CUP	28.0	2906	47,000 CUP
75 GR. SPR HP	Hodgdon	BL-C(2)	.243"	2.115"	28.5	2788	43,400 CUP	30.5	2974	47,800 CUP
75 GR. SPR HP	Hodgdon	H335	.243"	2.115"	24.5	2712	44,000 CUP	27.0	2990	49,000 CUP
75 GR. SPR HP	Hodgdon	H4895	.243"	2.115"	25.5	2740	43,500 CUP	27.5	2981	48,500 CUP
75 GR. SPR HP	IMR	IMR 8208 XBR	.243"	2.115"	26.0	2817	38,400 CUP	28.7	3089	51,200 CUP

75 GR. SPR HP	Hodgdon	Benchmark	.243"	2.115"	25.5	2749	38,900 CUP	28.5	3037	50,100 CUP
75 GR. SPR HP	Hodgdon	H322	.243"	2.115"	24.5	2809	45,000 CUP	26.0	2974	49,500 CUP
75 GR. SPR HP	Hodgdon	H4198	.243"	2.115"	20.0	2661	45,500 CUP	21.0	2780	49,000 CUP
80 GR. SPR SP	Hodgdon	CFE 223	.243"	2.115"	28.0	2763	36,300 CUP	31.0	3042	49,100 CUP
80 GR. SPR SP	Hodgdon	Varget	.243"	2.115"	26.0	2689	38,200 CUP	28.0	2843	44,400 CUP
80 GR. SPR SP	Hodgdon	BL-C(2)	.243"	2.115"	28.0	2748	42,500 CUP	30.0	2904	47,500 CUP
80 GR. SPR SP	Hodgdon	H335	.243"	2.115"	24.0	2650	42,000 CUP	26.0	2822	48,500 CUP
80 GR. SPR SP	Hodgdon	H4895	.243"	2.115"	25.0	2641	40,400 CUP	27.0	2904	47,500 CUP
80 GR. SPR SP	IMR	IMR 8208 XBR	.243"	2.115"	26.0	2811	39,700 CUP	28.3	3023	51,400 CUP
80 GR. SPR SP	Hodgdon	Benchmark	.243"	2.115"	25.0	2674	36,400 CUP	28.0	2970	50,400 CUP
80 GR. SPR SP	Hodgdon	H322	.243"	2.115"	23.5	2658	42,000 CUP	25.5	2866	47,500 CUP
80 GR. SPR SP	Hodgdon	H4198	.243"	2.115"	19.0	2359	37,600 CUP	21.0	2641	49,500 CUP
85 GR. SIE HPBT	Hodgdon	CFE 223	.243"	2.080"	27.0	2618	34,800 CUP	30.0	2920	46.900 CUP
85 GR. SIE HPBT	Hodgdon	Varget	.243"	2.080"	26.0	2671	43,400 CUP	28.0	2848	50,000 CUP
85 GR. SIE HPBT	Hodgdon	BL-C(2)	.243"	2.080"	27.0	2639	43,000 CUP	29.0	2818	48,000 CUP
85 GR. SIE HPBT	Hodgdon	H335	.243"	2.080"	23.5	2560	42,500 CUP	25.0	2739	47,500 CUP
85 GR. SIE HPBT	Hodgdon	H4895	.243"	2.080"	24.0	2540	41,500 CUP	26.0	2782	48,000 CUP
85 GR. SIE HPBT	IMR	IMR 8208 XBR	.243"	2.080"	25.0	2719	41,700 CUP	27.5	2928	52,200 CUP
85 GR. SIE HPBT	Hodgdon	Benchmark	.243"	2.080"	24.5	2619	38,300 CUP	27.0	2860	50,000 CUP
85 GR. SIE HPBT	Hodgdon	H322	.243"	2.080"	23.0	2571	44,000 CUP	25.0	2794	49,000 CUP
107 GR. SIE HPBT	Hodgdon	CFE 223	.243"	2.240"	26.0	2476	38,700 CUP	28.5	2702	48,600 CUP
107 GR. SIE HPBT	Hodgdon	Varget	.243"	2.240"	26.0	2503	44,900 CUP	27.7C	2626	50,000 CUP
107 GR. SIE HPBT	Hodgdon	BL-C(2)	.243"	2.240"	26.3	2463	41,800 CUP	28.0	2599	48,700 CUP
107 GR. SIE HPBT	Hodgdon	H335	.243"	2.240"	23.1	2359	39,900 CUP	26.0	2582	51,100 CUP
107 GR. SIE HPBT	Hodgdon	H4895	.243"	2.240"	24.5	2426	41,500 CUP	26.8C	2631	49,700 CUP
107 GR. SIE HPBT	IMR	IMR 8208 XBR	.243"	2.240"	23.0	2403	42,400 CUP	25.3	2584	51,300 CUP
107 GR. SIE HPBT	Hodgdon	Benchmark	.243"	2.240"	24.0	2437	43,400 CUP	25.8	2584	51,200 CUP
107 GR. SIE HPBT	Hodgdon	H322	.243"	2.240"	22.0	2351	42,000 CUP	24.5	2553	51,100 CUP

Cartridge: 6mm BR Remington Load Type: Rifle					Starting Loads			Maximum Loads		
Bullet Weight (Gr.)	Manufacturer	Powder	Bullet Diam.	C.O.L.	Grs.	Vel. (ft/s)	Pressure	Grs.	Vel. (ft/s)	Pressure
55 GR. NOS BT	Hodgdon	CFE 223	.243"	2.080"	34.0	3260	37,300 CUP	36.0	3440	42,500 CUP
55 GR. NOS BT	Hodgdon	Varget	.243"	2.080"	31.0	3043	31,600 CUP	34.0C	3347	41,800 CUP
55 GR. NOS BT	Hodgdon	BL-C(2)	.243"	2.080"	34.0	3234	40,400 CUP	36.0	3406	46,400 CUP
55 GR. NOS BT	Hodgdon	H335	.243"	2.080"	30.0	3201	37,900 CUP	32.5	3464	50,600 CUP
55 GR. NOS BT	Hodgdon	H4895	.243"	2.080"	31.0	3233	37,300 CUP	33.0C	3449	45,300 CUP
55 GR. NOS BT	IMR	IMR 8208 XBR	.243"	2.080"	30.0	3204	33,900 CUP	33.5C	3546	44,800 CUP
55 GR. NOS BT	Hodgdon	Benchmark	.243"	2.080"	31.0	3322	41,200 CUP	33.5C	3557	50,300 CUP
55 GR. NOS BT	Hodgdon	H322	.243"	2.080"	30.0	3333	38,800 CUP	32.5	3604	51,100 CUP

55 GR. NOS BT	Hodgdon	H4198	.243"	2.080"	26.0	3230	37,600 CUP	28.8	3542	51,000 CUP
58 GR. HDY V-MAX	Hodgdon	CFE 223	.243"	2.140"	34.0	3271	38,500 CUP	36.0	3484	46,500 CUP
58 GR. HDY V-MAX	Hodgdon	Varget	.243"	2.140"	31.0	3052	34,300 CUP	34.0C	3355	46,100 CUP
58 GR. HDY V-MAX	Hodgdon	BL-C(2)	.243"	2.140"	33.0	3203	41,900 CUP	35.0	3386	48,600 CUP
58 GR. HDY V-MAX	Hodgdon	H335	.243"	2.140"	30.0	3209	41,500 CUP	32.2	3409	51,200 CUP
58 GR. HDY V-MAX	Hodgdon	H4895	.243"	2.140"	31.5	3250	38,000 CUP	33.5	3415	45,100 CUP
58 GR. HDY V-MAX	IMR	IMR 8208 XBR	.243"	2.140"	30.0	3207	36,800 CUP	33.5C	3552	50,000 CUP
58 GR. HDY V-MAX	Hodgdon	Benchmark	.243"	2.140"	30.0	3241	42,000 CUP	32.0	3450	50,600 CUP
58 GR. HDY V-MAX	Hodgdon	H322	.243"	2.140"	29.5	3240	40,100 CUP	31.3	3415	48,400 CUP
58 GR. HDY V-MAX	Hodgdon	H4198	.243"	2.140"	26.0	3205	38,000 CUP	28.5	3454	49,900 CUP
60 GR. SIE HP	Hodgdon	CFE 223	.243"	2.080"	34.0	3275	39,800 CUP	36.0	3472	48,000 CUP
60 GR. SIE HP	Hodgdon	Varget	.243"	2.080"	31.0	3161	36,000 CUP	34.0C	3442	48,500 CUP
60 GR. SIE HP	Hodgdon	BL-C(2)	.243"	2.080"	34.0	3154	38,700 CUP	36.0	3375	47,500 CUP
60 GR. SIE HP	Hodgdon	H335	.243"	2.080"	30.0	3184	41,500 CUP	32.0	3411	49,000 CUP
60 GR. SIE HP	Hodgdon	H4895	.243"	2.080"	31.0	3177	42,000 CUP	33.0C	3384	47,000 CUP
60 GR. SIE HP	IMR	IMR 8208 XBR	.243"	2.080"	29.0	3121	36,800 CUP	32.7	3475	48,900 CUP
60 GR. SIE HP	Hodgdon	Benchmark	.243"	2.080"	30.0	3165	41,400 CUP	32.0	3373	49,900 CUP
60 GR. SIE HP	Hodgdon	H322	.243"	2.080"	30.0	3281	42,000 CUP	32.0	3481	49,500 CUP
60 GR. SIE HP	Hodgdon	H4198	.243"	2.080"	25.0	3137	39,600 CUP	27.5	3378	50,700 CUP
62 GR. BAR VG FB	Hodgdon	CFE 223	.243"	2.140"	32.0	3033	39,600 CUP	34.0	3183	46,000 CUP
62 GR. BAR VG FB	Hodgdon	Varget	.243"	2.140"	28.7	3102	45,200 CUP	31.5C	3258	49,200 CUP
62 GR. BAR VG FB	Hodgdon	BL-C(2)	.243"	2.140"	31.1	2963	42,300 CUP	33.0	3130	48,800 CUP
62 GR. BAR VG FB	Hodgdon	H335	.243"	2.140"	28.5	2971	41,000 CUP	30.3	3120	48,400 CUP
62 GR. BAR VG FB	Hodgdon	H4895	.243"	2.140"	29.6	3166	41,500 CUP	31.5C	3349	49,300 CUP
62 GR. BAR VG FB	IMR	IMR 8208 XBR	.243"	2.140"	29.6	3146	41,600 CUP	31.5C	3307	47,900 CUP
62 GR. BAR VG FB	Hodgdon	Benchmark	.243"	2.140"	29.1	3060	40,300 CUP	31.0C	3265	48,300 CUP
62 GR. BAR VG FB	Hodgdon	H322	.243"	2.140"	27.8	3070	42,000 CUP	29.6	3190	47,600 CUP
62 GR. BAR VG FB	Hodgdon	H4198	.243"	2.140"	24.4	3028	41,800 CUP	26.0	3145	47,700 CUP
65 GR. HDY V-MAX	Hodgdon	CFE 223	.243"	2.140"	33.0	3159	37,800 CUP	35.0	3350	46,700 CUP
65 GR. HDY V-MAX	Hodgdon	Varget	.243"	2.140"	31.0	3021	42,200 CUP	33.0	3268	49,900 CUP
65 GR. HDY V-MAX	Hodgdon	BL-C(2)	.243"	2.140"	31.5	3012	38,200 CUP	34.0	3254	48,800 CUP
65 GR. HDY V-MAX	Hodgdon	H335	.243"	2.140"	27.5	2907	36,800 CUP	30.5	3177	48,100 CUP
65 GR. HDY V-MAX	Hodgdon	H4895	.243"	2.140"	30.0	3064	37,700 CUP	33.0	3366	49,300 CUP
65 GR. HDY V-MAX	IMR	IMR 8208 XBR	.243"	2.140"	29.0	3084	36,300 CUP	32.3	3397	48,700 CUP
65 GR. HDY V-MAX	Hodgdon	Benchmark	.243"	2.140"	27.0	2997	36,000 CUP	30.5	3205	46,400 CUP
65 GR. HDY V-MAX	Hodgdon	H322	.243"	2.140"	27.0	2978	36,800 CUP	30.5	3303	49,600 CUP
65 GR. HDY V-MAX	Hodgdon	H4198	.243"	2.140"	25.0	3071	42,200 CUP	27.0	3242	49,100 CUP
70 GR. NOS BT	Hodgdon	Varget	.243"	2.100"	31.0	3101	38,900 CUP	34.0C	3342	49,400 CUP
70 GR. NOS BT	Hodgdon	BL-C(2)	.243"	2.100"	33.0	3118	42,500 CUP	35.0	3289	48,000 CUP

70 GR. NOS BT	Hodgdon	H335	.243"	2.100"	29.0	3050	43,000 CUP	31.0	3287	47,000 CUP
70 GR. NOS BT	Hodgdon	H4895	.243"	2.100"	29.0	2895	38,200 CUP	31.0	3188	47,000 CUP
70 GR. NOS BT	IMR	IMR 8208 XBR	.243"	2.100"	29.5	3045	37,100 CUP	32.7	3361	51,600 CUP
70 GR. NOS BT	Hodgdon	Benchmark	.243"	2.100"	29.7	3019	39,900 CUP	31.6	3227	49,000 CUP
70 GR. NOS BT	Hodgdon	H322	.243"	2.100"	28.0	2976	38,700 CUP	30.0	3200	47,000 CUP
75 GR. SPR HP	Hodgdon	CFE 223	.243"	2.115"	33.0	3071	40,900 CUP	35.0	3242	48,000 CUP
75 GR. SPR HP	Hodgdon	Varget	.243"	2.115"	30.5	3057	42,200 CUP	32.5	3239	50,000 CUP
75 GR. SPR HP	Hodgdon	BL-C(2)	.243"	2.115"	31.0	2883	38,200 CUP	33.0	3113	46,000 CUP
75 GR. SPR HP	Hodgdon	H335	.243"	2.115"	28.0	2928	43,000 CUP	30.0	3103	47,000 CUP
75 GR. SPR HP	Hodgdon	H4895	.243"	2.115"	28.5	2980	40,000 CUP	30.5	3129	47,000 CUP
75 GR. SPR HP	IMR	IMR 8208 XBR	.243"	2.115"	28.0	2926	38,900 CUP	30.8	3167	48,800 CUP
75 GR. SPR HP	Hodgdon	Benchmark	.243"	2.115"	29.0	2959	41,700 CUP	31.0	3127	49,600 CUP
75 GR. SPR HP	Hodgdon	H322	.243"	2.115"	26.0	2756	37,100 CUP	28.0	3096	47,000 CUP
80 GR. SPR SP	Hodgdon	CFE 223	.243"	2.115"	33.0	3046	44,200 CUP	35.0	3225	49,900 CUP
80 GR. SPR SP	Hodgdon	Varget	.243"	2.115"	30.5	2999	43,100 CUP	32.5	3159	50,700 CUP
80 GR. SPR SP	Hodgdon	BL-C(2)	.243"	2.115"	31.0	2894	42,500 CUP	33.0	3089	47,500 CUP
80 GR. SPR SP	Hodgdon	H335	.243"	2.115"	28.0	2957	42,000 CUP	30.0	3090	48,000 CUP
80 GR. SPR SP	Hodgdon	H4895	.243"	2.115"	28.0	2945	40,400 CUP	30.0	3100	47,000 CUP
80 GR. SPR SP	IMR	IMR 8208 XBR	.243"	2.115"	27.0	2823	39,800 CUP	30.4	3107	49,500 CUP
80 GR. SPR SP	Hodgdon	Benchmark	.243"	2.115"	28.5	2872	40,900 CUP	30.5	3048	49,400 CUP
80 GR. SPR SP	Hodgdon	H322	.243"	2.115"	26.0	2787	39,300 CUP	28.0	3005	47,000 CUP
85 GR. SPR SP	Hodgdon	CFE 223	.243"	2.115"	33.0	2996	43,300 CUP	35.0	3159	49,900 CUP
85 GR. SPR SP	Hodgdon	Varget	.243"	2.115"	29.0	2840	43,100 CUP	31.0	3007	50,800 CUP
85 GR. SPR SP	Hodgdon	BL-C(2)	.243"	2.115"	29.0	2821	43,000 CUP	31.0	2947	48,500 CUP
85 GR. SPR SP	Hodgdon	H335	.243"	2.115"	24.5	2600	41,000 CUP	26.5	2809	49,000 CUP
85 GR. SPR SP	Hodgdon	H4895	.243"	2.115"	24.5	2590	38,100 CUP	26.5	2770	49,500 CUP
85 GR. SPR SP	IMR	IMR 8208 XBR	.243"	2.115"	27.0	2782	41,400 CUP	29.8	3016	49,900 CUP
85 GR. SPR SP	Hodgdon	Benchmark	.243"	2.115"	27.7	2792	42,100 CUP	29.7	2960	49,800 CUP
85 GR. SPR SP	Hodgdon	H322	.243"	2.115"	22.0	2472	40,400 CUP	24.0	2632	47,000 CUP
90 GR. SPR SP	Hodgdon	CFE 223	.243"	2.115"	30.0	2759	45,100 CUP	32.0	2910	50,600 CUP
90 GR. SPR SP	Hodgdon	Varget	.243"	2.115"	27.5	2674	39,500 CUP	30.2	2886	47,500 CUP
90 GR. SPR SP	Hodgdon	BL-C(2)	.243"	2.115"	29.0	2738	44,000 CUP	31.0	2921	48,800 CUP
90 GR. SPR SP	Hodgdon	H335	.243"	2.115"	24.0	2432	38,200 CUP	26.0	2688	49,000 CUP
90 GR. SPR SP	Hodgdon	H4895	.243"	2.115"	24.5	2560	40,400 CUP	27.0	2743	48,000 CUP
90 GR. SPR SP	IMR	IMR 8208 XBR	.243"	2.115"	25.0	2599	41,500 CUP	28.0	2813	50,000 CUP
90 GR. SPR SP	Hodgdon	Benchmark	.243"	2.115"	27.0	2703	43,200 CUP	29.0	2868	49,300 CUP
90 GR. SPR SP	Hodgdon	H322	.243"	2.115"	22.0	2423	40,600 CUP	24.0	2607	48,000 CUP
100 GR. HDY SP	Hodgdon	CFE 223	.243"	2.150"	28.0	2497	40,000 CUP	30.0	2661	45,200 CUP
100 GR. HDY SP	Hodgdon	Varget	.243"	2.150"	26.0	2491	43,000 CUP	28.0	2649	48,900 CUP
100 GR. HDY SP	Hodgdon	BL-C(2)	.243"	2.150"	27.0	2379	41,500 CUP	29.0	2599	47,000 CUP

Bullet Weight (Gr.)	Manufacturer	Powder	Bullet Diam.	C.O.L.	Grs.	Vel. (ft/s)	Pressure	Grs.	Vel. (ft/s)	Pressure
100 GR. HDY SP	Hodgdon	H335	.243"	2.150"	24.0	2339	43,000 CUP	26.0	2537	50,000 CUP
100 GR. HDY SP	Hodgdon	H4895	.243"	2.150"	24.5	2423	42,500 CUP	27.0	2603	49,000 CUP
100 GR. HDY SP	IMR	IMR 8208 XBR	.243"	2.150"	24.0	2388	40,500 CUP	27.0	2630	49,800 CUP
100 GR. HDY SP	Hodgdon	Benchmark	.243"	2.150"	26.0	2485	43,100 CUP	28.0	2670	49,500 CUP
100 GR. HDY SP	Hodgdon	H322	.243"	2.150"	22.0	2275	42,000 CUP	23.5	2519	50,000 CUP
107 GR. SIE HPBT	Hodgdon	CFE 223	.243"	2.250"	28.0	2491	44,200 CUP	30.0	2632	49,000 CUP
107 GR. SIE HPBT	Hodgdon	Varget	.243"	2.250"	26.0	2367	39,800 CUP	29.0C	2620	50,100 CUP
107 GR. SIE HPBT	Hodgdon	BL-C(2)	.243"	2.250"	28.0	2454	38,100 CUP	30.0	2644	44,200 CUP
107 GR. SIE HPBT	Hodgdon	H335	.243"	2.250"	26.0	2482	43,200 CUP	28.0	2649	50,400 CUP
107 GR. SIE HPBT	Hodgdon	H4895	.243"	2.250"	24.5	2329	37,900 CUP	27.5	2605	49,800 CUP
107 GR. SIE HPBT	IMR	IMR 8208 XBR	.243"	2.250"	24.0	2380	42,700 CUP	26.7	2555	50,400 CUP
107 GR. SIE HPBT	Hodgdon	Benchmark	.243"	2.250"	26.0	2466	42,000 CUP	28.0	2613	49,800 CUP
107 GR. SIE HPBT	Hodgdon	H322	.243"	2.250"	23.0	2325	40,800 CUP	25.5	2525	49,200 CUP

Cartridge:6mm-250 Load Type:Rifle						Starting Loads			Maximum Loads	
Bullet Weight (Gr.)	Manufacturer	Powder	Bullet Diam.	C.O.L.	Grs.	Vel. (ft/s)	Pressure	Grs.	Vel. (ft/s)	Pressure
55 GR. NOS BT	Hodgdon	Varget	.243"	2.500"	38.0	3515	43,900 CUP	40.5C	3720	50,900 CUP
55 GR. NOS BT	Hodgdon	BL-C(2)	.243"	2.500"	38.0	3430	39,600 CUP	42.0	3812	51,500 CUP
55 GR. NOS BT	Hodgdon	H335	.243"	2.500"	35.0	3463	39,800 CUP	38.0	3718	51,100 CUP
55 GR. NOS BT	Hodgdon	H4895	.243"	2.500"	37.0	3544	41,100 CUP	39.7C	3766	51,000 CUP
55 GR. NOS BT	Hodgdon	Benchmark	.243"	2.500"	34.0	3452	43,700 CUP	37.0	3684	52,000 CUP
60 GR. SIE HP	Hodgdon	H414	.243"	2.400"	39.0	3190	38,700 CUP	42.0	3494	48,900 CUP
60 GR. SIE HP	Hodgdon	H380	.243"	2.400"	39.0	3315	39,100 CUP	42.0	3513	46,400 CUP
60 GR. SIE HP	Hodgdon	Varget	.243"	2.400"	37.0	3398	44,300 CUP	39.3	3601	51,400 CUP
60 GR. SIE HP	Hodgdon	BL-C(2)	.243"	2.400"	37.0	3357	40,300 CUP	40.0	3629	51,700 CUP
60 GR. SIE HP	Hodgdon	H335	.243"	2.400"	34.0	3337	42,500 CUP	36.4	3537	50,600 CUP
60 GR. SIE HP	Hodgdon	H4895	.243"	2.400"	36.0	3417	40,500 CUP	38.5	3674	51,400 CUP
60 GR. SIE HP	Hodgdon	Benchmark	.243"	2.400"	33.0	3337	44,500 CUP	35.5	3525	51,000 CUP
70 GR. SIE HPBT	Hodgdon	H414	.243"	2.400"	38.0	3099	39,900 CUP	40.8	3358	51,100 CUP
70 GR. SIE HPBT	Hodgdon	H380	.243"	2.400"	38.0	3208	41,900 CUP	40.0	3348	47,200 CUP
70 GR. SIE HPBT	Hodgdon	Varget	.243"	2.400"	35.0	3166	40,200 CUP	37.5	3383	50,900 CUP
70 GR. SIE HPBT	Hodgdon	BL-C(2)	.243"	2.400"	36.0	3264	42,700 CUP	38.0	3410	51,500 CUP
70 GR. SIE HPBT	Hodgdon	H335	.243"	2.400"	33.0	3177	42,800 CUP	35.3	3385	51,600 CUP
70 GR. SIE HPBT	Hodgdon	H4895	.243"	2.400"	34.0	3228	40,900 CUP	37.0	3436	51,300 CUP
70 GR. SIE HPBT	Hodgdon	Benchmark	.243"	2.400"	31.0	3149	47,000 CUP	34.3	3311	49,000 CUP
80 GR. SIE BTSP	Hodgdon	H4350	.243"	2.400"	39.0	3082	40,400 CUP	41.0C	3211	45,000 CUP
80 GR. SIE BTSP	Hodgdon	H414	.243"	2.400"	37.0	2974	39,800 CUP	40.0	3231	51,400 CUP
80 GR. SIE BTSP	Hodgdon	H380	.243"	2.400"	37.0	3055	39,600 CUP	40.0	3268	48,900 CUP

80 GR. SIE BTSP	Hodgdon	Varget	.243"	2.400"	34.0	3104	44,800 CUP	36.7	3274	51,400 CUP
80 GR. SIE BTSP	Hodgdon	BL-C(2)	.243"	2.400"	35.0	3111	43,100 CUP	37.2	3296	51,700 CUP
80 GR. SIE BTSP	Hodgdon	H335	.243"	2.400"	32.0	3005	41,600 CUP	34.5	3221	51,100 CUP
80 GR. SIE BTSP	Hodgdon	H4895	.243"	2.400"	34.0	3185	45,800 CUP	36.0	3304	51,000 CUP
85 GR. SPR SPBT	Hodgdon	H4350	.243"	2.450"	38.5	3059	42,800 CUP	41.0C	3223	48,900 CUP
85 GR. SPR SPBT	Hodgdon	H414	.243"	2.450"	37.0	2978	41,700 CUP	39.6	3188	51,400 CUP
85 GR. SPR SPBT	Hodgdon	H380	.243"	2.450"	37.0	3020	43,500 CUP	40.0	3260	51,200 CUP
85 GR. SPR SPBT	Hodgdon	Varget	.243"	2.450"	33.0	3011	44,100 CUP	35.4	3171	51,700 CUP
85 GR. SPR SPBT	Hodgdon	BL-C(2)	.243"	2.450"	34.5	3056	43,500 CUP	36.6	3220	50,500 CUP
85 GR. SPR SPBT	Hodgdon	H335	.243"	2.450"	31.6	2982	43,600 CUP	33.7	3141	51,000 CUP
85 GR. SPR SPBT	Hodgdon	H4895	.243"	2.450"	32.7	3070	45,300 CUP	34.8	3191	50,700 CUP
90 GR. SPR SP	Hodgdon	H4350	.243"	2.400"	38.5	2985	44,900 CUP	41.0C	3126	49,900 CUP
90 GR. SPR SP	Hodgdon	H414	.243"	2.400"	36.6	2911	42,400 CUP	39.0	3088	51,600 CUP
90 GR. SPR SP	Hodgdon	H380	.243"	2.400"	37.0	2952	46,200 CUP	39.5	3131	51,700 CUP
90 GR. SPR SP	Hodgdon	Varget	.243"	2.400"	33.3	2923	44,900 CUP	35.5	3053	51,300 CUP
90 GR. SPR SP	Hodgdon	BL-C(2)	.243"	2.400"	34.4	2941	44,100 CUP	36.6	3093	51,400 CUP
90 GR. SPR SP	Hodgdon	H335	.243"	2.400"	31.4	2846	42,500 CUP	33.5	3030	51,100 CUP
90 GR. SPR SP	Hodgdon	H4895	.243"	2.400"	32.4	2939	46,000 CUP	34.5	3060	51,400 CUP
95 GR. NOS PART	Hodgdon	H4350	.243"	2.500"	36.5	2887	44,800 CUP	39.0C	3045	50,700 CUP
95 GR. NOS PART	Hodgdon	H414	.243"	2.500"	35.5	2830	42,800 CUP	38.0	3008	51,200 CUP
95 GR. NOS PART	Hodgdon	H380	.243"	2.500"	35.0	2842	45,500 CUP	37.5	3010	51,200 CUP
95 GR. NOS PART	Hodgdon	Varget	.243"	2.500"	31.7	2819	43,900 CUP	33.8	2962	50,800 CUP
95 GR. NOS PART	Hodgdon	BL-C(2)	.243"	2.500"	33.0	2877	45,300 CUP	35.3	3046	50,900 CUP
95 GR. NOS PART	Hodgdon	H335	.243"	2.500"	30.5	2805	44,400 CUP	32.6	2963	50,600 CUP
95 GR. NOS PART	Hodgdon	H4895	.243"	2.500"	31.0	2830	45,900 CUP	33.0	2935	50,600 CUP
100 GR. HDY SP	Hodgdon	H4350	.243"	2.500"	35.5	2769	45,300 CUP	37.9C	2890	50,900 CUP
100 GR. HDY SP	Hodgdon	H414	.243"	2.500"	35.0	2719	42,000 CUP	37.5	2901	50,600 CUP
100 GR. HDY SP	Hodgdon	H380	.243"	2.500"	34.0	2681	44,400 CUP	36.3	2835	50,400 CUP
100 GR. HDY SP	Hodgdon	Varget	.243"	2.500"	31.5	2741	46,000 CUP	33.5	2851	50,800 CUP
100 GR. HDY SP	Hodgdon	BL-C(2)	.243"	2.500"	32.0	2718	44,900 CUP	34.5	2886	51,200 CUP
100 GR. HDY SP	Hodgdon	H335	.243"	2.500"	30.0	2674	46,500 CUP	32.2	2817	51,200 CUP
100 GR. HDY SP	Hodgdon	H4895	.243"	2.500"	29.8	2710	46,500 CUP	31.8	2835	50,200 CUP
105 GR. HDY A-MAX	Hodgdon	H4831	.243"	2.600"	37.6	2692	45,400 CUP	40.0C	2800	48,700 CUP
105 GR. HDY A-MAX	Hodgdon	H4350	.243"	2.600"	34.7	2724	45,700 CUP	37.0C	2883	52,200 CUP
105 GR. HDY A-MAX	Hodgdon	H414	.243"	2.600"	34.6	2710	43,500 CUP	36.8	2878	51,000 CUP
105 GR. HDY A-MAX	Hodgdon	H380	.243"	2.600"	32.9	2651	46,200 CUP	35.0	2812	51,800 CUP
105 GR. HDY A-MAX	Hodgdon	Varget	.243"	2.600"	30.8	2726	48,600 CUP	32.8	2822	51,400 CUP
105 GR. HDY A-MAX	Hodgdon	BL-C(2)	.243"	2.600"	31.7	2676	44,400 CUP	33.8	2838	50,600 CUP
105 GR. HDY A-MAX	Hodgdon	H335	.243"	2.600"	29.6	2660	47,700 CUP	31.5	2782	52,000 CUP
105 GR. HDY A-MAX	Hodgdon	H4895	.243"	2.600"	28.9	2646	46,000 CUP	30.8	2731	51,700 CUP

Bullet Weight (Gr.)	Manufacturer	Powder	Bullet Diam.	C.O.L.	Grs.	Vel. (ft/s)	Pressure	Grs.	Vel. (ft/s)	Pressure
107 GR. SIE HPBT	Hodgdon	H4831	.243'	2.600"	37.6	2606	40,600 CUP	40.0C	2738	45,500 CUP
107 GR. SIE HPBT	Hodgdon	H4350	.243"	2.600"	35.2	2720	45,000 CUP	37.5	2844	50,300 CUP
107 GR. SIE HPBT	Hodgdon	H414	.243"	2.600"	35.2	2720	43,800 CUP	37.5	2886	51,000 CUP
107 GR. SIE HPBT	Hodgdon	H380	.243"	2.600"	33.5	2621	45,000 CUP	35.7	2815	51,800 CUP
107 GR. SIE HPBT	Hodgdon	Varget	.243"	2.600"	31.2	2716	47,400 CUP	33.2	2817	51,800 CUP
107 GR. SIE HPBT	Hodgdon	BL-C(2)	.243"	2.600"	32.6	2698	44,900 CUP	34.7	2843	51,300 CUP
107 GR. SIE HPBT	Hodgdon	H335	.243"	2.600"	30.0	2651	46,100 CUP	32.0	2788	51,400 CUP
107 GR. SIE HPBT	Hodgdon	H4895	.243"	2.600"	29.7	2659	45,900 CUP	31.6	2783	51,700 CUP

Cartridge: 243 Winchester Load Type: Rifle					Starting Loads			Maximum Loads		
Bullet Weight (Gr.)	Manufacturer	Powder	Bullet Diam.	C.O.L.	Grs.	Vel. (ft/s)	Pressure	Grs.	Vel. (ft/s)	Pressure
55 GR. NOS BT	Hodgdon	H414	.243"	2.650"	45.0	3611	37,400 CUP	50.0	3950	51,600 CUP
55 GR. NOS BT	Winchester	760	.243"	2.650"	45.0	3611	37,400 CUP	50.0	3950	51,600 CUP
55 GR. NOS BT	IMR	IMR 4007 SSC	.243"	2.650"	45.6	3515	38,800 CUP	48.5C	3834	48,300 CUP
55 GR. NOS BT	Hodgdon	H380	.243"	2.650"	46.0	3704	40,600 CUP	51.0	4010	48,700 CUP
55 GR. NOS BT	Hodgdon	CFE 223	.243"	2.650"	41.0	3684	49,500 PSI	45.3	3941	58,700 PSI
55 GR. NOS BT	Hodgdon	Varget	.243"	2.650"	41.0	3776	42,000 CUP	45.0	4000	50,000 CUP
55 GR. NOS BT	IMR	IMR 4320	.243"	2.650"	40.0	3603	48,600 CUP	45.5	3876	49,800 CUP
55 GR. NOS BT	IMR	IMR 4064	.243"	2.650"	39.5	3554	41,300 CUP	44.0	3875	51,200 CUP
55 GR. NOS BT	Hodgdon	BL-C(2)	.243"	2.650"	43.0	3779	42,600 CUP	47.0	4025	49,400 CUP
55 GR. NOS BT	IMR	IMR 4895	.243"	2.650"	40.0	3599	42,100 CUP	44.0	3877	50,200 CUP
55 GR. NOS BT	Hodgdon	H4895	.243"	2.650"	40.0	3638	35,100 CUP	44.5	4058	49,300 CUP
55 GR. NOS BT	IMR	IMR 8208 XBR	.243"	2.650"	40.0	3687	47,700 PSI	43.0	3931	58,600 PSI
55 GR. NOS BT	IMR	IMR 3031	.243"	2.650"	37.0	3520	38,300 CUP	40.5	3864	50,900 CUP
55 GR. NOS BT	Hodgdon	Benchmark	.243"	2.650"	39.0	3575	42,600 CUP	41.5	3815	50,100 CUP
55 GR. NOS BT LF	Hodgdon	H414	.243"	2.710"	44.5	3687	50,700 PSI	48.4	3896	57,800 PSI
55 GR. NOS BT LF	Winchester	760	.243"	2.710"	44.5	3687	50,700 PSI	48.4	3896	57,800 PSI
55 GR. NOS BT LF	IMR	IMR 4007 SSC	.243"	2.710"	39.9	3560	51,400 PSI	44.3C	3789	58,200 PSI
55 GR. NOS BT LF	Hodgdon	H380	.243"	2.710"	41.7	3654	52,700 PSI	45.3	3826	57,500 PSI
55 GR. NOS BT LF	Hodgdon	Varget	.243"	2.710"	37.1	3646	53,000 PSI	39.5	3782	57,700 PSI
55 GR. NOS BT LF	IMR	IMR 4320	.243"	2.710"	38.2	3497	48,200 PSI	41.0	3757	56,500 PSI
55 GR. NOS BT LF	IMR	IMR 4064	.243"	2.710"	37.6	3606	50,000 PSI	40.0	3801	57,800 PSI
55 GR. NOS BT LF	Hodgdon	BL-C(2)	.243"	2.710"	40.9	3689	50,700 PSI	43.5	3868	58,300 PSI
55 GR. NOS BT LF	IMR	IMR 4895	.243"	2.710"	38.4	3585	50,000 PSI	40.8	3783	57,700 PSI
55 GR. NOS BT LF	Hodgdon	H4895	.243"	2.710"	35.7	3621	50,700 PSI	38.0	3777	57,100 PSI
58 GR. HDY V-MAX	Hodgdon	H414	.243"	2.600"	46.0	3633	43,600 CUP	49.0	3806	49,100 CUP
58 GR. HDY V-MAX	Winchester	760	.243"	2.600"	46.0	3633	43,600 CUP	49.0	3806	49,000 CUP
58 GR. HDY V-MAX	IMR	IMR 4007 SSC	.243"	2.600"	46.0	3550	42,800 CUP	49.0C	3794	49,200 CUP

58 GR. HDY V-MAX	Hodgdon	H380	.243"	2.600"	46.0	3721	47,500 CUP	49.5	3874	51,000 CUP
58 GR. HDY V-MAX	Hodgdon	CFE 223	.243"	2.600"	41.0	3634	50,200 PSI	44.9	3850	57,800 PSI
58 GR. HDY V-MAX	Hodgdon	Varget	.243"	2.600"	41.0	3617	44,800 CUP	44.0	3790	49,800 CUP
58 GR. HDY V-MAX	IMR	IMR 4320	.243"	2.600"	40.5	3448	41,800 CUP	44.8	3822	50,100 CUP
58 GR. HDY V-MAX	IMR	IMR 4064	.243"	2.600"	39.6	3388	39,400 CUP	44.0	3780	50,200 CUP
58 GR. HDY V-MAX	IMR	IMR 4895	.243"	2.600"	40.5	3551	42,300 CUP	44.7	3819	50,000 CUP
58 GR. HDY V-MAX	Hodgdon	H335	.243"	2.600"	39.5	3714	47,800 CUP	41.5	3812	50,600 CUP
58 GR. HDY V-MAX	Hodgdon	H4895	.243"	2.600"	40.0	3643	43,300 CUP	43.0	3851	49,900 CUP
58 GR. HDY V-MAX	IMR	IMR 8208 XBR	.243"	2.600"	39.0	3581	47,300 PSI	42.3	3825	58,300 PSI
58 GR. HDY V-MAX	IMR	IMR 3031	.243"	2.600"	36.5	3467	40,700 CUP	41.0	3815	50,500 CUP
58 GR. HDY V-MAX	Hodgdon	Benchmark	.243"	2.600"	35.0	3417	41,800 CUP	37.5	3607	50,000 CUP
60 GR. SIE HP	Hodgdon	H414	.243"	2.600"	43.0	3423	38,600 CUP	47.5	3724	49,600 CUP
60 GR. SIE HP	Winchester	760	.243"	2.600"	43.0	3423	38,600 CUP	47.5	3724	49,600 CUP
60 GR. SIE HP	IMR	IMR 4007 SSC	.243"	2.600"	45.7	3544	45,900 CUP	48.5C	3752	51,300 CUP
60 GR. SIE HP	Hodgdon	H380	.243"	2.600"	43.0	3514	38,900 CUP	48.0	3781	47,400 CUP
60 GR. SIE HP	Hodgdon	CFE 223	.243"	2.600"	41.0	3541	49,400 PSI	45.0	3785	58,600 PSI
60 GR. SIE HP	Hodgdon	Varget	.243"	2.600"	40.0	3671	45,400 CUP	42.7	3816	50,400 CUP
60 GR. SIE HP	IMR	IMR 4320	.243"	2.600"	40.0	3431	42,500 CUP	44.4	3716	50,500 CUP
60 GR. SIE HP	IMR	IMR 4064	.243"	2.600"	40.0	3476	43,600 CUP	43.8	3766	50,400 CUP
60 GR. SIE HP	IMR	IMR 4895	.243"	2.600"	39.6	3464	43,500 CUP	43.3	3785	50,800 CUP
60 GR. SIE HP	Hodgdon	H335	.243"	2.600"	35.0	3445	41,400 CUP	39.0	3717	50,300 CUP
60 GR. SIE HP	Hodgdon	H4895	.243"	2.600"	38.0	3521	40,500 CUP	42.0	3812	50,600 CUP
60 GR. SIE HP	IMR	IMR 8208 XBR	.243"	2.600"	37.0	3505	50,000 PSI	40.2	3702	58,500 PSI
60 GR. SIE HP	IMR	IMR 3031	.243"	2.600"	36.8	3448	43,000 CUP	40.5	3714	50,500 CUP
60 GR. SIE HP	Hodgdon	Benchmark	.243"	2.600"	38.5	3587	47,000 CUP	41.2	3713	50,700 CUP
62 GR. BAR VG FB	Hodgdon	H414	.243"	2.620"	43.5	3427	50,600 PSI	46.3	3631	58,600 PSI
62 GR. BAR VG FB	Winchester	760	.243"	2.620"	43.5	3427	50,600 PSI	46.3	3631	58,600 PSI
62 GR. BAR VG FB	IMR	IMR 4007 SSC	.243"	2.620"	42.0	3408	51,400 PSI	44.7	3600	58,600 PSI
62 GR. BAR VG FB	Hodgdon	H380	.243"	2.620"	41.9	3450	50,100 PSI	44.5	3625	57,900 PSI
62 GR. BAR VG FB	Hodgdon	CFE 223	.243"	2.620"	34.0	3328	54,200 PSI	38.0	3517	59,300 PSI
62 GR. BAR VG FB	Hodgdon	Varget	.243"	2.620"	39.3	3476	50,900 PSI	41.4	3620	57,100 PSI
62 GR. BAR VG FB	IMR	IMR 4320	.243"	2.620"	39.0	3425	49,600 PSI	41.4	3602	56,900 PSI
62 GR. BAR VG FB	IMR	IMR 4064	.243"	2.620"	38.1	3480	51,400 PSI	40.5	3652	58,000 PSI
62 GR. BAR VG FB	IMR	IMR 4895	.243"	2.620"	38.1	3460	50,600 PSI	40.5	3658	58,300 PSI
62 GR. BAR VG FB	Hodgdon	H4895	.243"	2.620"	36.7	3478	51,200 PSI	39.0	3622	57,400 PSI
62 GR. BAR VG FB	IMR	IMR 8208 XBR	.243"	2.620"	35.0	3321	46,500 PSI	39.0	3598	58,800 PSI
62 GR. BAR VG FB	IMR	IMR 3031	.243"	2.620"	34.8	3392	49,600 PSI	37.0	3573	58,100 PSI
62 GR. BAR VG FB	Hodgdon	Benchmark	.243"	2.620"	36.1	3442	52,000 PSI	38.0	3586	58,600 PSI
65 GR. HDY V-MAX	Hodgdon	Suprform	.243"	2.600"	49.0	3530	52,100 PSI	51.9C	3773	57,300 PSI
65 GR. HDY V-MAX	Hodgdon	H414	.243"	2.600"	45.0	3521	41,400 CUP	48.0	3746	49,400 CUP

65 GR. HDY V-MAX	Winchester	760	.243"	2.600"	45.0	3521	41,400 CUP	48.0	3746	49,400 CUP
65 GR. HDY V-MAX	IMR	IMR 4007 SSC	.243"	2.600"	44.6	3391	44,200 CUP	47.4	3646	51,000 CUP
65 GR. HDY V-MAX	Hodgdon	H380	.243"	2.600"	42.0	3448	45,200 CUP	45.0	3627	50,000 CUP
65 GR. HDY V-MAX	Hodgdon	CFE 223	.243"	2.600"	38.0	3360	47,400 PSI	43.0	3632	57,300 PSI
65 GR. HDY V-MAX	Hodgdon	Varget	.243"	2.600"	38.0	3494	43,100 CUP	41.0	3682	49,600 CUP
65 GR. HDY V-MAX	IMR	IMR 4320	.243"	2.600"	40.5	3448	43,800 CUP	43.9	3670	49,500 CUP
65 GR. HDY V-MAX	IMR	IMR 4064	.243"	2.600"	40.0	3415	43,000 CUP	43.4	3698	50,000 CUP
65 GR. HDY V-MAX	Hodgdon	BL-C(2)	.243"	2.600"	39.0	3493	47,300 CUP	42.0	3612	49,500 CUP
65 GR. HDY V-MAX	IMR	IMR 4895	.243"	2.600"	38.5	3392	42,300 CUP	42.7	3664	50,600 CUP
65 GR. HDY V-MAX	Hodgdon	H4895	.243"	2.600"	38.0	3522	44,500 CUP	41.0	3677	49,200 CUP
65 GR. HDY V-MAX	IMR	IMR 8208 XBR	.243"	2.600"	37.0	3363	45,800 PSI	41.0	3666	58,500 PSI
65 GR. HDY V-MAX	IMR	IMR 3031	.243"	2.600"	36.5	3397	43,800 CUP	39.8	3624	50,200 CUP
65 GR. HDY V-MAX	Hodgdon	Benchmark	.243"	2.600"	37.0	3417	44,300 CUP	40.0	3598	50,600 CUP
70 GR. SPR HP	Hodgdon	Suprform	.243"	2.625"	46.0	3332	43,600 PSI	51.0C	3661	57,900 PSI
70 GR. SPR HP	Hodgdon	H414	.243"	2.625"	42.0	3314	41,600 CUP	46.0	3568	49,800 CUP
70 GR. SPR HP	Winchester	760	.243"	2.625"	42.0	3314	41,600 CUP	46.0	3568	49,800 CUP
70 GR. SPR HP	IMR	IMR 4007 SSC	.243"	2.625"	43.7	3320	46,200 CUP	46.5	3515	50,900 CUP
70 GR. SPR HP	Hodgdon	H380	.243"	2.625"	42.0	3349	42,900 CUP	46.0	3567	48,900 CUP
70 GR. SPR HP	Hodgdon	CFE 223	.243"	2.625"	36.0	3266	51,800 PSI	41.5	3487	57,400 PSI
70 GR. SPR HP	Hodgdon	Varget	.243"	2.625"	38.0	3433	45,500 CUP	40.5	3574	50,100 CUP
70 GR. SPR HP	IMR	IMR 4320	.243"	2.625"	38.5	3325	43,800 CUP	42.5	3541	50,300 CUP
70 GR. SPR HP	IMR	IMR 4064	.243"	2.625"	38.5	3316	43,700 CUP	42.5	3541	50,000 CUP
70 GR. SPR HP	Hodgdon	BL-C(2)	.243"	2.625"	35.0	3228	47,900 CUP	39.0	3384	50,400 CUP
70 GR. SPR HP	IMR	IMR 4895	.243"	2.625"	38.5	3349	44,300 CUP	42.6	3558	50,000 CUP
70 GR. SPR HP	Hodgdon	H4895	.243"	2.625"	36.0	3286	42,700 CUP	39.5	3477	49,200 CUP
70 GR. SPR HP	IMR	IMR 8208 XBR	.243"	2.625"	35.0	3232	47,600 PSI	38.6	3461	58,100 PSI
70 GR. SPR HP	IMR	IMR 3031	.243"	2.625"	35.5	3218	41,500 CUP	39.0	3485	51,100 CUP
70 GR. SPR HP	Hodgdon	Benchmark	.243"	2.625"	36.5	3128	45,100 CUP	39.3	3491	50,300 CUP
75 GR. HDY HP	Hodgdon	Suprform	.243"	2.640"	45.0	3280	47,400 PSI	49.0	3510	57,900 PSI
75 GR. HDY HP	Hodgdon	H414	.243"	2.640"	42.0	3203	41,100 CUP	46.0	3447	50,100 CUP
75 GR. HDY HP	Winchester	760	.243"	2.640"	42.0	3203	41,100 CUP	46.0	3447	50,100 CUP
75 GR. HDY HP	IMR	IMR 4007 SSC	.243"	2.640"	42.3	3198	45,700 CUP	45.0	3391	51,100 CUP
75 GR. HDY HP	Hodgdon	H380	.243"	2.640"	40.0	3127	42,700 CUP	44.5	3393	48,600 CUP
75 GR. HDY HP	Hodgdon	CFE 223	.243"	2.640"	34.0	3080	50,600 PSI	37.7	3274	57,600 PSI
75 GR. HDY HP	Hodgdon	Varget	.243"	2.640"	36.0	3246	45,000 CUP	38.5	3408	50,500 CUP
75 GR. HDY HP	IMR	IMR 4320	.243"	2.640"	37.7	3180	43,500 CUP	41.5	3420	50,600 CUP
75 GR. HDY HP	IMR	IMR 4064	.243"	2.640"	37.5	3183	43,300 CUP	41.2	3419	50,300 CUP
75 GR. HDY HP	Hodgdon	BL-C(2)	.243"	2.640"	34.0	3041	45,100 CUP	37.5	3185	49,200 CUP
75 GR. HDY HP	IMR	IMR 4895	.243"	2.640"	37.5	3198	44,200 CUP	41.7	3423	50,400 CUP

75 GR. HDY HP	Hodgdon	H4895	.243"	2.640"	34.0	3101	40,900 CUP	38.0	3354	49,400 CUP
75 GR. HDY HP	IMR	IMR 8208 XBR	.243"	2.640"	34.5	3114	48,200 PSI	37.8	3316	57,900 PSI
75 GR. HDY HP	IMR	IMR 3031	.243"	2.640"	33.2	3061	41,800 CUP	36.7	3298	49,800 CUP
80 GR. HDY GMX	Hodgdon	Hybrid 100V	.243"	2.610"	39.1	3083	48,600 PSI	42.5	3318	58,100 PSI
80 GR. HDY GMX	Hodgdon	H4350	.243"	2.610"	38.3	3045	52,600 PSI	40.7	3183	58,500 PSI
80 GR. HDY GMX	Hodgdon	H414	.243"	2.610"	38.9	3022	48,400 PSI	42.3	3231	57,300 PSI
80 GR. HDY GMX	Winchester	760	.243"	2.610"	38.9	3022	48,400 PSI	42.3	3231	57,300 PSI
80 GR. HDY GMX	IMR	IMR 4007 SSC	.243"	2.610"	35.7	2964	51,900 PSI	38.0	3101	57,000 PSI
80 GR. HDY GMX	Hodgdon	H380	.243"	2.610"	36.9	3022	54,600 PSI	39.3	3135	57,300 PSI
80 GR. HDY GMX	Hodgdon	Varget	.243"	2.610"	34.1	2986	51,200 PSI	36.3	3137	58,700 PSI
80 GR. HDY GMX	IMR	IMR 4320	.243"	2.610"	35.7	3011	49,800 PSI	38.0	3182	58,200 PSI
80 GR. HDY GMX	IMR	IMR 4064	.243"	2.610"	34.0	2966	49,500 PSI	36.3	3134	57,600 PSI
80 GR. HDY GMX	Hodgdon	BL-C(2)	.243"	2.610"	36.5	3057	49,600 PSI	39.2	3220	57,000 PSI
80 GR. HDY GMX	IMR	IMR 4895	.243"	2.610"	35.3	3032	51,500 PSI	37.5	3165	58,100 PSI
80 GR. HDY GMX	Hodgdon	H4895	.243"	2.610"	32.7	2982	51,900 PSI	34.8	3123	58,100 PSI
80 GR. HDY GMX	IMR	IMR 8208 XBR	.243"	2.610"	33.0	2961	51,400 PSI	35.1	3109	58,800 PSI
80 GR. SIE BTSP	Hodgdon	Suprform	.243"	2.635"	44.0	3236	49,300 PSI	48.7	3460	58,400 PSI
80 GR. SIE BTSP	Hodgdon	Hybrid 100V	.243"	2.635"	41.0	3072	40,100 CUP	45.0C	3330	48,400 CUP
80 GR. SIE BTSP	Hodgdon	H414	.243"	2.635"	42.0	3249	46,300 CUP	45.0	3404	50,100 CUP
80 GR. SIE BTSP	Winchester	760	.243"	2.635"	42.0	3249	46,300 CUP	45.0	3404	50,100 CUP
80 GR. SIE BTSP	IMR	IMR 4007 SSC	.243"	2.635"	40.0	2990	40,200 CUP	45.0	3319	50,400 CUP
80 GR. SIE BTSP	Hodgdon	H380	.243"	2.635"	38.0	3047	44,700 CUP	41.2	3223	50,300 CUP
80 GR. SIE BTSP	Hodgdon	Varget	.243"	2.635"	36.0	3193	45,400 CUP	38.5	3355	50,300 CUP
80 GR. SIE BTSP	IMR	IMR 4320	.243"	2.635"	37.0	3132	44,000 CUP	40.5	3339	50,600 CUP
80 GR. SIE BTSP	IMR	IMR 4064	.243"	2.635"	37.5	3141	45,000 CUP	41.0	3320	50,800 CUP
80 GR. SIE BTSP	Hodgdon	BL-C(2)	.243"	2.635"	35.0	3083	47,100 CUP	38.5	3242	50,600 CUP
80 GR. SIE BTSP	IMR	IMR 4895	.243"	2.635"	36.5	3094	43,300 CUP	40.2	3290	50,300 CUP
80 GR. SIE BTSP	Hodgdon	H4895	.243"	2.635"	35.0	3123	45,800 CUP	38.0	3307	50,100 CUP
80 GR. SIE BTSP	IMR	IMR 8208 XBR	.243"	2.600"	34.0	3013	45,400 PSI	38.0	3269	57,500 PSI
85 GR. BAR TSX	Hodgdon	Hybrid 100V	.243"	2.620"	38.3	3022	47,500 PSI	42.5C	3267	58,100 PSI
85 GR. BAR TSX	IMR	IMR 4831	.243"	2.620"	38.3	3014	49,900 PSI	42.6C	3233	58,500 PSI
85 GR. BAR TSX	Hodgdon	H4350	.243"	2.620"	37.3	2972	49,600 PSI	40.5	3141	57,300 PSI
85 GR. BAR TSX	Hodgdon	H414	.243"	2.620"	38.4	2981	50,300 PSI	41.7	3165	57,300 PSI
85 GR. BAR TSX	IMR	IMR 4350	.243"	2.620"	37.4	2980	48,900 PSI	40.7	3176	57,800 PSI
85 GR. BAR TSX	Winchester	760	.243"	2.620"	38.4	2981	50,300 PSI	41.7	3165	57,300 PSI
85 GR. BAR TSX	Hodgdon	H380	.243"	2.620"	36.4	2987	55,700 PSI	38.7	3074	57,300 PSI
85 GR. BAR TSX	Hodgdon	Varget	.243"	2.620"	34.3	2997	52,200 PSI	36.5	3121	58,000 PSI
85 GR. BAR TSX	IMR	IMR 4320	.243"	2.620"	35.3	2996	49,700 PSI	37.6	3158	58,100 PSI
85 GR. BAR TSX	IMR	IMR 4064	.243"	2.620"	33.8	2964	49,200 PSI	36.0	3112	56,700 PSI
85 GR. BAR TSX	IMR	IMR 4895	.243"	2.620"	34.6	3010	50,700 PSI	36.8	3146	58,000 PSI

85 GR. BAR TSX	Hodgdon	H4895	.243"	2.620"	32.6	2955	51,800 PSI	34.7	3089	57,500 PSI
90 GR. SPR SP	IMR	IMR 7828	.243"	2.625"	45.0	2950	46,100 CUP	48.0C*	3130	50,600 CUP
90 GR. SPR SP	Hodgdon	H4831	.243"	2.625"	45.0	3010	43,700 CUP	48.0C	3203	50,800 CUP
90 GR. SPR SP	Hodgdon	Hybrid 100V	.243"	2.625"	40.0	2934	43,000 CUP	44.0C	3204	50,100 CUP
90 GR. SPR SP	IMR	IMR 4831	.243"	2.625"	40.5	2858	43,700 CUP	43.9	3050	50,700 CUP
90 GR. SPR SP	Hodgdon	H4350	.243"	2.625"	42.0	3039	44,400 CUP	44.5	3185	50,600 CUP
90 GR. SPR SP	Hodgdon	H414	.243"	2.625"	41.0	3024	43,600 CUP	43.5	3185	49,600 CUP
90 GR. SPR SP	IMR	IMR 4350	.243"	2.625"	39.5	2856	42,700 CUP	43.0	3096	50,800 CUP
90 GR. SPR SP	Winchester	760	.243"	2.625"	41.0	3024	43,600 CUP	43.5	3185	49,600 CUP
90 GR. SPR SP	IMR	IMR 4007 SSC	.243"	2.625"	39.0	2917	46,300 CUP	41.5	3062	49,900 CUP
90 GR. SPR SP	Hodgdon	H380	.243"	2.625"	38.0	2892	43,100 CUP	40.5	3060	49,500 CUP
90 GR. SPR SP	Hodgdon	Varget	.243"	2.625"	34.0	2964	44,800 CUP	36.5	3106	50,400 CUP
90 GR. SPR SP	IMR	IMR 4064	.243"	2.625"	33.5	2796	41,600 CUP	37.0	3020	50,200 CUP
90 GR. SPR SP	IMR	IMR 4895	.243"	2.625"	33.5	2815	41,800 CUP	36.9	3033	50,200 CUP
90 GR. SPR SP	Hodgdon	H4895	.243"	2.625"	34.0	2967	44,900 CUP	36.5	3114	50,800 CUP
95 GR. NOS PART	Hodgdon	H1000	.243"	2.650"	45.0	2946	44,900 CUP	48.0C	3077	50,000 CUP
95 GR. NOS PART	IMR	IMR 7828	.243"	2.650"	41.5	2780	42,300 CUP	45.8C*	3030	50,600 CUP
95 GR. NOS PART	Winchester	Supreme 780	.243"	2.650"	45.1	2943	44,100 CUP	48.0	3138	49,800 CUP
95 GR. NOS PART	Hodgdon	H4831	.243"	2.650"	42.0	2930	47,000 CUP	44.5C	3052	50,700 CUP
95 GR. NOS PART	Hodgdon	Hybrid 100V	.243"	2.650"	39.0	2866	42,200 CUP	43.0C	3113	50,200 CUP
95 GR. NOS PART	IMR	IMR 4831	.243"	2.650"	39.5	2793	43,900 CUP	42.8	2985	50,200 CUP
95 GR. NOS PART	Hodgdon	H4350	.243"	2.650"	39.0	2917	45,800 CUP	42.0	3087	50,500 CUP
95 GR. NOS PART	Hodgdon	H414	.243"	2.650"	39.0	2933	43,800 CUP	42.0	3138	50,700 CUP
95 GR. NOS PART	IMR	IMR 4350	.243"	2.650"	38.0	2792	43,200 CUP	41.8	2993	50,200 CUP
95 GR. NOS PART	Winchester	760	.243"	2.650"	39.0	2933	43,800 CUP	42.0	3138	50,700 CUP
95 GR. NOS PART	IMR	IMR 4007 SSC	.243"	2.650"	37.0	2822	46,100 CUP	39.5	2937	49,600 CUP
95 GR. NOS PART	Hodgdon	H380	.243"	2.650"	36.0	2779	43,000 CUP	38.0	2922	49,100 CUP
95 GR. NOS PART	Hodgdon	Varget	.243"	2.650"	33.0	2870	45,000 CUP	35.0	2996	50,200 CUP
95 GR. NOS PART	IMR	IMR 4064	.243"	2.650"	33.0	2745	43,500 CUP	36.5	2967	51,100 CUP
95 GR. NOS PART	IMR	IMR 4895	.243"	2.650"	32.0	2687	41,800 CUP	35.5	2908	50,400 CUP
95 GR. NOS PART	Hodgdon	H4895	.243"	2.650"	33.0	2865	45,000 CUP	35.0	2990	50,700 CUP
100 GR. SPR BTSP	Hodgdon	H1000	.243"	2.650"	44.0	2876	45,700 CUP	47.0C	3000	49,800 CUP
100 GR. SPR BTSP	IMR	IMR 7828	.243"	2.650"	42.5	2796	43,700 CUP	46.0C*	3009	51,100 CUP
100 GR. SPR BTSP	Winchester	Supreme 780	.243"	2.650"	45.7	2927	45,600 CUP	47.5	3046	49,300 CUP
100 GR. SPR BTSP	Hodgdon	H4831	.243"	2.650"	39.0	2761	44,400 CUP	42.0	2924	50,100 CUP
100 GR. SPR BTSP	Hodgdon	Hybrid 100V	.243"	2.650"	40.0	2868	45,400 CUP	43.7C	3100	51,700 CUP
100 GR. SPR BTSP	IMR	IMR 4831	.243"	2.650"	39.2	2733	43,500 CUP	43.0	2947	50,800 CUP
100 GR. SPR BTSP	Hodgdon	H4350	.243"	2.650"	37.0	2806	45,100 CUP	40.0	2973	51,000 CUP
100 GR. SPR BTSP	Hodgdon	H414	.243"	2.650"	37.0	2800	44,500 CUP	40.0	2963	50,600 CUP

Bullet	Mfg	Powder	Dia	COL	Charge	Vel	Pressure	Charge	Vel	Pressure
100 GR. SPR BTSP	IMR	IMR 4350	.243"	2.650"	38.5	2760	43,000 CUP	42.0	2958	50,100 CUP
100 GR. SPR BTSP	Winchester	760	.243"	2.650"	37.0	2800	44,500 CUP	40.0	2963	50,600 CUP
100 GR. SPR BTSP	IMR	IMR 4007 SSC	.243"	2.650"	37.2	2784	47,000 CUP	39.5	2905	50,400 CUP
100 GR. SPR BTSP	Hodgdon	H380	.243"	2.650"	34.0	2639	43,600 CUP	36.0	2770	50,100 CUP
100 GR. SPR BTSP	Hodgdon	Varget	.243"	2.650"	31.0	2674	42,700 CUP	33.7	2838	50,400 CUP
100 GR. SPR BTSP	IMR	IMR 4064	.243"	2.650"	33.0	2672	42,200 CUP	36.5	2902	51,100 CUP
100 GR. SPR BTSP	IMR	IMR 4895	.243"	2.650"	32.8	2683	42,300 CUP	35.7	2862	50,100 CUP
100 GR. SPR BTSP	Hodgdon	H4895	.243"	2.650"	31.0	2683	44,900 CUP	33.0	2818	50,100 CUP
100 GR. SPR BTSP	IMR	Trail Boss	.243"	2.650"	8.0	1045	27,300 CUP	15.3	1603	39,100 CUP
105 GR. HDY A-MAX	Hodgdon	Retumbo	.243"	2.760"	46.0	2772	44,200 CUP	49.0C	2986	49,700 CUP
105 GR. HDY A-MAX	Hodgdon	H1000	.243"	2.760"	43.0	2798	45,400 CUP	46.0C	2930	50,200 CUP
105 GR. HDY A-MAX	IMR	IMR 7828	.243"	2.760"	40.6	2721	44,500 CUP	44.0C	2894	50,300 CUP
105 GR. HDY A-MAX	Winchester	Supreme 780	.243"	2.760"	44.2	2872	46,900 CUP	47.0	3036	50,300 CUP
105 GR. HDY A-MAX	Hodgdon	H4831	.243"	2.760"	38.0	2687	43,900 CUP	41.0	2846	50,200 CUP
105 GR. HDY A-MAX	Hodgdon	Hybrid 100V	.243"	2.760"	37.0	2721	43,800 CUP	41.0C	2959	49,300 CUP
105 GR. HDY A-MAX	IMR	IMR 4831	.243"	2.760"	38.0	2661	43,700 CUP	41.5	2870	50,800 CUP
105 GR. HDY A-MAX	Hodgdon	H4350	.243"	2.760"	35.0	2663	44,300 CUP	37.5	2799	49,500 CUP
105 GR. HDY A-MAX	Hodgdon	H414	.243"	2.760"	36.0	2692	43,700 CUP	39.0	2862	50,100 CUP
105 GR. HDY A-MAX	IMR	IMR 4350	.243"	2.760"	36.7	2648	43,000 CUP	40.2	2870	50,800 CUP
105 GR. HDY A-MAX	Winchester	760	.243"	2.760"	36.0	2692	43,700 CUP	39.0	2862	50,100 CUP
105 GR. HDY A-MAX	IMR	IMR 4007 SSC	.243"	2.760"	35.7	2665	43,600 CUP	38.0	2797	49,800 CUP
105 GR. HDY A-MAX	Hodgdon	H380	.243"	2.760"	33.0	2589	43,700 CUP	35.0	2687	49,800 CUP
105 GR. HDY A-MAX	Hodgdon	Varget	.243"	2.760"	31.0	2631	45,600 CUP	33.0	2769	50,800 CUP
105 GR. HDY A-MAX	Hodgdon	H4895	.243"	2.760"	30.5	2619	44,900 CUP	32.5	2724	50,100 CUP
107 GR. SIE BTHP	Hodgdon	Retumbo	.243"	2.850"	46.0	2785	42,800 CUP	49.0C	2974	48,500 CUP
107 GR. SIE BTHP	Hodgdon	H1000	.243"	2.850"	43.0	2787	44,700 CUP	46.0C	2918	50,100 CUP
107 GR. SIE BTHP	IMR	IMR 7828	.243"	2.850"	40.0	2675	43,000 CUP	43.5	2878	50,100 CUP
107 GR. SIE BTHP	Winchester	Supreme 780	.243"	2.850"	44.0	2869	46,300 CUP	47.0	3016	50,500 CUP
107 GR. SIE BTHP	Hodgdon	H4831	.243"	2.850"	38.0	2678	43,700 CUP	41.0	2835	50,100 CUP
107 GR. SIE BTHP	Hodgdon	Hybrid 100V	.243"	2.850"	38.0	2760	45,300 CUP	41.5C	2957	50,900 CUP
107 GR. SIE BTHP	IMR	IMR 4831	.243"	2.850"	37.5	2662	43,900 CUP	40.9	2844	50,400 CUP
107 GR. SIE BTHP	Hodgdon	H4350	.243"	2.850"	35.0	2671	43,100 CUP	37.5	2800	50,200 CUP
107 GR. SIE BTHP	Hodgdon	H414	.243"	2.850"	35.0	2664	43,400 CUP	38.0	2809	49,500 CUP
107 GR. SIE BTHP	IMR	IMR 4350	.243"	2.850"	36.5	2661	42,100 CUP	39.8	2853	50,600 CUP
107 GR. SIE BTHP	Winchester	760	.243"	2.850"	35.0	2664	43,400 CUP	38.0	2809	49,500 CUP
107 GR. SIE BTHP	IMR	IMR 4007 SSC	.243"	2.850"	36.0	2707	47,300 CUP	38.0	2807	50,700 CUP
107 GR. SIE BTHP	Hodgdon	H380	.243"	2.850"	33.0	2570	44,400 CUP	34.8	2682	50,100 CUP
107 GR. SIE BTHP	Hodgdon	Varget	.243"	2.850"	31.0	2630	45,300 CUP	33.0	2749	50,400 CUP
107 GR. SIE BTHP	Hodgdon	H4895	.243"	2.850"	30.5	2613	45,900 CUP	32.5	2719	49,900 CUP

Cartridge: 6mm Remington Load Type: Rifle					Starting Loads			Maximum Loads		
Bullet Weight (Gr.)	Manufacturer	Powder	Bullet Diam.	C.O.L.	Grs.	Vel. (ft/s)	Pressure	Grs.	Vel. (ft/s)	Pressure
55 GR. NOS BT	Hodgdon	H414	.243"	2.800"	46.0	3626	43,900 PSI	51.0	4016	58,800 PSI
55 GR. NOS BT	Winchester	760	.243"	2.800"	46.0	3626	43,900 PSI	51.0	4016	58,800 PSI
55 GR. NOS BT	Hodgdon	H380	.243"	2.800"	48.0	3793	49,900 PSI	53.0	4083	60,700 PSI
55 GR. NOS BT	Hodgdon	Varget	.243"	2.800"	43.0	3678	45,700 PSI	47.5	4023	58,800 PSI
55 GR. NOS BT	IMR	IMR 4320	.243"	2.800"	43.0	3603	43,900 PSI	47.8	4047	60,300 PSI
55 GR. NOS BT	Hodgdon	BL-C(2)	.243"	2.800"	44.0	3680	44,800 PSI	48.8	4094	60,100 PSI
55 GR. NOS BT	Hodgdon	H4895	.243"	2.800"	42.0	3656	43,700 PSI	46.5	4066	59,300 PSI
55 GR. NOS BT	IMR	IMR 8208 XBR	.243"	2.800"	40.0	3533	39,700 PSI	45.0	4044	59,300 PSI
55 GR. NOS BT	IMR	IMR 3031	.243"	2.800"	40.0	3656	44,500 PSI	45.0	4090	61,200 PSI
55 GR. NOS BT	Hodgdon	Benchmark	.243"	2.800"	40.0	3656	44,800 PSI	44.5	4028	59,600 PSI
55 GR. NOS BT LF	Hodgdon	H380	.243"	2.825"	48.0	3770	50,900 PSI	53.0	4018	59,100 PSI
55 GR. NOS BT LF	Hodgdon	Varget	.243"	2.825"	43.0	3679	46,900 PSI	47.0	4027	60,700 PSI
55 GR. NOS BT LF	IMR	IMR 4320	.243"	2.825"	43.0	3594	45,400 PSI	47.5	4030	61,500 PSI
55 GR. NOS BT LF	Winchester	748	.243"	2.825"	43.0	3645	46,100 PSI	48.0	4036	60,500 PSI
55 GR. NOS BT LF	Hodgdon	BL-C(2)	.243"	2.825"	44.0	3686	46,400 PSI	48.8	4041	59,300 PSI
55 GR. NOS BT LF	IMR	IMR 4895	.243"	2.825"	43.0	3695	47,800 PSI	47.0	4061	61,100 PSI
55 GR. NOS BT LF	Hodgdon	H4895	.243"	2.825"	41.0	3598	43,200 PSI	46.0	4071	61,800 PSI
55 GR. NOS BT LF	IMR	IMR 8208 XBR	.243"	2.825"	40.0	3540	42,200 PSI	44.6	4013	60,800 PSI
55 GR. NOS BT LF	IMR	IMR 3031	.243"	2.825"	39.0	3609	45,200 PSI	43.7	4043	61,100 PSI
55 GR. NOS BT LF	Hodgdon	Benchmark	.243"	2.825"	40.0	3584	44,900 PSI	44.0	4005	61,700 PSI
58 GR. HDY V-MAX	Hodgdon	H414	.243"	2.775"	45.0	3534	43,200 PSI	49.7	3925	59,100 PSI
58 GR. HDY V-MAX	Winchester	760	.243"	2.775"	45.0	3534	43,200 PSI	49.7	3925	59,100 PSI
58 GR. HDY V-MAX	IMR	IMR 4007 SSC	.243"	2.775"	46.0	3543	45,100 PSI	51.0C	3913	59,100 PSI
58 GR. HDY V-MAX	Hodgdon	H380	.243"	2.775"	46.0	3627	47,300 PSI	50.0	3898	56,700 PSI
58 GR. HDY V-MAX	Hodgdon	Varget	.243"	2.775"	42.0	3571	44,600 PSI	46.7	3953	59,600 PSI
58 GR. HDY V-MAX	IMR	IMR 4320	.243"	2.775"	43.0	3616	46,800 PSI	47.0	3974	61,100 PSI
58 GR. HDY V-MAX	IMR	IMR 4064	.243"	2.775"	42.0	3599	44,500 PSI	46.3C	3970	58,400 PSI
58 GR. HDY V-MAX	Hodgdon	BL-C(2)	.243"	2.775"	42.0	3502	41,800 PSI	46.5	3939	60,000 PSI
58 GR. HDY V-MAX	IMR	IMR 4895	.243"	2.775"	42.0	3597	44,900 PSI	46.7	4029	62,100 PSI
58 GR. HDY V-MAX	Hodgdon	H4895	.243"	2.775"	41.0	3590	44,500 PSI	46.0	3972	58,900 PSI
58 GR. HDY V-MAX	IMR	IMR 8208 XBR	.243"	2.775"	40.0	3537	42,700 PSI	44.5	3939	58,600 PSI
58 GR. HDY V-MAX	IMR	IMR 3031	.243"	2.775"	40.0	3642	46,900 PSI	44.2	3981	61,100 PSI
58 GR. HDY V-MAX	Hodgdon	Benchmark	.243"	2.775"	39.0	3500	42,200 PSI	43.0	3896	59,000 PSI
60 GR. SIE HP	Hodgdon	H414	.243"	2.700"	45.0	3466	43,800 PSI	50.0	3877	60,300 PSI
60 GR. SIE HP	Winchester	760	.243"	2.700"	45.0	3435	37,100 CUP	50.0	3877	60,300 PSI
60 GR. SIE HP	IMR	IMR 4007 SSC	.243"	2.700"	46.0	3514	46,800 PSI	50.5C	3894	61,200 PSI

60 GR. SIE HP	Hodgdon	H380	.243"	2.700"	45.0	3546	47,400 PSI	50.0	3874	59,700 PSI
60 GR. SIE HP	Hodgdon	Varget	.243"	2.700"	42.0	3565	47,200 PSI	46.5	3900	60,200 PSI
60 GR. SIE HP	IMR	IMR 4320	.243"	2.700"	42.0	3488	45,100 PSI	47.2	3899	61,100 PSI
60 GR. SIE HP	IMR	IMR 4064	.243"	2.700"	42.0	3570	46,400 PSI	46.2C	3930	60,400 PSI
60 GR. SIE HP	Winchester	748	.243"	2.700"	41.0	3532	47,500 PSI	46.5	3870	61,100 PSI
60 GR. SIE HP	Hodgdon	BL-C(2)	.243"	2.700"	41.0	3454	42,600 PSI	46.7	3870	59,200 PSI
60 GR. SIE HP	IMR	IMR 4895	.243"	2.700"	42.0	3609	49,100 PSI	46.5	3955	62,500 PSI
60 GR. SIE HP	Hodgdon	H4895	.243"	2.700"	41.0	3544	45,300 PSI	46.0	3934	61,400 PSI
60 GR. SIE HP	IMR	IMR 8208 XBR	.243"	2.700"	40.0	3488	43,000 PSI	44.5	3907	60,500 PSI
60 GR. SIE HP	IMR	IMR 3031	.243"	2.700"	40.0	3584	47,800 PSI	44.3	3925	62,200 PSI
60 GR. SIE HP	Hodgdon	Benchmark	.243"	2.700"	39.0	3478	44,400 PSI	43.0	3826	59,000 PSI
65 GR. HDY V-MAX	Hodgdon	Suprform	.243"	2.825"	49.0	3495	44,700 PSI	54.5	3927	62,700 PSI
65 GR. HDY V-MAX	Hodgdon	H4350	.243"	2.825"	48.0	3564	50,900 PSI	51.5C	3763	58,900 PSI
65 GR. HDY V-MAX	Hodgdon	H414	.243"	2.825"	44.0	3388	44,900 PSI	49.2	3777	60,700 PSI
65 GR. HDY V-MAX	Winchester	760	.243"	2.825"	44.0	3388	44,900 PSI	49.2	3777	60,700 PSI
65 GR. HDY V-MAX	IMR	IMR 4007 SSC	.243"	2.825"	45.0	3453	48,300 PSI	50.0C	3787	61,000 PSI
65 GR. HDY V-MAX	Hodgdon	H380	.243"	2.825"	44.0	3438	47,800 PSI	49.0	3763	60,000 PSI
65 GR. HDY V-MAX	Hodgdon	Varget	.243"	2.825"	41.0	3468	47,600 PSI	45.5	3775	60,200 PSI
65 GR. HDY V-MAX	IMR	IMR 4320	.243"	2.825"	40.0	3380	44,900 PSI	45.3	3794	61,700 PSI
65 GR. HDY V-MAX	IMR	IMR 4064	.243"	2.825"	40.0	3450	46,500 PSI	45.0	3839	61,800 PSI
65 GR. HDY V-MAX	Winchester	748	.243"	2.825"	40.0	3465	50,300 PSI	44.5	3739	61,000 PSI
65 GR. HDY V-MAX	Hodgdon	BL-C(2)	.243"	2.825"	40.0	3379	45,000 PSI	44.7	3723	60,000 PSI
65 GR. HDY V-MAX	IMR	IMR 4895	.243"	2.825"	40.0	3457	46,900 PSI	45.3	3856	63,100 PSI
65 GR. HDY V-MAX	Hodgdon	H4895	.243"	2.825"	39.0	3460	47,100 PSI	44.0	3797	60,600 PSI
65 GR. HDY V-MAX	IMR	IMR 8208 XBR	.243"	2.825"	39.0	3412	45,000 PSI	43.5	3777	60,900 PSI
65 GR. HDY V-MAX	IMR	IMR 3031	.243"	2.825"	38.0	3426	46,700 PSI	42.2	3765	61,600 PSI
65 GR. HDY V-MAX	Hodgdon	Benchmark	.243"	2.825"	39.0	3472	49,000 PSI	41.3	3694	60,200 PSI
70 GR. SIE HPBT	Hodgdon	Suprform	.243"	2.810"	50.0	3509	48,600 PSI	54.0	3812	61,000 PSI
70 GR. SIE HPBT	Hodgdon	H4350	.243"	2.810"	46.0	3360	46,700 PSI	50.8C	3671	59,800 PSI
70 GR. SIE HPBT	Hodgdon	H414	.243"	2.810"	44.0	3305	44,600 PSI	49.0	3693	60,900 PSI
70 GR. SIE HPBT	Winchester	760	.243"	2.810"	44.0	3305	44,600 PSI	49.0	3693	60,900 PSI
70 GR. SIE HPBT	IMR	IMR 4007 SSC	.243"	2.810"	44.0	3332	47,000 PSI	48.0	3632	58,900 PSI
70 GR. SIE HPBT	Hodgdon	H380	.243"	2.810"	43.0	3334	47,900 PSI	48.0	3653	61,000 PSI
70 GR. SIE HPBT	Hodgdon	Varget	.243"	2.810"	40.0	3355	47,800 PSI	44.5	3639	59,500 PSI
70 GR. SIE HPBT	IMR	IMR 4320	.243"	2.810"	40.0	3342	47,400 PSI	45.3	3718	63,400 PSI
70 GR. SIE HPBT	IMR	IMR 4064	.243"	2.810"	40.0	3355	45,600 PSI	44.5	3710	61,200 PSI
70 GR. SIE HPBT	Winchester	748	.243"	2.810"	40.0	3324	46,300 PSI	45.0	3691	63,400 PSI
70 GR. SIE HPBT	IMR	IMR 4895	.243"	2.810"	40.0	3364	46.500 PSI	44.6	3735	63,200 PSI
70 GR. SIE HPBT	Hodgdon	H4895	.243"	2.810"	39.0	3435	51,200 PSI	43.0	3653	60,100 PSI
70 GR. SIE HPBT	IMR	IMR 8208 XBR	.243"	2.810"	38.0	3236	43,000 PSI	42.7	3616	59,500 PSI

70 GR. SIE HPBT	IMR	IMR 3031	.243"	2.810"	38.0	3335	46,500 PSI	42.0	3673	62,400 PSI
70 GR. SIE HPBT	Hodgdon	Benchmark	.243"	2.810"	38.0	3315	46,800 PSI	41.0	3579	59,300 PSI
75 GR. HDY HP	Hodgdon	Suprform	.243"	2.825"	47.0	3297	47,500 PSI	52.0	3637	60,700 PSI
75 GR. HDY HP	Hodgdon	Hybrid 100V	.243"	2.825"	44.0	3213	47,700 PSI	48.0C	3491	57,900 PSI
75 GR. HDY HP	Hodgdon	H4350	.243"	2.825"	44.0	3262	48,600 PSI	49.0	3563	61,200 PSI
75 GR. HDY HP	Hodgdon	H414	.243"	2.825"	42.0	3151	44,400 PSI	47.0	3513	58,800 PSI
75 GR. HDY HP	IMR	IMR 4350	.243"	2.825"	44.0	3206	47,300 PSI	48.5C	3509	58,600 PSI
75 GR. HDY HP	Winchester	760	.243"	2.825"	42.0	3151	44,400 PSI	47.0	3513	58,800 PSI
75 GR. HDY HP	IMR	IMR 4007 SSC	.243"	2.825"	44.0	3323	51,900 PSI	48.0C	3554	61,200 PSI
75 GR. HDY HP	Hodgdon	H380	.243"	2.825"	41.0	3154	47,200 PSI	45.5	3465	59,800 PSI
75 GR. HDY HP	Hodgdon	Varget	.243"	2.825"	38.0	3207	48,500 PSI	42.6	3480	59,500 PSI
75 GR. HDY HP	IMR	IMR 4320	.243"	2.825"	38.0	3185	47,800 PSI	43.0	3508	60,900 PSI
75 GR. HDY HP	IMR	IMR 4064	.243"	2.825"	39.0	3275	50,600 PSI	43.0	3553	62,100 PSI
75 GR. HDY HP	Winchester	748	.243"	2.825"	39.0	3244	50,600 PSI	43.0	3502	61,900 PSI
75 GR. HDY HP	IMR	IMR 4895	.243"	2.825"	38.0	3255	50,600 PSI	43.0	3558	63,100 PSI
75 GR. HDY HP	Hodgdon	H4895	.243"	2.825"	37.0	3230	49,900 PSI	41.5	3482	60,500 PSI
75 GR. HDY HP	IMR	IMR 8208 XBR	.243"	2.825"	37.0	3184	48,100 PSI	41.5	3470	59,700 PSI
75 GR. HDY HP	IMR	IMR 3031	.243"	2.825"	36.0	3217	50,500 PSI	40.0	3494	63,200 PSI
80 GR. BAR TTSX BT	Hodgdon	Suprform	.243"	2.810"	46.0	3202	45,000 PSI	51.0C	3581	59,600 PSI
80 GR. BAR TTSX BT	Hodgdon	H4350	.243"	2.810"	42.0	3065	43,900 PSI	47.5	3427	58,800 PSI
80 GR. BAR TTSX BT	Hodgdon	H414	.243"	2.810"	42.0	3134	46,400 PSI	47.0	3471	60,700 PSI
80 GR. BAR TTSX BT	IMR	IMR 4350	.243"	2.810"	43.0	3086	43,300 PSI	48.0C	3484	58,800 PSI
80 GR. BAR TTSX BT	Winchester	760	.243"	2.810"	42.0	3134	46,400 PSI	47.0	3471	60,700 PSI
80 GR. BAR TTSX BT	Hodgdon	H380	.243"	2.810"	41.0	3115	47,100 PSI	45.5	3411	59,500 PSI
80 GR. BAR TTSX BT	Hodgdon	Varget	.243"	2.810"	38.0	3140	47,900 PSI	42.5	3416	59,800 PSI
80 GR. BAR TTSX BT	IMR	IMR 4320	.243"	2.810"	39.0	3112	46,400 PSI	43.5	3441	60,800 PSI
80 GR. BAR TTSX BT	IMR	IMR 4064	.243"	2.810"	38.0	3094	44,700 PSI	42.0	3415	58,700 PSI
80 GR. BAR TTSX BT	Winchester	748	.243"	2.810"	38.0	3075	45,800 PSI	43.0	3431	61,300 PSI
80 GR. BAR TTSX BT	IMR	IMR 4895	.243"	2.810"	38.0	3129	47,500 PSI	42.3	3418	59,400 PSI
80 GR. BAR TTSX BT	Hodgdon	H4895	.243"	2.810"	37.0	3169	49,500 PSI	41.3	3419	60,500 PSI
80 GR. BAR TTSX BT	IMR	IMR 8208 XBR	.243"	2.810"	36.0	3068	46,400 PSI	40.3	3363	60,100 PSI
80 GR. BAR TTSX BT	IMR	IMR 3031	.243"	2.810"	35.0	3039	45,100 PSI	39.2	3356	59,300 PSI
80 GR. SPR SP	Hodgdon	Suprform	.243"	2.775"	46.0	3207	49,100 PSI	51.4	3536	61,000 PSI
80 GR. SPR SP	Hodgdon	Hybrid 100V	.243"	2.775"	44.0	3186	50,500 PSI	48.0C	3458	61,500 PSI
80 GR. SPR SP	Hodgdon	H4350	.243"	2.775"	42.0	3123	46,700 PSI	47.0	3430	59,400 PSI
80 GR. SPR SP	Hodgdon	H414	.243"	2.775"	42.0	3134	47,400 PSI	46.7	3439	59,600 PSI
80 GR. SPR SP	IMR	IMR 4350	.243"	2.775"	41.0	3108	52,000 PSI	46.5	3410	62,800 PSI
80 GR. SPR SP	Winchester	760	.243"	2.775"	42.0	3134	47,400 PSI	46.7	3439	59,600 PSI
80 GR. SPR SP	IMR	IMR 4007 SSC	.243"	2.775"	42.0	3180	50,400 PSI	46.3	3437	60,700 PSI

Bullet	Manufacturer	Powder	Diameter	COAL	Load	Velocity	Pressure	Load	Velocity	Pressure
80 GR. SPR SP	Hodgdon	H380	.243"	2.775"	40.0	3068	47,800 PSI	44.5	3358	58,900 PSI
80 GR. SPR SP	Hodgdon	Varget	.243"	2.775"	38.0	3148	49,400 PSI	41.8	3376	59,400 PSI
80 GR. SPR SP	IMR	IMR 4320	.243"	2.775"	36.0	3079	50,400 PSI	39.8	3321	61,700 PSI
80 GR. SPR SP	IMR	IMR 4064	.243"	2.775"	35.0	3066	51,600 PSI	39.6	3346	61,800 PSI
80 GR. SPR SP	Winchester	748	.243"	2.775"	35.0	3132	58,800 PSI	39.2	3297	61,800 PSI
80 GR. SPR SP	IMR	IMR 4895	.243"	2.775"	35.0	3067	50,800 PSI	39.4	3337	61,800 PSI
80 GR. SPR SP	Hodgdon	H4895	.243"	2.775"	37.0	3167	50,900 PSI	40.5	3377	59,900 PSI
80 GR. SPR SP	IMR	IMR 8208 XBR	.243"	2.775"	37.0	3156	51,600 PSI	40.7	3353	59,800 PSI
80 GR. SPR SP	IMR	IMR 3031	.243"	2.775"	33.0	3006	48,900 PSI	37.2	3296	61,600 PSI
85 GR. NOS PART	Hodgdon	Hybrid 100V	.243"	2.825"	43.0	3143	51,700 PSI	47.5C	3411	62,200 PSI
85 GR. NOS PART	IMR	IMR 4831	.243"	2.825"	44.0	3058	49,300 PSI	48.5C	3379	62,400 PSI
85 GR. NOS PART	Hodgdon	H4350	.243"	2.825"	42.0	3075	48,200 PSI	46.5	3350	59,300 PSI
85 GR. NOS PART	Hodgdon	H414	.243"	2.825"	41.0	3007	45,900 PSI	45.8	3329	59,500 PSI
85 GR. NOS PART	IMR	IMR 4350	.243"	2.825"	42.0	2996	48,900 PSI	47.0	3335	62,100 PSI
85 GR. NOS PART	Winchester	760	.243"	2.825"	41.0	3007	45,900 PSI	45.8	3329	59,500 PSI
85 GR. NOS PART	IMR	IMR 4007 SSC	.243"	2.825"	42.0	3047	47,600 PSI	46.3	3365	60,500 PSI
85 GR. NOS PART	Hodgdon	H380	.243"	2.825"	39.0	2937	46,800 PSI	43.5	3243	59,000 PSI
85 GR. NOS PART	Hodgdon	Varget	.243"	2.825"	37.0	3020	49,200 PSI	41.0	3270	59,100 PSI
85 GR. NOS PART	IMR	IMR 4320	.243"	2.825"	36.0	2945	49,300 PSI	40.5	3249	62,900 PSI
85 GR. NOS PART	IMR	IMR 4064	.243"	2.825"	37.0	3006	49,700 PSI	41.0	3277	61,700 PSI
85 GR. NOS PART	Winchester	748	.243"	2.825"	36.0	3020	54,800 PSI	40.2	3235	61,200 PSI
85 GR. NOS PART	IMR	IMR 4895	.243"	2.825"	36.5	2998	50,500 PSI	40.7	3261	61,800 PSI
85 GR. NOS PART	Hodgdon	H4895	.243"	2.825"	35.5	3003	48,400 PSI	39.5	3253	59,200 PSI
87 GR. HDY HPBT	IMR	IMR 7828 SSC	.243"	2.825"	45.0	2941	48,700 PSI	50.0C*	3250	61,900 PSI
87 GR. HDY HPBT	Hodgdon	H4831	.243"	2.825"	44.0	2871	41,900 PSI	49.5C	3164	53,200 PSI
87 GR. HDY HPBT	Hodgdon	Hybrid 100V	.243"	2.825"	43.0	3149	53,300 PSI	47.0C	3386	63,300 PSI
87 GR. HDY HPBT	IMR	IMR 4831	.243"	2.825"	43.0	2985	47,400 PSI	48.0C	3327	61,300 PSI
87 GR. HDY HPBT	Hodgdon	H4350	.243"	2.825"	42.0	3051	48,100 PSI	46.7	3317	59,500 PSI
87 GR. HDY HPBT	Hodgdon	H414	.243"	2.825"	41.0	3000	47,200 PSI	45.2	3291	59,900 PSI
87 GR. HDY HPBT	IMR	IMR 4350	.243"	2.825"	42.0	2990	49,000 PSI	46.5C	3306	62,500 PSI
87 GR. HDY HPBT	Winchester	760	.243"	2.825"	41.0	3000	47,200 PSI	45.2	3291	59,900 PSI
87 GR. HDY HPBT	IMR	IMR 4007 SSC	.243"	2.825"	41.0	3018	47,800 PSI	45.5	3302	59,600 PSI
87 GR. HDY HPBT	Hodgdon	H380	.243"	2.825"	39.0	2940	47,300 PSI	43.0	3206	59,200 PSI
87 GR. HDY HPBT	Hodgdon	Varget	.243"	2.825"	37.0	3011	49,100 PSI	41.0	3243	59,300 PSI
87 GR. HDY HPBT	IMR	IMR 4320	.243"	2.825"	36.0	2962	51,000 PSI	40.0	3215	62,900 PSI
87 GR. HDY HPBT	IMR	IMR 4064	.243"	2.825"	36.0	2945	48,900 PSI	40.3	3217	61,200 PSI
87 GR. HDY HPBT	Winchester	748	.243"	2.825"	36.0	2944	52,000 PSI	39.8	3174	62,100 PSI
87 GR. HDY HPBT	IMR	IMR 4895	.243"	2.825"	36.0	2982	51,200 PSI	40.2	3236	62,800 PSI
87 GR. HDY HPBT	Hodgdon	H4895	.243"	2.825"	35.5	2986	49,100 PSI	39.5	3214	60,300 PSI
95 GR. NOS BT	Hodgdon	H1000	.243"	2.825"	47.0	2835	43,000 PSI	50.5C	3056	52,900 PSI

95 GR. NOS BT	IMR	IMR 7828 SSC	.243"	2.825"	44.0	2818	48,400 PSI	48.7C	3130	61,800 PSI
95 GR. NOS BT	Winchester	Supreme 780	.243"	2.825"	46.3	2960	52,500 PSI	49.2	3169	62,600 PSI
95 GR. NOS BT	Hodgdon	H4831	.243"	2.825"	44.0	2798	43,700 PSI	49.5C	3125	57,600 PSI
95 GR. NOS BT	Hodgdon	Hybrid 100V	.243"	2.825"	41.0	2930	50,700 PSI	45.5	3226	63,100 PSI
95 GR. NOS BT	IMR	IMR 4831	.243"	2.825"	42.0	2887	49,000 PSI	47.0C	3218	63,000 PSI
95 GR. NOS BT	Hodgdon	H4350	.243"	2.825"	41.0	2909	48,100 PSI	45.5	3167	59,200 PSI
95 GR. NOS BT	Hodgdon	H414	.243"	2.825"	40.0	2847	45,900 PSI	44.5	3164	60,100 PSI
95 GR. NOS BT	IMR	IMR 4350	.243"	2.825"	41.0	2867	49,900 PSI	45.5C	3153	61,500 PSI
95 GR. NOS BT	Winchester	760	.243"	2.825"	40.0	2847	45,900 PSI	44.5	3164	60,100 PSI
95 GR. NOS BT	IMR	IMR 4007 SSC	.243"	2.825"	40.0	2877	47,600 PSI	44.0	3164	60,400 PSI
95 GR. NOS BT	Hodgdon	Varget	.243"	2.825"	36.0	2843	47,800 PSI	40.0	3091	58,900 PSI
95 GR. NOS BT	IMR	IMR 4064	.243"	2.825"	35.5	2828	51,000 PSI	39.5	3069	62,000 PSI
95 GR. NOS BT	Winchester	748	.243"	2.825"	36.0	2750	48,600 PSI	39.7	3042	62,200 PSI
95 GR. NOS BT	IMR	IMR 4895	.243"	2.825"	36.0	2835	51,300 PSI	40.0	3095	63,300 PSI
95 GR. NOS BT	Hodgdon	H4895	.243"	2.825"	35.0	2855	50,100 PSI	38.7	3076	60,100 PSI
100 GR. SPR BT	Hodgdon	H1000	.243"	2.775"	47.0	2779	41,500 PSI	50.0C	2955	48,900 PSI
100 GR. SPR BT	IMR	IMR 7828 SSC	.243"	2.775"	43.0	2778	49,500 PSI	47.5C*	3048	60,900 PSI
100 GR. SPR BT	Winchester	Supreme 780	.243"	2.775"	45.5	2912	51,600 PSI	48.4	3131	62,300 PSI
100 GR. SPR BT	Hodgdon	H4831	.243"	2.775"	45.0	2794	43,900 PSI	49.0C	3064	56,100 PSI
100 GR. SPR BT	Hodgdon	Hybrid 100V	.243"	2.775"	40.0	2909	53,400 PSI	44.5	3142	61,500 PSI
100 GR. SPR BT	IMR	IMR 4831	.243"	2.775"	42.0	2889	50,500 PSI	46.2C	3149	62,100 PSI
100 GR. SPR BT	Hodgdon	H4350	.243"	2.775"	41.0	2879	47,900 PSI	45.5	3137	59,800 PSI
100 GR. SPR BT	Hodgdon	H414	.243"	2.775"	39.0	2774	44,400 PSI	43.5	3093	58,500 PSI
100 GR. SPR BT	IMR	IMR 4350	.243"	2.775"	40.0	2842	50,200 PSI	44.6C	3126	62,600 PSI
100 GR. SPR BT	Winchester	760	.243"	2.775"	39.0	2774	44,400 PSI	43.5	3093	58,500 PSI
100 GR. SPR BT	IMR	IMR 4007 SSC	.243"	2.775"	40.0	2827	46,200 PSI	44.0	3122	59,200 PSI
100 GR. SPR BT	Hodgdon	Varget	.243"	2.775"	36.0	2843	49,800 PSI	40.2	3055	59,200 PSI
100 GR. SPR BT	IMR	IMR 4064	.243"	2.775"	34.0	2765	50,000 PSI	38.0	2982	61,000 PSI
100 GR. SPR BT	Winchester	748	.243"	2.775"	34.5	2766	55,300 PSI	38.5	2964	61,500 PSI
100 GR. SPR BT	IMR	IMR 4895	.243"	2.775"	34.0	2737	48,800 PSI	38.5	3016	62,400 PSI
100 GR. SPR BT	Hodgdon	H4895	.243"	2.775"	34.0	2749	45,900 PSI	38.5	3035	59,900 PSI
105 GR. HDY A-MAX	Hodgdon	H1000	.243"	2.825"	47.0	2817	45,800 PSI	50.0C	2980	53,300 PSI
105 GR. HDY A-MAX	Winchester	Supreme 780	.243"	2.825"	44.7	2854	52,400 PSI	47.5	3046	61,600 PSI
105 GR. HDY A-MAX	Hodgdon	H4831	.243"	2.825"	44.0	2839	49,400 PSI	47.5C	3028	57,900 PSI
105 GR. HDY A-MAX	Hodgdon	Hybrid 100V	.243"	2.825"	40.0	2849	51,900 PSI	43.7C	3078	62,500 PSI
105 GR. HDY A-MAX	IMR	IMR 4831	.243"	2.825"	41.0	2785	48,800 PSI	45.7C	3075	62,100 PSI
105 GR. HDY A-MAX	Hodgdon	H4350	.243"	2.825"	40.0	2838	49,700 PSI	43.5	3029	58,800 PSI
105 GR. HDY A-MAX	Hodgdon	H414	.243"	2.825"	40.0	2826	50,700 PSI	43.0	3009	58,600 PSI
105 GR. HDY A-MAX	IMR	IMR 4350	.243"	2.825"	39.0	2713	48,200 PSI	43.8	3027	62,600 PSI

Bullet	Manufacturer	Powder	Bullet Diam.	C.O.L.	Grs.	Vel.	Pressure	Grs.	Vel.	Pressure
105 GR. HDY A-MAX	Winchester	760	.243"	2.825"	40.0	2826	50,700 PSI	43.0	3009	58,600 PSI
105 GR. HDY A-MAX	IMR	IMR 4007 SSC	.243"	2.825"	38.0	2740	47,800 PSI	42.7	3032	60,000 PSI
105 GR. HDY A-MAX	Hodgdon	Varget	.243"	2.825"	34.0	2711	47,400 PSI	38.0	2946	58,800 PSI
105 GR. HDY A-MAX	IMR	IMR 4064	.243"	2.825"	33.0	2659	49,200 PSI	37.2	2894	60,700 PSI
107 GR. SIE HPBT	Hodgdon	Retumbo	.243"	2.950"	47.0	2836	44,900 PSI	50.0C	3033	55,200 PSI
107 GR. SIE HPBT	Hodgdon	H1000	.243"	2.950"	47.0	2818	47,400 PSI	50.0C	2980	55,100 PSI
107 GR. SIE HPBT	IMR	IMR 7828 SSC	.243"	2.950"	42.0	2739	50,300 PSI	47.0C*	3023	63,000 PSI
107 GR. SIE HPBT	Winchester	Supreme 780	.243"	2.950"	44.2	2816	51,200 PSI	47.0	3023	61,800 PSI
107 GR. SIE HPBT	Hodgdon	H4831	.243"	2.950"	43.0	2779	48,300 PSI	48.0C	3042	59,600 PSI
107 GR. SIE HPBT	Hodgdon	Hybrid 100V	.243"	2.950"	40.0	2870	54,400 PSI	43.5	3053	62,800 PSI
107 GR. SIE HPBT	IMR	IMR 4831	.243"	2.950"	40.0	2772	48,800 PSI	44.5	3080	63,600 PSI
107 GR. SIE HPBT	Hodgdon	H4350	.243"	2.950"	39.0	2779	48,800 PSI	43.5	3016	59,600 PSI
107 GR. SIE HPBT	Hodgdon	H414	.243"	2.950"	39.0	2757	49,800 PSI	43.0	3001	60,400 PSI
107 GR. SIE HPBT	IMR	IMR 4350	.243"	2.950"	39.0	2750	49,300 PSI	43.5	3044	63,800 PSI
107 GR. SIE HPBT	Winchester	760	.243"	2.950"	39.0	2757	49,800 PSI	43.0	3001	60,400 PSI
107 GR. SIE HPBT	IMR	IMR 4007 SSC	.243"	2.950"	39.0	2767	49,200 PSI	43.0	3005	60,000 PSI
107 GR. SIE HPBT	Hodgdon	Varget	.243"	2.950"	34.0	2652	46,300 PSI	38.5	2930	60,200 PSI
107 GR. SIE HPBT	IMR	IMR 4064	.243"	2.950"	33.0	2650	48,900 PSI	37.0	2869	60,800 PSI
115 GR. BAR RN	Hodgdon	Retumbo	.243"	2.825"	47.0	2711	43,200 CUP	50.0C	2878	49,000 CUP
115 GR. BAR RN	Hodgdon	H1000	.243"	2.825"	43.0	2665	43,800 CUP	45.5	2793	49,600 CUP
115 GR. BAR RN	Hodgdon	H4831	.243"	2.825"	39.0	2598	43,800 CUP	42.0	2761	49,800 CUP
115 GR. BAR RN	Hodgdon	H4350	.243"	2.825"	36.0	2537	43,200 CUP	39.0	2696	49,700 CUP

Cartridge: 243 Winchester Super Short Magnum
Load Type: Rifle

Bullet Weight (Gr.)	Manufacturer	Powder	Bullet Diam.	C.O.L.	Starting Loads			Maximum Loads		
					Grs.	Vel. (ft/s)	Pressure	Grs.	Vel. (ft/s)	Pressure
58 GR. HDY V-MAX	Hodgdon	H414	.243"	2.220"	49.0	3704	50,200 PSI	52.0	3947	60,800 PSI
58 GR. HDY V-MAX	Winchester	760	.243"	2.220"	49.0	3704	50,200 PSI	52.0	3947	60,800 PSI
58 GR. HDY V-MAX	IMR	IMR 4007 SSC	.243"	2.220"	45.0	3372	41,300 PSI	48.5C	3684	51,500 PSI
58 GR. HDY V-MAX	Hodgdon	H380	.243"	2.220"	47.5	3688	48,700 PSI	50.5	3872	56,300 PSI
58 GR. HDY V-MAX	Hodgdon	CFE 223	.243"	2.220"	44.0	3759	53,300 PSI	48.5	4030	62,900 PSI
58 GR. HDY V-MAX	Hodgdon	Varget	.243"	2.220"	44.0	3739	52,000 PSI	47.0	3975	62,800 PSI
58 GR. HDY V-MAX	IMR	IMR 4320	.243"	2.220"	44.0	3661	49,300 PSI	47.5	3977	62,500 PSI
58 GR. HDY V-MAX	IMR	IMR 4064	.243"	2.220"	42.5	3698	49,300 PSI	45.5	3966	60,400 PSI
58 GR. HDY V-MAX	Hodgdon	BL-C(2)	.243"	2.220"	46.0	3841	52,600 PSI	49.2	4068	62,700 PSI
58 GR. HDY V-MAX	IMR	IMR 4895	.243"	2.220"	43.0	3716	49,500 PSI	46.2	4017	62,600 PSI
58 GR. HDY V-MAX	Hodgdon	H4895	.243"	2.220"	42.0	3756	51,700 PSI	45.3	4021	63,100 PSI
58 GR. HDY V-MAX	IMR	IMR 8208 XBR	.243"	2.200"	40.0	3677	50,200 PSI	44.3	3985	63,200 PSI
58 GR. HDY V-MAX	IMR	IMR 3031	.243"	2.220"	40.0	3642	46,900 PSI	44.0	4013	63,300 PSI
62 GR. BAR VG FB	Hodgdon	H414	.243"	2.240"	47.0	3551	54,200 PSI	50.0	3751	62,600 PSI

62 GR. BAR VG FB	Winchester	760	.243"	2.240"	47.0	3551	54,200 PSI	50.0	3751	62,600 PSI
62 GR. BAR VG FB	IMR	IMR 4007 SSC	.243"	2.240"	44.4	3508	57,000 PSI	47.2	3681	63,500 PSI
62 GR. BAR VG FB	Hodgdon	H380	.243"	2.240"	45.1	3455	53,100 PSI	48.0	3666	61,900 PSI
62 GR. BAR VG FB	Hodgdon	CFE 223	.243"	2.240"	37.0	3500	56,900 PSI	40.0	3669	62,500 PSI
62 GR. BAR VG FB	Hodgdon	Varget	.243"	2.240"	39.9	3441	54,900 PSI	42.4	3637	61,900 PSI
62 GR. BAR VG FB	IMR	IMR 4320	.243"	2.240"	40.6	3469	54,900 PSI	43.2	3658	62,600 PSI
62 GR. BAR VG FB	IMR	IMR 4064	.243"	2.240"	38.8	3498	56,600 PSI	41.3	3671	63,100 PSI
62 GR. BAR VG FB	Hodgdon	BL-C(2)	.243"	2.240"	43.5	3596	56,200 PSI	46.3	3759	62,500 PSI
62 GR. BAR VG FB	IMR	IMR 4895	.243"	2.240"	40.3	3559	58,400 PSI	41.5	3653	62,400 PSI
62 GR. BAR VG FB	Hodgdon	H4895	.243"	2.240"	38.0	3497	55,700 PSI	40.0	3641	62,800 PSI
62 GR. BAR VG FB	IMR	IMR 8208 XBR	.243"	2.240"	38.5	3562	54,800 PSI	40.9	3726	62,300 PSI
62 GR. BAR VG FB	IMR	IMR 3031	.243"	2.240"	36.6	3473	56,500 PSI	38.5	3632	62,300 PSI
70 GR. NOS BT	Hodgdon	Suprform	.243"	2.230"	50.0	3541	49,700 PSI	54.0C	3821	61,000 PSI
70 GR. NOS BT	Hodgdon	H4350	.243"	2.280"	45.0	3385	48,000 PSI	48.7C	3614	58,400 PSI
70 GR. NOS BT	Hodgdon	H414	.243"	2.280"	46.0	3420	48,800 PSI	49.0	3618	58,900 PSI
70 GR. NOS BT	IMR	IMR 4350	.243"	2.280"	45.0	3374	48,500 PSI	48.0C	3566	56,400 PSI
70 GR. NOS BT	Winchester	760	.243"	2.280"	46.0	3420	48,800 PSI	49.0	3618	58,900 PSI
70 GR. NOS BT	IMR	IMR 4007 SSC	.243"	2.280"	45.0	3368	49,500 PSI	48.0C	3616	59,800 PSI
70 GR. NOS BT	Hodgdon	H380	.243"	2.280"	45.0	3420	51,100 PSI	48.0	3602	60,200 PSI
70 GR. NOS BT	Hodgdon	CFE 223	.243"	2.280"	42.0	3519	57,500 PSI	46.0	3710	62,600 PSI
70 GR. NOS BT	Hodgdon	Varget	.243"	2.280"	41.0	3474	54,500 PSI	43.7	3655	63,400 PSI
70 GR. NOS BT	IMR	IMR 4320	.243"	2.280"	42.0	3439	51,900 PSI	45.0	3663	62,600 PSI
70 GR. NOS BT	IMR	IMR 4064	.243"	2.280"	40.0	3420	49,100 PSI	43.5	3672	61,900 PSI
70 GR. NOS BT	Hodgdon	BL-C(2)	.243"	2.280"	43.0	3528	55,100 PSI	46.2	3707	62,900 PSI
70 GR. NOS BT	IMR	IMR 4895	.243"	2.280"	40.0	3419	50,500 PSI	43.5	3681	62,100 PSI
70 GR. NOS BT	Hodgdon	H4895	.243"	2.280"	39.0	3434	52,500 PSI	42.0	3618	62,500 PSI
70 GR. NOS BT	IMR	IMR 8208 XBR	.243"	2.200"	38.0	3445	54,000 PSI	41.5	3646	62,900 PSI
70 GR. NOS BT	IMR	IMR 3031	.243"	2.280"	38.0	3428	53,100 PSI	40.8	3627	62,400 PSI
80 GR. SIE BTSP	Hodgdon	Suprform	.243"	2.220"	47.0	3404	54,800 PSI	52.0C	3648	64,200 PSI
80 GR. SIE BTSP	Hodgdon	H4350	.243"	2.220"	45.0	3323	52,600 PSI	48.7C	3545	63,000 PSI
80 GR. SIE BTSP	Hodgdon	H414	.243"	2.220"	45.0	3349	54,600 PSI	48.0	3514	63,100 PSI
80 GR. SIE BTSP	IMR	IMR 4350	.243"	2.220"	44.0	3267	51,700 PSI	47.8C	3507	62,500 PSI
80 GR. SIE BTSP	Winchester	760	.243"	2.220"	45.0	3349	54,600 PSI	48.0	3514	63,100 PSI
80 GR. SIE BTSP	IMR	IMR 4007 SSC	.243"	2.220"	42.0	3135	46,900 PSI	47.0	3490	62,900 PSI
80 GR. SIE BTSP	Hodgdon	H380	.243"	2.220"	44.0	3331	56,300 PSI	46.7	3487	63,600 PSI
80 GR. SIE BTSP	Hodgdon	CFE 223	.243"	2.200"	36.0	3165	54,500 PSI	39.0	3338	62,600 PSI
80 GR. SIE BTSP	Hodgdon	Varget	.243"	2.220"	39.0	3288	54,400 PSI	42.0	3462	63,300 PSI
80 GR. SIE BTSP	IMR	IMR 4320	.243"	2.220"	40.0	3233	51,200 PSI	43.8	3474	63,200 PSI
80 GR. SIE BTSP	IMR	IMR 4064	.243"	2.220"	39.0	3250	51,700 PSI	42.2	3458	62,400 PSI

80 GR. SIE BTSP	Hodgdon	BL-C(2)	.243"	2.220"	40.0	3309	55,300 PSI	43.5	3493	63,600 PSI
80 GR. SIE BTSP	IMR	IMR 4895	.243"	2.220"	39.0	3263	52,600 PSI	42.0	3449	62,500 PSI
80 GR. SIE BTSP	Hodgdon	H4895	.243"	2.220"	38.5	3255	53,300 PSI	41.0	3409	62,500 PSI
80 GR. SIE BTSP	IMR	IMR 8208 XBR	.243"	2.200"	35.0	3137	50,500 PSI	39.0	3394	62,400 PSI
80 GR. SIE BTSP	IMR	IMR 3031	.243"	2.220"	36.0	3188	52,000 PSI	39.0	3379	62,400 PSI
90 GR. SFT SCIR	IMR	IMR 7828	.243"	2.300"	44.0	3002	51,900 PSI	48.5C*	3280	63,900 PSI
90 GR. SFT SCIR	Winchester	Supreme 780	.243"	2.300"	47.0	2981	49,000 PSI	50.0	3159	56,600 PSI
90 GR. SFT SCIR	Hodgdon	Suprform	.243"	2.300"	42.0	3183	59,500 PSI	47.6C	3362	63,800 PSI
90 GR. SFT SCIR	Hodgdon	H4831	.243"	2.300"	44.0	3045	55,800 PSI	47.0C	3200	63,200 PSI
90 GR. SFT SCIR	Hodgdon	Hybrid 100V	.243"	2.300"	40.0	2887	45,700 PSI	44.0C	3157	55,400 PSI
90 GR. SFT SCIR	IMR	IMR 4831	.243"	2.300"	43.0	3089	55,400 PSI	46.0C	3255	62,800 PSI
90 GR. SFT SCIR	Hodgdon	H4350	.243"	2.300"	41.0	3087	56,200 PSI	44.0C	3245	62,900 PSI
90 GR. SFT SCIR	Hodgdon	H414	.243"	2.300"	41.5	3042	51,300 PSI	44.5	3216	59,300 PSI
90 GR. SFT SCIR	IMR	IMR 4350	.243"	2.300"	42.0	3084	55,100 PSI	44.9C	3263	63,100 PSI
90 GR. SFT SCIR	Winchester	760	.243"	2.300"	41.5	3042	51,300 PSI	44.5	3216	59,300 PSI
90 GR. SFT SCIR	IMR	IMR 4007 SSC	.243"	2.300"	41.4	3057	53,700 PSI	44.0	3224	62,300 PSI
90 GR. SFT SCIR	Hodgdon	H380	.243"	2.300"	40.0	3000	52,500 PSI	43.5	3196	62,100 PSI
90 GR. SFT SCIR	Hodgdon	Varget	.243"	2.300"	36.0	2979	53,200 PSI	39.2	3175	63,200 PSI
90 GR. SFT SCIR	IMR	IMR 4320	.243"	2.300"	37.0	2972	52,900 PSI	39.8	3147	61,700 PSI
90 GR. SFT SCIR	IMR	IMR 4064	.243"	2.300"	36.0	2995	54,900 PSI	38.3	3138	61,600 PSI
90 GR. SFT SCIR	Hodgdon	BL-C(2)	.243"	2.300"	38.0	3033	53,200 PSI	41.0	3198	62,000 PSI
90 GR. SFT SCIR	IMR	IMR 4895	.243"	2.300"	35.5	2956	52,500 PSI	38.5	3153	61,900 PSI
90 GR. SFT SCIR	Hodgdon	H4895	.243"	2.300"	35.0	2954	52,000 PSI	37.7	3124	61,900 PSI
90 GR. SFT SCIR	IMR	IMR 8208 XBR	.243"	2.300"	32.0	2866	52,200 PSI	35.8	3098	63,600 PSI
100 GR. SPR BTSP	IMR	IMR 7828	.243"	2.300"	43.0	2909	53,500 PSI	47.0C*	3136	63,500 PSI
100 GR. SPR BTSP	Winchester	Supreme 780	.243"	2.300"	47.0	2960	52,300 PSI	50.0	3117	60,100 PSI
100 GR. SPR BTSP	Hodgdon	H4831	.243"	2.300"	41.5	2878	54,000 PSI	45.0	3058	63,000 PSI
100 GR. SPR BTSP	Hodgdon	Hybrid 100V	.243"	2.300"	41.0	2907	51,600 PSI	45.0C	3153	63,200 PSI
100 GR. SPR BTSP	IMR	IMR 4831	.243"	2.300"	40.5	2897	53,200 PSI	44.2	3098	62,800 PSI
100 GR. SPR BTSP	Hodgdon	H4350	.243"	2.300"	39.0	2938	55,400 PSI	41.7	3074	62,300 PSI
100 GR. SPR BTSP	Hodgdon	H414	.243"	2.300"	39.0	2909	54,300 PSI	41.8	3059	62,100 PSI
100 GR. SPR BTSP	IMR	IMR 4350	.243"	2.300"	40.0	2898	52,600 PSI	43.5C	3104	62,600 PSI
100 GR. SPR BTSP	Winchester	760	.243"	2.300"	39.0	2909	54,300 PSI	41.8	3059	62,100 PSI
100 GR. SPR BTSP	IMR	IMR 4007 SSC	.243"	2.300"	39.5	2900	53,500 PSI	42.0	3067	62,000 PSI
100 GR. SPR BTSP	Hodgdon	H380	.243"	2.300"	37.0	2810	52,600 PSI	40.0	2989	62,400 PSI
100 GR. SPR BTSP	Hodgdon	Varget	.243"	2.300"	34.0	2829	53,600 PSI	36.6	2981	62,100 PSI
100 GR. SPR BTSP	IMR	IMR 4320	.243"	2.300"	36.5	2869	54,300 PSI	39.5	3046	63,300 PSI
100 GR. SPR BTSP	IMR	IMR 4064	.243"	2.300"	35.0	2847	53,000 PSI	38.0	3029	62,300 PSI
100 GR. SPR BTSP	Hodgdon	BL-C(2)	.243"	2.300"	35.0	2840	54,300 PSI	37.5	2980	62,500 PSI
100 GR. SPR BTSP	IMR	IMR 4895	.243"	2.300"	35.0	2840	52,300 PSI	38.0	3020	61,900 PSI

| 100 GR. SPR BTSP | Hodgdon | H4895 | .243" | 2.300" | 33.0 | 2809 | 55,100 PSI | 35.5 | 2946 | 63,600 PSI |
| 100 GR. SPR BTSP | IMR | IMR 8208 XBR | .243" | 2.300" | 31.5 | 2764 | 52,500 PSI | 35.0 | 2982 | 63,100 PSI |

Cartridge:6mm - 284 Load Type:Rifle					Starting Loads			Maximum Loads		
Bullet Weight (Gr.)	Manufacturer	Powder	Bullet Diam.	C.O.L.	Grs.	Vel. (ft/s)	Pressure	Grs.	Vel. (ft/s)	Pressure
55 GR. NOS BT	Hodgdon	H4350	.243"	2.780"	55.0	3738	42,300 CUP	59.0C	4039	51,600 CUP
55 GR. NOS BT	Hodgdon	H414	.243"	2.780"	53.0	3847	46,300 CUP	56.5	4038	52,000 CUP
55 GR. NOS BT	Winchester	760	.243"	2.780"	53.0	3847	46,300 CUP	56.5	4038	52,000 CUP
55 GR. NOS BT	IMR	IMR 4007 SSC	.243"	2.780"	51.0	3680	43,400 CUP	55.5	3966	52,300 CUP
55 GR. NOS BT	Hodgdon	H380	.243"	2.780"	52.0	3833	44,000 CUP	56.0	4082	51,800 CUP
55 GR. NOS BT	Hodgdon	Varget	.243"	2.780"	47.0	3779	47,500 CUP	50.5	3921	51,600 CUP
55 GR. NOS BT	Hodgdon	H4895	.243"	2.780"	47.0	3837	47,100 CUP	50.0	4050	51,700 CUP
60 GR. SIE HP	Hodgdon	H4831	.243"	2.680"	56.0	3584	46,400 CUP	60.0C	3756	51,400 CUP
60 GR. SIE HP	Hodgdon	H4350	.243"	2.680"	54.0	3719	44,800 CUP	58.0	3976	52,300 CUP
60 GR. SIE HP	Hodgdon	H414	.243"	2.680"	51.0	3654	45,300 CUP	54.5	3881	51,700 CUP
60 GR. SIE HP	Winchester	760	.243"	2.680"	51.0	3654	45,300 CUP	54.5	3881	51,700 CUP
60 GR. SIE HP	IMR	IMR 4007 SSC	.243"	2.680"	48.0	3525	42,800 CUP	53.0	3826	51,900 CUP
60 GR. SIE HP	Hodgdon	H380	.243"	2.680"	51.0	3726	46,700 CUP	54.0	3910	52,000 CUP
60 GR. SIE HP	Hodgdon	Varget	.243"	2.680"	45.0	3672	47,700 CUP	49.0	3855	52,400 CUP
60 GR. SIE HP	Hodgdon	H4895	.243"	2.680"	45.0	3740	47,200 CUP	48.5	3910	52,100 CUP
62 GR. BAR VG FB	Hodgdon	H4831	.243"	2.775"	55.0	3607	46,400 CUP	59.0C	3777	50,300 CUP
62 GR. BAR VG FB	IMR	IMR 4831	.243"	2.775"	49.5	3487	44,100 CUP	55.0C	3849	51,800 CUP
62 GR. BAR VG FB	Hodgdon	H4350	.243"	2.775"	48.0	3489	41,600 CUP	54.3C	3863	52,500 CUP
62 GR. BAR VG FB	Hodgdon	H414	.243"	2.775"	49.0	3578	43,100 CUP	53.0	3833	51,600 CUP
62 GR. BAR VG FB	IMR	IMR 4350	.243"	2.775"	49.0	3474	40,400 CUP	54.0C	3843	50,700 CUP
62 GR. BAR VG FB	IMR	IMR 4007 SSC	.243"	2.775"	48.0	3518	42,900 CUP	53.0	3838	51,300 CUP
62 GR. BAR VG FB	Hodgdon	H380	.243"	2.775"	47.0	3470	43,300 CUP	50.5	3724	50,700 CUP
62 GR. BAR VG FB	Hodgdon	Varget	.243"	2.775"	44.0	3583	44,500 CUP	48.5	3851	51,800 CUP
62 GR. BAR VG FB	Hodgdon	H4895	.243"	2.775"	40.0	3408	40,600 CUP	44.5	3707	50,800 CUP
65 GR. HDY V-MAX	Hodgdon	H4831	.243"	2.735"	54.0	3481	43,800 CUP	57.5	3678	51,300 CUP
65 GR. HDY V-MAX	IMR	IMR 4831	.243"	2.735"	50.0	3379	43,100 CUP	54.4	3675	52,000 CUP
65 GR. HDY V-MAX	Hodgdon	H4350	.243"	2.735"	51.7	3584	44,500 CUP	55.0	3767	49,800 CUP
65 GR. HDY V-MAX	Hodgdon	H414	.243"	2.735"	49.8	3558	44,200 CUP	53.0	3740	50,000 CUP
65 GR. HDY V-MAX	IMR	IMR 4350	.243"	2.735"	49.0	3333	42,300 CUP	53,5	2669	52,000 CUP
65 GR. HDY V-MAX	Winchester	760	.243"	2.735"	49.8	3558	44,200 CUP	53.0	3740	50,000 CUP
65 GR. HDY V-MAX	IMR	IMR 4007 SSC	.243"	2.735"	48.0	2469	43,400 CUP	53.0	3783	52,100 CUP
65 GR. HDY V-MAX	Hodgdon	H380	.243"	2.735"	47.0	3480	44,700 CUP	50.0	3660	50,600 CUP
65 GR. HDY V-MAX	Hodgdon	Varget	.243"	2.735"	44.0	3532	45,200 CUP	47.0	3688	49,800 CUP

65 GR. HDY V-MAX	Hodgdon	H4895	.243"	2.735"	43.0	3528	42,800 CUP	46.0	3724	50,400 CUP
70 GR. HDY SP	IMR	IMR 7828 SSC	.243"	2.730"	51.0	3240	44,400 CUP	55.8	3496	51,400 CUP
70 GR. HDY SP	Hodgdon	H4831	.243"	2.730"	55.0	3442	45,900 CUP	58.5C	3632	51,900 CUP
70 GR. HDY SP	Hodgdon	Hybrid 100V	.243"	2.730"	49.0	3447	46,300 CUP	53.0	3691	52,400 CUP
70 GR. HDY SP	IMR	IMR 4831	.243"	2.730"	50.0	3296	42,000 CUP	54.0	3619	51,900 CUP
70 GR. HDY SP	Hodgdon	H4350	.243"	2.730"	52.0	3550	46,300 CUP	55.0	3731	52,200 CUP
70 GR. HDY SP	Hodgdon	H414	.243"	2.730"	49.0	3496	45,500 CUP	52.5	3717	51,800 CUP
70 GR. HDY SP	IMR	IMR 4350	.243"	2.730"	48.0	3268	42,500 CUP	53.0	3601	52,200 CUP
70 GR. HDY SP	Winchester	760	.243"	2.730"	49.0	3496	45,500 CUP	52.5	3717	51,800 CUP
70 GR. HDY SP	IMR	IMR 4007 SSC	.243"	2.750"	48.0	3425	43,700 CUP	52.5	3691	52,100 CUP
70 GR. HDY SP	Hodgdon	H380	.243"	2.730"	46.5	3419	45,500 CUP	49.5	3585	51,900 CUP
75 GR. HDY V-MAX	IMR	IMR 7828 SSC	.243"	2.750"	50.0	3188	43,800 CUP	54.3	3406	50,900 CUP
75 GR. HDY V-MAX	Hodgdon	H4831	.243"	2.750"	53.0	3331	45,200 CUP	56.5	3566	52,200 CUP
75 GR. HDY V-MAX	Hodgdon	Hybrid 100V	.243"	2.750"	46.0	3255	43,000 CUP	50.7	3583	52,300 CUP
75 GR. HDY V-MAX	IMR	IMR 4831	.243"	2.640"	50.0	3322	45,300 CUP	53.3	3560	52,500 CUP
75 GR. HDY V-MAX	Hodgdon	H4350	.243"	2.750"	49.0	3466	46,800 CUP	53.0	3644	52,300 CUP
75 GR. HDY V-MAX	Hodgdon	H414	.243"	2.750"	48.0	3420	45,900 CUP	51.0	3571	51,800 CUP
75 GR. HDY V-MAX	IMR	IMR 4350	.243"	2.750"	48.0	3191	42,100 CUP	52.3	3534	52,100 CUP
75 GR. HDY V-MAX	Winchester	760	.243"	2.750"	48.0	3420	45,900 CUP	51.0	3571	51,800 CUP
75 GR. HDY V-MAX	IMR	IMR 4007 SSC	.243"	2.750"	47.0	3364	44,800 CUP	51.5	3614	52,500 CUP
75 GR. HDY V-MAX	Hodgdon	H380	.243"	2.750"	44.0	3278	45,600 CUP	47.0	3441	51,800 CUP
80 GR. SPR SP	Hodgdon	H1000	.243"	2.730"	55.0	3296	46,700 CUP	59.0C	3467	52,000 CUP
80 GR. SPR SP	IMR	IMR 7828 SSC	.243"	2.730"	49.0	3166	45,900 CUP	53.5	3407	51,600 CUP
80 GR. SPR SP	Winchester	Supreme 780	.243"	2.730"	52.6	3315	45,800 CUP	56.0	3475	51,900 CUP
80 GR. SPR SP	Hodgdon	H4831	.243"	2.730"	52.0	3306	47,100 CUP	55.0	3440	52,000 CUP
80 GR. SPR SP	Hodgdon	Hybrid 100V	.243"	2.730"	46.0	3262	45,400 CUP	49.7	3469	52,000 CUP
80 GR. SPR SP	IMR	IMR 4831	.243"	2.739"	48.0	3234	43,300 CUP	52.3	3511	52,000 CUP
80 GR. SPR SP	Hodgdon	H4350	.243"	2.730"	47.5	3259	45,600 CUP	50.5	3447	51,800 CUP
80 GR. SPR SP	Hodgdon	H414	.243"	2.730"	47.0	3293	45,900 CUP	50.0	3460	52,200 CUP
80 GR. SPR SP	IMR	IMR 4350	.243"	2.730"	47.0	3186	42,300 CUP	51.2	3451	52,100 CUP
80 GR. SPR SP	Winchester	760	.243"	2.730"	47.0	3293	45,900 CUP	50.0	3460	52,200 CUP
80 GR. SPR SP	IMR	IMR 4007 SSC	.243"	2.730"	45.0	3258	45,400 CUP	49.0	3471	52,100 CUP
85 GR. BAR TSX	Hodgdon	Retumbo	.243"	2.750"	55.0	3272	44,300 CUP	57.0C	3398	49,000 CUP
85 GR. BAR TSX	Hodgdon	H1000	.243"	2.750"	51.0	3234	48,200 CUP	55.5C	3374	51,700 CUP
85 GR. BAR TSX	IMR	IMR 7828 SSC	.243"	2.750"	48.0	3176	46,200 CUP	51.8	3362	51,900 CUP
85 GR. BAR TSX	Winchester	Supreme 780	.243"	2.750"	50.8	3215	45,600 CUP	54.0	3390	50,900 CUP
85 GR. BAR TSX	Hodgdon	H4831	.243"	2.750"	46.0	3137	46,200 CUP	50.0	3332	51,700 CUP
85 GR. BAR TSX	Hodgdon	Hybrid 100V	.243"	2.750"	45.0	3194	43,900 CUP	49.8	3434	52,200 CUP
85 GR. BAR TSX	IMR	IMR 4831	.243"	2.750"	47.0	3215	45,100 CUP	50.5	3422	51,700 CUP
85 GR. BAR TSX	Hodgdon	H4350	.243"	2.750"	43.0	3116	43,100 CUP	47.5	3343	51,800 CUP

85 GR. BAR TSX	Hodgdon	H414	.243"	2.750"	44.5	3190	45,100 CUP	47.5	3333	51.200 CUP
85 GR. BAR TSX	IMR	IMR 4350	.243"	2.750"	47.0	3195	43,800 CUP	50.7	3407	51,700 CUP
85 GR. BAR TSX	IMR	IMR 4007 SSC	.243"	2.750"	42.0	3130	46,700 CUP	45.8	3320	52,100 CUP
90 GR. NOS E-TIP	Hodgdon	Retumbo	.243"	2.800"	52.0	3035	39,500 CUP	57.0C	3278	46,800 CUP
90 GR. NOS E-TIP	Hodgdon	H1000	.243"	2.800"	52.0	3001	41,200 CUP	57.0C	3236	48,200 CUP
90 GR. NOS E-TIP	IMR	IMR 7828 SSC	.243"	2.800"	50.0	2967	39,600 CUP	56.0C*	3340	49,900 CUP
90 GR. NOS E-TIP	Winchester	Supreme 780	.243"	2.800"	48.0	2922	39,000 CUP	52.0	3162	48,600 CUP
90 GR. NOS E-TIP	Hodgdon	H4831	.243"	2.800"	49.0	2986	41,100 CUP	54.5C	3267	50,100 CUP
90 GR. NOS E-TIP	Hodgdon	Hybrid 100V	.243"	2.800"	46.0	3064	41,300 CUP	51.0C	3387	50,000 CUP
90 GR. NOS E-TIP	IMR	IMR 4831	.243"	2.800"	47.0	2963	38,100 CUP	52.5C	3340	48,500 CUP
90 GR. NOS E-TIP	Hodgdon	H4350	.243"	2.800"	46.0	3064	43,700 CUP	50.0C	3244	49,100 CUP
90 GR. NOS E-TIP	Hodgdon	H414	.243"	2.800"	45.0	2940	40,000 CUP	49.5	3227	49,400 CUP
90 GR. NOS E-TIP	IMR	IMR 4350	.243"	2.800"	47.0	3029	40,800 CUP	51.5C	3316	50,100 CUP
90 GR. NOS E-TIP	IMR	IMR 4007 SSC	.243"	2.800"	44.0	3012	43,300 CUP	49.2	3297	51,400 CUP
90 GR. SPR SP	Hodgdon	Retumbo	.243"	2.750"	55.5	3185	46,300 CUP	59.0C	3338	51,900 CUP
90 GR. SPR SP	Hodgdon	H1000	.243"	2.750"	52.0	3072	45,900 CUP	55.5	3241	51,900 CUP
90 GR. SPR SP	IMR	IMR 7828 SSC	.243"	2.750"	47.0	3036	44,500 CUP	51.5	3306	52,100 CUP
90 GR. SPR SP	Winchester	Supreme 780	.243"	2.750"	48.9	3111	45,600 CUP	52.0	3263	50,300 CUP
90 GR. SPR SP	Hodgdon	H4831	.243"	2.750"	49.0	3101	47,100 CUP	52.5	3272	52,200 CUP
90 GR. SPR SP	Hodgdon	Hybrid 100V	.243"	2.750"	44.0	3134	45,400 CUP	48.0	3330	51,700 CUP
90 GR. SPR SP	IMR	IMR 4831	.243"	2.750"	46.0	3109	45,100 CUP	49.5	3316	52,700 CUP
90 GR. SPR SP	Hodgdon	H4350	.243"	2.750"	44.5	3077	46,300 CUP	47.5	3223	51,800 CUP
90 GR. SPR SP	Hodgdon	H414	.243"	2.750"	44.0	3046	45,500 CUP	47.0	3193	51,800 CUP
90 GR. SPR SP	IMR	IMR 4350	.243"	2.750"	46.0	3099	44,200 CUP	50.0	3337	52,200 CUP
90 GR. SPR SP	Winchester	760	.243"	2.750"	44.0	3046	45,500 CUP	47.0	3193	51,800 CUP
90 GR. SPR SP	IMR	IMR 4007 SSC	.243"	2.750"	41.0	2981	44,000 CUP	45.0	3186	51,900 CUP
100 GR. NOS PART	Hodgdon	Retumbo	.243"	2.760"	54.0	3018	44,400 CUP	57.5	3219	51,800 CUP
100 GR. NOS PART	Hodgdon	H1000	.243"	2.760"	52.0	3007	47,300 CUP	55.0	3145	52,200 CUP
100 GR. NOS PART	IMR	IMR 7828 SSC	.243"	2.760"	47.0	2904	43,500 CUP	52.0	3189	51,200 CUP
100 GR. NOS PART	Winchester	Supreme 780	.243"	2.760"	49.4	3047	46,100 CUP	52.5	3196	51,000 CUP
100 GR. NOS PART	Hodgdon	H4831	.243"	2.760"	48.0	2960	46,400 CUP	51.0	3108	52,100 CUP
100 GR. NOS PART	Hodgdon	Hybrid 100V	.243"	2.760"	44.0	2971	44,700 CUP	48.5	3242	52,800 CUP
100 GR. NOS PART	IMR	IMR 4831	.243"	2.760"	46.0	2991	43,600 CUP	50.3	3231	51,900 CUP
100 GR. NOS PART	Hodgdon	H4350	.243"	2.760"	43.0	2925	46,300 CUP	46.0	3066	52,000 CUP
100 GR. NOS PART	IMR	IMR 4350	.243"	2.760"	46.0	3015	44,900 CUP	50.0	3249	52,300 CUP
100 GR. NOS PART	IMR	IMR 4007 SSC	.243"	2.760"	41.0	2843	43,200 CUP	45.5	3076	51,100 CUP
105 GR. SPR SP	Hodgdon	Retumbo	.243"	2.800"	51.0	2901	45,700 CUP	54.5C	3070	52,000 CUP
105 GR. SPR SP	Hodgdon	H1000	.243"	2.800"	47.0	2794	45,700 CUP	50.0	2913	51,600 CUP
105 GR. SPR SP	Winchester	Supreme 780	.243"	2.800"	48.9	2995	49,200 CUP	52.0	3128	52,300 CUP

61

Bullet Weight (Gr.)	Manufacturer	Powder	Bullet Diam.	C.O.L.	Grs.	Vel. (ft/s)	Pressure	Grs.	Vel. (ft/s)	Pressure
105 GR. SPR SP	Hodgdon	H4831	.243"	2.800"	45.0	2804	47,700 CUP	48.0	2978	52,200 CUP
107 GR. SIE HPBT	Hodgdon	Retumbo	.243"	2.800"	53.0	2972	45,700 CUP	56.5C	3138	51,800 CUP
107 GR. SIE HPBT	Hodgdon	H1000	.243"	2.800"	51.0	2879	45,700 CUP	54.5	3069	52,400 CUP
107 GR. SIE HPBT	Winchester	Supreme 780	.243"	2.800"	48.4	2933	44,400 CUP	51.5	3107	51,000 CUP
107 GR. SIE HPBT	Hodgdon	H4831	.243"	2.800"	48.0	2946	48,000 CUP	51.0	3049	52,200 CUP
115 GR. BAR SP	Hodgdon	Retumbo	.243"	2.650"	50.0	2805	47,500 CUP	53.0C	2934	51,900 CUP
115 GR. BAR SP	Hodgdon	H1000	.243"	2.650"	46.0	2682	46,400 CUP	49.0	2805	52,200 CUP
115 GR. BAR SP	Hodgdon	H4831	.243"	2.650"	43.0	2670	46,500 CUP	46.0	2797	51,800 CUP

Cartridge: 240 Weatherby Magnum
Load Type: Rifle

Bullet Weight (Gr.)	Manufacturer	Powder	Bullet Diam.	C.O.L.	Starting Loads			Maximum Loads		
					Grs.	Vel. (ft/s)	Pressure	Grs.	Vel. (ft/s)	Pressure
60 GR. SIE HP	Hodgdon	H4831	.243"	3.060"				57.0	3488	
60 GR. SIE HP	Hodgdon	H414	.243"	3.060"				54.0	3817	
60 GR. SIE HP	Hodgdon	H380	.243"	3.060"				51.0	3775	
60 GR. SIE HP	Hodgdon	H4895	.243"	3.060"				47.0	3521	
70 GR. HDY SP	IMR	IMR 7828	.243"	3.063"				56.0C	3505	47,500 CUP
75 GR. HDY HP	Hodgdon	H4831	.243"	3.075"				56.0	3453	
75 GR. HDY HP	Hodgdon	H414	.243"	3.075"				53.0	3555	
75 GR. HDY HP	Hodgdon	H380	.243"	3.075"				49.0	3531	
75 GR. HDY HP	Hodgdon	H4895	.243"	3.075"				46.0	3445	
80 GR. SPR SP	Hodgdon	H1000	.243"	3.060"	57.0	3082		59.0	3207	
80 GR. SPR SP	Hodgdon	H4831	.243"	3.060"				56.0	3481	
80 GR. SPR SP	Hodgdon	H414	.243"	3.060"				52.0	3514	
80 GR. SPR SP	Hodgdon	H380	.243"	3.060"				48.0	3451	
80 GR. SPR SP	Hodgdon	H4895	.243"	3.060"				44.0	3359	
85 GR. SIE HPBT	Hodgdon	H1000	.243"	3.060"	57.0	3043		59.0	3167	
85 GR. SIE HPBT	Hodgdon	H4831	.243"	3.060"				56.0	3460	
85 GR. SIE HPBT	Hodgdon	H414	.243"	3.060"				51.0	3409	
85 GR. SIE HPBT	Hodgdon	H380	.243"	3.060"				47.0	3344	
87 GR. HDY SP	IMR	IMR 7828	.243"	3.063"				54.5C	3360	50,700 CUP
90 GR. SPR SP	Hodgdon	H1000	.243"	3.060"	57.0	3037		59.0	3140	
90 GR. SPR SP	Hodgdon	H4831	.243"	3.060"				55.0	3394	
90 GR. SPR SP	Hodgdon	H414	.243"	3.060"				49.0	3307	
90 GR. SPR SP	Hodgdon	H380	.243"	3.060"				46.0	3287	
100 GR. NOS PART	Hodgdon	H1000	.243"	3.060"	57.0	3018		59.0	3122	
100 GR. NOS PART	IMR	IMR 7828	.243"	3.060"				53.5C	3240	52,000 CUP
100 GR. NOS PART	Hodgdon	H4831	.243"	3.060"				53.0	3202	
100 GR. NOS PART	Hodgdon	H414	.243"	3.060"				47.0	3080	
100 GR. NOS PART	Hodgdon	H380	.243"	3.060"				44.0	3010	

115 GR. BAR SP	Hodgdon	H870	.243"	3.050"				55.0	2880	
115 GR. BAR SP	Hodgdon	H1000	.243"	3.050"	56.0	2971		58.0	3066	
115 GR. BAR SP	Hodgdon	H4831	.243"	3.050"				46.0	2779	

Cartridge:25-20 Winchester Load Type:Rifle					Starting Loads			Maximum Loads		
Bullet Weight (Gr.)	Manufacturer	Powder	Bullet Diam.	C.O.L.	Grs.	Vel. (ft/s)	Pressure	Grs.	Vel. (ft/s)	Pressure
60 GR. HDY FP	Hodgdon	H322	.257"	1.600"	14.0	1799	23,600 CUP	15.0C	1900	25,700 CUP
60 GR. HDY FP	Hodgdon	H4198	.257"	1.600"	12.0	1814	20,200 CUP	14.2C	2101	25,800 CUP
60 GR. HDY FP	Hodgdon	H4227	.257"	1.600"	9.6	1854	24,200 CUP	10.2	1962	26,700 CUP
60 GR. HDY FP	Hodgdon	H110	.257"	1.600"	8.5	1831	23,500 CUP	9.3	1931	26,600 CUP
71 GR. LRNFP	Hodgdon	H4227	.258"	1.545"	6.0	1146	13,700 CUP	7.0	1346	18,200 CUP
71 GR. LRNFP	Hodgdon	HS-6	.258"	1.545"	4.3	1206	18,700 CUP	5.3	1428	21,900 CUP
75 GR. SPR FP	Hodgdon	H322	.257"	1.575"	12.0	1523	22,300 CUP	13.5	1702	26,700 CUP
75 GR. SPR FP	Hodgdon	H4198	.257"	1.575"	10.5	1530	18,100 CUP	12.8	1877	27,300 CUP
75 GR. SPR FP	Hodgdon	H4227	.257"	1.575"	8.3	1521	21,000 CUP	9.3	1741	27,900 CUP
75 GR. SPR FP	Hodgdon	H110	.257"	1.575"	7.4	1513	23,700 CUP	8.4	1691	28,000 CUP
85 GR. LRNFP	Hodgdon	H4227	.258"	1.600"	6.0	1129	18,500 CUP	7.0	1317	20,500 CUP
85 GR. LRNFP	Hodgdon	HS-6	.258"	1.600"	4.5	1261	19,600 CUP	5.3	1391	25,300 CUP
86 GR. REM SP	Hodgdon	H322	.257"	1.600"	11.3	1358	22,100 CUP	12.0	1517	26,300 CUP
86 GR. REM SP	Hodgdon	H4198	.257"	1.600"	10.5	1576	24,500 CUP	11.5	1673	26,500 CUP
86 GR. REM SP	Hodgdon	H4227	.257"	1.600"	8.0	1444	23,700 CUP	8.6	1545	27,600 CUP
86 GR. REM SP	Hodgdon	H110	.257"	1.600"	7.0	1422	23,900 CUP	7.5	1502	27,100 CUP

Cartridge:256 Winchester Magnum Load Type:Rifle					Starting Loads			Maximum Loads		
Bullet Weight (Gr.)	Manufacturer	Powder	Bullet Diam.	C.O.L.	Grs.	Vel. (ft/s)	Pressure	Grs.	Vel. (ft/s)	Pressure
60 GR. HDY SP	Hodgdon	H4198	.257"	1.560"	17.0	2686		18.0	2794	
60 GR. HDY SP	Hodgdon	H110	.257"	1.560"	13.0	2616		14.0	2724	
75 GR. SPR FP	Hodgdon	H4198	.257"	1.540"	14.0	2019		16.0	2327	
87 GR. HDY SP	Hodgdon	H4198	.257"	1.775"	14.0	2081		15.0	2192	

Cartridge:25-35 Winchester Load Type:Rifle					Starting Loads			Maximum Loads		
Bullet Weight (Gr.)	Manufacturer	Powder	Bullet Diam.	C.O.L.	Grs.	Vel. (ft/s)	Pressure	Grs.	Vel. (ft/s)	Pressure
60 GR. HDY JFP	Hodgdon	CFE 223	.257"	2.300"	32.0	2731	23,900 CUP	35.0	2951	26,200 CUP
60 GR. HDY JFP	Hodgdon	Varget	.257"	2.300"	28.0	2677	27,900 CUP	31.5C	2972	36,200 CUP
60 GR. HDY JFP	Hodgdon	BL-C(2)	.257"	2.300"	32.0	2797	24,600 CUP	35.0	3023	29,800 CUP
60 GR. HDY JFP	Hodgdon	H335	.257"	2.300"	27.0	2865	31,800 CUP	30.0	3026	36,200 CUP

Bullet Weight (Gr.)	Manufacturer	Powder	Bullet Diam.	C.O.L.	Grs.	Vel. (ft/s)	Pressure	Grs.	Vel. (ft/s)	Pressure
60 GR. HDY JFP	Hodgdon	H4895	.257"	2.300"	26.0	2796	32,300 CUP	30.5C	3014	36,200 CUP
60 GR. HDY JFP	IMR	IMR 8208 XBR	.257"	2.300"	25.0	2838	34,500 CUP	27.5	2913	36,300 CUP
60 GR. HDY JFP	Hodgdon	Benchmark	.257"	2.300"	23.0	2626	29,700 CUP	25.7	2867	36,600 CUP
60 GR. HDY JFP	Hodgdon	H322	.257"	2.300"	22.0	2522	27,700 CUP	24.5	2793	35,900 CUP
60 GR. HDY JFP	Hodgdon	H4198	.257"	2.300"	20.0	2626	29,700 CUP	21.7	2827	36,100 CUP
75 GR. SPR JFP	Hodgdon	LVR	.257"	2.280"	30.0	2707	27,800 CUP	34.0C	2992	33,100 CUP
75 GR. SPR JFP	Hodgdon	CFE 223	.257"	2.280"	30.0	2611	27,100 CUP	33.0	2802	30,100 CUP
75 GR. SPR JFP	Hodgdon	Varget	.257"	2.280"	26.5	2487	29,800 CUP	29.0	2672	36,300 CUP
75 GR. SPR JFP	Hodgdon	BL-C(2)	.257"	2.280"	31.5	2680	29,700 CUP	34.0	2815	32,600 CUP
75 GR. SPR JFP	Hodgdon	H335	.257"	2.280"	23.0	2440	31,000 CUP	25.5	2595	36,400 CUP
75 GR. SPR JFP	Hodgdon	H4895	.257"	2.280"	25.0	2471	32,000 CUP	27.4	2689	36,500 CUP
75 GR. SPR JFP	IMR	IMR 8208 XBR	.257"	2.280"	23.0	2444	29,200 CUP	25.7	2660	34,200 CUP
75 GR. SPR JFP	Hodgdon	Benchmark	.257"	2.280"	21.0	2305	28,600 CUP	23.0	2502	36,400 CUP
75 GR. SPR JFP	Hodgdon	H322	.257"	2.280"	21.0	2256	25,900 CUP	23.5	2543	35,900 CUP
75 GR. SPR JFP	Hodgdon	H4198	.257"	2.280"	19.0	2422	32,300 CUP	20.5	2515	35,500 CUP
90 GR. LFP W/GCK	IMR	Trail Boss	.257"	2.320"	5.5	1224	22,000 CUP	8.0	1414	23,200 CUP
90 GR. LFP W/GCK	Hodgdon	Titegroup	.257"	2.320"	5.0	1369	18,000 CUP	7.0	1513	28,900 CUP
90 GR. LFP W/GCK	Hodgdon	Clays	.257"	2.320"	5.0	1284	25,100 CUP	6.0	1344	34,000 CUP
117 GR. HDY RN	Hodgdon	H380	.257"	2.550"	27.0	2172	30,100 CUP	30.0	2357	34,900 CUP
117 GR. HDY RN	Hodgdon	CFE 223	.257"	2.550"	25.0	2179	27,100 CUP	28.5	2404	36,100 CUP
117 GR. HDY RN	Hodgdon	Varget	.257"	2.550"	21.0	1916	25,800 CUP	24.5	2244	36,600 CUP
117 GR. HDY RN	Hodgdon	BL-C(2)	.257"	2.550"	24.0	2082	27,000 CUP	27.0	2327	35,800 CUP
117 GR. HDY RN	Hodgdon	H335	.257"	2.550"	20.0	1951	27,700 CUP	22.5	2174	35,900 CUP
117 GR. HDY RN	Hodgdon	H4895	.257"	2.550"	19.5	1875	25,000 CUP	22.5	2168	36,000 CUP
117 GR. HDY RN	IMR	IMR 8208 XBR	.257"	2.550"	20.0	1985	28,800 CUP	22.5	2257	35,700 CUP
117 GR. HDY RN	Hodgdon	Benchmark	.257"	2.550"	19.0	1902	27,200 CUP	21.0	2063	32,500 CUP
117 GR. HDY RN	Hodgdon	H322	.257"	2.550"	19.0	1916	27,900 CUP	21.0	2127	36,000 CUP
117 GR. HDY RN	Hodgdon	H4198	.257"	2.550"	16.8	1889	29,100 CUP	18.8	2065	36,100 CUP

Cartridge: 257 Kimber
Load Type: Rifle

Bullet Weight (Gr.)	Manufacturer	Powder	Bullet Diam.	C.O.L.	Starting Loads			Maximum Loads		
					Grs.	Vel. (ft/s)	Pressure	Grs.	Vel. (ft/s)	Pressure
75 GR. HDY HP	Hodgdon	H335	.257"	2.335"	28.0	2769		31.5	3195	
75 GR. HDY HP	Hodgdon	H4895	.257"	2.335"	28.0	2756		31.5	3192	
75 GR. HDY HP	Hodgdon	H322	.257"	2.335"	27.0	2806		30.0	3198	
87 GR. HDY SP	Hodgdon	H335	.257"	2.375"	29.0	2870		31.0	3030	
87 GR. HDY SP	Hodgdon	H4895	.257"	2.375"	29.0	2824		31.0	3056	
87 GR. HDY SP	Hodgdon	H322	.257"	2.375"	25.0	2604		28.0	2868	
100 GR. SPR SP	Hodgdon	H4895	.257"	2.390"	26.0	2527		28.0	2760	
117 GR. SIE SPBT	Hodgdon	H4895	.257"	2.455"	22.0	2017		24.0	2223	

Cartridge:250-3000 Savage Load Type:Rifle					Starting Loads			Maximum Loads		
Bullet Weight (Gr.)	Manufacturer	Powder	Bullet Diam.	C.O.L.	Grs.	Vel. (ft/s)	Pressure	Grs.	Vel. (ft/s)	Pressure
75 GR. HDY V-MAX	Hodgdon	CFE 223	.257"	2.475"	36.0	3096	36,300 CUP	39.0	3339	40,900 CUP
75 GR. HDY V-MAX	Hodgdon	Varget	.257"	2.475"	36.0	3061	36,700 CUP	38.5	3254	43,200 CUP
75 GR. HDY V-MAX	Hodgdon	BL-C(2)	.257"	2.475"	35.0	3001	36,200 CUP	37.5	3216	43,700 CUP
75 GR. HDY V-MAX	Hodgdon	H335	.257"	2.475"	33.0	3018	37,200 CUP	35.0	3209	43,800 CUP
75 GR. HDY V-MAX	Hodgdon	H4895	.257"	2.475"	34.0	3088	39,400 CUP	36.5	3256	43,500 CUP
75 GR. HDY V-MAX	IMR	IMR 8208 XBR	.257"	2.475"	34.0	3103	37,500 CUP	37.0	3341	43,200 CUP
75 GR. HDY V-MAX	Hodgdon	Benchmark	.257"	2.475"	31.0	2981	38,300 CUP	33.0	3102	43,900 CUP
80 GR. BAR TTSX BT	Hodgdon	Varget	.257"	2.500"	35.0	2977	38,300 CUP	37.3C	3149	43,500 CUP
80 GR. BAR TTSX BT	IMR	IMR 4064	.257"	2.500"	34.0	2910	38,300 CUP	36.5C	3113	43,200 CUP
80 GR. BAR TTSX BT	Winchester	748	.257"	2.500"	33.0	2863	38,500 CUP	35.8	3066	43,600 CUP
80 GR. BAR TTSX BT	Hodgdon	BL-C(2)	.257"	2.500"	33.0	2821	38,100 CUP	35.0	3008	43,600 CUP
80 GR. BAR TTSX BT	IMR	IMR 4895	.257"	2.500"	34.0	2888	38,500 CUP	36.5	3078	43,500 CUP
80 GR. BAR TTSX BT	Hodgdon	H335	.257"	2.500"	31.0	2879	39,200 CUP	33.0	3026	43,700 CUP
80 GR. BAR TTSX BT	Hodgdon	H4895	.257"	2.500"	33.0	2963	36,600 CUP	35.0	3121	42,800 CUP
80 GR. BAR TTSX BT	IMR	IMR 8208 XBR	.257"	2.500"	32.0	2868	36,000 CUP	34.5	3112	43,100 CUP
80 GR. BAR TTSX BT	IMR	IMR 3031	.257"	2.500"	32.0	2902	38,300 CUP	34.5C	3111	43,600 CUP
80 GR. BAR TTSX BT	Hodgdon	Benchmark	.257"	2.500"	32.0	2949	39,300 CUP	34.0	3090	43,700 CUP
85 GR. NOS BT	Hodgdon	CFE 223	.257"	2.500"	33.0	2873	34,500 CUP	36.5	3136	43,900 CUP
85 GR. NOS BT	Hodgdon	Varget	.257"	2.500"	34.0	2854	35,300 CUP	37.0	3090	43,500 CUP
85 GR. NOS BT	Hodgdon	BL-C(2)	.257"	2.500"	34.0	2859	36,200 CUP	36.0	3039	43,200 CUP
85 GR. NOS BT	Hodgdon	H335	.257"	2.500"	32.0	2872	38,800 CUP	34.0	3038	44,000 CUP
85 GR. NOS BT	Hodgdon	H4895	.257"	2.500"	33.0	2929	38,100 CUP	35.0	3084	43,600 CUP
85 GR. NOS BT	IMR	IMR 8208 XBR	.257"	2.500"	32.0	2897	34,600 CUP	35.3	3162	44,600 CUP
85 GR. NOS BT	Hodgdon	Benchmark	.257"	2.500"	29.5	2793	38,200 CUP	31.5	2943	43,200 CUP
87 GR. SPR SP	IMR	IMR 4350	.257"	2.450"				39.0C	2905	39,500 CUP
87 GR. SPR SP	Winchester	760	.257"	2.450"				39.5	2985	43,500 CUP
87 GR. SPR SP	Hodgdon	CFE 223	.257"	2.450"	34.0	2908	36,400 CUP	37.5	3151	44,500 CUP
87 GR. SPR SP	Hodgdon	Varget	.257"	2.450"	35.0	2947	40,200 CUP	37.0	3074	43,200 CUP
87 GR. SPR SP	IMR	IMR 4320	.257"	2.450"				35.5	2975	45,000 CUP
87 GR. SPR SP	IMR	IMR 4064	.257"	2.450"				35.5	3075	45,000 CUP
87 GR. SPR SP	Winchester	748	.257"	2.450"				36.0	2940	41,000 CUP
87 GR. SPR SP	Hodgdon	BL-C(2)	.257"	2.450"	34.5	2907	36,700 CUP	36.5	3080	43,900 CUP
87 GR. SPR SP	IMR	IMR 4895	.257"	2.450"				34.5	3000	44,900 CUP
87 GR. SPR SP	Hodgdon	H335	.257"	2.450"	32.0	2863	39,800 CUP	34.0	2969	43,100 CUP
87 GR. SPR SP	Hodgdon	H4895	.257"	2.450"	33.0	2913	39,100 CUP	35.5	3068	43,700 CUP

Bullet	Mfr	Powder	Diameter	COAL	Charge	Velocity	Pressure	Charge	Velocity	Pressure
87 GR. SPR SP	IMR	IMR 8208 XBR	.257"	2.450"	31.5	2864	35,300 CUP	35.0	3103	44,800 CUP
87 GR. SPR SP	IMR	IMR 3031	.257"	2.450"				34.0	3055	44,200 CUP
87 GR. SPR SP	Hodgdon	Benchmark	.257"	2.450"	30.5	2804	39,000 CUP	32.5	2937	43,000 CUP
87 GR. SPR SP	IMR	SR 4759	.257"	2.450"				20.5	2515	44,700 CUP
90 GR. SIE HPBT	Hodgdon	CFE 223	.257"	2.425"	34.0	2855	35,400 CUP	37.5	3128	44,600 CUP
90 GR. SIE HPBT	Hodgdon	Varget	.257"	2.425"	34.0	2860	37,300 CUP	36.5	3021	43,300 CUP
90 GR. SIE HPBT	Hodgdon	BL-C(2)	.257"	2.425"	34.5	2864	36,600 CUP	36.5	3012	43,500 CUP
90 GR. SIE HPBT	Hodgdon	H335	.257"	2.425"	31.5	2808	37,100 CUP	33.5	2960	43,500 CUP
90 GR. SIE HPBT	Hodgdon	H4895	.257"	2.425"	33.0	2901	39,000 CUP	35.5	3060	43,900 CUP
90 GR. SIE HPBT	IMR	IMR 8208 XBR	.257"	2.425"	32.0	2913	38,100 CUP	35.0	3002	44,200 CUP
90 GR. SIE HPBT	Hodgdon	Benchmark	.257"	2.425"	31.0	2831	39,200 CUP	33.0	2965	43,900 CUP
100 GR. HDY SP	Hodgdon	H4350	.257"	2.500"	38.0	2773	38,500 CUP	40.5C	2936	44,100 CUP
100 GR. HDY SP	Hodgdon	H414	.257"	2.500"	35.0	2697	36,700 CUP	37.2	2852	43,900 CUP
100 GR. HDY SP	IMR	IMR 4350	.257"	2.500"				38.5C	2780	41,400 CUP
100 GR. HDY SP	Winchester	760	.257"	2.500"				38.8	2820	42,000 CUP
100 GR. HDY SP	Hodgdon	H380	.257"	2.500"	35.0	2673	35,300 CUP	37.0	2834	43,500 CUP
100 GR. HDY SP	Hodgdon	CFE 223	.257"	2.500"	32.0	2675	35,500 CUP	35.0	2902	44,400 CUP
100 GR. HDY SP	Hodgdon	Varget	.257"	2.500"	33.0	2750	40,000 CUP	35.2	2877	43,700 CUP
100 GR. HDY SP	IMR	IMR 4320	.257"	2.500"				34.5	2785	45,000 CUP
100 GR. HDY SP	IMR	IMR 4064	.257"	2.500"				34.5	2875	44,100 CUP
100 GR. HDY SP	Winchester	748	.257"	2.500"				35.5	2820	43,500 CUP
100 GR. HDY SP	IMR	IMR 4895	.257"	2.500"				34.0	2845	45,000 CUP
100 GR. HDY SP	Hodgdon	H4895	.257"	2.500"	31.0	2698	38,500 CUP	33.5	2849	43,600 CUP
100 GR. HDY SP	IMR	IMR 8208 XBR	.257"	2.500"	30.0	2687	38,300 CUP	33.0	2862	44,200 CUP
100 GR. HDY SP	IMR	IMR 3031	.257"	2.500"				33.0	2865	44,500 CUP
100 GR. HDY SP	IMR	SR 4759	.257"	2.500"				20.0	2290	43,700 CUP
115 GR. NOS BT	Hodgdon	H4350	.257"	2.525"	34.5	2497	36,800 CUP	36.8C	2642	43,400 CUP
115 GR. NOS BT	Hodgdon	H414	.257"	2.525"	34.0	2504	35,900 CUP	36.0	2652	43,200 CUP
115 GR. NOS BT	Hodgdon	H380	.257"	2.525"	34.0	2504	40,100 CUP	35.5	2606	44,000 CUP
115 GR. NOS BT	Hodgdon	Varget	.257"	2.525"	30.5	2494	39,400 CUP	32.5	2611	43,500 CUP
115 GR. NOS BT	Hodgdon	H4895	.257"	2.525"	28.5	2440	38,400 CUP	30.5	2567	43,400 CUP
115 GR. NOS BT	IMR	IMR 8208 XBR	.257"	2.525"	28.0	2770	39,000 CUP	31.0	2614	44,400 CUP
117 GR. SIE SPBT	Hodgdon	H4831	.257"	2.475"	38.0	2453	35,900 CUP	39.0C	2519	39,600 CUP
117 GR. SIE SPBT	Hodgdon	H4350	.257"	2.475"	35.0	2518	37,900 CUP	37.0C	2637	43,400 CUP
117 GR. SIE SPBT	Hodgdon	H414	.257"	2.475"	34.0	2529	40,900 CUP	36.0	2646	43,500 CUP
117 GR. SIE SPBT	Hodgdon	H380	.257"	2.475"	32.5	2457	39,300 CUP	34.5	2565	43,600 CUP
117 GR. SIE SPBT	Hodgdon	Varget	.257"	2.475"	30.0	2493	41,100 CUP	32.0	2594	43,700 CUP
117 GR. SIE SPBT	Hodgdon	H4895	.257"	2.475"	28.5	2447	38,000 CUP	30.5	2579	43,800 CUP
117 GR. SIE SPBT	IMR	IMR 8208 XBR	.257"	2.475"	27.5	2429	38,200 CUP	30.6	2594	45,000 CUP
120 GR. SFT SP	Hodgdon	H4831	.257"	2.525"	37.5	2470	39,100 CUP	39.0C	2537	42,200 CUP

Bullet Weight (Gr.)	Manufacturer	Powder	Bullet Diam.	C.O.L.	Grs.	Vel. (ft/s)	Pressure	Grs.	Vel. (ft/s)	Pressure
120 GR. SFT SP	Hodgdon	H4350	.257"	2.525"	33.5	2443	38,000 CUP	35.5	2577	43,300 CUP
120 GR. SFT SP	Hodgdon	H414	.257"	2.525"	32.5	2450	37,900 CUP	34.5	2599	43,400 CUP
120 GR. SFT SP	Hodgdon	H380	.257"	2.525"	32.0	2423	38,700 CUP	33.5	2490	43,300 CUP
120 GR. SFT SP	Hodgdon	Varget	.257"	2.525"	29.0	2397	37,200 CUP	31.0	2508	43,200 CUP
120 GR. SFT SP	Hodgdon	H4895	.257"	2.525"	27.5	2331	37,500 CUP	29.0	2467	43,400 CUP
120 GR. SFT SP	IMR	IMR 8208 XBR	.257"	2.525"	26.0	2296	35,000 CUP	28.8	2480	44,200 CUP

Cartridge: 257 Roberts Load Type: Rifle					Starting Loads			Maximum Loads		
Bullet Weight (Gr.)	Manufacturer	Powder	Bullet Diam.	C.O.L.	Grs.	Vel. (ft/s)	Pressure	Grs.	Vel. (ft/s)	Pressure
60 GR. HDY SP	Hodgdon	H4831	.257"	2.535"	49.0	2847	23,700 CUP	53.0	3382	33,600 CUP
60 GR. HDY SP	Hodgdon	H4350	.257"	2.535"	48.0	3290	36,200 CUP	51.0	3612	44,700 CUP
60 GR. HDY SP	Hodgdon	H414	.257"	2.535"	49.5	3566	36,000 CUP	54.0	3818	43,800 CUP
60 GR. HDY SP	Winchester	760	.257"	2.535"	49.5	3566	36,000 CUP	54.0	3818	43,800 CUP
60 GR. HDY SP	Hodgdon	H380	.257"	2.535"	45.0	3497	39,000 CUP	49.0	3752	46,200 CUP
60 GR. HDY SP	Hodgdon	CFE 223	.257"	2.535"	44.0	3551	37,200 CUP	47.5	3760	43,600 CUP
60 GR. HDY SP	Hodgdon	BL-C(2)	.257"	2.535"	44.0	3469	30,000 CUP	48.0	3834	45,900 CUP
60 GR. HDY SP	Hodgdon	H335	.257"	2.535"	44.0	3467	29,400 CUP	48.0	3885	46,400 CUP
60 GR. HDY SP	Hodgdon	H4895	.257"	2.535"	42.0	3376	36,600 CUP	46.0	3805	45,000 CUP
60 GR. HDY SP	Hodgdon	Benchmark	.257"	2.535"	41.0	3453	42,200 CUP	43.7	3671	45,000 CUP
75 GR. HDY HP	Hodgdon	Hybrid 100V	.257"	2.795"	45.0	3145	36,500 CUP	49.0C	3380	42,900 CUP
75 GR. HDY HP	IMR	IMR 4831	.257"	2.795"	46.5	3017	34,100 CUP	51.5C	3403	43,500 CUP
75 GR. HDY HP	Hodgdon	H4350	.257"	2.795"	47.0	3129	35,200 CUP	50.0	3422	44,000 CUP
75 GR. HDY HP	Hodgdon	H414	.257"	2.795"	48.0	3343	37,200 CUP	52.0	3555	45,300 CUP
75 GR. HDY HP	IMR	IMR 4350	.257"	2.795"	47.8	3254	41,700 CUP	52.0C	3496	46,600 CUP
75 GR. HDY HP	Winchester	760	.257"	2.795"	48.0	3343	37,200 CUP	52.0	3555	45,300 CUP
75 GR. HDY HP	IMR	IMR 4007 SSC	.257"	2.795"	45.6	3215	41,200 CUP	48.5	3512	47,200 CUP
75 GR. HDY HP	Hodgdon	H380	.257"	2.795"	44.0	3258	37,800 CUP	48.0	3563	45,600 CUP
75 GR. HDY HP	Hodgdon	CFE 223	.257"	2.795"	38.0	3160	38,500 CUP	42.0	3369	44,800 CUP
75 GR. HDY HP	Hodgdon	Varget	.257"	2.795"	37.0	3155	34,700 CUP	41.0	3453	43,700 CUP
75 GR. HDY HP	IMR	IMR 4064	.257"	2.795"	41.7	3320	39,700 CUP	44.3	3517	46,400 CUP
75 GR. HDY HP	Hodgdon	BL-C(2)	.257"	2.795"	42.0	3094	31,800 CUP	46.0	3531	46,700 CUP
75 GR. HDY HP	IMR	IMR 4895	.257"	2.795"	40.9	3288	39,700 CUP	43.5	3496	46,500 CUP
75 GR. HDY HP	Hodgdon	H335	.257"	2.795"	42.0	3161	31,200 CUP	46.0	3548	45,000 CUP
75 GR. HDY HP	Hodgdon	H4895	.257"	2.795"	40.5	3201	34,800 CUP	44.0	3561	47,300 CUP
75 GR. HDY HP	IMR	IMR 8208 XBR	.257"	2.795"	40.5	3390	39,300 CUP	43.0	3456	44,900 CUP
75 GR. HDY HP	Hodgdon	Benchmark	.257"	2.795"	39.0	3226	39,200 CUP	41.7	3434	45,000 CUP
80 GR. BAR TTSX BT	Hodgdon	H4350	.257"	2.780"	44.0	2999	36,000 CUP	48.5	3290	45,000 CUP
80 GR. BAR TTSX BT	Hodgdon	H414	.257"	2.780"	43.0	3047	37,300 CUP	48.0	3377	45,000 CUP

80 GR. BAR TTSX BT	IMR	IMR 4350	.257"	2.780"	45.0	3008	35,100 CUP	49.2C	3326	43,600 CUP
80 GR. BAR TTSX BT	Winchester	760	.257"	2.780"	43.0	3047	37,300 CUP	48.0	3377	45,000 CUP
80 GR. BAR TTSX BT	IMR	IMR 4007 SSC	.257"	2.780"	42.0	3012	36,200 CUP	46.7	3300	45,000 CUP
80 GR. BAR TTSX BT	Hodgdon	H380	.257"	2.780"	41.0	2988	36,700 CUP	45.0	3257	44,600 CUP
80 GR. BAR TTSX BT	Hodgdon	CFE 223	.257"	2.780"	35.0	3038	40,700 CUP	39.0	3243	44,300 CUP
80 GR. BAR TTSX BT	Hodgdon	Varget	.257"	2.780"	39.0	3061	37,500 CUP	43.0	3287	45,000 CUP
80 GR. BAR TTSX BT	IMR	IMR 4064	.257"	2.780"	39.0	3071	35,300 CUP	43.5	3419	45,000 CUP
80 GR. BAR TTSX BT	Winchester	748	.257"	2.780"	39.0	3094	41,300 CUP	42.5	3248	44,700 CUP
80 GR. BAR TTSX BT	Hodgdon	BL-C(2)	.257"	2.780"	39.0	3114	42,300 CUP	43.0	3277	45,000 CUP
80 GR. BAR TTSX BT	IMR	IMR 4895	.257"	2.780"	39.0	3058	37,000 CUP	43.0	3357	45,900 CUP
80 GR. BAR TTSX BT	Hodgdon	H4895	.257"	2.780"	37.0	3090	38,800 CUP	40.8	3281	44,600 CUP
80 GR. BAR TTSX BT	IMR	IMR 8208 XBR	.257"	2.780"	36.0	3062	38,400 CUP	39.8	3284	44,700 CUP
80 GR. BAR TTSX BT	IMR	IMR 3031	.257"	2.780"	36.0	3036	35,800 CUP	40.3	3343	44,900 CUP
80 GR. BAR TTSX BT	Hodgdon	Benchmark	.257"	2.780"	35.5	2990	36,900 CUP	39.5	3285	45,000 CUP
90 GR. HDY GMX	IMR	IMR 7828 SSC	.257"	2.880"	44.0	2847	41,000 CUP	49.0C	3038	44,600 CUP
90 GR. HDY GMX	Hodgdon	H4831	.257"	2.880"	40.0	2645	35,200 CUP	44.5	2925	44,600 CUP
90 GR. HDY GMX	Hodgdon	Hybrid 100V	.257"	2.880"	40.0	2823	37,100 cUP	44.5	3128	44,300 CUP
90 GR. HDY GMX	IMR	IMR 4831	.257"	2.880"	41.0	2841	38,800 CUP	45.3	3031	44,600 CUP
90 GR. HDY GMX	Hodgdon	H4350	.257"	2.880"	38.0	2729	36,000 CUP	42.0	2968	44,200 CUP
90 GR. HDY GMX	Hodgdon	H414	.257"	2.880"	39.0	2832	39,200 CUP	42.5	2984	43,700 CUP
90 GR. HDY GMX	IMR	IMR 4350	.257"	2.880"	40.0	2837	39,400 CUP	44.0	3025	44,200 CUP
90 GR. HDY GMX	IMR	IMR 4007 SSC	.257"	2.880"	35.0	2740	41,700 CUP	38.0	2832	43,800 CUP
90 GR. HDY GMX	Hodgdon	H380	.257"	2.880"	36.0	2661	38,500 CUP	40.0	2862	44,100 CUP
90 GR. HDY GMX	Hodgdon	Varget	.257"	2.880"	35.0	2788	39,100 CUP	38.0	2968	44,600 CUP
90 GR. HDY GMX	IMR	IMR 4064	.257"	2.880"	35.0	2773	36,900 CUP	38.5	2973	44,500 CUP
90 GR. HDY GMX	Hodgdon	BL-C(2)	.257"	2.880"	35.0	2749	39,800 CUP	38.0	2916	44,500 CUP
90 GR. HDY GMX	IMR	IMR 4895	.257"	2.880"	36.0	2787	37,500 CUP	39.8	3023	44,500 CUP
90 GR. HDY GMX	Hodgdon	H4895	.257"	2.880"	33.0	2739	37,700 CUP	36.5	2943	44,800 CUP
90 GR. HDY GMX	IMR	IMR 8208 XBR	.257"	2.880"	33.0	2739	38,300 CUP	36.3	2927	44,100 CUP
90 GR. SIE HPBT	Hodgdon	H4831	.257"	2.775"	48.0	2786	27,600 CUP	52.0	3236	39,500 CUP
90 GR. SIE HPBT	Hodgdon	Hybrid 100V	.257"	2.775"	45.0	3061	38,800 CUP	49.0C	3282	44,800 CUP
90 GR. SIE HPBT	IMR	IMR 4831	.257"	2.775"	47.4	3049	37,500 CUP	51.5C	3313	45,800 CUP
90 GR. SIE HPBT	Hodgdon	H4350	.257"	2.775"	44.0	2890	36,100 CUP	46.0	3040	43,700 CUP
90 GR. SIE HPBT	Hodgdon	H414	.257"	2.775"	46.0	3107	34,800 CUP	50.0	3368	44,400 CUP
90 GR. SIE HPBT	IMR	IMR 4350	.257"	2.775"	47.0	3084	41,800 CUP	50.0C	3299	47,900 CUP
90 GR. SIE HPBT	Winchester	760	.257"	2.775"	46.0	3107	34,800 CUP	50.0	3368	44,400 CUP
90 GR. SIE HPBT	IMR	IMR 4007 SSC	.257"	2.775"	42.8	3027	39,800 CUP	45.5	3215	47,300 CUP
90 GR. SIE HPBT	Hodgdon	H380	.257"	2.775"	43.0	3083	38,400 CUP	47.0	3364	45,400 CUP
90 GR. SIE HPBT	Hodgdon	Varget	.257"	2.775"	36.0	2990	36,300 CUP	40.0	3269	44,900 CUP
90 GR. SIE HPBT	IMR	IMR 4064	.257"	2.775"	39.8	3040	39,600 CUP	42.3	3211	46,300 CUP

Bullet	Mfr	Powder	Dia	COL						
90 GR. SIE HPBT	Hodgdon	BL-C(2)	.257"	2.775"	40.0	2864	30,600 CUP	43.5	3231	45,000 CUP
90 GR. SIE HPBT	IMR	IMR 4895	.257"	2.775"	39.5	3042	39,800 CUP	42.0	3238	46,400 CUP
90 GR. SIE HPBT	Hodgdon	H335	.257"	2.775"	39.0	2951	30,600 CUP	43.0	3300	44,400 CUP
90 GR. SIE HPBT	Hodgdon	H4895	.257"	2.775"	38.5	2954	33,600 CUP	42.0	3372	47,600 CUP
90 GR. SIE HPBT	IMR	IMR 8208 XBR	.257"	2.775"	39.4	3129	40,200 CUP	42.0	3314	46,800 CUP
100 GR. SPR SPBT	Hodgdon	H4831	.257"	2.770"	45.0	2660	29,100 CUP	49.0	3010	44,100 CUP
100 GR. SPR SPBT	Hodgdon	Hybrid 100V	.257"	2.770"	44.0	2968	38,800 CUP	48.0C	3205	45,400 CUP
100 GR. SPR SPBT	IMR	IMR 4831	.257"	2.770"	46.3	2965	41,000 CUP	49.2C	3134	47,100 CUP
100 GR. SPR SPBT	Hodgdon	H4350	.257"	2.770"	43.0	2833	34,200 CUP	45.0	2970	45,400 CUP
100 GR. SPR SPBT	Hodgdon	H414	.257"	2.770"	44.0	2919	33,600 CUP	45.0	3098	44,500 CUP
100 GR. SPR SPBT	IMR	IMR 4350	.257"	2.770"	44.8	2896	38,400 CUP	47.7	3077	47,000 CUP
100 GR. SPR SPBT	Winchester	760	.257"	2.770"	44.0	2919	33,600 CUP	45.0	3098	44,500 CUP
100 GR. SPR SPBT	IMR	IMR 4007 SSC	.257"	2.770"	41.4	2894	41,800 CUP	44.0	3059	47,300 CUP
100 GR. SPR SPBT	Hodgdon	H380	.257"	2.770"	40.5	2868	37,800 CUP	44.0	3108	46,600 CUP
100 GR. SPR SPBT	Hodgdon	Varget	.257"	2.770"	34.0	2724	34,400 CUP	38.0	2981	44,900 CUP
100 GR. SPR SPBT	IMR	IMR 4064	.257"	2.770"	38.8	2904	40,900 CUP	41.3	3076	47,300 CUP
100 GR. SPR SPBT	Hodgdon	BL-C(2)	.257"	2.770"	36.0	2692	32,400 CUP	39.0	2958	45,400 CUP
100 GR. SPR SPBT	IMR	IMR 4895	.257"	2.770"	39.0	2921	41,200 CUP	41.0	3061	45,900 CUP
100 GR. SPR SPBT	Hodgdon	H335	.257"	2.770"	36.0	2776	37,200 CUP	39.0	3042	47,800 CUP
100 GR. SPR SPBT	Hodgdon	H4895	.257"	2.770"	35.0	2661	30,600 CUP	38.0	2990	46,100 CUP
100 GR. SPR SPBT	IMR	IMR 8208 XBR	.257"	2.770"	37.1	2991	39,400 CUP	39.5	3085	44,700 CUP
115 GR. NOS PART	IMR	IMR 7828 SSC	.257"	2.890"	42.0	2480	35,500 CUP	46.3	2724	43,700 CUP
115 GR. NOS PART	Hodgdon	H4831	.257"	2.780"	43.0	2479	30,400 CUP	46.0	2760	46,000 CUP
115 GR. NOS PART	Hodgdon	Hybrid 100V	.257"	2.780"	42.0	2845	40,700 CUP	46.0C	3049	46,600 CUP
115 GR. NOS PART	IMR	IMR 4831	.257"	2.890"	42.6	2670	37,900 CUP	46.3	2867	46,000 CUP
115 GR. NOS PART	Hodgdon	H4350	.257"	2.780"	41.0	2660	40,600 CUP	43.0	2777	44,400 CUP
115 GR. NOS PART	Hodgdon	H414	.257"	2.780"	39.5	2574	36,000 CUP	43.0	2720	44,200 CUP
115 GR. NOS PART	IMR	IMR 4350	.257"	2.890"	41.9	2666	39,800 CUP	45.5	2866	46,600 CUP
115 GR. NOS PART	Winchester	760	.257"	2.780"	39.5	2574	36,000 CUP	43.0	2720	44,200 CUP
115 GR. NOS PART	IMR	IMR 4007 SSC	.257"	2.890"	36.5	2521	38,600 CUP	40.0	2706	44,500 CUP
115 GR. NOS PART	Hodgdon	H380	.257"	2.780"	37.0	2567	39,600 CUP	40.0	2754	45,900 CUP
115 GR. NOS PART	Hodgdon	Varget	.257"	2.780"	31.0	2462	34,300 CUP	35.0	2701	44,900 CUP
115 GR. NOS PART	IMR	IMR 4064	.257"	2.890"	36.1	2650	39,400 CUP	38.4	2756	46,300 CUP
115 GR. NOS PART	Hodgdon	BL-C(2)	.257"	2.780"	33.0	2402	33,600 CUP	36.0	2673	47,100 CUP
115 GR. NOS PART	IMR	IMR 4895	.257"	2.890"	36.7	2667	40,500 CUP	38.6	2770	46,500 CUP
115 GR. NOS PART	Hodgdon	H4895	.257"	2.780"	33.0	2433	31,200 CUP	36.0	2702	45,100 CUP
115 GR. NOS PART	IMR	IMR 8208 XBR	.257"	2.780"	34.8	2707	39,200 CUP	37.0	2798	45,000 CUP
120 GR. SIE HPBT	IMR	IMR 7828	.257"	2.775"				47.0C	2745	43,900 CUP
120 GR. SIE HPBT	IMR	IMR 4831	.257"	2.775"				44.0	2810	45,000 CUP

Bullet Weight	Manufacturer	Powder	Bullet Diam.	C.O.L.	Grs.	Vel. (ft/s)	Pressure
120 GR. SIE HPBT	IMR	IMR 4350	.257"	2.775"	41.5	2780	45,000 CUP
120 GR. SIE HPBT	IMR	IMR 4064	.257"	2.775"	35.5	2695	44,000 CUP
120 GR. SIE HPBT	IMR	IMR 4895	.257"	2.775"	33.5	2615	45,000 CUP

Cartridge:25-284
Load Type:Rifle

Bullet Weight (Gr.)	Manufacturer	Powder	Bullet Diam.	C.O.L.	Starting Loads Grs.	Vel. (ft/s)	Pressure	Maximum Loads Grs.	Vel. (ft/s)	Pressure
75 GR. HDY HP	Hodgdon	H4831	.257"	2.795"	53.5	3330		58.0	3604	
75 GR. HDY HP	Hodgdon	H4350	.257"	2.795"	48.0	3429		52.0	3640	
75 GR. HDY HP	Hodgdon	H414	.257"	2.795"	48.0	3464		52.0	3632	
75 GR. HDY HP	Hodgdon	H380	.257"	2.795"	46.0	3438		50.0	3538	
87 GR. SIE SP	Hodgdon	H4831	.257"	2.795"	52.5	3347		57.0	3544	
87 GR. SIE SP	Hodgdon	H4350	.257"	2.795"	46.0	3180		50.0	3400	
87 GR. SIE SP	Hodgdon	H414	.257"	2.795"	45.0	3163		49.0	3352	
87 GR. SIE SP	Hodgdon	H380	.257"	2.795"	44.0	3082		48.0	3335	
100 GR. SPR SP	Hodgdon	H4831	.257"	2.795"	49.5	3068		54.0	3369	
100 GR. SPR SP	Hodgdon	H4350	.257"	2.795"	43.0	2860		48.0	3129	
100 GR. SPR SP	Hodgdon	H414	.257"	2.795"	40.5	2971		44.0	3120	
117 GR. HDY BTSP	Hodgdon	H4831	.257"	2.775"	48.0	2882		52.0	3025	
120 GR. NOS PART	Hodgdon	H4831	.257"	2.795"	45.0	2871		49.0	2978	
120 GR. NOS PART	Hodgdon	H4350	.257"	2.795"	41.0	2642		44.0	2916	

Cartridge:25-06 Remington
Load Type:Rifle

Bullet Weight (Gr.)	Manufacturer	Powder	Bullet Diam.	C.O.L.	Starting Loads Grs.	Vel. (ft/s)	Pressure	Maximum Loads Grs.	Vel. (ft/s)	Pressure
75 GR. HDY V-MAX	Hodgdon	H1000	.257"	3.100"	58.0	3135	35,300 CUP	62.0C	3339	40,000 CUP
75 GR. HDY V-MAX	IMR	IMR 7828 SSC	.257"	3.100"	56.0	3252	44,300 CUP	59.7C*	3486	50,600 CUP
75 GR. HDY V-MAX	Winchester	Supreme 780	.257"	3.100"	56.4	3390	46,900 PSI	60.0	3642	58,600 PSI
75 GR. HDY V-MAX	Hodgdon	H4831	.257"	3.100"	58.0	3393	41,800 CUP	62.0C	3599	49,300 CUP
75 GR. HDY V-MAX	Hodgdon	Hybrid 100V	.257"	3.100"	51.0	3395	44,300 CUP	55.5	3625	50,900 CUP
75 GR. HDY V-MAX	IMR	IMR 4831	.257"	3.100"	53.0	3197	43,200 CUP	58.0C	3540	51,600 CUP
75 GR. HDY V-MAX	Hodgdon	H4350	.257"	3.100"	54.0	3460	43,300 CUP	58.5	3700	50,900 CUP
75 GR. HDY V-MAX	Hodgdon	H414	.257"	3.100"	51.0	3471	44,500 CUP	55.0	3626	50,100 CUP
75 GR. HDY V-MAX	IMR	IMR 4350	.257"	3.100"	50.0	3195	41,800 CUP	55.0	3493	51,000 CUP
75 GR. HDY V-MAX	Winchester	760	.257"	3.100"	51.0	3471	44,500 CUP	55.0	3626	50,100 CUP
75 GR. HDY V-MAX	IMR	IMR 4007 SSC	.257"	3.100"	50.0	3299	43,200 CUP	54.5	3565	50,900 CUP
75 GR. HDY V-MAX	Hodgdon	H380	.257"	3.100"	47.0	3331	45,000 CUP	51.0	3494	49,900 CUP
75 GR. HDY V-MAX	Hodgdon	Varget	.257"	3.100"	46.0	3454	43,400 CUP	49.7	3660	51,200 CUP
75 GR. HDY V-MAX	IMR	IMR 4064	.257"	3.100"	44.0	3322	43,600 CUP	48.5	3566	51,200 CUP
75 GR. HDY V-MAX	IMR	IMR 4895	.257"	3.100"	43.0	3250	44,100 CUP	48.0	3529	50,900 CUP

75 GR. HDY V-MAX	Hodgdon	H4895	.257"	3.100"	45.0	3474	45,000 CUP	48.5	3642	50,800 CUP
80 GR. BAR TTSX BT	IMR	IMR 7828 SSC	.257"	3.075"	57.0	3350	49,900 PSI	61.0C*	3582	58,500 PSI
80 GR. BAR TTSX BT	Hodgdon	Hybrid 100V	.257"	3.075"	50.0	3353	46,400 PSI	54.0C	3624	56,600 PSI
80 GR. BAR TTSX BT	IMR	IMR 4831	.257"	3.075"	52.0	3301	45,600 PSI	56.0C	3569	55,200 PSI
80 GR. BAR TTSX BT	Hodgdon	H4350	.257"	3.075"	51.0	3347	48,500 PSI	55.0C	3560	56,900 PSI
80 GR. BAR TTSX BT	Hodgdon	H414	.257"	3.075"	48.0	3379	52,800 PSI	53.0	3586	60,300 PSI
80 GR. BAR TTSX BT	IMR	IMR 4350	.257"	3.075"	51.0	3372	49,300 PSI	55.0C	3600	57,300 PSI
80 GR. BAR TTSX BT	Winchester	760	.257"	3.075"	48.0	3379	52,800 PSI	53.0	3586	60,300 PSI
80 GR. BAR TTSX BT	IMR	IMR 4007 SSC	.257"	3.075"	50.0	3425	52,700 PSI	54.0	3653	61,800 PSI
80 GR. BAR TTSX BT	Hodgdon	H380	.257"	3.075"	49.0	3394	52,800 PSI	52.5	3597	60,800 PSI
80 GR. BAR TTSX BT	Hodgdon	Varget	.257"	3.075"	45.0	3389	51,800 PSI	49.0	3613	60,900 PSI
80 GR. BAR TTSX BT	IMR	IMR 4064	.257"	3.075"	45.0	3377	49,500 PSI	49.5	3645	61,400 PSI
80 GR. BAR TTSX BT	IMR	IMR 4895	.257"	3.075"	45.0	3385	50,500 PSI	49.5	3661	61,900 PSI
80 GR. BAR TTSX BT	Hodgdon	H4895	.257"	3.075"	43.0	3408	52,100 PSI	47.5	3630	61,500 PSI
85 GR. NOS BT	Hodgdon	H1000	.257"	3.230"	58.0	3218	41,000 CUP	62.0C	3442	48,100 CUP
85 GR. NOS BT	IMR	IMR 7828 SSC	.257"	3.230"	55.0	3186	46,200 CUP	59.2C*	3417	51,900 CUP
85 GR. NOS BT	Winchester	Supreme 780	.257"	3.230"	54.5	3321	52,700 CUP	58.0	3470	59,200 PSI
85 GR. NOS BT	Hodgdon	H4831	.257"	3.230"	54.0	3302	46,000 CUP	58.0	3473	51,700 CUP
85 GR. NOS BT	Hodgdon	Hybrid 100V	.257"	3.230"	49.0	3223	44,100 CUP	54.0	3490	51,200 CUP
85 GR. NOS BT	IMR	IMR 4831	.257"	3.230"	49.0	3021	42,400 CUP	55.0	3417	51,600 CUP
85 GR. NOS BT	Hodgdon	H4350	.257"	3.230"	49.0	3255	44,400 CUP	53.0	3445	50,700 CUP
85 GR. NOS BT	Hodgdon	H414	.257"	3.230"	48.0	3248	45,000 CUP	52.0	3443	50,600 CUP
85 GR. NOS BT	IMR	IMR 4350	.257"	3.230"	48.0	3107	43,700 CUP	53.0	3398	50,800 CUP
85 GR. NOS BT	Winchester	760	.257"	3.230"	48.0	3248	45,000 CUP	52.0	3443	50,600 CUP
85 GR. NOS BT	IMR	IMR 4007 SSC	.257"	3.230"	47.0	3147	45,000 CUP	52.0	3453	51,600 CUP
85 GR. NOS BT	Hodgdon	H380	.257"	3.230"	45.0	3130	43,700 CUP	49.0	3321	51,200 CUP
85 GR. NOS BT	Hodgdon	Varget	.257"	3.230"	43.0	3271	45,000 CUP	46.5	3449	50,900 CUP
85 GR. NOS BT	IMR	IMR 4064	.257"	3.230"	42.0	3149	45,700 CUP	45.7	3353	50,200 CUP
85 GR. NOS BT	IMR	IMR 4895	.257"	3.230"	41.0	3063	43,300 CUP	45.5	3297	50,100 CUP
85 GR. NOS BT	Hodgdon	H4895	.257"	3.230"	41.0	3176	44,600 CUP	44.5	3369	51,600 CUP
87 GR. SPR HP	Hodgdon	H1000	.257"	3.115"	58.0	3176	36,200 CUP	62.0C	3296	43,700 CUP
87 GR. SPR HP	IMR	IMR 7828 SSC	.257"	3.115"	55.0	3133	43,600 CUP	59.5C*	3398	51,600 CUP
87 GR. SPR HP	Winchester	Supreme 780	.257"	3.115"	55.5	3255	49,700 PSI	59.0	3454	58,500 PSI
87 GR. SPR HP	Hodgdon	H4831	.257"	3.115"	56.0	3232	43,500 CUP	60.0	3421	50,500 CUP
87 GR. SPR HP	Hodgdon	Hybrid 100V	.257"	3.115"	50.0	3214	42,400 CUP	55.0	3499	49,300 CUP
87 GR. SPR HP	IMR	IMR 4831	.257"	3.115"	52.0	3099	41,900 CUP	56.5	3398	50,600 CUP
87 GR. SPR HP	Hodgdon	H4350	.257"	3.115"	50.0	3234	45,600 CUP	54.5	3409	50,800 CUP
87 GR. SPR HP	Hodgdon	H414	.257"	3.115"	47.0	3138	43,800 CUP	50.5	3327	51,100 CUP
87 GR. SPR HP	IMR	IMR 4350	.257"	3.115"	50.0	3086	41,800 CUP	54.8	3378	50,900 CUP

87 GR. SPR HP	Winchester	760	.257"	3.115"	47.0	3138	43,800 CUP	50.5	3327	51,100 CUP
87 GR. SPR HP	IMR	IMR 4007 SSC	.257"	3.115"	49.0	3162	42,900 CUP	53.5	3421	50,400 CUP
87 GR. SPR HP	Hodgdon	Varget	.257"	3.115"	43.0	3231	44,900 CUP	46.0	3382	50,500 CUP
87 GR. SPR HP	IMR	IMR 4064	.257"	3.115"	42.0	3091	42,000 CUP	46.5	3344	50,600 CUP
87 GR. SPR HP	IMR	IMR 4895	.257"	3.115"	42.0	3148	45,800 CUP	46.0	3341	51,000 CUP
87 GR. SPR HP	Hodgdon	H4895	.257"	3.115"	43.0	3243	47,700 CUP	45.5	3364	51,600 CUP
90 GR. HDY GMX	Hodgdon	Retumbo	.257"	3.115"	56.0	3250	51,000 PSI	60.0C	3432	58,700 PSI
90 GR. HDY GMX	Hodgdon	H1000	.257"	3.115"	56.0	3248	54,900 PSI	60.0C	3377	59,300 PSI
90 GR. HDY GMX	IMR	IMR 7828 SSC	.257"	3.115"	52.0	3198	52,300 PSI	57.0C	3437	61,500 PSI
90 GR. HDY GMX	Winchester	Supreme 780	.257"	3.115"	54.0	3255	50,600 PSI	57.5	3429	57,100 PSI
90 GR. HDY GMX	Hodgdon	H4831	.257"	3.115"	50.0	3205	56,200 PSI	54.5C	3363	61,000 PSI
90 GR. HDY GMX	Hodgdon	Hybrid 100V	.257"	3.115"	46.0	3152	49,100 PSI	50.7	3436	59,500 PSI
90 GR. HDY GMX	IMR	IMR 4831	.257"	3.115"	48.0	3219	53,400 PSI	52.8	3437	60,400 PSI
90 GR. HDY GMX	Hodgdon	H4350	.257"	3.115"	45.0	3117	51,300 PSI	49.5	3344	60,600 PSI
90 GR. HDY GMX	Hodgdon	H414	.257"	3.115"	45.0	3122	51,900 PSI	49.5	3339	59,800 PSI
90 GR. HDY GMX	IMR	IMR 4350	.257"	3.115"	47.0	3223	54,800 PSI	52.0	3437	61,800 PSI
90 GR. HDY GMX	IMR	IMR 4007 SSC	.257"	3.115"	44.0	3147	55,400 PSI	49.0	3368	61,600 PSI
90 GR. HDY GMX	Hodgdon	Varget	.257"	3.115"	41.0	3098	51,600 PSI	44.0	3261	58,800 PSI
90 GR. HDY GMX	IMR	IMR 4064	.257"	3.115"	40.0	3043	48,900 PSI	44.0	3253	57,300 PSI
90 GR. HDY GMX	IMR	IMR 4895	.257"	3.115"	41.0	3070	49,200 PSI	46.0	3351	59,900 PSI
90 GR. HDY GMX	Hodgdon	H4895	.257"	3.115"	39.0	3053	50,800 PSI	43.0	3281	60,200 PSI
90 GR. SIE HPBT	Hodgdon	H1000	.257"	3.100"	58.0	3142	40,300 CUP	62.0C	3330	47,500 CUP
90 GR. SIE HPBT	IMR	IMR 7828 SSC	.257"	3.100"	55.0	3145	46,400 CUP	59.5C*	3374	52,900 CUP
90 GR. SIE HPBT	Winchester	Supreme 780	.257"	3.100"	53.6	3162	45,200 CUP	57.0	3331	50,300 CUP
90 GR. SIE HPBT	Hodgdon	H4831	.257"	3.100"	54.0	3213	46,000 CUP	58.0	3481	50,400 CUP
90 GR. SIE HPBT	Hodgdon	Hybrid 100V	.257"	3.100"	50.0	3217	46,400 CUP	54.0	3404	51,500 CUP
90 GR. SIE HPBT	IMR	IMR 4831	.257"	3.100"	51.0	3095	42,900 CUP	55.5	3374	51,100 CUP
90 GR. SIE HPBT	Hodgdon	H4350	.257"	3.100"	49.0	3191	44,000 CUP	53.0	3370	50,700 CUP
90 GR. SIE HPBT	Hodgdon	H414	.257"	3.100"	47.0	3135	44,300 CUP	51.0	3315	50,200 CUP
90 GR. SIE HPBT	IMR	IMR 4350	.257"	3.100"	49.0	3088	42,800 CUP	53.5	3348	51,400 CUP
90 GR. SIE HPBT	Winchester	760	.257"	3.100"	47.0	3135	44,300 CUP	51.0	3315	50,200 CUP
90 GR. SIE HPBT	IMR	IMR 4007 SSC	.257"	3.100"	48.0	3158	44,700 CUP	52.7	3430	51,700 CUP
90 GR. SIE HPBT	Hodgdon	Varget	.257"	3.100"	42.0	3165	45,000 CUP	45.0	3312	50,400 CUP
90 GR. SIE HPBT	IMR	IMR 4064	.257"	3.100"	42.0	3117	45,100 CUP	45.8	3298	51,100 CUP
90 GR. SIE HPBT	IMR	IMR 4895	.257"	3.100"	42.0	3106	46,000 CUP	45.9	3269	49,200 CUP
90 GR. SIE HPBT	Hodgdon	H4895	.257"	3.100"	41.0	3128	44,100 CUP	44.0	3257	51,000 CUP
100 GR. NOS PART	Hodgdon	H1000	.257"	3.200"	56.0	3055	44,600 CUP	59.7C	3212	50,700 CUP
100 GR. NOS PART	IMR	IMR 7828 SSC	.257"	3.200"	53.0	2940	40,700 CUP	57.2C	3203	51,300 CUP
100 GR. NOS PART	Winchester	Supreme 780	.257"	3.200"	52.2	3074	45,400 CUP	55.5	3229	50,000 CUP
100 GR. NOS PART	Hodgdon	H4831	.257"	3.200"	51.0	3025	46,800 CUP	54.3	3172	51,400 CUP

100 GR. NOS PART	Hodgdon	Hybrid 100V	.257"	3.200"	48.0	3034	44,200 CUP	52.5	3295	51,800 CUP
100 GR. NOS PART	IMR	IMR 4831	.257"	3.200"	49.0	2981	41,700 CUP	54.0	3233	51,400 CUP
100 GR. NOS PART	Hodgdon	H4350	.257"	3.200"	47.0	3038	47,800 CUP	50.0	3155	51,500 CUP
100 GR. NOS PART	Hodgdon	H414	.257"	3.200"	42.0	2843	44,600 CUP	47.0	3059	50,700 CUP
100 GR. NOS PART	IMR	IMR 4350	.257"	3.200"	48.0	2975	43,200 CUP	52.8	3257	51,200 CUP
100 GR. NOS PART	Winchester	760	.257"	3.200"	42.0	2843	44,600 CUP	47.0	3059	50,700 CUP
100 GR. NOS PART	IMR	IMR 4007 SSC	.257"	3.200"	46.0	2992	42,900 CUP	50.8	3256	51,100 CUP
100 GR. NOS PART	Hodgdon	Varget	.257"	3.200"	41.0	2974	45,600 CUP	44.0	3125	51,400 CUP
100 GR. NOS PART	IMR	IMR 4064	.257"	3.200"	40.0	2904	40,400 CUP	44.0	3122	50,800 CUP
100 GR. NOS PART	IMR	IMR 4895	.257"	3.200"	42.0	3009	46,000 CUP	45.3	3155	50,400 CUP
100 GR. NOS PART	Hodgdon	H4895	.257"	3.200"	40.0	2921	44,200 CUP	43.0	3072	51,000 CUP
100 GR. NOS PART	IMR	Trail Boss	.257"	3.200"	13.4	1454	25,500 PSI	19.2	1712	30,600 PSI
117 GR. HDY SPBT	Hodgdon	Retumbo	.257"	3.165"	56.0	2876	44,600 CUP	60.5C	3079	50,700 CUP
117 GR. HDY SPBT	Hodgdon	H1000	.257"	3.165"	55.0	2936	47,200 CUP	58.5C	3046	51,000 CUP
117 GR. HDY SPBT	IMR	IMR 7828 SSC	.257"	3.165"	51.0	2879	46,600 CUP	55.0	3037	51,200 CUP
117 GR. HDY SPBT	Winchester	Supreme 780	.257"	3.165"	51.2	2962	54,500 PSI	54.5	3095	61,200 PSI
117 GR. HDY SPBT	Hodgdon	H4831	.257"	3.165"	48.0	2748	43,000 CUP	52.0	2937	50,900 CUP
117 GR. HDY SPBT	Hodgdon	Hybrid 100V	.257"	3.165"	46.0	2981	43,100 CUP	50.5	3111	50,400 CUP
117 GR. HDY SPBT	IMR	IMR 4831	.257"	3.165"	48.0	2839	42,600 CUP	53.0	3137	51,400 CUP
117 GR. HDY SPBT	Hodgdon	H4350	.257"	3.165"	44.0	2737	44,300 CUP	47.7	2923	50,800 CUP
117 GR. HDY SPBT	IMR	IMR 4350	.257"	3.165"	47.0	2851	42,700 CUP	52.0	3106	51,300 CUP
117 GR. HDY SPBT	IMR	IMR 4007 SSC	.257"	3.165"	46.0	2901	45,100 CUP	50.0	3091	51,400 CUP
117 GR. HDY SPBT	Hodgdon	Varget	.257"	3.165"	37.0	2637	42,900 CUP	41.0	2838	50,100 CUP
117 GR. HDY SPBT	Hodgdon	H4895	.257"	3.165"	37.0	2641	44,500 CUP	40.0	2797	50,600 CUP
120 GR. SFT SP	Hodgdon	Retumbo	.257"	3.150"	56.0	2806	43,700 CUP	60.0C	2991	50,300 CUP
120 GR. SFT SP	Hodgdon	H1000	.257"	3.150"	52.0	2772	44,900 CUP	55.5	2902	50,600 CUP
120 GR. SFT SP	IMR	IMR 7828 SSC	.257"	3.150"	50.0	2752	44,400 CUP	54.0	2923	50,300 CUP
120 GR. SFT SP	Winchester	Supreme 780	.257"	3.150"	49.8	2821	44,600 CUP	53.0	2984	50,000 CUP
120 GR. SFT SP	Hodgdon	H4831	.257"	3.150"	48.0	2705	45,800 CUP	51.5	2856	51,200 CUP
120 GR. SFT SP	Hodgdon	Hybrid 100V	.257"	3.150"	46.0	2796	44,500 CUP	50.0	3009	51,200 CUP
120 GR. SFT SP	IMR	IMR 4831	.257"	3.150"	48.0	2787	42,200 CUP	53.0C	3065	50,900 CUP
120 GR. SFT SP	Hodgdon	H4350	.257"	3.150"	44.0	2643	42,900 CUP	47.5	2816	50,900 CUP
120 GR. SFT SP	IMR	IMR 4350	.257"	3.150"	48.0	2831	43,500 CUP	52.0C	3049	50,800 CUP
120 GR. SFT SP	IMR	IMR 4007 SSC	.257"	3.150"	45.0	2805	43,900 CUP	49.0	3005	50,300 CUP
120 GR. SFT SP	Hodgdon	Varget	.257"	3.150"	38.0	2584	45,100 CUP	41.0	2755	51,900 CUP
120 GR. SFT SP	Hodgdon	H4895	.257"	3.150"	37.0	2541	45,400 CUP	40.0	2694	51,700 CUP

Cartridge: 25 Winchester Super Short Magnum Load Type: Rifle					Starting Loads			Maximum Loads		
Bullet Weight (Gr.)	Manufacturer	Powder	Bullet Diam.	C.O.L.	Grs.	Vel. (ft/s)	Pressure	Grs.	Vel. (ft/s)	Pressure
75 GR. HDY V-MAX	Hodgdon	CFE 223	.257"	2.350"	46.0	3506	54,300 PSI	50.0	3762	63,500 PSI
75 GR. HDY V-MAX	Hodgdon	Varget	.257"	2.350"	43.0	3437	49,700 PSI	46.5	3677	62,200 PSI
75 GR. HDY V-MAX	IMR	IMR 4320	.257"	2.350"	44.0	3447	51,200 PSI	47.4	3671	62,000 PSI
75 GR. HDY V-MAX	IMR	IMR 4064	.257"	2.350"	43.0	3471	50,300 PSI	46.7C	3740	62,200 PSI
75 GR. HDY V-MAX	Hodgdon	BL-C(2)	.257"	2.350"	45.0	3482	48,000 PSI	49.3	3775	61,000 PSI
75 GR. HDY V-MAX	IMR	IMR 4895	.257"	2.350"	43.0	3477	50,400 PSI	46.3	3703	62,100 PSI
75 GR. HDY V-MAX	Hodgdon	H4895	.257"	2.350"	42.0	3473	49,700 PSI	45.2	3708	61,800 PSI
75 GR. HDY V-MAX	IMR	IMR 8208 XBR	.257"	2.350"	40.0	3341	47,200 PSI	45.0	3687	62,700 PSI
85 GR. NOS BT	IMR	IMR 4007 SSC	.257"	2.350"	44.0	3143	48,700 PSI	48.0C	3440	62,300 PSI
85 GR. NOS BT	Hodgdon	H380	.257"	2.350"	45.0	3216	47,700 PSI	48.0	3405	56,100 PSI
85 GR. NOS BT	Hodgdon	CFE 223	.257"	2.350"	43.0	3277	54,200 PSI	46.3	3454	62,300 PSI
85 GR. NOS BT	Hodgdon	Varget	.257"	2.350"	40.0	3180	46,200 PSI	44.9	3497	62,200 PSI
85 GR. NOS BT	IMR	IMR 4320	.257"	2.350"	43.0	3267	50,200 PSI	46.0	3491	62,000 PSI
85 GR. NOS BT	IMR	IMR 4064	.257"	2.350"	41.0	3237	47,600 PSI	45.0C	3532	62,200 PSI
85 GR. NOS BT	Hodgdon	BL-C(2)	.257"	2.350"	44.0	3361	51,500 PSI	47.5	3547	61,600 PSI
85 GR. NOS BT	IMR	IMR 4895	.257"	2.350"	41.0	3226	47,100 PSI	45.0	3545	62,800 PSI
85 GR. NOS BT	Hodgdon	H4895	.257"	2.350"	40.0	3268	50,700 PSI	43.3	3475	62,100 PSI
85 GR. NOS BT	IMR	IMR 8208 XBR	.257"	2.350"	38.0	3174	48,900 PSI	42.4	3456	62,600 PSI
87 GR. SIE SP	IMR	IMR 4831	.257"	2.300"	45.0	3130	54,100 PSI	48.2C	3284	60,600 PSI
87 GR. SIE SP	Hodgdon	H414	.257"	2.300"	45.0	3171	50,600 PSI	48.0	3342	58,200 PSI
87 GR. SIE SP	IMR	IMR 4350	.257"	2.300"	44.0	3090	50,600 PSI	47.0C	3276	58,500 PSI
87 GR. SIE SP	Winchester	760	.257"	2.300"	45.0	3171	50,600 PSI	48.0	3342	58,200 PSI
87 GR. SIE SP	IMR	IMR 4007 SSC	.257"	2.300"	44.2	3159	52,100 PSI	47.0	3353	61,300 PSI
87 GR. SIE SP	Hodgdon	H380	.257"	2.300"	44.0	3183	54,200 PSI	47.5	3363	62,200 PSI
87 GR. SIE SP	Hodgdon	CFE 223	.257"	2.300"	43.0	3307	59,700 PSI	46.3	3449	63,600 PSI
87 GR. SIE SP	Hodgdon	Varget	.257"	2.300"	40.0	3189	49,800 PSI	44.0	3431	62,600 PSI
87 GR. SIE SP	IMR	IMR 4064	.257"	2.300"	40.0	3179	47,800 PSI	43.3	3412	60,700 PSI
87 GR. SIE SP	IMR	IMR 4895	.257"	2.300"	40.0	3195	48,100 PSI	43.9	3452	61,700 PSI
87 GR. SIE SP	Hodgdon	H4895	.257"	2.300"	40.0	3271	53,000 PSI	43.3	3456	62,300 PSI
87 GR. SIE SP	IMR	IMR 8208 XBR	.257"	2.300"	38.0	3152	49,500 PSI	42.7	3423	62,100 PSI
100 GR. SPR BT	IMR	IMR 7828	.257"	2.300"	46.0	2931	51,400 PSI	49.5C*	3125	60,600 PSI
100 GR. SPR BT	Hodgdon	Suprform	.257"	2.300"	48.0	3155	49,900 PSI	52.0C	3381	59,700 PSI
100 GR. SPR BT	Hodgdon	Hybrid 100V	.257"	2.300"	42.0	3000	47,400 PSI	45.0C	3177	54,000 PSI
100 GR. SPR BT	IMR	IMR 4831	.257"	2.300"	45.0	3025	54,200 PSI	48.0C	3183	62,900 PSI
100 GR. SPR BT	Hodgdon	H4350	.257"	2.300"	45.0	3035	51,400 PSI	48.5C	3233	61,300 PSI
100 GR. SPR BT	Hodgdon	H414	.257"	2.300"	44.0	3015	50,400 PSI	47.5	3221	60,800 PSI
100 GR. SPR BT	IMR	IMR 4350	.257"	2.300"	44.0	3018	54,600 PSI	47.0C	3198	61,400 PSI

100 GR. SPR BT	Winchester	760	.257"	2.300"	44.0	3015	50,400 PSI	47.5	3221	60,800 PSI
100 GR. SPR BT	IMR	IMR 4007 SSC	.257"	2.300"	42.8	3025	53,700 PSI	45.5	3187	61,700 PSI
100 GR. SPR BT	Hodgdon	H380	.257"	2.300"	43.0	3010	53,500 PSI	46.5	3190	62,800 PSI
100 GR. SPR BT	Hodgdon	CFE 223	.257"	2.300"	39.0	3018	57,100 PSI	43.2	3190	63,900 PSI
100 GR. SPR BT	Hodgdon	Varget	.257"	2.300"	39.0	3022	50,000 PSI	42.8	3248	62,700 PSI
100 GR. SPR BT	IMR	IMR 4320	.257"	2.300"	40.0	3022	50,700 PSI	43.0	3227	61,600 PSI
100 GR. SPR BT	IMR	IMR 4064	.257"	2.300"	39.0	3065	52,600 PSI	42.0	3245	62,400 PSI
100 GR. SPR BT	Hodgdon	BL-C(2)	.257"	2.300"	42.0	3136	52,400 PSI	44.5	3264	58,900 PSI
100 GR. SPR BT	IMR	IMR 4895	.257"	2.300"	39.0	3055	51,900 PSI	42.5	3259	62,400 PSI
100 GR. SPR BT	Hodgdon	H4895	.257"	2.300"	38.0	3042	50,500 PSI	41.5	3243	61,700 PSI
100 GR. SPR BT	IMR	IMR 8208 XBR	.257"	2.300"	36.0	2954	51,200 PSI	40.0	3166	62,100 PSI
115 GR. NOS BT	IMR	IMR 7828	.257"	2.350"	44.0	2728	52,100 PSI	47.0C*	2910	61,600 PSI
115 GR. NOS BT	Winchester	Supreme 780	.257"	2.350"	44.0	2639	43,700 PSI	48.0C	2881	53,100 PSI
115 GR. NOS BT	Hodgdon	Suprform	.257"	2.350"	44.0	2845	48,800 PSI	48.5C	3081	60,300 PSI
115 GR. NOS BT	Hodgdon	H4831	.257"	2.350"	44.0	2733	52,100 PSI	47.0C	2883	60,900 PSI
115 GR. NOS BT	Hodgdon	Hybrid 100V	.257"	2.350"	40.0	2782	48,100 PSI	43.5C	2986	56,700 PSI
115 GR. NOS BT	IMR	IMR 4831	.257"	2.350"	42.0	2767	53,900 PSI	44.7C	2919	61,300 PSI
115 GR. NOS BT	Hodgdon	H4350	.257"	2.350"	42.0	2806	52,800 PSI	45.3C	2999	63,000 PSI
115 GR. NOS BT	Hodgdon	H414	257"	2.350"	42.0	2810	52,900 PSI	44.7	2958	62,300 PSI
115 GR. NOS BT	IMR	IMR 4350	.257"	2.350"	41.0	2733	50,400 PSI	44.5C	2944	61,300 PSI
115 GR. NOS BT	Winchester	760	.257"	2.350"	42.0	2810	52,900 PSI	44.7	2958	62,300 PSI
115 GR. NOS BT	IMR	IMR 4007 SSC	.257"	2.350"	39.0	2722	50,900 PSI	42.0C	2929	62,000 PSI
115 GR. NOS BT	Hodgdon	H380	.257"	2.350"	40.0	2722	51,200 PSI	43.2	2910	62,700 PSI
115 GR. NOS BT	Hodgdon	Varget	.257"	2.350"	36.0	2726	53,700 PSI	38.7	2871	62,600 PSI
115 GR. NOS BT	IMR	IMR 4320	.257"	2.350"	37.0	2695	51,100 PSI	40.4	2883	60,300 PSI
115 GR. NOS BT	IMR	IMR 4064	.257"	2.350"	36.0	2692	50,700 PSI	39.0	2877	61,900 PSI
115 GR. NOS BT	Hodgdon	BL-C(2)	.257"	2.350"	38.0	2778	55,600 PSI	41.0	2913	62,600 PSI
115 GR. NOS BT	IMR	IMR 4895	.257"	2.350"	37.0	2754	53,800 PSI	39.5	2890	62,300 PSI
115 GR. NOS BT	Hodgdon	H4895	.257"	2.350"	34.0	2658	51,600 PSI	37.0	2830	62,200 PSI
115 GR. NOS BT	IMR	IMR 8208 XBR	.257"	2.350"	33.0	2648	51,000 PSI	37.0	2877	63,000 PSI
117 GR. HDY BTSP	IMR	IMR 7828	.257"	2.335"	44.0	2737	53,200 PSI	47.0C*	2906	62,200 PSI
117 GR. HDY BTSP	Winchester	Supreme 780	.257"	2.335"	44.0	2658	43,800 PSI	48.0C	2878	52,600 PSI
117 GR. HDY BTSP	Hodgdon	Suprform	.257"	2.335"	45.0	2870	49,500 PSI	49.0C	3097	60,300 PSI
117 GR. HDY BTSP	Hodgdon	H4831	.257"	2.335"	44.0	2731	51,100 PSI	47.5C	2901	61,300 PSI
117 GR. HDY BTSP	Hodgdon	Hybrid 100V	.257"	2.335"	40.0	2775	48,000 PSI	43.5C	2977	56,500 PSI
117 GR. HDY BTSP	IMR	IMR 4831	.257"	2.335"	42.0	2771	52,600 PSI	44.7C	2924	61,900 PSI
117 GR. HDY BTSP	Hodgdon	H4350	.257"	2.335"	42.0	2796	52,300 PSI	45.0	2965	62,300 PSI
117 GR. HDY BTSP	Hodgdon	H414	.257"	2.335"	42.0	2821	53,700 PSI	44.7	2947	59,900 PSI
117 GR. HDY BTSP	IMR	IMR 4350	.257"	2.335"	41.0	2770	52,400 PSI	44.1C	2951	61,600 PSI

Bullet Weight (Gr.)	Manufacturer	Powder	Bullet Diam.	C.O.L.	Grs.	Vel. (ft/s)	Pressure	Grs.	Vel. (ft/s)	Pressure
117 GR. HDY BTSP	Winchester	760	.257"	2.335"	42.0	2821	53,700 PSI	44.7	2947	59,900 PSI
117 GR. HDY BTSP	IMR	IMR 4007 SSC	.257"	2.335"	39.0	2754	52,900 PSI	42.2C	2921	61,600 PSI
117 GR. HDY BTSP	Hodgdon	H380	.257"	2.335"	40.0	2709	50,900 PSI	43.2	2905	61,000 PSI
117 GR. HDY BTSP	Hodgdon	Varget	.257"	2.335"	36.0	2725	52,700 PSI	39.0	2888	62,200 PSI
117 GR. HDY BTSP	IMR	IMR 4320	.257"	2.335"	37.0	2723	52,100 PSI	39.5	2862	61,100 PSI
117 GR. HDY BTSP	IMR	IMR 4064	.257"	2.335"	36.0	2737	53,000 PSI	38.7	2889	61,800 PSI
117 GR. HDY BTSP	Hodgdon	BL-C(2)	.257"	2.335"	39.0	2804	54,800 PSI	41.5	2926	61,200 PSI
117 GR. HDY BTSP	IMR	IMR 4895	.257"	2.335"	36.0	2731	53,200 PSI	38.6	2885	61,700 PSI
117 GR. HDY BTSP	Hodgdon	H4895	.257"	2.335"	35.0	2723	53,800 PSI	37.5	2858	62,200 PSI
117 GR. HDY BTSP	IMR	IMR 8208 XBR	.257"	2.335"	33.0	2629	49,200 PSI	36.7	2851	61,700 PSI
120 GR. SFT SP	IMR	IMR 7828	.257"	2.330"	44.0	2686	50,000 PSI	47.8C*	2931	62,600 PSI
120 GR. SFT SP	Winchester	Supreme 780	.257"	2.330"	44.0	2606	43,800 PSI	47.5C	2820	52,800 PSI
120 GR. SFT SP	Hodgdon	Suprform	.257"	2.330"	44.0	2817	49,900 PSI	48.7C	3062	61,800 PSI
120 GR. SFT SP	Hodgdon	H4831	.257"	2.330"	45.0	2744	51,600 PSI	48.0C	2902	61,100 PSI
120 GR. SFT SP	Hodgdon	Hybrid 100V	.257"	2.330"	40.0	2768	50,200 PSI	43.0C	2932	57,200 PSI
120 GR. SFT SP	IMR	IMR 4831	.257"	2.330"	42.0	2712	52,400 PSI	45.2C	2910	63,600 PSI
120 GR. SFT SP	Hodgdon	H4350	.257"	2.330"	42.0	2793	51,000 PSI	45.5C	2981	62,400 PSI
120 GR. SFT SP	Hodgdon	H414	.257"	2.330"	42.0	2839	55,200 PSI	44.7	2985	63,100 PSI
120 GR. SFT SP	IMR	IMR 4350	.257"	2.330"	41.0	2713	51,600 PSI	44.3C	2912	62,000 PSI
120 GR. SFT SP	Winchester	760	.257"	2.330"	42.0	2839	55,200 PSI	44.7	2985	63,100 PSI
120 GR. SFT SP	IMR	IMR 4007 SSC	.257"	2.330"	39.5	2712	52,200 PSI	42.0	2863	61,300 PSI
120 GR. SFT SP	Hodgdon	H380	.257"	2.330"	40.0	2745	53,300 PSI	43.0	2900	61,200 PSI
120 GR. SFT SP	Hodgdon	Varget	.257"	2.330"	36.0	2702	53,200 PSI	39.0	2878	63,500 PSI
120 GR. SFT SP	IMR	IMR 4320	.257"	2.330"	36.0	2667	52,800 PSI	39.2	2846	63,200 PSI
120 GR. SFT SP	IMR	IMR 4064	.257"	2.330"	36.0	2681	52,000 PSI	38.5	2840	62,000 PSI
120 GR. SFT SP	Hodgdon	BL-C(2)	.257"	2.330"	38.0	2742	52,700 PSI	41.0	2908	62,200 PSI
120 GR. SFT SP	IMR	IMR 4895	.257"	2.330"	36.0	2686	52,800 PSI	39.0	2862	62,600 PSI
120 GR. SFT SP	Hodgdon	H4895	.257"	2.330"	35.0	2700	53,300 PSI	37.7	2840	61,700 PSI
120 GR. SFT SP	IMR	IMR 8208 XBR	.257"	2.330"	32.0	2542	48,300 PSI	36.3	2800	62,900 PSI

Cartridge: 257 Weatherby Magnum
Load Type: Rifle

Bullet Weight (Gr.)	Manufacturer	Powder	Bullet Diam.	C.O.L.	Starting Loads Grs.	Vel. (ft/s)	Pressure	Maximum Loads Grs.	Vel. (ft/s)	Pressure
75 GR. HDY V-MAX	Hodgdon	H1000	.257"	3.250"	76.0	3517	37,700 CUP	80.0C	3649	42,000 CUP
75 GR. HDY V-MAX	Hodgdon	H4831	.257"	3.250"	71.0	3652	45,200 CUP	75.0	3841	51,900 CUP
75 GR. HDY V-MAX	Hodgdon	H4350	.257"	3.250"	65.0	3715	43,100 CUP	70.0	3905	51,800 CUP
75 GR. HDY V-MAX	Hodgdon	H414	.257"	3.250"	65.0	3717	44,200 CUP	69.5	3971	52,400 CUP
85 GR. NOS BT	Hodgdon	H1000	.257"	3.250"	76.0	3548	44,600 CUP	80.0C	3665	47,900 CUP
85 GR. NOS BT	IMR	IMR 7828	.257"	3.170"				74.5	3775	53,500 CUP
85 GR. NOS BT	Hodgdon	H4831	.257"	3.250"	68.0	3498	45,000 CUP	72.0	3664	52,200 CUP

Bullet Weight (Gr.)	Manufacturer	Powder	Bullet Diam.	C.O.L.	Grs.	Vel. (ft/s)	Pressure	Grs.	Vel. (ft/s)	Pressure
85 GR. NOS BT	Hodgdon	H4350	.257"	3.250"	63.0	3544	44,400 CUP	67.0	3739	51,600 CUP
85 GR. NOS BT	Hodgdon	H414	.257"	3.250"	62.5	3543	44,800 CUP	66.5	3746	51,700 CUP
90 GR. SIE HPBT	Hodgdon	H1000	.257"	3.150"	76.0	3494	43,800 CUP	80.0C	3671	50,000 CUP
90 GR. SIE HPBT	Hodgdon	H4831	.257"	3.150"	67.0	3420	44,400 CUP	71.0	3611	52,500 CUP
90 GR. SIE HPBT	Hodgdon	H4350	.257"	3.150"	62.5	3524	46,600 CUP	66.5	3685	52,400 CUP
90 GR. SIE HPBT	Hodgdon	H414	.257"	3.150"	62.0	3458	44,000 CUP	66.0	3671	52,200 CUP
100 GR. SPR SPBT	Hodgdon	H1000	.257"	3.200"	73.0	3410	45,800 CUP	78.0	3575	52,400 CUP
100 GR. SPR SPBT	IMR	IMR 7828	.257"	3.200"				73.0	3655	53,100 CUP
100 GR. SPR SPBT	Hodgdon	H4831	.257"	3.200"	64.0	3312	45,800 CUP	68.0	3462	52,500 CUP
100 GR. SPR SPBT	Hodgdon	H4350	.257"	3.200"	59.0	3312	44,900 CUP	63.0	3500	52,400 CUP
100 GR. SPR SPBT	Hodgdon	H414	.257"	3.200"	59.0	3294	45,300 CUP	62.5	3449	51,800 CUP
115 GR. BAR XFB	Hodgdon	H1000	.257"	3.250"	67.0	3147	50,000 CUP	71.0	3265	52,700 CUP
115 GR. BAR XFB	Hodgdon	H4831	.257"	3.250"	60.0	3030	46,200 CUP	64.0	3170	52,000 CUP
115 GR. BAR XFB	Hodgdon	H4350	.257"	3.250"	56.0	2988	46,900 CUP	60.0	3188	52,500 CUP
117 GR. HDY SPBT	Hodgdon	H1000	.257"	3.220"	70.0	3169	45,200 CUP	74.0	3321	51,800 CUP
117 GR. HDY SPBT	IMR	IMR 7828	.257"	3.220"				70.0	3390	52,600 CUP
117 GR. HDY SPBT	Hodgdon	H4831	.257"	3.220"	62.0	3099	44,800 CUP	66.0	3252	52,300 CUP
117 GR. HDY SPBT	Hodgdon	H4350	.257"	3.220"	57.0	3112	46,000 CUP	60.5	3266	52,000 CUP
120 GR. SFT SP	Hodgdon	H1000	.257"	3.220"	69.0	3103	45,700 CUP	73.0	3256	51,800 CUP
120 GR. SFT SP	IMR	IMR 7828	.257"	3.220"				69.0	3325	53,000 CUP
120 GR. SFT SP	Hodgdon	H4831	.257"	3.220"	61.0	3013	44,600 CUP	65.0	3184	51,800 CUP
120 GR. SFT SP	Hodgdon	H4350	.257"	3.220"	56.0	3000	44,400 CUP	60.0	3189	51,800 CUP

Cartridge: 6.5mm Grendel
Load Type: Rifle

Bullet Weight (Gr.)	Manufacturer	Powder	Bullet Diam.	C.O.L.	Starting Loads			Maximum Loads		
					Grs.	Vel. (ft/s)	Pressure	Grs.	Vel. (ft/s)	Pressure
85 GR. SIE HP	Hodgdon	H335	.264"	2.240"	29.0	2705	37,700 PSI	32.0	2956	49,300 PSI
85 GR. SIE HP	Hodgdon	H322	.264"	2.240"	27.0	2625	36,600 PSI	30.1C	2927	49,400 PSI
85 GR. SIE HP	IMR	IMR 4198	.264"	2.240"	24.0	2645	38,100 PSI	26.4C	2898	50,000 PSI
85 GR. SIE HP	Hodgdon	H4198	.264"	2.240"	24.5	2674	38,500 PSI	27.2C	2919	49,500 PSI
90 GR. SPR TNT HP	Hodgdon	H335	.264"	2.200"	28.5	2613	35,200 PSI	31.7	2912	49,400 PSI
90 GR. SPR TNT HP	IMR	IMR 8208 XBR	.264"	2.220"	29.0	2580	34,700 PSI	31.0C	2794	42,400 PSI
90 GR. SPR TNT HP	Hodgdon	Benchmark	.264"	2.200"	28.5	2662	37,700 PSI	30.5C	2870	47,000 PSI
90 GR. SPR TNT HP	Hodgdon	H322	.264"	2.200"	26.5	2534	34,600 PSI	29.5C	2863	49,500 PSI
90 GR. SPR TNT HP	IMR	IMR 4198	.264"	2.200"	23.5	2562	36,600 PSI	26.2C	2844	49,900 PSI
90 GR. SPR TNT HP	Hodgdon	H4198	.264"	2.200"	24.0	2594	36,800 PSI	26.8C	2854	49,400 PSI
95 GR. HDY V-MAX	Hodgdon	H335	.264"	2.230"	28.0	2570	37,400 PSI	31.2	2841	50,200 PSI
95 GR. HDY V-MAX	IMR	IMR 8208 XBR	.264"	2.230"	28.0	2527	35,600 PSI	31.0C	2840	49,600 PSI
95 GR. HDY V-MAX	Hodgdon	Benchmark	.264"	2.230"	27.0	2476	33,900 PSI	30.0C	2807	49,700 PSI

Bullet Weight (Gr.)	Manufacturer	Powder	Bullet Diam.	C.O.L.	Grs.	Vel. (ft/s)	Pressure	Grs.	Vel. (ft/s)	Pressure
95 GR. HDY V-MAX	Hodgdon	H322	.264"	2.230"	26.0	2477	35,900 PSI	28.8C	2768	49,300 PSI
95 GR. HDY V-MAX	IMR	IMR 4198	.264"	2.230"	22.5	2470	36,700 PSI	25.2C	2740	49,900 PSI
95 GR. HDY V-MAX	Hodgdon	H4198	.264"	2.230"	23.0	2483	36,600 PSI	25.8C	2750	49,300 PSI
100 GR. NOS BT	Hodgdon	H335	.264"	2.200"	28.0	2509	38,200 PSI	30.7	2744	49,700 PSI
100 GR. NOS BT	IMR	IMR 8208 XBR	.264"	2.200"	29.0	2542	38,300 PSI	30.8C	2732	47,600 PSI
100 GR. NOS BT	Hodgdon	Benchmark	.264"	2.200"	27.0	2460	36,300 PSI	29.9C	2739	49,900 PSI
100 GR. NOS BT	Hodgdon	H322	.264"	2.200"	26.0	2420	36,700 PSI	29.0C	2716	49,800 PSI
100 GR. NOS BT	IMR	IMR 4198	.264"	2.200"	22.0	2334	34,400 PSI	25.1C	2646	49,600 PSI
100 GR. NOS BT	Hodgdon	H4198	.264"	2.200"	23.0	2414	36,800 PSI	25.6C	2666	49,800 PSI
107 GR. SIE HPBT	Hodgdon	H335	.264"	2.250"	27.0	2413	36,900 PSI	30.0	2677	49,500 PSI
107 GR. SIE HPBT	IMR	IMR 8208 XBR	.264"	2.250"	27.0	2356	34,600 PSI	29.8C	2667	49,300 PSI
107 GR. SIE HPBT	Hodgdon	Benchmark	.264"	2.250"	26.0	2355	34,800 PSI	29.0C	2653	49,600 PSI
107 GR. SIE HPBT	Hodgdon	H322	.264"	2.250"	25.0	2325	35,900 PSI	27.7C	2607	49,800 PSI
107 GR. SIE HPBT	IMR	IMR 4198	.264"	2.250"	21.5	2298	35,900 PSI	24.3C	2567	49,700 PSI
107 GR. SIE HPBT	Hodgdon	H4198	.264"	2.250"	22.0	2324	37,000 PSI	24.8	2576	49,900 PSI
120 GR. BAR TSX	Hodgdon	H335	.264"	2.200"	25.0	2142	37,400 PSI	28.0	2415	48,400 PSI
120 GR. BAR TSX	IMR	IMR 8208 XBR	.264"	2.200"	25.0	2094	34,600 PSI	28.0C	2419	50,000 PSI
120 GR. BAR TSX	Hodgdon	Benchmark	.264"	2.200"	24.5	2133	36,900 PSI	27.3	2401	50,200 PSI
120 GR. BAR TSX	Hodgdon	H322	.264"	2.200"	23.0	2074	37,700 PSI	25.8C	2347	50,000 PSI
120 GR. BAR TSX	IMR	IMR 4198	.264"	2.200"	20.3	2062	40,600 PSI	22.7C	2280	50,100 PSI
120 GR. BAR TSX	Hodgdon	H4198	.264"	2.200"	20.5	2074	41,000 PSI	22.9C	2272	49,700 PSI
123 GR. SIE HPBT	Hodgdon	H335	.264"	2.250"	26.0	2288	37,800 PSI	28.7	2508	49,800 PSI
123 GR. SIE HPBT	IMR	IMR 8208 XBR	.264"	2.250"	25.5	2180	33,900 PSI	28.5C	2497	50,000 PSI
123 GR. SIE HPBT	Hodgdon	Benchmark	.264"	2.250"	25.0	2225	36,900 PSI	27.5C	2460	49,900 PSI
123 GR. SIE HPBT	Hodgdon	H322	.264"	2.250"	24.0	2192	36,600 PSI	26.6C	2434	49,900 PSI
123 GR. SIE HPBT	IMR	IMR 4198	.264"	2.250"	22.0	2263	43,300 PSI	24.2C	2385	50,500 PSI
123 GR. SIE HPBT	Hodgdon	H4198	.264"	2.250"	21.0	2153	37,700 PSI	23.7C	2375	50,000 PSI

Cartridge: 6.5mm BR Load Type: Rifle					Starting Loads			Maximum Loads		
Bullet Weight (Gr.)	Manufacturer	Powder	Bullet Diam.	C.O.L.	Grs.	Vel. (ft/s)	Pressure	Grs.	Vel. (ft/s)	Pressure
90 GR. SPR TNT HP	Hodgdon	CFE 223	.264"	2.140"	33.0	2716	38,700 CUP	35.0	2917	45,900 CUP
90 GR. SPR TNT HP	Hodgdon	Varget	.264"	2.140"	31.0	2670	35,400 CUP	33.0C	2835	41,500 CUP
90 GR. SPR TNT HP	Hodgdon	BL-C(2)	.264"	2.140"	32.0	2588	34,000 CUP	34.0	2774	40,000 CUP
90 GR. SPR TNT HP	Hodgdon	H335	.264"	2.140"	30.5	2793	43,400 CUP	32.5	2919	49,600 CUP
90 GR. SPR TNT HP	Hodgdon	H4895	.264"	2.140"	31.0	2714	35,800 CUP	33.0C	2923	44,100 CUP
90 GR. SPR TNT HP	IMR	IMR 8208 XBR	.264"	2.140"	31.0	2799	39,800 CUP	33.2C	3017	46,500 CUP
90 GR. SPR TNT HP	Hodgdon	Benchmark	.264"	2.140"	29.7	2807	42,300 CUP	31.7	2953	49,100 CUP
90 GR. SPR TNT HP	Hodgdon	H322	.264"	2.140"	29.0	2749	39,400 CUP	31.0	2919	49,100 CUP
95 GR. HDY V-MAX	Hodgdon	CFE 223	.264"	2.220"	33.0	2720	40,200 CUP	35.0	2915	47,700 CUP

95 GR. HDY V-MAX	Hodgdon	Varget	.264"	2.220"	31.0	2698	40,000 CUP	33.0C	2843	45,900 CUP
95 GR. HDY V-MAX	Hodgdon	BL-C(2)	.264"	2.220"	32.0	2647	41,800 CUP	34.0	2822	49,500 CUP
95 GR. HDY V-MAX	Hodgdon	H335	.264"	2.220"	29.6	2683	42,400 CUP	31.5	2846	50,200 CUP
95 GR. HDY V-MAX	Hodgdon	H4895	.264"	2.220"	31.0	2774	40,000 CUP	33.0C	2946	48,500 CUP
95 GR. HDY V-MAX	IMR	IMR 8208 XBR	.264"	2.220"	30.0	2725	38,700 CUP	33.0C	2992	50,100 CUP
95 GR. HDY V-MAX	Hodgdon	Benchmark	.264"	2.220"	29.0	2740	43,200 CUP	31.0	2871	49,000 CUP
95 GR. HDY V-MAX	Hodgdon	H322	.264"	2.220"	28.8	2722	40,300 CUP	30.7	2894	50,000 CUP
100 GR. NOS BT	Hodgdon	CFE 223	.264"	2.220"	32.0	2620	39,500 CUP	34.0	2792	47,200 CUP
100 GR. NOS BT	Hodgdon	Varget	.264"	2.220"	31.0	2635	39,600 CUP	33.0C	2797	48,700 CUP
100 GR. NOS BT	Hodgdon	BL-C(2)	.264"	2.220"	31.7	2593	41,800 CUP	33.8	2760	50,100 CUP
100 GR. NOS BT	Hodgdon	H335	.264"	2.220"	29.0	2590	43,100 CUP	31.0	2731	51,300 CUP
100 GR. NOS BT	Hodgdon	H4895	.264"	2.220"	31.0	2702	41,700 CUP	33.0C	2878	49,100 CUP
100 GR. NOS BT	IMR	IMR 8208 XBR	.264"	2.220"	29.0	2624	38,400 CUP	32.0C	2887	50,000 CUP
100 GR. NOS BT	Hodgdon	Benchmark	.264"	2.220"	28.3	2584	41,700 CUP	30.2	2748	49,400 CUP
100 GR. NOS BT	Hodgdon	H322	.264"	2.220"	28.0	2601	39,400 CUP	29.7	2772	50,200 CUP
107 GR. SIE HPBT	Hodgdon	CFE 223	.264"	2.340"	31.0	2533	38,000 CUP	33.5	2747	48,000 CUP
107 GR. SIE HPBT	Hodgdon	Varget	.264"	2.340"	30.5	2658	41,800 CUP	32.5C	2798	48,500 CUP
107 GR. SIE HPBT	Hodgdon	BL-C(2)	.264"	2.340"	31.0	2596	41,900 CUP	33.0	2733	47,800 CUP
107 GR. SIE HPBT	Hodgdon	H335	.264"	2.340"	28.2	2541	41,000 CUP	30.1	2704	49,800 CUP
107 GR. SIE HPBT	Hodgdon	H4895	.264"	2.340"	29.8	2623	38,900 CUP	31.8C	2811	47,900 CUP
107 GR. SIE HPBT	IMR	IMR 8208 XBR	.264"	2.340"	28.0	2532	37,600 CUP	31.3	2817	49,500 CUP
107 GR. SIE HPBT	Hodgdon	Benchmark	.264"	2.340"	27.8	2587	40,200 CUP	29.6	2741	49,400 CUP
107 GR. SIE HPBT	Hodgdon	H322	.264"	2.340"	27.2	2563	39,100 CUP	29.0	2738	49,800 CUP
120 GR. NOS BT	Hodgdon	CFE 223	.264"	2.250"	31.0	2435	40,700 CUP	33.0	2611	47,800 CUP
120 GR. NOS BT	Hodgdon	Varget	.264"	2.250"	29.0	2409	39,400 CUP	31.0C	2542	45,100 CUP
120 GR. NOS BT	Hodgdon	BL-C(2)	.264"	2.250"	30.3	2407	40,500 CUP	32.2	2556	49,400 CUP
120 GR. NOS BT	Hodgdon	H335	.264"	2.250"	27.6	2353	41,700 CUP	29.4	2514	49,500 CUP
120 GR. NOS BT	Hodgdon	H4895	.264"	2.250"	29.0	2475	41,300 CUP	31.0C	2624	47,700 CUP
120 GR. NOS BT	IMR	IMR 8208 XBR	.264"	2.250"	27.0	2375	37,500 CUP	30.2	2623	50,200 CUP
120 GR. NOS BT	Hodgdon	Benchmark	.264"	2.250"	27.2	2445	43,800 CUP	29.0	2569	50,000 CUP
120 GR. NOS BT	Hodgdon	H322	.264"	2.250"	26.7	2403	40,800 CUP	28.5	2549	49,500 CUP
129 GR. HDY SP	Hodgdon	CFE 223	.264"	2.280"	29.0	2284	36,200 CUP	31.0	2442	42,400 CUP
129 GR. HDY SP	Hodgdon	Varget	.264"	2.280"	29.0	2371	44,200 CUP	31.0C	2494	49,900 CUP
129 GR. HDY SP	Hodgdon	BL-C(2)	.264"	2.280"	29.7	2341	39,800 CUP	31.7	2466	48,100 CUP
129 GR. HDY SP	Hodgdon	H335	.264"	2.280"	27.4	2306	41,500 CUP	29.2	2430	50,200 CUP
129 GR. HDY SP	Hodgdon	H4895	.264"	2.280"	28.4	2378	44,200 CUP	30.3C	2502	49,400 CUP
129 GR. HDY SP	IMR	IMR 8208 XBR	.264"	2.280"	27.0	2314	39,100 CUP	29.8	2514	49,600 CUP
129 GR. HDY SP	Hodgdon	Benchmark	.264"	2.280"	26.3	2285	43,800 CUP	28.0	2411	49,600 CUP
129 GR. HDY SP	Hodgdon	H322	.264"	2.280"	26.0	2293	44,500 CUP	27.7	2417	49,200 CUP

					Starting Loads			Maximum Loads		
140 GR. SPR SP	Hodgdon	CFE 223	.264"	2.300"	28.0	2179	35,300 CUP	30.0	2319	41,300 CUP
140 GR. SPR SP	Hodgdon	Varget	.264"	2.300"	28.3	2278	42,100 CUP	30.2C	2415	49,000 CUP
140 GR. SPR SP	Hodgdon	BL-C(2)	.264"	2.300"	29.6	2290	42,000 CUP	31.5	2419	49,600 CUP
140 GR. SPR SP	Hodgdon	H335	.264"	2.300"	27.2	2243	44,400 CUP	29.0	2365	50,600 CUP
140 GR. SPR SP	Hodgdon	H4895	.264"	2.300"	28.2	2298	44,200 CUP	30.0C	2421	49,000 CUP
140 GR. SPR SP	IMR	IMR 8208 XBR	.264"	2.300"	26.0	2186	39,200 CUP	28.8	2391	50,300 CUP
140 GR. SPR SP	Hodgdon	Benchmark	.264"	2.300"	26.3	2233	44,200 CUP	28.0	2362	49,800 CUP
140 GR. SPR SP	Hodgdon	H322	.264"	2.300"	25.0	2199	43,900 CUP	26.7	2299	50,200 CUP
142 GR. SIE HPBT	Hodgdon	CFE 223	.264"	2.350"	28.0	2178	35,900 CUP	30.0	2340	40,800 CUP
142 GR. SIE HPBT	Hodgdon	Varget	.264"	2.350"	27.9	2250	40,900 CUP	29.7C	2396	49,600 CUP
142 GR. SIE HPBT	Hodgdon	BL-C(2)	.264"	2.350"	29.0	2245	39,500 CUP	31.0	2389	48,500 CUP
142 GR. SIE HPBT	Hodgdon	H335	.264"	2.350"	26.8	2228	43,800 CUP	28.5	2333	49,800 CUP
142 GR. SIE HPBT	Hodgdon	H4895	.264"	2.350"	27.3	2271	41,900 CUP	29.0	2395	49,300 CUP
142 GR. SIE HPBT	IMR	IMR 8208 XBR	.264"	2.350"	26.0	2231	40,000 CUP	28.8	2426	49,800 CUP
142 GR. SIE HPBT	Hodgdon	Benchmark	.264"	2.350"	25.2	2232	45,500 CUP	26.9	2326	49,900 CUP
142 GR. SIE HPBT	Hodgdon	H322	.264"	2.350"	24.5	2199	44,200 CUP	26.1	2293	49,400 CUP

Cartridge:6.5 x 50mm Japanese Load Type:Rifle					Starting Loads			Maximum Loads		
Bullet Weight (Gr.)	Manufacturer	Powder	Bullet Diam.	C.O.L.	Grs.	Vel. (ft/s)	Pressure	Grs.	Vel. (ft/s)	Pressure
100 GR. SIE SP	Hodgdon	H4831	.264"	2.700"	39.0	2350		41.0	2424	
100 GR. SIE SP	Hodgdon	H380	.264"	2.700"	39.0	2449		42.0	2686	
100 GR. SIE SP	Hodgdon	BL-C(2)	.264"	2.700"	36.0	2502		38.0	2642	
100 GR. SIE SP	Hodgdon	H335	.264"	2.700"	36.0	2514		38.0	2670	
100 GR. SIE SP	Hodgdon	H4895	.264"	2.700"	35.0	2408		37.0	2717	
120 GR. SPR SP	Hodgdon	H4831	.264"	2.920"	39.0	2300		41.0	2429	
120 GR. SPR SP	Hodgdon	H380	.264"	2.920"	38.0	2424		41.0	2595	
120 GR. SPR SP	Hodgdon	BL-C(2)	.264"	2.920"	35.0	2439		37.0	2566	
120 GR. SPR SP	Hodgdon	H335	.264"	2.920"	35.0	2441		37.0	2597	
120 GR. SPR SP	Hodgdon	H4895	.264"	2.920"	33.0	2368		35.0	2505	
140 GR. NOS PART	Hodgdon	H4831	.264"	2.920"	38.0	2222		41.0	2392	
140 GR. NOS PART	Hodgdon	H380	.264"	2.920"	36.0	2249		39.0	2396	
140 GR. NOS PART	Hodgdon	BL-C(2)	.264"	2.920"	33.0	2191		35.0	2388	
140 GR. NOS PART	Hodgdon	H335	.264"	2.920"	33.0	2219		35.0	2414	
140 GR. NOS PART	Hodgdon	H4895	.264"	2.920"	32.0	2186		34.0	2407	
160 GR. HDY RN	Hodgdon	H4831	.264"	2.855"	36.0	2201		38.0	2393	
160 GR. HDY RN	Hodgdon	H380	.264"	2.855"	33.0	2214		35.0	2366	
160 GR. HDY RN	Hodgdon	BL-C(2)	.264"	2.855"	31.0	2081		33.0	2337	
160 GR. HDY RN	Hodgdon	H335	.264"	2.855"	31.0	2090		33.0	2341	
160 GR. HDY RN	Hodgdon	H4895	.264"	2.855"	30.0	2118		32.0	2334	

Cartridge: 6.5mm Carcano Load Type: Rifle					Starting Loads			Maximum Loads		
Bullet Weight (Gr.)	Manufacturer	Powder	Bullet Diam.	C.O.L.	Grs.	Vel. (ft/s)	Pressure	Grs.	Vel. (ft/s)	Pressure
100 GR. HDY SP	Hodgdon	H4831	.264"	2.835"	40.0	2189		43.0	2414	
100 GR. HDY SP	Hodgdon	H380	.264"	2.835"	34.0	2317		36.0	2451	
100 GR. HDY SP	Hodgdon	BL-C(2)	.264"	2.835"	31.0	2170		33.0	2357	
100 GR. HDY SP	Hodgdon	H335	.264"	2.835"	31.0	2181		33.0	2369	
100 GR. HDY SP	Hodgdon	H4895	.264"	2.835"	31.0	2204		33.0	2394	
120 GR. HDY SP	Hodgdon	H4831	.264"	2.835"	38.0	2019		41.0	2224	
120 GR. HDY SP	Hodgdon	H380	.264"	2.835"	30.0	1997		33.0	2192	
120 GR. HDY SP	Hodgdon	BL-C(2)	.264"	2.835"	29.0	2019		31.0	2207	
120 GR. HDY SP	Hodgdon	H335	.264"	2.835"	29.0	2021		31.0	2204	
120 GR. HDY SP	Hodgdon	H4895	.264"	2.835"	28.0	1959		30.0	2147	
140 GR. NOS PART	Hodgdon	H4831	.264"	2.900"	37.0	1919		40.0	2192	
140 GR. NOS PART	Hodgdon	H380	.264"	2.900"	29.0	1923		32.0	2127	
140 GR. NOS PART	Hodgdon	BL-C(2)	.264"	2.900"	28.0	1960		30.0	2097	
140 GR. NOS PART	Hodgdon	H335	.264"	2.900"	28.0	1967		30.0	2109	
140 GR. NOS PART	Hodgdon	H4895	.264"	2.900"	28.0	1904		30.0	2089	
160 GR. HDY RN	Hodgdon	H4831	.264"	2.935"	37.0	1891		39.0	2086	
160 GR. HDY RN	Hodgdon	H380	.264"	2.935"	28.0	1797		31.0	2009	
160 GR. HDY RN	Hodgdon	BL-C(2)	.264"	2.935"	27.0	1830		30.0	2047	
160 GR. HDY RN	Hodgdon	H335	.264"	2.935"	27.0	1824		30.0	2060	
160 GR. HDY RN	Hodgdon	H4895	.264"	2.935"	27.0	1804		30.0	1992	

Cartridge: 6.5 Creedmoor Load Type: Rifle					Starting Loads			Maximum Loads		
Bullet Weight (Gr.)	Manufacturer	Powder	Bullet Diam.	C.O.L.	Grs.	Vel. (ft/s)	Pressure	Grs.	Vel. (ft/s)	Pressure
95 GR. HDY V-MAX	Hodgdon	H4350	.264"	2.670"	43.0	2972	45,000 PSI	47.0C	3224	56,100 PSI
95 GR. HDY V-MAX	Hodgdon	H414	.264"	2.670"	42.0	2991	46,100 PSI	46.5	3243	57,100 PSI
95 GR. HDY V-MAX	Winchester	760	.264"	2.670"	42.0	2991	46,100 PSI	46.5	3243	57,100 PSI
95 GR. HDY V-MAX	IMR	IMR 4007 SSC	.264"	2.670"	41.0	2964	45,400 PSI	45.5C	3288	59,800 PSI
95 GR. HDY V-MAX	Hodgdon	CFE 223	.264"	2.670"	40.4	3152	54,500 PSI	43.0	3274	60,000 PSI
95 GR. HDY V-MAX	Hodgdon	Varget	.264"	2.670"	39.0	3051	49,000 PSI	43.0	3286	60,100 PSI
95 GR. HDY V-MAX	IMR	IMR 4064	.264"	2.670"	38.0	3009	45,800 PSI	41.6	3281	58,700 PSI
95 GR. HDY V-MAX	Winchester	748	.264"	2.670"	39.0	3050	50,200 PSI	43.0	3259	59,000 PSI
95 GR. HDY V-MAX	Hodgdon	BL-C(2)	.264"	2.670"	40.0	3082	49,800 PSI	44.0	3313	60,300 PSI
95 GR. HDY V-MAX	IMR	IMR 4895	.264"	2.670"	38.0	3006	46,600 PSI	42.2	3295	60,400 PSI
95 GR. HDY V-MAX	Hodgdon	H4895	.264"	2.670"	37.0	3059	50,400 PSI	41.0	3276	60,300 PSI

95 GR. HDY V-MAX	IMR	IMR 8208 XBR	.264"	2.670"	36.0	3041	50,800 PSI	40.0	3228	58,900 PSI
100 GR. BAR TTSX BT	Hodgdon	H4350	.264"	2.655"	39.9	2895	49,200 PSI	44.7	3133	60,300 PSI
100 GR. BAR TTSX BT	Hodgdon	H414	.264"	2.655"	39.7	2893	47,100 PSI	44.5	3163	60,400 PSI
100 GR. BAR TTSX BT	Winchester	760	.264"	2.655"	39.7	2893	47,100 PSI	44.5	3163	60,400 PSI
100 GR. BAR TTSX BT	IMR	IMR 4007 SSC	.264"	2.655"	38.3	2929	52,900 PSI	43.1	3143	60,800 PSI
100 GR. BAR TTSX BT	Hodgdon	Varget	.264"	2.655"	34.8	2867	50,700 PSI	39.0	3101	62,100 PSI
100 GR. BAR TTSX BT	IMR	IMR 4064	.264"	2.655"	35.1	2847	47,300 PSI	39.5	3116	60,400 PSI
100 GR. BAR TTSX BT	IMR	IMR 4895	.264"	2.655"	35.4	2819	46,600 PSI	39.8	3103	59,800 PSI
100 GR. BAR TTSX BT	Hodgdon	H4895	.264"	2.655"	33.1	2819	49,100 PSI	37.3	3063	61,000 PSI
100 GR. BAR TTSX BT	IMR	IMR 8208 XBR	.264"	2.655"	33.2	2812	49,300 PSI	37.4	3056	60,900 PSI
100 GR. NOS BT	Hodgdon	H4350	.264"	2.760"	40.5	2905	48,500 PSI	45.0C	3156	59,800 PSI
100 GR. NOS BT	Hodgdon	H414	.264"	2.760"	40.0	2923	48,700 PSI	43.8	3143	58,700 PSI
100 GR. NOS BT	Winchester	760	.264"	2.760"	40.0	2923	48,700 PSI	43.8	3143	58,700 PSI
100 GR. NOS BT	IMR	IMR 4007 SSC	.264"	2.760"	39.0	2906	49,800 PSI	43.0	3138	59,800 PSI
100 GR. NOS BT	Hodgdon	CFE 223	.264"	2.760"	41.0	3074	56,000 PSI	43.4	3200	60,700 PSI
100 GR. NOS BT	Hodgdon	Varget	.264"	2.760"	36.5	2888	48,900 PSI	40.5	3122	60,300 PSI
100 GR. NOS BT	IMR	IMR 4064	.264"	2.760"	36.0	2873	46,500 PSI	40.0	3135	59,400 PSI
100 GR. NOS BT	Hodgdon	BL-C(2)	.264"	2.760"	37.5	2912	48,800 PSI	41.8	3163	60,100 PSI
100 GR. NOS BT	IMR	IMR 4895	.264"	2.760"	36.5	2899	48,400 PSI	40.5	3151	60,300 PSI
100 GR. NOS BT	Hodgdon	H4895	.264"	2.760"	35.0	2878	49,400 PSI	38.5	3097	59,300 PSI
100 GR. NOS BT	IMR	IMR 8208 XBR	.264"	2.760"	34.0	2850	48,700 PSI	38.0	3087	60,000 PSI
107 GR. SIE HPBT	Hodgdon	H4350	.264"	2.780"	41.0	2829	45,300 PSI	46.0C	3139	60,900 PSI
107 GR. SIE HPBT	Hodgdon	H414	.264"	2.780"	40.0	2832	45,300 PSI	45.0	3127	58,800 PSI
107 GR. SIE HPBT	Winchester	760	.264"	2.780"	40.0	2832	45,300 PSI	45.0	3127	58,800 PSI
107 GR. SIE HPBT	IMR	IMR 4007 SSC	.264"	2.780"	39.0	2782	44,200 PSI	43.0	3073	58,600 PSI
107 GR. SIE HPBT	Hodgdon	CFE 223	.264"	2.780"	39.0	2960	53,600 PSI	41.5	3076	59,000 PSI
107 GR. SIE HPBT	Hodgdon	Varget	.264"	2.780"	37.0	2863	48,600 PSI	41.0	3093	60,200 PSI
107 GR. SIE HPBT	IMR	IMR 4064	.264"	2.780"	36.0	2799	44,100 PSI	39.7	3081	58,500 PSI
107 GR. SIE HPBT	Winchester	748	.264"	2.780"	37.0	2848	49,000 PSI	41.3	3086	59,300 PSI
107 GR. SIE HPBT	Hodgdon	BL-C(2)	.264"	2.780"	38.0	2912	50,300 PSI	42.0	3103	59,000 PSI
107 GR. SIE HPBT	IMR	IMR 4895	.264"	2.780"	36.0	2816	45,800 PSI	40.0	3083	59,700 PSI
107 GR. SIE HPBT	Hodgdon	H4895	.264"	2.780"	35.0	2846	49,400 PSI	39.0	3073	60,900 PSI
107 GR. SIE HPBT	IMR	IMR 8208 XBR	.264"	2.780"	34.0	2812	48,900 PSI	37.8	3027	59,700 PSI
120 GR. HDY A-MAX	Hodgdon	H4350	.264"	2.670"	40.5	2709	47,700 PSI	45.0C	2965	60,800 PSI
120 GR. HDY A-MAX	Hodgdon	H414	.264"	2.670"	40.0	2684	47,100 PSI	44.5	2960	61,500 PSI
120 GR. HDY A-MAX	Winchester	760	.264"	2.670"	40.0	2684	47,100 PSI	44.5	2960	61,500 PSI
120 GR. HDY A-MAX	IMR	IMR 4007 SSC	.264"	2.670"	39.0	2665	46,400 PSI	42.5	2907	58,700 PSI
120 GR. HDY A-MAX	Hodgdon	Varget	.264"	2.670"	36.0	2668	49,600 PSI	40.2	2891	60,400 PSI
120 GR. HDY A-MAX	IMR	IMR 4064	.264"	2.670"	35.0	2666	47,200 PSI	38.9	2903	59,800 PSI
120 GR. HDY A-MAX	Winchester	748	.264"	2.670"	36.0	2650	56,900 PSI	40.4	2899	59,900 PSI

120 GR. HDY A-MAX	Hodgdon	BL-C(2)	.264"	2.670"	37.0	2678	46,600PSI	41.3	2941	60,500 PSI
120 GR. HDY A-MAX	IMR	IMR 4895	.264"	2.670"	35.0	2670	48,600 PSI	39.0	2895	59,300 PSI
120 GR. HDY A-MAX	Hodgdon	H4895	.264"	2.670"	34.0	2672	50,500 PSI	37.4	2858	60,400 PSI
120 GR. HDY A-MAX	IMR	IMR 8208 XBR	.264"	2.670"	32.0	2564	45,800 PSI	36.0	2818	60,300 PSI
123 GR. SIE HPBT	Hodgdon	H4350	.264"	2.670"	40.0	2680	45,500 PSI	44.8	2951	59,700 PSI
123 GR. SIE HPBT	Hodgdon	H414	.264"	2.670"	40.0	2670	45,200 PSI	44.2	2938	58,900 PSI
123 GR. SIE HPBT	Winchester	760	.264"	2.670"	40.0	2670	45,200 PSI	44.2	2938	58,900 PSI
123 GR. SIE HPBT	IMR	IMR 4007 SSC	.264"	2.670"	38.0	2622	44,000 PSI	42.5	2917	59,200 PSI
123 GR. SIE HPBT	Hodgdon	Varget	.264"	2.670"	36.0	2712	51,100 PSI	39.8	2887	59,200 PSI
123 GR. SIE HPBT	IMR	IMR 4064	.264"	2.670"	35.0	2673	48,300 PSI	38.8	2882	58,300 PSI
123 GR. SIE HPBT	Winchester	748	.264"	2.670"	37.0	2650	45,600 PSI	40.8	2900	58,900 PSI
123 GR. SIE HPBT	Hodgdon	BL-C(2)	.264"	2.670"	37.0	2640	43,800 PSI	41.3	2916	58,600 PSI
123 GR. SIE HPBT	IMR	IMR 4895	.264"	2.670"	35.0	2663	47,700 PSI	39.2	2896	59,900 PSI
123 GR. SIE HPBT	IMR	IMR 8208 XBR	.264"	2.670"	32.0	2570	46,100 PSI	36.0	2806	59,000 PSI
130 GR. NOS AB	Hodgdon	H4350	.264"	2.750"	35.2	2464	49,300 PSI	39.2	2687	60,400 PSI
130 GR. NOS AB	Hodgdon	H414	.264"	2.750"	35.4	2490	50,500 PSI	39.3	2693	60,000 PSI
130 GR. NOS AB	Winchester	760	.264"	2.750"	35.4	2490	50,500 PSI	39.3	2693	60,000 PSI
130 GR. NOS AB	IMR	IMR 4007 SSC	.264"	2.750"	34.0	2437	49,900 PSI	38.0	2662	60,300 PSI
130 GR. NOS AB	Hodgdon	Varget	.264"	2.750"	31.4	2414	51,500 PSI	34.9	2610	61,400 PSI
130 GR. NOS AB	IMR	IMR 4064	.264"	2.750"	31.0	2352	47,600 PSi	34.9	2585	59,600 PSI
130 GR. NOS AB	Winchester	748	.264"	2.750"	33.0	2494	56,200 PSI	34.8	2586	60,500 PSI
130 GR. NOS AB	Hodgdon	BL-C(2)	.264"	2.750"	31.2	2358	52,600 PSI	34.9	2529	60,400 PSI
130 GR. NOS AB	IMR	IMR 4895	.264"	2.750"	32.9	2435	49,600 PSI	37.0	2668	61,000 PSI
130 GR. NOS AB	Hodgdon	H4895	.264"	2.750"	30.1	2361	48,500 PSI	33.8	2583	61,200 PSI
130 GR. NOS AB	IMR	IMR 8208 XBR	.264"	2.750"	30.5	2378	49,700 PSI	34.0	2589	61,200 PSI
140 GR. HDY A-MAX	Hodgdon	Hybrid 100V	.264"	2.820"	36.0	2451	45,300 PSI	40.9C	2736	59,600 PSI
140 GR. HDY A-MAX	Hodgdon	H4350	.264"	2.820"	36.0	2464	49,200 PSI	40.0C	2660	59,200 PSI
140 GR. HDY A-MAX	Hodgdon	H414	.264"	2.820"	36.0	2460	50,100 PSI	40.2	2672	60,300 PSI
140 GR. HDY A-MAX	IMR	IMR 4350	.264"	2.820"	37.0	2460	47,500 PSI	41.0C	2607	59,800 PSI
140 GR. HDY A-MAX	Winchester	760	.264"	2.820"	36.0	2460	50,100 PSI	40.2	2672	60,300 PSI
140 GR. HDY A-MAX	IMR	IMR 4007 SSC	.264"	2.820"	35.0	2449	49,500 PSI	39.0C	2656	59,800 PSI
140 GR. HDY A-MAX	Hodgdon	H380	.264"	2.820"	34.5	2388	47,800 PSI	38.5	2605	59,500 PSI
140 GR. HDY A-MAX	Hodgdon	Varget	.264"	2.820"	32.0	2371	47,400 PSI	35.8	2598	59,900 PSI
140 GR. HDY A-MAX	IMR	IMR 4064	.264"	2.820"	32.0	2393	48,700 PSI	35.7	2603	60,800 PSI
140 GR. HDY A-MAX	IMR	IMR 4895	.264"	2.820"	33.7	2491	52,700 PSI	35.9	2609	60,200 PSI
140 GR. HDY A-MAX	Hodgdon	H4895	.264"	2.820"	30.0	2316	46,800 PSI	34.0	2555	60,400 PSI
140 GR. HDY A-MAX	IMR	IMR 8208 XBR	.264"	2.820"	30.0	2335	49,200 PSI	32.8	2511	59,300 PSI
142 GR. SIE HPBT	Hodgdon	Hybrid 100V	.264"	2.780"	39.0	2581	50,200 PSI	41.5	2737	58,900 PSI
142 GR. SIE HPBT	Hodgdon	H4350	.264"	2.780"	38.8	2573	52,300 PSI	41.5	2694	59,800 PSI

142 GR. SIE HPBT	Hodgdon	H414	.264"	2.780"	36.5	2470	50,900 PSI	40.2	2634	58,300 PSI
142 GR. SIE HPBT	IMR	IMR 4350	.264"	2.780"	39.2	2511	48,300 PSI	41.7C	2687	58,600 PSI
142 GR. SIE HPBT	Winchester	760	.264"	2.780"	36.5	2470	50,900 PSI	40.2	2634	58,300 PSI
142 GR. SIE HPBT	IMR	IMR 4007 SSC	.264"	2.780"	37.9	2536	52,100 PSI	40.3	2677	60,000 PSI
142 GR. SIE HPBT	Hodgdon	H380	.264"	2.780"	35.5	2399	47,000 PSI	39.2	2618	59,100 PSI
142 GR. SIE HPBT	Hodgdon	Varget	.264"	2.780"	34.5	2489	52,600 PSI	36.3	2598	60,100 PSI
142 GR. SIE HPBT	IMR	IMR 4064	.264"	2.780"	34.6	2503	52,400 PSI	36.8	2614	59,500 PSI
142 GR. SIE HPBT	IMR	IMR 4895	.264"	2.780"	33.8	2479	51,200 PSI	36.0	2599	59,500 PSI
142 GR. SIE HPBT	Hodgdon	H4895	.264"	2.780"	32.4	2426	49,800 PSI	34.5	2551	58,000 PSI
142 GR. SIE HPBT	IMR	IMR 8208 XBR	.264"	2.780"	32.2	2431	51,500 PSI	33.5	2518	58,000 PSI

Cartridge: 260 Remington Load Type: Rifle					Starting Loads			Maximum Loads		
Bullet Weight (Gr.)	Manufacturer	Powder	Bullet Diam.	C.O.L.	Grs.	Vel. (ft/s)	Pressure	Grs.	Vel. (ft/s)	Pressure
95 GR. HDY V-MAX	Hodgdon	H4350	.264"	2.780"	47.0	3135	51,200 PSI	49.7	3284	58,100 PSI
95 GR. HDY V-MAX	Hodgdon	H414	.264"	2.780"	46.0	3136	50,700 PSI	49.0	3313	58,600 PSI
95 GR. HDY V-MAX	Winchester	760	.264"	2.780"	46.0	3136	50,700 PSI	49.0	3313	58,600 PSI
95 GR. HDY V-MAX	Hodgdon	H380	.264"	2.780"	44.0	3088	51,300 PSI	47.0	3262	59,500 PSI
95 GR. HDY V-MAX	Hodgdon	CFE 223	.264"	2.780"	40.4	3081	51,200 PSI	43.0	3240	58,500 PSI
95 GR. HDY V-MAX	Hodgdon	Varget	.264"	2.780"	39.0	3070	50,200 PSI	42.0	3244	58,500 PSI
95 GR. HDY V-MAX	Hodgdon	BL-C(2)	.264"	2.780"	41.0	3093	51,900 PSI	43.5	3236	58,300 PSI
95 GR. HDY V-MAX	Hodgdon	H335	.264"	2.780"	34.5	2968	55,700 PSI	38.3	3114	58,000 PSI
95 GR. HDY V-MAX	Hodgdon	H4895	.264"	2.780"	38.0	3069	51,300 PSI	40.8	3225	58,500 PSI
95 GR. HDY V-MAX	IMR	IMR 8208 XBR	.264"	2.780"	37.6	3038	51,900 PSI	40.0	3166	58,200 PSI
95 GR. HDY V-MAX	Hodgdon	Benchmark	.264"	2.780"	40.0	3190	51,400 PSI	43.5	3391	59,600 PSI
100 GR. BAR XFB	Hodgdon	H4831	.264"	2.750"	46.0	2925	52,800 PSI	48.8C	3055	58,600 PSI
100 GR. BAR XFB	Hodgdon	H4350	.264"	2.750"	42.0	2946	52,900 PSI	45.0	3077	58,200 PSI
100 GR. BAR XFB	Hodgdon	H414	.264"	2.750"	43.0	2929	50,600 PSI	46.0	3101	58,000 PSI
100 GR. BAR XFB	Winchester	760	.264"	2.750"	43.0	2929	50,600 PSI	46.0	3101	58,000 PSI
100 GR. BAR XFB	Hodgdon	H380	.264"	2.750"	41.0	2860	52,000 PSI	43.5	3004	58,200 PSI
100 GR. BAR XFB	Hodgdon	Varget	.264"	2.750"	36.5	2861	52,000 PSI	39.5	3027	58,900 PSI
100 GR. BAR XFB	Hodgdon	BL-C(2)	.264"	2.750"	37.0	2804	50,700 PSI	40.5	3002	59,100 PSI
100 GR. BAR XFB	Hodgdon	H335	.264"	2.750"	33.0	2685	50,300 PSI	36.0	2878	58,400 PSI
100 GR. BAR XFB	Hodgdon	H4895	.264"	2.750"	35.0	2810	51,300 PSI	38.0	2974	58,800 PSI
100 GR. BAR XFB	Hodgdon	Benchmark	.264"	2.750"	38.0	2981	50,700 PSI	41.0	3171	59,900 PSI
107 GR. SIE HPBT	Hodgdon	H4831	.264"	2.780"	50.0	2963	50,300 PSI	51.0C	3027	54,000 PSI
107 GR. SIE HPBT	Hodgdon	Hybrid 100V	.264"	2.780"	42.0	2835	46,600 PSI	46.0C	3071	56,100 PSI
107 GR. SIE HPBT	Hodgdon	H4350	.264"	2.780"	46.0	2997	50,400 PSI	49.0	3164	58,700 PSI
107 GR. SIE HPBT	Hodgdon	H414	.264"	2.780"	43.5	2917	46,900 PSI	46.5	3151	58,100 PSI
107 GR. SIE HPBT	Winchester	760	.264"	2.780"	43.5	2917	46,900 PSI	46.5	3151	58,100 PSI

107 GR. SIE HPBT	Hodgdon	H380	.264"	2.780"	43.0	2908	48,500 PSI	46.0	3107	58,200 PSI
107 GR. SIE HPBT	Hodgdon	CFE 223	.264'	2.780"	39.7	2955	54,900 PSI	42.2	3081	58,900 PSI
107 GR. SIE HPBT	Hodgdon	Varget	.264"	2.780"	38.5	2947	49,800 PSI	41.5	3125	58,700 PSI
107 GR. SIE HPBT	Hodgdon	BL-C(2)	.264"	2.780"	40.0	2951	50,400 PSI	42.7	3097	57,800 PSI
107 GR. SIE HPBT	Hodgdon	H335	.264"	2.780"	37.0	2862	50,300 PSI	39.2	3014	58,400 PSI
107 GR. SIE HPBT	Hodgdon	H4895	.264"	2.780"	38.0	2950	51,900 PSI	40.7	3074	58,000 PSI
107 GR. SIE HPBT	IMR	IMR 8208 XBR	.264"	2.780"	37.2	2900	52,300 PSI	39.1	3001	57,900 PSI
107 GR. SIE HPBT	Hodgdon	Benchmark	.264"	2.780"	40.0	3158	50,900 PSI	42.5	3227	59,500 PSI
120 GR. SPR SP	Hodgdon	H1000	.264"	2.780"	49.0	2710	44,600 PSI	51.0C	2810	49,300 PSI
120 GR. SPR SP	IMR	IMR 7828	.264"	2.780"				47.0C	2895	57,800 PSI
120 GR. SPR SP	Winchester	Supreme 780	.264"	2.780"	45.6	2701	49,800 PSI	48.5	2862	57,800 PSI
120 GR. SPR SP	Hodgdon	H4831	.264"	2.780"	47.0	2812	52,100 PSI	50.0C	2954	59,200 PSI
120 GR. SPR SP	Hodgdon	Hybrid 100V	.264"	2.780"	41.0	2738	50,200 PSI	45.0C	2934	58,500 PSI
120 GR. SPR SP	IMR	IMR 4831	.264"	2.780"				44.0	2885	58,400 PSI
120 GR. SPR SP	Hodgdon	H4350	.264"	2.780"	43.5	2814	51,400 PSI	46.5	2960	58,200 PSI
120 GR. SPR SP	Hodgdon	H414	.264"	2.780"	42.5	2802	51,000 PSI	45.5	2968	58,600 PSI
120 GR. SPR SP	IMR	IMR 4350	.264"	2.780"				43.0	2885	58,000 PSI
120 GR. SPR SP	Winchester	760	.264"	2.780"	42.5	2802	51,000 PSI	45.5	2968	58,600 PSI
120 GR. SPR SP	Hodgdon	H380	.264"	2.780"	40.0	2686	51,500 PSI	43.0	2844	58,100 PSI
120 GR. SPR SP	Hodgdon	Varget	.264"	2.780"	36.0	2716	50,300 PSI	39.0	2877	58,300 PSI
120 GR. SPR SP	IMR	IMR 4320	.264"	2.780"				37.5	2805	58,400 PSI
120 GR. SPR SP	IMR	IMR 4064	.264"	2.780"				37.0	2805	57,700 PSI
120 GR. SPR SP	Hodgdon	BL-C(2)	.264"	2.780"	37.0	2686	52,800 PSI	40.0	2840	58,900 PSI
120 GR. SPR SP	IMR	IMR 4895	.264"	2.780"				36.0	2770	57,100 PSI
120 GR. SPR SP	Hodgdon	H335	.264"	2.780"	34.0	2613	51,600 PSI	36.7	2755	58,600 PSI
120 GR. SPR SP	Hodgdon	H4895	.264"	2.780"	35.0	2664	51,900 PSI	38.0	2813	58,900 PSI
120 GR. SPR SP	IMR	IMR 3031	.264"	2.780"				34.0	2720	57,600 PSI
120 GR. SPR SP	Hodgdon	Benchmark	.264"	2.780"	37.0	2768	51,200 PSI	40.0	2935	59,500 PSI
120 GR. SPR SP	IMR	SR 4759	.264"	2.780"				23.5	2280	57,600 PSI
125 GR. NOS PART	Hodgdon	H1000	.264"	2.780"	48.0	2685	46,300 PSI	51.0C	2821	53,300 PSI
125 GR. NOS PART	Winchester	Supreme 780	.264"	2.780"	44.2	2635	49,500 PSI	47.0	2815	59,300 PSI
125 GR. NOS PART	Hodgdon	H4831	.264"	2.780"	45.0	2725	51,600 PSI	48.0C	2862	58,000 PSI
125 GR. NOS PART	Hodgdon	Hybrid 100V	.264"	2.780"	40.0	2657	48,600 PSI	44.0C	2876	58,600 PSI
125 GR. NOS PART	Hodgdon	H4350	.264"	2.780"	41.0	2714	50,900 PSI	44.3	2867	57,900 PSI
125 GR. NOS PART	Hodgdon	H414	.264"	2.780"	40.0	2691	50,500 PSI	43.0	2852	58,100 PSI
125 GR. NOS PART	Winchester	760	.264"	2.780"	40.0	2691	50,500 PSI	43.0	2852	58,100 PSI
125 GR. NOS PART	Hodgdon	H380	.264"	2.780"	39.0	2641	50,300 PSI	42.0	2806	58,900 PSI
125 GR. NOS PART	Hodgdon	Varget	.264"	2.780"	34.5	2624	51,200 PSI	37.5	2785	58,400 PSI
125 GR. NOS PART	Hodgdon	BL-C(2)	.264"	2.780"	36.5	2623	51,600 PSI	38.5	2746	58,200 PSI

125 GR. NOS PART	Hodgdon	H4895	.264"	2.780"	34.0	2623	54,300 PSI	37.0	2743	58,900 PSI
140 GR. NOS PART	Hodgdon	H1000	.264"	2.780"	48.0	2619	51,200 PSI	50.5	2730	57,000 PSI
140 GR. NOS PART	IMR	IMR 7828	.264"	2.780"				47.0C	2755	57,200 PSI
140 GR. NOS PART	Winchester	Supreme 780	.264"	2.780"	42.0	2494	51,100 PSI	44.6	2633	58,300 PSI
140 GR. NOS PART	Hodgdon	H4831	.264"	2.780"	43.0	2568	53,000 PSI	45.7	2686	59,000 PSI
140 GR. NOS PART	Hodgdon	Hybrid 100V	.264"	2.780"	37.0	2464	49,500 PSI	41.0C	2670	58,400 PSI
140 GR. NOS PART	IMR	IMR 4831	.264"	2.780"				44.0	2715	57,000 PSI
140 GR. NOS PART	Hodgdon	H4350	.264"	2.780"	39.0	2530	51,900 PSI	42.0	2677	58,800 PSI
140 GR. NOS PART	Hodgdon	H414	.264"	2.780"	38.0	2496	50,700 PSI	41.0	2656	58,800 PSI
140 GR. NOS PART	IMR	IMR 4350	.264"	2.780"				43.0	2715	57,000 PSI
140 GR. NOS PART	Winchester	760	.264"	2.780"	38.0	2496	50,700 PSI	41.0	2656	58,800 PSI
140 GR. NOS PART	Hodgdon	H380	.264"	2.780"	37.0	2434	51,200 PSI	40.0	2594	58,900 PSI
140 GR. NOS PART	Hodgdon	Varget	.264"	2.780"	34.0	2469	53,300 PSI	36.0	2578	59,400 PSI
140 GR. NOS PART	IMR	IMR 4320	.264"	2.780"				36.0	2600	57.600 PSI
140 GR. NOS PART	IMR	IMR 4064	.264"	2.780"				36.0	2615	56,900 PSI
140 GR. NOS PART	Hodgdon	BL-C(2)	.264"	2.780"	34.0	2412	52,800 PSI	36.6	2557	59,000 PSI
140 GR. NOS PART	IMR	IMR 4895	.264"	2.780"				35.5	2605	57,600 PSI
140 GR. NOS PART	Hodgdon	H4895	.264"	2.780"	32.0	2367	50,500 PSI	34.3	2517	58,400 PSI
140 GR. NOS PART	IMR	IMR 3031	.264"	2.780"				32.5	2505	56,200 PSI
140 GR. NOS PART	IMR	SR 4759	.264"	2.780"				23.0	2135	56,500 PSI
142 GR. SIE HPBT	Winchester	Supreme 780	.264"	2.780"	43.1	2502	49,300 PSI	45.8	2678	59,100 PSI
142 GR. SIE HPBT	Hodgdon	H4831	.264"	2.780"	45.0	2601	50,900 PSI	48.0C	2747	58,700 PSI
142 GR. SIE HPBT	Hodgdon	Hybrid 100V	.264"	2.780"	38.0	2464	46,800 PSI	42.0C	2690	57,500 PSI
142 GR. SIE HPBT	Hodgdon	H4350	.264"	2.780"	41.5	2590	50,100 PSI	44.5	2735	58,000 PSI
142 GR. SIE HPBT	Hodgdon	H414	.264"	2.780"	41.0	2588	50,400 PSI	43.5	2734	58,800 PSI
142 GR. SIE HPBT	Winchester	760	.264"	2.780"	41.0	2588	50,400 PSI	43.5	2734	58,800 PSI
142 GR. SIE HPBT	Hodgdon	H380	.264"	2.780"	39.0	2490	50,100 PSI	41.5	2636	58,300 PSI
142 GR. SIE HPBT	Hodgdon	Varget	.264"	2.780"	35.0	2541	54,000 PSI	37.5	2645	59,100 PSI
142 GR. SIE HPBT	Hodgdon	H4895	.264"	2.780"	34.0	2486	52,000 PSI	36.2	2597	58,200 PSI
160 GR. HDY RN	Hodgdon	H1000	.264"	2.860"	48.0	2498	50,500 PSI	50.0C	2595	56,400 PSI
160 GR. HDY RN	IMR	IMR 7828	.264"	2.860"				45.0	2580	58,100 PSi
160 GR. HDY RN	Winchester	Supreme 780	.264"	2.860"	43.0	2414	50,900 PSI	45.7	2545	57,800 PSI
160 GR. HDY RN	Hodgdon	H4831	.264"	2.860"	43.0	2419	50,900 PSI	46.0	2540	58,100 PSI
160 GR. HDY RN	Hodgdon	Hybrid 100V	.264"	2.860"	38.0	2346	47,400 PSI	42.0C	2539	56.900 PSI
160 GR. HDY RN	IMR	IMR 4831	.264"	2.860"				41.5	2520	57,200 PSI
160 GR. HDY RN	Hodgdon	H4350	.264"	2.860"	40.0	2417	52,100 PSI	43.0	2538	58,200 PSI
160 GR. HDY RN	Hodgdon	H414	.264"	2.860"	39.0	2365	51,200 PSI	42.0	2514	58,800 PSI
160 GR. HDY RN	IMR	IMR 4350	.264"	2.860"				40.5	2520	57,400 PSI
160 GR. HDY RN	Winchester	760	.264"	2.860"	39.0	2365	51,200 PSI	42.0	2514	58,800 PSI

Cartridge:6.5 x 55mm Swedish Mauser Load Type:Rifle					Starting Loads			Maximum Loads		
Bullet Weight (Gr.)	Manufacturer	Powder	Bullet Diam.	C.O.L.	Grs.	Vel. (ft/s)	Pressure	Grs.	Vel. (ft/s)	Pressure
85 GR. SIE HP	Hodgdon	H4350	.264"	2.800"	47.0	2909	31,600 CUP	52.0C	3283	42,100 CUP
85 GR. SIE HP	Hodgdon	H414	.264"	2.800"	45.0	3071	35,500 CUP	50.0	3265	40,900 CUP
85 GR. SIE HP	IMR	IMR 4350	.264"	2.800"	46.0	2896	37,500 CUP	49.0C	3117	43,100 CUP
85 GR. SIE HP	Winchester	760	.264"	2.800"	45.0	3071	35,500 CUP	50.0	3265	40,900 CUP
85 GR. SIE HP	IMR	IMR 4007 SSC	.264"	2.800"	45.0	2956	38,000 CUP	49.0	3255	45,600 CUP
85 GR. SIE HP	Hodgdon	H380	.264"	2.800"	43.0	2932	33,400 CUP	48.0	3231	42,900 CUP
85 GR. SIE HP	Hodgdon	CFE 223	.264"	2.800"	44.0	3003	37,000 CUP	48.0	3301	44,800 CUP
85 GR. SIE HP	Hodgdon	Varget	.264"	2.800"	40.0	3128	36,600 CUP	44.0	3350	42,300 CUP
85 GR. SIE HP	IMR	IMR 4064	.264"	2.800"	40.0	2993	39,000 CUP	43.5	3205	44,900 CUP
85 GR. SIE HP	Hodgdon	BL-C(2)	.264"	2.800"	43.0	2931	33,400 CUP	47.5	3261	44,500 CUP
85 GR. SIE HP	IMR	IMR 4895	.264"	2.800"	40.0	2979	39,200 CUP	43.5	3183	45,000 CUP
85 GR. SIE HP	Hodgdon	H335	.264"	2.800"	40.0	3023	36,800 CUP	44.5	3314	45,200 CUP
85 GR. SIE HP	Hodgdon	H4895	.264"	2.800"	40.0	3031	34,600 CUP	44.0	3370	45,100 CUP
100 GR. SIE HP	IMR	IMR 7828 SSC	.264"	2.850"	48.0	2772	39,500 CUP	51.5C*	2987	45,500 CUP
100 GR. SIE HP	Hodgdon	H4831	.264"	2.850"	46.0	2552	27,800 CUP	51.0C	2883	37,500 CUP
100 GR. SIE HP	IMR	IMR 4831	.264"	2.850"	46.5	2827	37,500 CUP	49.5C	3014	43,200 CUP
100 GR. SIE HP	Hodgdon	H4350	.264"	2.850"	45.0	2724	31,400 CUP	50.0C	3172	46,000 CUP
100 GR. SIE HP	Hodgdon	H414	.264"	2.850"	44.5	2879	36,500 CUP	49.5	3183	45,400 CUP
100 GR. SIE HP	IMR	IMR 4350	.264"	2.850"	45.0	2842	40,100 CUP	48.5C	3032	45,200 CUP
100 GR. SIE HP	Winchester	760	.264"	2.850"	44.5	2879	36,500 CUP	49.5	3183	45,400 CUP
100 GR. SIE HP	IMR	IMR 4007 SSC	.264"	2.850"	44.0	2863	39,400 CUP	47.5	3091	45,300 CUP
100 GR. SIE HP	Hodgdon	H380	.264"	2.850"	43.0	2845	36,000 CUP	48.0	3092	43,000 CUP
100 GR. SIE HP	Hodgdon	CFE 223	.264"	2.850"	41.0	2793	37,900 CUP	45.0	3037	44,900 CUP
100 GR. SIE HP	Hodgdon	Varget	.264"	2.850"	38.0	2892	37,800 CUP	42.0	3177	45,800 CUP
100 GR. SIE HP	IMR	IMR 4064	.264"	2.850"	39.0	2894	41,000 CUP	42.7	3074	46,000 CUP
100 GR. SIE HP	Hodgdon	BL-C(2)	.264"	2.850"	39.5	2734	38,900 CUP	43.8	2948	45,200 CUP
100 GR. SIE HP	IMR	IMR 4895	.264"	2.850"	39.0	2847	40,800 CUP	42.5	3024	45,600 CUP
100 GR. SIE HP	Hodgdon	H335	.264"	2.850"	37.0	2686	36,300 CUP	41.0	2991	46,000 CUP
100 GR. SIE HP	Hodgdon	H4895	.264"	2.850"	37.0	2820	38,800 CUP	41.0	3033	46,000 CUP
107 GR. SIE HPBT	IMR	IMR 7828 SSC	.264"	3.050"	46.5	2721	39,700 CUP	50.5C*	2915	45,300 CUP
107 GR. SIE HPBT	Hodgdon	H4831	.264"	3.050"	46.0	2590	34,500 CUP	51.0C	2911	42,700 CUP
107 GR. SIE HPBT	Hodgdon	Hybrid 100V	.264"	3.050"	43.0	2724	41,300 CUP	47.0C	2946	46,100 CUP
107 GR. SIE HPBT	IMR	IMR 4831	.264"	3.050"	46.0	2795	38,900 CUP	49.0C	2997	44,800 CUP
107 GR. SIE HPBT	Hodgdon	H4350	.264"	3.050"	43.0	2706	36,000 CUP	48.0C	3035	45,600 CUP
107 GR. SIE HPBT	Hodgdon	H414	.264"	3.050"	43.0	2743	36,100 CUP	47.5	3036	45,900 CUP
107 GR. SIE HPBT	IMR	IMR 4350	.264"	3.050"	44.0	2773	39,400 CUP	47.8	2994	45,600 CUP

107 GR. SIE HPBT	Winchester	760	.264"	3.050"	43.0	2743	36,100 CUP	47.5	3036	45,900 CUP
107 GR. SIE HPBT	IMR	IMR 4007 SSC	.264"	3.050"	43.0	2828	39,500 CUP	46.5C	3028	45,500 CUP
107 GR. SIE HPBT	Hodgdon	H380	.264"	3.050"	41.0	2749	39,200 CUP	45.0	2941	45,800 CUP
107 GR. SIE HPBT	Hodgdon	CFE 223	.264"	3.050"	41.0	2836	40,700 CUP	45.6	3004	45,900 CUP
107 GR. SIE HPBT	Hodgdon	Varget	.264"	3.050"	38.0	2742	39,800 CUP	42.0	2952	45,600 CUP
107 GR. SIE HPBT	IMR	IMR 4064	.264"	3.050"	38.0	2791	39,500 CUP	41.5	2982	45,200 CUP
107 GR. SIE HPBT	Hodgdon	BL-C(2)	.264"	3.050"	41.0	2784	37,300 CUP	44.5	3050	45,600 CUP
107 GR. SIE HPBT	IMR	IMR 4895	.264"	3.050"	37.5	2776	40,600 CUP	40.8	2955	45,500 CUP
107 GR. SIE HPBT	Hodgdon	H335	.264"	3.050"	36.0	2660	37,800 CUP	40.0	2948	45,800 CUP
107 GR. SIE HPBT	Hodgdon	H4895	.264"	3.050"	37.0	2777	39,600 CUP	39.7	2943	45,900 CUP
120 GR. NOS BT	IMR	IMR 7828 SSC	.264"	3.000"	45.5	2590	40,200 CUP	49.5C	2802	45,600 CUP
120 GR. NOS BT	Hodgdon	H4831	.264"	3.000"	44.5	2528	36,200 CUP	49.5C	2802	45,900 CUP
120 GR. NOS BT	Hodgdon	Hybrid 100V	.264"	3.000"	41.0	2553	39,300 CUP	45.5	2787	46,000 CUP
120 GR. NOS BT	IMR	IMR 4831	.264"	3.000"	44.5	2674	38,400 CUP	48.5C	2913	46,200 CUP
120 GR. NOS BT	Hodgdon	H4350	.264"	3.000"	41.5	2545	36,800 CUP	46.0	2792	45,800 CUP
120 GR. NOS BT	Hodgdon	H414	.264"	3.000"	40.0	2528	37,000 CUP	44.5	2783	46,000 CUP
120 GR. NOS BT	IMR	IMR 4350	.264"	3.000"	43.0	2631	39,500 CUP	46.8C	2863	46,000 CUP
120 GR. NOS BT	Winchester	760	.264"	3.000"	40.0	2528	37,000 CUP	44.5	2783	46,000 CUP
120 GR. NOS BT	IMR	IMR 4007 SSC	.264"	3.000"	41.0	2603	37,900 CUP	44.2	2788	45,100 CUP
120 GR. NOS BT	Hodgdon	H380	.264"	3.000"	40.0	2555	38,200 CUP	44.3	2784	46,000 CUP
120 GR. NOS BT	Hodgdon	Varget	.264"	3.000"	35.0	2579	36,800 CUP	39.0	2812	45,300 CUP
120 GR. NOS BT	IMR	IMR 4064	.264"	3.000"	37.0	2625	41,300 CUP	40.0	2764	45,100 CUP
120 GR. NOS BT	IMR	IMR 4895	.264"	3.000"	36.0	2569	39,200 CUP	39.6	2767	45,900 CUP
120 GR. NOS BT	Hodgdon	H4895	.264"	3.000"	34.0	2571	43,000 CUP	37.8	2715	46,000 CUP
129 GR. HDY SP	IMR	IMR 7828 SSC	.264"	2.935"	45.0	2537	38,900 CUP	49.0C*	2734	45,000 CUP
129 GR. HDY SP	Hodgdon	H4831	.264"	2.935"	44.0	2449	35,600 CUP	48.5C	2689	45,000 CUP
129 GR. HDY SP	Hodgdon	Hybrid 100V	.264"	2.935"	41.0	2504	39,300 CUP	45.5	2743	46,400 CUP
129 GR. HDY SP	IMR	IMR 4831	.264"	2.935"	43.0	2549	37,200 CUP	47.0C	2792	45,100 CUP
129 GR. HDY SP	Hodgdon	H4350	.264"	2.935"	40.0	2430	35,100 CUP	45.5	2703	45,500 CUP
129 GR. HDY SP	Hodgdon	H414	.264"	2.935"	39.5	2460	37,900 CUP	43.5	2677	45,700 CUP
129 GR. HDY SP	IMR	IMR 4350	.264"	2.935"	42.0	2584	40,000 CUP	46.0	2793	45,800 CUP
129 GR. HDY SP	Winchester	760	.264"	2.935"	39.5	2460	37,900 CUP	43.5	2677	45,700 CUP
129 GR. HDY SP	IMR	IMR 4007 SSC	.264"	2.935"	40.0	2548	39,000 CUP	43.4	2718	45,600 CUP
129 GR. HDY SP	Hodgdon	H380	.264"	2.935"	38.5	2440	38,400 CUP	42.5	2654	45,500 CUP
129 GR. HDY SP	Hodgdon	Varget	.264"	2.935"	34.0	2472	36,900 CUP	37.5	2664	46,000 CUP
129 GR. HDY SP	IMR	IMR 4064	.264"	2.935"	36.0	2534	39,800 CUP	39.2	2704	45,800 CUP
129 GR. HDY SP	IMR	IMR 4895	.264"	2.935"	35.0	2488	38,400 CUP	39.0	2703	45,600 CUP
129 GR. HDY SP	Hodgdon	H4895	.264"	2.935"	33.0	2373	38,200 CUP	36.3	2561	45,600 CUP
140 GR. SPR SP	Hodgdon	H1000	.264"	3.030"	46.5	2423	37,600 CUP	51.5C	2651	46,000 CUP
140 GR. SPR SP	IMR	IMR 7828 SSC	.264"	3.030"	44.0	2460	38,300 CUP	48.2	2678	45,800 CUP

140 GR. SPR SP	Winchester	Supreme 780	.264"	3.030"	45.0	2451	40,600 CUP	47.8	2592	45,300 CUP
140 GR. SPR SP	Hodgdon	H4831	.264"	3.030"	42.5	2382	38,100 CUP	47.0	2586	45,700 CUP
140 GR. SPR SP	Hodgdon	Hybrid 100V	.264"	3.030"	40.0	2418	38,300 CUP	44.5	2642	45,200 CUP
140 GR. SPR SP	IMR	IMR 4831	.264"	3.030"	43.0	2507	39,100 CUP	46.3	2700	45,400 CUP
140 GR. SPR SP	Hodgdon	H4350	.264"	3.030"	39.5	2418	38,600 CUP	44.0	2617	45,700 CUP
140 GR. SPR SP	Hodgdon	H414	.264"	3.030"	37.5	2393	40,000 CUP	41.5	2565	45,600 CUP
140 GR. SPR SP	IMR	IMR 4350	.264"	3.030"	41.0	2486	39,300 CUP	45.0	2677	46,000 CUP
140 GR. SPR SP	Winchester	760	.264"	3.030"	37.5	2393	40,000 CUP	41.5	2565	45,600 CUP
140 GR. SPR SP	IMR	IMR 4007 SSC	.264"	3.030"	39.0	2400	38,600 CUP	42.8	2591	45,300 CUP
140 GR. SPR SP	Hodgdon	H380	.264"	3.030"	36.5	2316	37,600 CUP	40.5	2520	45,100 CUP
140 GR. SPR SP	Hodgdon	Varget	.264"	3.030"	32.5	2312	37,500 CUP	36.0	2528	46,000 CUP
140 GR. SPR SP	IMR	IMR 4064	.264"	3.030"	35.0	2394	39,500 CUP	38.0	2563	45,800 CUP
140 GR. SPR SP	IMR	IMR 4895	.264"	3.030"	34.5	2364	38,900 CUP	37.8	2550	45,500 CUP
140 GR. SPR SP	Hodgdon	H4895	.264"	3.030"	32.5	2305	38,100 CUP	35.8	2493	45,700 CUP
142 GR. SIE HPBT	Hodgdon	H1000	.264"	3.050"	48.0	2453	37,500 CUP	51.5C	2601	41,600 CUP
142 GR. SIE HPBT	IMR	IMR 7828 SSC	264"	3.050"	44.0	2457	38,600 CUP	47.7	2671	45,500 CUP
142 GR. SIE HPBT	Winchester	Supreme 780	.264"	3.050"	44.6	2461	41,100 CUP	47.5	2640	45,900 CUP
142 GR. SIE HPBT	Hodgdon	H4831	.264"	3.050"	42.5	2383	37,300 CUP	47.0	2604	45,300 CUP
142 GR. SIE HPBT	Hodgdon	Hybrid 100V	.264"	3.050"	40.0	2420	39,300 CUP	44.0	2658	46,200 CUP
142 GR. SIE HPBT	IMR	IMR 4831	.264"	3.050"	43.0	2500	38,400 CUP	46.5	2704	44,900 CUP
142 GR. SIE HPBT	Hodgdon	H4350	.264"	3.050"	39.0	2427	38,400 CUP	43.7	2653	45,800 CUP
142 GR. SIE HPBT	Hodgdon	H414	.264"	3.050"	39.0	2399	37,200 CUP	43.0	2653	45,300 CUP
142 GR. SIE HPBT	IMR	IMR 4350	.264"	3.050"	41.0	2452	38,000 CUP	44.8	2667	45,100 CUP
142 GR. SIE HPBT	Winchester	760	.264"	3.050"	39.0	2399	37,200 CUP	43.0	2653	45,300 CUP
142 GR. SIE HPBT	IMR	IMR 4007 SSC	.264"	3.050"	39.0	2441	38,400 CUP	42.8	2638	45,900 CUP
142 GR. SIE HPBT	Hodgdon	H380	.264"	3.050"	35.0	2239	35,600 CUP	38.5	2437	45,300 CUP
142 GR. SIE HPBT	Hodgdon	Varget	.264"	3.050"	34.0	2334	38,100 CUP	38.0	2559	45,700 CUP
142 GR. SIE HPBT	IMR	IMR 4064	.264"	3.050"	35.0	2430	40,300 CUP	38.0	2582	45,600 CUP
142 GR. SIE HPBT	IMR	IMR 4895	.264"	3.050"	35.0	2416	40,000 CUP	38.3	2574	45,700 CUP
142 GR. SIE HPBT	Hodgdon	H4895	.264"	3.050"	32.5	2311	37,800 CUP	35.8	2511	45,800 CUP
160 GR. HDY RN	Hodgdon	H1000	.264"	3.000"	45.0	2265	35,000 CUP	50.0C	2517	45,300 CUP
160 GR. HDY RN	IMR	IMR 7828 SSC	.264"	3.300"	43.0	2335	40,100 CUP	47.0	2512	45,600 CUP
160 GR. HDY RN	Winchester	Supreme 780	.264"	3.000"	44.2	2333	39,800 CUP	47.0	2455	44,600 CUP
160 GR. HDY RN	Hodgdon	H4831	.264"	3.000"	44.0	2327	36,600 CUP	48.0C	2524	46,000 CUP
160 GR. HDY RN	Hodgdon	Hybrid 100V	.264"	3.000"	40.0	2317	39,300 CUP	43.5	2490	45,600 CUP
160 GR. HDY RN	IMR	IMR 4831	.264"	3.300"	42.0	2362	38,900 CUP	45.5	2503	45,100 CUP
160 GR. HDY RN	Hodgdon	H4350	.264"	3.000"	40.0	2317	38,800 CUP	43.0	2445	44,900 CUP
160 GR. HDY RN	Hodgdon	H414	.264"	3.000"	38.5	2262	38,400 CUP	41.0	2383	44,700 CUP
160 GR. HDY RN	IMR	IMR 4350	.264"	3.300"	40.0	2320	39,800 CUP	43.8	2513	45,900 CUP

Bullet Weight	Manufacturer	Powder	Bullet Diam.	C.O.L.	Grs.	Vel. (ft/s)	Pressure	Grs.	Vel. (ft/s)	Pressure
160 GR. HDY RN	Winchester	760	.264"	3.000"	38.5	2262	38,400 CUP	41.0	2383	44,700 CUP
160 GR. HDY RN	IMR	IMR 4007 SSC	.264"	3.300"	38.0	2284	40,000 CUP	41.5	2438	45,600 CUP
160 GR. HDY RN	Hodgdon	Varget	.264"	3.000"	32.5	2173	38,200 CUP	36.0	2354	45,600 CUP
160 GR. HDY RN	IMR	IMR 4064	.264"	3.300"	34.0	2243	39,500 CUP	36.5	2360	44,700 CUP
160 GR. HDY RN	IMR	IMR 4895	.264"	3.300"	33.0	2189	37,700 CUP	36.0	2346	44,600 CUP

Cartridge:6.5mm-06
Load Type:Rifle

Bullet Weight (Gr.)	Manufacturer	Powder	Bullet Diam.	C.O.L.	Starting Loads			Maximum Loads		
					Grs.	Vel. (ft/s)	Pressure	Grs.	Vel. (ft/s)	Pressure
85 GR. SIE HP	IMR	IMR 7828 SSC	.264"	3.140"	54.0	3114	47,400 PSI	60.5	3455	61,900 PSI
85 GR. SIE HP	Hodgdon	Hybrid 100V	.264"	3.140"	52.0	3372	50,200 PSI	56.5	3582	59,400 PSI
85 GR. SIE HP	IMR	IMR 4831	.264"	3.140"	51.0	3145	45,900 PSI	57.0	3526	62,400 PSI
85 GR. SIE HP	Hodgdon	H4350	.264"	3.140"	53.0	3336	52,300 PSI	57.5	3574	62,300 PSI
85 GR. SIE HP	Hodgdon	H414	.264"	3.140"	50.0	3276	48,500 PSI	55.0	3558	60,600 PSI
85 GR. SIE HP	IMR	IMR 4350	.264"	3.140"	50.0	3176	48,000 PSI	56.0	3542	63,800 PSI
85 GR. SIE HP	IMR	IMR 4007 SSC	264"	3.140"	48.0	3223	52,500 PSI	53.0	3484	62,600 PSI
85 GR. SIE HP	Hodgdon	H380	.264"	3.140"	50.0	3333	53,700 PSI	55.0	3552	63,000 PSI
85 GR. SIE HP	Hodgdon	Varget	.264"	3.140"	48.0	3453	58,400 PSI	52.0	3588	62,500 PSI
85 GR. SIE HP	IMR	IMR 4064	.264"	3.140"	45.0	3334	56,100 PSI	49.0	3515	63,900 PSI
85 GR. SIE HP	Hodgdon	H4895	.264"	3.140"	43.0	3245	49,900 PSI	46.5	3442	60,600 PSI
95 GR. HDY V-MAX	IMR	IMR 7828 SSC	.264"	3.200"	53.0	3056	50,100 PSI	59.0	3368	63,500 PSI
95 GR. HDY V-MAX	Hodgdon	Hybrid 100V	.264"	3.200"	52.0	3319	52,500 PSI	56.5C	3540	63,100 PSI
95 GR. HDY V-MAX	IMR	IMR 4831	.264"	3.200"	50.0	3094	48,800 PSI	56.0	3442	63,600 PSI
95 GR. HDY V-MAX	Hodgdon	H4350	.264"	3.200"	50.0	3204	52,100 PSI	54.5	3436	63,300 PSI
95 GR. HDY V-MAX	Hodgdon	H414	.264"	3.200"	49.0	3226	52,700 PSI	52.5	3418	61,900 PSI
95 GR. HDY V-MAX	IMR	IMR 4350	.264"	3.200"	49.0	3116	50,200 PSI	54.0	3410	63,300 PSI
95 GR. HDY V-MAX	IMR	IMR 4007 SSC	.264"	3.200"	46.0	3076	51,100 PSI	51.0	3348	63,200 PSI
95 GR. HDY V-MAX	Hodgdon	H380	.264"	3.200"	47.0	3182	55,400 PSI	50.5	3347	62,900 PSI
95 GR. HDY V-MAX	Hodgdon	Varget	.264"	3.200"	44.0	3167	51,600 PSI	49.0	3414	63,100 PSI
95 GR. HDY V-MAX	IMR	IMR 4064	.264"	3.200"	42.0	3090	52,000 PSI	47.0	3342	63,800 PSI
95 GR. HDY V-MAX	Hodgdon	H4895	.264"	3.200"	43.0	3209	55,400 PSI	46.0	3359	63,000 PSI
100 GR. NOS BT	IMR	IMR 7828 SSC	.264"	3.200"	51.0	2960	50,300 PSI	56.7	3257	62,800 PSI
100 GR. NOS BT	Hodgdon	H4831	.264"	3.200"	53.0	3085	53,200 PSI	57.7	3304	63,400 PSI
100 GR. NOS BT	Hodgdon	Hybrid 100V	.264"	3.200"	51.5	3225	53,400 PSI	56.0C	3427	62,300 PSI
100 GR. NOS BT	IMR	IMR 4831	.264"	3.200"	49.0	3068	51,400 PSI	54.0	3338	63,400 PSI
100 GR. NOS BT	Hodgdon	H4350	.264"	3.200"	49.0	3119	53,800 PSI	53.0	3315	63,300 PSI
100 GR. NOS BT	Hodgdon	H414	.264"	3.200"	46.0	3057	52,400 PSI	50.0	3260	62,200 PSI
100 GR. NOS BT	IMR	IMR 4350	.264"	3.200"	47.0	3000	49,700 PSI	52.5	3293	62,400 PSI
100 GR. NOS BT	IMR	IMR 4007 SSC	.264"	3.200"	45.0	3029	54,100 PSI	49.5	3235	62,700 PSI
100 GR. NOS BT	Hodgdon	H380	.264"	3.200"	44.0	2963	51,300 PSI	47.8	3172	62,500 PSI

100 GR. NOS BT	Hodgdon	Varget	.264"	3.200"	43.0	3070	53,000 PSI	47.0	3268	63,300 PSI
100 GR. NOS BT	IMR	IMR 4064	.264"	3.200"	41.0	2962	51,000 PSI	45.4	3198	62,100 PSI
100 GR. NOS BT	Hodgdon	H4895	.264"	3.200"	42.0	3083	56,400 PSI	44.0	3205	62,900 PSI
107 GR. SIE HPBT	Hodgdon	H1000	.264"	3.300"	56.0	2945	49,300 PSI	60.0C	3141	58,700 PSI
107 GR. SIE HPBT	IMR	IMR 7828 SSC	.264"	3.300"	50.0	2909	50,800 PSI	55.3	3172	62,400 PSI
107 GR. SIE HPBT	Winchester	Supreme 780	.264"	3.300"	53.8	3104	55,300 PSI	57.2	3252	62,600 PSI
107 GR. SIE HPBT	Hodgdon	H4831	.264"	3.300"	51.0	2985	51,800 PSI	55.5	3200	62,500 PSI
107 GR. SIE HPBT	Hodgdon	Hybrid 100V	.264"	3.300"	49.0	3136	52,700 PSI	53.0	3309	60,600 PSI
107 GR. SIE HPBT	IMR	IMR 4831	.264"	3.300"	48.0	2985	51,200 PSI	53.0	3246	62,900 PSI
107 GR. SIE HPBT	Hodgdon	H4350	.264"	3.300"	47.0	3022	52,600 PSI	51.5	3234	62,700 PSI
107 GR. SIE HPBT	Hodgdon	H414	.264"	3.300"	46.0	3031	53,400 PSI	49.5	3215	62,600 PSI
107 GR. SIE HPBT	IMR	IMR 4350	.264"	3.300"	46.0	2921	49,400 PSI	51.5	3209	63,000 PSI
107 GR. SIE HPBT	IMR	IMR 4007 SSC	.264"	3.300"	44.0	2900	50,700 PSI	48.5	3140	62,200 PSI
107 GR. SIE HPBT	Hodgdon	H380	.264"	3.300"	43.0	2891	50,000 PSI	47.5	3132	62,700 PSI
107 GR. SIE HPBT	Hodgdon	Varget	.264"	3.300"	42.0	2993	52,700 PSI	45.8	3185	62,700 PSI
120 GR. SFT SP	Hodgdon	H1000	.264"	3.150"	55.0	2837	53,900 PSI	58.5C	2986	62,700 PSI
120 GR. SFT SP	IMR	IMR 7828 SSC	.264"	3.150"	47.0	2676	50,800 PSI	52.0	2931	62,600 PSI
120 GR. SFT SP	Winchester	Supreme 780	.264"	3.150"	49.8	2836	52,900 PSI	53.0	2993	61,600 PSI
120 GR. SFT SP	Hodgdon	H4831	.264"	3.150"	48.0	2765	51,400 PSI	52.5	2970	62,300 PSI
120 GR. SFT SP	Hodgdon	Hybrid 100V	.264"	3.150"	46.0	2822	48,300 PSI	50.0	3035	60,300 PSI
120 GR. SFT SP	IMR	IMR 4831	.264"	3.150"	44.0	2716	51,500 PSI	48.7	2941	62,600 PSI
120 GR. SFT SP	Hodgdon	H4350	.264"	3.150"	45.0	2823	54,300 PSI	49.0	2996	63,300 PSI
120 GR. SFT SP	Hodgdon	H414	.264"	3.150"	42.0	2706	49,700 PSI	46.0	2925	62,800 PSI
120 GR. SFT SP	IMR	IMR 4350	.264"	3.150"	42.5	2683	51,400 PSI	47.2	2913	62,900 PSI
120 GR. SFT SP	IMR	IMR 4007 SSC	.264"	3.150"	40.0	2665	52,600 PSI	43.5	2833	60,500 PSI
120 GR. SFT SP	Hodgdon	H380	.264"	3.150"	39.0	2604	49,900 PSI	42.5	2812	62,000 PSI
129 GR. HDY SP	Hodgdon	H1000	.264"	3.245"	51.0	2683	53,800 PSI	55.5C	2885	62,700 PSI
129 GR. HDY SP	IMR	IMR 7828 SSC	.264"	3.245"	45.0	2603	50,800 PSI	50.5	2879	63,700 PSI
129 GR. HDY SP	Winchester	Supreme 780	.264"	3.245"	48.9	2739	53,900 PSI	52.0	2888	61,800 PSI
129 GR. HDY SP	Hodgdon	H4831	.264"	3.245"	47.0	2721	54,100 PSI	51.0	2889	62,900 PSI
129 GR. HDY SP	Hodgdon	Hybrid 100V	.264"	3.245"	45.0	2742	50,600 PSI	49.0	2925	60,400 PSI
129 GR. HDY SP	IMR	IMR 4831	.264"	3.245"	42.0	2611	51,000 PSI	47.0	2857	62,700 PSI
129 GR. HDY SP	Hodgdon	H4350	.264"	3.245"	43.0	2676	51,400 PSI	47.0	2876	62,500 PSI
129 GR. HDY SP	IMR	IMR 4350	.264"	3.245"	41.0	2609	52,400 PSI	45.9	2834	62,900 PSI
130 GR. NOS AB	Hodgdon	H1000	.264"	3.265"	47.7	2670	51,400 PSI	53.0	2880	61,600 PSI
130 GR. NOS AB	IMR	IMR 7828 SSC	.264"	3.265"	47.0	2637	49,300 PSI	52.2	2904	61,700 PSI
130 GR. NOS AB	Winchester	Supreme 780	.264"	3.265"	48.2	2672	46,700 PSI	53.5	2939	60,300 PSI
130 GR. NOS AB	Hodgdon	H4831	.264"	3.265"	44.0	2638	54,700 PSI	48.8	2824	62,300 PSI
130 GR. NOS AB	Hodgdon	Hybrid 100V	.264"	3.265"	45.0	2752	55,800 PSI	47.3	2867	62,300 PSI

Bullet Weight (Gr.)	Manufacturer	Powder	Bullet Diam.	C.O.L.	Grs.	Vel. (ft/s)	Pressure	Grs.	Vel. (ft/s)	Pressure
130 GR. NOS AB	IMR	IMR 4831	.264"	3.265"	43.5	2609	50,800 PSI	48.3	2845	61,900 PSI
130 GR. NOS AB	Hodgdon	H4350	.264"	3.265"	42.1	2615	51,300 PSI	46.7	2821	61,500 PSI
130 GR. NOS AB	IMR	IMR 4350	.264"	3.265"	43.4	2607	49,700 PSI	48.2	2867	62,300 PSI
140 GR. SPR GS-SP	Hodgdon	H1000	.264"	3.200"	49.0	2570	52,900 PSI	53.5C	2761	62,600 PSI
140 GR. SPR GS-SP	IMR	IMR 7828 SSC	.264"	3.200"	45.0	2482	48,600 PSI	50.5	2766	62,000 PSI
140 GR. SPR GS-SP	Winchester	Supreme 780	.264"	3.200"	48.6	2669	54,600 PSI	51.7	2801	61,300 PSI
140 GR. SPR GS-SP	Hodgdon	H4831	.264"	3.200"	45.0	2542	52,300 PSI	49.5	2731	62,300 PSI
140 GR. SPR GS-SP	Hodgdon	Hybrid 100V	.264'	3.200"	45.0	2635	48,900 PSI	49.0	2848	61,600 PSI
140 GR. SPR GS-SP	IMR	IMR 4831	.264"	3.200"	43.0	2532	49,500 PSI	47.8	2772	62,300 PSI
140 GR. SPR GS-SP	Hodgdon	H4350	.264"	3.200"	42.0	2558	52,400 PSI	45.5	2737	62,700 PSI
140 GR. SPR GS-SP	IMR	IMR 4350	.264"	3.200"	42.0	2521	51,000 PSI	46.8	2742	62,300 PSI
142 GR. SIE HPBT	Hodgdon	H1000	.264"	3.300"	49.0	2555	49,800 PSI	55.0C	2816	63,300 PSI
142 GR. SIE HPBT	IMR	IMR 7828 SSC	.264"	3.300"	45.0	2530	51,100 PSI	50.0	2761	62,800 PSI
142 GR. SIE HPBT	Winchester	Supreme 780	.264"	3.300"	48.4	2666	52,900 PSI	51.5	2816	61,400 PSI
142 GR. SIE HPBT	Hodgdon	H4831	.264"	3.300"	45.0	2559	50,000 PSI	50.3	2795	62,900 PSI
142 GR. SIE HPBT	Hodgdon	Hybrid 100V	.264"	3.300"	45.0	2678	50,500 PSI	49.5	2889	63,200 PSI
142 GR. SIE HPBT	IMR	IMR 4831	.264"	3.300"	41.0	2449	49,300 PSI	46.2	2702	63,000 PSI
142 GR. SIE HPBT	Hodgdon	H4350	.264"	3.300"	42.0	2572	51,300 PSI	46.0	2768	62,900 PSI
160 GR. HDY RN	Hodgdon	H1000	.264"	3.300"	51.0	2492	53,600 PSI	55.0	2650	62,400 PSI
160 GR. HDY RN	IMR	IMR 7828 SSC	.264"	3.300"	45.0	2351	51,200 PSI	49.5	2558	62,400 PSI
160 GR. HDY RN	Winchester	Supreme 780	.264"	3.300"	48.2	2505	52,900 PSI	51.3	2648	61,100 PSI
160 GR. HDY RN	Hodgdon	H4831	.264"	3.300"	46.0	2461	52,700 PSI	50.0	2625	62,600 PSI
160 GR. HDY RN	Hodgdon	Hybrid 100V	.264"	3.300"	45.0	2507	49,600 PSI	49.5	2702	62,700 PSI
160 GR. HDY RN	IMR	IMR 4831	.264"	3.300"	42.0	2347	50,500 PSI	46.3	2546	62,000 PSI

Cartridge:6.5-284
Load Type:Rifle

Bullet Weight (Gr.)	Manufacturer	Powder	Bullet Diam.	C.O.L.	Starting Loads Grs.	Vel. (ft/s)	Pressure	Maximum Loads Grs.	Vel. (ft/s)	Pressure
85 GR. SIE HP	IMR	IMR 7828 SSC	.264"	2.750"	54.0	3089		60.5C*	3542	
85 GR. SIE HP	IMR	IMR 4831	.264"	2.750"	51.0	3144		57.0	3602	
85 GR. SIE HP	Hodgdon	H4350	.264"	2.750"	53.0	3260		57.5	3531	
85 GR. SIE HP	Hodgdon	H414	.264"	2.750"	50.0	3158		55.0	3504	
85 GR. SIE HP	IMR	IMR 4350	.264"	2.750"	50.0	3123		56.0	3585	
85 GR. SIE HP	IMR	IMR 4007 SSC	.264"	2.750"	48.0	3173		53.0	3463	
85 GR. SIE HP	Hodgdon	H380	.264"	2.750"	50.0	3254		55.0	3527	
85 GR. SIE HP	Hodgdon	Varget	.264"	2.750"	48.0	3378		52.0	3587	
85 GR. SIE HP	IMR	IMR 4064	.264"	2.750"	45.0	3314		49.0	3535	
85 GR. SIE HP	Hodgdon	H4895	.264"	2.750"	43.0	3210		46.5	3417	
95 GR. HDY V-MAX	IMR	IMR 7828 SSC	.264"	2.820"	53.0	2977		59.0	3370	
95 GR. HDY V-MAX	Hodgdon	Hybrid 100V	.264"	2.820"	52.0	3294		56.5	3505	

95 GR. HDY V-MAX	IMR	IMR 4831	.264"	2.820"	50.0	3051	56.0	3486
95 GR. HDY V-MAX	Hodgdon	H4350	.264"	2.820"	50.0	3088	54.5	3349
95 GR. HDY V-MAX	Hodgdon	H414	.264"	2.820"	49.0	3122	52.5	3346
95 GR. HDY V-MAX	IMR	IMR 4350	.264"	2.820"	49.0	3059	54.0	3418
95 GR. HDY V-MAX	IMR	IMR 4007 SSC	.264"	2.820"	46.0	3019	51.0	3325
95 GR. HDY V-MAX	Hodgdon	H380	.264"	2.820"	47.0	3066	50.5	3291
95 GR. HDY V-MAX	Hodgdon	Varget	.264"	2.820"	44.0	3165	49.0	3380
95 GR. HDY V-MAX	IMR	IMR 4064	.264"	2.820"	42.0	3096	47.0	3341
95 GR. HDY V-MAX	Hodgdon	H4895	.264"	2.820"	43.0	3195	46.0	3318
100 GR. NOS BT	IMR	IMR 7828 SSC	.264"	2.800"	51.0	2860	56.7	3201
100 GR. NOS BT	Hodgdon	H4831	.264"	2.800"	53.0	2969	57.7	3211
100 GR. NOS BT	Hodgdon	Hybrid 100V	.264"	2.800"	51.5	3211	56.0C	3435
100 GR. NOS BT	IMR	IMR 4831	.264"	2.800"	49.0	2950	54.0	3318
100 GR. NOS BT	Hodgdon	H4350	.264"	2.800"	49.0	3003	53.0	3242
100 GR. NOS BT	Hodgdon	H414	.264"	2.800"	46.0	2893	50.0	3115
100 GR. NOS BT	IMR	IMR 4350	.264"	2.800"	47.0	2936	52.5	3291
100 GR. NOS BT	IMR	IMR 4007 SSC	.264"	2.800"	45.0	2895	49.5	3158
100 GR. NOS BT	Hodgdon	H380	.264"	2.800"	44.0	2814	47.8	3039
100 GR. NOS BT	Hodgdon	Varget	.264"	2.800"	43.0	3083	47.0	3227
100 GR. NOS BT	IMR	IMR 4064	.264"	2.800"	41.0	3003	45.4	3221
100 GR. NOS BT	Hodgdon	H4895	.264"	2.800"	42.0	3058	44.0	3143
107 GR. SIE HPBT	Hodgdon	H1000	.264"	2.920"	56.0	2808	60.0C	2985
107 GR. SIE HPBT	IMR	IMR 7828 SSC	.264"	2.920"	50.0	2779	55.3	3105
107 GR. SIE HPBT	Winchester	Supreme 780	.264"	2.920"	53.8	3066	57.2	3245
107 GR. SIE HPBT	Hodgdon	H4831	.264"	2.920"	51.0	2842	55.5	3084
107 GR. SIE HPBT	Hodgdon	Hybrid 100V	.264"	2.920"	49.0	3167	53.0	3358
107 GR. SIE HPBT	IMR	IMR 4831	.264"	2.920"	48.0	2888	53.0	3222
107 GR. SIE HPBT	Hodgdon	H4350	.264"	2.920"	47.0	2898	51.5	3118
107 GR. SIE HPBT	Hodgdon	H414	.264"	2.920"	46.0	2883	49.5	3110
107 GR. SIE HPBT	IMR	IMR 4350	.264"	2.920"	46.0	2845	51.5	3191
107 GR. SIE HPBT	IMR	IMR 4007 SSC	.264"	2.920"	44.0	2836	48.5	3094
107 GR. SIE HPBT	Hodgdon	H380	.264"	2.920"	43.0	2735	47.5	3020
107 GR. SIE HPBT	Hodgdon	Varget	.264"	2.920"	42.0	2970	45.8	3125
107 GR. SIE HPBT	IMR	IMR 4064	.264"	2.920"	40.0	2916	43.5	3105
120 GR. SFT SP	Hodgdon	H1000	.264"	2.780"	55.0	2743	58.5C	2901
120 GR. SFT SP	IMR	IMR 7828 SSC	.264"	2.780"	47.0	2636	52.0	2899
120 GR. SFT SP	Winchester	Supreme 780	.264"	2.780"	49.8	2728	53.0	2943
120 GR. SFT SP	Hodgdon	H4831	.264"	2.780"	48.0	2651	52.5	2871
120 GR. SFT SP	Hodgdon	Hybrid 100V	.264"	2.780"	46.0	2739	50.0	2979

120 GR. SFT SP	IMR	IMR 4831	.264"	2.780"	44.0	2671	48.7	2920
120 GR. SFT SP	Hodgdon	H4350	.264"	2.780"	45.0	2744	49.0	2897
120 GR. SFT SP	Hodgdon	H414	.264"	2.780"	42.0	2577	46.0	2797
120 GR. SFT SP	IMR	IMR 4350	.264"	2.780"	42.5	2624	47.2	2878
120 GR. SFT SP	IMR	IMR 4007 SSC	.264"	2.780"	40.0	2569	43.5	2750
120 GR. SFT SP	Hodgdon	H380	.264"	2.780"	39.0	2463	42.5	2626
129 GR. HDY SP	Hodgdon	H1000	.264"	2.935"	51.0	2638	55.5C	2820
129 GR. HDY SP	IMR	IMR 7828 SSC	.264"	2.935"	45.0	2536	50.5	2832
129 GR. HDY SP	Winchester	Supreme 780	.264"	2.935"	48.9	2688	52.0	2835
129 GR. HDY SP	Hodgdon	H4831	.264"	2.935"	47.0	2670	51.0	2859
129 GR. HDY SP	Hodgdon	Hybrid 100V	.264"	2.935"	45.0	2731	49.0	2910
129 GR. HDY SP	IMR	IMR 4831	.264"	2.935"	42.0	2559	47.0	2832
129 GR. HDY SP	Hodgdon	H4350	.264"	2.935"	43.0	2670	47.0	2863
129 GR. HDY SP	IMR	IMR 4350	.264"	2.935"	41.0	2574	45.9	2821
130 GR. NOS AB	Hodgdon	H1000	.264"	2.950"	47.7	2570	53.0	2812
130 GR. NOS AB	IMR	IMR 7828 SSC	.264"	2.950"	47.0	2589	52.2	2872
130 GR. NOS AB	Winchester	Supreme 780	.264"	2.950"	48.2	2672	53.5	2969
130 GR. NOS AB	Hodgdon	H4831	.264"	2.950"	44.0	2541	48.8	2779
130 GR. NOS AB	Hodgdon	Hybrid 100V	.264"	2.950"	45.0	2746	47.3	2884
130 GR. NOS AB	IMR	IMR 4831	.264"	2.950"	43.5	2628	48.3	2898
130 GR. NOS AB	Hodgdon	H4350	.264"	2.950"	42.1	2645	46.7	2874
130 GR. NOS AB	IMR	IMR 4350	.264"	2.950"	43.4	2667	48.2	2935
140 GR. SPR GS-SP	Hodgdon	H1000	.264"	2.910"	49.0	2503	53.5C	2694
140 GR. SPR GS-SP	IMR	IMR 7828 SSC	.264"	2.910"	45.0	2462	50.5	2718
140 GR. SPR GS-SP	Winchester	Supreme 780	.264"	2.910"	48.6	2606	51.7	2797
140 GR. SPR GS-SP	Hodgdon	H4831	.264"	2.910"	45.0	2520	49.5	2722
140 GR. SPR GS-SP	Hodgdon	Hybrid 100V	.264"	2.910"	45.0	2696	49.0	2895
140 GR. SPR GS-SP	IMR	IMR 4831	.264"	2.910"	43.0	2536	47.8	2762
140 GR. SPR GS-SP	Hodgdon	H4350	.264"	2.910"	42.0	2548	45.5	2720
140 GR. SPR GS-SP	IMR	IMR 4350	.264"	2.910"	42.0	2539	46.8	2753
142 GR. SIE HPBT	Hodgdon	H1000	.264"	2.900"	49.0	2436	55.0C	2700
142 GR. SIE HPBT	IMR	IMR 7828 SSC	.264"	2.900"	45.0	2484	50.0	2719
142 GR. SIE HPBT	Winchester	Supreme 780	.264"	2.900"	48.4	2580	51.5	2753
142 GR. SIE HPBT	Hodgdon	H4831	.264"	2.900"	45.0	2479	50.3	2714
142 GR. SIE HPBT	Hodgdon	Hybrid 100V	.264"	2.900"	45.0	2666	49.5	2901
142 GR. SIE HPBT	IMR	IMR 4831	.264"	2.900"	41.0	2460	46.2	2692
142 GR. SIE HPBT	Hodgdon	H4350	.264"	2.900"	42.0	2583	46.0	2735
160 GR. HDY RN	Hodgdon	H1000	.264"	2.980"	51.0	2454	55.0	2622
160 GR. HDY RN	IMR	IMR 7828 SSC	.264"	2.980"	45.0	2376	49.5	2557
160 GR. HDY RN	Winchester	Supreme 780	.264"	2.980"	48.2	2489	51.3	2657

	Manufacturer	Powder	Bullet Diam.	C.O.L.	Grs.	Vel. (ft/s)		Grs.	Vel. (ft/s)	
160 GR. HDY RN	Hodgdon	H4831	.264"	2.980"	46.0	2433		50.0	2582	
160 GR. HDY RN	Hodgdon	Hybrid 100V	.264"	2.980"	45.0	2548		49.5	2755	
160 GR. HDY RN	IMR	IMR 4831	.264"	2.980"	42.0	2367		46.3	2567	

Cartridge: 6.5mm Remington Magnum **Load Type:** Rifle					Starting Loads			Maximum Loads		
Bullet Weight (Gr.)	Manufacturer	Powder	Bullet Diam.	C.O.L.	Grs.	Vel. (ft/s)	Pressure	Grs.	Vel. (ft/s)	Pressure
85 GR. SIE HP	Hodgdon	H4831	.264"	2.800"	56.0	3201	34,800 CUP	61.0	3570	46,700 CUP
85 GR. SIE HP	Hodgdon	H4350	.264"	2.800"	54.0	3220	43,000 CUP	57.0	3564	50,700 CUP
85 GR. SIE HP	Hodgdon	H414	.264"	2.800"	55.0	3451	42,600 CUP	60.0	3755	51,700 CUP
85 GR. SIE HP	Hodgdon	H380	.264"	2.800"	52.5	3339	41,400 CUP	57.0	3681	50,500 CUP
85 GR. SIE HP	Hodgdon	H4895	.264"	2.800"	47.0	3322	39,000 CUP	51.0	3613	49,600 CUP
100 GR. HDY SP	Hodgdon	H4831	.264"	2.940"	55.0	3071	37,200 CUP	60.0	3416	48,100 CUP
100 GR. HDY SP	IMR	IMR 4831	.264"	2.940"				58.0	3335	52,300 CUP
100 GR. HDY SP	Hodgdon	H4350	.264"	2.940"	51.0	3071	44,000 CUP	55.0	3327	51,700 CUP
100 GR. HDY SP	Hodgdon	H414	.264"	2.940"	51.5	3168	44,400 CUP	56.0	3466	52,600 CUP
100 GR. HDY SP	IMR	IMR 4350	.264"	2.940"				56.0	3300	52,500 CUP
100 GR. HDY SP	Hodgdon	H380	.264"	2.940"	50.0	3111	41,400 CUP	54.0	3459	52,800 CUP
100 GR. HDY SP	IMR	IMR 4320	.264"	2.940"				49.0	3210	51,700 CUP
100 GR. HDY SP	IMR	IMR 4064	.264"	2.940"				51.0	3330	52,900 CUP
100 GR. HDY SP	IMR	IMR 4895	.264"	2.940"				48.0	3255	52,600 CUP
100 GR. HDY SP	Hodgdon	H4895	.264"	2.940"	46.0	3186	42,600 CUP	50.0	3475	52,200 CUP
100 GR. HDY SP	IMR	SR 4759	.264"	2.940"				32.5	2740	52,900 CUP
120 GR. SPR SP	Hodgdon	H4831	.264"	2.790"	54.0	2985	42,600 CUP	59.0	3286	51,000 CUP
120 GR. SPR SP	IMR	IMR 4831	.264"	2.790"				54.0	3060	52,900 CUP
120 GR. SPR SP	Hodgdon	H4350	.264"	2.790"	49.0	2780	43,700 CUP	52.0	3080	51,200 CUP
120 GR. SPR SP	Hodgdon	H414	.264"	2.790"	47.0	2792	40,800 CUP	51.0	3099	51,700 CUP
120 GR. SPR SP	IMR	IMR 4350	.264"	2.790"				51.0	3000	52,200 CUP
120 GR. SPR SP	Hodgdon	H380	.264"	2.790"	45.0	2843	45,900 CUP	49.0	3059	50,900 CUP
120 GR. SPR SP	IMR	IMR 4320	.264"	2.790"				46.5	2965	52,500 CUP
120 GR. SPR SP	IMR	IMR 4064	.264"	2.790"				46.5	2975	52,000 CUP
120 GR. SPR SP	IMR	IMR 4895	.264"	2.790"				45.0	2960	53,000 CUP
120 GR. SPR SP	Hodgdon	H4895	.264"	2.790"	42.5	2872	42,000 CUP	46.0	3081	50,900 CUP
120 GR. SPR SP	IMR	SR 4759	.264"	2.790"				32.0	2575	52,900 CUP
129 GR. HDY SP	Hodgdon	H4831	.264"	3.040"	53.5	2854	40,200 CUP	58.0	3155	50,800 CUP
129 GR. HDY SP	Hodgdon	H4350	.264"	3.040"	47.0	2709	41,400 CUP	51.0	2994	50,700 CUP
129 GR. HDY SP	Hodgdon	H414	.264"	3.040"	46.0	2673	39,000 CUP	50.0	2954	51,300 CUP
129 GR. HDY SP	Hodgdon	H380	.264"	3.040"	43.5	2636	45,500 CUP	47.0	2950	51,300 CUP
129 GR. HDY SP	Hodgdon	H4895	.264"	3.040"	40.5	2709	39,600 CUP	44.0	2936	49,900 CUP

140 GR. NOS PART	Hodgdon	H4831	.264"	2.790"	49.5	2708	44,400 CUP	54.0	2943	51,400 CUP
140 GR. NOS PART	Hodgdon	H4350	.264"	2.790"	45.0	2514	42,000 CUP	49.0	2780	51,200 CUP
140 GR. NOS PART	Hodgdon	H414	.264"	2.790"	42.0	2502	40,200 CUP	46.0	2743	51,100 CUP
140 GR. NOS PART	Hodgdon	H380	.264"	2.790"	40.5	2475	40,800 CUP	44.0	2666	51,200 CUP
140 GR. NOS PART	Hodgdon	H4895	.264"	2.790"	38.5	2569	43,800 CUP	42.0	2752	49,200 CUP

Cartridge: 264 Winchester Magnum Load Type: Rifle					Starting Loads			Maximum Loads		
Bullet Weight (Gr.)	Manufacturer	Powder	Bullet Diam.	C.O.L.	Grs.	Vel. (ft/s)	Pressure	Grs.	Vel. (ft/s)	Pressure
85 GR. SIE HP	Hodgdon	H1000	.264"	3.100"	74.0	3270	37,600 CUP	78.0	3480	48,000 CUP
85 GR. SIE HP	Winchester	Supreme 780	.264"	3.100"	70.5	3605	56,300 PSI	75.0	3811	57,600 PSI
85 GR. SIE HP	Hodgdon	H4831	.264"	3.100"	67.0	3304	39,000 CUP	73.0	3812	54,100 CUP
85 GR. SIE HP	Hodgdon	Hybrid 100V	.264"	3.100"	65.0	3646	53,300 PSI	69.0	3863	62,500 PSI
85 GR. SIE HP	Hodgdon	H4350	.264"	3.100"	59.0	3396	43,600 CUP	61.0	3669	52,400 CUP
85 GR. SIE HP	Hodgdon	H414	.264"	3.100"	57.0	3310	40,200 CUP	62.0	3633	52,200 CUP
85 GR. SIE HP	Hodgdon	H380	.264"	3.100"	54.5	3295	44,100 CUP	58.0	3612	50,600 CUP
85 GR. SIE HP	Hodgdon	H4895	.264"	3.100"	50.5	3264	44,600 CUP	55.0	3625	52,900 CUP
100 GR. HDY SP	Hodgdon	H1000	.264"	3.230"	72.0	3164	42,500 CUP	77.0	3428	47,500 CUP
100 GR. HDY SP	Winchester	Supreme 780	.264"	3.230"	64.4	3343	51,100 PSI	68.5	3525	60,800 PSI
100 GR. HDY SP	Hodgdon	H4831	.264"	3.230"	65.5	3239	45,900 CUP	71.0	3680	53,900 CUP
100 GR. HDY SP	Hodgdon	Hybrid 100V	.264"	3.230"	59.5	3427	54,500 PSI	63.3	3548	61,100 PSI
100 GR. HDY SP	Hodgdon	H4350	.264"	3.230"	56.0	3194	44,100 CUP	59.0	3570	52,600 CUP
100 GR. HDY SP	Hodgdon	H414	.264"	3.230"	54.0	3202	45,000 CUP	59.0	3389	52,600 CUP
100 GR. HDY SP	Hodgdon	H380	.264"	3.230"	51.5	3039	44,100 CUP	56.0	3374	51,000 CUP
100 GR. HDY SP	Hodgdon	H4895	.264"	3.230"	49.0	2970	44,100 CUP	53.0	3405	54,200 CUP
120 GR. SPR SP	Hodgdon	Retumbo	.264"	3.250"	66.3	3091	50,400 PSI	70.5	3299	61,700 PSI
120 GR. SPR SP	Hodgdon	H1000	.264"	3.250"	65.5	3050	49,100 PSI	69.7	3267	62,100 PSI
120 GR. SPR SP	Winchester	Supreme 780	.264"	3.250"	61.1	3079	54,300 PSI	65.0	3235	61,700 PSI
120 GR. SPR SP	Hodgdon	H4831	.264"	3.250"	60.6	3027	49,100 PSI	64.5	3254	62,000 PSI
120 GR. SPR SP	Hodgdon	Hybrid 100V	.264"	3.250"	56.4	3080	53,500 PSI	60.0	3232	60,600 PSI
120 GR. SPR SP	IMR	IMR 4831	.264"	3.250"	58.0	3105	56,400 PSI	60.7	3212	61,600 PSI
120 GR. SPR SP	Hodgdon	H4350	.264"	3.250"	54.5	3045	53,000 PSI	58.0	3185	61.200 PSI
120 GR. SPR SP	IMR	IMR 4350	.264"	3.250"	56.5	3075	54,700 PSI	60.0	3226	61,900 PSI
129 GR. HDY SP	Hodgdon	Retumbo	.264"	3.250"	63.5	3005	51,900 PSI	67.5	3171	61,500 PSI
129 GR. HDY SP	Hodgdon	H1000	.264"	3.250"	60.2	2942	54,500 PSI	64.0	3064	60,700 PSI
129 GR. HDY SP	IMR	IMR 7828 SSC	.264"	3.250"	58.7	2925	52,100 PSI	62.4	3109	60,800 PSI
129 GR. HDY SP	Winchester	Supreme 780	.264"	3.250"	63.0	3140	55,000 PSI	67.0	3269	59,500 PSI
129 GR. HDY SP	Hodgdon	H4831	.264"	3.250"	58.3	2927	52,500 PSI	62.0	3101	61,400 PSI
129 GR. HDY SP	Hodgdon	Hybrid 100V	.264"	3.250"	53.0	2922	51,000 PSI	56.7	3045	59,700 PSI
129 GR. HDY SP	IMR	IMR 4831	.264"	3.250"	55.5	2931	52,300 PSI	59.0	3090	60,700 PSI

Bullet Weight (Gr.)	Manufacturer	Powder	Bullet Diam.	C.O.L.	Grs.	Vel. (ft/s)	Pressure	Grs.	Vel. (ft/s)	Pressure
129 GR. HDY SP	Hodgdon	H4350	.264"	3.250"	53.6	2929	53,500 PSI	57.0	3067	60,900 PSI
129 GR. HDY SP	IMR	IMR 4350	.264"	3.250"	54.4	2913	51,800 PSI	57.8	3081	61,000 PSI
140 GR. NOS PART	Hodgdon	Retumbo	.264"	3.260"	59.7	2904	57,000 PSI	63.5	3026	63,000 PSI
140 GR. NOS PART	Hodgdon	H1000	.264"	3.260"	55.0	2810	58,600 PSI	58.5	2900	61,800 PSI
140 GR. NOS PART	IMR	IMR 7828 SSC	.264"	3.260"	54.5	2769	54,000 PSI	58.0	2927	60,700 PSI
140 GR. NOS PART	Winchester	Supreme 780	.264"	3.260"	55.5	2788	54,500 PSI	59.0	2927	60,900 PSI
140 GR. NOS PART	Hodgdon	H4831	.264"	3.260"	51.7	2753	55,600 PSI	55.0	2853	59,400 PSi
140 GR. NOS PART	Hodgdon	Hybrid 100V	.264"	3.260"	51.2	2787	55,700 PSI	54.5	2912	61,800 PSI
140 GR. NOS PART	IMR	IMR 4831	.264"	3.260"	51.9	2755	54,700 PSI	55.2	2907	61,700 PSI
140 GR. NOS PART	Hodgdon	H4350	.264"	3.260"	48.9	2713	55,300 PSI	52.0	2829	60,800 PSI
140 GR. NOS PART	IMR	IMR 4350	.264"	3.260"	51.2	2752	53,500 PSI	54.5	2903	61.400 PSI
160 GR. HDY RN	Hodgdon	Retumbo	.264"	3.350"	60.2	2703	54,800 PSI	64.0	2846	61.000 PSI
160 GR. HDY RN	Hodgdon	H1000	.264"	3.350"	61.5	2730	55,500 PSI	65.4	2857	62,200 PSI
160 GR. HDY RN	IMR	IMR 7828 SSC	.264"	3.350"	58.6	2764	56,500 PSI	62.3	2861	61,200 PSI
160 GR. HDY RN	Winchester	Supreme 780	.264"	3.350"	58.8	2733	56,800 PSI	62.5	2848	62,500 PSI
160 GR. HDY RN	Hodgdon	H4831	.264"	3.350"	58.1	2725	54,800 PSI	61.8	2847	61,500 PSI
160 GR. HDY RN	Hodgdon	Hybrid 100V	.264"	3.350"	52.7	2690	57,400 PSI	56.0	2784	61,500 PSI
160 GR. HDY RN	IMR	IMR 4831	.264"	3.350"	55.5	2680	54,000 PSI	59.0	2810	60,900 PSI
160 GR. HDY RN	Hodgdon	H4350	.264"	3.350"	53.4	2675	56,600 PSI	56.8	2784	61,500 PSI
160 GR. HDY RN	IMR	IMR 4350	.264"	3.350"	54.5	2696	53,800 PSI	58.0	2834	62,100 PSI

Cartridge: 6.8 mm Remington SPC Load Type: Rifle					Starting Loads			Maximum Loads		
Bullet Weight (Gr.)	Manufacturer	Powder	Bullet Diam.	C.O.L.	Grs.	Vel. (ft/s)	Pressure	Grs.	Vel. (ft/s)	Pressure
85 GR. BAR TAC-X FB	Hodgdon	Benchmark	.277"	2.230"	27.9	2595	31,800 PSI	31.0C	2848	40,000 PSI
85 GR. BAR TAC-X FB	Hodgdon	H322	.277"	2.230"	28.0	2637	33,600 PSI	31.0C	2949	45,600 PSI
85 GR. BAR TAC-X FB	IMR	IMR 4198	.277"	2.230"	24.8	2770	39,200 PSI	27.5C	3025	51,800 PSI
85 GR. BAR TAC-X FB	Hodgdon	H4198	.277"	2.230"	25.2	2829	40,400 PSI	27.4	3030	50,900 PSI
85 GR. BAR TAC-X FB	Hodgdon	Lil'Gun	.277"	2.230"	19.7	2836	49,500 PSI	21.0	2927	52,400 PSI
90 GR. SPR HP	Hodgdon	Benchmark	.277"	2.255"	29.0	2705	38,900 PSI	31.0C	2853	45,900 PSI
90 GR. SPR HP	Hodgdon	H322	.277"	2.255"	29.0	2765	42,100 PSI	31.0C	2929	49,500 PSI
90 GR. SPR HP	IMR	IMR 4198	.277"	2.255"	24.0	2669	37,800 PSI	27.3C	2970	52,000 PSI
90 GR. SPR HP	Hodgdon	H4198	.277"	2.255"	26.0	2810	47,700 PSI	28.6C	3012	54,000 PSI
90 GR. SPR HP	IMR	IMR 4227	.277"	2.255"	21.0	2590	44,200 PSI	23.9	2795	51,000 PSI
90 GR. SPR HP	Hodgdon	Lil'Gun	.277"	2.255"	20.0	2784	46,500 PSI	22.7	2923	53,500 PSI
100 GR. BAR X	Hodgdon	Benchmark	.277"	2.260"	28.0	2588	42,000 PSI	30.0C	2755	51,200 PSI
100 GR. BAR X	Hodgdon	H322	.277"	2.260"	27.0	2502	37,700 PSI	30.0C	2803	52,300 PSI
100 GR. BAR X	IMR	IMR 4198	.227"	2.260"	23.0	2525	40,500 PSI	25.3C	2755	52,400 PSI
100 GR. BAR X	Hodgdon	H4198	.277"	2.260"	24.0	2542	40,500 PSI	26.5	2791	52,900 PSI

Bullet Weight (Gr.)	Manufacturer	Powder	Bullet Diam.	C.O.L.	Grs.	Vel. (ft/s)	Pressure	Grs.	Vel. (ft/s)	Pressure
100 GR. BAR X	IMR	IMR 4227	.277"	2.260"	20.0	2431	46,800 PSI	22.9	2643	53,000 PSI
110 GR. HDY V-MAX	Hodgdon	H335	.277"	2.260"	27.0	2487	41,700 PSI	29.5	2694	53,600 PSI
110 GR. HDY V-MAX	Hodgdon	H4895	.277"	2.260"	27.0	2335	33,900 PSI	29.0C	2550	42,400 PSI
110 GR. HDY V-MAX	IMR	IMR 8208 XBR	.277"	2.260"	28.0	2496	38,500 PSI	30.0C	2690	48,600 PSI
110 GR. HDY V-MAX	IMR	IMR 3031	.277"	2.260"	26.0	2450	42,100 PSI	28.0C	2605	48,700 PSI
110 GR. HDY V-MAX	Hodgdon	Benchmark	.277"	2.260"	27.0	2518	44,000 PSI	28.8C	2665	52,000 PSI
110 GR. HDY V-MAX	Hodgdon	H322	.277"	2.260"	27.0	2571	47,600 PSI	29.0C	2697	53,600 PSI
110 GR. HDY V-MAX	IMR	IMR 4198	.277"	2.260"	22.0	2422	41,700 PSI	24.2C	2619	51,300 PSI
110 GR. HDY V-MAX	Hodgdon	H4198	.277"	2.260"	23.0	2431	40,600 PSI	25.3C	2651	52,000 PSI
115 GR. SIE HPBT	Hodgdon	H335	.277"	2.260"	27.0	2415	40,800 PSI	29.0	2569	48,500 PSI
115 GR. SIE HPBT	Hodgdon	H4895	.277"	2.260"	27.0	2302	34,300 PSI	29.0C	2495	42,800 PSI
115 GR. SIE HPBT	IMR	IMR 8208 XBR	.277"	2.260"	28.0	2483	41,800 PSI	30.0C	2647	51,400 PSI
115 GR. SIE HPBT	Hodgdon	Benchmark	.277"	2.260"	26.0	2400	42,400 PSI	28.5C	2581	51,800 PSI
115 GR. SIE HPBT	Hodgdon	H322	.277"	2.260"	26.0	2421	43,500 PSI	28.2C	2608	53,300 PSI
115 GR. SIE HPBT	IMR	IMR 4198	.277"	2.260"	22.0	2386	43,100 PSI	23.5C	2515	50,000 PSI
115 GR. SIE HPBT	Hodgdon	H4198	.277"	2.260"	22.0	2413	47,800 PSI	24.0C	2534	52,300 PSI

Cartridge: 270 Winchester Load Type: Rifle					Starting Loads			Maximum Loads		
Bullet Weight (Gr.)	Manufacturer	Powder	Bullet Diam.	C.O.L.	Grs.	Vel. (ft/s)	Pressure	Grs.	Vel. (ft/s)	Pressure
90 GR. SIE HP	Hodgdon	H4350	.277"	3.200"	58.0	3401	43,700 CUP	62.0C	3603	49,800 CUP
90 GR. SIE HP	Hodgdon	H414	.277"	3.200"	55.0	3361	42,200 CUP	59.0	3585	50,700 CUP
90 GR. SIE HP	IMR	IMR 4350	.277"	3.200"	56.0	3251	41,900 CUP	60.3	3516	50,800 CUP
90 GR. SIE HP	Winchester	760	.277"	3.200"	55.0	3361	42,200 CUP	59.0	3585	50,700 CUP
90 GR. SIE HP	IMR	IMR 4007 SSC	.277"	3.200"	53.0	3293	54,600 PSI	57.5	3508	63,300 PSI
90 GR. SIE HP	Hodgdon	H380	.277"	3.200"	53.0	3344	45,600 CUP	56.3	3462	50,900 CUP
90 GR. SIE HP	Hodgdon	CFE 223	.277"	3.200"	52.6	3408	54,200 PSI	56.0	3579	62,200 PSI
90 GR. SIE HP	Hodgdon	Varget	.277"	3.200"	51.0	3409	46,000 CUP	55.0	3596	51,400 CUP
90 GR. SIE HP	IMR	IMR 4320	.277"	3.200"	48.5	3220	46,800 CUP	52.7	3425	51,500 CUP
90 GR. SIE HP	IMR	IMR 4064	.277"	3.200"	49.6	3295	44,400 CUP	54.0	3538	50,500 CUP
90 GR. SIE HP	Hodgdon	BL-C(2)	.277"	3.200"	49.0	3328	45,400 CUP	52.0	3475	50,100 CUP
90 GR. SIE HP	IMR	IMR 4895	.277"	3.200"	49.0	3268	43,700 CUP	53.3	3507	50,300 CUP
90 GR. SIE HP	Hodgdon	H335	.277"	3.200"	46.0	3313	46,100 CUP	49.0	3459	50,900 CUP
90 GR. SIE HP	Hodgdon	H4895	.277"	3.200"	50.0	3482	48,100 CUP	53.0	3595	50,400 CUP
90 GR. SIE HP	IMR	IMR 8208 XBR	.277"	3.200"	45.6	3380	57,900 PSI	48.0	3476	61,900 PSI
90 GR. SIE HP	IMR	IMR 3031	.277"	3.200"	46.0	3299	45,000 CUP	50.2	3487	50,600 CUP
100 GR. SPR SP	Hodgdon	H4350	.277"	3.145"	56.0	3258	44,000 CUP	59.4	3401	50,200 CUP
100 GR. SPR SP	Hodgdon	H414	.277"	3.145"	53.0	3262	46,000 CUP	56.0	3383	50,700 CUP
100 GR. SPR SP	IMR	IMR 4350	.277"	3.145"	54.0	3072	40,100 CUP	59.5	3383	50,200 CUP
100 GR. SPR SP	Winchester	760	.277"	3.145"	53.0	3262	46,000 CUP	56.0	3383	50,700 CUP

100 GR. SPR SP	IMR	IMR 4007 SSC	.277"	3.145"	52.0	3108	52,800 PSI	57.0	3357	64,000 PSI
100 GR. SPR SP	Hodgdon	H380	.277"	3.145"	50.0	3160	46,200 CUP	53.7	3274	50,300 CUP
100 GR. SPR SP	Hodgdon	CFE 223	.277"	3.145"	53.0	3356	54,900 PSI	55.8	3514	62,900 PSI
100 GR. SPR SP	Hodgdon	Varget	.277"	3.145"	48.0	3232	44,400 CUP	52.0	3397	50,200 CUP
100 GR. SPR SP	IMR	IMR 4320	.277"	3.145"	46.2	3066	47,100 CUP	50.0	3220	51,000 CUP
100 GR. SPR SP	IMR	IMR 4064	.277"	3.145"	48.0	3116	40,800 CUP	52.7	3380	50,100 CUP
100 GR. SPR SP	Hodgdon	BL-C(2)	.277"	3.145"	45.0	3144	47,300 CUP	47.3	3243	50,500 CUP
100 GR. SPR SP	IMR	IMR 4895	.277"	3.145"	48.0	3180	47,900 CUP	52.2	3367	51,500 CUP
100 GR. SPR SP	Hodgdon	H335	.277"	3.145"	41.0	3058	45,300 CUP	43.5	3185	50,200 CUP
100 GR. SPR SP	Hodgdon	H4895	.277"	3.145"	47.0	3298	47,000 CUP	50.0	3401	50,200 CUP
100 GR. SPR SP	IMR	IMR 3031	.277"	3.145"	45.5	3139	44,700 CUP	49.0	3339	50,400 CUP
110 GR. HDY HP	Hodgdon	H4831	.277"	3.250"	58.0	3057	42,600 CUP	62.0C	3214	48,200 CUP
110 GR. HDY HP	Hodgdon	Hybrid 100V	.277"	3.250"	53.0	3072	49,500 PSI	57.0C	3240	56,100 PSI
110 GR. HDY HP	Hodgdon	H4350	.277"	3.250"	54.0	3164	46,900 CUP	57.0	3267	50,100 CUP
110 GR. HDY HP	Hodgdon	H414	.277"	3.250"	51.0	3058	43,500 CUP	55.0	3241	50,700 CUP
110 GR. HDY HP	IMR	IMR 4350	.277"	3.250"	52.5	2997	43,000 CUP	57.8	3308	50,900 CUP
110 GR. HDY HP	Winchester	760	.277"	3.250"	51.0	3058	43,500 CUP	55.0	3241	50,700 CUP
110 GR. HDY HP	IMR	IMR 4007 SSC	.277"	3.250"	50.0	2931	50,900 PSI	54.5	3185	63,200 PSI
110 GR. HDY HP	Hodgdon	H380	.277"	3.250"	48.0	2976	46,000 CUP	52.0	3124	50,500 CUP
110 GR. HDY HP	Hodgdon	CFE 223	.277"	3.250"	50.4	3142	53,500 PSI	53.6	3304	61,700 PSI
110 GR. HDY HP	Hodgdon	Varget	.277"	3.250"	43.0	3072	44,100 CUP	48.7	3248	50,800 CUP
110 GR. HDY HP	IMR	IMR 4320	.277"	3.250"	45.5	3031	48,700 CUP	49.7	3152	50,100 CUP
110 GR. HDY HP	IMR	IMR 4064	.277"	3.250"	46.0	3036	45,800 CUP	50.7	3223	50,300 CUP
110 GR. HDY HP	Hodgdon	BL-C(2)	.277"	3.250"	45.0	2971	47,300 CUP	47.5	3089	50,200 CUP
110 GR. HDY HP	IMR	IMR 4895	.277"	3.250"	46.0	3045	43,400 CUP	50.2	3269	51,100 CUP
110 GR. HDY HP	Hodgdon	H335	.277"	3.250"	42.0	2958	46,800 CUP	45.0	3081	50,800 CUP
110 GR. HDY HP	Hodgdon	H4895	.277"	3.250"	45.0	3113	46,700 CUP	47.5	3215	50,800 CUP
110 GR. HDY HP	IMR	IMR 8208 XBR	.277"	3.250"	44.1	3064	56,400 PSI	46.4	3146	59,500 PSI
110 GR. HDY HP	IMR	IMR 3031	.277"	3.250"	44.0	3024	46,000 CUP	47.2	3159	49,500 CUP
120 GR. BAR XFB	Hodgdon	H4831	.277"	3.270"	58.0	2918	45,800 CUP	62.0C	3112	51,200 CUP
120 GR. BAR XFB	IMR	IMR 4831	.277"	3.270"	51.5	2793	40,600 CUP	56.7	3112	50,100 CUP
120 GR. BAR XFB	Hodgdon	H4350	.277"	3.270"	51.0	2886	44,700 CUP	55.0	3069	51,200 CUP
120 GR. BAR XFB	Hodgdon	H414	.277"	3.270"	49.0	2814	43,100 CUP	53.0	3017	51,100 CUP
120 GR. BAR XFB	IMR	IMR 4350	.277"	3.270"	50.5	2836	42,300 CUP	56.0	3131	50,500 CUP
120 GR. BAR XFB	Winchester	760	.277"	3.270"	49.0	2814	43,100 CUP	53.0	3017	51,100 CUP
120 GR. BAR XFB	Hodgdon	H380	.277"	3.270"	46.0	2698	43,200 CUP	49.5	2980	51,000 CUP
120 GR. BAR XFB	Hodgdon	Varget	.277"	3.270"	44.0	2858	46,300 CUP	47.0	3010	51,000 CUP
120 GR. BAR XFB	IMR	IMR 4320	.277"	3.270"	44.2	2782	43,800 CUP	48.5	3029	51,000 CUP
120 GR. BAR XFB	IMR	IMR 4064	.277"	3.270"	45.5	2937	45,600 CUP	49.2	3096	51,000 CUP

120 GR. BAR XFB	IMR	IMR 4895	.277"	3.270"	44.0	2883	44,900 CUP	48.2	3057	50,600 CUP
120 GR. BAR XFB	Hodgdon	H4895	.277"	3.270"	42.0	2799	45,000 CUP	45.0	2950	50,400 CUP
120 GR. BAR XFB	IMR	IMR 3031	.277"	3.270"	42.5	2864	48,000 CUP	45.0	2976	49,300 CUP
130 GR. BAR TSX	Hodgdon	H1000	.277"	3.230"	57.0	2716	42,100 PSI	60.0C	2846	48,200 PSI
130 GR. BAR TSX	IMR	IMR 7828 SSC	.277"	3.230"	55.0	2815	48,700 PSI	60.2C	3083	62,400 PSI
130 GR. BAR TSX	Winchester	Supreme 780	.277"	3.240"	55.5	2882	52,900 PSI	59.0	3028	60,000 PSI
130 GR. BAR TSX	Hodgdon	H4831	.277"	3.230"	54.0	2747	45,500 PSI	60.0C	3025	59,000 PSI
130 GR. BAR TSX	Hodgdon	Hybrid 100V	.277"	3.240"	52.2	2994	55,700 PSI	55.5	3144	63,100 PSI
130 GR. BAR TSX	IMR	IMR 4831	.277"	3.230"	52.0	2822	46,600 PSI	57.0C	3113	61,700 PSI
130 GR. BAR TSX	Hodgdon	H4350	.277"	3.230"	51.0	2905	52,500 PSI	55.5	3111	63,500 PSI
130 GR. BAR TSX	Hodgdon	H414	.277"	3.230"	48.0	2840	50,400 PSI	52.5	3059	62,100 PSI
130 GR. BAR TSX	IMR	IMR 4350	.277"	3.230"	50.0	2824	48,900 PSI	55.0C	3104	62,800 PSI
130 GR. BAR TSX	Winchester	760	.277"	3.230"	48.0	2840	50,400 PSI	52.5	3059	62,100 PSI
130 GR. BAR TSX	IMR	IMR 4007 SSC	.277"	3.230"	48.0	2810	49,300 PSI	52.0	3037	61,500 PSI
130 GR. BAR TSX	Hodgdon	H380	.277"	3.230"	47.0	2810	51,900 PSI	50.8	2989	61,600 PSI
130 GR. BAR TSX	Hodgdon	Varget	.277"	3.230"	44.0	2849	54,800 PSI	48.0	3013	63,200 PSI
130 GR. BAR TSX	IMR	IMR 4064	.277"	3.230"	42.0	2760	49,400 PSI	47.3	3013	62,900 PSI
130 GR. BAR TSX	IMR	IMR 8208 XBR	.277"	3.230"	42.3	2798	55,700 PSI	45.0	2922	62,400 PSI
130 GR. HDY SP	Hodgdon	H1000	.277"	3.180"	61.0	2900	42,900 CUP	64.0C	3025	48,100 CUP
130 GR. HDY SP	IMR	IMR 7828	.277"	3.180"	56.0	2862	43,800 CUP	60.2	3085	50,300 CUP
130 GR. HDY SP	Winchester	Supreme 780	.277"	3.180"	56.4	2906	55,000 PSI	60.0	3043	61,900 PSI
130 GR. HDY SP	Hodgdon	H4831	.277"	3.180"	56.0	2843	44,400 CUP	60.0C	3019	51,000 CUP
130 GR. HDY SP	Hodgdon	Hybrid 100V	.277"	3.180"	51.0	2845	51,000 PSI	56.0C	3066	61,800 PSI
130 GR. HDY SP	IMR	IMR 4831	.277"	3.180"	51.0	2759	42,900 CUP	55.8	3002	50,300 CUP
130 GR. HDY SP	Hodgdon	H4350	.277"	3.180"	51.0	2865	45,200 CUP	54.3	3012	50,500 CUP
130 GR. HDY SP	Hodgdon	H414	.277"	3.180"	50.0	2843	44,700 CUP	53.5	3003	50,800 CUP
130 GR. HDY SP	IMR	IMR 4350	.277"	3.180"	50.2	2806	43,700 CUP	55.0	3028	49,900 CUP
130 GR. HDY SP	Winchester	760	.277"	3.180"	50.0	2843	44,700 CUP	53.5	3003	50,800 CUP
130 GR. HDY SP	IMR	IMR 4007 SSC	.277	3.180"	47.0	2718	51,400 PSI	51.5	2949	63,700 PSI
130 GR. HDY SP	Hodgdon	H380	.277"	3.180"	47.0	2744	46,400 CUP	49.8	2884	51,000 CUP
130 GR. HDY SP	Hodgdon	Varget	.277"	3.180"	43.0	2797	43,900 CUP	46.0	2931	49,600 CUP
130 GR. HDY SP	IMR	IMR 4320	.277"	3.180"	45.6	2850	48,600 CUP	47.0	2916	50,200 CUP
130 GR. HDY SP	IMR	IMR 4064	.277"	3.180"	43.0	2745	43,100 CUP	47.5	2932	50,000 CUP
130 GR. HDY SP	IMR	IMR 4895	.277"	3.180"	43.0	2768	43,000 CUP	46.9	2957	50,600 CUP
130 GR. HDY SP	Hodgdon	H4895	.277"	3.180"	42.0	2782	44,700 CUP	45.0	2922	51,000 CUP
130 GR. HDY SP	IMR	IMR 8208 XBR	.277"	3.180"	42.8	2840	57,600 PSI	45.0	2934	62,800 PSI
130 GR. HDY SP	IMR	Trail Boss	.277"	3.180"	14.0	1318	22,800 PSI	19.7	1537	27,100 PSI
135 GR. SIE BT	Hodgdon	H1000	.277"	3.340"	61.0	2915	43,100 CUP	63.0C	3011	47,600 CUP
135 GR. SIE BT	IMR	IMR 7828	.277"	3.340"	54.0	2696	40,200 CUP	60.0	3046	50,000 CUP
135 GR. SIE BT	Winchester	Supreme 780	.277"	3.340"	55.9	2827	53,000 PSI	59.5	2994	62,000 PSI

Bullet	Manufacturer	Powder	Diameter	OAL	Start Load	Start Velocity	Start Pressure	Max Load	Max Velocity	Max Pressure
135 GR. SIE BT	Hodgdon	H4831	.277"	3.340"	55.0	2812	43,600 CUP	59.5C	3010	51,000 CUP
135 GR. SIE BT	Hodgdon	Hybrid 100V	.277"	3.340"	50.0	2830	49,900 PSI	55.0	3056	61,600 PSI
135 GR. SIE BT	IMR	IMR 4831	.277"	3.340"	51.0	2774	40,400 CUP	55.8	2990	51,100 CUP
135 GR. SIE BT	Hodgdon	H4350	.277"	3.340"	50.0	2834	44,400 CUP	53.5	2994	50,700 CUP
135 GR. SIE BT	Hodgdon	H414	.277"	3.340"	47.0	2785	45,400 CUP	50.0	2910	50,500 CUP
135 GR. SIE BT	IMR	IMR 4350	.277"	3.340"	50.0	2772	41,700 CUP	54.9	3007	50,000 CUP
135 GR. SIE BT	Winchester	760	.277"	3.340"	47.0	2785	45,400 CUP	50.0	2910	50,500 CUP
135 GR. SIE BT	IMR	IMR 4007 SSC	.277"	3.340"	46.0	2674	49,600 PSI	51.2	2925	62,800 PSI
135 GR. SIE BT	Hodgdon	H380	.277"	3.340"	44.0	2667	43,600 CUP	47.0	2803	50,500 CUP
135 GR. SIE BT	Hodgdon	Varget	.277"	3.340"	41.0	2701	40,800 CUP	45.0	2902	50,200 CUP
135 GR. SIE BT	IMR	IMR 4320	.277"	3.340"	43.0	2718	43,500 CUP	46.5	2887	50,300 CUP
135 GR. SIE BT	IMR	IMR 4064	.277"	3.340"	43.5	2775	44,500 CUP	47.3	2934	50,700 CUP
135 GR. SIE BT	IMR	IMR 4895	.277"	3.340"	43.0	2755	43,400 CUP	47.7	2972	51,100 CUP
135 GR. SIE BT	Hodgdon	H4895	.277"	3.340"	41.0	2735	44,300 CUP	44.0	2879	50,600 CUP
140 GR. SFT SP	Hodgdon	H1000	.277"	3.280"	59.0	2771	41,800 CUP	63.0C	2979	50,800 CUP
140 GR. SFT SP	IMR	IMR 7828	.277"	3.280"	52.0	2628	40,500 CUP	57.2	2939	50,600 CUP
140 GR. SFT SP	Winchester	Supreme 780	.277"	3.280"	54.5	2758	51,500 PSI	58.0	2925	60,100 PSI
140 GR. SFT SP	Hodgdon	H4831	.277"	3.280"	54.0	2716	43,900 CUP	58.0C	2888	50,100 CUP
140 GR. SFT SP	Hodgdon	Hybrid 100V	.277"	3.280"	50.0	2787	53,600 PSI	54.2C	2964	62,300 PSI
140 GR. SFT SP	IMR	IMR 4831	.277"	3.280"	50.6	2738	44,400 CUP	54.0	2896	50,700 CUP
140 GR. SFT SP	Hodgdon	H4350	.277"	3.280"	49.0	2737	44,500 CUP	52.0	2870	50,400 CUP
140 GR. SFT SP	Hodgdon	H414	.277"	3.280"	46.0	2644	42,900 CUP	48.9	2788	49,800 CUP
140 GR. SFT SP	IMR	IMR 4350	.277"	3.280"	49.0	2712	43,800 CUP	53.2	2916	51,000 CUP
140 GR. SFT SP	Winchester	760	.277"	3.280"	46.0	2644	42,900 CUP	48.9	2788	49,800 CUP
140 GR. SFT SP	Hodgdon	Varget	.277"	3.280"	41.0	2623	44,300 CUP	43.7	2772	50,500 CUP
140 GR. SFT SP	IMR	IMR 4320	.277"	3.280"	41.5	2614	42,700 CUP	44.5	2775	50,000 CUP
140 GR. SFT SP	IMR	IMR 4064	.277"	3.280"	42.0	2608	43,300 CUP	46.1	2828	50,800 CUP
140 GR. SFT SP	IMR	IMR 4895	.277"	3.280"	42.0	2650	44,600 CUP	45.6	2828	50,100 CUP
140 GR. SFT SP	Hodgdon	H4895	.277"	3.280"	40.0	2627	45,300 CUP	42.6	2768	50,600 CUP
150 GR. HDY SP	Hodgdon	H1000	.277"	3.285"	55.0	2689	44,900 CUP	59.0C	2831	51,000 CUP
150 GR. HDY SP	IMR	IMR 7828	.277"	3.285"	51.2	2536	39,800 CUP	56.8	2850	50,400 CUP
150 GR. HDY SP	Winchester	Supreme 780	.277"	3.285"	53.4	2673	53,500 PSI	56.8	2774	61,200 PSI
150 GR. HDY SP	Hodgdon	H4831	.277"	3.285"	52.0	2651	46,300 CUP	55.7	2804	51,200 CUP
150 GR. HDY SP	Hodgdon	Hybrid 100V	.277"	3.285"	48.0	2650	53,600 PSI	52.0	2811	61,900 PSI
150 GR. HDY SP	IMR	IMR 4831	.277"	3.285"	46.3	2498	40,500 CUP	53.0	2815	50,900 CUP
150 GR. HDY SP	Hodgdon	H4350	.277"	3.285"	46.0	2575	43,400 CUP	49.0	2724	51,000 CUP
150 GR. HDY SP	Hodgdon	H414	.277"	3.285"	45.0	2569	45,000 CUP	48.0	2706	51,200 CUP
150 GR. HDY SP	IMR	IMR 4350	.277"	3.285"	48.0	2642	44,600 CUP	51.6	2809	50,900 CUP
150 GR. HDY SP	Winchester	760	.277"	3.285"	45.0	2569	45,000 CUP	48.0	2706	51,200 CUP

Bullet Weight	Manufacturer	Powder	Bullet Diam.	C.O.L.	Grs.	Vel. (ft/s)	Pressure	Grs.	Vel. (ft/s)	Pressure
150 GR. HDY SP	IMR	IMR 4064	.277"	3.285"	42.0	2584	44,000 CUP	45.0	2719	50,700 CUP
150 GR. HDY SP	IMR	IMR 4895	.277"	3.285"	41.5	2560	44,500 CUP	44.5	2704	50,600 CUP
160 GR. NOS PART	Hodgdon	H1000	.277"	3.340"	55.0	2614	44,200 CUP	59.0C	2765	50,900 CUP
160 GR. NOS PART	IMR	IMR 7828	.277"	3.340"	50.5	2450	38,900 CUP	56.0	2758	50,300 CUP
160 GR. NOS PART	Winchester	Supreme 780	.277"	3.340"	54.5	2704	56,000 PSI	58.0	2833	62,000 PSI
160 GR. NOS PART	Hodgdon	H4831	.277"	3.340"	50.0	2510	43,000 CUP	54.0	2673	50,500 CUP
160 GR. NOS PART	Hodgdon	Hybrid 100V	.277"	3.340"	48.0	2578	49,900 PSI	53.0C	2796	63,300 PSI
160 GR. NOS PART	IMR	IMR 4831	.277"	3.340"	48.5	2481	41,800 CUP	52.9	2680	50,300 CUP
160 GR. NOS PART	Hodgdon	H4350	.277"	3.340"	46.0	2501	43,600 CUP	49.0	2646	51,100 CUP
160 GR. NOS PART	IMR	IMR 4350	.277"	3.340"	46.5	2483	42,100 CUP	51.0	2706	50,500 CUP
160 GR. NOS PART	IMR	IMR 4320	.277"	3.340"	40.0	2453	44,500 CUP	42.8	2584	51,000 CUP
160 GR. NOS PART	IMR	IMR 4064	.277"	3.340"	40.0	2401	42,200 CUP	43.3	2580	50,400 CUP
160 GR. NOS PART	IMR	IMR 4895	.277"	3.340"	40.0	2334	44,100 CUP	43.2	2573	50,100 CUP
180 GR. BAR JRN	Hodgdon	H1000	.277"	3.300"	50.0	2404	45,100 CUP	54.0	2540	50,600 CUP
180 GR. BAR JRN	IMR	IMR 7828	.277"	3.300"	48.0	2307	40,900 CUP	52.8	2529	50,400 CUP
180 GR. BAR JRN	Hodgdon	H4831	.277"	3.300"	47.0	2358	46,000 CUP	50.5	2501	51,100 CUP

Cartridge: 270 Winchester Short Magnum
Load Type: Rifle

Bullet Weight (Gr.)	Manufacturer	Powder	Bullet Diam.	C.O.L.	Starting Loads			Maximum Loads		
					Grs.	Vel. (ft/s)	Pressure	Grs.	Vel. (ft/s)	Pressure
90 GR. SIE HP	Hodgdon	H4831	.277"	2.700"	69.0	3525	54,900 PSI	73.0C	3703	63,400 PSI
90 GR. SIE HP	Hodgdon	H4350	.277"	2.700"	64.0	3568	55,000 PSI	67.5	3733	62,800 PSI
90 GR. SIE HP	Hodgdon	H414	.277"	2.700"	64.0	3609	54,800 PSI	68.0	3789	63,400 PSI
90 GR. SIE HP	Winchester	760	.277"	2.700"	64.0	3609	54,800 PSI	68.0	3789	63,400 PSI
90 GR. SIE HP	IMR	IMR 4007 SSC	.277"	2.700"	60.0	3323	47,600 PSI	66.5	3708	63,700 PSI
90 GR. SIE HP	Hodgdon	H380	.277"	2.700"	62.0	3561	56,200 PSI	65.5	3711	62,900 PSI
90 GR. SIE HP	Hodgdon	Varget	.277"	2.700"	57.0	3610	57,600 PSI	60.5	3734	62,800 PSI
90 GR. SIE HP	Hodgdon	H4895	.277"	2.700"	53.0	3508	52,900 PSI	56.5	3690	62,500 PSI
100 GR. SPR HP	Hodgdon	H4831	.277"	2.700"	67.0	3352	52,900 PSI	71.0C	3542	62,700 PSI
100 GR. SPR HP	Hodgdon	Hybrid 100V	.277"	2.700"	61.0	3293	51,600 PSI	66.5	3543	61,700 PSI
100 GR. SPR HP	Hodgdon	H4350	.277"	2.700"	62.0	3458	55,000 PSI	65.5	3585	62,900 PSI
100 GR. SPR HP	Hodgdon	H414	.277"	2.700"	62.0	3451	54,600 PSI	65.0	3613	63,000 PSI
100 GR. SPR HP	Winchester	760	.277"	2.700"	62.0	3451	54,600 PSI	65.0	3613	63,000 PSI
100 GR. SPR HP	IMR	IMR 4007 SSC	.277"	2.700"	58.0	3185	47,300 PSI	64.5	3526	62,100 PSI
100 GR. SPR HP	Hodgdon	H380	.277"	2.700"	60.0	3361	54,300 PSI	63.5	3518	62,600 PSI
100 GR. SPR HP	Hodgdon	Varget	.277"	2.700"	55.0	3416	55,700 PSI	58.5	3573	63,300 PSI
100 GR. SPR HP	Hodgdon	H4895	.277"	2.700"	51.0	3338	53,200 PSI	54.5	3505	62,500 PSI
110 GR. HDY HP	Hodgdon	H1000	.277"	2.800"	71.0	3279	55,400 PSI	73.0C	3360	60,400 PSI
110 GR. HDY HP	Hodgdon	H4831	.277"	2.800"	64.0	3265	56,300 PSI	67.5	3404	63,000 PSI
110 GR. HDY HP	Hodgdon	Hybrid 100V	.277"	2.800"	59.0	3115	49,800 PSI	65.0C	3426	62,300 PSI

110 GR. HDY HP	Hodgdon	H4350	.277"	2.800"	59.0	3287	55,900 PSI	63.0	3436	63,200 PSI
110 GR. HDY HP	Hodgdon	H414	.277"	2.800"	59.0	3283	55,600 PSI	62.5	3435	62,800 PSI
110 GR. HDY HP	Winchester	760	.277"	2.800"	59.0	3283	55,600 PSI	62.5	3435	62,800 PSI
110 GR. HDY HP	IMR	IMR 4007 SSC	.277"	2.800"	57.0	3108	49,500 PSI	63.5	3416	63,200 PSI
110 GR. HDY HP	Hodgdon	H380	.277"	2.800"	55.0	3173	56,300 PSI	59.0	3327	62,900 PSI
110 GR. HDY HP	Hodgdon	Varget	.277"	2.800"	53.0	3276	57,000 PSI	56.0	3406	63,200 PSI
130 GR. BAR TSX	Hodgdon	H1000	.277"	2.800"	69.0	3066	55,100 PSI	73.0C	3196	61,100 PSI
130 GR. BAR TSX	IMR	IMR 7828	.277"	2.800"	63.0	2938	49,200 PSI	67.5C	3160	58,700 PSI
130 GR. BAR TSX	Winchester	Supreme 780	.277"	2.800"	61.1	2905	56,300 PSI	65.0	3037	61,900 PSI
130 GR. BAR TSX	Hodgdon	H4831	.277"	2.800"	63.0	3002	53,200 PSI	67.0C	3160	60,700 PSI
130 GR. BAR TSX	Hodgdon	Hybrid 100V	.277"	2.800"	55.0	2927	56,700 PSI	58.5	3074	62,800 PSI
130 GR. BAR TSX	IMR	IMR 4831	.277"	2.800"	60.0	2966	51,800 PSI	65.5C	3232	63,700 PSI
130 GR. BAR TSX	Hodgdon	H4350	.277"	2.800"	57.0	3041	55,700 PSI	61.5	3191	62,900 PSI
130 GR. BAR TSX	Hodgdon	H414	.277"	2.800"	56.0	2976	52,900 PSI	60.0	3178	62,900 PSI
130 GR. BAR TSX	IMR	IMR 4350	.277"	2.800"	57.0	2966	51,200 PSI	63.0	3222	62,900 PSI
130 GR. BAR TSX	IMR	IMR 4007 SSC	.277"	2.800"	55.0	2943	51,000 PSI	60.0	3170	62,000 PSI
130 GR. BAR TSX	Hodgdon	H380	.277"	2.800"	55.0	2996	56,900 PSI	59.0	3122	62,800 PSI
130 GR. BAR TSX	Hodgdon	Varget	.277"	2.800"	48.0	2900	51,600 PSI	52.5	3106	62,500 PSI
130 GR. BAR TSX	IMR	IMR 4064	.277"	2.800"	49.0	2952	53,900 PSI	53.5	3128	63,000 PSI
130 GR. BAR TSX	IMR	IMR 4895	.277"	2.800"	49.0	2940	53,100 PSI	53.8	3136	62,900 PSI
130 GR. HDY SP	Hodgdon	H1000	.277"	2.730"	71.0	3100	55,400 PSI	73.0C	3168	58,700 PSI
130 GR. HDY SP	IMR	IMR 7828	.277"	2.730"	63.0	3031	55,000 PSI	67.0	3201	63,000 PSI
130 GR. HDY SP	Winchester	Supreme 780	.277"	2.730"	64.9	3030	50,200 PSI	69.0	3273	62,800 PSI
130 GR. HDY SP	Hodgdon	H4831	.277"	2.730"	63.0	3085	56,300 PSI	67.0	3228	63,400 PSI
130 GR. HDY SP	Hodgdon	Hybrid 100V	.277"	2.730"	57.0	2992	52,400 PSI	63.0C	3259	64,600 PSI
130 GR. HDY SP	IMR	IMR 4831	.277"	2.730"	59.0	3022	54,800 PSI	63.5	3208	63,300 PSI
130 GR. HDY SP	Hodgdon	H4350	.277"	2.730"	57.0	3093	56,600 PSI	60.5	3226	63,500 PSI
130 GR. HDY SP	Hodgdon	H414	.277"	2.730"	57.0	3065	53,800 PSI	61.0	3235	62,700 PSI
130 GR. HDY SP	IMR	IMR 4350	.277"	2.730"	58.0	3022	53,200 PSI	62.5	3230	63,000 PSI
130 GR. HDY SP	Winchester	760	.277"	2.730"	57.0	3065	53,800 PSI	61.0	3235	62,700 PSI
130 GR. HDY SP	IMR	IMR 4007 SSC	.277"	2.730"	53.0	2897	51,400 PSI	59.5	3159	63,400 PSI
130 GR. HDY SP	Hodgdon	H380	.277"	2.730"	56.0	3032	56,100 PSI	59.5	3174	63,200 PSI
130 GR. HDY SP	Hodgdon	Varget	.277"	2.730"	51.0	3040	56,400 PSI	54.0	3169	63,200 PSI
130 GR. HDY SP	IMR	IMR 4064	.277"	2.730"	51.0	3005	56,400 PSI	54.3	3140	63,800 PSI
130 GR. HDY SP	IMR	IMR 4895	.277"	2.730"	50.0	2953	53,500 PSI	54.0	3120	62,500 PSI
130 GR. HDY SP	IMR	Trail Boss	.277"	2.730"	16.0	1516	38,100 PSI	22.5	1832	47,900 PSI
135 GR. SIE HPBT	Hodgdon	H1000	.277"	2.840"	69.0	3056	54,400 PSI	73.0C	3205	62,600 PSI
135 GR. SIE HPBT	IMR	IMR 7828	.277"	2.840"	62.0	2986	52,000 PSI	67.0C	3211	62,900 PSI
135 GR. SIE HPBT	Winchester	Supreme 780	.277"	2.840"	63.9	3012	52,800 PSI	68.0	3214	62,900 PSI

135 GR. SIE HPBT	Hodgdon	H4831	.277"	2.840"	62.0	3056	55,400 PSI	65.5	3192	62,900 PSI
135 GR. SIE HPBT	Hodgdon	Hybrid 100V	.277"	2.840"	54.0	2826	54,400 PSI	59.5	3055	63,900 PSI
135 GR. SIE HPBT	IMR	IMR 4831	.277"	2.840"	60.0	3032	54,700 PSI	64.0C	3198	62,700 PSI
135 GR. SIE HPBT	Hodgdon	H4350	.277"	2.840"	58.0	3093	57,000 PSI	61.5	3211	63,100 PSI
135 GR. SIE HPBT	Hodgdon	H414	.277"	2.840"	57.0	3041	54,000 PSI	61.0	3208	63,200 PSI
135 GR. SIE HPBT	IMR	IMR 4350	.277"	2.840"	58.0	3003	51,800 PSI	62.5	3210	61,600 PSI
135 GR. SIE HPBT	Winchester	760	.277"	2.840"	57.0	3041	54,000 PSI	61.0	3208	63,200 PSI
135 GR. SIE HPBT	IMR	IMR 4007 SSC	.277"	2.840"	54.0	2897	50,900 PSI	59.5	3123	62,400 PSI
135 GR. SIE HPBT	Hodgdon	H380	.277"	2.840"	55.0	2943	52,800 PSI	58.0	3116	63,000 PSI
135 GR. SIE HPBT	Hodgdon	Varget	.277"	2.840"	51.0	3000	54,800 PSI	54.0	3134	63,000 PSI
135 GR. SIE HPBT	IMR	IMR 4064	.277"	2.840"	50.0	2947	54,500 PSI	54.3	3108	62,800 PSI
135 GR. SIE HPBT	IMR	IMR 4895	.277"	2.840"	50.0	2933	53,600 PSI	54.0	3093	62,100 PSI
140 GR. SFT SP	Hodgdon	Retumbo	.277"	2.800"	68.0	3016	53,200 PSI	71.0C	3165	61,300 PSI
140 GR. SFT SP	Hodgdon	H1000	.277"	2.800"	66.0	2984	55,700 PSI	70.0C	3137	63,500 PSI
140 GR. SFT SP	IMR	IMR 7828	.277"	2.800"	61.0	2922	54,100 PSI	64.5	3081	61,900 PSI
140 GR. SFT SP	Winchester	Supreme 780	.277"	2.800"	63.5	3000	54,800 PSI	67.4	3163	63,000 PSI
140 GR. SFT SP	Hodgdon	H4831	.277"	2.800"	59.0	2974	57,000 PSI	62.5	3085	63,000 PSI
140 GR. SFT SP	Hodgdon	Hybrid 100V	.277"	2.800"	55.0	2862	52,900 PSI	60.0	3071	61,600 PSI
140 GR. SFT SP	IMR	IMR 4831	.277"	2.800"	57.0	2860	53,100 PSI	61.5	3059	62,600 PSI
140 GR. SFT SP	Hodgdon	H4350	.277"	2.800"	54.0	2928	54,500 PSI	58.0	3087	63,100 PSI
140 GR. SFT SP	Hodgdon	H414	.277"	2.800"	55.0	2932	53,700 PSI	58.0	3068	62,600 PSI
140 GR. SFT SP	IMR	IMR 4350	.277"	2.800"	56.0	2876	52,300 PSI	60.5	3081	62,200 PSI
140 GR. SFT SP	Winchester	760	.277"	2.800"	55.0	2932	53,700 PSI	58.0	3068	62,600 PSI
140 GR. SFT SP	IMR	IMR 4007 SSC	.277"	2.800"	52.0	2820	51,700 PSI	57.5	3043	63,000 PSI
140 GR. SFT SP	Hodgdon	H380	.277"	2.800"	53.0	2865	55,500 PSI	56.5	3005	62,700 PSI
150 GR. HDY SP	Hodgdon	Retumbo	.277"	2.740"	66.0	2908	53,300 PSI	70.0C	3071	63,000 PSI
150 GR. HDY SP	Hodgdon	H1000	.277"	2.740"	64.0	2864	54,600 PSI	67.5C	3001	62,800 PSI
150 GR. HDY SP	IMR	IMR 7828	.277"	2.740"	59.0	2785	55,400 PSI	63.1	2952	63,200 PSI
150 GR. HDY SP	Winchester	Supreme 780	.277"	2.850"	62.5	2883	44,400 PSI	66.6	3066	58,400 PSI
150 GR. HDY SP	Hodgdon	H4831	.277"	2.740"	56.0	2804	54,500 PSI	60.0	2962	63,100 PSI
150 GR. HDY SP	Hodgdon	Hybrid 100V	.277"	2.850"	54.0	2752	52,100 PSI	59.0	2954	61,800 PSI
150 GR. HDY SP	IMR	IMR 4831	.277"	2.740"	55.0	2739	54,400 PSI	59.3	2916	63,000 PSI
150 GR. HDY SP	Hodgdon	H4350	.277"	2.740"	53.0	2846	55,600 PSI	56.5	2978	63,000 PSI
150 GR. HDY SP	Hodgdon	H414	.277"	2.740"	54.0	2845	55,400 PSI	57.5	2991	63,200 PSI
150 GR. HDY SP	IMR	IMR 4350	.277"	2.740"	54.0	2754	52,900 PSI	58.5	2934	62,200 PSI
150 GR. HDY SP	Winchester	760	.277"	2.740"	54.0	2845	55,400 PSI	57.5	2991	63,200 PSI
150 GR. HDY SP	IMR	IMR 4007 SSC	.277"	2.740"	50.0	2665	51,500 PSI	56.0	2892	63,900 PSI
150 GR. HDY SP	Hodgdon	H380	.277"	2.740"	51.0	2749	56,700 PSI	54.5	2885	63,100 PSI
160 GR. NOS PART	Hodgdon	Retumbo	.277"	2.830"	65.0	2826	53,400 PSI	68.5	2989	62,600 PSI
160 GR. NOS PART	Hodgdon	H1000	.277"	2.830"	63.0	2802	57,400 PSI	66.5	2913	63,200 PSI

Bullet Weight (Gr.)	Manufacturer	Powder	Bullet Diam.	C.O.L.	Grs.	Vel. (ft/s)	Pressure	Grs.	Vel. (ft/s)	Pressure
160 GR. NOS PART	IMR	IMR 7828	.277"	2.830"	57.0	2663	52,700 PSI	61.5	2858	62,600 PSI
160 GR. NOS PART	Winchester	Supreme 780	.277"	2.830"	62.0	2801	49,100 PSI	66.0	2993	59,300 PSI
160 GR. NOS PART	Hodgdon	H4831	.277"	2.830"	57.0	2784	58,400 PSI	60.0	2877	63,300 PSI
160 GR. NOS PART	Hodgdon	Hybrid 100V	.277"	2.830"	51.0	2551	53,900 PSI	56.0	2747	62,500 PSI
160 GR. NOS PART	IMR	IMR 4831	.277"	2.830"	54.0	2650	53,000 PSI	58.2	2829	62,500 PSI
160 GR. NOS PART	Hodgdon	H4350	.277"	2.830"	52.0	2735	56,100 PSI	55.0	2834	62,600 PSI
160 GR. NOS PART	Hodgdon	H414	.277"	2.830"	52.0	2718	56,100 PSI	55.5	2844	63,100 PSI
160 GR. NOS PART	IMR	IMR 4350	.277"	2.830"	54.0	2692	53,900 PSI	57.5	2850	63,000 PSI
160 GR. NOS PART	Winchester	760	.277"	2.830"	52.0	2718	56,100 PSI	55.5	2844	63,100 PSI

Cartridge: 270 Weatherby Magnum
Load Type: Rifle

Bullet Weight (Gr.)	Manufacturer	Powder	Bullet Diam.	C.O.L.	Starting Loads Grs.	Vel. (ft/s)	Pressure	Maximum Loads Grs.	Vel. (ft/s)	Pressure
90 GR. SIE HP	Hodgdon	H1000	.277"	3.150"	78.0	3183		81.0	3269	
90 GR. SIE HP	Hodgdon	H4831	.277"	3.150"	72.0	3386		78.0	3631	
90 GR. SIE HP	Hodgdon	H4350	.277"	3.150"	66.0	3317		70.0	3631	
90 GR. SIE HP	Hodgdon	H414	.277"	3.150"	65.0	3304		68.0	3592	
90 GR. SIE HP	Hodgdon	H4895	.277"	3.150"	63.0	3388		67.0	3647	
100 GR. SPR SP	Hodgdon	H1000	.277"	3.250"	77.0	3062		81.0	3287	
100 GR. SPR SP	IMR	IMR 7828	.277"	3.250"				78.5C	3645	48,200 CUP
100 GR. SPR SP	Hodgdon	H4831	.277"	3.250"	74.0	3482		77.0	3666	
100 GR. SPR SP	Hodgdon	H4350	.277"	3.250"	65.0	3282		69.0	3509	
100 GR. SPR SP	Hodgdon	H414	.277"	3.250"	65.0	3231		68.0	3450	
100 GR. SPR SP	Hodgdon	H4895	.277"	3.250"	63.0	3377		66.0	3597	
110 GR. HDY HP	Hodgdon	H1000	.277"	3.290"	76.0	3045		81.0	3242	
110 GR. HDY HP	Hodgdon	H4831	.277"	3.290"	73.0	3397		76.0	3482	
110 GR. HDY HP	Hodgdon	H4350	.277"	3.290"	64.0	3214		68.0	3477	
110 GR. HDY HP	Hodgdon	H414	.277"	3.290"	63.0	3187		66.0	3334	
130 GR. SPR SP	Hodgdon	H1000	.277"	3.250"	76.0	2941		81.0	3259	
130 GR. SPR SP	IMR	IMR 7828	.277"	3.250"				76.0	3500	53,000 CUP
130 GR. SPR SP	Hodgdon	H4831	.277"	3.250"	67.0	3087		70.0	3205	
130 GR. SPR SP	Hodgdon	H4350	.277"	3.250"	62.0	3110		66.0	3262	
140 GR. HDY BTSP	Hodgdon	H1000	.277"	3.280"	75.0	2849		80.0	3145	
140 GR. HDY BTSP	IMR	IMR 7828	.277"	3.280"				73.5	3325	53,000 CUP
140 GR. HDY BTSP	Hodgdon	H4831	.277"	3.280"	65.0	2904		68.0	3112	
140 GR. HDY BTSP	Hodgdon	H4350	.277"	3.280"	60.0	2926		64.0	3140	
150 GR. NOS PART	Hodgdon	H1000	.277"	3.250"	75.0	2902		79.0	3132	
150 GR. NOS PART	IMR	IMR 7828	.277"	3.250"				72.0	3215	53,600 CUP
150 GR. NOS PART	Hodgdon	H4831	.277"	3.250"	65.0	2872		68.0	3057	

150 GR. NOS PART	Hodgdon	H4350	.277"	3.250"	60.0	2846		63.0	2986	
160 GR. NOS PART	Hodgdon	H1000	.277"	3.250"	74.0	2872		78.0	3051	
160 GR. NOS PART	Hodgdon	H4831	.277"	3.250"	62.0	2674		65.0	2901	
160 GR. NOS PART	Hodgdon	H4350	.277"	3.250"	58.0	2666		61.0	2738	

Cartridge:7mm BR Remington
Load Type: Rifle

Bullet Weight (Gr.)	Manufacturer	Powder	Bullet Diam.	C.O.L.	Grs.	Vel. (ft/s)	Pressure	Grs.	Vel. (ft/s)	Pressure
						Starting Loads			**Maximum Loads**	
100 GR. BAR XFB	Hodgdon	H335	.284"	2.125"	29.0	2476	41,000 CUP	32.0	2694	50,700 CUP
100 GR. BAR XFB	Hodgdon	H4895	.284"	2.125"	31.0	2582	40,900 CUP	33.0C	2706	45,300 CUP
100 GR. BAR XFB	Hodgdon	Benchmark	.284"	2.125"	29.0	2439	38,800 CUP	32.0C	2719	50,100 CUP
100 GR. BAR XFB	Hodgdon	H322	.284"	2.125"	29.0	2516	37,700 CUP	31.5C	2738	49,800 CUP
100 GR. BAR XFB	Hodgdon	H4198	.284"	2.125"	26.0	2524	36,600 CUP	28.5	2743	49,900 CUP
115 GR. SPR HP	Hodgdon	H335	.284"	2.150"	30.0	2449	40,000 CUP	32.5	2648	49,800 CUP
115 GR. SPR HP	Hodgdon	H4895	.284"	2.150"	31.0	2497	38,900 CUP	33.0C	2644	45,300 CUP
115 GR. SPR HP	IMR	IMR 8208 XBR	.284"	2.150"	30.0	2455	34,400 CUP	33.0C	2737	45,300 CUP
115 GR. SPR HP	Hodgdon	Benchmark	.284"	2.150"	30.0	2524	41,600 CUP	32.0C	2674	49,800 CUP
115 GR. SPR HP	Hodgdon	H322	.284"	2.150"	29.0	2476	37,200 CUP	31.5C	2693	49,800 CUP
115 GR. SPR HP	IMR	IMR 4198	.284"	2.150"	25.0	2485	38,900 CUP	27.3	2678	49,200 CUP
115 GR. SPR HP	Hodgdon	H4198	.284"	2.150"	26.0	2498	41,500 CUP	28.5	2685	50,500 CUP
120 GR. HDY V-MAX	Hodgdon	H335	.284"	2.300"	29.5	2421	43,100 CUP	31.5	2555	50,400 CUP
120 GR. HDY V-MAX	Hodgdon	H4895	.284"	2.300"	30.0	2437	39,600 CUP	32.7C	2650	49,800 CUP
120 GR. HDY V-MAX	IMR	IMR 8208 XBR	.284"	2.300"	30.0	2479	36,400 CUP	33.0C	2726	49,200 CUP
120 GR. HDY V-MAX	Hodgdon	Benchmark	.284"	2.300"	29.0	2457	43,100 CUP	31.0	2590	49,900 CUP
120 GR. HDY V-MAX	Hodgdon	H322	.284"	2.300"	28.0	2430	39,800 CUP	30.8	2636	50,400 CUP
120 GR. HDY V-MAX	IMR	IMR 4198	.284"	2.300"	24.0	2372	40,100 CUP	26.5	2584	49,800 CUP
120 GR. HDY V-MAX	Hodgdon	H4198	.284"	2.300"	25.5	2399	40,200 CUP	27.5	2597	49,500 CUP
130 GR. SIE HPBT	Hodgdon	H335	.284"	2.250"	28.5	2315	39,700 CUP	30.5	2475	49,500 CUP
130 GR. SIE HPBT	Hodgdon	H4895	.284"	2.250"	30.0	2431	43,900 CUP	32.0C	2560	49,200 CUP
130 GR. SIE HPBT	IMR	IMR 8208 XBR	.284"	2.250"	29.0	2379	37,500 CUP	32.0C	2625	50,400 CUP
130 GR. SIE HPBT	Hodgdon	Benchmark	.284"	2.250"	28.0	2361	40,700 CUP	30.2C	2517	50,000 CUP
130 GR. SIE HPBT	Hodgdon	H322	.284"	2.250"	28.0	2376	40,500 CUP	30.0C	2543	50,600 CUP
130 GR. SIE HPBT	IMR	IMR 4198	.284"	2.250"	23.0	2257	39,100 CUP	25.5C	2475	48,700 CUP
130 GR. SIE HPBT	Hodgdon	H4198	.284"	2.250"	25.0	2347	40,000 CUP	27.0	2514	50,500 CUP
139 GR. HDY SST	Hodgdon	H335	.284"	2.260"	28.0	2221	41,300 CUP	30.0	2380	50,500 CUP
139 GR. HDY SST	Hodgdon	H4895	.284"	2.260"	29.0	2320	41,200 CUP	31.0C	2448	47,000 CUP
139 GR. HDY SST	IMR	IMR 8208 XBR	.284"	2.250"	29.0	2359	41,300 CUP	31.0C	2510	46,700 CUP
139 GR. HDY SST	Hodgdon	Benchmark	.284"	2.260"	27.5	2278	41,200 CUP	29.7C	2420	49,900 CUP
139 GR. HDY SST	Hodgdon	H322	.284"	2.260"	26.5	2265	40,100 CUP	28.5C	2426	49,700 CUP
139 GR. HDY SST	IMR	IMR 4198	.284"	2.250"	23.0	2209	40,600 CUP	25.5C	2413	49,700 CUP

Bullet Weight (Gr.)	Manufacturer	Powder	Bullet Diam.	C.O.L.	Grs.	Vel. (ft/s)	Pressure	Grs.	Vel. (ft/s)	Pressure
139 GR. HDY SST	Hodgdon	H4198	.284"	2.260"	24.0	2275	42,500 CUP	26.0	2390	49,800 CUP
145 GR. SPR SPBT	Hodgdon	H335	.284"	2.200"	28.0	2218	41,300 CUP	30.0	2362	49,600 CUP
145 GR. SPR SPBT	Hodgdon	H4895	.284"	2.200"	29.0	2320	42,400 CUP	31.0C	2453	47,500 CUP
145 GR. SPR SPBT	IMR	IMR 8208 XBR	.284"	2.200"	28.5	2290	38,500 CUP	31.0C	2492	47,000 CUP
145 GR. SPR SPBT	Hodgdon	Benchmark	.284"	2.200"	27.5	2270	40,400 CUP	29.7C	2432	50,400 CUP
145 GR. SPR SPBT	Hodgdon	H322	.284"	2.200"	27.0	2220	37,400 CUP	28.5C	2349	47,500 CUP
145 GR. SPR SPBT	IMR	IMR 4198	.284"	2.200"	23.0	2176	38,900 CUP	25.3C	2357	49,200 CUP
150 GR. NOS BT	Hodgdon	H335	.284"	2.340"	27.5	2154	40,300 CUP	29.5	2297	49,700 CUP
150 GR. NOS BT	Hodgdon	H4895	.284"	2.340"	28.5	2247	39,600 CUP	30.5C	2385	48,300 CUP
150 GR. NOS BT	IMR	IMR 8208 XBR	.284"	2.340"	28.5	2289	39,600 CUP	31.0C	2475	50,200 CUP
150 GR. NOS BT	Hodgdon	Benchmark	.284"	2.340"	27.0	2232	41,900 CUP	29.5C	2385	50,200 CUP
150 GR. NOS BT	Hodgdon	H322	.284"	2.340"	26.5	2215	40,400 CUP	28.5C	2366	49,600 CUP
162 GR. HDY A-MAX	Hodgdon	H335	.284"	2.400"	27.5	2143	41,900 CUP	29.5	2278	47,800 CUP
162 GR. HDY A-MAX	Hodgdon	H4895	.284"	2.400"	27.5	2132	37,500 CUP	29.5C	2296	49,600 CUP
162 GR. HDY A-MAX	IMR	IMR 8208 XBR	.284"	2.400"	28.0	2209	40,600 CUP	30.5C	2387	48,600 CUP
162 GR. HDY A-MAX	Hodgdon	Benchmark	.284"	2.400"	27.0	2144	41,200 CUP	29.0C	2285	49,500 CUP
162 GR. HDY A-MAX	Hodgdon	H322	.284"	2.400"	26.0	2132	39,800 CUP	28.3	2292	49,800 CUP
168 GR. SIE HPBT	Hodgdon	H335	.284"	2.320"	27.5	2129	43,100 CUP	29.2	2252	49,800 CUP
168 GR. SIE HPBT	Hodgdon	H4895	.284"	2.320"	28.0	2154	42,300 CUP	30.0C	2287	49,200 CUP
168 GR. SIE HPBT	IMR	IMR 8208 XBR	.284"	2.320"	28.0	2165	41,300 CUP	30.5C	2354	49,800 CUP
168 GR. SIE HPBT	Hodgdon	Benchmark	.284"	2.320"	26.5	2118	41,400 CUP	28.5	2246	49,700 CUP
168 GR. SIE HPBT	Hodgdon	H322	.284"	2.320"	26.0	2112	40,300 CUP	28.0	2247	49,600 CUP

Cartridge: 7-30 Waters Load Type: Rifle					Starting Loads			Maximum Loads		
Bullet Weight (Gr.)	Manufacturer	Powder	Bullet Diam.	C.O.L.	Grs.	Vel. (ft/s)	Pressure	Grs.	Vel. (ft/s)	Pressure
100 GR. HDY HP	Hodgdon	Varget	.284"	2.700"	35.0	2660	31,400 CUP	38.0C	2814	35,000 CUP
100 GR. HDY HP	Hodgdon	BL-C(2)	.284"	2.700"	39.0	2858	33,500 CUP	41.0	2965	35,500 CUP
100 GR. HDY HP	Hodgdon	H335	.284"	2.700"	33.0	2743	33,900 CUP	36.0	2913	39,300 CUP
100 GR. HDY HP	Hodgdon	H4895	.284"	2.700"	34.0	2707	33,500 CUP	37.0C	2908	39,200 CUP
100 GR. HDY HP	Hodgdon	Benchmark	.284"	2.700"	27.0	2407	29,600 CUP	30.5	2646	39,300 CUP
100 GR. HDY HP	Hodgdon	H322	.284"	2.700"	27.0	2447	30,500 CUP	30.0	2679	40,200 CUP
120 GR. NOS FP	Hodgdon	Varget	.284"	2.550"	34.0	2480	31,100 CUP	37.0C	2653	40,000 CUP
120 GR. NOS FP	Hodgdon	BL-C(2)	.284"	2.550"	35.0	2484	28,800 CUP	38.0	2689	38,900 CUP
120 GR. NOS FP	Hodgdon	H335	.284"	2.550"	31.0	2407	29,600 CUP	34.0	2606	39,700 CUP
120 GR. NOS FP	Hodgdon	H4895	.284"	2.550"	31.0	2413	33,200 CUP	34.5	2654	39,400 CUP
120 GR. NOS FP	Hodgdon	Benchmark	.284"	2.550"	26.5	2267	31,500 CUP	29.5	2474	40,200 CUP
120 GR. NOS FP	Hodgdon	H322	.284"	2.550"	26.0	2274	29,500 CUP	29.0	2497	40,200 CUP
130 GR. SIE HPBT	Hodgdon	Varget	.284"	2.720"	32.0	2336	30,600 CUP	35.6C	2561	40,100 CUP

Bullet Weight (Gr.)	Manufacturer	Powder	Bullet Diam.	C.O.L.	Grs.	Vel. (ft/s)	Pressure	Grs.	Vel. (ft/s)	Pressure
130 GR. SIE HPBT	Hodgdon	BL-C(2)	.284"	2.720"	33.0	2353	30,500 CUP	35.5	2548	38,700 CUP
130 GR. SIE HPBT	Hodgdon	H335	.284"	2.720"	29.0	2221	28,800 CUP	32.0	2457	39,600 CUP
130 GR. SIE HPBT	Hodgdon	H4895	.284"	2.720"	31.0	2360	31,000 CUP	33.4C	2528	39,500 CUP
130 GR. SIE HPBT	Hodgdon	Benchmark	.284"	2.720"	25.0	2078	28,900 CUP	28.0	2314	40,100 CUP
130 GR. SIE HPBT	Hodgdon	H322	.284"	2.720"	25.0	2142	31,600 CUP	27.3	2320	39,300 CUP
139 GR. HDY FP	Hodgdon	Varget	.284"	2.550"	32.0	2251	30,900 CUP	35.5C	2472	39,100 CUP
139 GR. HDY FP	Hodgdon	BL-C(2)	.284"	2.550"	33.0	2299	31,800 CUP	35.5	2468	39,800 CUP
139 GR. HDY FP	Hodgdon	H335	.284"	2.550"	29.0	2207	31,900 CUP	31.5	2355	39,800 CUP
139 GR. HDY FP	Hodgdon	H4895	.284"	2.550"	30.0	2250	32,900 CUP	33.0	2435	39,800 CUP
139 GR. HDY FP	Hodgdon	Benchmark	.284"	2.550"	25.0	2048	31,000 CUP	28.0	2220	39,600 CUP
139 GR. HDY FP	Hodgdon	H322	.284"	2.550	24.0	1981	28,500 CUP	27.0	2217	39,400 CUP
145 GR. SPR SP	Hodgdon	Varget	.284"	2.720"	31.0	2217	33,600 CUP	34.2	2439	39,700 CUP
145 GR. SPR SP	Hodgdon	BL-C(2)	.284"	2.720"	31.0	2208	31,300 CUP	34.0	2415	39,300 CUP
145 GR. SPR SP	Hodgdon	H335	.284"	2.720"	28.5	2183	32,400 CUP	30.5	2310	40,000 CUP
145 GR. SPR SP	Hodgdon	H4895	.284"	2.720"	29.0	2238	35,100 CUP	32.0	2369	39,900 CUP
145 GR. SPR SP	Hodgdon	Benchmark	.284"	2.720"	25.0	2037	30,200 CUP	28.0	2235	40,100 CUP
150 GR. NOS BT	Hodgdon	Varget	.284"	2.780"	31.0	2215	32,900 CUP	34.2C	2388	40,000 CUP
150 GR. NOS BT	Hodgdon	BL-C(2)	.284"	2.780"	31.0	2165	29,000 CUP	34.0	2368	39,900 CUP
150 GR. NOS BT	Hodgdon	H335	.284"	2.780"	28.5	2147	30,300 CUP	30.5	2268	39,400 CUP
150 GR. NOS BT	Hodgdon	H4895	.284"	2.780"	29.0	2192	33,300 CUP	32.0C	2347	39,600 CUP
150 GR. NOS BT	Hodgdon	Benchmark	.284"	2.780"	23.0	1929	30,400 CUP	26.0	2144	39,200 CUP
168 GR. SIE HPBT	Hodgdon	Varget	.284"	2.780"	29.0	2089	33,000 CUP	32.0C	2229	39,200 CUP
168 GR. SIE HPBT	Hodgdon	BL-C(2)	.284"	2.780"	31.0	2131	32,000 CUP	33.6	2315	40,000 CUP
168 GR. SIE HPBT	Hodgdon	H335	.284"	2.780"	28.5	2112	34,000 CUP	30.2	2221	39,600 CUP
168 GR. SIE HPBT	Hodgdon	H4895	.284"	2.780"	28.0	2132	34,400 CUP	30.2	2222	38,600 CUP
168 GR. SIE HPBT	Hodgdon	Benchmark	.284"	2.780"	23.0	1897	31,600 CUP	25.5C	2055	39,800 CUP

Cartridge: 7mm-08 Remington Load Type: Rifle					Starting Loads			Maximum Loads		
Bullet Weight (Gr.)	Manufacturer	Powder	Bullet Diam.	C.O.L.	Grs.	Vel. (ft/s)	Pressure	Grs.	Vel. (ft/s)	Pressure
100 GR. BAR XFB	Hodgdon	H414	.284"	2.650"	47.0	3041	44,900 CUP	49.5	3157	50,100 CUP
100 GR. BAR XFB	Winchester	760	.284"	2.650"	47.0	3041	44,900 CUP	49.5	3157	50,100 CUP
100 GR. BAR XFB	Hodgdon	H380	.284"	2.650"	47.0	3080	42,100 CUP	49.0	3171	46,300 CUP
100 GR. BAR XFB	Hodgdon	Varget	.284"	2.650"	42.0	3060	40,800 CUP	45.7	3277	49,600 CUP
100 GR. BAR XFB	Hodgdon	BL-C(2)	.284"	2.650"	43.0	3109	44,600 CUP	46.5	3231	50,000 CUP
100 GR. BAR XFB	Hodgdon	H335	.284"	2.650"	39.0	2977	44,600 CUP	41.2	3123	49,700 CUP
100 GR. BAR XFB	Hodgdon	H4895	.284"	2.650"	41.0	3037	41,000 CUP	45.0	3286	49,900 CUP
100 GR. BAR XFB	Hodgdon	Benchmark	.284"	2.650"	40.0	2968	41,400 CUP	42.5	3144	49,600 CUP
100 GR. BAR XFB	Hodgdon	H322	.284"	2.650"	37.5	2917	40,300 CUP	40.0	3105	49,000 CUP
115 GR. SPR HP	Hodgdon	H414	.284"	2.655"	46.5	2906	41,400 CUP	49.5	3062	47,900 CUP

115 GR. SPR HP	Winchester	760	.284"	2.655"	46.5	2906	41,400 CUP	49.5	3062	47,900 CUP
115 GR. SPR HP	IMR	IMR 4007 SSC	.284"	2.655"	46.0	2941	39,200 CUP	49.0C	3080	46,400 CUP
115 GR. SPR HP	Hodgdon	H380	.284"	2.655"	47.0	2925	40,200 CUP	49.0	3046	44,700 CUP
115 GR. SPR HP	Hodgdon	CFE 223	.284"	2.655"	45.4	2924	35,800 CUP	50.4	3231	49,700 CUP
115 GR. SPR HP	Hodgdon	Varget	.284"	2.655"	43.0	3019	41,200 CUP	46.3	3216	50,100 CUP
115 GR. SPR HP	IMR	IMR 4320	.284"	2.655"	43.2	2933	45,100 CUP	46.0	3074	50,500 CUP
115 GR. SPR HP	IMR	IMR 4064	.284"	2.655"	42.0	2918	41,100 CUP	44.5	3101	49,900 CUP
115 GR. SPR HP	Hodgdon	BL-C(2)	.284"	2.655"	45.0	3055	43,200 CUP	48.0	3219	49,900 CUP
115 GR. SPR HP	IMR	IMR 4895	.284"	2.655"	41.7	2871	41,000 CUP	45.0	3062	49,400 CUP
115 GR. SPR HP	Hodgdon	H335	.284"	2.655"	39.0	2900	42,300 CUP	42.0	3067	50,100 CUP
115 GR. SPR HP	Hodgdon	H4895	.284"	2.655"	42.0	3007	42,400 CUP	45.0	3172	49,900 CUP
115 GR. SPR HP	IMR	IMR 8208 XBR	.284"	2.655"	40.6	2866	40,100 CUP	43.2	3022	48,400 CUP
115 GR. SPR HP	IMR	IMR 3031	.284"	2.655"	39.0	2922	44,300 CUP	41.8	3066	50,500 CUP
115 GR. SPR HP	Hodgdon	Benchmark	.284"	2.655"	40.0	2887	42,000 CUP	43.5	3103	50,500 CUP
115 GR. SPR HP	Hodgdon	H322	.284"	2.655"	39.0	2951	44,800 CUP	41.0	3053	49,800 CUP
120 GR. NOS BT	Hodgdon	H4350	.284"	2.800"	48.0	2895	39,300 CUP	50.0C	3039	44,600 CUP
120 GR. NOS BT	Hodgdon	H414	.284"	2.800"	46.5	2867	40,600 CUP	49.0	3023	47,600 CUP
120 GR. NOS BT	Winchester	760	.284"	2.800"	46.5	2867	40,600 CUP	49.0	3023	47,600 CUP
120 GR. NOS BT	IMR	IMR 4007 SSC	.284"	2.800"	45.0	2875	38,600 CUP	49.0C	3118	49,000 CUP
120 GR. NOS BT	Hodgdon	H380	.284"	2.800"	46.0	2881	40,200 CUP	48.0	2977	43,400 CUP
120 GR. NOS BT	Hodgdon	CFE 223	.284"	2.800"	46.0	2944	40,700 CUP	49.5	3151	50,000 CUP
120 GR. NOS BT	Hodgdon	Varget	.284"	2.800"	42.5	2996	43,800 CUP	45.0	3117	49,900 CUP
120 GR. NOS BT	IMR	IMR 4320	.284"	2.800"	42.0	2861	45,400 CUP	44.7	3001	50,400 CUP
120 GR. NOS BT	IMR	IMR 4064	.284"	2.800"	41.0	2839	41,500 CUP	43.9	3017	50,000 CUP
120 GR. NOS BT	Hodgdon	BL-C(2)	.284"	2.800"	43.5	2932	41,400 CUP	46.5	3109	50,100 CUP
120 GR. NOS BT	IMR	IMR 4895	.284"	2.800"	41.5	2861	43,900 CUP	44.0	3022	49,800 CUP
120 GR. NOS BT	Hodgdon	H335	.284"	2.800"	39.5	2810	42,100 CUP	42.0	2984	49,400 CUP
120 GR. NOS BT	Hodgdon	H4895	.284"	2.800"	41.0	2931	42,200 CUP	43.7	3085	49,700 CUP
120 GR. NOS BT	IMR	IMR 8208 XBR	.284"	2.800"	40.1	2830	40,500 CUP	42.7	2997	48,900 CUP
120 GR. NOS BT	IMR	IMR 3031	.284"	2.800"	38.5	2826	42,700 CUP	41.0	2987	50,500 CUP
120 GR. NOS BT	Hodgdon	Benchmark	.284"	2.800"	39.0	2812	40,900 CUP	41.3	2968	49,000 CUP
130 GR. SIE HPBT	Hodgdon	H4350	.284"	2.800"	47.0	2871	43,000 CUP	50.0C	2998	47,400 CUP
130 GR. SIE HPBT	Hodgdon	H414	.284"	2.800"	44.0	2761	40,900 CUP	47.0	2925	50,000 CUP
130 GR. SIE HPBT	IMR	IMR 4350	.284"	2.800"	45.0	2730	41,200 CUP	47.0C	2846	46,300 CUP
130 GR. SIE HPBT	Winchester	760	.284"	2.800"	44.0	2761	40,900 CUP	47.0	2925	50,000 CUP
130 GR. SIE HPBT	IMR	IMR 4007 SSC	.284"	2.800"	43.0	2739	37,000 CUP	47.5C	3040	50,300 CUP
130 GR. SIE HPBT	Hodgdon	H380	.284"	2.800"	45.0	2804	41,900 CUP	47.0	2934	45,700 CUP
130 GR. SIE HPBT	Hodgdon	CFE 223	.284"	2.800"	41.9	2765	37,300 CUP	45.5	2957	47,800 CUP
130 GR. SIE HPBT	Hodgdon	Varget	.284"	2.800"	40.0	2830	43,400 CUP	43.5	3004	50,100 CUP

130 GR. SIE HPBT	IMR	IMR 4320	.284"	2.800"	40.0	2709	43,200 CUP	42.5	2863	50,100 CUP
130 GR. SIE HPBT	IMR	IMR 4064	.284"	2.800"	39.0	2711	39,600 CUP	41.7	2890	49,900 CUP
130 GR. SIE HPBT	Hodgdon	BL-C(2)	.284"	2.800"	41.5	2857	44,000 CUP	44.2	2989	49,800 CUP
130 GR. SIE HPBT	IMR	IMR 4895	.284"	2.800"	40.0	2759	43,300 CUP	42.4	2801	50,000 CUP
130 GR. SIE HPBT	Hodgdon	H335	.284"	2.800"	37.0	2690	44,800 CUP	39.0	2809	49,500 CUP
130 GR. SIE HPBT	Hodgdon	H4895	.284"	2.800"	39.5	2824	43,500 CUP	42.0	2957	50,200 CUP
130 GR. SIE HPBT	IMR	IMR 8208 XBR	.284"	2.800"	39.1	2755	42,600 CUP	41.6	2922	50,400 CUP
130 GR. SIE HPBT	IMR	IMR 3031	.284"	2.800"	37.0	2709	42,400 CUP	39.5	2860	50,000 CUP
130 GR. SIE HPBT	Hodgdon	Benchmark	.284"	2.800"	37.0	2701	41,500 CUP	39.8	2861	50,200 CUP
139 GR. HDY SP	Hodgdon	H4350	.284"	2.800"	47.0	2729	40,400 CUP	50.0C	2906	47,500 CUP
139 GR. HDY SP	Hodgdon	H414	.284"	2.800"	45.5	2710	40,400 CUP	47.0	2810	44,100 CUP
139 GR. HDY SP	IMR	IMR 4350	.284"	2.800"	45.5	2646	39,700 CUP	48.0C	2793	45,200 CUP
139 GR. HDY SP	Winchester	760	.284"	2.800"	45.5	2710	40,400 CUP	47.0	2810	44,100 CUP
139 GR. HDY SP	IMR	IMR 4007 SSC	.284"	2.800"	43.0	2688	39,800 CUP	46.5C	2874	48,600 CUP
139 GR. HDY SP	Hodgdon	H380	.284"	2.800"	44.0	2674	41,800 CUP	47.0	2807	46,800 CUP
139 GR. HDY SP	Hodgdon	CFE 223	.284"	2.800"	41.4	2666	38,900 CUP	45.0	2847	48,900 CUP
139 GR. HDY SP	Hodgdon	Varget	.284"	2.800"	40.5	2721	44,700 CUP	43.5	2877	50,000 CUP
139 GR. HDY SP	IMR	IMR 4320	.284"	2.800"	40.7	2643	43,700 CUP	43.3	2772	49,200 CUP
139 GR. HDY SP	IMR	IMR 4064	.284"	2.800"	40.0	2682	42,500 CUP	42.5	2847	49,900 CUP
139 GR. HDY SP	Hodgdon	BL-C(2)	.284"	2.800"	41.0	2641	41,200 CUP	44.7	2857	49,900 CUP
139 GR. HDY SP	IMR	IMR 4895	.284"	2.800"	40.5	2706	43,600 CUP	43.2	2851	49,900 CUP
139 GR. HDY SP	Hodgdon	H335	.284"	2.800"	37.5	2585	42,700 CUP	40.0	2730	49,400 CUP
139 GR. HDY SP	Hodgdon	H4895	.284"	2.800"	39.0	2678	42,500 CUP	42.5	2857	50,200 CUP
139 GR. HDY SP	IMR	IMR 8208 XBR	.284"	2.800"	39.0	2642	41,200 CUP	41.5	2783	49,000 CUP
139 GR. HDY SP	IMR	IMR 3031	.284"	2.800"	38.0	2633	42,000 CUP	40.3	2797	49,900 CUP
139 GR. HDY SP	Hodgdon	Benchmark	.284"	2.800"	37.5	2624	40,300 CUP	40.5	2799	49,600 CUP
140 GR. SFT SP	Hodgdon	H4350	.284"	2.750"	45.0	2692	42,300 CUP	48.0C	2868	49,800 CUP
140 GR. SFT SP	Hodgdon	H414	.284"	2.750"	43.5	2624	41,900 CUP	46.0	2791	49,500 CUP
140 GR. SFT SP	IMR	IMR 4350	.284"	2.750"	43.7	2616	38,600 CUP	46.5C	2826	50,000 CUP
140 GR. SFT SP	Winchester	760	.284"	2.750"	43.5	2624	41,900 CUP	46.0	2791	49,500 CUP
140 GR. SFT SP	IMR	IMR 4007 SSC	.284"	2.750"	41.0	2533	36,300 CUP	46.0	2847	49,600 CUP
140 GR. SFT SP	Hodgdon	H380	.284"	2.750"	43.0	2645	44,200 CUP	45.7	2775	49,400 CUP
140 GR. SFT SP	Hodgdon	CFE 223	.284"	2.750"	39.7	2577	38,400 CUP	43.2	2796	48,800 CUP
140 GR. SFT SP	Hodgdon	Varget	.284"	2.750"	39.5	2695	43,700 CUP	42.2	2819	49,800 CUP
140 GR. SFT SP	IMR	IMR 4320	.284"	2.750"	39.0	2588	41,400 CUP	41.4	2749	49,800 CUP
140 GR. SFT SP	IMR	IMR 4064	.284"	2.750"	38.0	2593	41,200 CUP	40.5	2770	50,300 CUP
140 GR. SFT SP	Hodgdon	BL-C(2)	.284"	2.750"	40.0	2660	44,800 CUP	42.5	2796	49,700 CUP
140 GR. SFT SP	IMR	IMR 4895	.284"	2.750"	38.5	2596	40,100 CUP	41.0	2752	49,600 CUP
140 GR. SFT SP	Hodgdon	H335	.284"	2.750"	35.5	2536	43,800 CUP	37.5	2647	49,800 CUP
140 GR. SFT SP	Hodgdon	H4895	.284"	2.750"	38.0	2618	42,000 CUP	40.5	2769	49,700 CUP

140 GR. SFT SP	IMR	IMR 8208 XBR	.284"	2.750"	37.3	2606	43,200 CUP	39.7	2732	48,800 CUP
140 GR. SFT SP	IMR	IMR 3031	.284"	2.750"	36.0	2537	40,700 CUP	38.3	2695	49,600 CUP
140 GR. SFT SP	Hodgdon	Benchmark	.284"	2.750"	36.0	2564	42,600 CUP	38.3	2688	49,300 CUP
140 GR. SFT SP	IMR	Trail Boss	.284"	2.750"	11.0	1211	36,200 CUP	16.0	1472	43,300 CUP
145 GR. SPR SP	Hodgdon	H4350	.284"	2.730"	45.0	2647	42,300 CUP	48.0C	2801	49,800 CUP
145 GR. SPR SP	Hodgdon	H414	.284"	2.730"	43.0	2589	41,200 CUP	46.0	2788	49,500 CUP
145 GR. SPR SP	IMR	IMR 4350	.284"	2.730"	45.0	2668	43,900 CUP	48.0C	2847	50,200 CUP
145 GR. SPR SP	Winchester	760	.284"	2.730"	43.0	2589	41,200 CUP	46.0	2788	49,500 CUP
145 GR. SPR SP	IMR	IMR 4007 SSC	.284"	2.730"	42.0	2596	40,800 CUP	45.5C	2817	50,000 CUP
145 GR. SPR SP	Hodgdon	H380	.284"	2.730"	43.0	2603	45,000 CUP	45.5	2716	49,900 CUP
145 GR. SPR SP	Hodgdon	CFE 223	.284"	2.730"	39.3	2519	36,000 CUP	42.7	2701	47,400 CUP
145 GR. SPR SP	Hodgdon	Varget	.284"	2.730"	39.0	2639	46,200 CUP	41.5	2745	50,200 CUP
145 GR. SPR SP	IMR	IMR 4320	.284"	2.730"	39.5	2606	44,700 CUP	42.0	2737	49,800 CUP
145 GR. SPR SP	IMR	IMR 4064	.284"	2.730"	38.5	2590	45,000 CUP	41.0	2728	50,300 CUP
145 GR. SPR SP	Hodgdon	BL-C(2)	.284"	2.730"	39.0	2516	41,700 CUP	41.7	2693	49,600 CUP
145 GR. SPR SP	IMR	IMR 4895	.284"	2.730"	40.0	2598	45,700 CUP	42.5	2753	50,700 CUP
145 GR. SPR SP	Hodgdon	H4895	.284"	2.730"	38.5	2599	44,400 CUP	41.0	2728	49,800 CUP
145 GR. SPR SP	IMR	IMR 8208 XBR	.284"	2.730"	37.8	2589	43,700 CUP	40.2	2721	50,200 CUP
145 GR. SPR SP	IMR	IMR 3031	.284"	2.730"	36.5	2512	44,000 CUP	38.8	2659	49,800 CUP
145 GR. SPR SP	Hodgdon	Benchmark	.284"	2.730"	36.0	2487	40,900 CUP	39.5	2693	50,700 CUP
150 GR. BAR TTSX BT	Hodgdon	H4350	.284"	2.770"	41.9	2475	40,100 CUP	45.5C	2659	50,400 CUP
150 GR. BAR TTSX BT	Hodgdon	H414	.284"	2.770"	43.4	2576	43,500 CUP	46.2	2733	50,400 CUP
150 GR. BAR TTSX BT	IMR	IMR 4350	.284"	2.770"	41.4	2380	37,600 CUP	46.0C	2633	46,100 CUP
150 GR. BAR TTSX BT	Winchester	760	.284"	2.770"	43.4	2576	43,500 CUP	46.2	2733	50,400 CUP
150 GR. BAR TTSX BT	IMR	IMR 4007 SSC	.284"	2.770"	40.1	2417	43,500 CUP	43.6C	2596	50,400 CUP
150 GR. BAR TTSX BT	Hodgdon	H380	.284"	2.770"	41.4	2441	41,400 CUP	45.0	2646	49,900 CUP
150 GR. BAR TTSX BT	Hodgdon	CFE 223	.284"	2.770"	39.5	2501	43,500 CUP	42.0	2668	49,200 CUP
150 GR. BAR TTSX BT	Hodgdon	Varget	.284"	2.770"	37.3	2448	43,400 CUP	39.7	2580	50,700 CUP
150 GR. BAR TTSX BT	IMR	IMR 4320	.284"	2.770"	38.5	2430	42,200 CUP	41.0	2609	49,800 CUP
150 GR. BAR TTSX BT	IMR	IMR 4064	.284"	2.770"	37.4	2468	43,900 CUP	39.8	2576	49,900 CUP
150 GR. BAR TTSX BT	Hodgdon	BL-C(2)	.284"	2.770"	38.5	2463	41,400 CUP	41.0	2630	48,800 CUP
150 GR. BAR TTSX BT	IMR	IMR 4895	.284"	2.770"	38.3	2512	44,800 CUP	41.0	2655	50,600 CUP
150 GR. BAR TTSX BT	Hodgdon	H335	.284"	2.770"	35.2	2373	43,500 CUP	37.4	2522	50,400 CUP
150 GR. BAR TTSX BT	Hodgdon	H4895	.284"	2.770"	34.8	2428	45,200 CUP	37.0	2561	50,700 CUP
150 GR. BAR TTSX BT	IMR	IMR 8208 XBR	.284"	2.770"	35.2	2404	44,600 CUP	37.4	2518	50,700 CUP
150 GR. BAR TTSX BT	IMR	IMR 3031	.284"	2.770"	34.8	2400	43,900 CUP	37.0	2553	49,000 CUP
150 GR. BAR TTSX BT	Hodgdon	Benchmark	.284"	2.770"	34.8	2369	45,900 CUP	37.0	2506	50,600 CUP
150 GR. SIE HPBT	Hodgdon	H4350	.284"	2.800"	42.0	2549	40,600 CUP	45.4	2724	51,500 CUP
150 GR. SIE HPBT	Hodgdon	H414	.284"	2.800"	44.0	2640	43,600 CUP	46.5	2776	50,000 CUP

150 GR. SIE HPBT	IMR	IMR 4350	.284"	2.800"	44.0	2637	41,800 CUP	46.5C	2746	46,600 CUP
150 GR. SIE HPBT	Winchester	760	.284"	2.800"	44.0	2640	43,600 CUP	46.5	2776	50,000 CUP
150 GR. SIE HPBT	IMR	IMR 4007 SSC	.284"	2.800"	41.0	2547	38,600 CUP	45.5	2804	50,400 CUP
150 GR. SIE HPBT	Hodgdon	H380	.284"	2.800"	42.0	2583	43,000 CUP	45.5	2748	49,900 CUP
150 GR. SIE HPBT	Hodgdon	CFE 223	.284"	2.800"	39.9	2529	41,500 CUP	42.5	2688	48,200 CUP
150 GR. SIE HPBT	Hodgdon	Varget	.284"	2.800"	38.5	2597	42,400 CUP	41.3	2731	50,000 CUP
150 GR. SIE HPBT	IMR	IMR 4320	.284"	2.800"	39.0	2587	43,000 CUP	41.5	2711	49,400 CUP
150 GR. SIE HPBT	IMR	IMR 4064	.284"	2.800"	38.0	2569	42,600 CUP	40.3	2723	48,800 CUP
150 GR. SIE HPBT	Hodgdon	BL-C(2)	.284"	2.800"	39.0	2559	43,000 CUP	41.5	2699	49,600 CUP
150 GR. SIE HPBT	IMR	IMR 4895	.284"	2.800"	39.0	2605	44,000 CUP	41.5	2737	50,700 CUP
150 GR. SIE HPBT	Hodgdon	H335	.284"	2.800"	35.0	2471	44,700 CUP	37.5	2605	49,900 CUP
150 GR. SIE HPBT	Hodgdon	H4895	.284"	2.800"	37.0	2546	43,300 CUP	40.5	2723	50,000 CUP
150 GR. SIE HPBT	IMR	IMR 8208 XBR	.284"	2.800"	36.9	2539	43,200 CUP	39.3	2677	49,900 CUP
150 GR. SIE HPBT	IMR	IMR 3031	.284"	2.800"	36.2	2533	43,000 CUP	38.5	2684	49,900 CUP
150 GR. SIE HPBT	Hodgdon	Benchmark	.284"	2.800"	36.0	2526	43,300 CUP	38.5	2667	50,200 CUP
154 GR. HDY SP	Hodgdon	H4831	.284"	2.800"	48.0	2550	40,900 CUP	49.5C	2625	44,500 CUP
154 GR. HDY SP	Hodgdon	Hybrid 100V	.284"	2.800"	42.5	2541	42,900 CUP	46.0C	2713	47,500 CUP
154 GR. HDY SP	IMR	IMR 4831	.284"	2.800"	44.2	2517	38,400 CUP	47.0C	2655	45,100 CUP
154 GR. HDY SP	Hodgdon	H4350	.284"	2.800"	42.3	2531	46,100 CUP	45.0	2645	51,300 CUP
154 GR. HDY SP	Hodgdon	H414	.284"	2.800"	43.0	2569	41,200 CUP	46.0	2731	49,600 CUP
154 GR. HDY SP	IMR	IMR 4350	.284"	2.800"	44.2	2595	43,100 CUP	47.0C	2744	50,200 CUP
154 GR. HDY SP	Winchester	760	.284"	2.800"	43.0	2569	41,200 CUP	46.0	2731	49,600 CUP
154 GR. HDY SP	IMR	IMR 4007 SSC	.284"	2.800"	41.0	2506	39,400 CUP	44.5C	2710	49,300 CUP
154 GR. HDY SP	Hodgdon	H380	.284"	2.800"	41.5	2462	42,400 CUP	44.0	2627	49,600 CUP
154 GR. HDY SP	Hodgdon	CFE 223	.284"	2.800"	38.7	2444	39,600 CUP	41.2	2696	47,000 CUP
154 GR. HDY SP	Hodgdon	Varget	.284"	2.800"	38.5	2530	44,100 CUP	41.2	2666	50,300 CUP
154 GR. HDY SP	IMR	IMR 4320	.284"	2.800"	39.0	2530	44,500 CUP	41.5	2698	50,400 CUP
154 GR. HDY SP	IMR	IMR 4064	.284"	2.800"	38.0	2552	45,600 CUP	40.5	2697	50,700 CUP
154 GR. HDY SP	Hodgdon	BL-C(2)	.284"	2.800"	38.0	2387	40,800 CUP	40.5	2566	49,500 CUP
154 GR. HDY SP	IMR	IMR 4895	.284"	2.800"	38.4	2532	45,500 CUP	40.8	2687	50,700 CUP
154 GR. HDY SP	Hodgdon	H335	.284"	2.800"	35.0	2374	41,700 CUP	37.5	2506	49,000 CUP
154 GR. HDY SP	Hodgdon	H4895	.284"	2.800"	37.0	2484	44,200 CUP	39.5	2592	49,900 CUP
154 GR. HDY SP	IMR	IMR 8208 XBR	.284"	2.800"	36.2	2482	43,200 CUP	38.5	2587	49,100 CUP
154 GR. HDY SP	IMR	IMR 3031	.284"	2.800"	36.7	2498	43,800 CUP	39.0	2624	50,400 CUP
154 GR. HDY SP	Hodgdon	Benchmark	.284"	2.800"	36.0	2467	42,900 CUP	38.5	2597	49,500 CUP
160 GR. SPR SPBT	Hodgdon	H4831	.284"	2.800"	47.5	2547	43,700 CUP	49.5C	2627	47,500 CUP
160 GR. SPR SPBT	Hodgdon	Hybrid 100V	.284"	2.800"	41.0	2486	41,300 CUP	45.0C	2690	48,900 CUP
160 GR. SPR SPBT	IMR	IMR 4831	.284"	2.800"	43.5	2474	41,300 CUP	46.0C	2626	47,200 CUP
160 GR. SPR SPBT	Hodgdon	H4350	.284"	2.800"	40.9	2471	45,400 CUP	43.5	2583	50,800 CUP
160 GR. SPR SPBT	Hodgdon	H414	.284"	2.800"	42.5	2566	43,300 CUP	45.5	2684	49,600 CUP

160 GR. SPR SPBT	IMR	IMR 4350	.284"	2.800"	43.0	2513	43,500 CUP	46.0C	2681	49,300 CUP
160 GR. SPR SPBT	Winchester	760	.284"	2.800"	42.5	2566	43,300 CUP	45.5	2684	49,600 CUP
160 GR. SPR SPBT	IMR	IMR 4007 SSC	.284"	2.800"	40.0	2462	39,400 CUP	43.5C	2653	49,200 CUP
160 GR. SPR SPBT	Hodgdon	H380	.284"	2.800"	40.5	2413	42,800 CUP	43.0	2566	49,700 CUP
160 GR. SPR SPBT	Hodgdon	CFE 223	.284"	2.800"	37.9	2421	42,000 CUP	40.3	2525	49,500 CUP
160 GR. SPR SPBT	Hodgdon	Varget	.284"	2.800"	36.5	2451	43,400 CUP	39.0	2562	49,900 CUP
160 GR. SPR SPBT	IMR	IMR 4320	.284"	2.800"	38.0	2485	44,900 CUP	40.4	2623	50,800 CUP
160 GR. SPR SPBT	IMR	IMR 4064	.284"	2.800"	36.5	2438	42,000 CUP	38.7	2564	49,000 CUP
160 GR. SPR SPBT	Hodgdon	BL-C(2)	.284"	2.800"	37.0	2382	43,900 CUP	39.5	2533	49,700 CUP
160 GR. SPR SPBT	IMR	IMR 4895	.284"	2.800"	37.5	2477	43,100 CUP	40.0	2601	50,300 CUP
160 GR. SPR SPBT	Hodgdon	H335	.284"	2.800"	34.0	2335	44,100 CUP	36.5	2468	49,900 CUP
160 GR. SPR SPBT	Hodgdon	H4895	.284"	2.800"	35.0	2420	44,400 CUP	38.5	2530	50,000 CUP
160 GR. SPR SPBT	IMR	IMR 8208 XBR	.284"	2.800"	35.5	2459	45,400 CUP	37.7	2554	49,900 CUP
160 GR. SPR SPBT	IMR	IMR 3031	.284"	2.800"	34.5	2378	43,000 CUP	36.7	2516	49,200 CUP
160 GR. SPR SPBT	Hodgdon	Benchmark	.284"	2.800"	36.0	2457	44,100 CUP	38.5	2592	50,700 CUP
162 GR. HDY A-MAX	Hodgdon	H4831	.284"	2.875"	47.5	2501	39,000 CUP	48.5C	2555	42,400 CUP
162 GR. HDY A-MAX	Hodgdon	Hybrid 100V	.284"	2.875"	41.0	2455	40,300 CUP	45.0C	2651	46,900 CUP
162 GR. HDY A-MAX	Hodgdon	H4350	.284"	2.875"	41.4	2443	40,400 CUP	45.0	2622	50,500 CUP
162 GR. HDY A-MAX	Hodgdon	H414	.284"	2.875"	43.0	2553	42,100 CUP	45.0	2632	44,500 CUP
162 GR. HDY A-MAX	IMR	IMR 4350	.284"	2.875"	44.0C	2494	40,000 CUP	46.0C	2655	46,900 CUP
162 GR. HDY A-MAX	Winchester	760	.284"	2.875"	43.0	2553	42,100 CUP	45.0	2632	44,500 CUP
162 GR. HDY A-MAX	IMR	IMR 4007 SSC	.284"	2.875"	40.0	2445	37,800 CUP	44.5C	2681	49,700 CUP
162 GR. HDY A-MAX	Hodgdon	H380	.284"	2.875"	42.5	2508	42,400 CUP	44.0	2590	45,800 CUP
162 GR. HDY A-MAX	Hodgdon	Varget	.284"	2.875"	38.5	2504	43,400 CUP	41.0	2644	49,800 CUP
162 GR. HDY A-MAX	IMR	IMR 4320	.284"	2.875"	38.5	2478	42,300 CUP	41.0	2635	49,900 CUP
162 GR. HDY A-MAX	IMR	IMR 4064	.284"	2.875"	37.0	2463	42,000 CUP	39.5	2624	49,900 CUP
162 GR. HDY A-MAX	IMR	IMR 4895	.284"	2.875"	38.0	2471	42,100 CUP	40.6	2650	49,300 CUP
162 GR. HDY A-MAX	Hodgdon	H335	.284"	2.875"	36.5	2467	45,200 CUP	38.2	2585	50,100 CUP
162 GR. HDY A-MAX	Hodgdon	H4895	.284"	2.875"	37.0	2462	43,700 CUP	39.5	2600	49,800 CUP
162 GR. HDY A-MAX	IMR	IMR 8208 XBR	.284"	2.875"	36.2	2499	41,000 CUP	40.2	2725	50,800 CUP
162 GR. HDY A-MAX	IMR	IMR 3031	.284"	2.875"	35.7	2452	43,200 CUP	38.0	2598	50,300 CUP
162 GR. HDY A-MAX	Hodgdon	Benchmark	.284"	2.875"	36.0	2441	43,100 CUP	38.0	2557	49,200 CUP
168 GR. SIE HPBT	IMR	IMR 7828	.284"*	2.800"	46.0	2385	40,700 CUP	49.0C*	2547	46,700 CUP
168 GR. SIE HPBT	Hodgdon	H4831	.284"	2.800"	47.0	2438	39,700 CUP	49.0C	2545	45,000 CUP
168 GR. SIE HPBT	Hodgdon	Hybrid 100V	.284"	2.800"	40.0	2443	42,800 CUP	44.0C	2623	48,200 CUP
168 GR. SIE HPBT	IMR	IMR 4831	.284"	2.800"	44.0	2402	38,500 CUP	46.0C	2517	42,900 CUP
168 GR. SIE HPBT	Hodgdon	H4350	.284"	2.800"	41.6	2431	42,500 CUP	44.2	2551	50,700 CUP
168 GR. SIE HPBT	Hodgdon	H414	.284"	2.800"	44.0	2557	44,600 CUP	46.5	2670	49,800 CUP
168 GR. SIE HPBT	IMR	IMR 4350	.284"	2.800"	43.7	2469	42,500 CUP	46.5C	2643	49,300 CUP

Bullet Weight (Gr.)	Manufacturer	Powder	Bullet Diam.	C.O.L.	Grs.	Vel. (ft/s)	Pressure	Grs.	Vel. (ft/s)	Pressure
168 GR. SIE HPBT	Winchester	760	.284"	2.800"	44.0	2557	44,600 CUP	46.5	2670	49,800 CUP
168 GR. SIE HPBT	IMR	IMR 4007 SSC	.284"	2.800"	39.0	2357	34,800 CUP	44.0C	2646	49,800 CUP
168 GR. SIE HPBT	Hodgdon	H380	.284"	2.800"	42.0	2458	45,800 CUP	44.5	2565	49,900 CUP
168 GR. SIE HPBT	Hodgdon	Varget	.284"	2.800"	37.5	2430	44,600 CUP	40.0	2540	50,100 CUP
168 GR. SIE HPBT	IMR	IMR 4320	.284"	2.800"	38.0	2430	41,300 CUP	40.5C	2565	48,700 CUP
168 GR. SIE HPBT	IMR	IMR 4064	.284"	2.800"	37.5	2466	43,200 CUP	39.8	2597	50,200 CUP
168 GR. SIE HPBT	Hodgdon	BL-C(2)	.284"	2.800"	38.0	2370	42,700 CUP	40.5	2492	49,500 CUP
168 GR. SIE HPBT	IMR	IMR 4895	.284"	2.800"	37.5	2439	42,300 CUP	40.0	2583	49,800 CUP
168 GR. SIE HPBT	Hodgdon	H335	.284"	2.800"	35.0	2328	44,700 CUP	37.0	2421	49,600 CUP
168 GR. SIE HPBT	Hodgdon	H4895	.284"	2.800"	36.5	2390	45,400 CUP	39.0	2504	49,700 CUP
168 GR. SIE HPBT	IMR	IMR 8208 XBR	.284"	2.800"	34.9	2414	46,400 CUP	37.1	2486	49,600 CUP
168 GR. SIE HPBT	IMR	IMR 3031	.284"	2.800"	36.0	2431	45,200 CUP	38.2	2565	50,100 CUP
168 GR. SIE HPBT	Hodgdon	Benchmark	.284"	2.800"	36.0	2389	43,500 CUP	38.0	2517	49,400 CUP
175 GR. NOS PART	Hodgdon	H4831	.284"	2.800"	47.0	2443	46,600 CUP	49.0C	2516	49,400 CUP
175 GR. NOS PART	Hodgdon	Hybrid 100V	.284"	2.800"	40.0	2359	41,500 CUP	44.0C	2568	48,300 CUP
175 GR. NOS PART	Hodgdon	H4350	.284"	2.800"	39.9	2303	41,900 CUP	42.4	2451	50,400 CUP
175 GR. NOS PART	Hodgdon	H414	.284"	2.800"	40.5	2322	40,600 CUP	43.0	2495	50,100 CUP
175 GR. NOS PART	IMR	IMR 4350	.284"	2.800"	41.4	2310	39,200 CUP	46.0C	2556	48,500 CUP
175 GR. NOS PART	Winchester	760	.284"	2.800"	40.5	2322	40,600 CUP	43.0	2495	50,100 CUP
175 GR. NOS PART	IMR	IMR 4007 SSC	.284"	2.800"	39.0	2310	37,300 CUP	42.7C	2523	49,100 CUP
175 GR. NOS PART	Hodgdon	H380	.284"	2.800"	40.0	2303	45,600 CUP	42.7	2415	49,900 CUP
175 GR. NOS PART	Hodgdon	Varget	.284"	2.800"	35.0	2231	43,400 CUP	37.5	2344	49,500 CUP
175 GR. NOS PART	IMR	IMR 4320	.284"	2.800"	38.5	2355	43,900 CUP	41.0	2464	49,700 CUP
175 GR. NOS PART	IMR	IMR 4064	.284"	2.800"	37.5	2308	43,300 CUP	40.0C	2433	49,700 CUP
175 GR. NOS PART	Hodgdon	BL-C(2)	.284"	2.800"	35.0	2154	40,000 CUP	37.0	2298	49,500 CUP
175 GR. NOS PART	IMR	IMR 4895	.284"	2.800"	38.0	2343	43,900 CUP	40.5	2466	49,400 CUP
175 GR. NOS PART	Hodgdon	H335	.284"	2.800"	34.0	2195	46,200 CUP	36.0	2276	49,800 CUP
175 GR. NOS PART	Hodgdon	H4895	.284"	2.800"	35.0	2240	44,500 CUP	37.5	2354	49,700 CUP
175 GR. NOS PART	IMR	IMR 8208 XBR	.284"	2.800"	33.4	2264	43,200 CUP	35.5	2372	48,200 CUP
175 GR. NOS PART	IMR	IMR 3031	.284"	2.800"	35.2	2270	44,900 CUP	37.5	2381	49,700 CUP
175 GR. NOS PART	Hodgdon	Benchmark	.284"	2.800"	34.0	2202	42,400 CUP	36.5	2333	49,700 CUP

| Cartridge: 7mm Shooting Times Easterner | | | | | Starting Loads | | | Maximum Loads | | |
| Load Type: Rifle | | | | | | | | | | |
Bullet Weight (Gr.)	Manufacturer	Powder	Bullet Diam.	C.O.L.	Grs.	Vel. (ft/s)	Pressure	Grs.	Vel. (ft/s)	Pressure
120 GR. NOS FP	Hodgdon	H4350	.284"	2.475"	44.0	2503		49.0	2873	
120 GR. NOS FP	Hodgdon	H414	.284"	2.475"	42.0	2581		47.0	2916	
120 GR. NOS FP	Hodgdon	H4895	.284"	2.475"	37.0	2529		41.0	2909	
139 GR. HDY FP	Hodgdon	H4350	.284"	2.500"	43.0	2271		48.0	2676	
139 GR. HDY FP	Hodgdon	H414	.284"	2.500"	40.0	2346		45.0	2706	

Cartridge: 7 x 57mm Mauser Load Type: Rifle					Starting Loads			Maximum Loads		
Bullet Weight (Gr.)	Manufacturer	Powder	Bullet Diam.	C.O.L.	Grs.	Vel. (ft/s)	Pressure	Grs.	Vel. (ft/s)	Pressure
100 GR. HDY HP	Hodgdon	Hybrid 100V	.284"	2.900"	45.0	2693	32,100 CUP	48.0C	2881	38,400 CUP
100 GR. HDY HP	Hodgdon	H4350	.284"	2.900"	51.0	2993	36,000 CUP	54.0C	3166	41,200 CUP
100 GR. HDY HP	Hodgdon	H414	.284"	2.900"	50.0	3072	38,400 CUP	54.0	3299	46,400 CUP
100 GR. HDY HP	IMR	IMR 4350	.284"	2.900"	46.1	2889	36,800 CUP	51.2C	3080	45,100 CUP
100 GR. HDY HP	Winchester	760	.284"	2.900"	50.0	3072	38,400 CUP	54.0	3299	46,400 CUP
100 GR. HDY HP	IMR	IMR 4007 SSC	.284"	2.900"	46.6	2931	39,700 CUP	50.6	3139	45,000 CUP
100 GR. HDY HP	Hodgdon	H380	.284"	2.900"	50.0	3077	41,800 CUP	52.5	3228	45,500 CUP
100 GR. HDY HP	Hodgdon	Varget	.284"	2.900"	45.0	3123	42,000 CUP	48.0	3250	45,600 CUP
100 GR. HDY HP	IMR	IMR 4064	.284"	2.900"	42.8	2986	40,800 CUP	45.5	3139	46,100 CUP
100 GR. HDY HP	Hodgdon	BL-C(2)	.284"	2.900"	46.0	3085	42,900 CUP	48.5	3205	45,900 CUP
100 GR. HDY HP	IMR	IMR 4895	.284"	2.900"	41.9	2967	43,300 CUP	45.5	3129	45,800 CUP
100 GR. HDY HP	Hodgdon	H4895	.284"	2.900"	44.0	3095	41,200 CUP	46.0	3208	45,400 CUP
100 GR. HDY HP	IMR	IMR 8208 XBR	.284"	2.900"	40.0	2939	40,500 CUP	44.0	3113	45,500 CUP
100 GR. HDY HP	Hodgdon	Benchmark	.284"	2.900"	41.5	2987	39,900 CUP	44.3	3138	45,800 CUP
110 GR. SPR HP	Hodgdon	H4350	.284"	2.980"	51.0	2865	36,000 CUP	54.0C	3046	41,900 CUP
110 GR. SPR HP	Hodgdon	H414	.284"	2.980"	50.0	2911	36,800 CUP	53.5	3101	44,100 CUP
110 GR. SPR HP	IMR	IMR 4350	.284"	2.890"	46.0	2660	35,000 CUP	52.0C	3016	45,600 CUP
110 GR. SPR HP	Winchester	760	.284"	2.980"	50.0	2911	36,800 CUP	53.5	3101	44,100 CUP
110 GR. SPR HP	IMR	IMR 4007 SSC	.284"	2.980"	46.0	2819	36,900 CUP	50.0	3063	45,600 CUP
110 GR. SPR HP	Hodgdon	H380	.284"	2.980"	49.0	2933	41,000 CUP	52.0	3085	45,300 CUP
110 GR. SPR HP	Hodgdon	Varget	.284"	2.980"	41.0	2902	40,900 CUP	45.5	3081	46,000 CUP
110 GR. SPR HP	IMR	IMR 4320	.284"	2.980"	41.4	2846	43,400 CUP	44.0	2915	44,600 CUP
110 GR. SPR HP	IMR	IMR 4064	.284"	2.980"	42.8	2860	38,400 CUP	46.0	3058	45,800 CUP
110 GR. SPR HP	IMR	IMR 4895	.284"	2.980"	41.8	2832	39,200 CUP	44.5	2955	42,500 CUP
110 GR. SPR HP	Hodgdon	H4895	.284"	2.980"	43.0	2939	39,600 CUP	46.0	3078	45,000 CUP
110 GR. SPR HP	IMR	IMR 8208 XBR	.284"	2.980"	39.0	2823	43,400 CUP	43.5	3006	45,900 CUP
110 GR. SPR HP	IMR	IMR 3031	.284"	2.980"	40.0	2833	40,300 CUP	43.0	2995	45,700 CUP
110 GR. SPR HP	Hodgdon	Benchmark	.284"	2.980"	41.0	2874	39,300 CUP	44.0	3034	45,700 CUP
120 GR. NOS BT	IMR	IMR 7828 SSC	.284"	3.000"	49.1	2571	36,600 CUP	54.5C*	2825	44,900 CUP
120 GR. NOS BT	Hodgdon	H4831	.284"	3.000"	50.0	2650	36,500 CUP	52.5C	2777	40,800 CUP
120 GR. NOS BT	Hodgdon	Hybrid 100V	.284"	3.000"	44.0	2615	35,300 CUP	48.0C	2806	41,700 CUP
120 GR. NOS BT	IMR	IMR 4831	.284"	3.000"	46.4	2602	34,800 CUP	51.5C	2896	44,400 CUP
120 GR. NOS BT	Hodgdon	H4350	.284"	3.000"	48.0	2790	40,300 CUP	51.0C	2945	45,800 CUP
120 GR. NOS BT	Hodgdon	H414	.284"	3.000"	48.0	2784	37,800 CUP	51.0	2938	45,600 CUP
120 GR. NOS BT	IMR	IMR 4350	.284"	3.000"	45.0	2622	36,900 CUP	50.0C	2896	45,700 CUP

120 GR. NOS BT	Winchester	760	.284"	3.000"	48.0	2784	37,800 CUP	51.0	2938	45,600 CUP
120 GR. NOS BT	IMR	IMR 4007 SSC	.284"	3.000"	42.5	2621	38,000 CUP	47.2	2873	45,200 CUP
120 GR. NOS BT	Hodgdon	H380	.284"	3.000"	44.5	2716	40,000 CUP	47.5	2860	46,000 CUP
120 GR. NOS BT	Hodgdon	Varget	.284"	3.000"	41.0	2820	41,700 CUP	44.0	2979	46,000 CUP
120 GR. NOS BT	IMR	IMR 4064	.284"	3.000"	39.9	2673	37,900 CUP	42.5	2807	43,400 CUP
120 GR. NOS BT	IMR	IMR 4895	.284"	3.000"	40.9	2744	40,100 CUP	43.5	2878	45,300 CUP
120 GR. NOS BT	Hodgdon	H4895	.284"	3.000"	40.0	2732	40,900 CUP	42.0	2859	45,400 CUP
120 GR. NOS BT	IMR	IMR 8208 XBR	.284"	3.000"	37.0	2652	42,800 CUP	41.0	2821	45,800 CUP
120 GR. NOS BT	IMR	IMR 3031	.284"	3.000"	38.6	2695	39,200 CUP	41.0	2828	45,400 CUP
120 GR. NOS BT	Hodgdon	Benchmark	.284"	3.000"	39.0	2743	42,900 CUP	41.5	2863	46,000 CUP
130 GR. SPR SP	IMR	IMR 7828 SSC	.284"	2.800"	48.9	2675	42,800 CUP	52.0C*	2802	45,700 CUP
130 GR. SPR SP	Hodgdon	Hybrid 100V	.284"	2.800"	43.0	2536	35,000 CUP	47.0C	2721	41,000 CUP
130 GR. SPR SP	IMR	IMR 4831	.284"	2.800"	45.1	2674	42,800 CUP	48.0	2776	45,700 CUP
130 GR. SPR SP	Hodgdon	H4350	.284"	2.800"	47.0	2682	40,500 CUP	50.0	2848	46,000 CUP
130 GR. SPR SP	IMR	IMR 4350	.284"	2.800"	43.7	2621	40,500 CUP	46.5	2749	45,600 CUP
130 GR. SPR SP	IMR	IMR 4007 SSC	.284"	2.800"	39.0	2496	39,600 CUP	41.5	2610	44,700 CUP
130 GR. SPR SP	Hodgdon	H380	.284"	2.800"	43.0	2575	41,500 CUP	46.5	2769	46,000 CUP
130 GR. SPR SP	Hodgdon	Varget	.284"	2.800"	39.0	2678	40,400 CUP	42.0	2800	45,700 CUP
130 GR. SPR SP	IMR	IMR 4320	.284"	2.800"	36.2	2461	38,700 CUP	38.5	2597	44,100 CUP
130 GR. SPR SP	IMR	IMR 4064	.284"	2.800"	37.6	2556	40,200 CUP	40.0	2680	45,300 CUP
130 GR. SPR SP	IMR	IMR 4895	.284"	2.800"	37.6	2556	40,700 CUP	40.0	2691	45,200 CUP
130 GR. SPR SP	Hodgdon	H4895	.284"	2.800"	38.0	2579	40,600 CUP	41.0	2704	46,000 CUP
130 GR. SPR SP	IMR	IMR 8208 XBR	.284"	2.800"	35.0	2488	41,700 CUP	39.0	2676	46,100 CUP
130 GR. SPR SP	IMR	IMR 3031	.284"	2.800"	34.0	2466	38,400 CUP	36.2	2578	44,700 CUP
130 GR. SPR SP	Hodgdon	Benchmark	.284"	2.800"	39.0	2674	43,300 CUP	41.2	2765	46,000 CUP
140 GR. NOS BT	IMR	IMR 7828 SSC	.284"	3.000"	47.3	2492	37,200 CUP	50.3C	2632	44,800 CUP
140 GR. NOS BT	Hodgdon	H4831	.284"	3.000"	47.0	2520	42,500 CUP	49.5C	2719	46,000 CUP
140 GR. NOS BT	Hodgdon	Hybrid 100V	.284"	3.000"	42.0	2466	35,900 CUP	46.5C	2654	43,300 CUP
140 GR. NOS BT	IMR	IMR 4831	.284"	3.000"	46.1	2604	40,700 CUP	49.0	2759	46,100 CUP
140 GR. NOS BT	Hodgdon	H4350	.284"	3.000"	43.0	2530	40,400 CUP	46.5	2682	46,000 CUP
140 GR. NOS BT	Hodgdon	H414	.284"	3.000"	44.0	2548	40,400 CUP	47.0	2715	46,000 CUP
140 GR. NOS BT	IMR	IMR 4350	.284"	3.000"	44.2	2534	39,600 CUP	47.0	2683	45,300 CUP
140 GR. NOS BT	Winchester	760	.284"	3.000"	44.0	2548	40,400 CUP	47.0	2715	46,000 CUP
140 GR. NOS BT	IMR	IMR 4007 SSC	.284"	3.000"	41.3	2470	40,600 CUP	44.5	2645	46,200 CUP
140 GR. NOS BT	Hodgdon	H380	.284"	3.000"	41.0	2467	41,500 CUP	44.0	2614	46,000 CUP
140 GR. NOS BT	Hodgdon	Varget	.284"	3.000"	35.0	2368	40,800 CUP	37.7	2516	46,000 CUP
140 GR. NOS BT	IMR	IMR 4320	.284"	3.000"	36.1	2378	37,400 CUP	38.4	2505	45,000 CUP
140 GR. NOS BT	IMR	IMR 4064	.284"	3.000"	38.1	2498	41,800 CUP	40.5	2615	45,600 CUP
140 GR. NOS BT	IMR	IMR 4895	.284"	3.000"	37.8	2454	40,000 CUP	40.2	2678	44,700 CUP
140 GR. NOS BT	Hodgdon	H4895	.284"	3.000"	35.0	2376	39,800 CUP	37.5	2530	45,800 CUP

140 GR. NOS BT	IMR	IMR 8208 XBR	.284"	3.000"	33.0	2335	44,100 CUP	37.0	2522	46,100 CUP
140 GR. NOS BT	IMR	IMR 3031	.284"	3.000"	35.0	2426	40,600 CUP	37.2	2528	45,400 CUP
140 GR. NOS BT	Hodgdon	Benchmark	.284"	3.000"	35.5	2441	40,900 CUP	38.0	2571	45,700 CUP
150 GR. BAR TTSX	IMR	IMR 7828 SSC	.284"	2.965"	43.0	2317	39,500 CUP	47.0C*	2492	45.000 CUP
150 GR. BAR TTSX	Hodgdon	H4831	.284"	2.965"	42.0	2318	39,000 CUP	46.0C	2495	45,000 CUP
150 GR. BAR TTSX	Hodgdon	Hybrid 100V	.284"	2.965"	38.0	2329	40,600 CUP	42.0C	2516	44,200 CUP
150 GR. BAR TTSX	IMR	IMR 4831	.284"	2.965"	40.0	2314	38,900 CUP	44.0C	2515	44,200 CUP
150 GR. BAR TTSX	Hodgdon	H4350	.284"	2.965"	38.0	2288	36,900 CUP	42.5C	2502	45,300 CUP
150 GR. BAR TTSX	Hodgdon	H414	.284"	2.965"	38.0	2321	40,900 CUP	42.0	2493	45,500 CUP
150 GR. BAR TTSX	IMR	IMR 4350	.284"	2.965"	39.0	2320	39,800 CUP	43.5C	2532	44,800 CUP
150 GR. BAR TTSX	Winchester	760	.284"	2.965"	38.0	2321	40,900 CUP	42.0	2493	45,500 CUP
150 GR. BAR TTSX	IMR	IMR 4007 SSC	.284"	2.965"	36.0	2305	40,700 CUP	40.0	2453	45,500 CUP
150 GR. BAR TTSX	Hodgdon	H380	.284"	2.965"	36.0	2216	36,700 CUP	40.5	2405	45,500 CUP
150 GR. BAR TTSX	Hodgdon	Varget	.284"	2.965"	32.0	2183	38,600 CUP	36.5	2415	45,900 CUP
150 GR. BAR TTSX	IMR	IMR 4320	.284"	2.965"	34.0	2232	42,100 CUP	37.5	2369	45,300 CUP
150 GR. BAR TTSX	IMR	IMR 4064	.284"	2.965"	34.0	2297	42,400 CUP	37.0	2423	45,600 CUP
150 GR. BAR TTSX	IMR	IMR 4895	.284"	2.965"	34.0	2261	39,900 CUP	38.0	2430	45,600 CUP
150 GR. BAR TTSX	Hodgdon	H4895	.284"	2.965"	31.0	2167	37,700 CUP	35.0	2403	45,700 CUP
150 GR. BAR TTSX	IMR	IMR 3031	.284"	2.965"	32.0	2246	42,200 CUP	36.0	2429	46,000 CUP
150 GR. BAR TTSX	Hodgdon	Benchmark	.284"	2.965"	31.0	2194	40,300 CUP	35.0	2356	45,000 CUP
150 GR. NOS BT	IMR	IMR 7828 SSC	.284"	3.000"	46.1	2381	37,800 CUP	49.0C	2517	44,700 CUP
150 GR. NOS BT	Hodgdon	H4831	.284"	3.000"	45.0	2411	41,700 CUP	48.0	2542	46,000 CUP
150 GR. NOS BT	Hodgdon	Hybrid 100V	.284"	3.000"	41.0	2374	35,100 CUP	44.5C	2530	40,200 CUP
150 GR. NOS BT	IMR	IMR 4831	.284"	3.000"	43.7	2437	39,900 CUP	46.5	2575	45,000 CUP
150 GR. NOS BT	Hodgdon	H4350	.284"	3.000"	41.0	2364	38,800 CUP	44.0	2513	45,500 CUP
150 GR. NOS BT	Hodgdon	H414	.284"	3.000"	42.0	2406	40,100 CUP	44.5	2532	45,400 CUP
150 GR. NOS BT	IMR	IMR 4350	.284"	3.000"	42.3	2403	40,200 CUP	45.0	2535	45,400 CUP
150 GR. NOS BT	Winchester	760	.284"	3.000"	42.0	2406	40,100 CUP	44.5	2532	45,400 CUP
150 GR. NOS BT	IMR	IMR 4007 SSC	.284"	3.000"	40.0	2358	41,700 CUP	42.5	2486	45,500 CUP
150 GR. NOS BT	Hodgdon	H380	.284"	3.000"	39.0	2298	40,200 CUP	42.0	2455	46,000 CUP
150 GR. NOS BT	Hodgdon	Varget	.284"	3.000"	34.0	2265	40,900 CUP	36.0	2372	45,600 CUP
150 GR. NOS BT	IMR	IMR 4320	.284"	3.000"	35.4	2286	40,500 CUP	37.7	2401	45,000 CUP
150 GR. NOS BT	IMR	IMR 4064	.284"	3.000"	36.3	2345	41,000 CUP	38.6	2448	45,300 CUP
150 GR. NOS BT	IMR	IMR 4895	.284"	3.000"	36.9	2381	40,600 CUP	39.3	2487	45,600 CUP
150 GR. NOS BT	Hodgdon	H4895	.284"	3.000"	34.0	2271	40,200 CUP	36.0	2383	46,000 CUP
150 GR. NOS BT	IMR	IMR 8208 XBR	.284"	3.000"	32.0	2206	39,500 CUP	36.0	2401	45,800 CUP
150 GR. NOS BT	IMR	IMR 3031	.284"	3.000"	34.5	2341	40,200 CUP	36.7	2441	45,600 CUP
150 GR. NOS BT	Hodgdon	Benchmark	.284"	3.000"	34.0	2291	40,900 CUP	36.0	2365	45,700 CUP
160 GR. NOS PART	IMR	IMR 7828 SSC	.284"	3.000"	45.1	2370	41,200 CUP	48.0	2483	45,400 CUP

160 GR. NOS PART	Hodgdon	H4831	.284"	3.000"	43.0	2311	41,500 CUP	46.0	2415	45,700 CUP
160 GR. NOS PART	Hodgdon	Hybrid 100V	.284"	3.000"	40.5	2337	36,600 CUP	43.5C	2468	41,600 CUP
160 GR. NOS PART	IMR	IMR 4831	.284"	3.000"	43.5	2416	42,400 CUP	46.2	2515	45,300 CUP
160 GR. NOS PART	Hodgdon	H4350	.284"	3.000"	40.0	2314	42,100 CUP	42.5	2399	45,400 CUP
160 GR. NOS PART	Hodgdon	H414	.284"	3.000"	40.0	2292	40,200 CUP	42.5	2405	45,400 CUP
160 GR. NOS PART	IMR	IMR 4350	.284"	3.000"	41.8	2389	42,000 CUP	44.4	2499	45,500 CUP
160 GR. NOS PART	Winchester	760	.284"	3.000"	40.0	2292	40,200 CUP	42.5	2405	45,400 CUP
160 GR. NOS PART	IMR	IMR 4007 SSC	.284"	3.000"	36.2	2194	40,000 CUP	38.5	2302	43,900 CUP
160 GR. NOS PART	Hodgdon	H380	.284"	3.000"	37.0	2186	40,800 CUP	39.5	2299	46,000 CUP
160 GR. NOS PART	Hodgdon	Varget	.284"	3.000"	33.0	2160	41,100 CUP	35.0	2261	45,900 CUP
160 GR. NOS PART	IMR	IMR 4320	.284"	3.000"	34.8	2212	39,100 CUP	37.0	2331	44,500 CUP
160 GR. NOS PART	IMR	IMR 4064	.284"	3.000"	35.4	2255	39,400 CUP	37.6	2357	45,000 CUP
160 GR. NOS PART	IMR	IMR 4895	.284"	3.000"	34.7	2227	38,300 CUP	37.0	2312	44,600 CUP
160 GR. NOS PART	Hodgdon	H4895	.284"	3.000"	33.0	2165	40,200 CUP	34.5	2245	44,700 CUP
160 GR. NOS PART	IMR	IMR 8208 XBR	.284"	3.000"	31.0	2106	38,000 CUP	34.5	2287	45,900 CUP
160 GR. NOS PART	IMR	IMR 3031	.284"	3.000"	33.2	2207	41,400 CUP	35.3	2337	45,500 CUP
160 GR. NOS PART	Hodgdon	Benchmark	.284"	3.000"	32.5	2174	40,800 CUP	34.7	2284	45,700 CUP
168 GR. SIE HPBT	Hodgdon	H1000	.284"	3.000"	49.0	2338	40,800 CUP	52.0C	2485	46,000 CUP
168 GR. SIE HPBT	IMR	IMR 7828 SSC	.284"	3.000"	45.0	2329	40,400 CUP	48.0	2567	45,200 CUP
168 GR. SIE HPBT	Hodgdon	H4831	.284"	3.000"	43.0	2244	38,100 CUP	46.0	2393	43,900 CUP
168 GR. SIE HPBT	Hodgdon	Hybrid 100V	.284"	3.300"	41.0	2338	37,400 CUP	45.5C	2534	45,000 CUP
168 GR. SIE HPBT	IMR	IMR 4831	.284"	3.000"	43.7	2392	40,100 CUP	46.5	2534	45,600 CUP
168 GR. SIE HPBT	Hodgdon	H4350	.284"	3.000"	40.0	2267	40,400 CUP	42.5	2378	44,100 CUP
168 GR. SIE HPBT	Hodgdon	H414	.284"	3.000"	40.0	2276	40,700 CUP	42.5	2378	45,000 CUP
168 GR. SIE HPBT	IMR	IMR 4350	.284"	3.000"	42.8	2363	40,100 CUP	45.6	2515	45,900 CUP
168 GR. SIE HPBT	Winchester	760	.284"	3.000"	40.0	2276	40,700 CUP	42.5	2378	45,000 CUP
168 GR. SIE HPBT	IMR	IMR 4007 SSC	.284"	3.000"	38.5	2253	39,200 CUP	41.0	2472	44,900 CUP
168 GR. SIE HPBT	Hodgdon	H380	.284"	3.000"	37.0	2149	38,600 CUP	39.5	2272	44,500 CUP
168 GR. SIE HPBT	Hodgdon	Varget	.284"	3.000"	34.5	2232	36,600 CUP	37.5	2404	45,500 CUP
168 GR. SIE HPBT	IMR	IMR 4320	.284"	3.000"	34.8	2212	38,100 CUP	37.0	2343	45,800 CUP
168 GR. SIE HPBT	IMR	IMR 4064	.284"	3.000"	36.6	2298	41,800 CUP	39.0	2397	45,600 CUP
168 GR. SIE HPBT	IMR	IMR 4895	.284"	3.000"	35.7	2245	39,500 CUP	38.0	2344	44,900 CUP
168 GR. SIE HPBT	Hodgdon	H4895	.284"	3.000"	33.0	2118	36,400 CUP	34.5	2211	42,600 CUP
168 GR. SIE HPBT	IMR	IMR 8208 XBR	.284"	3.000"	31.0	3100	39,100 CUP	34.0	2260	45,800 CUP
168 GR. SIE HPBT	IMR	IMR 3031	.284"	3.000"	33.8	2227	41,400 CUP	36.0	2318	45,500 CUP
168 GR. SIE HPBT	Hodgdon	Benchmark	.284"	3.000"	33.5	2212	40,900 CUP	36.0	2336	46,000 CUP
175 GR. NOS PART	Hodgdon	H1000	.284"	3.025"	42.0	2038	41,000 CUP	44.5	2239	45,500 CUP
175 GR. NOS PART	IMR	IMR 7828 SSC	.284"	3.025"	41.6	2180	40,400 CUP	44.3	2299	44,700 CUP
175 GR. NOS PART	Hodgdon	H4831	.284"	3.025"	37.0	2098	41,300 CUP	40.0	2201	45,700 CUP
175 GR. NOS PART	Hodgdon	Hybrid 100V	.284"	3.025"	38.0	2163	34,800 CUP	41.0C	2300	40,800 CUP

	Manufacturer	Powder	Bullet Diam.	C.O.L.	Grs.	Vel. (ft/s)	Pressure	Grs.	Vel. (ft/s)	Pressure
175 GR. NOS PART	IMR	IMR 4831	.284"	3.025"	37.8	2124	39,500 CUP	40.2	2229	44,400 CUP
175 GR. NOS PART	Hodgdon	H4350	.284"	3.025"	35.0	2066	39,700 CUP	37.0	2159	43,400 CUP
175 GR. NOS PART	Hodgdon	H414	.284"	3.025"	35.0	2033	40,100 CUP	37.0	2119	44,500 CUP
175 GR. NOS PART	IMR	IMR 4350	.284"	3.025"	37.0	2076	35,800 CUP	40.0	2231	44,600 CUP
175 GR. NOS PART	Winchester	760	.284"	3.025"	35.0	2033	40,100 CUP	37.0	2119	44,500 CUP
175 GR. NOS PART	IMR	IMR 4007 SSC	.284"	3.025"	34.3	2085	40,200 CUP	36.5	2167	45,100 CUP
175 GR. NOS PART	Hodgdon	Varget	.284"	3.025"	31.0	2005	34,200 CUP	35.0	2178	45,500 CUP
175 GR. NOS PART	IMR	IMR 4320	.284"	3.025"	34.0	2103	39,100 CUP	36.2	2213	44,900 CUP
175 GR. NOS PART	IMR	IMR 4064	.284'	3.025"	33.1	2063	40,400 CUP	35.2	2161	44,700 CUP

Cartridge:280 Remington Load Type:Rifle					Starting Loads			Maximum Loads		
Bullet Weight (Gr.)	Manufacturer	Powder	Bullet Diam.	C.O.L.	Grs.	Vel. (ft/s)	Pressure	Grs.	Vel. (ft/s)	Pressure
100 GR. SIE HP	Hodgdon	H4831	.284"	3.180"	59.0	3053	38,900 CUP	63.0C	3266	46,000 CUP
100 GR. SIE HP	Hodgdon	H4350	.284"	3.180"	56.0	3167	41,400 CUP	60.5	3379	49,200 CUP
100 GR. SIE HP	Hodgdon	H414	.284"	3.180"	54.0	3243	42,100 CUP	57.5	3395	47,100 CUP
100 GR. SIE HP	Winchester	760	.284"	3.180"	54.0	3243	42,100 CUP	57.5	3395	47,100 CUP
100 GR. SIE HP	Hodgdon	H380	.284"	3.180"	52.0	3231	42,200 CUP	55.5	3368	47,800 CUP
100 GR. SIE HP	Hodgdon	Varget	.284"	3.180"	48.0	3254	42,400 CUP	51.3	3433	48,300 CUP
100 GR. SIE HP	Hodgdon	BL-C(2)	.284"	3.180"	49.0	3226	41,700 CUP	53.0	3409	48,300 CUP
100 GR. SIE HP	Hodgdon	H4895	.284"	3.180"	47.0	3226	42,800 CUP	50.5	3418	49,000 CUP
115 GR. SPR HP	Hodgdon	H4831	.284"	3.180"	58.0	3014	40,600 CUP	62.0C	3190	47,300 CUP
115 GR. SPR HP	Hodgdon	H4350	.284"	3.180"	54.0	3017	40,200 CUP	58.5	3234	48,100 CUP
115 GR. SPR HP	Hodgdon	H414	.284"	3.180"	52.0	3012	40,300 CUP	56.0	3192	47,400 CUP
115 GR. SPR HP	Winchester	760	.284"	3.180"	52.0	3012	40,300 CUP	56.0	3192	47,400 CUP
115 GR. SPR HP	Hodgdon	H380	.284"	3.180"	48.0	2902	42,200 CUP	52.0	3090	48,600 CUP
115 GR. SPR HP	Hodgdon	Varget	.284"	3.180"	46.0	3040	43,500 CUP	49.0	3170	47,700 CUP
115 GR. SPR HP	Hodgdon	BL-C(2)	.284"	3.180"	45.0	2927	42,300 CUP	49.0	3118	48,400 CUP
115 GR. SPR HP	Hodgdon	H4895	.284"	3.180"	46.0	3033	42,600 CUP	49.0	3175	48,300 CUP
120 GR. BAR TSX	IMR	IMR 7828 SSC	.284"	3.230"	60.2	3054	50,000 PSI	64.0C*	3234	58,300 PSI
120 GR. BAR TSX	Hodgdon	Suprform	.284"	3.230"	54.0	3072	48,900 PSI	60.0	3304	57,300 PSI
120 GR. BAR TSX	Hodgdon	H4831	.284"	3.230"	58.0	2923	43.600 PSI	63.0C	3124	53,100 PSI
120 GR. BAR TSX	IMR	IMR 4831	.284"	3.230"	57.0	3060	49,500 PSI	61.0C	3259	57,400 PSI
120 GR. BAR TSX	Hodgdon	H4350	.284"	3.230"	55.5	3093	49,100 PSI	59.0C	3254	57,400 PSI
120 GR. BAR TSX	Hodgdon	H414	.284:	3.230"	53.0	3033	49,700 PSI	56.2	3191	56,900 PSI
120 GR. BAR TSX	IMR	IMR 4350	.284"	3.230"	55.5	3038	49,500 PSI	59.0C	3210	56,800 PSI
120 GR. BAR TSX	IMR	IMR 4007 SSC	.284"	3.230"	52.9	3077	50,500 PSI	56.3	3230	57,400 PSI
120 GR. BAR TSX	Hodgdon	H380	.284"	3.230"	51.7	3044	50,700 PSI	55.0	3210	58,000 PSI
120 GR. BAR TSX	Hodgdon	Varget	.284"	3.230"	47.7	3007	48,800 PSI	50.7	3177	57,200 PSI

120 GR. BAR TSX	IMR	IMR 4064	.284"	3.230"	47.6	2994	48,700 PSI	50.6	3160	57,000 PSI
120 GR. BAR TSX	Winchester	748	.284"	3.230"	47.0	2935	49,600 PSI	50.0	3061	56,400 PSI
120 GR. BAR TSX	Hodgdon	BL-C(2)	.284"	3.230"	48.0	3002	50,000 PSI	50.6	3125	55,800 PSI
120 GR. BAR TSX	Hodgdon	H4895	.284"	3.230"	46.9	3067	54,300 PSI	49.9	3171	57,200 PSI
140 GR. NOS PART	Hodgdon	Suprform	.284"	3.230"	54.0	2905	55,400 PSI	57.0	2983	58,600 PSI
140 GR. NOS PART	Hodgdon	H4831	.284"	3.230"	54.0	2732	41,000 CUP	58.5	2927	48,500 CUP
140 GR. NOS PART	Hodgdon	Hybrid 100V	.284"	3.230"	50.0	2669	41,300 CUP	54.0C	2847	47,000 CUP
140 GR. NOS PART	Hodgdon	H4350	.284"	3.230"	50.0	2756	41,900 CUP	53.5	2918	48,500 CUP
140 GR. NOS PART	Hodgdon	H414	.284"	3.230"	47.0	2710	41,800 CUP	51.0	2867	47,900 CUP
140 GR. NOS PART	Winchester	760	.284"	3.230"	47.0	2710	41,800 CUP	51.0	2867	47,900 CUP
140 GR. NOS PART	Hodgdon	Varget	.284"	3.230"	42.0	2674	41,400 CUP	45.5	2838	48,100 CUP
140 GR. NOS PART	Hodgdon	H4895	.284"	3.230"	42.0	2711	43,200 CUP	45.2	2830	48,400 CUP
145 GR. SPR SP	Hodgdon	H4831	.284"	3.160"	48.0	2579	46,900 CUP	53.0	2727	50,000 CUP
145 GR. SPR SP	Hodgdon	Hybrid 100V	.284"	3.160"	50.0	2691	43,000 CUP	54.0C	2866	49,100 CUP
145 GR. SPR SP	Hodgdon	H4350	.284"	3.160"	45.0	2553	44,500 CUP	48.8	2714	49,900 CUP
145 GR. SPR SP	Hodgdon	H414	.284"	3.160"	43.0	2491	44,700 CUP	46.5	2639	48,900 CUP
145 GR. SPR SP	Winchester	760	.284"	3.160"	43.0	2491	44,700 CUP	46.5	2639	48,900 CUP
145 GR. SPR SP	Hodgdon	Varget	.284"	3.160"	39.0	2469	44,900 CUP	43.0	2690	48,000 CUP
145 GR. SPR SP	Hodgdon	H4895	.284"	3.160"	38.0	2434	43,800 CUP	41.0	2596	48,400 CUP
150 GR. NOS PART	Hodgdon	H1000	.284"	3.300"	56.0	2647	43,500 CUP	60.0C	2797	49,300 CUP
150 GR. NOS PART	Hodgdon	H4831	.284"	3.300"	50.0	2579	45,100 CUP	53.7	2709	49,500 CUP
150 GR. NOS PART	Hodgdon	H4350	.284"	3.300"	46.0	2550	42,500 CUP	49.7	2700	49,300 CUP
150 GR. NOS PART	Hodgdon	H414	.284"	3.300"	43.0	2456	41,500 CUP	47.3	2640	49,400 CUP
150 GR. NOS PART	Winchester	760	.284"	3.300"	43.0	2456	41,500 CUP	47.3	2640	49,400 CUP
150 GR. NOS PART	Hodgdon	Varget	.284"	3.300"	39.0	2485	44,000 CUP	42.0	2611	49,800 CUP
150 GR. NOS PART	Hodgdon	H4895	.284"	3.300"	38.0	2430	43,700 CUP	41.5	2588	50,000 CUP
160 GR. SFT SP	Hodgdon	H1000	.284"	3.240"	57.0	2517	40,700 CUP	61.0C	2714	47,500 CUP
160 GR. SFT SP	Winchester	Supreme 780	.284"	3.240"	53.3	2546	44,800 CUP	56.7	2718	49,500 CUP
160 GR. SFT SP	Hodgdon	H4831	.284"	3.240"	51.0	2464	40,600 CUP	55.0	2660	49,500 CUP
160 GR. SFT SP	Hodgdon	Hybrid 100V	.284"	3.240"	47.0	2451	38,900 CUP	52.0C	2712	48,600 CUP
160 GR. SFT SP	Hodgdon	H4350	.284"	3.240"	46.0	2441	40,900 CUP	49.5	2610	48,900 CUP
160 GR. SFT SP	Hodgdon	H414	.284"	3.240"	43.0	2348	40,300 CUP	47.5	2558	49,700 CUP
160 GR. SFT SP	Winchester	760	.284"	3.240"	43.0	2348	40,300 CUP	47.5	2558	49,700 CUP
160 GR. SFT SP	Hodgdon	Varget	.284"	3.240"	39.0	2384	43,000 CUP	42.5	2555	49,300 CUP
160 GR. SFT SP	Hodgdon	H4895	.284"	3.240"	38.0	2341	40,300 CUP	41.5	2535	49,500 CUP
162 GR. HDY A-MAX	Hodgdon	H1000	.284"	3.330"	56.0	2526	40,300 CUP	60.0C	2711	47,200 CUP
162 GR. HDY A-MAX	Winchester	Supreme 780	.284"	3.330"	52.2	2548	42,700 CUP	55.5	2735	49,400 CUP
162 GR. HDY A-MAX	Hodgdon	H4831	.284"	3.330"	51.0	2517	44,100 CUP	54.5	2644	49,300 CUP
162 GR. HDY A-MAX	Hodgdon	Hybrid 100V	.284"	3.330"	47.5	2528	39,800 CUP	51.5C	2746	47,500 CUP
162 GR. HDY A-MAX	Hodgdon	H4350	.284"	3.330"	46.0	2468	42,300 CUP	49.5	2614	49,900 CUP

Bullet Weight (Gr.)	Manufacturer	Powder	Bullet Diam.	C.O.L.	Grs.	Vel. (ft/s)	Pressure	Grs.	Vel. (ft/s)	Pressure
162 GR. HDY A-MAX	Hodgdon	H414	.284"	3.330"	43.0	2400	41,400 CUP	47.5	2669	49,900 CUP
162 GR. HDY A-MAX	Winchester	760	.284"	3.330"	43.0	2400	41,400 CUP	47.5	2669	49,900 CUP
162 GR. HDY A-MAX	Hodgdon	Varget	.284"	3.330"	39.0	2443	44,100 CUP	42.0	2573	49,500 CUP
162 GR. HDY A-MAX	Hodgdon	H4895	.284"	3.330"	38.0	2396	42,800 CUP	41.5	2567	50,000 CUP
168 GR. SIE HPBT	Hodgdon	H1000	.284"	3.330"	56.0	2506	39,400 CUP	60.0C	2700	49,300 CUP
168 GR. SIE HPBT	Winchester	Supreme 780	.284"	3.330"	51.7	2537	43,000 CUP	55.0	2701	49,100 CUP
168 GR. SIE HPBT	Hodgdon	H4831	.284"	3.330"	51.0	2462	42,400 CUP	54.5	2605	49,200 CUP
168 GR. SIE HPBT	Hodgdon	Hybrid 100V	.284"	3.330"	47.0	2537	42,100 CUP	51.0C	2704	48,100 CUP
168 GR. SIE HPBT	Hodgdon	H4350	.284"	3.330"	46.0	2422	41,300 CUP	50.0	2586	49,400 CUP
168 GR. SIE HPBT	Hodgdon	Varget	.284"	3.330"	40.0	2424	45,800 CUP	42.2	2523	49,900 CUP
168 GR. SIE HPBT	Hodgdon	H4895	.284"	3.330"	38.0	2329	45,900 CUP	41.2	2468	49,600 CUP
175 GR. HDY SP	Hodgdon	H1000	.284"	3.300"	54.0	2502	47,000 CUP	57.0C	2583	49,600 CUP
175 GR. HDY SP	Winchester	Supreme 780	.284"	3.300"	52.0	2479	44,300 CUP	55.0	2593	49,200 CUP
175 GR. HDY SP	Hodgdon	H4831	.284"	3.300"	48.0	2362	44,400 CUP	51.0	2477	49,800 CUP
175 GR. HDY SP	Hodgdon	Hybrid 100V	.284"	3.300"	45.5	2374	39,400 CUP	49.5C	2569	47,400 CUP
175 GR. HDY SP	Hodgdon	H4350	.284"	3.300"	44.0	2343	44,600 CUP	46.5	2447	49,300 CUP

Cartridge: 284 Winchester
Load Type: Rifle

Bullet Weight (Gr.)	Manufacturer	Powder	Bullet Diam.	C.O.L.	Starting Loads			Maximum Loads		
					Grs.	Vel. (ft/s)	Pressure	Grs.	Vel. (ft/s)	Pressure
100 GR. SIE HP	Hodgdon	H4350	.284"	2.800"	55.0	3096	39,600 CUP	60.0C	3368	49,000 CUP
100 GR. SIE HP	Hodgdon	H414	.284"	2.800"	54.0	3157	41,800 CUP	58.5	3393	49,900 CUP
100 GR. SIE HP	Winchester	760	.284"	2.800"	54.0	3157	41,800 CUP	58.5	3393	49,900 CUP
100 GR. SIE HP	IMR	IMR 4007 SSC	.284"	2.800"	54.3	3134	40,300 CUP	59.0C	3438	50,200 CUP
100 GR. SIE HP	Hodgdon	Varget	.284"	2.800"	51.0	3242	45,900 CUP	54.0	3435	52,900 CUP
100 GR. SIE HP	IMR	IMR 4320	.284"	2.800"	50.0	3170	43,600 CUP	53.2	3354	50,900 CUP
100 GR. SIE HP	IMR	IMR 4064	.284"	2.800"	49.5	3123	39,500 CUP	53.2	3419	51,700 CUP
100 GR. SIE HP	IMR	IMR 4895	.284"	2.800"	49.8	3220	43,100 CUP	53.0	3422	51,900 CUP
100 GR. SIE HP	Hodgdon	H4895	.284"	2.800"	47.0	3213	45,800 CUP	51.5	3428	51,600 CUP
100 GR. SIE HP	IMR	IMR 8208 XBR	.284"	2.800"	48.9	3322	44,800 CUP	52.0	3478	52,000 CUP
100 GR. SIE HP	IMR	IMR 3031	.284"	2.800"	47.0	3198	42,900 CUP	50.0	3390	51,900 CUP
115 GR. SPR SP	Hodgdon	H4350	.284"	2.800"	54.0	3008	40,200 CUP	59.0C	3305	52,200 CUP
115 GR. SPR SP	Hodgdon	H414	.284"	2.800"	52.0	2963	41,000 CUP	57.4	3273	51,700 CUP
115 GR. SPR SP	Winchester	760	.284"	2.800"	52.0	2963	41,000 CUP	57.4	3273	51, 700 CUP
115 GR. SPR SP	Hodgdon	Varget	.284"	2.800"	49.0	3096	46,900 CUP	53.0	3281	53,400 CUP
115 GR. SPR SP	Hodgdon	H4895	.284"	2.800"	45.0	3000	43,500 CUP	50.0	3245	52,400 CUP
120 GR. HDY V-MAX	Hodgdon	H4831	.284"	2.825"	56.0	2846	38,900 CUP	60.0C	3018	45,200 CUP
120 GR. HDY V-MAX	Hodgdon	Hybrid 100V	.284"	2.825"	51.0	2909	39,400 CUP	55.0C	3050	44,700 CUP
120 GR. HDY V-MAX	Hodgdon	H4350	.284"	2.825"	53.0	3017	44,700 CUP	57.0C	3174	49,600 CUP

120 GR. HDY V-MAX	Hodgdon	H414	.284"	2.825"	50.0	2897	42,800 CUP	54.8	3191	52,200 CUP
120 GR. HDY V-MAX	IMR	IMR 4350	.284"	2.825"	51.8	2878	38,000 CUP	57.5C	3168	46,500 CUP
120 GR. HDY V-MAX	Winchester	760	.284"	2.825"	50.0	2897	42,800 CUP	54.8	3191	52,200 CUP
120 GR. HDY V-MAX	IMR	IMR 4007 SSC	84"	2.825"	50.1	2871	38,500 CUP	56.5C	3245	52,400 CUP
120 GR. HDY V-MAX	Hodgdon	Varget	.284"	2.825"	45.0	2919	43,200 CUP	50.5	3158	52,200 CUP
120 GR. HDY V-MAX	IMR	IMR 4320	.284"	2.825"	48.4	3039	46,300 CUP	51.5	3187	52,100 CUP
120 GR. HDY V-MAX	IMR	IMR 4064	.284"	2.825"	47.0	2924	40,100 CUP	50.2	3202	51,500 CUP
120 GR. HDY V-MAX	IMR	IMR 4895	.284"	2.825"	47.9	2991	42,900 CUP	50.9	3192	51,800 CUP
120 GR. HDY V-MAX	Hodgdon	H4895	.284"	2.825"	43.0	2880	41,400 CUP	48.0	3120	51,600 CUP
120 GR. HDY V-MAX	IMR	IMR 8208 XBR	.284"	2.825"	45.1	3032	45,600 CUP	48.0	3134	52,600 CUP
130 GR. BAR XBT	Hodgdon	H4831	.284"	2.850"	56.0	2788	40,500 CUP	60.0C	2923	46,300 CUP
130 GR. BAR XBT	Hodgdon	H4350	.284"	2.850"	53.0	2920	45,700 CUP	57.0C	3095	50,900 CUP
130 GR. BAR XBT	Hodgdon	H414	.284"	2.850"	50.0	2780	41,000 CUP	55.0	3080	51,200 CUP
130 GR. BAR XBT	Winchester	760	.284"	2.850"	50.0	2780	41,000 CUP	55.0	3080	51,200 CUP
130 GR. BAR XBT	Hodgdon	Varget	.284"	2.850"	45.0	2844	47,400 CUP	49.7	3026	52,700 CUP
130 GR. BAR XBT	Hodgdon	H4895	.284"	2.850"	44.0	2853	47,300 CUP	47.5	2984	52,100 CUP
130 GR. SPR SP	IMR	IMR 4831	.284"	2.800"				59.0C	3100	50,600 CUP
130 GR. SPR SP	IMR	IMR 4350	.284"	2.800"				57.0	3130	53,600 CUP
130 GR. SPR SP	IMR	IMR 4064	.284"	2.800"				50.0	3085	54,000 CUP
130 GR. SPR SP	IMR	IMR 4895	.284"	2.800"				45.0	2905	52,800 CUP
130 GR. SPR SP	IMR	IMR 3031	.284"	2.800"				48.0	3055	54,000 CUP
130 GR. SPR SP	IMR	SR 4759	.284"	2.800"				30.0	2425	51,900 CUP
139 GR. HDY SST	Hodgdon	H4831	.284"	2.915"	56.0	2760	40,000 CUP	60.0C	2923	46,900 CUP
139 GR. HDY SST	Hodgdon	Hybrid 100V	.284"	2.915"	51.0	2835	42,000 CUP	55.0C	2996	46,800 CUP
139 GR. HDY SST	IMR	IMR 4831	.284"	2.915"	54.1	2813	41,100 CUP	57.5C	2969	45,700 CUP
139 GR. HDY SST	Hodgdon	H4350	.284"	2.915"	52.0	2840	44,300 CUP	57.0C	3079	52,400 CUP
139 GR. HDY SST	Hodgdon	H414	.284"	2.915"	50.0	2792	39,800 CUP	55.0	3075	51,200 CUP
139 GR. HDY SST	IMR	IMR 4350	.284"	2.915"	51.3	2671	37,800 CUP	57.0C	2985	48,100 CUP
139 GR. HDY SST	Winchester	760	.284"	2.915"	50.0	2792	39,800 CUP	55.0	3075	51,200 CUP
139 GR. HDY SST	IMR	IMR 4007 SSC	.284"	2.915"	50.1	2799	40,500 CUP	54.0C	3022	51,900 CUP
139 GR. HDY SST	Hodgdon	Varget	.284"	2.915"	45.0	2777	44,400 CUP	49.5	2996	52,600 CUP
139 GR. HDY SST	IMR	IMR 4320	.284"	2.915"	47.7	2742	43,100 CUP	50.7	3035	52,400 CUP
139 GR. HDY SST	IMR	IMR 4064	.284"	2.915"	46.6	2845	43,500 CUP	49.5	3018	51,400 CUP
139 GR. HDY SST	IMR	IMR 4895	.284"	2.915"	46.5	2812	42,500 CUP	49.6	2986	51,400 CUP
139 GR. HDY SST	Hodgdon	H4895	.284"	2.915"	43.0	2811	48,000 CUP	47.0	2943	51,700 CUP
139 GR. HDY SST	IMR	IMR 8208 XBR	.284"	2.915"	42.8	2772	43,900 CUP	45.5	2914	51,900 CUP
145 GR. SPR SP	IMR	IMR 7828 SSC	.284"	2.800"	54.0	2614	38,900 CUP	60.0C*	2902	50,700 CUP
145 GR. SPR SP	Hodgdon	H4831	.284"	2.800"	55.0	2733	45,200 CUP	60.0C	2945	52,500 CUP
145 GR. SPR SP	Hodgdon	Hybrid 100V	.284"	2.800"	51.0	2811	43,900 CUP	55.0C	2950	48,500 CUP
145 GR. SPR SP	IMR	IMR 4831	.284"	2.800"	52.5	2721	41,600 CUP	57.0C	2941	50,900 CUP

145 GR. SPR SP	Hodgdon	H4350	.284"	2.800"	50.0	2743	45,600 CUP	55.0	2964	53,200 CUP
145 GR. SPR SP	Hodgdon	H414	.284"	2.800"	49.0	2735	43,100 CUP	54.0	2985	52,800 CUP
145 GR. SPR SP	IMR	IMR 4350	.284"	2.800"	51.5	2713	42,700 CUP	56.0C	2935	52,000 CUP
145 GR. SPR SP	Winchester	760	.284"	2.800"	49.0	2735	43,100 CUP	54.0	2985	52,800 CUP
145 GR. SPR SP	IMR	IMR 4007 SSC	.284"	2.800"	48.3	2703	44,100 CUP	51.4	2865	51,500 CUP
145 GR. SPR SP	Hodgdon	Varget	.284"	2.800"	45.0	2771	48,300 CUP	49.0	2905	52,500 CUP
145 GR. SPR SP	IMR	IMR 4320	.284"	2.800"	46.3	2717	44,500 CUP	49.3	2858	51,500 CUP
145 GR. SPR SP	IMR	IMR 4064	.284"	2.800"	45.1	2696	44,800 CUP	48.0	2831	50,800 CUP
145 GR. SPR SP	IMR	IMR 4895	.284"	2.800"	44.9	2656	43,400 CUP	47.8	2828	50,400 CUP
145 GR. SPR SP	Hodgdon	H4895	.284"	2.800"	43.0	2736	47,500 CUP	46.5	2856	51,600 CUP
150 GR. SFT SCIR	IMR	IMR 7828 SSC	.284"	2.950"	53.1	2573	38,700 CUP	59.0C*	2861	49,900 CUP
150 GR. SFT SCIR	Hodgdon	H4831	.284"	2.950"	55.0	2682	45,200 CUP	59.0C	2852	50,100 CUP
150 GR. SFT SCIR	Hodgdon	Hybrid 100V	.284"	2.950"	49.0	2713	44,200 CUP	54.0C	2900	49,200 CUP
150 GR. SFT SCIR	IMR	IMR 4831	.284"	2.950"	52.0	2652	39,600 CUP	56.5C	2865	48,100 CUP
150 GR. SFT SCIR	Hodgdon	H4350	.284"	2.950"	50.0	2721	46,100 CUP	54.7C	2913	52,300 CUP
150 GR. SFT SCIR	Hodgdon	H414	.284"	2.950"	50.0	2801	45,600 CUP	53.5	2968	50,900 CUP
150 GR. SFT SCIR	IMR	IMR 4350	.284"	2.950"	50.6	2634	39,400 CUP	55.0C	2872	49,900 CUP
150 GR. SFT SCIR	Winchester	760	.284"	2.950"	50.0	2801	45,600 CUP	53.5	2968	50,900 CUP
150 GR. SFT SCIR	IMR	IMR 4007 SSC	.284"	2.950"	48.3	2662	41,300 CUP	51.4	2823	51,200 CUP
150 GR. SFT SCIR	Hodgdon	Varget	.284"	2.950"	44.0	2674	45,400 CUP	48.7	2863	52,800 CUP
150 GR. SFT SCIR	IMR	IMR 4320	.284"	2.950"	45.9	2666	43,200 CUP	48.8	2816	51,800 CUP
150 GR. SFT SCIR	IMR	IMR 4064	.284"	2.950"	45.0	2643	43,200 CUP	47.9	2810	51,900 CUP
150 GR. SFT SCIR	IMR	IMR 4895	.284"	2.950"	44.7	2644	43,700 CUP	47.6	2775	51,000 CUP
150 GR. SFT SCIR	Hodgdon	H4895	.284"	2.950"	43.0	2719	48,100 CUP	46.5	2818	52,300 CUP
160 GR. BAR TSX	Hodgdon	Hybrid 100V	.284"	2.870"	48.0	2474	39,900 CUP	52.0C	2648	44,200 CUP
160 GR. BAR TSX	IMR	IMR 7828 SSC	.284"	2.870"	53.1	2491	41,000 CUP	59.0C*	2810	52,000 CUP
160 GR. BAR TSX	Winchester	Supreme 780	.284"	2.870"	55.5	2672	44,800 CUP	59.0	2808	49,700 CUP
160 GR. BAR TSX	Hodgdon	H4831	.284"	2.870"	50.0	2391	38,300 CUP	55.5C	2629	47,400 CUP
160 GR. BAR TSX	IMR	IMR 4831	.284"	2.870"	51.5	2520	41,900 CUP	56.0C	2771	51,500 CUP
160 GR. BAR TSX	Hodgdon	H4350	.284"	2.870"	47.0	2497	43,700 CUP	52.0C	2672	50,400 CUP
160 GR. BAR TSX	Hodgdon	H414	.284"	2.870"	47.0	2495	40,300 CUP	51.0	2702	47,700 CUP
160 GR. BAR TSX	IMR	IMR 4350	.284"	2.870"	49.7	2496	42,100 CUP	54.0C	2705	51,300 CUP
160 GR. BAR TSX	Winchester	760	.284"	2.870"	47.0	2472	47,700 CUP	50.7	2657	51,900 CUP
160 GR. BAR TSX	IMR	IMR 4007 SSC	.284"	2.870"	48.0	2510	43,600 CUP	51.1	2697	52,100 CUP
160 GR. BAR TSX	Hodgdon	Varget	.284"	2.870"	42.0	2397	43,100 CUP	46.5	2632	51,800 CUP
160 GR. BAR TSX	IMR	IMR 4320	.284"	2.870"	45.2	2527	45,100 CUP	48.1	2678	51,500 CUP
160 GR. BAR TSX	IMR	IMR 4064	.284"	2.870"	44.2	2527	48,100 CUP	47.0	2648	52,100 CUP
160 GR. BAR TSX	IMR	IMR 4895	.284"	2.870"	44.0	2501	45,100 CUP	46.8	2620	51,000 CUP
160 GR. BAR TSX	Hodgdon	H4895	.284"	2.870"	40.0	2374	42,800 CUP	45.0	2593	51,500 cUP

162 GR. HDY BTSP	IMR	IMR 7828 SSC	.284"	2.970"	53.5	2601	42,100 CUP	58.2C*	2852	51,600 CUP
162 GR. HDY BTSP	Winchester	Supreme 780	.284"	2.970"	53.6	2643	43,500 CUP	57.0	2820	50,400 CUP
162 GR. HDY BTSP	Hodgdon	H4831	.284"	2.970"	53.0	2617	44,500 CUP	58.0C	2816	50,900 CUP
162 GR. HDY BTSP	Hodgdon	Hybrid 100V	.284"	2.970"	49.0	2666	40,900 CUP	54.0C	2864	48,900 CUP
162 GR. HDY BTSP	IMR	IMR 4831	.284"	2.970"	50.6	2580	39,000 CUP	55.0C	2823	50,800 CUP
162 GR. HDY BTSP	Hodgdon	H4350	.284"	2.970"	50.0	2712	47,600 CUP	53.5C	2847	53,000 CUP
162 GR. HDY BTSP	Hodgdon	H414	.284"	2.970"	48.0	2610	42,900 CUP	52.5	2822	50,700 CUP
162 GR. HDY BTSP	IMR	IMR 4350	.284"	2.970"	49.9	2605	41,600 CUP	53.7C	2797	51,400 CUP
162 GR. HDY BTSP	Winchester	760	.284"	2.970"	48.0	2610	42,900 CUP	52.5	2822	50,700 CUP
162 GR. HDY BTSP	IMR	IMR 4007 SSC	.284"	2.970"	47.9	2588	41,000 CUP	51.0	2774	51,100 CUP
162 GR. HDY BTSP	Hodgdon	Varget	.284"	2.970"	42.0	2557	43,800 CUP	47.0	2764	52,500 CUP
162 GR. HDY BTSP	IMR	IMR 4320	.284"	2.970"	45.1	2648	43,600 CUP	48.0	2758	50,400 CUP
162 GR. HDY BTSP	IMR	IMR 4064	.284"	2.970"	44.3	2585	42,300 CUP	47.1	2764	51,600 CUP
162 GR. HDY BTSP	IMR	IMR 4895	.284"	2.970"	44.7	2613	43,800 CUP	47.6	2770	51,500 CUP
162 GR. HDY BTSP	Hodgdon	H4895	.284"	2.970"	40.0	2502	42,900 CUP	44.2	2703	51,600 CUP
168 GR. SIE HPBT	IMR	IMR 7828 SSC	.284"	2.990"	53.5	2578	43,800 CUP	58.5C*	2801	52,200 CUP
168 GR. SIE HPBT	Winchester	Supreme 780	.284"	2.900"	53.3	2651	43,800 CUP	56.7	2813	51,200 CUP
168 GR. SIE HPBT	Hodgdon	H4831	.284"	2.900"	53.0	2602	45,100 CUP	58.0C	2807	52,700 CUP
168 GR. SIE HPBT	Hodgdon	Hybrid 100V	.284"	2.900"	49.0	2610	42,200 CUP	54.0C	2829	49,200 CUP
168 GR. SIE HPBT	IMR	IMR 4831	.284"	2.990"	50.9	2595	42,600 CUP	55.3C	2807	51,900 CUP
168 GR. SIE HPBT	Hodgdon	H4350	.284"	2.900"	50.0	2668	47,400 CUP	53.5C	2822	53,000 CUP
168 GR. SIE HPBT	Hodgdon	H414	.284"	2.900"	48.0	2585	42,500 CUP	52.5	2830	51,900 CUP
168 GR. SIE HPBT	IMR	IMR 4350	.284"	2.990"	49.2	2542	40,600 CUP	53.5	2793	52,700 CUP
168 GR. SIE HPBT	Winchester	760	.284"	2.900"	48.0	2585	42,500 CUP	52.5	2830	51,900 CUP
168 GR. SIE HPBT	IMR	IMR 4007 SSC	.284"	2.990"	46.9	2539	41,400 CUP	49.9	2693	51,400 CUP
168 GR. SIE HPBT	Hodgdon	Varget	.284"	2.900"	42.0	2576	45,400 CUP	47.0	2736	52,500 CUP
168 GR. SIE HPBT	IMR	IMR 4320	.284"	2.990"	44.0	2506	48,600 CUP	46.8	2685	51,600 CUP
168 GR. SIE HPBT	IMR	IMR 4064	.284"	2.990"	43.7	2536	44,300 CUP	46.5	2690	52,500 CUP
168 GR. SIE HPBT	IMR	IMR 4895	.284"	2.990"	43.7	2543	44,300 CUP	46.5	2683	51,600 CUP
168 GR. SIE HPBT	Hodgdon	H4895	.284"	2.900"	40.0	2531	46,200 CUP	44.0	2689	52,300 CUP
175 GR. SFT SP	IMR	IMR 7828 SSC	.284"	2.930"	52.5	2428	40,800 CUP	57.0C*	2664	49,800 CUP
175 GR. SFT SP	Winchester	Supreme 780	.284"	2.930"	54.0	2579	43,300 CUP	56.7	2664	47,000 CUP
175 GR. SFT SP	Hodgdon	H4831	.284"	2.930"	52.0	2482	44,500 CUP	57.0C	2695	52,900 CUP
175 GR. SFT SP	Hodgdon	Hybrid 100V	.284"	2.930"	48.0	2472	40,300 CUP	53.0C	2702	47,400 CUP
175 GR. SFT SP	IMR	IMR 4831	.284"	2.930"	49.1	2417	39,600 CUP	54.0C	2674	49,900 CUP
175 GR. SFT SP	Hodgdon	H4350	.284"	2.930"	47.0	2483	44,900 CUP	51.5C	2649	52,000 CUP
175 GR. SFT SP	Hodgdon	H414	.284"	2.930"	48.0	2494	45,100 CUP	52.0	2722	52,600 CUP
175 GR. SFT SP	IMR	IMR 4350	.284"	2.930"	48.5	2433	40,500 CUP	52.7C	2633	49,600 CUP
175 GR. SFT SP	Winchester	760	.284"	2.930"	48.0	2494	45,100 CUP	52.0	2722	52,600 CUP
175 GR. SFT SP	IMR	IMR 4007 SSC	.284"	2.930"	46.6	2469	44,600 CUP	49.5	2590	50,900 CUP

Bullet Weight (Gr.)	Manufacturer	Powder	Bullet Diam.	C.O.L.	Grs.	Vel. (ft/s)	Pressure	Grs.	Vel. (ft/s)	Pressure
175 GR. SFT SP	Hodgdon	Varget	.284"	2.930"	42.0	2413	45,800 CUP	46.0	2582	52,600 CUP
175 GR. SFT SP	IMR	IMR 4320	.284"	2.930"	43.6	2496	47,100 CUP	46.4	2609	51,400 CUP

Cartridge: 280 Ackley Improved
Load Type: Rifle

Bullet Weight (Gr.)	Manufacturer	Powder	Bullet Diam.	C.O.L.	Starting Loads Grs.	Vel. (ft/s)	Pressure	Maximum Loads Grs.	Vel. (ft/s)	Pressure
120 GR. NOS BT	Hodgdon	H1000	.284"	3.320"	62.0	2924	45,100 PSI	66.0C	3120	54,400 PSI
120 GR. NOS BT	IMR	IMR 7828 SSC	.284"	3.320"	59.2	2997	52,500 PSI	63.0	3219	62,200 PSI
120 GR. NOS BT	Hodgdon	H4831	.284"	3.320"	61.1	3024	52,200 PSI	65.0C	3240	60,900 PSI
120 GR. NOS BT	IMR	IMR 4831	.284"	3.320"	56.4	2967	48,900 PSI	60.0	3223	60,100 PSI
120 GR. NOS BT	Hodgdon	H4350	.284"	3.320"	55.5	3120	54,000 PSI	59.0	3271	61,400 PSI
120 GR. NOS BT	Hodgdon	H414	.284"	3.320"	53.1	3059	52,700 PSI	56.5	3237	62,000 PSI
120 GR. NOS BT	IMR	IMR 4350	.284"	3.320"	55.0	3056	53,100 PSI	58.5	3222	60,900 PSI
120 GR. NOS BT	Winchester	760	.284"	3.320"	53.1	3059	52,700 PSI	56.5	3237	62,000 PSI
120 GR. NOS BT	IMR	IMR 4007 SSC	.284"	3.320"	53.2	3028	51,800 PSI	56.7	3222	62,100 PSI
120 GR. NOS BT	Hodgdon	Varget	.284"	3.320"	47.0	2988	52,200 PSI	50.0	3153	61,300 PSI
120 GR. NOS BT	IMR	IMR 4320	.284"	3.320"	47.5	2970	51,000 PSI	50.5	3141	60,300 PSI
120 GR. NOS BT	IMR	IMR 4064	.284"	3.320"	47.8	3046	54,200 PSI	50.9	3180	60,400 PSI
120 GR. NOS BT	Winchester	748	.284"	3.320"	48.0	3005	52,800 PSI	51.0	3177	60,600 PSI
120 GR. NOS BT	Hodgdon	BL-C(2)	.284"	3.320"	50.3	3089	55,800 PSI	53.5	3242	61,900 PSI
120 GR. NOS BT	IMR	IMR 4895	.284"	3.320"	47.7	3039	54,100 PSI	50.7	3174	60,800 PSI
120 GR. NOS BT	Hodgdon	H4895	.284"	3.320"	44.7	2974	51,800 PSI	47.5	3128	60,700 PSI
120 GR. NOS BT	IMR	IMR 3031	.284"	3.320"	45.1	3014	55,700 PSI	48.0	3120	60,200 PSI
130 GR. SIE HPBT	Hodgdon	H1000	.284"	3.320"	60.6	2910	51,600 PSI	64.5C	3065	59,800 PSI
130 GR. SIE HPBT	IMR	IMR 7828 SSC	.284"	3.320"	56.4	2907	52,800 PSI	60.0	3079	61,300 PSI
130 GR. SIE HPBT	Hodgdon	H4831	.284"	3.320"	57.3	2910	53,800 PSI	61.0	3060	61,300 PSI
130 GR. SIE HPBT	IMR	IMR 4831	.284"	3.320"	54.8	2939	52,800 PSI	58.3	3128	62,000 PSI
130 GR. SIE HPBT	Hodgdon	H4350	.284"	3.320"	50.8	2913	53,300 PSI	54.0	3051	60,000 PSI
130 GR. SIE HPBT	Hodgdon	H414	.284"	3.320"	50.3	2932	53,500 PSI	53.5	3071	61,700 PSI
130 GR. SIE HPBT	IMR	IMR 4350	.284"	3.320"	51.3	2901	53,200 PSI	54.6	3067	61,200 PSI
130 GR. SIE HPBT	Winchester	760	.284"	3.320"	50.3	2932	53,500 PSI	53.5	3071	61,700 PSI
130 GR. SIE HPBT	IMR	IMR 4007 SSC	.284"	3.320"	49.4	2878	51,200 PSI	52.5	3048	60,500 PSI
130 GR. SIE HPBT	Hodgdon	Varget	.284"	3.320"	44.7	2855	53,500 PSI	47.5	2991	60,800 PSI
130 GR. SIE HPBT	IMR	IMR 4320	.284"	3.320"	43.2	2787	51,000 PSI	46.0	2948	60,400 PSI
130 GR. SIE HPBT	IMR	IMR 4064	.284"	3.320"	44.2	2859	52,400 PSI	47.0	3007	61,800 PSI
130 GR. SIE HPBT	Winchester	748	.284"	3.320"	44.8	2851	52,000 PSI	47.7	2994	60,600 PSI
130 GR. SIE HPBT	Hodgdon	BL-C(2)	.284"	3.320"	46.5	2888	52,600 PSI	49.5	3026	61,300 PSI
130 GR. SIE HPBT	IMR	IMR 4895	.284"	3.320"	44.7	2867	52,300 PSI	47.5	2982	58,000 PSI
130 GR. SIE HPBT	Hodgdon	H4895	.284"	3.320"	42.8	2813	51,200 PSI	45.5	2953	60,300 PSI

130 GR. SIE HPBT	IMR	IMR 3031	.284"	3.320"	42.0	2830	53,800 PSI	44.6	2941	60,300 PSI
140 GR. NOS BT	Hodgdon	H1000	.284"	3.330"	60.0	2778	48,200 PSI	64.0C	2972	58,700 PSI
140 GR. NOS BT	IMR	IMR 7828 SSC	.284"	3.330"	56.2	2738	48,600 PSI	59.8	2967	60,200 PSI
140 GR. NOS BT	Hodgdon	H4831	.284"	3.330"	58.3	2841	53,600 PSI	62.0C	3012	61,100 PSI
140 GR. NOS BT	IMR	IMR 4831	.384"	3.330"	54.5	2821	51,200 PSI	58.0	3025	60,900 PSI
140 GR. NOS BT	Hodgdon	H4350	.284"	3.330"	52.2	2893	55,200 PSI	55.5	3012	61,600 PSI
140 GR. NOS BT	Hodgdon	H414	.284"	3.330"	50.3	2830	52,700 PSI	53.5	2991	62,200 PSI
140 GR. NOS BT	IMR	IMR 4350	.284"	3.330"	52.0	2814	52,700 PSI	55.4	2992	61,800 PSI
140 GR. NOS BT	Winchester	760	.284"	3.330"	50.3	2830	52,700 PSI	53.5	2991	62,200 PSI
140 GR. NOS BT	IMR	IMR 4007 SSC	.284"	3.330"	49.8	2772	51,600 PSI	53.0	2936	60,100 PSI
140 GR. NOS BT	Hodgdon	Varget	.284"	3.330"	44.6	2754	54,100 PSI	47.4	2903	60,400 PSI
140 GR. NOS BT	IMR	IMR 4064	.284"	3.330"	43.7	2728	52,300 PSI	46.5	2876	61,200 PSI
140 GR. NOS BT	IMR	IMR 4895	.284"	3.330"	44.2	2737	52,800 PSI	47.0	2870	60,500 PSI
140 GR. NOS BT	Hodgdon	H4895	.284"	3.330"	42.8	2737	53,600 PSI	45.5	2876	61,600 PSI
150 GR. BAR TSX	Hodgdon	H1000	.284"	3.230"	54.5	2592	54,100 PSI	61.0C	2826	56,900 PSI
150 GR. BAR TSX	IMR	IMR 7828 SSC	.284"	3.230"	54.0	2737	53,900 PSI	57.5	2863	59,200 PSI
150 GR. BAR TSX	Hodgdon	H4831	.284"	3.230"	54.1	2705	51,900 PSI	57.5C	2840	59,900 PSI
150 GR. BAR TSX	IMR	IMR 4831	.284"	3.230"	51.2	2756	53,500 PSI	54.5	2881	60,800 PSI
150 GR. BAR TSX	Hodgdon	H4350	.284"	3.230"	49.5	2736	55,600 PSI	52.7	2855	61,600 PSI
150 GR. BAR TSX	Hodgdon	H414	.284"	3.230"	47.3	2689	53,200 PSI	50.3	2818	60,100 PSI
150 GR. BAR TSX	IMR	IMR 4350	.284"	3.230"	51.0	2746	52,600 PSI	54.5	2893	60,100 PSI
150 GR. BAR TSX	Winchester	760	.284"	3.230"	47.3	2689	53,200 PSI	50.3	2818	60,100 PSI
150 GR. BAR TSX	IMR	IMR 4007 SSC	.284"	3.230"	49.0	2714	54,000 PSI	52.0	2843	61,600 PSI
150 GR. BAR TSX	Hodgdon	Varget	.284"	3.230"	43.0	2632	53,800 PSI	45.8	2750	60,900 PSI
150 GR. BAR TSX	IMR	IMR 4064	.284"	3.230"	44.2	2686	54,600 PSI	47.0	2799	61,900 PSI
150 GR. BAR TSX	IMR	IMR 4895	.284"	3.230"	44.7	2665	51,600 PSI	47.5	2805	62,000 PSI
150 GR. BAR TSX	Hodgdon	H4895	.284"	3.230"	41.4	2598	52,800 PSI	44.0	2716	59,900 PSI
150 GR. SFT SCIR	Hodgdon	H1000	.284"	3.330"	58.5	2724	57,100 PSI	62.2C	2883	60,300 PSI
150 GR. SFT SCIR	IMR	IMR 7828 SSC	.284"	3.330"	54.0	2668	51,600 PSI	59.0	2902	60,600 PSI
150 GR. SFT SCIR	Hodgdon	H4831	.284"	3.330"	53.6	2657	51,500 PSI	57.0	2773	61,200 PSI
150 GR. SFT SCIR	IMR	IMR 4831	.284"	3.330"	51.0	2650	50,600 PSI	56.0	2922	60,000 PSI
150 GR. SFT SCIR	Hodgdon	H4350	.284"	3.330"	48.0	2676	51,900 PSI	54.5	2908	61,700 PSI
150 GR. SFT SCIR	Hodgdon	H414	.284"	3.330"	46.1	2601	52,900 PSI	51.5	2808	56,000 PSI
150 GR. SFT SCIR	IMR	IMR 4350	.284"	3.330"	52.0	2739	50,800 PSI	55.3	2932	61,200 PSI
150 GR. SFT SCIR	Winchester	760	.284"	3.330"	46.1	2601	52,900 PSI	51.5	2808	56,000 PSI
150 GR. SFT SCIR	IMR	IMR 4007 SSC	.284"	3.330"	47.5	2638	52,300 PSI	50.5	2790	61,400 PSI
150 GR. SFT SCIR	Hodgdon	Varget	.284"	3.330"	43.5	2647	51,700 PSI	46.3	2796	59,300 PSI
150 GR. SFT SCIR	IMR	IMR 4064	.284"	3.330"	44.0	2665	50,700 PSI	46.5	2834	61,100 PSI
150 GR. SFT SCIR	IMR	IMR 4895	.284"	3.330"	45.1	2764	55,900 PSI	48.0	2850	60,400 PSI
150 GR. SFT SCIR	Hodgdon	H4895	.284"	3.330"	42.0	2633	52,100 PSI	44.6	2773	61,200 PSI

160 GR. NOS AB	Hodgdon	H1000	.284"	3.330"	57.3	2672	54,200 PSI	61.0C	2808	61,100 PSI
160 GR. NOS AB	IMR	IMR 7828 SSC	.284"	3.330"	54.5	2667	51,900 PSI	58.0	2849	61,300 PSI
160 GR. NOS AB	Hodgdon	H4831	.284"	3.330"	54.0	2674	55,000 PSI	57.5C	2812	62,000 PSI
160 GR. NOS AB	IMR	IMR 4831	.284"	3.330"	52.2	2663	53,100 PSI	55.5	2847	61,900 PSI
160 GR. NOS AB	Hodgdon	H4350	.284"	3.330"	48.4	2633	54,100 PSI	51.5	2747	60,700 PSI
160 GR. NOS AB	Hodgdon	H414	.284"	3.330"	47.5	2594	52,700 PSI	50.5	2736	60,800 PSI
160 GR. NOS AB	IMR	IMR 4350	.284"	3.330"	50.5	2647	53,600 PSI	53.7	2813	61,600 PSI
160 GR. NOS AB	Winchester	760	.284"	3.330"	47.5	2594	52,700 PSI	50.5	2736	60,800 PSI
160 GR. NOS AB	IMR	IMR 4007 SSC	.284"	3.330"	47.8	2587	53,100 PSI	50.8	2741	61,400 PSI
160 GR. NOS AB	Hodgdon	Varget	.284"	3.330"	43.2	2551	53,200 PSI	46.0	2685	62,000 PSI
160 GR. NOS AB	IMR	IMR 4064	.284"	3.330"	42.3	2517	52,900 PSI	45.0	2668	61,400 PSI
160 GR. NOS AB	IMR	IMR 4895	.284"	3.330"	43.0	2532	51,300 PSI	45.8	2670	60,000 PSI
160 GR. NOS AB	Hodgdon	H4895	.284"	3.330"	40.9	2496	52,300 PSI	43.5	2615	59,500 PSI
162 GR. HDY BTSP	Hodgdon	H1000	.284"	3.325"	56.8	2653	52,300 PSI	60.4	2797	61,300 PSI
162 GR. HDY BTSP	IMR	IMR 7828 SSC	.284"	3.325"	54.0	2678	53,600 PSI	57.3	2824	61,900 PSI
162 GR. HDY BTSP	Hodgdon	H4831	.284"	3.325"	53.0	2662	54,200 PSI	56.4	2788	61,400 PSI
162 GR. HDY BTSP	IMR	IMR 4831	.284"	3.325"	51.5	2697	54,700 PSI	54.8	2850	62,000 PSI
162 GR. HDY BTSP	Hodgdon	H4350	.284"	3.325"	47.6	2629	52,900 PSI	50.6	2755	60,800 PSI
162 GR. HDY BTSP	Hodgdon	H414	.284"	3.325"	47.0	2610	52,600 PSI	50.0	2730	60,300 PSI
162 GR. HDY BTSP	IMR	IMR 4350	.284"	3.325"	49.4	2677	54,400 PSI	52.5	2797	60,800 PSI
162 GR. HDY BTSP	Winchester	760	.284"	3.325"	47.0	2610	52,600 PSI	50.0	2730	60,300 PSI
162 GR. HDY BTSP	IMR	IMR 4007 SSC	.284"	3.325"	48.0	2641	53,100 PSI	51.0	2782	61,100 PSI
162 GR. HDY BTSP	Hodgdon	Varget	.284"	3.325"	42.6	2570	54,600 PSI	45.3	2690	62,000 PSI
162 GR. HDY BTSP	IMR	IMR 4064	.284"	3.325"	42.0	2556	53,700 PSI	44.5	2673	61,000 PSI
162 GR. HDY BTSP	IMR	IMR 4895	.284"	3.325"	42.3	2547	53,100 PSI	45.0	2675	61,100 PSI
162 GR. HDY BTSP	Hodgdon	H4895	.284"	3.325"	40.9	2535	53,800 PSI	43.5	2651	61,400 PSI
168 GR. SIE HPBT	Hodgdon	Retumbo	.284"	3.330"	59.0	2652	49,000 PSI	63.0C	2831	59,300 PSI
168 GR. SIE HPBT	Hodgdon	H1000	.284"	3.330"	57.8	2641	52,500 PSI	61.5C	2789	61,100 PSI
168 GR. SIE HPBT	IMR	IMR 7828 SSC	.284"	3.330"	53.8	2618	52,600 PSI	57.2	2776	61,000 PSI
168 GR. SIE HPBT	Hodgdon	H4831	.284"	3.330"	54.0	2653	55,100 PSI	57.7	2779	62,000 PSI
168 GR. SIE HPBT	IMR	IMR 4831	.284"	3.330"	52.0	2633	51,400 PSI	55.3	2798	61,400 PSI
168 GR. SIE HPBT	Hodgdon	H4350	.284"	3.330"	48.4	2621	54,500 PSI	51.5	2734	61,800 PSI
168 GR. SIE HPBT	Hodgdon	H414	.284"	3.330"	47.0	2571	53,200 PSI	50.3	2717	61,600 PSI
168 GR. SIE HPBT	IMR	IMR 4350	.284"	3.330"	49.8	2632	53,100 PSI	53.0	2762	61,100 PSI
168 GR. SIE HPBT	Winchester	760	.284"	3.330"	47.0	2571	53,200 PSI	50.3	2717	61,600 PSI
168 GR. SIE HPBT	IMR	IMR 4007 SSC	.284"	3.330"	47.0	2590	53,000 PSI	50.0	2711	60,900 PSI
168 GR. SIE HPBT	Hodgdon	Varget	.284"	3.330"	43.0	2518	53,700 PSI	46.0	2667	62,100 PSI
168 GR. SIE HPBT	IMR	IMR 4064	.284"	3.330"	42.3	2532	55,900 PSI	45.0	2643	62,300 PSI
168 GR. SIE HPBT	IMR	IMR 4895	.284"	3.330"	42.8	2530	53,700 PSI	45.5	2650	61,300 PSI

Bullet Weight (Gr.)	Manufacturer	Powder	Bullet Diam.	C.O.L.	Grs.	Vel. (ft/s)	Pressure	Grs.	Vel. (ft/s)	Pressure
168 GR. SIE HPBT	Hodgdon	H4895	.284"	3.330"	40.4	2474	52,300 PSI	43.0	2595	60,900 PSI
175 GR. SFT SP	Hodgdon	Retumbo	.284"	3.270"	56.7	2604	52,400 PSI	60.3C	2743	59,800 PSI
175 GR. SFT SP	Hodgdon	H1000	.284"	3.270"	55.5	2544	52,700 PSI	59.0C	2675	61,100 PSI
175 GR. SFT SP	IMR	IMR 7828 SSC	.284"	3.270"	53.1	2505	51,400 PSI	56.5	2686	61,700 PSI
175 GR. SFT SP	Hodgdon	H4831	.284"	3.270"	52.0	2496	51,900 PSI	55.5	2651	62,000 PSI
175 GR. SFT SP	IMR	IMR 4831	.284"	3.270"	51.7	2545	51,200 PSI	55.0	2702	61,400 PSI
175 GR. SFT SP	Hodgdon	H4350	.284"	3.270"	47.7	2515	54,700 PSI	50.7	2626	62,100 PSI
175 GR. SFT SP	Hodgdon	H414	.284"	3.270"	45.9	2469	52,600 PSI	48.8	2594	59,700 PSI
175 GR. SFT SP	IMR	IMR 4350	.284"	3.270"	50.0	2529	51,300 PSI	53.3	2681	60,700 PSI
175 GR. SFT SP	Winchester	760	.284"	3.270"	45.9	2469	52,600 PSI	48.8	2594	59,700 PSI
175 GR. SFT SP	IMR	IMR 4007 SSC	.284"	3.270"	46.1	2485	52,700 PSI	49.0	2598	59,900 PSI

Cartridge: 7mm Rem. S.A. Ultra Mag.					Starting Loads			Maximum Loads		
Load Type: Rifle										
Bullet Weight (Gr.)	Manufacturer	Powder	Bullet Diam.	C.O.L.	Grs.	Vel. (ft/s)	Pressure	Grs.	Vel. (ft/s)	Pressure
100 GR. HDY HP	Hodgdon	H4350	.284"	2.700"	63.0	3424	52,500 PSI	66.5C	3622	63,100 PSI
100 GR. HDY HP	Hodgdon	H414	.284"	2.700"	62.0	3472	52,800 PSI	66.0	3656	62,700 PSI
100 GR. HDY HP	Winchester	760	.284"	2.700"	62.0	3472	52,800 PSI	66.0	3656	62,700 PSI
100 GR. HDY HP	Hodgdon	H380	.284"	2.700"	60.0	3403	52,000 PSI	64.0	3613	62,900 PSI
100 GR. HDY HP	Hodgdon	Varget	.284"	2.700"	56.0	3418	52,600 PSI	60.0	3626	63,000 PSI
100 GR. HDY HP	Hodgdon	H4895	.284"	2.700"	53.0	3450	53,900 PSI	57.0	3631	62,800 PSI
110 GR. SPR TNT HP	Hodgdon	H4350	.284"	2.730"	61.0	3263	49,400 PSI	65.0	3499	62,600 PSI
110 GR. SPR TNT HP	Hodgdon	H414	.284"	2.730"	62.0	3381	53,200 PSI	65.5	3578	63,200 PSI
110 GR. SPR TNT HP	Winchester	760	.284"	2.730"	62.0	3381	53,200 PSI	65.5	3578	63,200 PSI
110 GR. SPR TNT HP	IMR	IMR 4007 SSC	.284"	2.730"	59.0	3299	51,500 PSI	63.0	3527	62,900 PSI
110 GR. SPR TNT HP	Hodgdon	H380	.284"	2.730"	59.0	3263	51,100 PSI	63.0	3492	62,900 PSI
110 GR. SPR TNT HP	Hodgdon	Varget	.284"	2.730"	54.0	3295	52,500 PSI	59.0	3513	63,200 PSI
110 GR. SPR TNT HP	Hodgdon	H4895	.284"	2.730"	53.0	3351	55,400 PSI	56.5	3494	62,700 PSI
115 GR. SPR HP	Hodgdon	H4831	.284"	2.650"	65.0	3212	53,800 PSI	68.0C	3342	61,400 PSI
115 GR. SPR HP	Hodgdon	H4350	.284"	2.650"	60.0	3196	51,100 PSI	64.0	3413	63,200 PSI
115 GR. SPR HP	Hodgdon	H414	.284"	2.650"	59.0	3235	51,700 PSI	63.0	3437	63,200 PSI
115 GR. SPR HP	Winchester	760	.284"	2.650"	59.0	3235	51,700 PSI	63.0	3437	63,200 PSI
115 GR. SPR HP	IMR	IMR 4007 SSC	.284"	2.650"	57.0	3196	50,300 PSI	61.5	3418	61,400 PSI
115 GR. SPR HP	Hodgdon	H380	.284"	2.650"	56.0	3159	53,700 PSI	59.5	3329	62,600 PSI
115 GR. SPR HP	Hodgdon	Varget	.284"	2.650"	54.0	3234	54,300 PSI	58.0	3402	62,800 PSI
115 GR. SPR HP	Hodgdon	H4895	.284"	2.650"	51.0	3211	55,700 PSI	54.0	3336	62,400 PSI
120 GR. BAR TSX	IMR	IMR 7828	.284"	2.725"	64.0	3154	52,400 PSI	68.0C	3339	61,400 PSI
120 GR. BAR TSX	Hodgdon	H4831	.284"	2.725"	63.0	3077	50,100 PSI	67.0C	3243	58,200 PSI
120 GR. BAR TSX	IMR	IMR 4831	.284"	2.725"	61.0	3166	50,400 PSI	65.0C	3350	58,600 PSI
120 GR. BAR TSX	Hodgdon	H4350	.284"	2.725"	58.0	3130	51,300 PSI	63.2	3375	63,700 PSI

Bullet	Mfg	Powder	Dia.	COL	Charge	Vel.	Pressure	Charge	Vel.	Pressure
120 GR. BAR TSX	Hodgdon	H414	.284"	2.725"	57.0	3122	50,700 PSI	61.0	3351	62,000 PSI
120 GR. BAR TSX	IMR	IMR 4350	.284"	2.725"	59.0	3125	49,200 PSI	64.5C	3420	63,400 PSI
120 GR. BAR TSX	IMR	IMR 4007 SSC	.284"	2.725"	56.0	3093	48,800 PSI	61.0	3363	61,800 PSI
120 GR. BAR TSX	Hodgdon	H380	.284"	2.725"	56.0	3132	52,800 PSI	59.5	3313	62,600 PSI
120 GR. BAR TSX	Hodgdon	Varget	.284"	2.725"	51.0	3120	52,900 PSI	55.5	3310	62,500 PSI
120 GR. BAR TSX	IMR	IMR 4064	.284"	2.725"	50.0	3081	48,000 PSI	55.2	3361	63,100 PSI
130 GR. SIE HPBT	Hodgdon	H4831	.284"	2.800"	61.0	3017	52,300 PSI	65.0	3192	62,600 PSI
130 GR. SIE HPBT	Hodgdon	Hybrid 100V	.284"	2.800"	57.0	3074	50,100 PSI	62.3C	3322	62,500 PSI
130 GR. SIE HPBT	Hodgdon	H4350	.284"	2.800"	57.0	3060	53,700 PSI	60.5	3222	62,600 PSI
130 GR. SIE HPBT	Hodgdon	H414	.284"	2.800"	57.0	3105	55,200 PSI	60.0	3230	62,600 PSI
130 GR. SIE HPBT	Winchester	760	.284"	2.800"	57.0	3105	55,200 PSI	60.0	3230	62,600 PSI
130 GR. SIE HPBT	IMR	IMR 4007 SSC	.284"	2.800"	54.0	3045	52,400 PSI	58.0	3227	62,000 PSI
130 GR. SIE HPBT	Hodgdon	H380	.284"	2.800"	54.0	2992	53,900 PSI	57.5	3148	62,500 PSI
130 GR. SIE HPBT	Hodgdon	Varget	.284"	2.800"	51.0	3057	55,700 PSI	54.0	3190	62,900 PSI
140 GR. NOS BT	IMR	IMR 7828	.284"	2.825"				65.0C*	3104	58,600 PSI
140 GR. NOS BT	Hodgdon	H4831	.284"	2.825"	61.0	2928	52,800 PSI	64.5C	3099	63,100 PSI
140 GR. NOS BT	Hodgdon	Hybrid 100V	.284"	2.825"	57.0	2980	50,200 PSI	62.0C	3217	62,400 PSI
140 GR. NOS BT	IMR	IMR 4831	.284"	2.825"				62.3	3173	62,700 PSI
140 GR. NOS BT	Hodgdon	H4350	.284"	2.825"	56.0	2910	50,600 PSI	60.0	3122	63,200 PSI
140 GR. NOS BT	Hodgdon	H414	.284"	2.825"	57.0	2982	52,700 PSI	60.0	3153	62,900 PSI
140 GR. NOS BT	IMR	IMR 4350	.284"	2.825"				61.2	3174	62,000 PSI
140 GR. NOS BT	Winchester	760	.284"	2.825"	57.0	2982	52,700 PSI	60.0	3153	62,900 PSI
140 GR. NOS BT	Hodgdon	H380	.284"	2.825"	54.0	2869	51,000 PSI	57.5	3069	62,600 PSI
140 GR. NOS BT	Hodgdon	Varget	.284"	2.825"	50.0	2945	56,500 PSI	53.5	3068	62,300 PSI
145 GR. SPR HPBT	Hodgdon	H4831	.284"	2.750"	59.0	2909	52,300 PSI	63.0	3094	63,100 PSI
145 GR. SPR HPBT	Hodgdon	Hybrid 100V	.284"	2.750"	56.0	2932	51,000 PSI	61.0	3159	62,500 PSI
145 GR. SPR HPBT	Hodgdon	H4350	.284"	2.750"	55.0	2943	54,000 PSI	58.5	3093	62,800 PSI
145 GR. SPR HPBT	Hodgdon	H414	.284"	2.750"	55.0	2885	53,000 PSI	58.5	3095	62,800 PSI
145 GR. SPR HPBT	Winchester	760	.284"	2.750"	55.0	2885	53,000 PSI	58.5	3095	62,800 PSI
145 GR. SPR HPBT	IMR	IMR 4007 SSC	.284"	2.750"	53.0	2864	50,700 PSI	57.0	3058	61,500 PSI
145 GR. SPR HPBT	Hodgdon	H380	.284"	2.750"	53.0	2849	56,500 PSI	56.0	2971	63,200 PSI
145 GR. SPR HPBT	Hodgdon	Varget	.284"	2.750"	49.0	2865	56,100 PSI	52.5	2999	63,400 PSI
150 GR. SFT SCIR	Hodgdon	H1000	.284"	2.825"	66.0	2873	53,500 PSI	68.0C	2967	59,300 PSI
150 GR. SFT SCIR	IMR	IMR 7828	.284"	2.825"	59.5	2895	58,000 PSI	63.5C	3028	61,700 PSI
150 GR. SFT SCIR	Winchester	Supreme 780	.284"	2.825"	61.1	2909	54,700 PSI	65.0	3065	62,800 PSI
150 GR. SFT SCIR	Hodgdon	H4831	.284"	2.825"	58.0	2823	52,800 PSI	61.5	2987	63,000 PSI
150 GR. SFT SCIR	Hodgdon	Hybrid 100V	.284"	2.825"	55.0	2867	51,400 PSI	59.5C	3081	62,100 PSI
150 GR. SFT SCIR	IMR	IMR 4831	.284"	2.825"	54.0	2767	49,900 PSI	59.3	3022	63,200 PSI
150 GR. SFT SCIR	Hodgdon	H4350	.284"	2.825"	53.5	2837	53,500 PSI	57.0	2984	62,800 PSI

150 GR. SFT SCIR	Hodgdon	H414	.284"	2.825"	54.0	2885	56,100 PSI	57.0	3018	63,100 PSI
150 GR. SFT SCIR	IMR	IMR 4350	.284"	2.825"	53.0	2753	49,500 PSI	57.8	3023	63,000 PSI
150 GR. SFT SCIR	Winchester	760	.284"	2.825"	54.0	2885	56,100 PSI	57.0	3018	63,100 PSI
150 GR. SFT SCIR	IMR	IMR 4007 SSC	.284"	2.825"	52.0	2770	51,600 PSI	56.0	2967	62,300 PSI
150 GR. SFT SCIR	Hodgdon	H380	.284"	2.825"	50.0	2714	52,800 PSI	53.5	2893	62,600 PSI
154 GR. HDY SP	Hodgdon	H1000	.284"	2.800"	65.0	2866	55,700 PSI	68.0C	2960	61,900 PSI
154 GR. HDY SP	IMR	IMR 7828	.284"	2.800"	59.0	2845	55,500 PSI	63.4	3016	63,400 PSI
154 GR. HDY SP	Winchester	Supreme 780	.284"	2.800"	61.6	2912	54,600 PSI	65.5	3059	62,400 PSI
154 GR. HDY SP	Hodgdon	H4831	.284"	2.800"	58.0	2824	55,000 PSI	61.5	2947	62,700 PSI
154 GR. HDY SP	Hodgdon	Hybrid 100V	.284"	2.800"	55.0	2869	52,300 PSI	60.0C	3067	62,300 PSI
154 GR. HDY SP	IMR	IMR 4831	.284"	2.800"	54.0	2788	52,500 PSI	58.7	2963	62,200 PSI
154 GR. HDY SP	Hodgdon	H4350	.284"	2.800"	53.0	2805	54,500 PSI	56.5	2947	62,900 PSI
154 GR. HDY SP	Hodgdon	H414	.284"	2.800"	54.0	2845	56,400 PSI	57.5	2971	63,200 PSI
154 GR. HDY SP	IMR	IMR 4350	.284"	2.800"	53.0	2783	52,600 PSI	57.3	2964	62,400 PSI
154 GR. HDY SP	Winchester	760	.284"	2.800"	54.0	2845	56,400 PSI	57.5	2971	63,200 PSI
154 GR. HDY SP	IMR	IMR 4007 SSC	.284"	2.800"	51.0	2740	51,400 PSI	55.7	2931	61,900 PSI
154 GR. HDY SP	Hodgdon	H380	.284"	2.800"	50.0	2736	56,600 PSI	53.5	2855	62,800 PSI
160 GR. NOS PART	Hodgdon	H1000	.284"	2.825"	63.0	2772	53,600 PSI	67.0C	2931	63,300 PSI
160 GR. NOS PART	IMR	IMR 7828	.284"	2.825"	58.5	2804	56,800 PSI	63.3	2996	63,600 PSI
160 GR. NOS PART	Winchester	Supreme 780	.284"	2.825"	60.2	2823	52,200 PSI	64.0	3003	62,900 PSI
160 GR. NOS PART	Hodgdon	H4831	.284"	2.825"	57.0	2730	53,800 PSI	60.5	2900	62,600 PSI
160 GR. NOS PART	Hodgdon	Hybrid 100V	.284"	2.825"	54.0	2781	50,000 PSI	59.0C	2993	61,200 PSI
160 GR. NOS PART	IMR	IMR 4831	.284"	2.825"	54.0	2742	52,700 PSI	58.6	2928	62,400 PSI
160 GR. NOS PART	Hodgdon	H4350	.284"	2.825"	53.0	2774	55,200 PSI	56.5	2914	63,100 PSI
160 GR. NOS PART	Hodgdon	H414	.284"	2.825"	53.0	2786	55,300 PSI	56.0	2905	62,700 PSI
160 GR. NOS PART	IMR	IMR 4350	.284"	2.825"	52.0	2695	51,200 PSI	56.9	2929	63,000 PSI
160 GR. NOS PART	Winchester	760	.284"	2.825"	53.0	2786	55,300 PSI	56.0	2905	62,700 PSI
160 GR. NOS PART	Hodgdon	H380	.284"	2.825"	50.0	2669	53,800 PSI	53.5	2824	62,700 PSI
162 GR. HDY SPBT	Hodgdon	H1000	.284"	2.825"	64.0	2793	54,400 PSI	67.0C	2902	60,900 PSI
162 GR. HDY SPBT	IMR	IMR 7828	.284"	2.825"	58.0	2761	54,500 PSI	62.0	2925	63,500 PSI
162 GR. HDY SPBT	Winchester	Supreme 780	.284"	2.825"	60.6	2831	51,800 PSI	64.5	3011	62,500 PSI
162 GR. HDY SPBT	Hodgdon	H4831	.284"	2.825"	56.5	2751	55,100 PSI	60.0	2887	63,100 PSI
162 GR. HDY SPBT	Hodgdon	Hybrid 100V	.284"	2.825"	54.0	2794	51,400 PSI	58.5C	2971	60,900 PSI
162 GR. HDY SPBT	IMR	IMR 4831	.284"	2.825"	55.0	2765	54,000 PSI	59.0	2939	63,800 PSI
162 GR. HDY SPBT	Hodgdon	H4350	.284"	2.825"	52.0	2760	54,700 PSI	55.5	2879	62,500 PSI
162 GR. HDY SPBT	Hodgdon	H414	.284"	2.825"	53.0	2785	56,600 PSI	56.0	2901	62,800 PSI
162 GR. HDY SPBT	IMR	IMR 4350	.284"	2.825"	54.0	2745	52,900 PSI	58.0	2918	62,500 PSI
162 GR. HDY SPBT	Winchester	760	.284"	2.825"	53.0	2785	56,600 PSI	56.0	2901	62,800 PSI
162 GR. HDY SPBT	IMR	IMR 4007 SSC	.284"	2.825"	50.0	2708	53,500 PSI	54.7	2880	63,000 PSI
162 GR. HDY SPBT	Hodgdon	H380	.284"	2.825"	50.0	2676	55,000 PSI	53.0	2814	63,000 PSI

Bullet Weight (Gr.)	Manufacturer	Powder	Bullet Diam.	C.O.L.	Grs.	Vel. (ft/s)	Pressure	Grs.	Vel. (ft/s)	Pressure
168 GR. SIE HPBT	Hodgdon	H1000	.284"	2.825"	64.0	2770	55,100 PSI	67.0C	2874	61,200 PSI
168 GR. SIE HPBT	IMR	IMR 7828	.284"	2.825"	57.0	2662	51,500 PSI	61.5	2875	63,800 PSI
168 GR. SIE HPBT	Winchester	Supreme 780	.284"	2.825"	59.9	2772	51,900 PSI	63.7	2946	62,400 PSI
168 GR. SIE HPBT	Hodgdon	H4831	.284"	2.825"	56.0	2682	52,400 PSI	60.5	2848	62,800 PSI
168 GR. SIE HPBT	Hodgdon	Hybrid 100V	.284"	2.825"	53.0	2721	50,800 PSI	57.7C	2905	60,400 PSI
168 GR. SIE HPBT	IMR	IMR 4831	.284"	2.825"	55.0	2680	52,300 PSI	59.0	2856	61,700 PSI
168 GR. SIE HPBT	Hodgdon	H4350	.284"	2.825"	51.0	2666	51,800 PSI	56.0	2855	62,900 PSI
168 GR. SIE HPBT	Hodgdon	H414	.284"	2.825"	53.0	2722	54,000 PSI	56.0	2871	63,000 PSI
168 GR. SIE HPBT	IMR	IMR 4350	.284"	2.825"	54.0	2712	53,400 PSI	57.5	2869	63,000 PSI
168 GR. SIE HPBT	Winchester	760	.284"	2.825"	53.0	2722	54,000 PSI	56.0	2871	63,000 PSI
168 GR. SIE HPBT	IMR	IMR 4007 SSC	.284"	2.825"	50.0	2635	51,600 PSI	54.3	2809	61,600 PSI
168 GR. SIE HPBT	Hodgdon	H380	.284"	2.825"	50.0	2623	53,800 PSI	53.3	2771	63,100 PSI
175 GR. HDY SP	Hodgdon	Retumbo	.284"	2.825"	62.0	2686	51,000 PSI	66.0C	2863	62,700 PSI
175 GR. HDY SP	Hodgdon	H1000	.284"	2.825"	61.0	2658	54,500 PSI	65.5C	2817	62,800 PSI
175 GR. HDY SP	IMR	IMR 7828	.284"	2.825"	55.0	2611	54,500 PSI	59.2	2784	63,500 PSI
175 GR. HDY SP	Winchester	Supreme 780	.284"	2.825"	56.4	2649	50,400 PSI	60.0	2818	61,700 PSI
175 GR. HDY SP	Hodgdon	H4831	.284"	2.825"	54.0	2627	54,300 PSI	58.0	2760	62,900 PSI
175 GR. HDY SP	Hodgdon	Hybrid 100V	.284"	2.825"	52.0	2630	50,500 PSI	57.3C	2844	62,400 PSI
175 GR. HDY SP	IMR	IMR 4831	.284"	2.825"	53.0	2619	54,900 PSI	56.5	2756	62,500 PSI
175 GR. HDY SP	Hodgdon	H4350	.284"	2.825"	50.0	2619	53,900 PSI	54.5	2775	63,100 PSI
175 GR. HDY SP	Hodgdon	H414	.284"	2.825"	51.0	2640	55,000 PSI	54.5	2778	63,200 PSI
175 GR. HDY SP	IMR	IMR 4350	.284"	2.825"	52.0	2616	54,100 PSI	55.5	2758	62,600 PSI
175 GR. HDY SP	Winchester	760	.284"	2.825"	51.0	2640	55,000 PSI	54.5	2778	63,200 PSI

Cartridge:7mm Winchester Short Magnum Load Type:Rifle					Starting Loads			Maximum Loads		
Bullet Weight (Gr.)	Manufacturer	Powder	Bullet Diam.	C.O.L.	Grs.	Vel. (ft/s)	Pressure	Grs.	Vel. (ft/s)	Pressure
100 GR. BAR XFB	Hodgdon	H4350	.284"	2.725"	65.0	3388	51,800 PSI	70.0	3647	63,200 PSI
100 GR. BAR XFB	Hodgdon	H414	.284"	2.725"	63.0	3408	53,000 PSI	68.0	3628	61,900 PSI
100 GR. BAR XFB	Winchester	760	.284"	2.725"	63.0	3408	53,000 PSI	68.0	3628	61,900 PSI
100 GR. BAR XFB	Hodgdon	H380	.284"	2.725"	62.0	3390	54,000 PSI	66.0	3591	62,700 PSI
100 GR. BAR XFB	Hodgdon	Varget	.284"	2.725"	56.0	3392	54,100 PSI	60.5	3588	62,400 PSI
100 GR. BAR XFB	Hodgdon	H4895	.284"	2.725"	54.0	3442	56,100 PSI	57.5	3590	62,500 PSI
110 GR. SPR TNT HP	Hodgdon	H4831	.284"	2.830"	68.0	3225	51,300 PSI	73.0	3465	62,600 PSI
110 GR. SPR TNT HP	Hodgdon	H4350	.284"	2.830"	65.0	3323	52,600 PSI	70.0	3553	63,300 PSI
110 GR. SPR TNT HP	Hodgdon	H414	.284"	2.830"	63.0	3366	55,600 PSI	67.8	3543	63,500 PSI
110 GR. SPR TNT HP	Winchester	760	.284"	2.830"	63.0	3366	55,600 PSI	67.8	3543	63,500 PSI
110 GR. SPR TNT HP	IMR	IMR 4007 SSC	.284"	2.830"	63.5	3245	50,200 PSI	67.6	3481	62,000 PSI
110 GR. SPR TNT HP	Hodgdon	H380	.284"	2.830"	62.0	3301	54,100 PSI	66.0	3464	62,900 PSI

110 GR. SPR TNT HP	Hodgdon	Varget	.284"	2.830"	56.0	3320	56,200 PSI	60.0	3458	62,500 PSI
110 GR. SPR TNT HP	Hodgdon	H4895	.284"	2.830"	53.0	3229	52,500 PSI	57.0	3417	62,300 PSI
110 GR. SPR TNT HP	IMR	IMR 8208 XBR	.284"	2.830"	53.3	3283	55,200 PSI	56.7	3435	63,400 PSI
115 GR. SPR HP	Hodgdon	H4831	.284"	2.770"	65.0	3179	53,700 PSI	70.0	3372	62,900 PSI
115 GR. SPR HP	Hodgdon	H4350	.284"	2.770"	62.0	3278	56,400 PSI	66.5	3441	63,500 PSI
115 GR. SPR HP	Hodgdon	H414	.284"	2.770"	60.0	3228	55,000 PSI	64.5	3385	62,300 PSI
115 GR. SPR HP	Winchester	760	.284"	2.770"	60.0	3228	55,000 PSI	64.5	3385	62,300 PSI
115 GR. SPR HP	IMR	IMR 4007 SSC	.284"	2.770"	61.6	3178	51,900 PSI	65.5	3409	63,500 PSI
115 GR. SPR HP	Hodgdon	H380	.284"	2.770"	57.0	3168	57,500 PSI	61.5	3304	61,900 PSI
115 GR. SPR HP	Hodgdon	Varget	.284"	2.770"	54.0	3220	57,000 PSI	57.5	3360	63,800 PSI
115 GR. SPR HP	Hodgdon	H4895	.284"	2.770"	51.0	3143	54,700 PSI	55.0	3309	62,700 PSI
115 GR. SPR HP	IMR	IMR 8208 XBR	.284"	2.770"	50.8	3147	54,400 PSI	54.0	3298	62,700 PSI
120 GR. HDY V-MAX	IMR	IMR 7828	.284"	2.825"	62.6	3094	53,800 PSI	68.0	3302	62,800 PSI
120 GR. HDY V-MAX	Hodgdon	H4831	.284"	2.825"	65.0	3159	55,100 PSI	69.5	3335	63,400 PSI
120 GR. HDY V-MAX	IMR	IMR 4831	.284"	2.825"	59.0	3082	52,300 PSI	63.5	3280	62,000 PSI
120 GR. HDY V-MAX	Hodgdon	H4350	.284"	2.825"	61.0	3206	54,800 PSI	65.5	3387	63,500 PSI
120 GR. HDY V-MAX	Hodgdon	H414	.284"	2.825"	60.0	3202	55,100 PSI	64.0	3371	63,000 PSI
120 GR. HDY V-MAX	IMR	IMR 4350	.284"	2.825"	57.5	3126	53,500 PSI	61.2	3301	62,000 PSI
120 GR. HDY V-MAX	Winchester	760	.284"	2.825"	60.0	3202	55,100 PSI	64.0	3371	63,000 PSI
120 GR. HDY V-MAX	IMR	IMR 4007 SSC	.284"	2.825"	59.0	3155	56,300 PSI	62.7	3293	63,100 PSI
120 GR. HDY V-MAX	Hodgdon	H380	.284"	2.825"	57.0	3074	52,300 PSI	61.5	3285	63,300 PSI
120 GR. HDY V-MAX	Hodgdon	Varget	.284"	2.825"	53.0	3155	56,300 PSI	57.0	3311	63,500 PSI
120 GR. HDY V-MAX	IMR	IMR 4320	.284"	2.825"	52.4	3097	56,800 PSI	55.7	3253	63,400 PSI
120 GR. HDY V-MAX	IMR	IMR 4064	.284"	2.825"	51.9	3117	56,100 PSI	55.2	3253	63,100 PSI
120 GR. HDY V-MAX	IMR	IMR 4895	.284"	2.825"	51.4	3088	54,300 PSI	54.7	3226	61,200 PSI
120 GR. HDY V-MAX	Hodgdon	H4895	.284"	2.825"	50.0	3059	51,600 PSI	54.0	3262	62,500 PSI
120 GR. HDY V-MAX	IMR	IMR 8208 XBR	.284"	2.825"	49.2	3052	54,800 PSI	52.3	3202	62,000 PSI
130 GR. SIE HPBT	Hodgdon	H1000	.284"	2.860"	67.0	3018	52,300 PSI	72.0C	3208	61,600 PSI
130 GR. SIE HPBT	IMR	IMR 7828	.284"	2.825"	63.0	3017	53,100 PSI	67.3	3228	62,600 PSI
130 GR. SIE HPBT	Winchester	Supreme 780	.284"	2.860"	67.7	3086	52,500 PSI	72.0	3272	61,800 PSI
130 GR. SIE HPBT	Hodgdon	H4831	.284"	2.860"	62.0	3041	55,000 PSI	66.0	3202	63,200 PSI
130 GR. SIE HPBT	IMR	IMR 4831	.284"	2.860"	60.0	3054	53,600 PSI	64.8	3253	63,300 PSI
130 GR. SIE HPBT	Hodgdon	H4350	.284"	2.860"	57.0	3048	54,500 PSI	61.0	3213	62,800 PSI
130 GR. SIE HPBT	Hodgdon	H414	.284"	2.860"	56.0	3025	55,100 PSI	60.3	3184	62,400 PSI
130 GR. SIE HPBT	IMR	IMR 4350	.284"	2.860"	59.0	3058	53,000 PSI	63.0	3243	62,400 PSI
130 GR. SIE HPBT	Winchester	760	.284"	2.860	56.0	3025	55,100 PSI	60.3	3184	62,400 PSI
130 GR. SIE HPBT	IMR	IMR 4007 SSC	.284"	2.860"	58.8	3038	54,000 PSI	62.5C	3209	62,700 PSI
130 GR. SIE HPBT	Hodgdon	H380	.284"	2.860"	55.0	2993	56,300 PSI	59.0	3142	63,000 PSI
130 GR. SIE HPBT	Hodgdon	Varget	.284"	2.860"	51.5	3029	56,200 PSI	55.2	3183	64,000 PSI
130 GR. SIE HPBT	IMR	IMR 4320	.384"	2.860"	51.0	2964	53,400 PSI	54.9	3141	63,100 PSI

130 GR. SIE HPBT	IMR	IMR 4064	.284"	2.860"	50.9	3005	55,000 PSI	54.2	3136	62,600 PSI
130 GR. SIE HPBT	IMR	IMR 4895	.284"	2.860"	51.0	2983	54,200 PSI	54.3	3121	61,600 PSI
130 GR. SIE HPBT	Hodgdon	H4895	.284"	2.860"	49.0	2969	54,500 PSI	53.0	3136	63,000 PSI
130 GR. SIE HPBT	IMR	IMR 8208 XBR	.284"	2.860"	48.7	2972	55,500 PSI	51.8	3109	63,000 PSI
140 GR. NOS PART	Hodgdon	Retumbo	.284"	2.850"	69.0	2888	47,100 PSI	72.0C	3046	54,300 PSI
140 GR. NOS PART	Hodgdon	H1000	.284"	2.850"	69.0	2995	53,400 PSI	72.0C	3091	59,000 PSI
140 GR. NOS PART	IMR	IMR 7828	.284"	2.850"	64.0	2997	55,700 PSI	68.2	3155	63,000 PSI
140 GR. NOS PART	Winchester	Supreme 780	.284"	2.850"	67.4	2962	51,500 PSI	71.7	3160	59,900 PSI
140 GR. NOS PART	Hodgdon	H4831	.284"	2.850"	62.0	2957	53,600 PSI	66.0	3116	62,000 PSI
140 GR. NOS PART	Hodgdon	Hybrid 100V	.284"	2.850"	58.0	2870	48,600 PSI	63.5	3116	60,200 PSI
140 GR. NOS PART	IMR	IMR 4831	.284"	2.850"	60.5	2994	55,300 PSI	64.6	3149	62,600 PSI
140 GR. NOS PART	Hodgdon	H4350	.284"	2.850"	58.0	2979	53,700 PSI	61.5	3133	61,900 PSI
140 GR. NOS PART	Hodgdon	H414	.284"	2.850"	57.0	2983	55,700 PSI	60.8	3130	62,600 PSI
140 GR. NOS PART	IMR	IMR 4350	.284"	2.850"	59.0	2974	53,500 PSI	63.2	3161	63,200 PSI
140 GR. NOS PART	Winchester	760	.184"	2.850"	57.0	2983	55,700 PSI	60.8	3130	62,600 PSI
140 GR. NOS PART	IMR	IMR 4007 SSC	.284"	2.850"	55.0	2836	49,100 PSI	62.0	3129	63,400 PSI
140 GR. NOS PART	Hodgdon	H380	.284"	2.850"	55.0	2890	53,800 PSI	59.0	3062	63,300 PSI
140 GR. NOS PART	Hodgdon	Varget	.284"	2.850"	51.0	2909	54,100 PSI	54.5	3063	62,600 PSI
140 GR. NOS PART	IMR	IMR 4320	.284"	2.850"	51.3	2898	54,000 PSI	54.3	3030	61,200 PSI
140 GR. NOS PART	IMR	IMR 4064	.284"	2.850"	51.0	2914	55,000 PSI	54.5	3058	62,900 PSI
140 GR. NOS PART	IMR	IMR 4895	.284"	2.850"	51.5	2933	55,800 PSI	55.0	3073	63,700 PSI
140 GR. NOS PART	Hodgdon	H4895	.284"	2.850"	49.0	2873	54,100 PSI	52.3	3024	63,000 PSI
140 GR. NOS PART	IMR	IMR 8208 XBR	.284"	2.850"	48.6	2895	55,700 PSI	51.7	3026	62,900 PSI
145 GR. SPR BTSP	Hodgdon	H1000	.284"	2.860"	65.0	2904	54,000 PSI	70.0C	3082	62,900 PSI
145 GR. SPR BTSP	IMR	IMR 7828	.284"	2.860"	63.5	2970	56,400 PSI	67.5C	3096	62,700 PSI
145 GR. SPR BTSP	Winchester	Supreme 780	.284"	2.860"	66.7	2958	52,600 PSI	71.0	3161	63,100 PSI
145 GR. SPR BTSP	Hodgdon	H4831	.284"	2.860"	59.0	2890	55,800 PSI	63.0	3044	63,400 PSI
145 GR. SPR BTSP	Hodgdon	Hybrid 100V	.284"	2.860"	58.0	2879	49,500 PSI	63.5C	3152	63,500 PSI
145 GR. SPR BTSP	IMR	IMR 4831	.284"	2.860"	60.0	2943	55,100 PSI	63.7	3096	62,700 PSI
145 GR. SPR BTSP	Hodgdon	H4350	.284"	2.860"	55.0	2898	55,700 PSI	58.7	3040	62,600 PSI
145 GR. SPR BTSP	Hodgdon	H414	.384"	2.860"	54.0	2847	54,900 PSI	58.0	3005	62,200 PSI
145 GR. SPR BTSP	IMR	IMR 4350	.284"	2.860"	58.5	2934	53,700 PSI	62.3	3101	63,200 PSI
145 GR. SPR BTSP	Winchester	760	.284"	2.860"	54.0	2847	54,900 PSI	58.0	3005	62,200 PSI
145 GR. SPR BTSP	IMR	IMR 4007 SSC	.284"	2.860"	57.9	2919	55,000 PSI	61.6	3079	63,800 PSI
145 GR. SPR BTSP	Hodgdon	H380	.284"	2.860"	53.0	2826	56,300 PSI	57.0	2970	62,800 PSI
145 GR. SPR BTSP	Hodgdon	Varget	.284"	2.860"	50.0	2872	57,100 PSI	53.3	3001	64,000 PSI
145 GR. SPR BTSP	IMR	IMR 4320	.284"	2.860"	51.7	2877	56,900 PSI	55.0	3000	63,600 PSI
145 GR. SPR BTSP	IMR	IMR 4064	.284"	2.860"	50.5	2839	54,800 PSI	54.0	2978	62,500 PSI
145 GR. SPR BTSP	IMR	IMR 4895	.284"	2.860"	50.8	2863	56,000 PSI	54.0	2977	62,000 PSI

145 GR. SPR BTSP	Hodgdon	H4895	.284"	2.860"	47.0	2779	55,100 PSI	50.5	2922	62,300 PSI
145 GR. SPR BTSP	IMR	IMR 8208 XBR	.284"	2.860"	47.4	2761	55,100 PSI	50.4	2885	62,400 PSI
150 GR. WIN SP	Hodgdon	Retumbo	.284"	2.840"	68.0	2824	45,600 PSI	72.0C	2987	53,000 PSI
150 GR. WIN SP	Hodgdon	H1000	.284"	2.840"	68.0	2899	51,300 PSI	72.0C	3031	58,600 PSI
150 GR. WIN SP	IMR	IMR 7828	.284"	2.840"	65.0	2886	51,400 PSI	69.5	3114	62,800 PSI
150 GR. WIN SP	Winchester	Supreme 780	.284"	2.840"	66.4	2824	43,400 PSI	70.6	3197	60,100 PSI
150 GR. WIN SP	Hodgdon	H4831	.284"	2.840"	63.0	2902	53,700 PSI	67.3	3066	62,500 PSI
150 GR. WIN SP	Hodgdon	Hybrid 100V	.284"	2.840"	59.0	2854	48,100 PSI	63.5C	3053	57,800 PSI
150 GR. WIN SP	IMR	IMR 4831	.284"	2.840"	63.0	2947	53,100 PSI	67.0	3116	62,800 PSI
150 GR. WIN SP	Hodgdon	H4350	.284"	2.840"	59.0	2923	54,600 PSI	63.0	3080	62,900 PSI
150 GR. WIN SP	Hodgdon	H414	.284"	2.840"	56.0	2886	55,600 PSI	59.7	3013	61,800 PSI
150 GR. WIN SP	IMR	IMR 4350	.284"	2.840"	61.0	2936	53,200 PSI	65.0	3120	63,100 PSI
150 GR. WIN SP	Winchester	760	.284"	2.840"	56.0	2886	55,600 PSI	59.7	3013	61,800 PSI
150 GR. WIN SP	IMR	IMR 4007 SSC	.284"	2.840"	57.8	2856	51,400 PSI	61.5	3040	61,700 PSI
150 GR. WIN SP	Hodgdon	H380	.284"	2.840"	55.5	2816	53,800 PSI	59.5	2991	63,400 PSI
150 GR. WIN SP	Hodgdon	Varget	.284"	2.840"	51.0	2852	55,700 PSI	55.0	3000	63,400 PSI
150 GR. WIN SP	IMR	IMR 4320	.284"	2.840"	52.6	2852	55,100 PSI	56.0	2977	62,200 PSI
150 GR. WIN SP	IMR	IMR 4064	.284"	2.840"	53.0	2870	55,700 PSI	56.2	2998	63,100 PSI
150 GR. WIN SP	Hodgdon	H4895	.284"	2.840"	48.0	2782	54,000 PSI	51.5	2930	62,300 PSI
150 GR. WIN SP	IMR	IMR 8208 XBR	.284"	2.850"	47.9	2803	55,500 PSI	51.0	2922	62,200 PSI
154 GR. HDY SP	Hodgdon	Retumbo	.284"	2.860"	66.0	2833	50,000 PSI	71.0C	3040	61,700 PSI
154 GR. HDY SP	Hodgdon	H1000	.284"	2.860"	64.0	2831	55,100 PSI	68.5C	2975	62,500 PSI
154 GR. HDY SP	IMR	IMR 7828	.284"	2.860"	61.5	2831	54,800 PSI	65.5	2986	62,600 PSI
154 GR. HDY SP	Winchester	Supreme 780	.284"	2.860"	63.5	2810	50,600 PSI	69.0	3063	61,400 PSI
154 GR. HDY SP	Hodgdon	H4831	.284"	2.860"	58.0	2779	54,100 PSI	62.5	2942	62,900 PSI
154 GR. HDY SP	Hodgdon	Hybrid 100V	.284"	2.860"	58.0	2848	53,000 PSI	62.5C	3040	63,000 PSI
154 GR. HDY SP	IMR	IMR 4831	.284"	2.860"	58.0	2804	53,900 PSI	61.7	2952	61,600 PSI
154 GR. HDY SP	Hodgdon	H4350	.284"	2.860"	54.0	2775	54,500 PSI	57.7	2920	62,600 PSI
154 GR. HDY SP	Hodgdon	H414	.284"	2.860"`	54.0	2762	56,000 PSI	58.5	2924	63,600 PSI
154 GR. HDY SP	IMR	IMR 4350	.284"	2.860"	57.0	2817	54,100 PSI	60.6	2956	61,800 PSI
154 GR. HDY SP	Winchester	760	.284"	2.860"	54.0	2762	56,000 PSI	58.5	2924	63,600 PSI
154 GR. HDY SP	IMR	IMR 4007 SSC	.284"	2.860"	53.0	2723	51,400 PSI	59.0	2954	63,800 PSI
154 GR. HDY SP	Hodgdon	H380	.284"	2.860"	52.0	2714	56,700 PSI	55.6	2834	63,100 PSI
154 GR. HDY SP	Hodgdon	Varget	.284"	2.860"	48.0	2705	55,000 PSI	52.0	2854	62,800 PSI
154 GR. HDY SP	IMR	IMR 4320	.284"	2.860"	49.5	2703	55,200 PSI	52.5	2829	62,700 PSI
154 GR. HDY SP	Hodgdon	H4895	.284"	2.860"	46.0	2658	55,200 PSI	49.5	2799	63,000 PSI
154 GR. HDY SP	IMR	IMR 8208 XBR	.284"	2.860"	46.2	2683	54,200 PSI	49.7	2824	63,200 PSI
160 GR. SFT SP	Hodgdon	Retumbo	.284"	2.850"	66.0	2793	51,200 PSI	70.0C	2958	59,800 PSI
160 GR. SFT SP	Hodgdon	H1000	.284"	2.850"	65.0	2801	54,300 PSI	69.5C	2956	62,800 PSI
160 GR. SFT SP	IMR	IMR 7828	.284"	2.850"	61.1	2780	54,400 PSI	65.0	2943	63,000 PSI

160 GR. SFT SP	Winchester	Supreme 780	.284"	2.850"	64.9	2788	49,700 PSI	69.0	2968	60,900 PSI
160 GR. SFT SP	Hodgdon	H4831	.284"	2.850"	59.0	2757	54,200 PSI	63.5	2921	62,600 PSI
160 GR. SFT SP	Hodgdon	Hybrid 100V	.284"	2.850"	57.0	2716	49,400 PSI	62.5C	2956	61,600 PSI
160 GR. SFT SP	IMR	IMR 4831	.284"	2.850"	57.7	2761	54,100 PSI	61.4	2907	62,100 PSI
160 GR. SFT SP	Hodgdon	H4350	.284"	2.850"	56.0	2782	54,600 PSI	59.5	2918	62,200 PSI
160 GR. SFT SP	Hodgdon	H414	.284"	2.850"	55.0	2743	54,300 PSI	58.7	2904	63,100 PSI
160 GR. SFT SP	IMR	IMR 4350	.284"	2.850"	58.0	2789	54,200 PSI	61.7	2946	63,400 PSI
160 GR. SFT SP	Winchester	760	.184"	2.850"	55.0	2743	54,300 PSI	58.7	2904	63,100 PSI
160 GR. SFT SP	IMR	IMR 4007 SSC	.284"	2.850"	53.0	2649	50,000 PSI	59.0	2884	61,900 PSI
160 GR. SFT SP	Hodgdon	H380	.284"	2.850"	53.0	2665	52,800 PSI	57.0	2832	61,900 PSI
160 GR. SFT SP	Hodgdon	Varget	.284"	2.850"	48.0	2676	54,100 PSI	51.3	2823	62,100 PSI
160 GR. SFT SP	IMR	IMR 4320	.284"	2.850"	49.4	2656	53,500 PSI	52.5	2803	62,000 PSI
160 GR. SFT SP	Hodgdon	H4895	.284"	2.850"	46.0	2614	52,500 PSI	49.0	2762	62,600 PSI
162 GR. HDY BTSP	Hodgdon	Retumbo	.284"	2.860"	66.0	2836	53,300 PSI	70.5C	3007	62,500 PSI
162 GR. HDY BTSP	Hodgdon	H1000	.284"	2.860"	64.0	2816	55,600 PSI	69.0C	2969	63,400 PSI
162 GR. HDY BTSP	IMR	IMR 7828	.284"	2.860"	62.0	2785	54,000 PSI	66.0	2959	62,800 PSI
162 GR. HDY BTSP	Winchester	Supreme 780	.284"	2.860"	64.9	2869	54,800 PSI	69.0	3036	63,700 PSI
162 GR. HDY BTSP	Hodgdon	H4831	.284"	2.860"	58.0	2772	55,500 PSI	62.0	2915	62,800 PSI
162 GR. HDY BTSP	Hodgdon	Hybrid 100V	.284"	2.860"	57.0	2778	52,000 PSI	61.5C	2959	61,800 PSI
162 GR. HDY BTSP	IMR	IMR 4831	.284"	2.860"	60.2	2834	55,500 PSI	64.0	2976	62,800 PSI
162 GR. HDY BTSP	Hodgdon	H4350	.284"	2.860"	54.0	2759	53,700 PSI	58.0	2909	62,900 PSI
162 GR. HDY BTSP	Hodgdon	H414	.284"	2.860"	54.0	2762	56,700 PSI	57.5	2892	63,200 PSI
162 GR. HDY BTSP	IMR	IMR 4350	.284"	2.860"	59.2	2817	54,700 PSI	63.0	2980	63,100 PSI
162 GR. HDY BTSP	Winchester	760	.284"	2.860"	54.0	2762	56,700 PSI	57.5	2892	63,200 PSI
162 GR. HDY BTSP	IMR	IMR 4007 SSC	.284"	2.860"	53.6	2728	54,500 PSI	57.0	2859	62,200 PSI
162 GR. HDY BTSP	Hodgdon	H380	.284"	2.860"	52.0	2700	55,700 PSI	56.0	2824	63,200 PSI
162 GR. HDY BTSP	Hodgdon	Varget	.284"	2.860"	48.0	2691	54,900 PSI	51.5	2830	62,900 PSI
162 GR. HDY BTSP	Hodgdon	H4895	.284"	2.860"	46.0	2645	54,800 PSI	49.0	2773	62,700 PSI
168 GR. SIE HPBT	Hodgdon	Retumbo	.284"	2.850"	66.0	2757	50,900 PSI	70.0C	2921	59,500 PSI
168 GR. SIE HPBT	Hodgdon	H1000	.284"	2.850"	65.0	2759	54,000 PSI	69.0C	2907	61,600 PSI
168 GR. SIE HPBT	IMR	IMR 7828	.284"	2.850"	62.0	2754	55,200 PSI	65.8	2921	62,900 PSI
168 GR. SIE HPBT	Winchester	Supreme 780	.284"	2.850"	64.0	2760	50,500 PSI	67.5	2940	61,300 PSI
168 GR. SIE HPBT	Hodgdon	H4831	.284"	2.850"	59.0	2759	56,200 PSI	63.0	2892	63,400 PSI
168 GR. SIE HPBT	Hodgdon	Hybrid 100V	.284"	2.850"	57.0	2755	53,600 PSI	61.0C	2895	61,000 PSI
168 GR. SIE HPBT	IMR	IMR 4831	.284"	2.850"	59.0	2734	53,300 PSI	62.7	2889	62,300 PSI
168 GR. SIE HPBT	Hodgdon	H4350	.284"	2.850"	55.0	2747	55,900 PSI	58.5	2865	62,300 PSI
168 GR. SIE HPBT	Hodgdon	H414	.284"	2.850"	53.0	2685	54,700 PSI	57.0	2834	62,800 PSI
168 GR. SIE HPBT	IMR	IMR 4350	.284"	2.850"	58.3	2743	53,900 PSI	62.0	2907	63,300 PSI
168 GR. SIE HPBT	Winchester	760	.284"	2.850"	53.0	2685	54,700 PSI	57.0	2834	62,800 PSI

135

Bullet Weight	Manufacturer	Powder	Bullet Diam.	C.O.L.	Grs.	Vel. (ft/s)	Pressure	Grs.	Vel. (ft/s)	Pressure
168 GR. SIE HPBT	IMR	IMR 4007 SSC	.284"	2.850"	54.5	2681	53,700 PSI	58.0	2833	62,700 PSI
168 GR. SIE HPBT	Hodgdon	H380	.284"	2.850"	52.0	2654	55,600 PSI	55.5	2781	63,000 PSI
168 GR. SIE HPBT	Hodgdon	Varget	.284"	2.850"	48.0	2666	55,100 PSI	51.0	2788	63,200 PSI
168 GR. SIE HPBT	Hodgdon	H4895	.284"	2.850"	46.0	2615	55,000 PSI	48.7	2732	62,600 PSI
175 GR. SPR MAG TIP	Hodgdon	Retumbo	.284"	2.760"	60.0	2651	53,000 PSI	64.0C	2800	61,200 PSI
175 GR. SPR MAG TIP	Hodgdon	H1000	.284"	2.760"	58.0	2635	56,600 PSI	62.0C	2764	63,100 PSI
175 GR. SPR MAG TIP	IMR	IMR 7828	.284"	2.760"	59.2	2636	55,800 PSI	63.0	2788	63,600 PSI
175 GR. SPR MAG TIP	Winchester	Supreme 780	.284"	2.760"	63.0	2649	49,900 PSI	68.0	2850	60,500 PSI
175 GR. SPR MAG TIP	Hodgdon	H4831	.284"	2.760"	54.0	2618	58,100 PSI	57.5	2733	63,900 PSI
175 GR. SPR MAG TIP	Hodgdon	Hybrid 100V	.284"	2.760"	53.0	2552	53,900 PSI	58.5	2738	63,200 PSI
175 GR. SPR MAG TIP	IMR	IMR 4831	.284"	2.760"	55.5	2600	54,300 PSI	59.0	2729	61,900 PSI
175 GR. SPR MAG TIP	Hodgdon	H4350	.284"	2.760"	49.0	2545	55,500 PSI	52.5	2672	62,200 PSI
175 GR. SPR MAG TIP	Hodgdon	H414	.284"	2.760"	48.0	2475	53,100 PSI	52.0	2636	61,300 PSI
175 GR. SPR MAG TIP	IMR	IMR 4350	.284"	2.760"	54.5	2595	53,800 PSI	58.0	2729	62,000 PSI
175 GR. SPR MAG TIP	Winchester	760	.284"	2.760"	48.0	2475	53,100 PSI	52.0	2636	61,300 PSI

Cartridge: 7mm Remington Magnum Load Type: Rifle					Starting Loads			Maximum Loads		
Bullet Weight (Gr.)	Manufacturer	Powder	Bullet Diam.	C.O.L.	Grs.	Vel. (ft/s)	Pressure	Grs.	Vel. (ft/s)	Pressure
100 GR. SIE HP	IMR	IMR 7828	.284"	3.150"	72.0	3267	48,900 PSI	75.0C	3421	54,100 PSI
100 GR. SIE HP	Hodgdon	H4831	.284"	3.150"	71.0	3316	43,300 CUP	75.0	3499	50,300 CUP
100 GR. SIE HP	Hodgdon	Hybrid 100V	.284"	3.150"	62.0	3290	49,500 PSI	68.0	3547	58,700 PSI
100 GR. SIE HP	IMR	IMR 4831	.284"	3.150"	67.0	3318	49,300 PSI	72.0	3592	59,400 PSI
100 GR. SIE HP	Hodgdon	H4350	.284"	3.150"	65.0	3334	44,800 CUP	69.0	3494	49,600 CUP
100 GR. SIE HP	Hodgdon	H414	.284"	3.150"	60.0	3216	39,900 CUP	66.0	3499	49,100 CUP
100 GR. SIE HP	IMR	IMR 4350	.284"	3.150"	66.0	3312	49,400 PSI	70.5	3569	59,000 PSI
100 GR. SIE HP	Hodgdon	Varget	.284"	3.150"	53.0	3193	39,600 CUP	59.0	3487	49,800 CUP
100 GR. SIE HP	IMR	IMR 4064	.284"	3.150"	57.0	3318	50,000 PSI	61.5	3528	58,600 PSI
100 GR. SIE HP	IMR	IMR 4895	.284"	3.150"	57.0	3288	49,200 PSI	61.2	3538	59,400 PSI
110 GR. SPR HP	IMR	IMR 7828	.284"	3.250"	72.0	3230	50,900 PSI	75.0C	3386	56,700 PSI
110 GR. SPR HP	Hodgdon	H4831	.284"	3.250"	68.0	3213	44,000 CUP	73.0	3367	49,700 CUP
110 GR. SPR HP	Hodgdon	Hybrid 100V	.284"	3.250"	62.0	3203	48,900 PSI	68.0	3465	59,500 PSI
110 GR. SPR HP	IMR	IMR 4831	.284"	3.250"	67.0	3249	51,200 PSI	71.3	3456	59,700 PSI
110 GR. SPR HP	Hodgdon	H4350	.284"	3.250"	65.0	3233	44,700 CUP	68.5	3357	49,500 CUP
110 GR. SPR HP	Hodgdon	H414	.284"	3.250"	62.0	3250	45,800 CUP	65.5	3395	50,400 CUP
110 GR. SPR HP	IMR	IMR 4350	.284"	3.250"	65.0	3205	49,700 PSI	69.8	3442	59,000 PSI
110 GR. SPR HP	IMR	IMR 4007 SSC	.284"	3.250"	63.5	3256	50,800 PSI	67.5	3452	60,000 PSI
110 GR. SPR HP	Hodgdon	Varget	.284"	3.250"	54.0	3174	44,600 CUP	58.5	3356	50,300 CUP
110 GR. SPR HP	IMR	IMR 4064	.284"	3.250"	56.0	3214	53,100 PSI	60.5	3369	59,400 PSI
110 GR. SPR HP	IMR	IMR 4895	.284"	3.250"	56.0	3210	52,600 PSI	59.9	3350	58,800 PSI

115 GR. SPR HP	Hodgdon	H4831	.284"	3.200"	65.0	3060	44,200 CUP	69.7	3257	50,600 CUP
115 GR. SPR HP	Hodgdon	Hybrid 100V	.284"	3.200"	60.0	3102	48,500 PSI	66.0	3354	58,500 PSI
115 GR. SPR HP	Hodgdon	H4350	.284"	3.200"	62.0	3089	43,800 CUP	66.0	3281	50,300 CUP
115 GR. SPR HP	Hodgdon	H414	.284"	3.200"	59.0	3071	45,100 CUP	63.5	3267	50,400 CUP
115 GR. SPR HP	IMR	IMR 4007 SSC	.284"	3.200"	60.6	3157	51,600 PSI	64.5	3320	59,500 PSI
115 GR. SPR HP	Hodgdon	Varget	.284"	3.200"	53.0	3068	44,800 CUP	56.5	3245	49,800 CUP
120 GR. HDY SP	IMR	IMR 7828	.284"	3.230"	68.0	3044	50,000 PSI	72.5C	3261	59,100 PSI
120 GR. HDY SP	Hodgdon	H4831	.284"	3.230"	65.0	3095	45,800 CUP	68.5	3236	50,600 CUP
120 GR. HDY SP	Hodgdon	Hybrid 100V	.284"	3.230"	60.0	3092	50,100 PSI	65.5	3327	59,600 PSI
120 GR. HDY SP	IMR	IMR 4831	.284"	3.230"	64.0	3040	51,300 PSI	68.2	3231	58,500 PSI
120 GR. HDY SP	Hodgdon	H4350	.284"	3.230"	62.0	3106	44,700 CUP	65.0	3226	50,100 CUP
120 GR. HDY SP	Hodgdon	H414	.284"	3.230"	61.0	3126	45,500 CUP	64.5	3261	50,700 CUP
120 GR. HDY SP	IMR	IMR 4350	.284"	3.230"	62.0	3050	49,900 PSI	66.5	3251	59,000 PSI
120 GR. HDY SP	IMR	IMR 4007 SSC	.284"	3.230"	60.0	3085	49,800 PSI	63.8	3278	59,500 PSI
120 GR. HDY SP	Hodgdon	Varget	.284"	3.230"	53.0	3021	45,200 CUP	57.0	3218	50,900 CUP
120 GR. HDY SP	IMR	IMR 4064	.284"	3.230"	54.0	3062	52,600 PSI	58.2	3212	59,400 PSI
120 GR. HDY SP	IMR	IMR 4895	.284"	3.230"	54.0	3049	52,200 PSI	57.9	3189	58,700 PSI
130 GR. SPR SP	IMR	IMR 7828	.284"	3.185"	65.0	2943	50,800 PSI	70.0	3159	59,300 PSI
130 GR. SPR SP	Hodgdon	H4831	.284"	3.185"	63.0	2952	46,300 CUP	66.0	3051	50,200 CUP
130 GR. SPR SP	Hodgdon	Hybrid 100V	.284"	3.185"	57.0	2931	49,400 PSI	62.5	3157	59,000 PSI
130 GR. SPR SP	IMR	IMR 4831	.284"	3.185"	62.0	2971	53,200 PSI	66.3	3125	59,800 PSI
130 GR. SPR SP	Hodgdon	H4350	.284"	3.185"	58.0	2953	45,100 CUP	61.5	3082	50,800 CUP
130 GR. SPR SP	Hodgdon	H414	.284"	3.185"	59.0	2985	46,500 CUP	61.0	3064	49,400 CUP
130 GR. SPR SP	IMR	IMR 4350	.284"	3.185"	60.0	2964	52,300 PSI	64.0	3131	59,300 PSI
130 GR. SPR SP	IMR	IMR 4007 SSC	.284"	3.185"	57.3	2964	53,100 PSI	61.0	3122	59,500 PSI
130 GR. SPR SP	Hodgdon	Varget	.284"	3.185"	51.0	2877	45,700 CUP	54.0	2998	49,400 CUP
130 GR. SPR SP	IMR	IMR 4064	.284"	3.185"	52.0	2904	52,200 PSI	55.4	3048	59,600 PSI
139 GR. HDY GMX	Hodgdon	Retumbo	.284"	3.290"	68.0	2869	45,500 PSI	74.0C	3128	58,400 PSI
139 GR. HDY GMX	Hodgdon	H1000	.284"	3.290"	67.5	2847	46,300 PSI	73.0C	3065	56,000 PSI
139 GR. HDY GMX	IMR	IMR 7828	.284"	3.290"	63.4	2841	45,800 PSI	70.0C	3191	59,400 PSI
139 GR. HDY GMX	Winchester	Supreme 780	.284"	3.290"	65.0	2934	48,300 PSI	70.5	3200	58,500 PSI
139 GR. HDY GMX	Hodgdon	H4831	.284"	3.290"	64.5	2878	50,200 PSI	68.8	3054	58,100 PSI
139 GR. HDY GMX	Hodgdon	Hybrid 100V	.284"	3.290"	58.5	2914	49,800 PSI	62.2	3114	59,500 PSI
139 GR. HDY GMX	IMR	IMR 4831	.284"	3.290"	61.6	2862	48,400 PSI	65.5	3085	58,400 PSI
139 GR. HDY GMX	Hodgdon	H4350	.284"	3.290"	56.1	2834	45,300 PSI	59.7	3007	57,800 PSI
139 GR. HDY GMX	Hodgdon	H414	.284"	3.290"	56.2	2820	51,300 PSI	59.8	3043	59,300 PSI
139 GR. HDY GMX	IMR	IMR 4350	.284"	3.290"	59.6	2902	49,300 PSI	63.4	3099	58,500 PSI
139 GR. HDY GMX	Winchester	760	.284"	3.290"	56.2	2820	51,300 PSI	59.8	3043	59,300 PSI
139 GR. HDY GMX	IMR	IMR 4007 SSC	.284"	3.290"	56.9	2873	51,600 PSI	60.5	3017	57,700 PSI

140 GR. NOS PART	Hodgdon	Retumbo	.284"	3.250"	71.0	2955	46,100 CUP	75.0C	3107	49,400 CUP
140 GR. NOS PART	Hodgdon	H1000	.284"	3.250"	67.0	2934	46,200 CUP	70.0	3036	50,600 CUP
140 GR. NOS PART	IMR	IMR 7828	.284"	3.250"	64.0	2867	50,000 PSI	69.0	3095	59,200 PSI
140 GR. NOS PART	Winchester	Supreme 780	.284"	3.250"	65.1	2976	50,500 PSI	69.3	3134	58,000 PSI
140 GR. NOS PART	Hodgdon	H4831	.284"	3.250"	61.0	2841	46,300 CUP	64.0	2950	50,200 CUP
140 GR. NOS PART	Hodgdon	Hybrid 100V	.284"	3.250"	57.0	2895	49,100 PSI	63.0	3138	59,800 PSI
140 GR. NOS PART	IMR	IMR 4831	.284"	3.250"	61.0	2880	52,200 PSI	65.4	3053	59,400 PSI
140 GR. NOS PART	Hodgdon	H4350	.284"	3.250"	56.0	2808	45,500 CUP	59.0	2927	50,000 CUP
140 GR. NOS PART	Hodgdon	H414	.284"	3.250"	58.0	2897	46,700 CUP	60.2	2967	49,300 CUP
140 GR. NOS PART	IMR	IMR 4350	.284"	3.250"	59.0	2877	51,400 PSI	62.8	3045	58,600 PSI
140 GR. NOS PART	Winchester	760	.284"	3.250"	58.0	2897	46,700 CUP	60.2	2967	49,300 CUP
140 GR. NOS PART	IMR	IMR 4007 SSC	.284"	3.250"	56.4	2867	50,900 PSI	60.0	3025	58,600 PSI
140 GR. NOS PART	IMR	Trail Boss	.284"	3.250"	17.2	1405	21,400 PSI	24.5	1724	31,000 PSI
150 GR. BAR TTSX BT	Hodgdon	Retumbo	.284"	3.225"	66.9	2895	47,900 PSI	73.5C	3115	57,200 PSI
150 GR. BAR TTSX BT	Hodgdon	H1000	.284"	3.225"	67.2	2847	49,200 PSI	73.8	3083	59,100 PSI
150 GR. BAR TTSX BT	IMR	IMR 7828	.284"	3.225"	63.4	2851	48,400 PSI	68.7	3100	59,200 PSI
150 GR. BAR TTSX BT	Winchester	Supreme 780	.284"	3.225"	62.3	2850	47,900 PSI	67.8	3113	59,500 PSI
150 GR. BAR TTSX BT	Hodgdon	H4831	.284"	3.225"	62.7	2852	50,600 PSI	68.0	3080	60,200 PSI
150 GR. BAR TTSX BT	Hodgdon	Hybrid 100V	.284"	3.225"	56.8	2829	47,800 PSI	60.7	3071	59,000 PSI
150 GR. BAR TTSX BT	IMR	IMR 4831	.284"	3.225"	60.4	2848	49,600 PSI	65.0	3075	59,600 PSI
150 GR. BAR TTSX BT	Hodgdon	H4350	.284"	3.225"	57.9	2836	50,800 PSI	62.5	3041	59,800 PSI
150 GR. BAR TTSX BT	IMR	IMR 4350	.284"	3.225"	58.9	2856	49,800 PSI	63.7	3059	59,300 PSI
150 GR. NOS PART	Hodgdon	Retumbo	.284"	3.270"	68.0	2818	43,300 CUP	72.5C	2998	50,300 CUP
150 GR. NOS PART	Hodgdon	H1000	.284"	3.270"	65.0	2835	46,200 CUP	68.0	2936	49,900 CUP
150 GR. NOS PART	IMR	IMR 7828	.284"	3.270"	62.0	2792	51,700 PSI	66.2	2952	58,500 PSI
150 GR. NOS PART	Winchester	Supreme 780	.284"	3.270"	63.9	2913	50,600 PSI	68.0	3081	58,800 PSI
150 GR. NOS PART	Hodgdon	H4831	.284"	3.270"	59.0	2775	45,300 CUP	62.0	2986	51,100 CUP
150 GR. NOS PART	Hodgdon	Hybrid 100V	.284"	3.270"	55.0	2746	48,800 PSI	60.0	2975	59,500 PSI
150 GR. NOS PART	IMR	IMR 4831	.284"	3.270"	58.0	2758	51,500 PSI	62.5	2925	59,400 PSI
150 GR. NOS PART	Hodgdon	H4350	.284"	3.270"	55.0	2781	45,700 CUP	57.0	2859	50,100 CUP
150 GR. NOS PART	IMR	IMR 4350	.284"	3.270"	57.0	2786	52,400 PSI	60.8	2931	59,400 PSI
160 GR. NOS PART	Hodgdon	US 869	.284"	3.290"	77.0	2786	52,300 PSI	80.0	2897	58,300 PSI
160 GR. NOS PART	Hodgdon	Retumbo	.284"	3.290"	65.0	2756	43,200 CUP	69.5C	2915	49,900 CUP
160 GR. NOS PART	Hodgdon	H1000	.284"	3.290"	63.0	2729	43,300 CUP	66.0	2839	49,600 CUP
160 GR. NOS PART	IMR	IMR 7828	.284"	3.290"	60.0	2709	50,500 PSI	64.0	2868	58,200 PSI
160 GR. NOS PART	Winchester	Supreme 780	.284"	3.290"	61.8	2829	52,400 PSI	65.7	2948	58,000 PSI
160 GR. NOS PART	Hodgdon	H4831	.284"	3.290"	58.0	2695	46,400 CUP	60.0	2787	49,800 CUP
160 GR. NOS PART	Hodgdon	Hybrid 100V	.284"	3.290"	53.0	2647	49,600 PSI	58.0	2839	58,300 PSI
160 GR. NOS PART	IMR	IMR 4831	.284"	3.290"	57.0	2707	50,600 PSI	61.0	2858	58,400 PSI
160 GR. NOS PART	Hodgdon	H4350	.284"	3.290"	53.0	2651	46,400 CUP	55.5	2745	49,800 CUP

160 GR. NOS PART	IMR	IMR 4350	.284"	3.290"	56.0	2697	49,700 PSI	59.5	2856	58,500 PSI
162 GR. HDY SPBT	Hodgdon	US 869	.284"	3.290"	77.0	2820	49,800 PSI	80.0	2921	54,400 PSI
162 GR. HDY SPBT	Hodgdon	Retumbo	.284"	3.290"	69.0	2787	43,900 CUP	73.5C	2963	50,500 CUP
162 GR. HDY SPBT	Hodgdon	H1000	.284"	3.290"	67.0	2800	45,400 CUP	70.0	2905	49,600 CUP
162 GR. HDY SPBT	IMR	IMR 7828	.284"	3.290"	61.0	2724	50,800 PSI	65.0	2882	59,000 PSI
162 GR. HDY SPBT	Winchester	Supreme 780	.284"	3.290"	61.6	2819	53,100 PSI	65.5	2953	59,700 PSI
162 GR. HDY SPBT	Hodgdon	H4831	.284"	3.290"	60.0	2731	43,300 CUP	64.0	2871	49,800 CUP
162 GR. HDY SPBT	Hodgdon	Hybrid 100V	.284"	3.290"	55.0	2725	49,700 PSI	60.0	2922	59,500 PSI
162 GR. HDY SPBT	IMR	IMR 4831	.284"	3.290"	58.0	2710	49,900 PSI	61.8	2877	59,500 PSI
162 GR. HDY SPBT	Hodgdon	H4350	.284"	3.290"	55.0	2677	43,400 CUP	58.0	2799	49,400 CUP
162 GR. HDY SPBT	IMR	IMR 4350	.284"	3.290"	56.0	2704	49,700 PSI	60.0	2861	58,100 PSI
170 GR. SIE RN	Hodgdon	US 869	.284"	3.270"	77.0	2688	44,700 PSI	79.0	2826	51,300 PSI
170 GR. SIE RN	Hodgdon	Retumbo	.284"	3.270"	71.0	2752	44,200 CUP	75.0C	2899	50,700 CUP
170 GR. SIE RN	Hodgdon	H1000	.284"	3.270"	69.0	2744	45,600 CUP	71.0	2806	49,400 CUP
170 GR. SIE RN	IMR	IMR 7828	.284"	3.270"	62.0	2680	50,400 PSI	66.0	2839	58,700 PSI
170 GR. SIE RN	Winchester	Supreme 780	.284"	3.270"	63.9	2746	49,900 PSI	68.0	2916	59,300 PSI
170 GR. SIE RN	Hodgdon	H4831	.284"	3.270"	63.0	2749	46,300 CUP	65.0	2806	48,900 CUP
170 GR. SIE RN	Hodgdon	Hybrid 100V	.284"	3.270"	54.0	2604	49,400 PSI	59.0	2807	59,500 PSI
170 GR. SIE RN	IMR	IMR 4831	.284"	3.270"	59.0	2672	50,500 PSI	63.0	2828	59,100 PSI
170 GR. SIE RN	Hodgdon	H4350	.284"	3.270"	58.0	2701	44,600 CUP	60.0	2767	48,500 CUP
170 GR. SIE RN	IMR	IMR 4350	.284"	3.270"	57.0	2669	50,700 PSI	61.5	2829	59,200 PSI
175 GR. NOS PART	Hodgdon	US 869	.284"	3.290"	74.0	2632	49,300 PSI	77.0	2758	56,200 PSI
175 GR. NOS PART	Hodgdon	Retumbo	.284"	3.290"	64.0	2650	45,400 CUP	68.0	2800	51,200 CUP
175 GR. NOS PART	Hodgdon	H1000	.284"	3.290"	61.0	2567	45,000 CUP	64.5	2692	50,400 CUP
175 GR. NOS PART	IMR	IMR 7828	.284"	3.290"	57.0	2549	49,800 PSI	61.0	2707	58,300 PSI
175 GR. NOS PART	Winchester	Supreme 780	.284"	3.290"	59.2	2639	51,300 PSI	63.0	2789	58,800 PSI
175 GR. NOS PART	Hodgdon	H4831	.284"	3.290"	55.0	2532	45,800 CUP	58.0	2660	50,200 CUP
175 GR. NOS PART	Hodgdon	Hybrid 100V	.284"	3.290"	53.0	2567	49,700 PSI	57.5	2740	58,200 PSI
175 GR. NOS PART	IMR	IMR 4831	.284"	3.290"	54.0	2540	50,100 PSI	58.0	2710	58,700 PSI
175 GR. NOS PART	Hodgdon	H4350	.284"	3.290"	51.0	2504	46,200 CUP	54.0	2617	51,400 CUP
175 GR. NOS PART	IMR	IMR 4350	.284"	3.290"	54.0	2586	52,600 PSI	57.0	2698	58,800 PSI
180 GR. BER VLD	Hodgdon	Retumbo	.284"	3.290"	64.4	2638	46,400 PSI	70.8C	2914	59,600 PSI
180 GR. BER VLD	Hodgdon	H1000	.284"	3.290"	63.2	2605	46,000 PSI	69.5C	2884	60,000 PSI
180 GR. BER VLD	IMR	IMR 7828	.284"	3.290"	59.6	2570	45,300 PSI	65.5	2874	58,900 PSI
180 GR. BER VLD	Winchester	Supreme 780	.284"	3.290"	59.1	2635	47,500 PSI	65.0	2894	60,100 PSI
180 GR. BER VLD	Hodgdon	H4831	.284"	3.290"	58.6	2652	51,800 PSI	64.5	2830	60,200 PSI
180 GR. BER VLD	Hodgdon	Hybrid 100V	.284"	3.290"	53.6	2594	48,800 PSI	59.0	2810	59,700 PSI
180 GR. BER VLD	IMR	IMR 4831	.284"	3.290"	56.4	2608	48,900 PSI	62.0	2841	59,500 PSI
180 GR. BER VLD	Hodgdon	H4350	.284"	3.290"	52.0	2553	48,000 PSI	56.0	2752	59,000 PSI

180 GR. BER VLD	IMR	IMR 4350	.284"	3.290"	55.5	2622	49,300 PSI	61.0	2837	59,400 PSI

Cartridge: 7mm Weatherby Magnum Load Type: Rifle						Starting Loads			Maximum Loads	
Bullet Weight (Gr.)	Manufacturer	Powder	Bullet Diam.	C.O.L.	Grs.	Vel. (ft/s)	Pressure	Grs.	Vel. (ft/s)	Pressure
140 GR. SFT SP	Hodgdon	H1000	.284"	3.250"	75.0	3104	42,800 CUP	79.0C	3273	49,900 CUP
140 GR. SFT SP	IMR	IMR 7828	.284"	3.250"	69.0	3098	45,100 CUP	74.0	3326	55,100 CUP
140 GR. SFT SP	Winchester	Supreme 780	.284"	3.250"	67.7	3044	46,800 CUP	72.0	3198	53,100 CUP
140 GR. SFT SP	Hodgdon	H4831	.284"	3.250"	69.0	3023	43,600 CUP	74.0C	3258	54,000 CUP
140 GR. SFT SP	Hodgdon	Hybrid 100V	.284"	3.250"	60.0	2931	44,800 CUP	66.0	3196	53,300 CUP
140 GR. SFT SP	IMR	IMR 4831	.284"	3.250"	65.0	3031	42,800 CUP	69.5	3255	52,800 CUP
140 GR. SFT SP	Hodgdon	H4350	.284"	3.250"	64.0	3046	43,800 CUP	68.5	3248	54,000 CUP
140 GR. SFT SP	IMR	IMR 4350	.284"	3.250"	62.0	3037	41,400 CUP	67.0	3261	53,100 CUP
140 GR. SFT SP	IMR	Trail Boss	.284"	3.250"	18.5	1365	22,700 CUP	26.5	1529	30,500 CUP
150 GR. NOS PART	Hodgdon	H1000	.284"	3.250"	75.0	3073	45,400 CUP	79.0C	3223	52,200 CUP
150 GR. NOS PART	IMR	IMR 7828	.284"	3.250"	67.0	2989	48,500 CUP	72.0	3212	54,100 CUP
150 GR. NOS PART	Winchester	Supreme 780	.284"	3.250"	68.2	2991	45,800 CUP	72.5	3157	52,300 CUP
150 GR. NOS PART	Hodgdon	H4831	.284"	3.250"	68.0	2973	44,800 CUP	72.0	3152	53,500 CUP
150 GR. NOS PART	Hodgdon	Hybrid 100V	.284"	3.250"	61.0	2967	41,500 CUP	65.5C	3133	53,900 CUP
150 GR. NOS PART	IMR	IMR 4831	.284"	3.250"	64.0	2957	44,300 CUP	69.0	3172	53,900 CUP
150 GR. NOS PART	Hodgdon	H4350	.284"	3.250"	64.0	3012	45,800 CUP	68.0	3180	54,000 CUP
150 GR. NOS PART	IMR	IMR 4350	.284"	3.250"	62.0	3003	44,000 CUP	66.5	3175	54,100 CUP
160 GR. BAR TTSX	Hodgdon	H1000	.284"	3.250"	68.0	2778	45,600 CUP	75.0C	3034	54,800 CUP
160 GR. BAR TTSX	IMR	IMR 7828 SSC	.284"	3.250"	62.0	2699	43,900 CUP	69.5C	2998	54,200 CUP
160 GR. BAR TTSX	Winchester	Supreme 780	.284"	3.250"	64.5	2751	43,800 CUP	68.6	2946	51,400 CUP
160 GR. BAR TTSX	Hodgdon	H4831	.284"	3.250"	62.0	2759	48,300 CUP	69.0C	3001	55,000 CUP
160 GR. BAR TTSX	Hodgdon	Hybrid 100V	.284"	3.250"	58.0	2664	43,200 CUP	63.5C	2888	50,700 CUP
160 GR. BAR TTSX	IMR	IMR 4831	.284"	3.250"	59.0	2750	44,300 CUP	65.0	2991	54,100 CUP
160 GR. BAR TTSX	Hodgdon	H4350	.284"	3.250"	55.0	2723	48,500 CUP	61.5	2960	55,300 CUP
160 GR. BAR TTSX	IMR	IMR 4350	.284"	3.250"	56.0	2715	46,900 CUP	62.0	2917	54,100 CUP
175 GR. HDY SP	Hodgdon	US 869	.284"	3.350"	78.0	2751	41,600 CUP	80.0	2862	45,200 CUP
175 GR. HDY SP	Hodgdon	H1000	.284"	3.350"	70.0	2844	45,000 CUP	74.7C	3022	54,000 CUP
175 GR. HDY SP	IMR	IMR 7828	.284"	3.350"	64.0	2773	45,000 CUP	67.5	2942	52,600 CUP
175 GR. HDY SP	Winchester	Supreme 780	.284"	3.350"	63.7	2714	45,800 CUP	67.8	2873	51,400 CUP
175 GR. HDY SP	Hodgdon	H4831	.284"	3.350"	63.0	2724	43,500 CUP	67.5	2895	53,400 CUP
175 GR. HDY SP	Hodgdon	Hybrid 100V	.284"	3.350"	57.0	2658	46,000 CUP	62.0C	2826	52,600 CUP
175 GR. HDY SP	IMR	IMR 4831	.284"	3.350"	60.0	2756	46,400 CUP	64.0	2880	53,000 CUP
175 GR. HDY SP	Hodgdon	H4350	.284"	3.350"	60.0	2755	45,900 CUP	63.7	2899	53,600 CUP
175 GR. HDY SP	IMR	IMR 4350	.284"	3.350"	59.0	2784	45,800 CUP	63.0	2885	53,400 CUP
180 GR. BER VLD	Hodgdon	US 869	.284"	3.350"	75.2	2698	42,800 CUP	81.8C	2927	50,900 CUP

Bullet Weight	Manufacturer	Powder	Bullet Diam.	C.O.L.	Grs.	Vel. (ft/s)	Pressure	Grs.	Vel. (ft/s)	Pressure
180 GR. BER VLD	Hodgdon	H1000	.284"	3.350"	66.3	2733	44,400 CUP	72.1C	2939	53,600 CUP
180 GR. BER VLD	IMR	IMR 7828	.284"	3.350"	62.6	2686	42,800 CUP	68.1C	2948	53,800 CUP
180 GR. BER VLD	Winchester	Supreme 780	.284"	3.350"	62.5	2676	42,200 CUP	67.2	2945	53,300 CUP
180 GR. BER VLD	Hodgdon	H4831	.284"	3.350"	60.3	2647	42,800 CUP	66.3	2877	53,600 CUP
180 GR. BER VLD	Hodgdon	Hybrid 100V	.284"	3.350"	56.4	2641	43,900 CUP	61.4	2832	52,600 CUP
180 GR. BER VLD	IMR	IMR 4831	.284"	3.350"	59.1	2705	45,700 CUP	64.3	2886	52,700 CUP
180 GR. BER VLD	Hodgdon	H4350	.284"	3.350"	55.4	2630	44,400 CUP	60.3	2840	53,900 CUP

Cartridge: 7mm Shooting Times Westerner Load Type: Rifle					Starting Loads			Maximum Loads		
Bullet Weight (Gr.)	Manufacturer	Powder	Bullet Diam.	C.O.L.	Grs.	Vel. (ft/s)	Pressure	Grs.	Vel. (ft/s)	Pressure
120 GR. SIE SP	Hodgdon	Retumbo	.284"	3.585"	85.0	3330	47,900 CUP	89.5C	3519	54,300 CUP
120 GR. SIE SP	Hodgdon	H1000	.284"	3.585"	82.0	3255	45,300 CUP	86.0	3405	51,800 CUP
120 GR. SIE SP	IMR	IMR 7828	.284"	3.585"	75.8	3289	50,800 CUP	80.6	3436	53,000 CUP
120 GR. SIE SP	Winchester	Supreme 780	.284"	3.585"	74.0	3188	44,300 CUP	80.5	3438	52,500 CUP
120 GR. SIE SP	Hodgdon	H4831	.284"	3.585"	75.0	3200	46,300 CUP	78.5	3348	51,900 CUP
120 GR. SIE SP	Hodgdon	Hybrid 100V	.284"	3.585"	69.0	3256	47,200 CUP	75.0	3498	53,800 CUP
120 GR. SIE SP	IMR	IMR 4831	.284"	3.585"	71.2	3257	46,100 CUP	75.7	3387	50,700 CUP
120 GR. SIE SP	Hodgdon	H4350	.284"	3.585"	69.0	3185	45,400 CUP	73.0	3350	52,300 CUP
120 GR. SIE SP	IMR	IMR 4350	.284"	3.585"	68.0	3236	44,000 CUP	72.5	3402	52,700 CUP
139 GR. HDY SPBT	Hodgdon	Retumbo	.284"	3.585"	83.0	3165	47,700 CUP	88.0C	3347	54,300 CUP
139 GR. HDY SPBT	Hodgdon	H1000	.284"	3.585"	81.0	3119	46,400 CUP	85.5	3284	52,300 CUP
139 GR. HDY SPBT	IMR	IMR 7828	.284"	3.585"	75.0	3190	49,700 CUP	79.7	3333	52,800 CUP
139 GR. HDY SPBT	Winchester	Supreme 780	.284"	3.585"	72.0	3000	42,700 CUP	78.5	3236	51,000 CUP
139 GR. HDY SPBT	Hodgdon	H4831	.284"	3.585"	72.0	3018	44,400 CUP	76.5	3181	51,900 CUP
139 GR. HDY SPBT	Hodgdon	Hybrid 100V	.284"	3.585"	67.0	3085	45,800 CUP	72.0	3264	52,500 CUP
139 GR. HDY SPBT	IMR	IMR 4831	.284"	3.585"	70.5	3156	48,500 CUP	75.0	3302	54,200 CUP
139 GR. HDY SPBT	Hodgdon	H4350	.284"	3.585"	69.0	3079	46,700 CUP	71.0	3183	52,300 CUP
139 GR. HDY SPBT	IMR	IMR 4350	.284"	3.585"	67.2	3125	46,000 CUP	71.5	3274	53,100 CUP
145 GR. SPR SP	Hodgdon	US 869	.284"	3.565"	86.0	3055	48,300 CUP	91.0	3209	52,900 CUP
145 GR. SPR SP	Hodgdon	Retumbo	.284"	3.565"	77.0	3052	48,000 CUP	81.5C	3195	53,700 CUP
145 GR. SPR SP	Hodgdon	H1000	.284"	3.565"	74.0	3023	47,400 CUP	77.0	3120	52,100 CUP
145 GR. SPR SP	IMR	IMR 7828	.284"	3.565"	69.5	2975	48,800 CUP	74.0	3136	53,700 CUP
145 GR. SPR SP	Winchester	Supreme 780	.284"	3.565"	69.0	2983	49,100 CUP	73.5	3117	52,900 CUP
145 GR. SPR SP	Hodgdon	H4831	.284"	3.565"	68.0	2937	47,800 CUP	72.0	3063	52,300 CUP
145 GR. SPR SP	Hodgdon	Hybrid 100V	.284"	3.565"	64.0	2959	46,600 CUP	69.0	3144	53,000 CUP
145 GR. SPR SP	IMR	IMR 4831	.284"	3.565"	64.5	2909	46,000 CUP	69.0	3048	52,200 CUP
145 GR. SPR SP	IMR	IMR 4350	.284"	3.565"	65.0	2965	47,800 CUP	69.0	3168	54,300 CUP
150 GR. BAR TSX	Hodgdon	US 869	.284"	3.530"	83.0	2930	43,600 CUP	88.0	3081	48,900 CUP

Bullet Weight (Gr.)	Manufacturer	Powder	Bullet Diam.	C.O.L.	Grs.	Vel. (ft/s)	Pressure	Grs.	Vel. (ft/s)	Pressure
150 GR. BAR TSX	Hodgdon	H50BMG	.284"	3.530"	80.0	2908	46,600 CUP	84.0C	3005	49,500 CUP
150 GR. BAR TSX	Hodgdon	Retumbo	.284"	3.530"	71.0	2929	46,200 CUP	77.0C	3140	53,500 CUP
150 GR. BAR TSX	Hodgdon	H1000	.284"	3.530"	71.0	2889	45,000 CUP	76.0C	3038	51,600 CUP
150 GR. BAR TSX	IMR	IMR 7828 SSC	.284"	3.530"	69.0	2909	46,600 CUP	72.0	3047	52,200 CUP
150 GR. BAR TSX	Winchester	Supreme 780	.284"	3.530"	69.0	2915	47,000 CUP	73.0	3056	51,800 CUP
150 GR. BAR TSX	Hodgdon	H4831	.284"	3.530"	65.0	2842	47,100 CUP	70.0	3022	53,100 CUP
150 GR. BAR TSX	Hodgdon	Hybrid 100V	.284"	3.530"	64.0	2910	47,300 CUP	68.5	3060	52,800 CUP
150 GR. BAR TSX	IMR	IMR 4831	.284"	3.530"	62.0	2849	44,500 CUP	66.5	3019	53,200 CUP
150 GR. BAR TSX	IMR	IMR 4350	.284"	3.530"	60.0	2813	46,100 CUP	65.5	3006	53,900 CUP
160 GR. SFT SP	Hodgdon	US 869	.284"	3.565"	85.0	2922	46,400 CUP	90.0	3041	50,800 CUP
160 GR. SFT SP	Hodgdon	H50BMG	.284"	3.565"	88.0	2929	46,100 CUP	90.0C	2970	46,600 CUP
160 GR. SFT SP	Hodgdon	Retumbo	.284"	3.565"	75.0	2909	46,700 CUP	80.2	3056	53,600 CUP
160 GR. SFT SP	Hodgdon	H1000	.284"	3.565"	76.0	2930	44,300 CUP	80.7	3084	51,500 CUP
160 GR. SFT SP	IMR	IMR 7828	.284"	3.565"	72.5	2900	48,400 CUP	77.0	3085	54,200 CUP
160 GR. SFT SP	Winchester	Supreme 780	.284"	3.565"	69.0	2838	45,800 CUP	73.0	2976	51,500 CUP
160 GR. SFT SP	Hodgdon	H4831	.284"	3.565"	70.0	2884	45,900 CUP	74.0	3037	52,300 CUP
160 GR. SFT SP	Hodgdon	Hybrid 100V	.284"	3.565"	64.0	2850	46,300 CUP	69.0	3013	52,500 CUP
160 GR. SFT SP	IMR	IMR 4831	.284"	3.565"	65.0	2730	41,600 CUP	69.5	2926	51,800 CUP
175 GR. NOS PART	Hodgdon	US 869	.284"	3.585"	84.0	2908	50,100 CUP	88.0	3020	53,200 CUP
175 GR. NOS PART	Hodgdon	H50BMG	.284"	3.585"	85.0	2851	46,900 CUP	89.0C	2973	52,300 CUP
175 GR. NOS PART	Hodgdon	Retumbo	.284"	3.585"	72.0	2819	48,300 CUP	77.0	2967	54,200 CUP
175 GR. NOS PART	Hodgdon	H1000	.284"	3.585"	70.0	2833	47,700 CUP	74.0	2944	51,900 CUP
175 GR. NOS PART	IMR	IMR 7828	.284"	3.585"	67.5	2770	47,700 CUP	71.7	2910	53,000 CUP
175 GR. NOS PART	Winchester	Supreme 780	.284"	3.585"	68.0	2758	47,100 CUP	72.0	2889	52,100 CUP
175 GR. NOS PART	Hodgdon	Hybrid 100V	.284"	3.585"	64.0	2771	47,900 CUP	68.0	2883	52,900 CUP
175 GR. NOS PART	IMR	IMR 4831	.284"	3.585"	63.5	2698	47,900 CUP	67.5	2831	53,900 CUP
180 GR. BER VLD	Hodgdon	US 869	.284"	3.655"	81.8	2822	46,200 CUP	87.0	2988	52,700 CUP
180 GR. BER VLD	Hodgdon	H50BMG	.284"	3.655"	80.8	2772	48,800 CUP	86.0C	2894	52,400 CUP
180 GR. BER VLD	Hodgdon	Retumbo	.284"	3.655"	69.3	2760	49,700 CUP	73.8	2876	53,500 CUP
180 GR. BER VLD	Hodgdon	H1000	.284"	3.655"	70.0	2771	48,800 CUP	74.5	2892	53,300 CUP
180 GR. BER VLD	IMR	IMR 7828	.284"	3.655"	67.8	2789	48,200 CUP	72.0	2920	53,600 CUP

Cartridge: 7mm Remington Ultra Magnum Load Type: Rifle					Starting Loads			Maximum Loads		
Bullet Weight (Gr.)	Manufacturer	Powder	Bullet Diam.	C.O.L.	Grs.	Vel. (ft/s)	Pressure	Grs.	Vel. (ft/s)	Pressure
100 GR. HDY HP	Hodgdon	H1000	.284"	3.500"	98.0	3515	52,200 PSI	104.0C	3750	62,700 PSI
100 GR. HDY HP	Hodgdon	H4831	.284"	3.500"	90.0	3585	55,900 PSI	95.0	3754	62,800 PSI
100 GR. HDY HP	Hodgdon	H4350	.284"	3.500"	82.0	3618	55,500 PSI	87.0	3804	63,300 PSI
110 GR. SPR TNT HP	Hodgdon	H1000	.284"	3.500"	96.0	3437	52,100 PSI	102.0	3676	62,600 PSI
110 GR. SPR TNT HP	Hodgdon	H4831	.284"	3.500"	88.0	3431	53,500 PSI	93.5	3652	63,000 PSI

110 GR. SPR TNT HP	Hodgdon	H4350	.284"	3.500"	82.0	3519	56,000 PSI	86.0	3675	63,200 PSI
115 GR. SPR HP	Hodgdon	Retumbo	.284"	3.450"	98.0	3398	54,100 PSI	104.0C	3683	64,100 PSI
115 GR. SPR HP	Hodgdon	H1000	.284"	3.450"	95.0	3380	54,500 PSI	101.0	3589	63,100 PSI
115 GR. SPR HP	Hodgdon	H4831	.284"	3.450"	87.0	3364	54,000 PSI	91.5	3565	62,800 PSI
115 GR. SPR HP	Hodgdon	H4350	.284"	3.450"	82.0	3472	57,600 PSI	85.5	3592	63,400 PSI
120 GR. NOS BT	Hodgdon	Retumbo	.284"	3.600"	96.0	3326	52,100 PSI	102.5C	3601	62,300 PSI
120 GR. NOS BT	Hodgdon	H1000	.284"	3.600"	94.0	3368	54,600 PSI	99.5	3572	63,100 PSI
120 GR. NOS BT	Hodgdon	H4831	.284"	3.600"	85.0	3344	54,600 PSI	90.0	3536	63,000 PSI
120 GR. NOS BT	Hodgdon	H4350	.284"	3.600"	81.0	3475	59,700 PSI	83.0	3552	62,900 PSI
130 GR. BAR XBT	Hodgdon	US 869	.284"	3.560"	105.0	3285	57,300 PSI	108.3	3405	63,800 PSI
130 GR. BAR XBT	Hodgdon	H50BMG	.284"	3.560"	102.0	3289	56,900 PSI	107.0C	3413	62,300 PSI
130 GR. BAR XBT	Hodgdon	Retumbo	.284"	3.560"	93.0	3223	52,400 PSI	99.5C	3514	63,600 PSI
130 GR. BAR XBT	Hodgdon	H1000	.284"	3.560"	90.0	3224	53,700 PSI	95.5	3430	62,900 PSI
130 GR. BAR XBT	Hodgdon	H4831	.284"	3.560"	83.0	3235	55,600 PSI	88.0	3412	63,100 PSI
140 GR. BAR XBT	Hodgdon	US 869	.284"	3.560"	102.0	3162	56,400 PSI	104.7	3275	62,400 PSI
140 GR. BAR XBT	Hodgdon	H50BMG	.284"	3.560"	101.0	3092	54,200 PSI	107.0C	3271	62,400 PSI
140 GR. BAR XBT	Hodgdon	Retumbo	.284"	3.560"	90.0	3142	55,200 PSI	96.5C	3353	62,900 PSI
140 GR. BAR XBT	Hodgdon	H1000	.284"	3.560"	90.0	3196	59,300 PSI	95.0	3277	62,700 PSI
140 GR. BAR XBT	IMR	IMR 7828	.284"	3.560"				86.8	3290	62,000 PSI
140 GR. BAR XBT	Hodgdon	H4831	.284"	3.560"	82.0	3123	56,200 PSI	87.0	3279	63,100 PSI
140 GR. BAR XBT	IMR	IMR 4831	.284"	3.560"				79.3	3220	62,000 PSI
145 GR. SPR GSSP	Hodgdon	US 869	.284"	3.580"	103.0	3172	56,600 PSI	106.0	3270	61,100 PSI
145 GR. SPR GSSP	Hodgdon	H50BMG	.284"	3.580"	101.0	3100	53,800 PSI	107.0C	3319	63,600 PSI
145 GR. SPR GSSP	Hodgdon	Retumbo	.284"	3.580"	93.0	3159	52,800 PSI	99.0	3388	63,400 PSI
145 GR. SPR GSSP	Hodgdon	H1000	.284"	3.580"	91.0	3157	55,300 PSI	97.0	3331	63,300 PSI
145 GR. SPR GSSP	IMR	IMR 7828 SSC	.284"	3.580"	81.0	3022	49,600 PSI	88.6	3341	63,800 PSI
145 GR. SPR GSSP	Winchester	Supreme 780	.284"	3.580"	83.0	3102	53,700 PSI	88.8	3311	63,200 PSI
145 GR. SPR GSSP	Hodgdon	H4831	.284"	3.580"	83.0	3125	55,400 PSI	88.0	3302	63,400 PSI
145 GR. SPR GSSP	Hodgdon	Hybrid 100V	.284"	3.580"	74.0	3045	50,500 PSI	80.7	3303	62,800 PSI
145 GR. SPR GSSP	IMR	IMR 4831	.284"	3.580"	79.0	3058	50,100 PSI	85.0	3322	62,100 PSI
150 GR. SFT SCIR	Hodgdon	US 869	.284"	3.600"	102.0	3137	58,800 PSI	104.5	3226	63,200 PSI
150 GR. SFT SCIR	Hodgdon	H50BMG	.284"	3.600"	97.0	3048	55,000 PSI	103.0C	3222	63,200 PSI
150 GR. SFT SCIR	Hodgdon	Retumbo	.284"	3.600"	89.0	3054	53,000 PSI	95.0C	3299	63,600 PSI
150 GR. SFT SCIR	Hodgdon	H1000	.284"	3.600"	87.0	3045	54,400 PSI	92.0	3230	63,100 PSI
150 GR. SFT SCIR	IMR	IMR 7828	.284"	3.600"	80.0	3035	53,600 PSI	86.0	3247	62,900 PSI
150 GR. SFT SCIR	Winchester	Supreme 780	.284"	3.600"	78.0	2952	51,500 PSI	85.3	3238	63,600 PSI
150 GR. SFT SCIR	Hodgdon	H4831	.284"	3.600"	82.0	3146	61,900 PSI	84.0	3187	63,100 PSI
150 GR. SFT SCIR	Hodgdon	Hybrid 100V	.284"	3.600"	72.0	3006	53,600 PSI	78.3	3207	62,900 PSI
150 GR. SFT SCIR	IMR	IMR 4831	.284"	3.600"	77.0	3007	52,700 PSI	83.0	3229	62,500 PSI

Bullet Weight	Manufacturer	Powder	Bullet Diam.	C.O.L.	Grs.	Vel.	Pressure	Grs.	Vel.	Pressure
154 GR. HDY SP	Hodgdon	US 869	.284"	3.630"	101.8	3060	56,400 PSI	104.5	3211	62,800 PSI
154 GR. HDY SP	Hodgdon	H50BMG	.284"	3.630"	94.0	2989	54,800 PSI	100.0C	3170	63,100 PSI
154 GR. HDY SP	Hodgdon	Retumbo	.284"	3.630"	90.0	3055	53,400 PSI	96.2	3289	63,900 PSI
154 GR. HDY SP	Hodgdon	H1000	.284"	3.630"	85.0	3051	56,700 PSI	90.0	3192	63,300 PSI
160 GR. NOS PART	Hodgdon	US 869	.284"	3.600"	97.0	2928	50,400 PSI	103.0	3192	62,900 PSI
160 GR. NOS PART	Hodgdon	H50BMG	.284"	3.600"	94.0	2985	55,600 PSI	100.0	3144	63,400 PSI
160 GR. NOS PART	Hodgdon	Retumbo	.284"	3.600"	88.0	3003	53,700 PSI	94.0	3212	62,800 PSI
160 GR. NOS PART	Hodgdon	H1000	.284"	3.600"	85.0	3007	56,500 PSI	91.0	3167	63,500 PSI
160 GR. NOS PART	IMR	IMR 7828	.284"	3.600"				84.5	3140	62,000 PSI
160 GR. NOS PART	IMR	IMR 4831	.284"	3.600"				76.5	3050	61,000 PSI
162 GR. HDY SPBT	Hodgdon	US 869	.284"	3.650"	100.5	3075	58,700 PSI	103.5	3173	62,800 PSI
162 GR. HDY SPBT	Hodgdon	H50BMG	.284"	3.650"	94.0	2979	56,000 PSI	100.0	3119	62,600 PSI
162 GR. HDY SPBT	Hodgdon	Retumbo	.284"	3.650"	89.0	3009	53,100 PSI	95.0	3223	62,700 PSI
162 GR. HDY SPBT	Hodgdon	H1000	.284"	3.650"	84.0	2993	55,600 PSI	89.0	3127	62,500 PSI
168 GR. SIE HPBT	Hodgdon	US 869	.284"	3.650"	96.0	2899	53,100 PSI	101.5	3089	61,900 PSI
168 GR. SIE HPBT	Hodgdon	H50BMG	.284"	3.650"	94.0	2942	55,600 PSI	100.0C	3118	63,400 PSI
168 GR. SIE HPBT	Hodgdon	Retumbo	.284"	3.650"	89.0	2986	54,400 PSI	94.0	3171	63,300 PSI
168 GR. SIE HPBT	Hodgdon	H1000	.284"	3.650"	85.0	2988	57,500 PSI	90.0	3116	63,500 PSI
175 GR. SFT SP	Hodgdon	US 869	.284"	3.600"	95.0	2851	51,800 PSI	102.0	3077	63,000 PSI
175 GR. SFT SP	Hodgdon	H50BMG	.284"	3.600"	91.0	2888	57,000 PSI	96.0	3019	63,100 PSI
175 GR. SFT SP	Hodgdon	Retumbo	.284"	3.600"	86.0	2919	57,300 PSI	91.5	3069	63,400 PSI
175 GR. SFT SP	Hodgdon	H1000	.284"	3.600"	82.0	2871	56,700 PSI	87.0	3021	63,500 PSI

Cartridge: 30 Carbine
Load Type: Rifle

Bullet Weight (Gr.)	Manufacturer	Powder	Bullet Diam.	C.O.L.	Starting Loads			Maximum Loads		
					Grs.	Vel. (ft/s)	Pressure	Grs.	Vel. (ft/s)	Pressure
85 GR. SIE RN	Hodgdon	H4227	.308"	1.625"	14.5	2054	25,200 CUP	15.5C	2181	30,700 CUP
85 GR. SIE RN	Winchester	296	.308"	1.625"	16.5	2293	26,000 CUP	17.5	2458	34,800 CUP
85 GR. SIE RN	Hodgdon	H110	.308"	1.625"	16.5	2293	26,000 CUP	17.5	2458	34,800 CUP
85 GR. SIE RN	Hodgdon	Lil'Gun	.308"	1.625"	16.0	2140	20,300 CUP	17.0	2285	24,800 CUP
100 GR. HDY SJ	IMR	IMR 4227	.308"	1.760"				16.0C	2005	40,000 CUP
100 GR. HDY SJ	IMR	SR 4759	.308"	1.760"				11.0C	1575	23,700 CUP
100 GR. SPR SP	Hodgdon	H4227	.308"	1.625"	13.0	1879	28,900 CUP	14.5C	2026	33,600 CUP
100 GR. SPR SP	Winchester	296	.308"	1.625"	14.5	2075	28,200 CUP	15.5	2202	36,100 CUP
100 GR. SPR SP	Hodgdon	H110	.308"	1.625"	14.5	2075	28,200 CUP	15.5	2202	36,100 CUP
100 GR. SPR SP	Hodgdon	Lil'Gun	.308"	1.625"	14.0	2032	26,700 CUP	15.0	2132	28,300 CUP
110 GR. HDY JRN	IMR	IMR 4227	.308"	1.680"	13.0	1826	30,100 CUP	14.5C	2003	38,800 CUP
110 GR. HDY JRN	IMR	SR 4759	.308"	1.680"				11.0C	1545	26,100 CUP
110 GR. HDY JRN	Hodgdon	H4227	.308"	1.680"	13.0	1826	30,100 CUP	14.5C	2003	38,800 CUP
110 GR. HDY JRN	Winchester	296	.308"	1.680"	14.0	2006	32,000 CUP	15.0	2106	36,500 CUP

| 110 GR. HDY JRN | Hodgdon | H110 | .308" | 1.680" | 14.0 | 2006 | 32,000 CUP | 15.0 | 2106 | 36,500 CUP |
| 110 GR. HDY JRN | Hodgdon | Lil'Gun | .308" | 1.680" | 14.0 | 1998 | 28,000 CUP | 15.0 | 2064 | 29,800 CUP |

Cartridge: 300 AAC Blackout
Load Type: Rifle

Bullet Weight (Gr.)	Manufacturer	Powder	Bullet Diam.	C.O.L.	Starting Loads			Maximum Loads		
					Grs.	Vel. (ft/s)	Pressure	Grs.	Vel. (ft/s)	Pressure
110 GR. HDY V-MAX	IMR	IMR 4227	.308"	2.040"	17.6	1942	36,500 CUP	19.5C	2130	46,700 CUP
110 GR. HDY V-MAX	Winchester	296	.308"	2.040"	18.8	2259	40,600 CUP	20.0	2382	50,600 CUP
110 GR. HDY V-MAX	Hodgdon	H110	.308"	2.040"	18.8	2259	40,600 CUP	20.0	2382	50,600 CUP
110 GR. HDY V-MAX	Hodgdon	Lil'Gun	.308"	2.040"	18.9	2248	31.000 CUP	20.0	2388	37,600 CUP
110 GR. HDY V-MAX	IMR	Trail Boss	.308"	2.040"	4.5	880	21,900 CUP	6.3	1046	20,200 CUP
115 GR. BER TGT FB	IMR	IMR 4227	.308"	2.050"	17.6	1934	36,800 CUP	19.5C	2110	47,000 CUP
115 GR. BER TGT FB	Winchester	296	.308"	2.050"	18.8	2220	39,300 CUP	20.0	2348	50,800 CUP
115 GR. BER TGT FB	Hodgdon	H110	.308"	2.050"	18.8	2220	39,300 CUP	20.0	2348	50,800 CUP
115 GR. BER TGT FB	Hodgdon	Lil'Gun	.308"	2.050"	18.9	2235	32,600 CUP	20.5	2393	39,900 CUP
115 GR. BER TGT FB	IMR	Trail Boss	.308"	2.050"	4.5	894	23,200 CUP	6.3	1044	19,900 CUP
125 GR. NOS BT	IMR	IMR 4227	.308"	2.060"	16.5	1818	38,000 CUP	17.7C	1965	49,800 CUP
125 GR. NOS BT	Winchester	296	.308"	2.060"	16.7	2020	40,200 CUP	17.8	2118	48,800 CUP
125 GR. NOS BT	Hodgdon	H110	.308"	2.060"	16.7	2020	40,200 CUP	17.8	2118	48,800 CUP
125 GR. NOS BT	Hodgdon	Lil'Gun	.308"	2.060"	16.9	2086	35,900 CUP	18.0	2185	40,800 CUP
130 GR. SPR HP	IMR	IMR 4227	.308"	2.005"	18.0	1902	41,900 cup	19.2	2008	47,600 CUP
130 GR. SPR HP	Winchester	296	.308"	2.005"	17.9	2056	40,400 CUP	19.0	2155	48,400 CUP
130 GR. SPR HP	Hodgdon	H110	.308"	2.005"	17.9	2056	40,400 CUP	19.0	2155	48,400 CUP
130 GR. SPR HP	Hodgdon	Lil'Gun	.308"	2.005"	18.3	2073	37,700 CUP	19.5	2213	41,900 CUP
135 GR. SIE HPBT	IMR	IMR 4227	.308"	2.120"	17.1	1818	39,700 CUP	18.2	1960	47,600 CUP
135 GR. SIE HPBT	Winchester	296	.308"	2.120"	17.3	2010	43,100 CUP	18.4	2109	51,200 CUP
135 GR. SIE HPBT	Hodgdon	H110	.308"	2.120"	17.3	2010	43,100 CUP	18.4	2109	51,200 CUP
135 GR. SIE HPBT	Hodgdon	Lil'Gun	.308"	2.120"	16.5	2017	37,800 CUP	18.0	2127	43,200 CUP
220 GR. SIE HPBT	IMR	IMR 4198	.308"	2.260"				11.5	1036	25,300 CUP
220 GR. SIE HPBT	Hodgdon	H4198	.308"	2.260"				11.5	1068	25,600 CUP
220 GR. SIE HPBT	IMR	IMR 4227	.308"	2.260"				10.5	1014	28,800 CUP
220 GR. SIE HPBT	Winchester	296	.308"	2.260"				9.9	1050	29,700 CUP
220 GR. SIE HPBT	Hodgdon	H110	.308"	2.260"				9.9	1050	29,700 CUP
220 GR. SIE HPBT	Hodgdon	Lil'Gun	.308"	2.260"				9.0	1077	31,100 CUP
230 GR. BER TACT	IMR	IMR 4227	.308"	2.260"				10.2	1065	37,100 CUP
230 GR. BER TACT	Winchester	296	.308"	2.260"				9.5	1085	34,500 CUP
230 GR. BER TACT	Hodgdon	H110	.308"	2.260"				9.5	1085	34,500 CUP
230 GR. BER TACT	Hodgdon	Lil'Gun	.308"	2.260"				8.7	1077	28,900 CUP

Cartridge: 30-30 Winchester Load Type: Rifle					Starting Loads			Maximum Loads		
Bullet Weight (Gr.)	Manufacturer	Powder	Bullet Diam.	C.O.L.	Grs.	Vel. (ft/s)	Pressure	Grs.	Vel. (ft/s)	Pressure
110 GR. SPR FP	Hodgdon	Varget	.308"	2.415"	34.5	2365	27,200 CUP	38.0C	2572	31,900 CUP
110 GR. SPR FP	IMR	IMR 4320	.308"	2.415"	34.3	2322	31,300 CUP	36.5	2435	36,100 CUP
110 GR. SPR FP	IMR	IMR 4064	.308"	2.415"	33.3	2342	31,800 CUP	35.5C	2506	36,100 CUP
110 GR. SPR FP	Winchester	748	.308"	2.415"				36.8	2595	33,000 CUP
110 GR. SPR FP	Hodgdon	BL-C(2)	.308"	2.415"	36.0	2351	24,500 CUP	39.0	2526	25,400 CUP
110 GR. SPR FP	IMR	IMR 4895	.308"	2.415"	33.8	2290	30,500 CUP	36.0C	2459	35,400 CUP
110 GR. SPR FP	Hodgdon	H335	.308"	2.415"	35.0	2487	28,800 CUP	38.0	2684	34,300 CUP
110 GR. SPR FP	Hodgdon	H4895	.308"	2.415"	34.0	2417	28,600 CUP	37.0	2605	31,100 CUP
110 GR. SPR FP	IMR	IMR 3031	.308"	2.415"	30.5	2281	22,400 CUP	32.5C	2445	33,700 CUP
110 GR. SPR FP	Hodgdon	Benchmark	.308"	2.415"	30.5	2406	36,400 CUP	32.5	2507	37,800 CUP
110 GR. SPR FP	IMR	IMR 4198	.308"	2.415"	22.5	2168	27,800 CUP	24.0	2302	35,400 CUP
110 GR. SPR FP	Hodgdon	H4198	.308"	2.415"	23.0	2174	27,100 CUP	25.5	2409	35,900 CUP
130 GR. SPR FP	Hodgdon	CFE 223	.308"	2.540"	32.8	2378	31,500 PSI	35.7	2533	37,000 PSI
130 GR. SPR FP	Hodgdon	Varget	.308"	2.540"	32.5	2312	30,200 CUP	36.0C	2496	35,700 CUP
130 GR. SPR FP	IMR	IMR 4320	.308"	2.540"	34.0	2201	33,700 CUP	36.3	2384	37,200 CUP
130 GR. SPR FP	IMR	IMR 4064	.308"	2.540"	33.3	2196	27,200 CUP	35.5C	2424	37,300 CUP
130 GR. SPR FP	Hodgdon	BL-C(2)	.308"	2.540"	34.0	2305	28,500 CUP	37.5	2473	32,800 CUP
130 GR. SPR FP	Hodgdon	H335	.308"	2.540"	30.5	2173	27,600 CUP	34.0	2423	34,700 CUP
130 GR. SPR FP	Hodgdon	H4895	.308"	2.540"	31.5	2248	27,600 CUP	35.0	2482	35,300 CUP
130 GR. SPR FP	IMR	IMR 3031	.308"	2.540"	29.6	2159	27,400 CUP	31.5	2323	33,500 CUP
130 GR. SPR FP	Hodgdon	Benchmark	.308"	2.540"	27.7	2165	33,700 CUP	29.7	2295	37,100 CUP
130 GR. SPR FP	IMR	IMR 4198	.308"	2.540"	22.0	2025	28,700 CUP	23.5	2187	36,200 CUP
130 GR. SPR FP	Hodgdon	H4198	.308"	2.540"	22.5	2082	29,200 CUP	24.5	2234	36,400 CUP
140 GR. HDY MFTX	Hodgdon	LVR	.308"	2.550"	29.0	2175	32,400 PSI	34.0C	2436	39,700 PSI
140 GR. HDY MFTX	Hodgdon	Varget	.308"	2.550"	27.0	1986	31,600 PSI	30.5C	2225	39,900 PSI
140 GR. HDY MFTX	IMR	IMR 4320	.308"	2.550"	26.0	1814	29,900 PSI	30.0C	2094	39,500 PSI
140 GR. HDY MFTX	IMR	IMR 4064	.308"	2.550"	26.0	1909	30,600 PSI	30.0C	2209	41,000 PSI
140 GR. HDY MFTX	Hodgdon	BL-C(2)	.308"	2.550"	29.0	2030	31,600 PSI	32.7	2239	39,900 PSI
140 GR. HDY MFTX	Hodgdon	H335	.308"	2.550"	25.0	1977	31,200 PSI	28.8	2224	40,600 PSI
140 GR. HDY MFTX	Hodgdon	H4895	.308"	2.550"	26.0	2077	36,800 PSI	29.7	2273	40,300 PSI
140 GR. HDY MFTX	IMR	IMR 3031	.308"	2.550"	25.0	1963	32,300 PSI	28.5	2216	41,600 PSI
140 GR. HDY MFTX	Hodgdon	Benchmark	.308"	2.550"	24.0	1839	26,400 PSI	28.0	2160	38,800 PSI
150 GR. SIE FN	Winchester	760	.308"	2.550"				35.9	2090	30,000 CUP
150 GR. SIE FN	Hodgdon	LVR	.308"	2.550"	35.0	2314	28,700 CUP	38.5C	2512	34,800 CUP
150 GR. SIE FN	Hodgdon	CFE 223	.308"	2.550"	33.9	2274	31,700 PSI	36.8	2409	36,700 PSI

150 GR. SIE FN	Hodgdon	Varget	.308"	2.550"	31.0	2172	31,100 CUP	34.5	2349	36,200 CUP
150 GR. SIE FN	IMR	IMR 4320	.308"	2.550"	30.5	2062	32,500 CUP	32.5	2127	36,500 CUP
150 GR. SIE FN	IMR	IMR 4064	.308"	2.550"	31.0	2106	33,300 CUP	33.3	2236	36,200 CUP
150 GR. SIE FN	Winchester	748	.308"	2.550"				34.5	2310	36,000 CUP
150 GR. SIE FN	Hodgdon	BL-C(2)	.308"	2.550"	33.0	2021	21,800 CUP	37.0	2358	33,900 CUP
150 GR. SIE FN	IMR	IMR 4895	.308"	2.550"	31.5	2071	32,200 CUP	33.5	2213	34,300 CUP
150 GR. SIE FN	Hodgdon	H335	.308"	2.550"	29.7	2098	28,700 CUP	33.0	2308	36,200 CUP
150 GR. SIE FN	Hodgdon	H4895	.308"	2.550"	30.5	2138	27,900 CUP	34.0	2390	36,700 CUP
150 GR. SIE FN	IMR	IMR 8208 XBR	.308"	2.550"	30.0	2213	35,000 CUP	32.0	2316	36,700 CUP
150 GR. SIE FN	IMR	IMR 3031	.308"	2.550"	28.7	2085	28,700 CUP	30.5	2192	36,000 CUP
150 GR. SIE FN	Hodgdon	Benchmark	.308"	2.550"	27.0	2042	32,100 CUP	29.0	2183	37,200 CUP
150 GR. SIE FN	IMR	IMR 4198	.308"	2.550"	21.5	1888	27,800 CUP	23.0	2055	35,500 CUP
150 GR. SIE FN	Hodgdon	H4198	.308"	2.550"	21.6	1924	26,900 CUP	24.0	2110	36,800 CUP
160 GR. CAST LFN	Hodgdon	H4895	.308"	2.485"	17.5	1351	15,200 CUP	21.0	1562	23,100 CUP
160 GR. CAST LFN	Hodgdon	H4198	.308"	2.485"	15.0	1420	15,000 CUP	17.0	1616	20,600 CUP
160 GR. CAST LFN	IMR	Trail Boss	.308"	2.485"	6.5	997	20,500 CUP	9.0	1195	29,100 CUP
160 GR. HDY FTX	Hodgdon	LVR	.308"	2.535"	32.0	2221	31,200 CUP	35.5C	2389	37,500 CUP
160 GR. HDY FTX	Hodgdon	CFE 223	.308"	2.540"	31.6	2170	30,700 PSI	34.0	2302	36,700 PSI
160 GR. HDY FTX	Hodgdon	Varget	.308"	2.550"	29.8	2081	31,700 CUP	32.4	2235	35,900 CUP
160 GR. HDY FTX	IMR	IMR 4320	.308"	2.550"	28.7	1900	30,900 CUP	31.2	2056	36,400 CUP
160 GR. HDY FTX	IMR	IMR 4064	.308"	2.550"	28.7	2000	33,700 CUP	30.5	2095	36,200 CUP
160 GR. HDY FTX	Winchester	748	.308"	2.550"	29.8	1994	31,500 CUP	31.7	2112	36,400 CUP
160 GR. HDY FTX	Hodgdon	BL-C(2)	.308"	2.550"	29.1	1863	27,400 CUP	31.0	2035	35,600 CUP
160 GR. HDY FTX	IMR	IMR 4895	.308"	2.550"	28.2	1912	31,700 CUP	30.0	2065	36,900 CUP
160 GR. HDY FTX	Hodgdon	H335	.308"	2.550"	28.2	2005	31,600 CUP	30.0	2131	37,100 CUP
160 GR. HDY FTX	Hodgdon	H4895	.308"	2.550"	27.8	2045	31,100 CUP	30.0	2200	35,500 CUP
160 GR. HDY FTX	IMR	IMR 8208 XBR	.308"	2.535"	27.0	2045	33,900 CUP	30.0	2207	37,000 CUP
160 GR. HDY FTX	IMR	IMR 3031	.308"	2.550"	26.8	1992	34,300 CUP	28.5	2094	36,800 CUP
160 GR. HDY FTX	Hodgdon	Benchmark	.308"	2.550"	26.1	1933	31,000 CUP	27.8	2045	35,400 CUP
170 GR. SIE FN	Hodgdon	CFE 223	.308"	2.540"	32.2	2115	30,600 PSI	35.0	2258	36,800 PSI
170 GR. SIE FP	Winchester	760	.308"	2.550"				33.6	1975	30,000 CUP
170 GR. SIE FP	Hodgdon	LVR	.308"	2.550"	33.0	2145	28,900 CUP	36.3C	2332	35,400 CUP
170 GR. SIE FP	Hodgdon	Varget	.308"	2.550"	29.5	1976	30,200 CUP	33.0	2168	36,500 CUP
170 GR. SIE FP	IMR	IMR 4320	.308"	2.550"	30.0	1976	35,400 CUP	32.5	2068	36,300 CUP
170 GR. SIE FP	IMR	IMR 4064	.308"	2.550"	29.8	1991	30,700 CUP	31.7	2090	35,300 CUP
170 GR. SIE FP	Winchester	748	.308"	2.550"				32.0	2145	36,000 CUP
170 GR. SIE FP	Hodgdon	BL-C(2)	.308"	2.550"	32.5	2048	27,900 CUP	36.0	2227	34,700 CUP
170 GR. SIE FP	IMR	IMR 4895	.308"	2.550"	29.8	1938	30,500 CUP	31.7	2068	35,300 CUP
170 GR. SIE FP	Hodgdon	H335	.308"	2.550"	27.5	1934	29,000 CUP	30.5	2086	36,300 CUP

Bullet Weight (Gr.)	Manufacturer	Powder	Bullet Diam.	C.O.L.	Grs.	Vel. (ft/s)	Pressure	Grs.	Vel. (ft/s)	Pressure
170 GR. SIE FP	Hodgdon	H4895	.308"	2.550"	27.5	1947	28,200 CUP	30.5	2138	35,200 CUP
170 GR. SIE FP	IMR	IMR 8208 XBR	.308"	2.550"	27.8	2052	36,400 CUP	30.9	2181	37,500 CUP
170 GR. SIE FP	IMR	IMR 3031	.308"	2.550"	27.5	1959	27,500 CUP	29.2	2085	35,800 CUP
170 GR. SIE FP	Hodgdon	Benchmark	.308"	2.550"	25.3	1894	32,200 CUP	27.0	2001	36,100 CUP
170 GR. SIE FP	IMR	IMR 4198	.308"	2.550"	21.0	1800	27,400 CUP	22.3	1896	32,100 CUP
170 GR. SIE FP	Hodgdon	H4198	.308"	2.550"	20.5	1764	27,300 CUP	22.5	1918	32,600 CUP

Cartridge: 30 AR Remington
Load Type: Rifle

Bullet Weight (Gr.)	Manufacturer	Powder	Bullet Diam.	C.O.L.	Starting Loads			Maximum Loads		
					Grs.	Vel. (ft/s)	Pressure	Grs.	Vel. (ft/s)	Pressure
110 GR. HDY V-MAX	IMR	IMR 4198	.308"	2.240"	32.0	2798	37,700 PSI	35.0C	3031	48,900 PSI
110 GR. HDY V-MAX	Hodgdon	H4198	.308"	2.240"	32.0	2794	37,700 PSI	35.5C	3076	50,800 PSI
115 GR. BER TGT FB	Hodgdon	H322	.308"	2.240"	37.0	2798	39,100 PSI	40.0C	3016	50,200 PSI
115 GR. BER TGT FB	IMR	IMR 4198	.308"	2.240"	31.0	2685	35,700 PSI	35.0C	3000	50,300 PSI
115 GR. BER TGT FB	Hodgdon	H4198	.308"	2.240"	32.0	2717	35,900 PSI	36.0	3035	50,900 PSI
125 GR. NOS BT	Hodgdon	H335	.308"	2.240"	37.0	2693	41,000 PSI	40.0	2871	50,000 PSI
125 GR. NOS BT	IMR	IMR 8208 XBR	.308"	2.240"	37.0	2676	37,600 PSI	40.0C	2875	46,400 PSI
125 GR. NOS BT	Hodgdon	Benchmark	.308"	2.240"	37.0	2740	47,000 PSI	40.0C	2931	51,400 PSI
125 GR. NOS BT	Hodgdon	H322	.308"	2.240"	34.5	2635	38,900 PSI	38.2C	2903	53,500 PSI
130 GR. BAR TTSX BT	Hodgdon	H335	.308"	2.230"	36.0	2595	40,800 PSI	39.0	2810	51,200 PSI
130 GR. BAR TTSX BT	IMR	IMR 8208 XBR	.308"	2.230"	36.0	2561	36,500 PSI	39.0C	2826	48,600 PSI
130 GR. BAR TTSX BT	Hodgdon	Benchmark	.308"	2.230"	36.0	2622	39,400 PSI	39.2C	2866	52,900 PSI
130 GR. BAR TTSX BT	Hodgdon	H322	.308"	2.230"	34.0	2557	38,600 PSI	37.5C	2818	52,800 PSI
135 GR. SIE HPBT	Hodgdon	H335	.308"	2.250"	37.0	2643	41,200 PSI	40.0	2831	50,700 PSI
135 GR. SIE HPBT	IMR	IMR 8208 XBR	.308"	2.250"	36.0	2557	34,600 PSI	39.0C	2790	46,700 PSI
135 GR. SIE HPBT	Hodgdon	Benchmark	.308"	2.250"	36.0	2605	38,800 PSI	39.5C	2859	51,800 PSI
135 GR. SIE HPBT	Hodgdon	H322	.308"	2.250"	34.0	2526	36,900 PSI	37.7C	2814	52,700 PSI
150 GR. NOS BT	IMR	IMR 4895	.308"	2.250"	34.5	2303	35,700 PSI	38.0C	2586	50,500 PSI
150 GR. NOS BT	Hodgdon	H335	.308"	2.250"	35.0	2442	39,500 PSI	38.0	2652	52,000 PSI
150 GR. NOS BT	Hodgdon	H4895	.308"	2.250"	34.0	2355	35,200 PSI	38.0C	2647	51,000 PSI
150 GR. NOS BT	IMR	IMR 8208 XBR	.308"	2.250"	34.0	2385	34,700 PSI	38.0C	2692	51,200 PSI
150 GR. NOS BT	Hodgdon	Benchmark	.308"	2.250"	34.5	2485	41,300 PSI	37.5C	2675	52,100 PSI
150 GR. NOS BT	Hodgdon	H322	.308"	2.250"	32.5	2393	38,900 PSI	35.5C	2614	51,700 PSI
160 GR. HDY FTX ME	Hodgdon	H335	.308"	2.200"	33.0	2316	37,200 PSI	37.0	2585	52,400 PSI
160 GR. HDY FTX ME	IMR	IMR 8208 XBR	.308"	2.200"	33.0	2315	35,600 PSI	36.0C	2535	47,300 PSI
160 GR. HDY FTX ME	Hodgdon	Benchmark	.308"	2.200"	33.0	2353	38,500 PSI	36.0C	2566	50,900 PSI
160 GR. HDY FTX ME	Hodgdon	H322	.308"	2.200"	31.0	2260	36,600 PSI	34.3C	2515	51,100 PSI

Cartridge:30-40 Krag Load Type:Rifle					Starting Loads			Maximum Loads		
Bullet Weight (Gr.)	Manufacturer	Powder	Bullet Diam.	C.O.L.	Grs.	Vel. (ft/s)	Pressure	Grs.	Vel. (ft/s)	Pressure
100 GR. HDY SP	Hodgdon	H4350	.308"	2.880"	48.0	2300		51.0	2492	
100 GR. HDY SP	Hodgdon	BL-C(2)	.308"	2.880"	42.0	2677		44.0	2894	
100 GR. HDY SP	Hodgdon	H335	.308"	2.880"	42.0	2669		44.0	2881	
100 GR. HDY SP	Hodgdon	H4895	.308"	2.880"	42.0	2707		44.0	2835	
100 GR. HDY SP	Hodgdon	H322	.308"	2.880"	39.0	2542		43.0	2898	
100 GR. HDY SP	Hodgdon	H4198	.308"	2.880"	30.0	2604		34.0	2886	
100 GR. HDY SP	Hodgdon	H4227	.308"	2.880"	13.0	1433		16.0	1706	
110 GR. SIE HP	Hodgdon	H414	.308"	2.875"	46.0	2552		50.0	2773	
110 GR. SIE HP	Hodgdon	H335	.308"	2.875"	41.0	2464		43.0	2806	
110 GR. SIE HP	Hodgdon	H322	.308"	2.875"	39.0	2497		43.0	2841	
110 GR. SIE HP	Hodgdon	H4198	.308"	2.875"	30.0	2417		34.0	2807	
130 GR. SPR HP	Hodgdon	H4350	.308"	2.865"	48.0	2330		51.0	2535	
130 GR. SPR HP	Hodgdon	H414	.308"	2.865"	45.0	2507		49.0	2746	
130 GR. SPR HP	Hodgdon	H335	.308"	2.865"	40.0	2414		42.0	2717	
130 GR. SPR HP	Hodgdon	H322	.308"	2.865"	38.0	2458		42.0	2698	
130 GR. SPR HP	Hodgdon	H4198	.308"	2.865"	29.0	2224		33.0	2565	
150 GR. NOS PART	Hodgdon	H4831	.308"	3.090"	45.0	2129		49.0	2306	
150 GR. NOS PART	Hodgdon	H4350	.308"	3.090"	46.0	2198		49.0	2388	
150 GR. NOS PART	Hodgdon	H414	.308"	3.090"	42.0	2403		47.0	2531	
150 GR. NOS PART	IMR	IMR 4350	.308"	3.090"				48.5C	2615	36,300 CUP
150 GR. NOS PART	Hodgdon	H380	.308"	3.090"	40.5	2311		44.0	2489	
150 GR. NOS PART	IMR	IMR 4320	.308"	3.090"				37.0	2420	39,700 CUP
150 GR. NOS PART	IMR	IMR 4064	.308"	3.090"				44.0	2695	39,000 CUP
150 GR. NOS PART	Hodgdon	BL-C(2)	.308"	3.090"	35.0	2351		37.0	2491	
150 GR. NOS PART	IMR	IMR 4895	.308"	3.090"				36.0	2435	39,700 CUP
150 GR. NOS PART	Hodgdon	H335	.308"	3.090"	35.0	2349		37.0	2508	
150 GR. NOS PART	Hodgdon	H4895	.308"	3.090"	38.5	2410		42.0	2575	
150 GR. NOS PART	IMR	IMR 3031	.308"	3.090"				42.0	2695	39,600 CUP
150 GR. NOS PART	Hodgdon	H322	.308"	3.090"	36.0	2369		40.0	2518	
150 GR. NOS PART	Hodgdon	H4198	.308"	3.090"	28.0	2220		32.0	2366	
150 GR. NOS PART	IMR	SR 4759	.308"	3.090"				24.5	2080	37,300 CUP
165 GR. HDY BTSP	Hodgdon	H4831	.308"	3.105"	44.0	1967		48.0	2176	
165 GR. HDY BTSP	Hodgdon	H4350	.308"	3.105"	45.0	2115		48.0	2242	
165 GR. HDY BTSP	Hodgdon	H335	.308"	3.105"	35.0	2242		36.0	2364	
165 GR. HDY BTSP	Hodgdon	H322	.308"	3.105"	35.0	2228		39.0	2402	
180 GR. SPR GS SP	IMR	IMR 4831	.308"	3.090"				49.0C	2425	35.900 CUP

Bullet Weight (Gr.)	Manufacturer	Powder	Bullet Diam.	C.O.L.	Grs.	Vel. (ft/s)	Pressure	Grs.	Vel. (ft/s)	Pressure
180 GR. SPR GS SP	Hodgdon	H4350	.308"	3.090"	43.0	2006		46.0	2110	
180 GR. SPR GS SP	Hodgdon	H414	.308"	3.090"	39.5	2225		43.0	2276	
180 GR. SPR GS SP	IMR	IMR 4350	.308"	3.090"				46.0C	2445	38,700 CUP
180 GR. SPR GS SP	Hodgdon	H380	.308"	3.090"	37.0	2057		40.0	2182	
180 GR. SPR GS SP	IMR	IMR 4320	.308"	3.090"				35.5	2210	38,100 CUP
180 GR. SPR GS SP	IMR	IMR 4064	.308"	3.090"				41.0	2435	39,000 CUP
180 GR. SPR GS SP	Hodgdon	BL-C(2)	.308"	3.090"	30.5	1951		33.0	2006	
180 GR. SPR GS SP	IMR	IMR 4895	.308"	3.090"				35.5	2270	38,800 CUP
180 GR. SPR GS SP	Hodgdon	H335	.308"	3.090"	31.0	1969		34.0	2049	
180 GR. SPR GS SP	Hodgdon	H4895	.308"	3.090"	35.0	2171		38.0	2265	
180 GR. SPR GS SP	IMR	IMR 3031	.308"	3.090"				38.0	2375	39,300 CUP
180 GR. SPR GS SP	Hodgdon	H322	.308"	3.090"	33.0	2111		37.0	2250	
180 GR. SPR GS SP	IMR	SR 4759	.308"	3.090"				24.0	1940	39,100 CUP
200 GR. SIE SPBT	Hodgdon	H4350	.308"	3.090"	42.0	1929		44.0	2018	
200 GR. SIE SPBT	Hodgdon	H414	.308"	3.090"	37.0	2013		40.0	2151	
200 GR. SIE SPBT	Hodgdon	H335	.308"	3.090"	30.0	1894		33.0	2106	
200 GR. SIE SPBT	Hodgdon	H322	.308"	3.090"	32.0	1915		35.0	2075	
220 GR. HDY RN	Hodgdon	H4350	.308"	3.080"	40.0	1874		42.0	1947	
220 GR. HDY RN	Hodgdon	H335	.308"	3.080"	30.0	1836		33.0	1974	
220 GR. HDY RN	Hodgdon	H322	.308"	3.080"	30.0	1852		33.0	1969	

Cartridge: 7.5 x 55mm Swiss
Load Type: Rifle

Bullet Weight (Gr.)	Manufacturer	Powder	Bullet Diam.	C.O.L.	Starting Loads			Maximum Loads		
					Grs.	Vel. (ft/s)	Pressure	Grs.	Vel. (ft/s)	Pressure
125 GR. SIE SP	Hodgdon	H4831	.308"	2.800"	49.0	2639		52.0	2811	
125 GR. SIE SP	Hodgdon	H4350	.308"	2.800"	47.0	2565		51.0	2839	
125 GR. SIE SP	Hodgdon	H414	.308"	2.800"	46.0	2652		48.0	2829	
125 GR. SIE SP	Hodgdon	H380	.308"	2.800"	44.0	2661		46.0	2797	
125 GR. SIE SP	Hodgdon	BL-C(2)	.308"	2.800"	41.0	2614		43.0	2739	
125 GR. SIE SP	Hodgdon	H335	.308"	2.800"	40.0	2587		42.0	2692	
125 GR. SIE SP	Hodgdon	H4895	.308"	2.800"	41.0	2639		43.0	2762	
150 GR. HDY SP	Hodgdon	H4831	.308"	2.790"	47.0	2493		51.0	2659	
150 GR. HDY SP	Hodgdon	H4350	.308"	2.790"	45.0	2420		49.0	2610	
150 GR. HDY SP	Hodgdon	H414	.308"	2.790"	44.0	2529		46.0	2689	
150 GR. HDY SP	Hodgdon	H380	.308"	2.790"	42.0	2536		44.0	2661	
150 GR. HDY SP	Hodgdon	BL-C(2)	.308"	2.790"	40.0	2450		42.0	2559	
150 GR. HDY SP	Hodgdon	H335	.308"	2.790"	40.0	2442		42.0	2541	
150 GR. HDY SP	Hodgdon	H4895	.308"	2.790"	40.0	2484		42.0	2578	
168 GR. SIE HPBT	Hodgdon	H4831	.308"	3.060"	45.0	2477		49.0	2578	
168 GR. SIE HPBT	Hodgdon	H4350	.308"	3.060"	44.0	2379		48.0	2524	

Bullet Weight (Gr.)	Manufacturer	Powder	Bullet Diam.	C.O.L.	Grs.	Vel. (ft/s)	Pressure	Grs.	Vel. (ft/s)	Pressure
168 GR. SIE HPBT	Hodgdon	H414	.308"	3.060"	42.0	2429		44.0	2519	
168 GR. SIE HPBT	Hodgdon	H380	.308"	3.060"	41.0	2414		43.0	2502	
168 GR. SIE HPBT	Hodgdon	BL-C(2)	.308"	3.060"	39.0	2363		41.0	2404	
168 GR. SIE HPBT	Hodgdon	H335	.308"	3.060"	39.0	2354		41.0	2399	
168 GR. SIE HPBT	Hodgdon	H4895	.308"	3.060"	39.0	2388		41.0	2432	
180 GR. HDY SP	Hodgdon	H4831	.308"	2.900"	43.0	2304		47.0	2424	
180 GR. HDY SP	Hodgdon	H4350	.308"	2.900"	42.0	2250		46.0	2566	
180 GR. HDY SP	Hodgdon	H414	.308"	2.900"	40.0	2237		42.0	2355	
180 GR. HDY SP	Hodgdon	H380	.308"	2.900"	38.0	2213		40.0	2323	
180 GR. HDY SP	Hodgdon	BL-C(2)	.308"	2.900"	37.0	2189		39.0	2284	
180 GR. HDY SP	Hodgdon	H335	.308"	2.900"	37.0	2184		39.0	2263	
180 GR. HDY SP	Hodgdon	H4895	.308"	2.900"	37.0	2201		39.0	2296	

Cartridge: 300 Savage
Load Type: Rifle

Bullet Weight (Gr.)	Manufacturer	Powder	Bullet Diam.	C.O.L.	Starting Loads			Maximum Loads		
					Grs.	Vel. (ft/s)	Pressure	Grs.	Vel. (ft/s)	Pressure
100 GR. SPR RN SP	Winchester	748	.308"	2.475"				45.2	2930	41,500 CUP
100 GR. SPR RN SP	Hodgdon	BL-C(2)	.308"	2.475"	41.0	2755		43.0	2959	
100 GR. SPR RN SP	Hodgdon	H335	.308"	2.475"	41.0	2741		43.0	2952	
100 GR. SPR RN SP	Hodgdon	H4895	.308"	2.475"	41.0	2819		43.0	3002	
100 GR. SPR RN SP	Hodgdon	H4198	.308"	2.475"	34.0	2914		37.0	3103	
110 GR. HDY SP	Hodgdon	BL-C(2)	.308"	2.450"	39.5	2652		43.0	2940	
110 GR. HDY SP	Hodgdon	H335	.308"	2.450"	39.0	2639		43.0	2947	
110 GR. HDY SP	Hodgdon	H4895	.308"	2.450"	39.5	2669		43.0	2944	
110 GR. HDY SP	Hodgdon	H4198	.308"	2.450"	34.0	2742		37.0	2978	
130 GR. HDY SP	Hodgdon	BL-C(2)	.308"	2.520"	38.0	2503		41.0	2634	
130 GR. HDY SP	Hodgdon	H335	.308"	2.520"	38.0	2494		41.0	2631	
130 GR. HDY SP	Hodgdon	H4895	.308"	2.520"	39.5	2324		43.0	2698	
130 GR. HDY SP	Hodgdon	H4198	.308"	2.520"	33.0	2624		36.0	2837	
150 GR. NOS PART	IMR	IMR 4320	308"	2.520"				41.5	2555	46,000 CUP
150 GR. NOS PART	IMR	IMR 4064	.308"	2.520"				40.0	2565	45,400 CUP
150 GR. NOS PART	Winchester	748	.308"	2.520"				40.9	2505	42,000 PSI
150 GR. NOS PART	Hodgdon	BL-C(2)	.308"	2.520"	36.0	2321		39.0	2574	
150 GR. NOS PART	IMR	IMR 4895	.308"	2.520"				40.0	2570	45,900 CUP
150 GR. NOS PART	Hodgdon	H335	.308"	2.520"	36.0	2303		39.0	2545	
150 GR. NOS PART	Hodgdon	H4895	.308"	2.520"	37.0	2187		40.0	2408	
150 GR. NOS PART	IMR	IMR 3031	.308"	2.520"				38.5	2575	44,500 CUP
150 GR. NOS PART	IMR	SR 4759	.308"	2.520"				23.5	2095	45,500 CUP
165 GR. SIE SPBT	Winchester	748	.308"	2.600"				39.5	2340	39,900 PSI

Bullet Weight	Manufacturer	Powder	Bullet Diam.	C.O.L.	Grs.	Vel. (ft/s)	Pressure	Grs.	Vel. (ft/s)	Pressure
165 GR. SIE SPBT	Hodgdon	BL-C(2)	.308"	2.600"	34.0	2204		37.0	2249	
165 GR. SIE SPBT	Hodgdon	H335	.308"	2.600"	34.0	2186		37.0	2240	
165 GR. SIE SPBT	Hodgdon	H4895	.308"	2.600"	35.0	2164		38.0	2341	
180 GR. HDY SP	IMR	IMR 4350	.308"	2.600"				44.0C	2350	46,000 CUP
180 GR. HDY SP	IMR	IMR 4320	.308"	2.600"				40.0	2390	46,000 CUP
180 GR. HDY SP	IMR	IMR 4064	.308"	2.600"				38.5	2395	45,900 CUP
180 GR. HDY SP	Winchester	748	.308"	2.600"				38.8	2350	45,600 PSI
180 GR. HDY SP	Hodgdon	BL-C(2)	.308"	2.600"	32.0	1987		35.0	2069	
180 GR. HDY SP	IMR	IMR 4895	.308"	2.600"				38.5	2390	45,700 CUP
180 GR. HDY SP	Hodgdon	H335	.308"	2.600"	32.0	1974		35.0	2074	
180 GR. HDY SP	Hodgdon	H4895	.308"	2.600"	34.0	2081		37.0	2130	
180 GR. HDY SP	IMR	IMR 3031	.308"	2.600"				37.0	2390	45,900 CUP
180 GR. HDY SP	IMR	SR 4759	.308"	2.600"				22.5	1910	45,500 CUP
200 GR. SPR SP	Hodgdon	H335	.308"	2.550"	31.0	1934		34.0	2047	
200 GR. SPR SP	Hodgdon	H4895	.308"	2.550"	32.0	1973		35.0	2089	

Cartridge: 7.62 x 54R Load Type: Rifle					Starting Loads			Maximum Loads		
Bullet Weight (Gr.)	Manufacturer	Powder	Bullet Diam.	C.O.L.	Grs.	Vel. (ft/s)	Pressure	Grs.	Vel. (ft/s)	Pressure
110 GR. HDY SP	Hodgdon	Varget	.308"	2.715"	51.0	3016	34,700 CUP	55.0C	3200	39,900 CUP
110 GR. HDY SP	Hodgdon	BL-C(2)	.308"	2.715"	56.0	3141	34,200 CUP	60.0	3376	42,300 CUP
110 GR. HDY SP	Hodgdon	H335	.308"	2.715"	51.0	3126	36,300 CUP	54.5	3332	45,200 CUP
110 GR. HDY SP	Hodgdon	H4895	.308"	2.715"	51.0	3150	35,500 CUP	55.0C	3345	43,400 CUP
110 GR. HDY SP	Hodgdon	Benchmark	.308"	2.715"	47.0	3060	39,700 CUP	50.5	3213	44,900 CUP
125 GR. SIE SP	Hodgdon	Varget	.308"	2.715"	51.0	2967	37,400 CUP	55.0C	3139	45,700 CUP
125 GR. SIE SP	Hodgdon	BL-C(2)	.308"	2.715"	56.0	3094	37,500 CUP	60.0	3298	45,100 CUP
125 GR. SIE SP	Hodgdon	H335	.308"	2.715"	50.0	2997	36,500 CUP	53.0	3193	45,100 CUP
125 GR. SIE SP	Hodgdon	H4895	.308"	2.715"	50.0	3036	36,700 CUP	54.0C	3236	45,700 CUP
150 GR. NOS BT	Hodgdon	Varget	.308"	2.875"	47.0	2721	38,000 CUP	50.5	2985	46,400 CUP
150 GR. NOS BT	Hodgdon	BL-C(2)	.308"	2.875"	52.0	2878	40,200 CUP	55.5	3027	46,300 CUP
150 GR. NOS BT	Hodgdon	H335	.308"	2.875"	46.0	2751	38,800 CUP	49.5	2918	45,900 CUP
150 GR. NOS BT	Hodgdon	H4895	.308"	2.875"	46.0	2769	38,000 CUP	49.5C	2938	46,300 CUP
165 GR. BAR XBTC	Hodgdon	H4350	.308"	2.950"	52.0	2608	36,300 CUP	55.0C	2740	41,500 CUP
165 GR. BAR XBTC	Hodgdon	H414	.308"	2.950"	49.0	2521	33,600 CUP	52.0	2669	41,400 CUP
165 GR. BAR XBTC	Hodgdon	H380	.308"	2.950"	47.0	2499	35,900 CUP	50.0	2629	40,800 CUP
165 GR. BAR XBTC	Hodgdon	Varget	.308"	2.950"	45.0	2581	39,800 CUP	48.3	2727	46,000 CUP
165 GR. BAR XBTC	Hodgdon	H4895	.308"	2.950"	44.0	2633	40,200 CUP	47.0	2761	45,800 CUP
180 GR. SFT SCIR	Hodgdon	H4831	.308"	2.975"	51.0	2281	31,900 CUP	55.0C	2484	39,200 CUP
180 GR. SFT SCIR	Hodgdon	H4350	.308"	2.975"	51.0	2493	37,600 CUP	55.0C	2692	44,700 CUP
180 GR. SFT SCIR	Hodgdon	H414	.308"	2.975"	49.0	2478	38,600 CUP	52.0	2622	45,600 CUP

Bullet Weight (Gr.)	Manufacturer	Powder	Bullet Diam.	C.O.L.	Grs.	Vel. (ft/s)	Pressure	Grs.	Vel. (ft/s)	Pressure
180 GR. SFT SCIR	Hodgdon	H380	.308"	2.975"	47.0	2430	38,200 CUP	50.0	2542	42,000 CUP
180 GR. SFT SCIR	Hodgdon	Varget	.308"	2.975"	43.0	2409	38,400 CUP	46.5C	2575	45,900 CUP
180 GR. SFT SCIR	Hodgdon	H4895	.308"	2.975"	42.0	2482	40,900 CUP	45.4C	2618	45,800 CUP
200 GR. SPR SP	Hodgdon	H4831	.308"	2.950"	52.0	2348	41,100 CUP	55.0C	2468	45,700 CUP
200 GR. SPR SP	Hodgdon	H4350	.308"	2.950"	48.0	2329	37,400 CUP	52.0	2529	46,500 CUP
200 GR. SPR SP	Hodgdon	H414	.308"	2.950"	48.0	2396	40,500 CUP	51.0	2526	45,500 CUP
200 GR. SPR SP	Hodgdon	H380	.308"	2.950"	46.0	2337	41,200 CUP	49.0	2432	46,600 CUP
200 GR. SPR SP	Hodgdon	Varget	.308"	2.950"	41.0	2304	41,500 CUP	44.0	2412	46,000 CUP
200 GR. SPR SP	Hodgdon	H4895	.308"	2.950"	39.0	2271	41,400 CUP	42.2	2411	46,400 CUP
220 GR. HDY JRN	Hodgdon	H4831	.308"	2.830"	50.0	2209	39,100 CUP	54.0C	2381	46,000 CUP
220 GR. HDY JRN	Hodgdon	H4350	.308"	2.830"	47.0	2227	37,600 CUP	50.5C	2396	45,900 CUP
220 GR. HDY JRN	Hodgdon	H414	.308"	2.830"	47.0	2296	40,200 CUP	49.5	2401	44,500 CUP
220 GR. HDY JRN	Hodgdon	H380	.308"	2.830"	43.0	2145	39,400 CUP	46.0	2274	45,900 CUP
220 GR. HDY JRN	Hodgdon	Varget	.308"	2.830"	40.0	2178	42,300 CUP	42.5	2269	46,000 CUP
220 GR. HDY JRN	Hodgdon	H4895	.308"	2.830"	38.0	2143	41,200 CUP	41.0	2263	46,600 CUP

Cartridge: 30 Remington
Load Type: Rifle

Bullet Weight (Gr.)	Manufacturer	Powder	Bullet Diam.	C.O.L.	Starting Loads			Maximum Loads		
					Grs.	Vel. (ft/s)	Pressure	Grs.	Vel. (ft/s)	Pressure
170 GR. SP	Winchester	760	.308"	2.525"				35.0	2095	35,000 CUP
170 GR. SP	Winchester	748	.308"	2.525"				30.0	2000	34,000 CUP

Cartridge: 307 Winchester
Load Type: Rifle

Bullet Weight (Gr.)	Manufacturer	Powder	Bullet Diam.	C.O.L.	Starting Loads			Maximum Loads		
					Grs.	Vel. (ft/s)	Pressure	Grs.	Vel. (ft/s)	Pressure
110 GR. SPR HP	Hodgdon	H4831	.308"	2.390"	48.0	2340		50.0	2451	
110 GR. SPR HP	Hodgdon	H4350	.308"	2.390"	47.0	2320		50.0	2589	
110 GR. SPR HP	Hodgdon	H414	.308"	2.390"	51.0	2688		53.0	2828	
110 GR. SPR HP	Hodgdon	H380	.308"	2.390"	50.0	2747		52.0	2939	
110 GR. SPR HP	Hodgdon	BL-C(2)	.308"	2.390"	47.0	2839		49.0	2950	
110 GR. SPR HP	Hodgdon	H335	.308"	2.390"	45.0	2769		47.0	2899	
110 GR. SPR HP	Hodgdon	H4895	.308"	2.390"	42.0	2724		45.0	2930	
110 GR. SPR HP	Hodgdon	H322	.308"	2.390"	41.0	2814		44.0	3000	
125 GR. SPR FP	Hodgdon	H4831	.308"	2.520"	48.0	2269		50.0	2400	
125 GR. SPR FP	Hodgdon	H4350	.308"	2.520"	47.0	2380		50.0	2522	
125 GR. SPR FP	Hodgdon	H414	.308"	2.520"	48.0	2489		50.0	2665	
125 GR. SPR FP	Hodgdon	H380	.308"	2.520"	47.0	2424		49.0	2639	
125 GR. SPR FP	Hodgdon	BL-C(2)	.308"	2.520"	44.0	2510		47.0	2732	
125 GR. SPR FP	Hodgdon	H335	.308"	2.520"	42.0	2439		45.0	2695	

Bullet Weight (Gr.)	Manufacturer	Powder	Bullet Diam.	C.O.L.	Grs.	Vel. (ft/s)	Pressure	Grs.	Vel. (ft/s)	Pressure
125 GR. SPR FP	Hodgdon	H4895	.308"	2.520"	40.0	2540		43.0	2762	
125 GR. SPR FP	Hodgdon	H322	.308"	2.520"	39.0	2481		42.0	2669	
150 GR. HDY RN	Winchester	748	.308"	2.520"				44.0	2625	
150 GR. HDY RN	Hodgdon	H4831	.308"	2.520"	47.0	2154		49.0	2349	
150 GR. HDY RN	Hodgdon	H4350	.308"	2.520"	46.0	2292		48.0	2453	
150 GR. HDY RN	Hodgdon	H414	.308"	2.520"	47.0	2347		49.0	2562	
150 GR. HDY RN	Winchester	760	.308"	2.520"	47.0	2347		49.0	2562	
150 GR. HDY RN	Hodgdon	H380	.308"	2.520"	46.0	2329		48.0	2543	
150 GR. HDY RN	Hodgdon	BL-C(2)	.308"	2.520"	43.0	2390		46.0	2593	
150 GR. HDY RN	Hodgdon	H335	.308"	2.520"	41.0	2377		44.0	2590	
150 GR. HDY RN	Hodgdon	H4895	.308"	2.520"	39.0	2402		42.0	2604	
150 GR. HDY RN	Hodgdon	H322	.308"	2.520"	38.0	2319		41.0	2513	
170 GR. HDY FP	Hodgdon	H4350	.308"	2.520"	45.0	2210		47.0	2380	
170 GR. HDY FP	Hodgdon	H414	.308"	2.520"	45.0	2333		47.0	2513	
170 GR. HDY FP	Winchester	760	.308"	2.520"	45.0	2333		47.0	2513	
170 GR. HDY FP	Hodgdon	H380	.308"	2.520"	44.0	2279		46.0	2429	
170 GR. HDY FP	Winchester	748	.308"	2.520"				41.2	2455	
170 GR. HDY FP	Hodgdon	BL-C(2)	.308"	2.520"	41.0	2351		44.0	2535	
170 GR. HDY FP	Hodgdon	H335	.308"	2.520"	38.0	2282		41.0	2432	
170 GR. HDY FP	Hodgdon	H4895	.308"	2.520"	37.0	2314		40.0	2474	
170 GR. HDY FP	Hodgdon	H322	.308"	2.520"	35.0	2234		38.0	2418	
180 GR. HDY RN	Hodgdon	H4350	.308"	2.730"	45.0	2290		47.0	2416	
180 GR. HDY RN	Hodgdon	H414	.308"	2.730"	44.0	2323		46.0	2470	
180 GR. HDY RN	Hodgdon	H380	.308"	2.730"	43.0	2311		45.0	2440	
180 GR. HDY RN	Hodgdon	BL-C(2)	.308"	2.730"	40.0	2290		43.0	2474	
180 GR. HDY RN	Hodgdon	H335	.308"	2.730"	37.0	2231		40.0	2417	
180 GR. HDY RN	Hodgdon	H4895	.308"	2.730"	36.0	2227		39.0	2373	
180 GR. HDY RN	Hodgdon	H322	.308"	2.730"	34.0	2169		37.0	2359	

Cartridge: 308 Marlin Express
Load Type: Rifle

Bullet Weight (Gr.)	Manufacturer	Powder	Bullet Diam.	C.O.L.	Starting Loads			Maximum Loads		
					Grs.	Vel. (ft/s)	Pressure	Grs.	Vel. (ft/s)	Pressure
125 GR. SIE HP FN	Hodgdon	Varget	.308"	2.300"	39.0	2525	37,500 PSI	42.3C	2700	42,800 PSI
125 GR. SIE HP FN	IMR	IMR 4320	.308"	2.300"	39.0	2476	36,900 PSI	42.0	2682	44,900 PSI
125 GR. SIE HP FN	IMR	IMR 4064	.308"	2.300"	38.5	2481	36,500 PSI	41.5C	2684	43,000 PSI
125 GR. SIE HP FN	Winchester	748	.308"	2.300"	39.0	2420	29,800 PSI	44.0	2751	42,100 PSI
125 GR. SIE HP FN	Hodgdon	BL-C(2)	.308"	2.300"	42.0	2543	34,900 PSI	46.0	2808	46,200 PSI
125 GR. SIE HP FN	IMR	IMR 4895	.308"	2.300"	38.0	2428	34,800 PSI	42.0	2717	45,600 PSI
125 GR. SIE HP FN	Hodgdon	H335	.308"	2.300"	39.0	2647	38,700 PSI	42.4	2820	45,400 PSI
125 GR. SIE HP FN	Hodgdon	H4895	.308"	2.300"	38.0	2527	35,900 PSI	42.0	2788	45,000 PSI

125 GR. SIE HP FN	IMR	IMR 8208 XBR	.308"	2.300"	37.0	2682	39,200 PSI	41.0	2868	44,900 PSI
125 GR. SIE HP FN	IMR	IMR 3031	.308"	2.300"	35.0	2446	34,600 PSI	38.8	2725	45,700 PSI
125 GR. SIE HP FN	Hodgdon	Benchmark	.308"	2.300"	34.0	2504	39,500 PSI	37.6	2680	45,200 PSI
125 GR. SIE HP FN	Hodgdon	H322	.308"	2.300"	34.0	2555	41,400 PSI	37.0	2704	46,200 PSI
130 GR. SPR FP	Hodgdon	Varget	.308"	2.420"	39.0	2502	37,500 PSI	42.5	2730	46,400 PSI
130 GR. SPR FP	IMR	IMR 4320	.308"	2.420"	38.0	2487	40,400 PSI	42.8	2670	45,900 PSI
130 GR. SPR FP	IMR	IMR 4064	.308"	2.420"	38.0	2441	36,400 PSI	41.5C	2686	45,400 PSI
130 GR. SPR FP	Winchester	748	.308"	2.420"	40.0	2531	35,800 PSI	43.0	2677	40,500 PSI
130 GR. SPR FP	Hodgdon	BL-C(2)	.308"	2.420"	42.0	2589	37,900 PSI	46.0	2799	45,600 PSI
130 GR. SPR FP	IMR	IMR 4895	.308"	2.420"	38.0	2414	35,700 PSI	41.7	2700	46,500 PSI
130 GR. SPR FP	Hodgdon	H335	.308"	2.420"	38.0	2569	37,800 PSI	41.5	2772	45,700 PSI
130 GR. SPR FP	Hodgdon	H4895	.308"	2.420"	38.0	2551	38,600 PSI	41.7	2762	46,000 PSI
130 GR. SPR FP	IMR	IMR 8208 XBR	.308"	2.420"	36.0	2627	40,700 PSI	40.0	2808	45,700 PSI
130 GR. SPR FP	IMR	IMR 3031	.308"	2.420"	35.0	2433	35,000 PSI	38.5	2700	45,800 PSI
130 GR. SPR FP	Hodgdon	Benchmark	.308"	2.420"	33.0	2428	38,800 PSI	36.5	2635	46,300 PSI
130 GR. SPR FP	Hodgdon	H322	.308"	2.420"	32.0	2388	36,500 PSI	35.3	2617	45,800 PSi
150 GR. BAR TSX FN	Hodgdon	LVR	.308"	2.350"	39.5	2500	39,100 PSI	42.0	2632	44,400 PSI
150 GR. BAR TSX FN	Hodgdon	Varget	.308"	2.350"	36.0	2268	39,500 PSI	39.5C	2458	46,500 PSI
150 GR. BAR TSX FN	IMR	IMR 4320	.308"	2.350"	36.0	2266	40,000 PSI	39.3	2433	45,900 PSI
150 GR. BAR TSX FN	IMR	IMR 4064	.308"	2.350"	36.0	2291	39,900 PSI	39.0C	2404	42,500 PSI
150 GR. BAR TSX FN	Winchester	748	.308"	2.350"	36.0	2245	35,300 PSI	40.0	2471	43,600 PSI
150 GR. BAR TSX FN	Hodgdon	BL-C(2)	.308"	2.350"	38.0	2282	36,600 PSI	41.0	2479	45,300 PSI
150 GR. BAR TSX FN	IMR	IMR 4895	.308"	2.350"	36.0	2140	35,400 PSI	39.0C	2452	45,600 PSI
150 GR. BAR TSX FN	Hodgdon	H335	.308"	2.350"	35.0	2303	36,900 PSI	38.0	2490	44,400 PSI
150 GR. BAR TSX FN	Hodgdon	H4895	.308"	2.350"	35.0	2279	38,800 PSI	38.3C	2498	46,800 PSI
150 GR. BAR TSX FN	IMR	IMR 8208 XBR	.308"	2.350"	34.0	2403	40,700 PSI	37.4C	2558	46,100 PSI
150 GR. BAR TSX FN	IMR	IMR 3031	.308"	2.350"	33.0	2238	37,600 PSI	36.0C	2437	46,100 PSI
150 GR. HDY RN	Hodgdon	Varget	.308"	2.430"	38.0	2405	39,100 PSI	41.5C	2572	46,100 PSI
150 GR. HDY RN	IMR	IMR 4320	.308"	2.430"	37.0	2300	37,200 PSI	41.0C	2533	46,400 PSI
150 GR. HDY RN	IMR	IMR 4064	.308"	2.430"	37.0	2328	36,100 PSI	41.0C	2574	45,700 PSI
150 GR. HDY RN	Winchester	748	.308"	2.430"	39.0	2368	34,700 PSI	42.0	2560	42,100 PSI
150 GR. HDY RN	Hodgdon	BL-C(2)	.308"	2.430"	40.0	2373	34,000 PSI	43.0	2544	41,200 PSI
150 GR. HDY RN	IMR	IMR 4895	.308"	2.430"	37.0	2301	35,400 PSI	41.0C	2575	46,500 PSI
150 GR. HDY RN	Hodgdon	H335	.308"	2.430"	37.0	2430	38,500 PSI	40.0C	2611	46,800 PSI
150 GR. HDY RN	Hodgdon	H4895	.308"	2.430"	37.0	2443	40,000 PSI	40.5	2607	45,900 PSI
150 GR. HDY RN	IMR	IMR 8208 XBR	.308"	2.430"	36.0	2537	42,600 PSI	39.5	2665	46,300 PSI
150 GR. HDY RN	IMR	IMR 3031	.308"	2.430"	34.0	2320	36,000 PSI	37.3C	2545	46,200 PSI
160 GR. HDY FTX ME	Hodgdon	LVR	.308"	2.590"	39.0	2495	38,400 PSI	41.5	2658	47,000 PSI
160 GR. HDY FTX ME	Hodgdon	Varget	.308"	2.590"	36.4	2361	38,900 PSI	39.6C	2547	46,800 PSI

155

Bullet Weight (Gr.)	Manufacturer	Powder	Bullet Diam.	C.O.L.	Grs.	Vel. (ft/s)	Pressure	Grs.	Vel. (ft/s)	Pressure
160 GR. HDY FTX ME	IMR	IMR 4320	.308"	2.590"	35.7	2322	39,100 PSI	38.0	2465	45,400 PSI
160 GR. HDY FTX ME	IMR	IMR 4064	.308"	2.590"	35.7	2280	34,400 PSI	38.0	2475	44,000 PSI
160 GR. HDY FTX ME	Winchester	748	.308"	2.590"	37.6	2356	34,400 PSI	40.0	2550	44,700 PSI
160 GR. HDY FTX ME	Hodgdon	BL-C(2)	.308"	2.590"	38.5	2386	36,100 PSI	41.0	2555	44,700 PSI
160 GR. HDY FTX ME	IMR	IMR 4895	.308"	2.590"	36.3	2345	37,700 PSI	38.6	2521	46,000 PSI
160 GR. HDY FTX ME	Hodgdon	H335	.308"	2.590"	35.3	2387	36,200 PSI	37.5	2545	45,200 PSI
160 GR. HDY FTX ME	Hodgdon	H4895	.308"	2.590"	34.8	2442	40,900 PSI	37.0	2555	46,800 PSI
160 GR. HDY FTX ME	IMR	IMR 8208 XBR	.308"	2.590"	35.0	2456	42,500 PSI	37.8	2570	46,700 PSI
160 GR. HDY FTX ME	IMR	IMR 3031	.308"	2.590"	32.9	2334	37,800 PSI	35.0	2459	44,300 PSI
170 GR. HDY FP	Hodgdon	LVR	.308"	2.400"	39.0	2392	37,400 PSI	41.4	2565	46,800 PSI
170 GR. HDY FP	Hodgdon	Varget	.308"	2.400"	36.0	2255	40,500 PSI	39.3C	2394	46,300 PSI
170 GR. HDY FP	IMR	IMR 4320	.308"	2.400"	36.0	2169	36,600 PSI	39.4	2383	45,800 PSI
170 GR. HDY FP	IMR	IMR 4064	.308"	2.400"	36.0	2202	36,400 PSI	39.3C	2416	46,100 PSI
170 GR. HDY FP	Winchester	748	.308"	2.400 "	37.0	2228	35,100 PSI	40.0	2432	45,400 PSI
170 GR. HDY FP	Hodgdon	BL-C(2)	.308"	2.400"	37.0	2200	34,300 PSI	40.6	2420	44,800 PSI
170 GR. HDY FP	IMR	IMR 4895	.308"	2.400"	35.0	2170	36,200 PSI	39.0C	2409	46,300 PSI
170 GR. HDY FP	Hodgdon	H335	.308"	2.400"	34.5	2219	36,200 PSI	37.5	2409	46,300 PSI
170 GR. HDY FP	Hodgdon	H4895	.308"	2.400"	35.0	2289	41,000 PSI	38.6C	2439	46,300 PSI
170 GR. HDY FP	IMR	IMR 8208 XBR	.308"	2.400"	33.0	2288	38,300 PSI	37.0	2473	46,600 PSI
170 GR. HDY FP	IMR	IMR 3031	.308"	2.400"	32.0	2157	36,100 PSI	35.6C	2372	45,800 PSI

Cartridge: 30 TC
Load Type: Rifle

Bullet Weight (Gr.)	Manufacturer	Powder	Bullet Diam.	C.O.L.	Starting Loads Grs.	Vel. (ft/s)	Pressure	Maximum Loads Grs.	Vel. (ft/s)	Pressure
125 GR. NOS BT	IMR	IMR 4320	.308"	2.640"	40.0	2606	35,400 PSI	48.8C	3102	57,100 PSI
125 GR. NOS BT	Hodgdon	H4895	.308"	2.640"	43.0	2895	42,700 PSI	47.8C	3177	57,700 PSI
125 GR. NOS BT	IMR	IMR 3031	.308"	2.640"	40.0	2794	41,100 PSI	44.8C	3128	59,300 PSI
125 GR. NOS BT	Hodgdon	Benchmark	.308"	2.640"	41.0	2860	43,500 PSI	46.0	3149	59,300 PSI
125 GR. NOS BT	Hodgdon	H322	.308"	2.640"	40.0	2925	52,000 PSI	44.8	3137	60,600 PSI
125 GR. NOS BT	IMR	IMR 4198	.308"	2.640"	34.0	2841	49,000 PSI	38.0	3035	58,700 PSI
125 GR. NOS BT	Hodgdon	H4198	.308"	2.640"	34.0	2800	46,500 PSI	38.4	3032	58,500 PSI
130 GR. BAR TSX BT	Hodgdon	Varget	.308"	2.640"	44.0	2839	45,200 PSI	48.0C	3051	55,900 PSI
130 GR. BAR TSX BT	IMR	IMR 4320	.308"	2.640"	45.0	2869	47,600 PSI	48.5C	3077	58,200 PSI
130 GR. BAR TSX BT	Hodgdon	BL-C(2)	.308"	2.640"	47.0	2879	43,900 PSI	50.5	3070	53,000 PSI
130 GR. BAR TSX BT	IMR	IMR 4895	.308"	2.640"	45.0	2881	47,100 PSI	48.0C	3093	57,200 PSI
130 GR. BAR TSX BT	Hodgdon	H335	.308"	2.640"	44.0	2948	47,000 PSI	47.5	3126	55,700 PSI
130 GR. BAR TSX BT	Hodgdon	H4895	.308"	2.640"	43.0	2875	44,800 PSI	47.5C	3133	59,200 PSI
130 GR. BAR TSX BT	IMR	IMR 3031	.308"	2.640"	40.0	2816	45,000 PSI	44.5C	3078	58,600 PSI
130 GR. BAR TSX BT	Hodgdon	Benchmark	.308"	2.640"	41.0	2841	44,800 PSI	45.7C	3104	59,600 PSI
130 GR. BAR TSX BT	Hodgdon	H322	.308"	2.640"	40.0	2869	49,500 PSI	44.5	3089	60,100 PSI

135 GR. SIE HPBT	Hodgdon	Varget	.308"	2.640"	44.0	2814	45,600 PSI	49.0C	3081	60,200 PSI
135 GR. SIE HPBT	IMR	IMR 4320	.308"	2.640"	43.0	2731	42,900 PSI	48.0C	3039	59,000 PSI
135 GR. SIE HPBT	Winchester	748	.308"	2.640"	44.0	2729	37,400 PSI	48.5	3035	53,300 PSI
135 GR. SIE HPBT	Hodgdon	BL-C(2)	.308"	2.640"	45.0	2758	39,200 PSI	50.0	3099	58,900 PSI
135 GR. SIE HPBT	IMR	IMR 4895	.308"	2.640"	43.0	2878	44,400 PSI	47.5C	3058	58,400 PSI
135 GR. SIE HPBT	Hodgdon	H335	.308"	2.640"	42.0	2838	43,600 PSI	47.0	3127	60,800 PSI
135 GR. SIE HPBT	Hodgdon	H4895	.308"	2.640"	42.0	2800	42,900 PSI	47.3C	3106	59,300 PSI
135 GR. SIE HPBT	IMR	IMR 8208 XBR	.308"	2.640"	42.0	2893	46,500 PSI	45.3	3095	59,700 PSI
135 GR. SIE HPBT	IMR	IMR 3031	.308"	2.640"	39.0	2716	41,400 PSI	43.8C	3044	60,100 PSI
135 GR. SIE HPBT	Hodgdon	Benchmark	.308"	2.640"	40.0	2758	42,200 PSI	45.0C	3057	59,900 PSI
135 GR. SIE HPBT	Hodgdon	H322	.308"	2.640"	39.0	2816	50,100 PSI	43.0	3002	59,300 PSI
150 GR. HDY IB	Hodgdon	Varget	.308"	2.640"	42.0	2631	45,700 PSI	45.8C	2830	56,100 PSI
150 GR. HDY IB	IMR	IMR 4320	.308"	2.640"	42.0	2612	46,100 PSI	46.5C	2861	58,800 PSI
150 GR. HDY IB	Winchester	748	.308"	2.640"	42.0	2580	39,700 PSI	46.0	2813	51,600 PSI
150 GR. HDY IB	Hodgdon	BL-C(2)	.308"	2.640"	44.0	2633	42,600 PSI	48.0	2856	55,300 PSI
150 GR. HDY IB	IMR	IMR 4895	.308"	2.640"	42.0	2658	46,800 PSI	45.8C	2863	57,500 PSI
150 GR. HDY IB	Hodgdon	H335	.308"	2.640"	40.0	2598	41,600 PSI	44.8	2907	59,200 PSI
150 GR. HDY IB	Hodgdon	H4895	.308"	2.640"	41.0	2652	44,300 PSI	45.5C	2901	58,900 PSI
150 GR. HDY IB	IMR	IMR 8208 XBR	.308"	2.640"	39.0	2646	43,400 PSI	43.7	2915	60,000 PSI
150 GR. HDY IB	IMR	IMR 3031	.308"	2.640"	38.0	2566	43,200 PSI	42.5C	2856	60,200 PSI
150 GR. HDY IB	Hodgdon	Benchmark	.308"	2.640"	38.0	2596	45,700 PSI	42.5C	2831	59,400 PSI
150 GR. HDY IB	Hodgdon	H322	.308"	2.640"	38.0	2683	53,600 PSI	42.5C	2857	60,700 PSI
155 GR. NOS HPBT	Hodgdon	Varget	.308"	2.640"	41.0	2594	43,700 PSI	46.0C	2861	59,100 PSI
155 GR. NOS HPBT	IMR	IMR 4320	.308"	2.640"	40.0	2502	40,200 PSI	45.2C	2830	58,600 PSI
155 GR. NOS HPBT	Winchester	748	.308"	2.640"	42.0	2589	39,500 PSI	45.0	2799	51,700 PSI
155 GR. NOS HPBT	Hodgdon	BL-C(2)	.308"	2.640"	43.0	2615	41,800 PSI	47.8	2916	59,800 PSI
155 GR. NOS HPBT	IMR	IMR 4895	.308"	2.640"	40.0	2534	40,600 PSI	45.0C	2856	58,600 PSI
155 GR. NOS HPBT	Hodgdon	H335	.308"	2.640"	39.0	2576	40,800 PSI	43.8	2865	58,800 PSI
155 GR. NOS HPBT	Hodgdon	H4895	.308"	2.640"	40.0	2648	45,500 PSI	44.4C	2871	58,300 PSI
155 GR. NOS HPBT	Hodgdon	Benchmark	.308"	2.640"	38.0	2549	40,800 PSI	42.6	2834	59,200 PSI
155 GR. NOS HPBT	Hodgdon	H322	.308"	2.640"	36.0	2590	49,400 PSI	40.5	2780	58,400 PSI
165 GR. BAR TSX	Hodgdon	Varget	.308"	2.630"	40.0	2465	43,700 PSI	45.0C	2748	60,500 PSI
165 GR. BAR TSX	IMR	IMR 4320	.308"	2.630"	40.0	2469	44,700 PSI	44.8C	2764	60,200 PSI
165 GR. BAR TSX	Winchester	748	.308"	2.630"	42.0	2547	45,600 PSI	46.0	2748	53,900 PSI
165 GR. BAR TSX	Hodgdon	BL-C(2)	.308"	2.630"	43.0	2554	44,300 PSI	47.5	2796	58,600 PSI
165 GR. BAR TSX	IMR	IMR 4895	.308"	2.630"	40.0	2478	44,600 PSI	45.0C	2764	59,800 PSI
165 GR. BAR TSX	Hodgdon	H335	.308"	2.630"	39.0	2500	43,900 PSI	43.5	2761	58,700 PSI
165 GR. BAR TSX	Hodgdon	H4895	.308"	2.630"	39.0	2491	43,900 PSI	43.4C	2755	59,700 PSI
165 GR. BAR TSX	IMR	IMR 8208 XBR	.308"	2.630"	38.0	2524	44,600 PSI	42.0C	2752	58,600 PSI

Bullet Weight (Gr.)	Manufacturer	Powder	Bullet Diam.	C.O.L.	Grs.	Vel. (ft/s)	Pressure	Grs.	Vel. (ft/s)	Pressure
165 GR. BAR TSX	IMR	IMR 3031	.308"	2.630"	37.0	2445	43,500 PSI	41.0C	2708	59,800 PSI
165 GR. BAR TSX	Hodgdon	Benchmark	.308"	2.630"	38.0	2486	44,000 PSI	42.0C	2719	58,800 PSI
165 GR. BAR TSX	Hodgdon	H322	.308"	2.630"	36.0	2536	54,500 PSI	40.5C	2691	59,600 PSI
168 GR. SIE HPBT	Hodgdon	Varget	.308"	2.640"	40.0	2476	42,800 PSI	45.2C	2748	59,100 PSI
168 GR. SIE HPBT	IMR	IMR 4320	.308"	2.640"	40.0	2448	42,700 PSI	44.6C	2727	59,100 PSI
168 GR. SIE HPBT	Winchester	748	.308"	2.640"	41.0	2483	39,400 PSI	46.0	2772	57,600 PSI
168 GR. SIE HPBT	Hodgdon	BL-C(2)	.308"	2.640"	42.0	2474	38,800 PSI	47.3	2784	58,000 PSI
168 GR. SIE HPBT	IMR	IMR 4895	.308"	2.640"	40.0	2492	44,200 PSI	44.8C	2767	60,300 PSI
168 GR. SIE HPBT	Hodgdon	H335	.308"	2.640"	39.0	2511	43,400 PSI	43.2	2746	58,600 PSI
168 GR. SIE HPBT	Hodgdon	H4895	.308"	2.640"	39.0	2514	45,100 PSI	43.5	2744	58,400 PSI
168 GR. SIE HPBT	IMR	IMR 3031	.308"	2.640"	37.0	2461	44,000 PSI	40.7C	2685	58,700 PSI
168 GR. SIE HPBT	Hodgdon	Benchmark	.308"	2.640"	38.0	2494	44,200 PSI	41.9	2716	59,700 PSI
168 GR. SIE HPBT	Hodgdon	H322	.308"	2.640"	36.0	2528	54,400 PSI	40.2	2678	60,200 PSI
180 GR. HDY SP	Hodgdon	Varget	.308"	2.640"	39.0	2345	45,600 PSI	43.8C	2579	59,100 PSI
180 GR. HDY SP	IMR	IMR 4320	.308"	2.640"	39.0	2336	45,500 PSI	43.9C	2601	59,800 PSI
180 GR. HDY SP	Winchester	748	.308"	2.640"	40.0	2344	39,800 PSI	44.5	2626	57,900 PSI
180 GR. HDY SP	Hodgdon	BL-C(2)	.308"	2.640"	41.0	2370	41,000 PSI	46.0	2652	59,200 PSI
180 GR. HDY SP	IMR	IMR 4895	.308"	2.640"	39.0	2352	43,700 PSI	43.5C	2599	58,800 PSI
180 GR. HDY SP	Hodgdon	H335	.308"	2.640"	38.0	2358	45,000 PSI	42.0	2580	59,400 PSI
180 GR. HDY SP	Hodgdon	H4895	.308"	2.640"	38.0	2379	47,200 PSI	42.5C	2596	59,400 PSI
180 GR. HDY SP	IMR	IMR 8208 XBR	.308"	2.640"	37.0	2416	49,000 PSI	41.5C	2620	59,900 PSI
180 GR. HDY SP	IMR	IMR 3031	.308"	2.640"	36.0	2302	42,400 PSI	39.9C	2544	59,000 PSI
180 GR. HDY SP	Hodgdon	Benchmark	.308"	2.640"	37.0	2353	45,600 PSI	41.0	2565	59,300 PSI

Cartridge: 308 Winchester Load Type: Rifle					Starting Loads			Maximum Loads		
Bullet Weight (Gr.)	Manufacturer	Powder	Bullet Diam.	C.O.L.	Grs.	Vel. (ft/s)	Pressure	Grs.	Vel. (ft/s)	Pressure
110 GR. BAR TSX FB	IMR	IMR 4895	.308"	2.690"	45.0	2831	36,100 PSI	50.0C	3128	46,600 PSI
110 GR. BAR TSX FB	Hodgdon	H335	.308"	2.690"	47.3	3078	40,800 PSI	52.5	3358	53,900 PSI
110 GR. BAR TSX FB	Hodgdon	H4895	.308"	2.690"	46.1	3055	40,300 PSI	49.0C	3212	46,200 PSI
110 GR. BAR TSX FB	IMR	IMR 8208 XBR	.308"	2.690"	45.5	2975	37,700 PSI	50.0C	3266	50,000 PSI
110 GR. BAR TSX FB	IMR	IMR 3031	.308"	2.690"	43.2	2913	37,700 PSI	47.0C	3170	47,700 PSI
110 GR. BAR TSX FB	Hodgdon	Benchmark	.308"	2.690"	45.2	3005	39,700 PSI	50.2C	3316	54,200 PSI
110 GR. BAR TSX FB	Hodgdon	H322	.308"	2.690"	46.1	3139	48,100 PSI	49.0C	3334	59,000 PSI
110 GR. BAR TSX FB	IMR	IMR 4198	.308"	2.690"	39.1	3064	46,200 PSI	41.6	3251	57,600 PSI
110 GR. BAR TSX FB	Hodgdon	H4198	.308"	2.690"	39.9	3124	48,800 PSI	42.5	3278	58,700 PSI
125 GR. SFIRE	IMR	IMR 4895	.308"	2.700"	43.0	2772	42,100 PSI	48.0	3068	55,000 PSI
125 GR. SFIRE	Hodgdon	H335	.308"	2.700"	42.0	2840	42,100 PSI	46.5	3075	52,300 PSI
125 GR. SFIRE	Hodgdon	H4895	.308"	2.700"	42.0	2796	39,500 PSI	46.0C	3034	49,600 PSI
125 GR. SFIRE	IMR	IMR 8208 XBR	.308"	2.700"	42.0	2830	41,200 PSI	46.5C	3110	54,100 PSI

125 GR. SFIRE	IMR	IMR 3031	.308"	2.700"	39.0	2741	40,600 PSI	43.5C	3007	51,400 PSI
125 GR. SFIRE	Hodgdon	Benchmark	.308"	2.700"	40.0	2736	38,200 PSI	44.5C	3019	52,000 PSI
125 GR. SFIRE	Hodgdon	H322	.308"	2.700"	38.0	2760	43,500 PSI	42.5C	2985	52,800 PSI
125 GR. SIE SP	Hodgdon	Varget	.308"	2.700"	48.0	3049	42,400 CUP	50.0C	3135	45,700 CUP
125 GR. SIE SP	IMR	IMR 4320	.308"	2.700"	48.7	2952	46,400 PSI	53.0C	3167	55,200 PSI
125 GR. SIE SP	IMR	IMR 4064	.308"	2.700"	46.0	2891	42,500 PSI	50.1C	3119	52,100 PSI
125 GR. SIE SP	Winchester	748	.308"	2.700"				52.0	3175	50,000 CUP
125 GR. SIE SP	Hodgdon	BL-C(2)	.308"	2.700"	48.0	2876	35,900 CUP	52.0	3069	42,600 CUP
125 GR. SIE SP	IMR	IMR 4895	.308"	2.700"	48.0	2969	45,600 PSI	51.8C	3185	55,200 PSI
125 GR. SIE SP	Hodgdon	H335	.308"	2.700"	44.0	2840	37,500 CUP	48.0	3080	48,200 CUP
125 GR. SIE SP	Hodgdon	H4895	.308"	2.700"	45.0	2891	36,800 CUP	49.0C	3127	48,400 CUP
125 GR. SIE SP	IMR	IMR 8208 XBR	.308"	2.700"	46.0	3000	50,200 PSI	49.2C	3174	60,100 PSI
125 GR. SIE SP	IMR	IMR 3031	.308"	2.700"	43.2	2866	40,200 PSI	48.0C	3194	58,100 PSI
125 GR. SIE SP	Hodgdon	Benchmark	.308"	2.700"	43.0	2821	40,600 CUP	47.5	3070	50,700 CUP
125 GR. SIE SP	Hodgdon	H322	.308"	2.700"	42.0	2888	43,400 CUP	45.0	3052	51,400 CUP
125 GR. SIE SP	Hodgdon	H4198	.308"	2.700"	36.0	2841	46,600 CUP	39.5	2988	49,800 CUP
130 GR. SPR HP	Hodgdon	CFE 223	.308"	2.615"	52.0	3054	49,600 PSI	54.0	3202	59,500 PSI
130 GR. SPR HP	Hodgdon	Varget	.308"	2.615"	47.0	2975	42,900 CUP	50.0C	3130	50,400 CUP
130 GR. SPR HP	IMR	IMR 4320	.308"	2.615"	46.8	2819	44,100 PSI	52.0C	3140	59,600 PSI
130 GR. SPR HP	IMR	IMR 4064	.308"	2.615"	45.0	2809	43,600 PSI	49.5C	3036	52,300 PSI
130 GR. SPR HP	Hodgdon	BL-C(2)	.308"	2.615"	48.0	2897	42,400 CUP	51.5	3089	49,700 CUP
130 GR. SPR HP	IMR	IMR 4895	.308"	2.615"	45.9	2867	44,500 PSI	51.0C	3153	57,800 PSI
130 GR. SPR HP	Hodgdon	H335	.308"	2.615"	43.0	2805	40,400 CUP	46.0	2980	49,700 CUP
130 GR. SPR HP	Hodgdon	H4895	.308"	2.615"	45.0	2903	41,800 CUP	49.0C	3099	50,100 CUP
130 GR. SPR HP	IMR	IMR 8208 XBR	.308"	2.615"	43.0	2834	46,900 PSI	48.0C	3110	62,100 PSI
130 GR. SPR HP	IMR	IMR 3031	.308"	2.615"	42.0	2827	42,600 PSI	46.7C	3130	59,800 PSI
130 GR. SPR HP	Hodgdon	Benchmark	.308"	2.615"	41.0	2704	38,800 CUP	46.0	2985	50,100 CUP
130 GR. SPR HP	Hodgdon	H322	.308"	2.615"	40.0	2754	41,200 CUP	43.0	2924	49,800 CUP
130 GR. SPR HP	Hodgdon	H4198	.308"	2.615"	35.0	2745	44,700 CUP	37.0	2837	49,700 CUP
150 GR. NOS BT	IMR	IMR 4007 SSC	.308"	2.800"	44.7	2578	44,700 PSI	48.0C	2742	51,300 PSI
150 GR. NOS BT	Hodgdon	CFE 223	.308"	2.800"	48.4	2764	44,500 PSI	51.5	2974	57,000 PSI
150 GR. NOS BT	Hodgdon	Varget	.308"	2.800"	44.0	2788	43,300 CUP	47.0C	2937	50,300 CUP
150 GR. NOS BT	IMR	IMR 4320	.308"	2.800"	44.1	2658	44,600 PSI	49.0C	2936	59,800 PSI
150 GR. NOS BT	IMR	IMR 4064	.308"	2.800"	43.0	2663	44,700 PSI	47.7C	2903	57,100 PSI
150 GR. NOS BT	Winchester	748	.308"	2.800"				48.5	2865	48,000 CUP
150 GR. NOS BT	Hodgdon	BL-C(2)	.308"	2.800"	45.0	2661	40,200 CUP	48.0	2839	50,000 CUP
150 GR. NOS BT	IMR	IMR 4895	.308"	2.800"	42.6	2631	42,300 PSI	47.3C	2920	57,700 PSI
150 GR. NOS BT	Hodgdon	H335	.308"	2.800"	41.0	2619	42,600 CUP	44.0	2787	51,200 CUP
150 GR. NOS BT	Hodgdon	H4895	.308"	2.800"	43.0	2742	43,200 CUP	45.5	2870	51,000 CUP

159

150 GR. NOS BT	IMR	IMR 8208 XBR	.308"	2.800"	40.0	2604	45,500 PSI	44.5C	2870	60,800 PSI
150 GR. NOS BT	IMR	IMR 3031	.308"	2.800"	40.2	2658	44,300 PSI	43.5C	2881	59,200 PSI
150 GR. NOS BT	Hodgdon	Benchmark	.308"	2.800"	39.0	2521	38,800 CUP	43.0	2752	49,900 CUP
150 GR. NOS BT	Hodgdon	H322	.308"	2.800"	37.0	2508	39,100 CUP	40.0	2702	50,500 CUP
150 GR. NOS BT	IMR	Trail Boss	.308"	2.800"	10.0	1176	25,800 PSI	14.0	1417	27,100 PSI
150 GR. NOS E-TIP	Hodgdon	CFE 223	.308"	2.800"	49.0	2865	52,300 PSI	51.1	2990	60,400 PSI
150 GR. NOS E-TIP	Hodgdon	Varget	.308"	2.800"	42.3	2670	46,700 PSI	46.5C	2914	60,400 PSI
150 GR. NOS E-TIP	IMR	IMR 4320	.308"	2.800"	43.7	2637	48,100 PSI	47.6	2876	60,100 PSI
150 GR. NOS E-TIP	IMR	IMR 4064	.308"	2.800"	42.9	2659	47,500 PSI	46.7C	2883	59,800 PSI
150 GR. NOS E-TIP	Winchester	748	.308"	2.800"	43.9	2762	50,800 PSI	47.3	2923	59,600 PSI
150 GR. NOS E-TIP	Hodgdon	BL-C(2)	.308"	2.800"	43.7	2654	47,800 PSI	47.0	2868	60,100 PSI
150 GR. NOS E-TIP	IMR	IMR 4895	.308"	2.800"	42.7	2684	48,800 PSI	46.5C	2899	60,100 PSI
150 GR. NOS E-TIP	Hodgdon	H335	.308"	2.800"	40.4	2551	46,500 PSI	43.4	2790	59,100 PSI
150 GR. NOS E-TIP	Hodgdon	H4895	.308"	2.800"	41.5	2677	48,700 PSI	45.6	2893	60,500 PSI
150 GR. NOS E-TIP	IMR	IMR 8208 XBR	.308"	2.800"	40.8	2659	45,900 PSI	44.3	2889	60,000 PSI
150 GR. NOS E-TIP	IMR	IMR 3031	.308"	2.800"	39.3	2628	48,500 PSI	42.8	2839	60,100 PSI
150 GR. NOS E-TIP	Hodgdon	Benchmark	.308"	2.800"	39.9	2629	47,300 PSI	43.0	2819	59,600 PSI
155 GR. SIE HPBT	Hodgdon	H414	.308"	2.775"	48.0	2625	40,500 CUP	51.0	2793	50,200 CUP
155 GR. SIE HPBT	Winchester	760	.308"	2.775"	48.0	2625	40,500 CUP	51.0	2793	50,200 CUP
155 GR. SIE HPBT	IMR	IMR 4007 SSC	.308"	2.775"	46.5	2592	41,700 PSI	49.5C	2751	49,900 PSI
155 GR. SIE HPBT	Hodgdon	CFE 223	.308"	2.775"	49.5	2846	50,900 PSI	51.0	2966	60,500 PSI
155 GR. SIE HPBT	Hodgdon	Varget	.308"	2.775"	44.0	2759	41,300 CUP	47.0C	2909	49,400 CUP
155 GR. SIE HPBT	IMR	IMR 4320	.308"	2.775"	44.0	2622	44,800 PSI	48.5C	2875	58,400 PSI
155 GR. SIE HPBT	IMR	IMR 4064	.308"	2.775"	43.0	2602	42,900 PSI	47.5C	2871	56,500 PSI
155 GR. SIE HPBT	Hodgdon	BL-C(2)	.308"	2.775"	45.0	2658	37,500 CUP	48.0	2867	49,600 CUP
155 GR. SIE HPBT	IMR	IMR 4895	.308"	2.775"	43.5	2664	45,100 PSI	47.5C	2897	58,200 PSI
155 GR. SIE HPBT	Hodgdon	H335	.308"	2.775"	41.0	2646	42,100 CUP	43.5	2779	49,900 CUP
155 GR. SIE HPBT	Hodgdon	H4895	.308"	2.775"	43.0	2735	42,000 CUP	46.0	2873	49,700 CUP
155 GR. SIE HPBT	IMR	IMR 8208 XBR	.308"	2.775"	41.0	2619	47,300 PSI	45.3	2854	60,900 PSI
155 GR. SIE HPBT	IMR	IMR 3031	.308"	2.775"	39.5	2594	43,400 PSI	43.2C	2832	58,500 PSI
155 GR. SIE HPBT	Hodgdon	Benchmark	.308"	2.775"	39.0	2538	41,900 CUP	43.0	2753	50,200 CUP
155 GR. SIE HPBT	Hodgdon	H322	.308"	2.775"	38.0	2588	42,400 CUP	41.0	2710	49,400 CUP
165 GR. HDY SP	Hodgdon	H414	.308"	2.750"	48.0	2537	43,500 CUP	52.0	2704	49,200 CUP
165 GR. HDY SP	Winchester	760	.308"	2.750"	48.0	2537	43,500 CUP	52.0	2704	49,200 CUP
165 GR. HDY SP	IMR	IMR 4007 SSC	.308"	2.750"	45.1	2539	45,500 PSI	48.0C	2656	51,100 PSI
165 GR. HDY SP	Hodgdon	CFE 223	.308"	2.750"	45.4	2649	46,700 PSI	48.3	2839	61,500 PSI
165 GR. HDY SP	Hodgdon	Varget	.308"	2.750"	42.0	2582	40,800 CUP	46.0C	2773	50,500 CUP
165 GR. HDY SP	IMR	IMR 4320	.308"	2.750"	43.0	2536	46,900 PSI	46.5C	2730	58,400 PSI
165 GR. HDY SP	IMR	IMR 4064	.308"	2.750"	42.0	2554	47,700 PSI	46.3C	2767	59,700 PSI
165 GR. HDY SP	Hodgdon	BL-C(2)	.308"	2.750"	44.0	2528	37,700 CUP	47.5	2738	49,700 CUP

165 GR. HDY SP	IMR	IMR 4895	.308"	2.750"	42.7	2584	49,200 PSI	45.5C	2745	58,800 PSI
165 GR. HDY SP	Hodgdon	H335	.308"	2.750"	39.0	2432	44,500 CUP	42.0	2608	49,100 CUP
165 GR. HDY SP	Hodgdon	H4895	.308"	2.750"	41.0	2525	38,600 CUP	43.5	2694	50,000 CUP
165 GR. HDY SP	IMR	IMR 8208 XBR	.308"	2.750"	38.5	2491	49,100 PSI	42.8	2691	60,200 PSI
165 GR. HDY SP	IMR	IMR 3031	.308"	2.750"	39.1	2537	49,600 PSI	41.6	2697	59,800 PSI
165 GR. HDY SP	Hodgdon	Benchmark	.308"	2.750"	38.5	2438	40,200 CUP	42.5	2647	50,500 CUP
168 GR. BAR TTSX BT	Hodgdon	CFE 223	.308"	2.800"	41.0	2444	39,600 PSI	45.0C	2664	49,800 PSI
168 GR. BAR TTSX BT	Hodgdon	Varget	.308	2.800"	41.0	2514	46,100 PSI	45.0C	2737	60,000 PSI
168 GR. BAR TTSX BT	IMR	IMR 4320	.308"	2.800"	42.0	2490	47,200 PSI	45.5C	2715	60,700 PSI
168 GR. BAR TTSX BT	IMR	IMR 4064	.308"	2.800"	43.0	2539	47,400 PSI	45.0C	2743	58,900 PSI
168 GR. BAR TTSX BT	Hodgdon	BL-C(2)	.308"	2.800"	43.0	2532	46,000 PSI	46.0	2697	55,000 PSI
168 GR. BAR TTSX BT	IMR	IMR 4895	.308"	2.800"	41.0	2514	47,400 PSI	44.0C	2692	57,800 PSI
168 GR. BAR TTSX BT	Hodgdon	H335	.308"	2.800"	39.0	2500	46,800 PSI	42.0	2661	56,100 PSI
168 GR. BAR TTSX BT	Hodgdon	H4895	.308"	2.800"	39.0	2497	45,100 PSI	43.0C	2727	59,900 PSI
168 GR. BAR TTSX BT	IMR	IMR 8208 XBR	.308"	2.800"	39.0	2505	46,500 PSI	43.0C	2724	60,700 PSI
168 GR. BAR TTSX BT	IMR	IMR 3031	.308"	2.800"	38.0	2493	46,600 PSI	41.5C	2693	58,600 PSI
168 GR. BAR TTSX BT	Hodgdon	Benchmark	.308"	2.800"	38.0	2458	44,500 PSI	42.0C	2686	59,500 PSI
168 GR. SIE HPBT	IMR	IMR 4007 SSC	.308"	2.800"	43.2	2466	44,300 PSI	48.0C	2729	58,300 PSI
168 GR. SIE HPBT	Hodgdon	CFE 223	.308"	2.800"	46.6	2662	48,200 PSI	49.0	2828	60,400 PSI
168 GR. SIE HPBT	Hodgdon	Varget	.308"	2.800"	42.0	2520	41,200 CUP	46.0C	2731	50,600 CUP
168 GR. SIE HPBT	IMR	IMR 4320	.308"	2.800"	41.5	2463	43,800 PSI	46.0	2733	59,300 PSI
168 GR. SIE HPBT	IMR	IMR 4064	.308"	2.800"	41.5	2518	43,800 PSI	45.9C	2766	58,800 PSI
168 GR. SIE HPBT	Hodgdon	BL-C(2)	.308"	2.800"	44.0	2569	39,400 CUP	47.0	2754	50,200 CUP
168 GR. SIE HPBT	IMR	IMR 4895	.308"	2.800"	41.0	2447	39,700 PSI	45.4C	2758	58,000 PSI
168 GR. SIE HPBT	Hodgdon	H335	.308"	2.800"	39.0	2451	37,700 CUP	42.0	2631	49,300 CUP
168 GR. SIE HPBT	Hodgdon	H4895	.308"	2.800"	41.0	2551	38,300 CUP	43.5	2703	49,500 CUP
168 GR. SIE HPBT	IMR	IMR 8208 XBR	.308"	2.800"	39.0	2493	49,000 PSI	43.3	2707	61,500 PSI
168 GR. SIE HPBT	IMR	IMR 3031	.308"	2.800"	39.0	2507	43,900 PSI	42.0	2710	58,900 PSI
168 GR. SIE HPBT	Hodgdon	Benchmark	.308"	2.800"	38.0	2416	38,100 CUP	42.0	2630	49,300 CUP
168 GR. SIE HPBT	Hodgdon	Titegroup	.308"	2.800"				8.0	1080	25,000 CUP
168 GR. SIE HPBT	Hodgdon	Clays	.308"	2.800"				8.0	1060	26,800 CUP
175 GR. SIE HPBT	Hodgdon	H414	.308"	2.800"	46.0	2484	40,300 CUP	49.0	2629	50,100 CUP
175 GR. SIE HPBT	Winchester	760	.308"	2.800"	46.0	2484	40,300 CUP	49.0	2629	50,100 CUP
175 GR. SIE HPBT	IMR	IMR 4007 SSC	.308"	2.800"	45.0	2489	46,100 PSI	48.0C	2666	56,500 PSI
175 GR. SIE HPBT	Hodgdon	CFE 223	.308"	2.800"	45.5	2612	49,600 PSI	47.5	2752	60,400 PSI
175 GR. SIE HPBT	Hodgdon	Varget	.308"	2.800"	42.0	2583	42,600 CUP	45.0C	2690	48,600 CUP
175 GR. SIE HPBT	IMR	IMR 4320	.308"	2.800"	42.0	2471	44,000 PSI	45.7C	2687	57,600 PSI
175 GR. SIE HPBT	IMR	IMR 4064	.308"	2.800"	41.5	2500	45,200 PSI	45.6C	2728	59,500 PSI
175 GR. SIE HPBT	Hodgdon	BL-C(2)	.308"	2.800"	43.0	2517	39,200 CUP	46.0	2706	50,300 CUP

175 GR. SIE HPBT	IMR	IMR 4895	.308"	2.800"	41.0	2463	42,800 PSI	45.0C	2704	57,800 PSI
175 GR. SIE HPBT	Hodgdon	H335	.308"	2.800"	38.0	2390	38,800 CUP	41.3	2592	50,100 CUP
175 GR. SIE HPBT	Hodgdon	H4895	.308"	2.800"	40.0	2489	39,100 CUP	42.7	2647	49,000 CUP
175 GR. SIE HPBT	IMR	IMR 8208 XBR	.308"	2.800"	39.0	2511	52,200 PSI	42.5	2664	61,800 PSI
175 GR. SIE HPBT	IMR	IMR 3031	.308"	2.800"	38.0	2427	42,000 PSI	41.3	2653	59,100 PSI
175 GR. SIE HPBT	Hodgdon	Benchmark	.308"	2.800"	38.0	2400	40,100 CUP	41.5	2590	50,800 CUP
180 GR. SPR SP	Hodgdon	H414	.308"	2.800"	46.0	2433	39,800 CUP	49.0	2573	47,500 CUP
180 GR. SPR SP	Winchester	760	.308"	2.800"	46.0	2433	39,800 CUP	49.0	2573	47,500 CUP
180 GR. SPR SP	IMR	IMR 4007 SSC	.308"	2.800"	45.0	2481	46,600 PSI	48.0C	2616	54,200 PSI
180 GR. SPR SP	Hodgdon	CFE 223	.308"	2.800"	42.9	2502	52,500 PSI	45.1	2615	61,100 PSI
180 GR. SPR SP	Hodgdon	Varget	.308"	2.800"	41.0	2470	41,200 CUP	45.0C	2661	49,600 CUP
180 GR. SPR SP	IMR	IMR 4320	.308"	2.800"	41.0	2407	43,500 PSI	45.4C	2665	57,900 PSI
180 GR. SPR SP	IMR	IMR 4064	.308"	2.800"	40.7	2445	44,100 PSI	45.2C	2683	58,200 PSI
180 GR. SPR SP	Winchester	748	.308"	2.800"				46.5	2610	48,500 CUP
180 GR. SPR SP	Hodgdon	BL-C(2)	.308"	2.800"	42.0	2460	40,300 CUP	46.0	2660	50,100 CUP
180 GR. SPR SP	IMR	IMR 4895	.308"	2.800"	40.5	2439	43,800 PSI	44.7C	2674	58,700 PSI
180 GR. SPR SP	Hodgdon	H335	.308"	2.800"	38.0	2374	41,100 CUP	41.0	2528	49,500 CUP
180 GR. SPR SP	Hodgdon	H4895	.308"	2.800"	40.0	2454	41,200 CUP	42.5	2595	49,700 CUP
180 GR. SPR SP	IMR	IMR 8208 XBR	.308"	2.800"	36.0	2340	51,600 PSI	40.0	2497	60,100 PSI
180 GR. SPR SP	IMR	IMR 3031	.308"	2.800"	37.0	2372	43,300 PSI	40.6	2594	58,000 PSI
180 GR. SPR SP	Hodgdon	Benchmark	.308"	2.800"	38.0	2363	40,700 CUP	41.3	2542	50,800 CUP
190 GR. HDY BTSP	Hodgdon	H414	.308"	2.740"	45.0	2368	42,100 CUP	48.0	2504	48,700 CUP
190 GR. HDY BTSP	Winchester	760	.308"	2.740"	45.0	2386	42,100 CUP	48.0	2504	48,700 CUP
190 GR. HDY BTSP	IMR	IMR 4007 SSC	.308"	2.740"	44.7	2446	49,900 PSI	47.5C	2570	58,000 PSI
190 GR. HDY BTSP	Hodgdon	CFE 223	.308"	2.740"	41.4	2388	46,500 PSI	45.0	2589	60,200 PSI
190 GR. HDY BTSP	Hodgdon	Varget	.308"	2.740"	41.0	2452	46,100 CUP	44.0C	2536	49,100 CUP
190 GR. HDY BTSP	IMR	IMR 4320	.308"	2.740"	41.0	2430	50,700 PSI	43.7C	2566	58,800 PSI
190 GR. HDY BTSP	IMR	IMR 4064	.308"	2.740"	39.4	2365	47,800 PSI	43.7C	2569	59,100 PSI
190 GR. HDY BTSP	Winchester	748	.308"	2.740"				42.0	2445	49,000 CUP
190 GR. HDY BTSP	Hodgdon	BL-C(2)	.308"	2.740"	42.0	2396	41,300 CUP	44.5	2543	48,700 CUP
190 GR. HDY BTSP	IMR	IMR 4895	.308"	2.740"	40.0	2363	46,000 PSI	43.9C	2571	59,100 PSI
190 GR. HDY BTSP	Hodgdon	H335	.308"	2.740"	37.0	2246	39,200 CUP	40.0	2449	49,800 CUP
190 GR. HDY BTSP	Hodgdon	H4895	.308"	2.740"	39.0	2359	40,400 CUP	42.0	2514	49,500 CUP
190 GR. HDY BTSP	IMR	IMR 8208 XBR	.308"	2.740"	36.0	2303	51,700 PSI	40.0	2459	59,800 PSI
190 GR. HDY BTSP	IMR	IMR 3031	.308"	2.740"	36.0	2273	43,800 PSI	39.6C	2483	57,700 PSI
190 GR. HDY BTSP	Hodgdon	Benchmark	.308"	2.740"	37.0	2288	41,100 CUP	39.5	2418	48,500 CUP
200 GR. SFT SP	Winchester	760	.308"	2.700"				45.7	2430	46,500 CUP
200 GR. SFT SP	IMR	IMR 4007 SSC	.308"	2.700"	41.4	2216	40,400 PSI	44.0C	2358	48,700 PSI
200 GR. SFT SP	Hodgdon	CFE 223	.308"	2.700"	41.7	2362	48,600 PSI	45.3	2582	60,600 PSI
200 GR. SFT SP	Hodgdon	Varget	.308"	2.700"	39.0	2288	43,100 CUP	42.0C	2441	50,100 CUP

Bullet Weight (Gr.)	Manufacturer	Powder	Bullet Diam.	C.O.L.	Grs.	Vel. (ft/s)	Pressure	Grs.	Vel. (ft/s)	Pressure
200 GR. SFT SP	IMR	IMR 4320	.308"	2.700"	38.3	2222	44,900 PSI	42.5C	2427	56,600 PSI
200 GR. SFT SP	IMR	IMR 4064	.308"	2.700"	39.0	2268	46,100 PSI	42.5C	2466	58,400 PSI
200 GR. SFT SP	Winchester	748	.308"	2.700"				43.0	2435	50,000 CUP
200 GR. SFT SP	Hodgdon	BL-C(2)	.308"	2.700"	41.0	2213	40,200 CUP	43.5	2514	49,800 CUP
200 GR. SFT SP	IMR	IMR 4895	.308"	2.700"	40.0	2302	47,500 PSI	43.2C	2476	59,000 PSI
200 GR. SFT SP	Hodgdon	H335	.308"	2.700"	37.0	2217	41,600 CUP	39.5	2400	50,400 CUP
200 GR. SFT SP	Hodgdon	H4895	.308"	2.700"	38.0	2256	42,400 CUP	41.0C	2403	49,400 CUP
200 GR. SFT SP	IMR	IMR 8208 XBR	.308"	2.700"	35.5	2250	51,900 PSI	39.5	2400	59,900 PSI
200 GR. SFT SP	IMR	IMR 3031	.308"	2.700"	36.0	2219	46,100 PSI	39.5C	2410	59,200 PSI
200 GR. SFT SP	Hodgdon	Benchmark	.308"	2.700"	37.5	2227	43,000 CUP	40.0	2355	50,100 CUP
208 GR. HDY A-MAX	Hodgdon	CFE 223	.308"	2.820"	40.6	2274	46,600 PSI	43.7	2474	57,500 PSI
208 GR. HDY A-MAX	Hodgdon	Varget	.308"	2.820"	38.1	2260	49,400 PSI	41.5C	2420	59,500 PSI
208 GR. HDY A-MAX	IMR	IMR 4320	.308"	2.820"	38.1	2220	47,900 PSI	41.5C	2416	59,600 PSI
208 GR. HDY A-MAX	IMR	IMR 4064	.308"	2.820"	37.7	2207	45,100 PSI	41.0C	2391	56,700 PSI
208 GR. HDY A-MAX	Winchester	748	.308"	2.820"	39.8	2279	47,000 PSI	42.8	2453	57,300 PSI
208 GR. HDY A-MAX	Hodgdon	BL-C(2)	.308"	2.820"	40.7	2273	48,300 PSI	43.8	2455	58,900 PSI
208 GR. HDY A-MAX	IMR	IMR 4895	.308"	2.820"	37.7	2229	47,200 PSI	41.0C	2425	59,400 PSI
208 GR. HDY A-MAX	Hodgdon	H335	.308"	2.820"	37.5	2264	52,600 PSI	39.5	2381	59,700 PSI
208 GR. HDY A-MAX	Hodgdon	H4895	.308"	2.820"	35.6	2218	49,900 PSI	38.8C	2359	58,600 PSI
208 GR. HDY A-MAX	IMR	IMR 8208 XBR	.308"	2.820"	36.4	2219	48,100 PSI	39.2	2373	59,300 PSI
208 GR. HDY A-MAX	IMR	IMR 3031	.308"	2.820"	35.2	2214	48,600 PSI	38.1	2363	58,700 PSI
208 GR. HDY A-MAX	Hodgdon	Benchmark	.308"	2.820"	35.2	2207	51,000 PSI	38.3	2346	59,300 PSI

Cartridge:30-06 Load Type:Rifle					Starting Loads			Maximum Loads		
Bullet Weight (Gr.)	Manufacturer	Powder	Bullet Diam.	C.O.L.	Grs.	Vel. (ft/s)	Pressure	Grs.	Vel. (ft/s)	Pressure
110 GR. HDY SP	Hodgdon	H414	.308"	3.170"	57.0	3044	39,200 CUP	62.5	3268	46,900 CUP
110 GR. HDY SP	Winchester	760	.308"	3.170"	57.0	3044	39,200 CUP	62.5	3268	46,900 CUP
110 GR. HDY SP	Hodgdon	CFE 223	.308"	3.170"	55.6	3224	50,600 PSI	59.0	3370	56,400 PSI
110 GR. HDY SP	Hodgdon	Varget	.308"	3.170"	55.0	3308	44,400 CUP	59.0	3452	48,500 CUP
110 GR. HDY SP	IMR	IMR 4320	.308"	3.170"	57.0	3285	49,400 PSI	60.5	3470	58,100 PSI
110 GR. HDY SP	IMR	IMR 4064	.308"	3.170"	55.0	3263	47,900 PSI	58.5	3453	56,400 PSI
110 GR. HDY SP	Winchester	748	.308"	3.170"				52.7	3320	47,000 CUP
110 GR. HDY SP	Hodgdon	BL-C(2)	.308"	3.170"	54.0	3108	36,200 CUP	60.0	3396	45,000 CUP
110 GR. HDY SP	IMR	IMR 4895	.308"	3.170"	56.0	3303	48,200 PSI	59.8	3505	57,300 PSI
110 GR. HDY SP	Hodgdon	H335	.308"	3.170"	50.0	3168	43,500 CUP	55.5	3367	48,100 CUP
110 GR. HDY SP	Hodgdon	H4895	.308"	3.170"	51.0	3155	39,000 CUP	57.0	3431	49,300 CUP
110 GR. HDY SP	IMR	IMR 8208 XBR	.308"	3.170"	52.6	3223	46,200 PSI	56.0	3415	57,500 PSI
110 GR. HDY SP	IMR	IMR 3031	.308"	3.170"	51.0	3252	47,200 PSI	54.9	3471	57,800 PSI

163

110 GR. HDY SP	Hodgdon	Benchmark	.308"	3.170"	51.5	3242	45,600 CUP	55.0	3396	49,800 CUP
125 GR. SIE SP	Hodgdon	H414	.308"	3.150"	57.0	2952	40,300 CUP	62.5	3181	46,700 CUP
125 GR. SIE SP	Winchester	760	.308"	3.150"	57.0	2952	40,300 CUP	62.5	3181	46,700 CUP
125 GR. SIE SP	IMR	IMR 4007 SSC	.308"	3.150"	55.0	2881	42,500 PSI	60.0C	3136	53,000 PSI
125 GR. SIE SP	Hodgdon	CFE 223	.308"	3.150"	54.5	3081	53,000 PSI	58.0	3212	58,900 PSI
125 GR. SIE SP	Hodgdon	Varget	.308"	3.150"	54.0	3159	45,500 CUP	57.2	3267	49,500 CUP
125 GR. SIE SP	IMR	IMR 4320	.308"	3.150"	54.0	3125	49,100 PSI	57.5	3307	57,900 PSI
125 GR. SIE SP	IMR	IMR 4064	.308"	3.150"	53.0	3129	47,400 PSI	56.5	3334	58,000 PSI
125 GR. SIE SP	Winchester	748	.308"	3.150"				51.0	3060	46,000 CUP
125 GR. SIE SP	Hodgdon	BL-C(2)	.308"	3.150"	53.0	3117	38,000 CUP	58.7	3273	48,700 CUP
125 GR. SIE SP	IMR	IMR 4895	.308"	3.150"	53.0	3137	47,800 PSI	57.2	3331	56,800 PSI
125 GR. SIE SP	Hodgdon	H335	.308"	3.150"	49.0	3046	43,000 CUP	54.0	3228	49,300 CUP
125 GR. SIE SP	Hodgdon	H4895	.308"	3.150"	48.0	2977	41,400 CUP	53.7	3229	49,300 CUP
125 GR. SIE SP	IMR	IMR 8208 XBR	.308"	3.150"	51.5	3100	50,400 PSI	54.7	3243	57,400 PSI
125 GR. SIE SP	IMR	IMR 3031	.308"	3.150"	49.0	3091	47,100 PSI	52.8	3298	58,400 PSI
125 GR. SIE SP	Hodgdon	Benchmark	.308"	3.150"	49.0	2996	40,700 CUP	52.0	3178	48,700 CUP
130 GR. SPR HP	Hodgdon	H414	.308"	3.060"	56.0	2862	40,600 CUP	62.0	3157	48,700 CUP
130 GR. SPR HP	IMR	IMR 4007 SSC	.308"	3.060"	54.0	2888	45,300 PSI	59.0C	- 3140	57,100 PSI
130 GR. SPR HP	Hodgdon	CFE 223	.308"	3.060"	54.0	3004	52,300 PSI	57.4	3145	59,100 PSI
130 GR. SPR HP	Hodgdon	Varget	.308"	3.060"	49.0	2979	41,300 CUP	53.5	3154	48,400 CUP
130 GR. SPR HP	IMR	IMR 4320	.308"	3.060"	51.0	3094	55,600 PSI	54.5	3197	57,700 PSI
130 GR. SPR HP	IMR	IMR 4064	.308"	3.060"	51.0	3070	49,500 PSI	54.5	3243	58,200 PSI
130 GR. SPR HP	Hodgdon	BL-C(2)	.308"	3.060"	52.0	2936	36,600 CUP	58.0	3179	48,300 CUP
130 GR. SPR HP	IMR	IMR 4895	.308"	3.060"	51.0	3074	50,800 PSI	54.7	3234	57,800 PSI
130 GR. SPR HP	Hodgdon	H335	.308"	3.060"	48.0	2912	39,600 CUP	53.5	3158	48,600 CUP
130 GR. SPR HP	Hodgdon	H4895	.308"	3.060"	48.0	2927	38,600 CUP	53.1	3144	46,100 CUP
130 GR. SPR HP	IMR	IMR 8208 XBR	.308"	3.060"	49.1	3021	52,100 PSI	51.7	3126	56,900 PSI
130 GR. SPR HP	IMR	IMR 3031	.308"	3.060"	47.0	3010	49,500 PSI	50.3	3176	58,300 PSI
130 GR. SPR HP	Hodgdon	Benchmark	.308"	3.060"	48.0	2986	44,900 CUP	51.0	3107	48,700 CUP
150 GR. NOS BT	Hodgdon	Suprform	.308"	3.250"	60.0	2850	43,100 PSI	65.0C	3072	53,000 PSI
150 GR. NOS BT	Hodgdon	H4350	.308"	3.250"	56.0	2792	37,100 CUP	62.0C	3068	48,400 CUP
150 GR. NOS BT	Hodgdon	H414	.308"	3.250"	54.0	2753	40,500 CUP	60.0	2992	48,600 CUP
150 GR. NOS BT	IMR	IMR 4350	.308"	3.250"	54.0	2745	47,400 PSI	58.0C	2942	57,200 PSI
150 GR. NOS BT	Winchester	760	.308"	3.250"	54.0	2792	40,500 CUP	60.0	2992	48,600 CUP
150 GR. NOS BT	IMR	IMR 4007 SSC	.308"	3.250"	52.4	2799	49,300 PSI	55.3	2972	58,000 PSI
150 GR. NOS BT	Hodgdon	H380	.308"	3.250"	53.0	2798	40,200 CUP	59.0	3005	45,900 CUP
150 GR. NOS BT	Hodgdon	CFE 223	.308"	3.250"	50.1	2763	50,500 PSI	54.2	2942	58,600 PSI
150 GR. NOS BT	Hodgdon	Varget	.308"	3.250"	47.0	2808	42,600 CUP	51.0	2975	50,000 CUP
150 GR. NOS BT	IMR	IMR 4320	.308"	3.250"	49.0	2850	51,600 PSI	52.3	3016	58,000 PSI
150 GR. NOS BT	IMR	IMR 4064	.308"	3.250"	47.0	2743	49,000 PSI	51.0	2928	58,600 PSI

150 GR. NOS BT	Winchester	748	.308"	3.250"				48.0	2810	46,000 CUP
150 GR. NOS BT	Hodgdon	BL-C(2)	.308"	3.250"	49.0	2759	39,700 CUP	54.0	2962	48,600 CUP
150 GR. NOS BT	IMR	IMR 4895	.308"	3.250"	49.0	2856	49,400 PSI	53.0	3009	56,700 PSI
150 GR. NOS BT	Hodgdon	H335	.308"	3.250"	47.0	2785	42,500 CUP	51.5	2982	49,200 CUP
150 GR. NOS BT	Hodgdon	H4895	.308"	3.250"	46.0	2806	44,400 CUP	51.0	2976	48,500 CUP
150 GR. NOS BT	IMR	IMR 8208 XBR	.308"	3.250"	47.0	2797	50,500 PSI	50.0	2935	58,400 PSI
150 GR. NOS BT	IMR	IMR 3031	.308"	3.250"	43.0	2697	47,600 PSI	46.7	2887	59,300 PSI
150 GR. NOS BT	Hodgdon	Benchmark	.308"	3.250"	46.5	2792	44,600 CUP	49.5	2944	49,300 CUP
150 GR. NOS BT	IMR	Trail Boss	.308"	3.250"	13.3	1061	14,700 PSI	19.0	1477	26,400 PSI
150 GR. NOS E-TIP	Hodgdon	H4350	.308"	3.300"	54.0	2747	47,000 PSI	57.8C	2927	57,700 PSI
150 GR. NOS E-TIP	Hodgdon	H414	.308"	3.300"	53.0	2779	49,300 PSI	57.0	2945	57,100 PSI
150 GR. NOS E-TIP	IMR	IMR 4350	.308"	3.300"	54.0	2744	48,800 PSI	57.5C	2930	57,300 PSI
150 GR. NOS E-TIP	Winchester	760	.308"	3.300"	53.0	2779	49,300 PSI	57.0	2945	57,100 PSI
150 GR. NOS E-TIP	IMR	IMR 4007 SSC	.308"	3.300"	52.0	2729	49,900 PSI	55.3C	2901	57,800 PSI
150 GR. NOS E-TIP	Hodgdon	H380	.308"	3.300"	53.0	2763	50,400 PSI	57.0	2921	57,300 PSI
150 GR. NOS E-TIP	Hodgdon	CFE 223	.308"	3.300"	49.0	2715	47,600 PSI	53.2	2927	58,600 PSI
150 GR. NOS E-TIP	Hodgdon	Varget	.308"	3.300"	46.0	2697	49,900 PSI	49.5	2860	58,000 PSI
150 GR. NOS E-TIP	IMR	IMR 4320	.308"	3.300"	48.0	2695	48,400 PSI	52.0	2897	58,100 PSI
150 GR. NOS E-TIP	IMR	IMR 4064	.308"	3.300"	47.0	2714	48,700 PSI	51.0	2926	59,500 PSI
150 GR. NOS E-TIP	Winchester	748	.308"	3.300"	48.0	2704	48,000 PSI	51.5	2859	55,400 PSI
150 GR. NOS E-TIP	Hodgdon	BL-C(2)	.308"	3.300"	50.0	2777	51,300 PSI	53.5	2915	57,900 PSI
150 GR. NOS E-TIP	IMR	IMR 4895	.308"	3.300"	47.0	2717	50,000 PSI	50.8	2900	58,700 PSI
150 GR. NOS E-TIP	Hodgdon	H335	.308"	3.300"	44.0	2671	51,600 PSI	48.0	2842	59,200 PSI
150 GR. NOS E-TIP	Hodgdon	H4895	.308"	3.300"	43.0	2658	49,000 PSI	47.5	2863	59,700 PSI
150 GR. NOS E-TIP	IMR	IMR 8208 XBR	.308"	3.300"	44.0	2677	50,100 PSI	47.7	2838	58,500 PSI
150 GR. NOS E-TIP	IMR	IMR 3031	.308"	3.300"	43.0	2644	47,600 PSI	46.0	2811	56,600 PSI
150 GR. NOS E-TIP	Hodgdon	Benchmark	.308"	3.300"	44.0	2631	46,400 PSI	48.0	2850	58,600 PSI
155 GR. SIE HPBT	Hodgdon	Suprform	.308"	3.225"	59.0	2843	43,400 PSI	65.2C	3125	58,800 PSI
155 GR. SIE HPBT	Hodgdon	H4350	.308"	3.225"	56.0	2757	36,000 CUP	62.0C	3038	47,500 CUP
155 GR. SIE HPBT	Hodgdon	H414	.308"	3.225"	54.0	2732	39,600 CUP	60.0	2956	46,200 CUP
155 GR. SIE HPBT	IMR	IMR 4350	.308"	3.225"	56.0	2784	45,800 PSI	60.0C	2959	53,800 PSI
155 GR. SIE HPBT	IMR	IMR 4007 SSC	.308"	3.225"	53.0	2766	48,800 PSI	57.2	2964	58,800 PSI
155 GR. SIE HPBT	Hodgdon	H380	.308"	3.225"	53.0	2789	40,100 CUP	59.0	3009	47,800 CUP
155 GR. SIE HPBT	Hodgdon	CFE 223	.308"	3.225"	49.2	2744	52,200 PSI	52.3	2879	59,500 PSI
155 GR. SIE HPBT	Hodgdon	Varget	.308"	3.225"	48.0	2822	44,600 CUP	50.7	2958	48,800 CUP
155 GR. SIE HPBT	IMR	IMR 4320	.308"	3.225"	49.0	2823	50,800 PSI	53.0	2976	57,900 PSI
155 GR. SIE HPBT	IMR	IMR 4064	.308"	3.225"	49.0	2811	46,800 PSI	53.0	3005	58,800 PSI
155 GR. SIE HPBT	Hodgdon	BL-C(2)	.308"	3.225"	49.0	2723	38,800 CUP	54.0	2912	46,300 CUP
155 GR. SIE HPBT	IMR	IMR 4895	.308"	3.225"	50.0	2851	49,800 PSI	53.8	3010	58,000 PSI

155 GR. SIE HPBT	Hodgdon	H335	.308"	3.225"	47.0	2776	42,200 CUP	51.5	2943	48,800 CUP
155 GR. SIE HPBT	Hodgdon	H4895	.308"	3.225"	46.0	2752	41,200 CUP	51.0	2925	45,600 CUP
155 GR. SIE HPBT	IMR	IMR 8208 XBR	.308"	3.225"	46.1	2747	50,400 PSI	49.0	2869	57,500 PSI
155 GR. SIE HPBT	IMR	IMR 3031	.308"	3.225"	46.0	2779	47,600 PSI	49.0	2944	58,600 PSI
155 GR. SIE HPBT	Hodgdon	Benchmark	.308"	3.225"	46.5	2779	40,500 CUP	49.5	2916	49,400 CUP
165 GR. HDY GMX	Hodgdon	Hybrid 100V	.308"	3.225"	52.5	2653	48,600 PSI	56.7C	2818	56,700 PSI
165 GR. HDY GMX	Hodgdon	H4350	.308"	3.225"	51.0	2587	48,600 PSI	55.4	2781	59,200 PSI
165 GR. HDY GMX	Hodgdon	H414	.308"	3.225"	50.0	2656	52,400 PSI	53.1	2773	58,500 PSI
165 GR. HDY GMX	IMR	IMR 4350	.308"	3.225"	52.0	2546	46,700 PSI	56.6	2770	58,200 PSI
165 GR. HDY GMX	Winchester	760	.308"	3.225"	50.0	2656	52,400 PSI	53.1	2773	58,500 PSI
165 GR. HDY GMX	IMR	IMR 4007 SSC	.308"	3.225"	49.0	2594	48,700 PSI	52.4	2762	57,600 PSI
165 GR. HDY GMX	Hodgdon	H380	.308"	3.225"	52.0	2652	52,700 PSI	56.0	2788	57,300 PSI
165 GR. HDY GMX	Hodgdon	CFE 223	.308"	3.225"	43.9	2531	51,200 PSI	46.7	2672	57,500 PSI
165 GR. HDY GMX	Hodgdon	Varget	.308"	3.225"	44.5	2526	46,600 PSI	48.3	2724	59,000 PSI
165 GR. HDY GMX	IMR	IMR 4320	.308"	3.225"	45.6	2515	45,800 PSI	49.6	2731	58,700 PSI
165 GR. HDY GMX	IMR	IMR 4064	.308"	3.225"	44.4	2510	44,900 PSI	48.2	2729	58,600 PSI
165 GR. HDY GMX	Hodgdon	BL-C(2)	.308"	3.225"	43.9	2511	49,200 PSI	47.5	2706	58,800 PSI
165 GR. HDY GMX	IMR	IMR 4895	.308"	3.225"	44.4	2535	45,100 PSI	47.8	2757	58,400 PSI
165 GR. HDY GMX	Hodgdon	H4895	.308"	3.225"	43.4	2595	50,300 PSI	46.7	2712	57,100 PSI
165 GR. HDY GMX	IMR	IMR 8208 XBR	.308"	3.225"	43.2	2572	50,800 PSI	47.0	2717	58,300 PSI
165 GR. HDY GMX	IMR	IMR 3031	.308"	3.225"	41.0	2510	46,400 PSI	44.1	2685	58,100 PSI
165 GR. SIE SPBT	Hodgdon	Suprform	.308"	3.300"	55.0	2724	45,100 PSI	61.0	2972	58,800 PSI
165 GR. SIE SPBT	Hodgdon	Hybrid 100V	.308"	3.300"	53.0	2648	46,000 PSI	57.0C	2801	52,800 PSI
165 GR. SIE SPBT	Hodgdon	H4350	.308"	3.300"	53.0	2678	38,400 CUP	59.0	2938	49,400 CUP
165 GR. SIE SPBT	Hodgdon	H414	.308"	3.300"	51.0	2678	41,900 CUP	56.5	2877	49,700 CUP
165 GR. SIE SPBT	IMR	IMR 4350	.308"	3.300"	56.0	2746	48,100 PSI	60.0C	2934	57,600 PSI
165 GR. SIE SPBT	Winchester	760	.308"	3.300"	51.0	2678	38,400 CUP	56.5	2877	49,700 CUP
165 GR. SIE SPBT	IMR	IMR 4007 SSC	.308"	3.300"	54.3	2800	54,300 PSI	55.9	2867	58,300 PSI
165 GR. SIE SPBT	Hodgdon	H380	.308"	3.300"	51.0	2669	41,700 CUP	56.5	2892	50,000 CUP
165 GR. SIE SPBT	Hodgdon	CFE 223	.308"	3.300"	46.5	2612	52,900 PSI	49.5	2731	58,700 PSI
165 GR. SIE SPBT	Hodgdon	Varget	.308"	3.300"	47.0	2726	44,500 CUP	50.5	2873	49,700 CUP
165 GR. SIE SPBT	IMR	IMR 4320	.308"	3.300"	48.0	2727	50,700 PSI	51.2	2869	58,600 PSI
165 GR. SIE SPBT	IMR	IMR 4064	.308"	3.300"	49.0	2752	50,400 PSI	52.5	2901	58,900 PSI
165 GR. SIE SPBT	Hodgdon	BL-C(2)	.308"	3.300"	46.0	2608	41,200 CUP	51.0	2805	49,800 CUP
165 GR. SIE SPBT	IMR	IMR 4895	.308"	3.300"	49.0	2768	50,500 PSI	52.0	2888	57,200 PSI
165 GR. SIE SPBT	Hodgdon	H335	.308"	3.300"	42.0	2515	38,500 CUP	47.0	2749	49,300 CUP
165 GR. SIE SPBT	Hodgdon	H4895	.308"	3.300"	43.0	2607	41,100 CUP	47.5	2782	49,000 CUP
165 GR. SIE SPBT	IMR	IMR 8208 XBR	.308"	3.300"	44.6	2667	55,100 PSI	46.5	2728	58,000 PSI
165 GR. SIE SPBT	IMR	IMR 3031	.308"	3.300"	45.0	2707	51,000 PSI	48.0	2825	57,500 PSI
165 GR. SIE SPBT	Hodgdon	Benchmark	.308"	3.300"	45.0	2686	45,600 CUP	47.7	2795	49,300 CUP

168 GR. HDY HPBT	Hodgdon	Hybrid 100V	.308"	3.230"	52.0	2645	50,400 PSI	57.0C	2817	57,400 PSI
168 GR. HDY HPBT	Hodgdon	H4350	.308"	3.230"	55.0	2695	40,400 CUP	59.0	2897	48,100 CUP
168 GR. HDY HPBT	Hodgdon	H414	.308"	3.230"	53.0	2686	40,300 CUP	56.5	2839	49,700 CUP
168 GR. HDY HPBT	IMR	IMR 4350	.308"	3.230"	54.0	2720	48,500 PSI	58.0C	2903	57,800 PSI
168 GR. HDY HPBT	Winchester	760	.308"	3.230"	53.0	2686	40,300 CUP	56.5	2839	49,700 CUP
168 GR. HDY HPBT	IMR	IMR 4007 SSC	.308"	3.230"	49.0	2574	46,400 PSI	53.5	2798	57,900 PSI
168 GR. HDY HPBT	Hodgdon	H380	.308"	3.230"	51.0	2648	42,800 CUP	56.5	2859	49,700 CUP
168 GR. HDY HPBT	Hodgdon	Varget	.308"	3.230"	47.0	2710	42,700 CUP	50.5	2859	49,200 CUP
168 GR. HDY HPBT	IMR	IMR 4320	.308"	3.230"	46.0	2646	48,900 PSI	49.7	2816	58,400 PSI
168 GR. HDY HPBT	IMR	IMR 4064	.308"	3.230"	47.0	2660	46,800 PSI	50.8	2850	57,900 PSI
168 GR. HDY HPBT	Hodgdon	BL-C(2)	.308"	3.230"	46.0	2555	39,100 CUP	51.0	2767	49,200 CUP
168 GR. HDY HPBT	IMR	IMR 4895	.308"	3.230"	48.0	2719	49,900 PSI	51.2	2859	58,200 PSI
168 GR. HDY HPBT	Hodgdon	H335	.308"	3.230"	42.0	2459	39,900 CUP	46.5	2656	49,500 CUP
168 GR. HDY HPBT	Hodgdon	H4895	.308"	3.230"	43.0	2574	41,200 CUP	47.5	2789	50,000 CUP
168 GR. HDY HPBT	IMR	IMR 8208 XBR	.308"	3.230"	45.1	2661	54,800 PSI	48.0	2748	58,700 PSI
168 GR. HDY HPBT	Hodgdon	Benchmark	.308"	3.230"	44.0	2614	42,900 CUP	47.2	2760	49,400 CUP
175 GR. SIE HPBT	Hodgdon	Suprform	.308"	3.300"	53.0	2609	42,600 PSI	58.7	2881	59,400 PSI
175 GR. SIE HPBT	Hodgdon	H4831	.308"	3.300"	57.0	2535	38,300 CUP	61.5C	2719	44,400 CUP
175 GR. SIE HPBT	Hodgdon	Hybrid 100V	.308"	3.300"	50.0	2543	47,400 PSI	55.0C	2757	57,600 PSI
175 GR. SIE HPBT	IMR	IMR 4831	.308"	3.300"	54.0	2615	48,100 PSI	57.5C	2781	56,900 PSI
175 GR. SIE HPBT	Hodgdon	H4350	.308"	3.300"	55.0	2661	42,100 CUP	59.0	2842	48,700 CUP
175 GR. SIE HPBT	Hodgdon	H414	.308"	3.300"	52.5	2622	40,700 CUP	56.2	2794	49,200 CUP
175 GR. SIE HPBT	IMR	IMR 4350	.308"	3.300"	52.0	2546	45,000 PSI	57.0C	2780	57,100 PSI
175 GR. SIE HPBT	Winchester	760	.308"	3.300"	52.5	2622	40,700 CUP	56.2	2794	49,200 CUP
175 GR. SIE HPBT	IMR	IMR 4007 SSC	.308"	3.300"	48.0	2526	46,700 PSI	53.0	2755	58,900 PSI
175 GR. SIE HPBT	Hodgdon	H380	.308"	3.300"	49.5	2564	43,400 CUP	53.0	2704	48,400 CUP
175 GR. SIE HPBT	Hodgdon	Varget	.308"	3.300"	45.0	2551	41,700 CUP	48.0	2694	49,000 CUP
175 GR. SIE HPBT	IMR	IMR 4320	.308"	3.300"	45.5	2533	48,000 PSI	48.5	2697	58,200 PSI
175 GR. SIE HPBT	IMR	IMR 4064	.308"	3.300"	46.5	2626	52,000 PSI	49.5	2741	58,000 PSI
175 GR. SIE HPBT	Hodgdon	BL-C(2)	.308"	3.300"	48.5	2644	44,100 CUP	51.5	2765	48,700 CUP
175 GR. SIE HPBT	IMR	IMR 4895	.308"	3.300"	46.0	2619	51,600 PSI	49.0	2741	58,100 PSI
175 GR. SIE HPBT	Hodgdon	H335	.308"	3.300"	43.0	2566	46,600 CUP	45.7	2667	49,400 CUP
175 GR. SIE HPBT	Hodgdon	H4895	.308"	3.300"	43.8	2584	44,100 CUP	46.7	2700	49,000 CUP
180 GR. SIE SPBT	Winchester	Supreme 780	.308"	3.300"	57.3	2545	47,300 PSI	61.0	2673	54,100 PSI
180 GR. SIE SPBT	Hodgdon	Suprform	.308"	3.300"	54.0	2628	46,200 PSI	59.7	2840	57,600 PSI
180 GR. SIE SPBT	Hodgdon	H4831	.308"	3.300"	54.0	2447	34,700 CUP	60.0C	2710	44,300 CUP
180 GR. SIE SPBT	Hodgdon	Hybrid 100V	.308"	3.300"	53.0	2585	47,000 PSI	57.0C	2742	55,200 PSI
180 GR. SIE SPBT	IMR	IMR 4831	.308"	3.300"	53.0	2563	47,300 PSI	56.8C	2749	57,100 PSI
180 GR. SIE SPBT	Hodgdon	H4350	.308"	3.300"	52.0	2543	37,800 CUP	57.5	2798	49,300 CUP

180 GR. SIE SPBT	Hodgdon	H414	.308"	3.300"	50.0	2528	39,200 CUP	55.5	2743	48,700 CUP
180 GR. SIE SPBT	IMR	IMR 4350	.308"	3.300"	53.0	2586	48,300 PSI	56.5C	2752	57,200 PSI
180 GR. SIE SPBT	Winchester	760	.308"	3.300"	50.0	2528	39,200 CUP	55.5	2743	48,700 CUP
180 GR. SIE SPBT	IMR	IMR 4007 SSC	.308"	3.300"	52.7	2698	55,600 PSI	53.5	2732	58,100 PSI
180 GR. SIE SPBT	Hodgdon	H380	.308"	3.300"	48.0	2490	39,900 CUP	53.0	2682	48,700 CUP
180 GR. SIE SPBT	Hodgdon	Varget	.308"	3.300"	44.0	2533	41,900 CUP	47.0	2668	50,000 CUP
180 GR. SIE SPBT	IMR	IMR 4320	.308"	3.300"	45.0	2525	49,900 PSI	47.8	2661	58,000 PSI
180 GR. SIE SPBT	IMR	IMR 4064	.308"	3.300"	45.5	2550	48,900 PSI	48.7	2700	58,200 PSI
180 GR. SIE SPBT	Hodgdon	BL-C(2)	.308"	3.300"	44.0	2456	39,200 CUP	48.5	2634	48,100 CUP
180 GR. SIE SPBT	IMR	IMR 4895	.308"	3.300"	45.0	2555	49,500 PSI	48.0	2680	56,800 PSI
180 GR. SIE SPBT	Hodgdon	H335	.308"	3.300"	42.0	2455	41,900 CUP	46.0	2621	49,200 CUP
180 GR. SIE SPBT	Hodgdon	H4895	.308"	3.300"	41.0	2427	38,100 CUP	46.0	2638	48,800 CUP
180 GR. SIE SPBT	Hodgdon	Benchmark	.308"	3.300"	43.0	2550	45,600 CUP	46.0	2660	49,000 CUP
190 GR. HDY BTSP	IMR	IMR 7828	.308"	3.220"	55.0	2429	46,200 PSI	59.8C*	2646	58,700 PSI
190 GR. HDY BTSP	Winchester	Supreme 780	.308"	3.220"	56.2	2512	52,300 PSI	59.8	2628	59,000 PSI
190 GR. HDY BTSP	Hodgdon	H4831	.308"	3.220"	57.0	2514	44,100 CUP	61.0C	2668	50,000 CUP
190 GR. HDY BTSP	Hodgdon	Hybrid 100V	.308"	3.220"	49.0	2456	49,300 PSI	53.5C	2639	58,300 PSI
190 GR. HDY BTSP	IMR	IMR 4831	.308	3.220"	51.0	2445	46,300 PSI	55.0C	2639	57,000 PSI
190 GR. HDY BTSP	Hodgdon	H4350	.308"	3.220"	51.0	2451	39,500 CUP	56.5	2692	49,200 CUP
190 GR. HDY BTSP	Hodgdon	H414	.308"	3.220"	48.0	2398	39,000 CUP	53.0	2640	49,500 CUP
190 GR. HDY BTSP	IMR	IMR 4350	.308"	3.220"	51.0	2466	47,200 PSI	54.5	2647	58,500 PSI
190 GR. HDY BTSP	Winchester	760	.308"	3.220"	48.0	2398	49,000 CUP	53.0	2640	49,500 CUP
190 GR. HDY BTSP	IMR	IMR 4007 SSC	.308"	3.220"	46.0	2389	46,700 PSI	50.5	2598	58,100 PSI
190 GR. HDY BTSP	Hodgdon	H380	.308"	3.220"	47.0	2369	40,900 CUP	51.5	2555	48,700 CUP
190 GR. HDY BTSP	Hodgdon	Varget	.308"	3.220"	43.5	2450	41,800 CUP	46.5	2608	49,700 CUP
190 GR. HDY BTSP	IMR	IMR 4064	.308"	3.220"	45.0	2485	50,900 PSI	47.7	2593	57,600 PSI
190 GR. HDY BTSP	Hodgdon	BL-C(2)	.308"	3.220"	43.0	2312	39,200 CUP	47.0	2510	48,600 CUP
190 GR. HDY BTSP	Hodgdon	H335	.308"	3.220"	40.0	2271	40,200 CUP	44.0	2465	48,400 CUP
190 GR. HDY BTSP	Hodgdon	H4895	.308"	3.220"	41.0	2380	41,400 CUP	45.5	2525	48,000 CUP
200 GR. NOS AB	Hodgdon	H1000	.308"	3.300"	57.0	2329	35,800 CUP	61.0C	2487	42,200 CUP
200 GR. NOS AB	IMR	IMR 7828	.308"	3.300"	53.0	2323	45,000 PSI	58.0C*	2559	58,100 PSI
200 GR. NOS AB	Winchester	Supreme 780	.308"	3.300"	53.6	2367	46,600 PSI	57.0	2555	58,500 PSI
200 GR. NOS AB	Hodgdon	H4831	.308"	3.300"	55.0	2427	42,100 CUP	59.0C	2586	49,300 CUP
200 GR. NOS AB	Hodgdon	Hybrid 100V	.308"	3.300"	48.0	2384	50,000 PSI	52.0C	2542	57,900 PSI
200 GR. NOS AB	IMR	IMR 4831	.308"	3.300"	51.0	2375	46,600 PSI	54.2C	2550	56,800 PSI
200 GR. NOS AB	Hodgdon	H4350	.308"	3.300"	50.0	2412	40,400 CUP	53.7	2580	48,400 CUP
200 GR. NOS AB	Hodgdon	H414	.308"	3.300"	48.0	2413	42,900 CUP	51.5	2579	49,400 CUP
200 GR. NOS AB	IMR	IMR 4350	.308"	3.300"	50.0	2364	45,900 PSI	53.5C	2550	57,200 PSI
200 GR. NOS AB	Winchester	760	.308"	3.300"	48.0	2413	42,900 CUP	51.5	2579	49,400 CUP
200 GR. NOS AB	IMR	IMR 4007 SSC	.308"	3.300"	45.0	2320	47,700 PSI	49.0	2506	58,500 PSI

200 GR. NOS AB	Hodgdon	H380	.308"	3.300"	45.5	2325	42,300 CUP	48.5	2463	48,800 CUP
200 GR. NOS AB	Hodgdon	Varget	.308"	3.300"	42.0	2337	41,900 CUP	47.0	2505	49,100 CUP
200 GR. NOS AB	IMR	IMR 4064	.308"	3.300"	43.0	2292	44,600 PSI	46.0	2469	57,400 PSI
200 GR. NOS AB	Hodgdon	H4895	.308"	3.300"	41.0	2355	43,700 CUP	44.0	2474	49,500 CUP
200 GR. SPR SP	Hodgdon	H1000	.308"	3.230"	55.0	2267	33,600 CUP	61.0C	2510	44,400 CUP
200 GR. SPR SP	Winchester	Supreme 780	.308"	3.230"	55.0	2440	51,000 PSI	58.5	2565	58,500 PSI
200 GR. SPR SP	Hodgdon	H4831	.308"	3.230"	54.0	2436	43,200 CUP	57.5C	2577	49,400 CUP
200 GR. SPR SP	Hodgdon	Hybrid 100V	.308"	3.230"	47.0	2335	48,100 PSI	51.5C	2532	58,600 PSI
200 GR. SPR SP	Hodgdon	H4350	.308"	3.230"	50.0	2431	44,500 CUP	53.0	2544	49,100 CUP
200 GR. SPR SP	Hodgdon	H414	.308"	3.230"	47.0	2351	40,700 CUP	52.0	2551	49,100 CUP
200 GR. SPR SP	IMR	IMR 4007 SSC	.308"	3.230"	45.0	2314	47,500 PSI	49.0	2497	57,800 PSI
200 GR. SPR SP	Hodgdon	H380	.308"	3.230"	44.0	2231	41,700 CUP	48.0	2395	49,600 CUP
200 GR. SPR SP	Hodgdon	Varget	.308"	3.230"	42.5	2373	44,700 CUP	45.5	2501	49,600 CUP
200 GR. SPR SP	Hodgdon	H4895	.308"	3.230"	39.0	2246	40,700 CUP	43.5	2421	49,200 CUP
208 GR. HDY A-MAX	IMR	IMR 7828	.308"	3.285"	52.2	2239	43,600 PSI	57.0C	2442	53,100 PSI
208 GR. HDY A-MAX	Winchester	Supreme 780	.308"	3.285"	52.2	2314	46,900 PSI	56.8	2476	54,000 PSI
208 GR. HDY A-MAX	Hodgdon	H4831	.308"	3.285"	52.1	2301	47,100 PSI	58.0C	2511	58,700 PSI
208 GR. HDY A-MAX	Hodgdon	Hybrid 100V	.308"	3.285"	47.3	2292	45,100 PSI	52.0C	2519	58,300 PSI
208 GR. HDY A-MAX	IMR	IMR 4831	.308"	3.285"	49.9	2291	46,100 PSI	54.9C	2538	59,500 PSI
208 GR. HDY A-MAX	Hodgdon	H4350	.308"	3.285"	47.6	2303	47,600 PSI	52.4	2499	59,600 PSI
208 GR. HDY A-MAX	Hodgdon	H414	.308"	3.285"	46.1	2307	49,300 PSI	49.6	2467	58,300 PSI
208 GR. HDY A-MAX	IMR	IMR 4350	.308"	3.285"	47.9	2259	45,000 PSI	52.7C	2503	58,600 PSI
208 GR. HDY A-MAX	Winchester	760	.308"	3.285"	46.1	2307	49,300 PSI	49.6	2467	58,300 PSI
208 GR. HDY A-MAX	IMR	IMR 4007 SSC	.308"	3.285"	46.4	2269	46,000 PSI	51.0	2498	60,000 PSI
208 GR. HDY A-MAX	Hodgdon	H380	.308"	3.285"	45.5	2231	45,600 PSI	49.5	2427	57,300 PSI
208 GR. HDY A-MAX	Hodgdon	Varget	.308"	3.285"	40.9	2226	47,900 PSI	45.0	2415	59,200 PSI
208 GR. HDY A-MAX	IMR	IMR 4064	.308"	3.285"	42.5	2250	47,400 PSI	45.5	2404	57,000 PSI
208 GR. HDY A-MAX	Hodgdon	H4895	.308"	3.285"	38.9	2203	48,700 PSI	43.2	2362	57,400 PSI
220 GR. HDY JRN	Hodgdon	H1000	.308"	3.230"	58.0	2293	36,500 CUP	61.0C	2412	43,600 CUP
220 GR. HDY JRN	IMR	IMR 7828	.308"	3.230"	53.0	2288	48,600 PSI	58.0	2476	59,700 PSI
220 GR. HDY JRN	Winchester	Supreme 780	.308"	3.230"	53.6	2310	47,800 PSI	57.0	2458	57,200 PSI
220 GR. HDY JRN	Hodgdon	H4831	.308"	3.230"	54.0	2342	43,300 CUP	57.5C	2458	48,600 CUP
220 GR. HDY JRN	Hodgdon	Hybrid 100V	.308"	3.230"	47.0	2258	48,100 PSI	52.0C	2448	58,600 PSI
220 GR. HDY JRN	IMR	IMR 4831	.308"	3.230"	50.0	2275	47,300 PSI	54.0	2438	57,200 PSI
220 GR. HDY JRN	Hodgdon	H4350	.308"	3.230"	50.0	2318	43,400 CUP	53.0	2435	49,200 CUP
220 GR. HDY JRN	Hodgdon	H414	.308"	3.230"	47.0	2215	39,000 CUP	52.0	2408	49,500 CUP
220 GR. HDY JRN	IMR	IMR 4350	.308"	3.230"	49.0	2287	49,500 PSI	52.5	2425	57,300 PSI
220 GR. HDY JRN	Winchester	760	.308"	3.230"	47.0	2215	39,000 CUP	52.0	2408	49,500 CUP
220 GR. HDY JRN	Hodgdon	Varget	.308"	3.230"	42.0	2279	44,000 CUP	45.0	2382	49,400 CUP

220 GR. HDY JRN	IMR	IMR 4064	.308"	3.230"	43.0	2241	52,200 PSI	45.5	2325	56,700 PSI

Cartridge: 300 H & H Magnum Load Type: Rifle					Starting Loads			Maximum Loads		
Bullet Weight (Gr.)	Manufacturer	Powder	Bullet Diam.	C.O.L.	Grs.	Vel. (ft/s)	Pressure	Grs.	Vel. (ft/s)	Pressure
130 GR. SPR HP	Hodgdon	H4831	.308"	3.440"	75.0	3186		81.0	3362	
130 GR. SPR HP	Hodgdon	H4350	.308"	3.440"	68.0	3142		72.0	3394	
130 GR. SPR HP	Hodgdon	H414	.308"	3.440"	62.0	3153		67.0	3301	
150 GR. HDY SP	Hodgdon	H4831	.308"	3.560"	72.0	3096		78.0	3313	
150 GR. HDY SP	IMR	IMR 4831	.308"	3.560"				75.5C	3200	53,100 CUP
150 GR. HDY SP	Hodgdon	H4350	.308"	3.560"	67.0	2998		71.0	3202	
150 GR. HDY SP	Hodgdon	H414	.308"	3.560"	60.0	2985		65.0	3247	
150 GR. HDY SP	IMR	IMR 4350	.308"	3.560"				73.0	3215	53,600 CUP
150 GR. HDY SP	IMR	IMR 4064	.308"	3.560"				64.0	3170	53,800 CUP
150 GR. HDY SP	IMR	SR 4759	.308"	3.560"				40.0	2455	53,600 CUP
165 GR. NOS PART	Hodgdon	H4831	.308"	3.560"	71.0	2949		77.0	3099	
165 GR. NOS PART	Hodgdon	H4350	.308"	3.560"	66.0	3018		69.0	3164	
165 GR. NOS PART	Hodgdon	H414	.308"	3.560"	59.0	2899		63.0	3046	
180 GR. SIE SPBT	IMR	IMR 4831	.308"	3.560"				73.0C	3035	53,500 CUP
180 GR. SIE SPBT	IMR	IMR 4350	.308"	3.560"				69.0	2990	54,000 CUP
200 GR. SIE HPBT	Hodgdon	H4831	.308"	3.655"	67.0	2737		72.0	2932	
200 GR. SIE HPBT	Hodgdon	H4350	.308"	3.655"	62.0	2747		66.0	2909	
200 GR. SIE HPBT	Hodgdon	H414	.308"	3.655"	52.0	2423		56.0	2649	
220 GR. HDY RN	Hodgdon	H4831	.308"	3.580"	65.0	2655		70.0	2714	
220 GR. HDY RN	IMR	IMR 4831	.308"	3.580"				67.0	2710	54,000 CUP
220 GR. HDY RN	Hodgdon	H4350	.308"	3.580"	60.0	2595		64.0	2717	
220 GR. HDY RN	IMR	IMR 4350	.308"	3.580"				65.0	2695	54,000 CUP
250 GR. BAR RN	Hodgdon	H4831	.308"	3.580"	63.0	2372		67.0	2563	
250 GR. BAR RN	Hodgdon	H4350	.308"	3.580"	59.0	2344		62.0	2493	

Cartridge: 308 Norma Magnum Load Type: Rifle					Starting Loads			Maximum Loads		
Bullet Weight (Gr.)	Manufacturer	Powder	Bullet Diam.	C.O.L.	Grs.	Vel. (ft/s)	Pressure	Grs.	Vel. (ft/s)	Pressure
100 GR. SPR RN SP	Hodgdon	H414	.308"	2.870"				55.0	2928	
100 GR. SPR RN SP	Hodgdon	H380	.308"	2.870"				54.0	3089	
100 GR. SPR RN SP	Hodgdon	H4895	.308"	2.870"				52.0	2997	
110 GR. SIE HP	Hodgdon	H4831	.308"	3.160"	73.0	3229	37,800 CUP	80.0	3563	50,100 CUP
110 GR. SIE HP	Hodgdon	H4350	.308"	3.160"	72.0	3202	39,400 CUP	77.0	3506	51,200 CUP
110 GR. SIE HP	Hodgdon	H414	.308"	3.160"	68.0	3508	45,500 CUP	74.0	3687	52,000 CUP
110 GR. SIE HP	Hodgdon	H380	.308"	3.160"	65.5	3452	45,500 CUP	71.0	3609	51,100 CUP

Bullet Weight (Gr.)	Manufacturer	Powder	Bullet Diam.	C.O.L.	Grs.	Vel. (ft/s)	Pressure	Grs.	Vel. (ft/s)	Pressure
110 GR. SIE HP	Hodgdon	H4895	.308"	3.160"	59.0	3339	41,400 CUP	64.0	3554	53,000 CUP
130 GR. HDY SP	Hodgdon	H1000	.308"	3.275"	80.0	3211	44,400 CUP	84.0	3333	46,400 CUP
130 GR. HDY SP	Hodgdon	H4831	.308"	3.275"	73.0	3201	40,800 CUP	79.0	3302	45,900 CUP
130 GR. HDY SP	Hodgdon	H4350	.308"	3.275"	71.0	3139	42,400 CUP	74.0	3292	51,400 CUP
130 GR. HDY SP	Hodgdon	H414	.308"	3.275"	66.0	3211	46,800 CUP	72.0	3449	52,300 CUP
130 GR. HDY SP	Hodgdon	H380	.308"	3.275"	64.5	3263	49,200 CUP	70.0	3415	50,900 CUP
130 GR. HDY SP	Hodgdon	H4895	.308"	3.275"	59.0	3166	42,600 CUP	64.0	3388	50,500 CUP
150 GR. NOS PART	Hodgdon	H1000	.308"	3.300"	79.0	3090	46,600 CUP	83.0	3279	50,800 CUP
150 GR. NOS PART	Hodgdon	H4831	.308"	3.300"	70.0	3157	47,800 CUP	76.0	3258	51,900 CUP
150 GR. NOS PART	Hodgdon	H4350	.308"	3.300"	69.0	2914	43,100 CUP	73.0	3188	51,200 CUP
150 GR. NOS PART	Hodgdon	H414	.308"	3.300"	62.5	3007	47,300 CUP	68.0	3226	52,400 CUP
150 GR. NOS PART	Hodgdon	H380	.308"	3.300"	63.5	3028	48,200 CUP	68.0	3221	52,400 CUP
150 GR. NOS PART	Hodgdon	H4895	.308"	3.300"	57.0	2940	42,000 CUP	62.0	3192	54,700 CUP
168 GR. SIE HPBT	Hodgdon	H1000	.308"	3.250"	75.0	2939	47,100 CUP	79.0	3123	52,000 CUP
168 GR. SIE HPBT	Hodgdon	H4831	.308"	3.250"	69.0	2944	43,800 CUP	75.0	3140	52,300 CUP
168 GR. SIE HPBT	Hodgdon	H4350	.308"	3.250"	68.0	2880	42,000 CUP	72.0	3114	51,000 CUP
168 GR. SIE HPBT	Hodgdon	H414	.308"	3.250"	61.0	2884	46,400 CUP	67.0	3087	54,000 CUP
168 GR. SIE HPBT	Hodgdon	H380	.308"	3.250"	62.0	2995	50,100 CUP	67.0	3079	52,100 CUP
168 GR. SIE HPBT	Hodgdon	H4895	.308"	3.250"	56.0	2859	48,200 CUP	61.0	3059	52,100 CUP
180 GR. HDY SP	Hodgdon	H1000	.308"	3.345"	72.0	2769	45,900 CUP	76.0	2940	51,900 CUP
180 GR. HDY SP	Hodgdon	H4831	.308"	3.345"	67.0	2865	43,200 CUP	73.0	3022	52,300 CUP
180 GR. HDY SP	Hodgdon	H4350	.308"	3.345"	65.0	2770	43,000 CUP	69.0	2999	52,800 CUP
180 GR. HDY SP	Hodgdon	H414	.308"	3.345"	58.0	2772	50,500 CUP	63.0	2908	54,300 CUP
180 GR. HDY SP	Hodgdon	H380	.308"	3.345"	58.0	2746	48,600 CUP	63.0	2847	51,400 CUP
180 GR. HDY SP	Hodgdon	H4895	.308"	3.345"	54.0	2732	48,200 CUP	59.0	2898	53,400 CUP
190 GR. HDY BTSP	Hodgdon	H1000	.308"	3.435"	70.0	2711	45,500 CUP	74.0	2891	51,100 CUP
200 GR. NOS PART	Hodgdon	H1000	.308"	3.400"	69.0	2674	47,400 CUP	73.0	2859	54,500 CUP
200 GR. NOS PART	Hodgdon	H4831	.308"	3.400"	64.5	2662	44,400 CUP	70.0	2889	52,700 CUP
200 GR. NOS PART	Hodgdon	H4350	.308"	3.400"	63.0	2740	44,700 CUP	67.0	2851	52,100 CUP
220 GR. HDY RN	Hodgdon	H1000	.308"	3.360"	66.0	2449	46,000 CUP	70.0	2672	52,000 CUP
220 GR. HDY RN	Hodgdon	H4831	.308"	3.360"	63.0	2437	42,600 CUP	68.0	2697	52,700 CUP
220 GR. HDY RN	Hodgdon	H4350	.308"	3.360"	61.0	2519	42,200 CUP	65.0	2707	52,800 CUP

Cartridge: 300 Ruger Compact Magnum
Load Type: Rifle

Bullet Weight (Gr.)	Manufacturer	Powder	Bullet Diam.	C.O.L.	Starting Loads			Maximum Loads		
					Grs.	Vel. (ft/s)	Pressure	Grs.	Vel. (ft/s)	Pressure
135 GR. SIE HPBT	Hodgdon	Hybrid 100V	.308"	2.820"	60.8	3081	50,300 PSI	64.0C	3224	56,200 PSI
135 GR. SIE HPBT	IMR	IMR 4007 SSC	.308"	2.820"	59.9	3022	49,300 PSI	63.7	3287	63,400 PSI
135 GR. SIE HPBT	Hodgdon	Varget	.308"	2.820"	55.2	3064	51,300 PSI	58.7	3267	63,200 PSI

135 GR. SIE HPBT	IMR	IMR 4064	.308"	2.820"	53.9	3076	51,200 PSI	57.3	3279	62,700 PSI
135 GR. SIE HPBT	IMR	IMR 4895	.308"	2.820"	54.5	3114	53,700 PSI	58.0	3268	61,000 PSI
135 GR. SIE HPBT	Hodgdon	H4895	.308"	2.820"	54.0	3090	50,900 PSI	57.4	3259	60,000 PSI
135 GR. SIE HPBT	IMR	IMR 3031	.308"	2.820"	51.3	3048	50,800 PSI	54.5	3243	62,600 PSI
150 GR. HDY IB	Hodgdon	Suprform	.308"	2.830"	62.0	3001	46,900 PSI	67.0C	3254	59,000 PSI
150 GR. HDY IB	Hodgdon	Hybrid 100V	.308"	2.830"	59.2	2965	51,300 PSI	63.0C	3131	58,800 PSI
150 GR. HDY IB	Hodgdon	H4350	.308"	2.830"	59.1	2901	50,300 PSI	63.5C	3118	61,800 PSI
150 GR. HDY IB	Hodgdon	H414	.308"	2.830"	58.8	2975	53,000 PSI	62.5	3121	61,800 PSI
150 GR. HDY IB	IMR	IMR 4350	.308"	2.830"	59.5	2919	52,600 PSI	63.0C	3081	60,800 PSI
150 GR. HDY IB	Winchester	760	.308"	2.830"	58.8	2975	53,000 PSI	62.5	3121	61,800 PSI
150 GR. HDY IB	IMR	IMR 4007 SSC	.308"	2.830"	57.9	2900	50,500 PSI	61.6	3121	63,200 PSI
150 GR. HDY IB	Hodgdon	H380	.308"	2.830"	58.3	2969	55,100 PSI	62.0	3123	62,400 PSI
150 GR. HDY IB	Hodgdon	Varget	.308"	2.830"	53.0	2918	53,600 PSI	56.4	3086	62,700 PSI
150 GR. HDY IB	IMR	IMR 4064	.308"	2.830"	52.8	2928	52,200 PSI	56.2	3114	62,900 PSI
150 GR. HDY IB	Winchester	748	.308"	2.830"	54.2	2920	52,100 PSI	57.7	3095	61,300 PSI
150 GR. HDY IB	IMR	IMR 4895	.308"	2.830"	52.6	2909	51,700 PSI	56.0	3081	60,600 PSI
150 GR. HDY IB	Hodgdon	H4895	.308"	2.830"	51.7	2922	52,000 PSI	55.0	3091	62,500 PSI
155 GR. NOS HPBT	Hodgdon	Suprform	.308"	2.830"	63.0	3034	49,600 PSI	67.5C	3250	60,800 PSI
155 GR. NOS HPBT	Hodgdon	Hybrid 100V	.308"	2.830"	59.0	2955	51,800 PSI	63.0C	3141	61,000 PSI
155 GR. NOS HPBT	Hodgdon	H4350	.308"	2.830"	58.6	2819	47,100 PSI	62.3	3062	60,800 PSI
155 GR. NOS HPBT	Hodgdon	H414	.308"	2.830"	59.0	2912	50,700 PSI	62.5	3066	59,200 PSI
155 GR. NOS HPBT	IMR	IMR 4350	.308"	2.830"	59.2	2889	51,800 PSI	63.0C	3085	63,100 PSI
155 GR. NOS HPBT	Winchester	760	.308"	2.830"	59.0	2912	50,700 PSI	62.5	3066	59,200 PSI
155 GR. NOS HPBT	IMR	IMR 4007 SSC	.308"	2.830"	57.1	2831	48,500 PSI	60.7	3074	62,100 PSI
155 GR. NOS HPBT	Hodgdon	H380	.308"	2.830"	57.8	2878	51,200 PSI	61.5	3068	61,600 PSI
155 GR. NOS HPBT	Hodgdon	Varget	.308"	2.830"	52.6	2896	53,800 PSI	56.0	3041	61,900 PSI
155 GR. NOS HPBT	IMR	IMR 4064	.308"	2.830"	52.0	2865	50,400 PSI	55.3	3069	62,900 PSI
155 GR. NOS HPBT	Winchester	748	.308"	2.830"	54.0	2888	51,600 PSI	57.5	3072	62,200 PSI
155 GR. NOS HPBT	IMR	IMR 4895	.308"	2.830"	51.7	2856	50,000 PSI	55.0	3047	62,000 PSI
155 GR. NOS HPBT	Hodgdon	H4895	.308"	2.830"	52.5	2929	54,700 PSI	55.0	3066	62,300 PSI
165 GR. BAR TSX	Hodgdon	Suprform	.308"	2.800"	60.0	2900	49,200 PSI	65.0C	3126	60,600 PSI
165 GR. BAR TSX	Hodgdon	Hybrid 100V	.308"	2.800"	57.3	2807	50,700 PSI	61.0C	2962	57,900 PSI
165 GR. BAR TSX	Hodgdon	H4350	.308"	2.800"	58.8	2843	55,600 PSI	62.5C	2979	62,700 PSI
165 GR. BAR TSX	Hodgdon	H414	.308"	2.800"	56.0	2832	55,300 PSI	59.5	2958	62,200 PSI
165 GR. BAR TSX	IMR	IMR 4350	.308"	2.800"	59.2	2826	55,900 PSI	63.0C	2967	62,300 PSI
165 GR. BAR TSX	Winchester	760	.308"	2.800"	56.0	2832	55,300 PSI	59.5	2958	62,200 PSI
165 GR. BAR TSX	IMR	IMR 4007 SSC	.308"	2.800"	56.9	2786	53,200 PSI	60.5C	2976	63,300 PSI
165 GR. BAR TSX	Hodgdon	H380	.308"	2.800"	55.5	2772	52,800 PSI	59.0	2951	62,900 PSI
165 GR. BAR TSX	Hodgdon	Varget	.308"	2.800"	50.1	2718	53,100 PSI	54.2	2908	62,600 PSI
165 GR. BAR TSX	IMR	IMR 4064	.308"	2.800"	50.8	2775	53,900 PSI	54.0	2920	61,400 PSI

165 GR. BAR TSX	Winchester	748	.308"	2.800"	51.0	2745	52,400 PSI	54.3	2921	62,500 PSI
165 GR. BAR TSX	IMR	IMR 4895	.308"	2.800"	50.8	2741	51,900 PSI	54.0	2902	60,700 PSI
165 GR. BAR TSX	Hodgdon	H4895	.308"	2.800"	49.8	2785	55,900 PSI	53.0	2917	62,700 PSI
168 GR. SIE HPBT	Hodgdon	Suprform	.308"	2.820"	61.0	2919	51,900 PSI	65.5C	3125	63,300 PSI
168 GR. SIE HPBT	Hodgdon	Hybrid 100V	.308"	2.820"	57.0	2810	50,600 PSI	62.0C	3039	62,600 PSI
168 GR. SIE HPBT	IMR	IMR 4831	.308"	2.820"	59.5	2731	47,300 PSI	64.0C	2987	61,000 PSI
168 GR. SIE HPBT	Hodgdon	H4350	.308"	2.820"	57.3	2736	47,900 PSI	61.0	2947	61,200 PSI
168 GR. SIE HPBT	Hodgdon	H414	.308"	2.820"	56.4	2782	50,900 PSI	60.0	2986	63,100 PSI
168 GR. SIE HPBT	IMR	IMR 4350	.308"	2.820"	57.4	2737	50,100 PSI	61.0C	2935	61,000 PSI
168 GR. SIE HPBT	Winchester	760	.308"	2.820"	56.4	2782	50,900 PSI	60.0	2986	63,100 PSI
168 GR. SIE HPBT	IMR	IMR 4007 SSC	.308"	2.820"	56.4	2772	51,100 PSI	60.0	2964	62,400 PSI
168 GR. SIE HPBT	Hodgdon	H380	.308"	2.820"	55.8	2761	51,900 PSI	59.4	2918	60,400 PSI
168 GR. SIE HPBT	Hodgdon	Varget	.308"	2.820"	51.0	2755	52,900 PSI	54.3	2890	60,500 PSI
168 GR. SIE HPBT	IMR	IMR 4064	.308"	2.820"	50.5	2725	49,400 PSI	53.7	2914	61,700 PSI
168 GR. SIE HPBT	Winchester	748	.308"	2.820"	51.7	2745	51,900 PSI	55.0	2902	60,500 PSI
168 GR. SIE HPBT	IMR	IMR 4895	.308"	2.820"	50.9	2763	52,600 PSI	54.1	2912	60,800 PSI
168 GR. SIE HPBT	Hodgdon	H4895	.308"	2.820"	50.3	2803	56,600 PSI	53.5	2907	61,700 PSI
178 GR. HDY A-MAX	Hodgdon	Hybrid 100V	.308"	2.840"	56.1	2744	51,500 PSI	61.0C	2916	59,500 PSI
178 GR. HDY A-MAX	IMR	IMR 4831	.308"	2.840"	58.0	2667	48,200 PSI	63.0C	2898	59,900 PSI
178 GR. HDY A-MAX	Hodgdon	H4350	.308"	2.840"	56.9	2729	53,600 PSI	60.5C	2886	62,200 PSI
178 GR. HDY A-MAX	Hodgdon	H414	.308"	2.840"	55.7	2691	51,400 PSI	59.2	2859	61,000 PSI
178 GR. HDY A-MAX	IMR	IMR 4350	.308"	2.840"	56.5	2703	51,800 PSI	61.3C	2910	62,900 PSI
178 GR. HDY A-MAX	Winchester	760	.308"	2.840"	55.7	2691	51,400 PSI	59.2	2859	61,000 PSI
178 GR. HDY A-MAX	IMR	IMR 4007 SSC	.308"	2.840"	55.6	2733	53,900 PSI	59.2	2896	62,200 PSI
178 GR. HDY A-MAX	Hodgdon	H380	.308"	2.840"	54.7	2709	55,300 PSI	58.2	2836	61,800 PSI
178 GR. HDY A-MAX	Hodgdon	Varget	.308"	2.840"	50.0	2701	55,500 PSI	53.2	2820	62,300 PSI
178 GR. HDY A-MAX	IMR	IMR 4064	.308"	2.840"	49.5	2676	54,100 PSI	52.7	2824	62,900 PSI
178 GR. HDY A-MAX	Winchester	748	.308"	2.840"	51.0	2671	52,600 PSI	54.3	2820	62,400 PSI
178 GR. HDY A-MAX	IMR	IMR 4895	.308"	2.840"	49.4	2664	53,000 PSI	52.5	2812	62,100 PSI
178 GR. HDY A-MAX	Hodgdon	H4895	.308"	2.840"	48.4	2685	54,000 PSI	51.5	2793	61,200 PSI
180 GR. HDY SP	Hodgdon	Hybrid 100V	.308"	2.820"	57.3	2747	53,800 PSI	61.0C	2922	62,800 PSI
180 GR. HDY SP	IMR	IMR 4831	.308"	2.820"	56.3	2527	44,200 PSI	62.5C	2840	59,700 PSI
180 GR. HDY SP	Hodgdon	H4350	.308"	2.820"	56.4	2648	50,700 PSI	60.0C	2826	62,600 PSI
180 GR. HDY SP	Hodgdon	H414	.308"	2.090"	54.7	2646	50,900 PSI	58.2	2813	61,100 PSI
180 GR. HDY SP	IMR	IMR 4350	.308"	2.820"	57.2	2662	52,000 PSI	60.8C	2850	62,500 PSI
180 GR. HDY SP	Winchester	760	.308"	2.820"	54.7	2646	50,900 PSI	58.2	2813	61,100 PSI
180 GR. HDY SP	IMR	IMR 4007 SSC	.308"	2.820"	55.7	2697	54,100 PSI	59.3	2835	62,000 PSI
180 GR. HDY SP	Hodgdon	H380	.308"	2.820"	55.0	2645	53,500 PSI	58.5	2812	62,900 PSI
180 GR. HDY SP	Hodgdon	Varget	.308"	2.820"	49.4	2625	54,800 PSI	52.6	2755	62,700 PSI

Bullet Weight	Manufacturer	Powder	Bullet Diam.	C.O.L.	Grs.	Vel. (ft/s)	Pressure	Grs.	Vel. (ft/s)	Pressure
180 GR. HDY SP	IMR	IMR 4064	.308"	2.820"	50.0	2625	52,500 PSI	53.2	2777	61,300 PSI
180 GR. HDY SP	Winchester	748	.308"	2.820"	51.2	2627	52,400 PSI	54.5	2766	60,600 PSI
180 GR. HDY SP	IMR	IMR 4895	.308"	2.820"	49.4	2605	52,400 PSI	52.5	2766	61,400 PSI
180 GR. HDY SP	Hodgdon	H4895	.308"	2.820"	47.2	2575	51,900 PSI	50.2	2711	60,400 PSI
200 GR. SFT AF/SS	Hodgdon	Hybrid 100V	.308"	2.775"	55.7	2608	52,500 PSI	59.3C	2767	62,100 PSI
200 GR. SFT AF/SS	IMR	IMR 4831	.308"	2.775"	56.4	2512	49,100 PSI	60.0C	2688	58,700 PSI
200 GR. SFT AF/SS	Hodgdon	H4350	.308"	2.775"	55.2	2544	53,300 PSI	58.7C	2710	62,600 PSI
200 GR. SFT AF/SS	Hodgdon	H414	.308"	2.775"	53.6	2521	51,200 PSI	57.0	2697	62,500 PSI
200 GR. SFT AF/SS	IMR	IMR 4350	.308"	2.775"	55.0	2502	51,000 PSI	58.5C	2688	61,700 PSI
200 GR. SFT AF/SS	IMR	IMR 4007 SSC	.308"	2.775"	53.7	2525	51,900 PSI	57.1C	2696	63,000 PSI
200 GR. SFT AF/SS	Hodgdon	H380	.308"	2.775"	53.6	2505	53,200 PSI	57.0	2650	61,700 PSI
200 GR. SFT AF/SS	Hodgdon	Varget	.308"	2.775"	48.3	2498	57,200 PSI	51.4	2586	61,700 PSI
200 GR. SFT AF/SS	IMR	IMR 4064	.308"	2.775"	48.0	2443	51,000 PSI	51.0	2588	60,700 PSI
200 GR. SFT AF/SS	Winchester	748	.308"	2.775"	48.9	2431	50,000 PSI	52.0	2595	60,000 PSI
200 GR. SFT AF/SS	IMR	IMR 4895	.308"	2.775"	47.4	2455	52,800 PSI	50.4	2580	60,100 PSI
200 GR. SFT AF/SS	Hodgdon	H4895	.308"	2.775"	45.6	2440	54,600 PSI	48.5	2546	61,800 PSI

Cartridge: 300 Remington S.A. Ultra Mag.
Load Type: Rifle

Bullet Weight (Gr.)	Manufacturer	Powder	Bullet Diam.	C.O.L.	Starting Loads Grs.	Vel. (ft/s)	Pressure	Maximum Loads Grs.	Vel. (ft/s)	Pressure
110 GR. SPR SP	Hodgdon	H414	.308"	2.600"	65.0	3295	44,800 PSI	69.0	3508	54,500 PSI
110 GR. SPR SP	Winchester	760	.308"	2.600"	65.0	3295	44,800 PSI	69.0	3508	54,500 PSI
110 GR. SPR SP	Hodgdon	Varget	.308"	2.600"	60.5	3391	51,100 PSI	64.5	3619	63,200 PSI
110 GR. SPR SP	Hodgdon	H4895	.308"	2.600"	58.0	3431	50,600 PSI	62.0	3663	63,000 PSI
125 GR. NOS BT	Hodgdon	H4350	.308"	2.825"	65.0	3172	47,800 PSI	69.0C	3374	58,300 PSI
125 GR. NOS BT	Hodgdon	H414	.308"	2.825"	65.0	3235	49,000 PSI	69.0	3426	57,500 PSI
125 GR. NOS BT	Winchester	760	.308"	2.825"	65.0	3235	49,000 PSI	69.0	3426	57,500 PSI
125 GR. NOS BT	IMR	IMR 4007 SSC	.308"	2.825"	64.5	3261	52,900 PSI	66.5C	3372	58,900 PSI
125 GR. NOS BT	Hodgdon	Varget	.308"	2.825"	60.0	3297	52,700 PSI	64.0	3511	64,200 PSI
125 GR. NOS BT	Hodgdon	H4895	.308"	2.825"	58.0	3341	54,700 PSI	62.0	3557	64,300 PSI
130 GR. HDY SP	Hodgdon	H4350	.308"	2.750"	65.0	3198	54,700 PSI	69.0C	3359	63,500 PSI
130 GR. HDY SP	Hodgdon	H414	.308"	2.750"	64.0	3195	51,600 PSI	68.0	3392	61,900 PSI
130 GR. HDY SP	Winchester	760	.308"	2.750"	64.0	3195	51,600 PSI	68.0	3392	61,900 PSI
130 GR. HDY SP	IMR	IMR 4007 SSC	.308"	2.750"	62.5	3151	52,200 PSI	66.5C	3364	63,400 PSI
130 GR. HDY SP	Hodgdon	Varget	.308"	2.750"	57.5	3165	53,600 PSI	61.0	3330	62,600 PSI
130 GR. HDY SP	Hodgdon	H4895	.308"	2.750"	55.5	3182	51,700 PSI	59.0	3360	62,800 PSI
135 GR. SIE SP	Hodgdon	H4350	.308"	2.750"	63.0	3090	51,900 PSI	67.0C	3283	63,500 PSI
135 GR. SIE SP	Hodgdon	H414	.308"	2.750"	63.0	3133	52,700 PSI	67.3	3334	64,000 PSI
135 GR. SIE SP	Winchester	760	.308"	2.750"	63.0	3133	52,700 PSI	67.3	3334	64,000 PSI
135 GR. SIE SP	IMR	IMR 4007 SSC	.308"	2.750"	62.0	3119	52,200 PSI	66.0C	3306	62,200 PSI

135 GR. SIE SP	Hodgdon	Varget	.308"	2.750"	56.5	3079	52,000 PSI	60.0	3272	63,100 PSI
135 GR. SIE SP	Hodgdon	H4895	.308"	2.750"	55.5	3166	52,700 PSI	59.0	3340	62,500 PSI
150 GR. SPR GSSP	IMR	IMR 4831	.308"	2.700"	59.0	2888	48,300 PSI	65.0C	3050	55,700 PSI
150 GR. SPR GSSP	Hodgdon	H4350	.308"	2.700"	62.0	2985	52,600 PSI	65.5C	3147	62,100 PSI
150 GR. SPR GSSP	Hodgdon	H414	.308"	2.700"	62.0	3038	53,600 PSI	65.5	3201	62,800 PSI
150 GR. SPR GSSP	IMR	IMR 4350	.308"	2.700"	61.1	2866	46,900 PSI	65.0C	3140	60,100 PSI
150 GR. SPR GSSP	Winchester	760	.308"	2.700"	62.0	3038	53,600 PSI	65.5	3201	62,800 PSI
150 GR. SPR GSSP	IMR	IMR 4007 SSC	.308"	2.700"	58.3	2910	50,800 PSI	62.0	3112	61,900 PSI
150 GR. SPR GSSP	Hodgdon	H380	.308"	2.700"	59.0	2946	51,200 PSI	63.0	3119	60,700 PSI
150 GR. SPR GSSP	Hodgdon	Varget	.308"	2.700"	55.0	2967	52,700 PSI	59.0	3148	63,200 PSI
150 GR. SPR GSSP	IMR	IMR 4064	.308	2.700"	54.0	2939	50,800 PSI	57.5	3148	62,100 PSI
150 GR. SPR GSSP	Hodgdon	H4895	.308"	2.700"	53.0	3007	55,900 PSI	57.0	3147	62,800 PSI
150 GR. SPR GSSP	IMR	IMR 3031	.308"	2.700"	50.3	2846	47,200 PSI	53.5	3085	62,400 PSI
155 GR. HDY A-MAX	Hodgdon	Hybrid 100V	.308"	2.825"	59.0	2848	47,400 PSI	63.0C	3016	54,900 PSI
155 GR. HDY A-MAX	Hodgdon	H4350	.308"	2.825"	60.5	2900	50,200 PSI	64.5	3112	63,500 PSI
155 GR. HDY A-MAX	Hodgdon	H414	.308"	2.825"	60.5	2972	53,300 PSI	64.5	3163	63,800 PSI
155 GR. HDY A-MAX	Winchester	760	.308"	2.825"	60.5	2972	53,300 PSI	64.5	3163	63,800 PSI
155 GR. HDY A-MAX	IMR	IMR 4007 SSC	.308"	2.825"	57.5	2895	51,600 PSI	61.0	3076	62,000 PSI
155 GR. HDY A-MAX	Hodgdon	H380	.308"	2.825"	59.0	2918	53,600 PSI	63.0	3093	62,800 PSI
155 GR. HDY A-MAX	Hodgdon	Varget	.308"	2.825"	54.5	2925	53,900 PSI	57.7	3082	63,200 PSI
155 GR. HDY A-MAX	Hodgdon	H4895	.308"	2.825"	52.0	2895	50,800 PSI	55.5	3064	61,700 PSI
165 GR. NOS PART	Hodgdon	Hybrid 100V	.308"	2.825"	59.0	2808	49,500 PSI	63.0C	2966	56,600 PSI
165 GR. NOS PART	Hodgdon	H4350	.308	2.825"	59.0	2797	50,200 PSI	63.0	2997	62,900 PSI
165 GR. NOS PART	Hodgdon	H414	.308	2.825"	59.0	2849	52,600 PSI	63.0	3031	63,600 PSI
165 GR. NOS PART	IMR	IMR 4350	.308"	2.825"	60.0	2824	51,800 PSI	64.0	3035	63,300 PSI
165 GR. NOS PART	Winchester	760	.308"	2.825"	59.0	2849	52,600 PSI	63.0	3031	63,600 PSI
165 GR. NOS PART	IMR	IMR 4007 SSC	.308"	2.825"	57.3	2839	54,300 PSI	61.0	2984	62,600 PSI
165 GR. NOS PART	Hodgdon	H380	.308	2.825"	57.0	2828	55,800 PSI	61.0	2963	62,600 PSI
165 GR. NOS PART	Hodgdon	Varget	.308	2.825"	53.0	2833	55,400 PSI	56.5	2967	63,100 PSI
165 GR. NOS PART	IMR	IMR 4064	.308"	2.825"	53.0	2830	54,200 PSI	56.0	2960	62,600 PSI
165 GR. NOS PART	IMR	IMR 4895	.308"	2.825"	53.0	2809	52,900 PSI	56.0	2965	63,000 PSI
165 GR. NOS PART	Hodgdon	H4895	.308	2.825"	50.5	2827	56,500 PSI	54.0	2946	63,000 PSI
168 GR. SIE HPBT	Hodgdon	H4831	.308"	2.825"	64.0	2801	53,200 PSI	68.0C	2950	62,600 PSI
168 GR. SIE HPBT	Hodgdon	Hybrid 100V	.308"	2.825"	59.0	2812	50,200 PSI	63.0C	2973	58,400 PSI
168 GR. SIE HPBT	Hodgdon	H4350	.308"	2.825"	58.0	2771	49,500 PSI	62.5	2985	63,000 PSI
168 GR. SIE HPBT	Hodgdon	H414	.308"	2.825'	58.5	2825	51,100 PSI	62.5	3016	62,800 PSI
168 GR. SIE HPBT	Winchester	760	.308"	2.825"	58.5	2825	51,100 PSI	62.5	3016	62,800 PSI
168 GR. SIE HPBT	IMR	IMR 4007 SSC	.308"	2.825"	56.9	2792	52,100 PSI	60.5	2950	61,300 PSI
168 GR. SIE HPBT	Hodgdon	H380	.308"	2.825"	57.0	2802	53,300 PSI	60.0	2916	59,400 PSI

168 GR. SIE HPBT	Hodgdon	Varget	.308"	2.825"	53.5	2835	55,600 PSI	56.5	2955	62,700 PSI
168 GR. SIE HPBT	Hodgdon	H4895	.308"	2.825"	51.0	2833	57,000 PSI	54.5	2948	63,100 PSI
175 GR. SIE HPBT	Hodgdon	H4831	.308"	2.825"	64.0	2785	54,800 PSI	68.0C	2924	62,600 PSI
175 GR. SIE HPBT	Hodgdon	Hybrid 100V	.308"	2.825"	59.0	2816	53,700 PSI	63.0C	2954	60,300 PSI
175 GR. SIE HPBT	Hodgdon	H4350	.308"	2.825"	59.0	2806	54,000 PSI	62.5	2945	62,700 PSI
175 GR. SIE HPBT	Hodgdon	H414	.308"	2.825"	59.0	2822	53,800 PSI	62.5	2979	63,300 PSI
175 GR. SIE HPBT	Winchester	760	.308"	2.825"	59.0	2822	53,800 PSI	62.5	2979	63,300 PSI
175 GR. SIE HPBT	IMR	IMR 4007 SSC	.308"	2.825"	56.4	2751	53,100 PSI	60.0	2907	62,900 PSI
175 GR. SIE HPBT	Hodgdon	H380	.308"	2.825"	56.0	2691	49,500 PSI	60.0	2885	61,600 PSI
180 GR. SFT SCIR	Winchester	Supreme 780	.308"	2.825"	63.0	2699	50,500 PSI	67.0	2844	58,600 PSI
180 GR. SFT SCIR	IMR	IMR 4831	.308"	2.825"	59.2	2671	47,900 PSI	63.0C	2836	58,500 PSI
180 GR. SFT SCIR	Hodgdon	H4350	.308"	2.825"	58.0	2772	55,600 PSI	61.6C	2907	63,500 PSI
180 GR. SFT SCIR	Hodgdon	H414	.308"	2.825"	57.0	2784	54,500 PSI	60.5	2935	63,400 PSI
180 GR. SFT SCIR	IMR	IMR 4350	.308"	2.825"	59.0	2771	55,100 PSI	62.7	2902	62,800 PSI
180 GR. SFT SCIR	Winchester	760	.308"	2.825"	57.0	2784	54,500 PSI	60.5	2935	63,400 PSI
180 GR. SFT SCIR	IMR	IMR 4007 SSC	.308"	2.825"	54.5	2683	53,500 PSI	58.0C	2836	62,900 PSI
180 GR. SFT SCIR	Hodgdon	Varget	.308"	2.825"	50.0	2680	53,600 PSI	54.0	2842	63,600 PSI
180 GR. SFT SCIR	IMR	IMR 4064	.308"	2.825"	51.5	2753	58,500 PSI	54.8	2822	62,400 PSI
180 GR. SFT SCIR	Hodgdon	H4895	.308"	2.825"	48.0	2693	57,000 PSI	51.5	2823	64,700 PSI
190 GR. SIE HPBT	Winchester	Supreme 780	.308"	2.825"	63.4	2664	52,000 PSI	67.5	2818	61,300 PSI
190 GR. SIE HPBT	Hodgdon	H4831	.308"	2.825"	61.0	2660	54,000 PSI	65.5C	2811	62,800 PSI
190 GR. SIE HPBT	Hodgdon	Hybrid 100V	.308"	2.825"	57.0	2708	52,300 PSI	61.5C	2867	62,600 PSI
190 GR. SIE HPBT	Hodgdon	H4350	.308"	2.825"	56.0	2660	52,100 PSI	60.0	2836	62,900 PSI
190 GR. SIE HPBT	Hodgdon	H414	.308"	2.825"	56.0	2680	52,200 PSI	60.0	2856	62,800 PSI
190 GR. SIE HPBT	Winchester	760	.308"	2.825"	56.0	2680	52,200 PSI	60.0	2856	62,800 PSI
200 GR. NOS PART	Winchester	Supreme 780	.308"	2.825"	63.0	2624	52,400 PSI	67.0	2771	61,500 PSI
200 GR. NOS PART	Hodgdon	H4831	.308"	2.825"	63.0	2639	55,500 PSI	66.0C	2755	63,300 PSI
200 GR. NOS PART	IMR	IMR 4831	.308"	2.825"	56.0	2475	44,600 PSI	59.5C	2649	56,300 PSI
200 GR. NOS PART	Hodgdon	H4350	.308"	2.825"	56.0	2584	51,600 PSI	59.5C	2751	63,200 PSI
200 GR. NOS PART	Hodgdon	H414	.308"	2.825"	56.0	2609	51,300 PSI	59.5	2788	64,100 PSI
200 GR. NOS PART	IMR	IMR 4350	.308"	2.825"	56.0	2524	48,200 PSI	59.5C	2732	61,800 PSI
200 GR. NOS PART	Winchester	760	.308"	2.825"	56.0	2609	51,300 PSI	59.5	2788	64,100 PSI
200 GR. NOS PART	IMR	IMR 4064	.308"	2.825"	49.5	2535	54,900 PSI	52.5	2663	63,100 PSI
220 GR. HDY RN	Winchester	Supreme 780	.308"	2.750"	61.1	2481	52,600 PSI	65.0	2647	63,900 PSI
220 GR. HDY RN	Hodgdon	H4831	.308"	2.750"	60.0	2497	55,800 PSI	63.5C	2614	63,500 PSI
220 GR. HDY RN	Hodgdon	Hybrid 100V	.308"	2.750"	55.0	2482	52,600 PSI	59.5C	2647	62,800 PSI
220 GR. HDY RN	Hodgdon	H4350	.308"	2.750"	54.0	2470	54,200 PSI	58.0	2608	63,700 PSI
220 GR. HDY RN	Hodgdon	H414	.308"	2.750"	55.0	2482	53,900 PSI	58.5	2625	64,000 PSI
220 GR. HDY RN	Winchester	760	.308"	2.750"	55.0	2482	53,900 PSI	58.5	2625	64,000 PSI

Cartridge: 300 Winchester Short Magnum Load Type: Rifle					Starting Loads			Maximum Loads		
Bullet Weight (Gr.)	Manufacturer	Powder	Bullet Diam.	C.O.L.	Grs.	Vel. (ft/s)	Pressure	Grs.	Vel. (ft/s)	Pressure
110 GR. SPR SP	Hodgdon	H4350	.308"	2.650"	70.0	3437	53,500 PSI	74.5C	3646	63,300 PSI
110 GR. SPR SP	Hodgdon	H414	.308"	2.650"	70.0	3538	55,800 PSI	73.5	3692	62,900 PSI
110 GR. SPR SP	Winchester	760	.308"	2.650"	70.0	3538	55,800 PSI	73.5	3692	62,900 PSI
110 GR. SPR SP	IMR	IMR 4007 SSC	.308"	2.650"	66.7	3426	52,300 PSI	71.0C	3643	62,800 PSI
110 GR. SPR SP	Hodgdon	H380	.308"	2.650"	68.0	3456	52,500 PSI	71.0	3600	60,200 PSI
110 GR. SPR SP	Hodgdon	Varget	.308"	2.650"	62.0	3454	54,300 PSI	66.0	3631	63,200 PSI
110 GR. SPR SP	Hodgdon	H4895	.308"	2.650"	60.0	3495	56,800 PSI	63.5	3647	63,600 PSI
110 GR. SPR SP	IMR	IMR 8208 XBR	.308"	2.650"	60.3	3555	54,400 PSI	63.5	3697	62,400 PSI
125 GR. NOS BT	Hodgdon	H4350	.308"	2.810"	69.0	3332	55,800 PSI	73.0	3481	63,000 PSI
125 GR. NOS BT	Hodgdon	H414	.308"	2.810"	68.0	3318	51,300 PSI	72.0	3540	63,300 PSI
125 GR. NOS BT	Winchester	760	.308"	2.810"	68.0	3318	51,300 PSI	72.0	3540	63,300 PSI
125 GR. NOS BT	IMR	IMR 4007 SSC	.308"	2.810"	65.8	3243	49,700 PSI	70.0C	3487	62,800 PSI
125 GR. NOS BT	Hodgdon	H380	.308"	2.810"	68.0	3346	55,100 PSI	71.0	3493	62,600 PSI
125 GR. NOS BT	Hodgdon	Varget	.308"	2.810"	61.0	3312	54,700 PSI	65.0	3478	63,100 PSI
125 GR. NOS BT	Hodgdon	H4895	.308"	2.810"	58.0	3314	56,600 PSI	61.0	3431	63,000 PSI
125 GR. NOS BT	IMR	IMR 8208 XBR	.308"	2.810"	58.3	3350	53,600 PSI	62.0	3496	61,700 PSI
130 GR. HDY SP	Hodgdon	Suprform	.308"	2.720"	69.0	3256	42,900 PSI	77.0C	3645	62,600 PSI
130 GR. HDY SP	Hodgdon	H4350	.308"	2.720"	67.0	3237	54,900 PSI	71.0	3393	63,200 PSI
130 GR. HDY SP	Hodgdon	H414	.308"	2.720"	66.0	3267	54,500 PSI	70.0	3437	63,700 PSI
130 GR. HDY SP	Winchester	760	.308"	2.720"	66.0	3267	54,500 PSI	70.0	3437	63,700 PSI
130 GR. HDY SP	IMR	IMR 4007 SSC	.308"	2.720"	64.4	3213	53,500 PSI	68.5	3393	63,000 PSI
130 GR. HDY SP	Hodgdon	H380	.308"	2.720"	66.0	3244	55,700 PSI	69.5	3497	63,300 PSI
130 GR. HDY SP	Hodgdon	Varget	.308"	2.720"	60.0	3269	58,100 PSI	63.5	3388	63,500 PSI
130 GR. HDY SP	Hodgdon	H4895	.308"	2.720"	56.0	3213	55,700 PSI	58.5	3318	63,000 PSI
130 GR. HDY SP	IMR	IMR 8208 XBR	.308"	2.720"	56.4	3272	56,600 PSI	60.0	3391	61,900 PSI
150 GR. SPR GSSP	Winchester	Supreme 780	.308"	2.780"	69.6	2940	48,900 PSI	74.0	3134	59,200 PSI
150 GR. SPR GSSP	Hodgdon	Suprform	.308"	2.780"	67.0	3129	50,000 PSI	74.0	3410	63,500 PSI
150 GR. SPR GSSP	Hodgdon	Hybrid 100V	.308"	2.780"	63.0	2948	49,400 PSI	67.0C	3127	57,700 PSI
150 GR. SPR GSSP	Hodgdon	H4350	.308"	2.780"	63.0	3040	55,700 PSI	67.0	3187	63,200 PSI
150 GR. SPR GSSP	Hodgdon	H414	.308"	2.780"	62.0	3025	53,400 PSI	66.0	3204	63,300 PSI
150 GR. SPR GSSP	IMR	IMR 4350	.308"	2.780"	64.0	3006	50,200 PSI	68.0	3221	62,100 PSI
150 GR. SPR GSSP	Winchester	760	.308"	2.780"	62.0	3025	53,400 PSI	66.0	3204	63,300 PSI
150 GR. SPR GSSP	IMR	IMR 4007 SSC	.308"	2.780"	61.8	3125	57,200 PSI	63.7	3220	63,100 PSI
150 GR. SPR GSSP	Hodgdon	H380	.308"	2.780"	60.0	2987	54,900 PSI	64.0	3141	63,600 PSI
150 GR. SPR GSSP	Hodgdon	Varget	.308"	2.780"	55.0	3008	56,800 PSI	58.5	3140	63,800 PSI
150 GR. SPR GSSP	IMR	IMR 4320	.308"	2.780"	57.0	3004	54,000 PSI	61.0	3172	63,900 PSI

150 GR. SPR GSSP	IMR	IMR 4064	.308"	2.780"	57.0	3012	52,100 PSI	61.0	3198	63,300 PSI
150 GR. SPR GSSP	IMR	IMR 4895	.308"	2.780"	56.0	2980	50,800 PSI	60.5	3176	62,300 PSI
150 GR. SPR GSSP	Hodgdon	H4895	.308"	2.780"	51.0	2919	53,400 PSI	54.5	3078	63,100 PSI
150 GR. SPR GSSP	IMR	IMR 8208 XBR	.308"	2.780"	52.6	2992	55,800 PSI	56.0	3115	62,300 PSI
150 GR. SPR GSSP	IMR	Trail Boss	.308"	2.780"	16.3	1473	26,400 PSI	23.3	1758	31,600 PSI
155 GR. HDY A-MAX	Winchester	Supreme 780	.308"	2.860"	70.0	3054	51,700 PSI	74.5	3201	60,800 PSI
155 GR. HDY A-MAX	Hodgdon	Suprform	.308"	2.860"	66.0	3065	45,700 PSI	73.5C	3405	63,500 PSI
155 GR. HDY A-MAX	Hodgdon	Hybrid 100V	.308"	2.860"	63.0	3060	51,800 PSI	68.5C	3269	62,300 PSI
155 GR. HDY A-MAX	Hodgdon	H4350	.308"	2.860"	63.0	3014	55,300 PSI	66.5	3156	63,200 PSI
155 GR. HDY A-MAX	Hodgdon	H414	.308"	2.860"	63.0	3023	53,300 PSI	66.5	3206	63,100 PSI
155 GR. HDY A-MAX	Winchester	760	.308"	2.860"	63.0	3023	53,300 PSI	66.5	3206	63,100 PSI
155 GR. HDY A-MAX	IMR	IMR 4007 SSC	.308"	2.860"	61.9	2990	53,700 PSI	65.8	3167	63,500 PSI
155 GR. HDY A-MAX	Hodgdon	H380	.308"	2.860"	60.0	2956	54,500 PSI	64.0	3117	63,100 PSI
155 GR. HDY A-MAX	Hodgdon	Varget	.308"	2.860"	55.0	2963	54,800 PSI	58.5	3110	63,600 PSI
155 GR. HDY A-MAX	Hodgdon	H4895	.308"	2.860"	52.0	2935	55,800 PSI	55.0	3061	63,600 PSI
155 GR. HDY A-MAX	IMR	IMR 8208 XBR	.308"	2.860"	53.0	2990	56,800 PSI	56.4	3110	63,400 PSI
165 GR. HDY GMX	Winchester	Supreme 780	.308"	2.840"	67.0	2933	54,400 PSI	70.0C	3038	59,500 PSI
165 GR. HDY GMX	Hodgdon	Suprform	.308"	2.840"	64.0	2952	51,600 PSI	69.0C	3169	62,700 PSI
165 GR. HDY GMX	Hodgdon	Hybrid 100V	.308"	2.840"	58.0	2867	51,600 PSI	63.0C	3099	63,300 PSI
165 GR. HDY GMX	Hodgdon	H4350	.308"	2.840"	58.0	2821	52,400 PSI	62.0C	2986	61,300 PSI
165 GR. HDY GMX	Hodgdon	H414	.308"	2.840"	58.0	2860	53,400 PSI	62.5	3043	62,900 PSI
165 GR. HDY GMX	Winchester	760	.308"	2.840"	58.0	2860	53,400 PSI	62.5	3043	62,900 PSI
165 GR. HDY GMX	Hodgdon	H380	.308"	2.840"	57.0	2800	52,500 PSI	61.8	2993	62,300 PSI
165 GR. HDY GMX	Hodgdon	Varget	.308"	2.840"	51.0	2810	56,700 PSI	54.5	2948	63,600 PSI
165 GR. HDY GMX	Hodgdon	H4895	.308"	2.840"	47.0	2700	51,900 PSI	51.0	2887	63,300 PSI
165 GR. HDY GMX	IMR	IMR 8208 XBR	.308"	2.840"	48.0	2743	55,600 PSI	52.0	2887	63,300 PSI
165 GR. NOS PART	Winchester	Supreme 780	.308"	2.860"	69.4	2951	50,300 PSI	73.8	3139	61,300 PSI
165 GR. NOS PART	Hodgdon	Suprform	.308"	2.860"	65.0	2987	47,800 PSI	72.0	3273	63,500 PSI
165 GR. NOS PART	Hodgdon	Hybrid 100V	.308"	2.860"	62.0	2957	51,600 PSI	68.0C	3175	63,100 PSI
165 GR. NOS PART	Hodgdon	H4350	.308"	2.860"	61.0	2898	54,800 PSI	65.5	3047	63,600 PSI
165 GR. NOS PART	Hodgdon	H414	.308"	2.860"	61.0	2915	54,200 PSI	65.0	3069	63,200 PSI
165 GR. NOS PART	Winchester	760	.308"	2.860"	61.0	2915	54,200 PSI	65.0	3069	63,200 PSI
165 GR. NOS PART	Hodgdon	H380	.308"	2.860"	59.0	2854	55,100 PSI	63.0	3012	63,600 PSI
165 GR. NOS PART	Hodgdon	Varget	.308"	2.860"	54.0	2859	56,400 PSI	57.5	2987	63,700 PSI
165 GR. NOS PART	Hodgdon	H4895	.308"	2.860"	51.0	2810	55,700 PSI	54.0	2929	63,200 PSI
165 GR. NOS PART	IMR	IMR 8208 XBR	.308"	2.860"	51.1	2849	55,600 PSI	54.4	2963	61,700 PSI
168 GR. SIE HPBT	Winchester	Supreme 780	.308"	2.840"	69.1	2936	50,900 PSI	73.5	3133	63,100 PSI
168 GR. SIE HPBT	Hodgdon	H4831	.308"	2.840"	65.0	2848	53,400 PSI	69.5C	3015	63,200 PSI
168 GR. SIE HPBT	Hodgdon	Hybrid 100V	.308"	2.840"	62.0	2921	49,800 PSI	67.7C	3144	61,100 PSI
168 GR. SIE HPBT	Hodgdon	H4350	.308"	2.840"	61.0	2908	56,000 PSI	64.5	3034	63,700 PSI

168 GR. SIE HPBT	Hodgdon	H414	.308"	2.840"	61.0	2919	54,600 PSI	65.0	3074	63,200 PSI
168 GR. SIE HPBT	Winchester	760	.308"	2.840"	61.0	2919	54,600 PSI	65.0	3074	63,200 PSI
168 GR. SIE HPBT	IMR	IMR 4007 SSC	.308"	2.840"	60.0	2848	51,300 PSI	63.8	3013	60,800 PSI
168 GR. SIE HPBT	Hodgdon	H380	.308"	2.840"	59.0	2865	56,000 PSI	62.0	2985	63,300 PSI
168 GR. SIE HPBT	IMR	IMR 8208 XBR	.308"	2.840"	51.5	2853	56,400 PSI	54.8	2970	63,400 PSI
175 GR. SIE HPBT	Winchester	Supreme 780	.308"	2.860"	67.7	2910	54,000 PSI	72.0	3069	63,000 PSI
175 GR. SIE HPBT	Hodgdon	H4831	.308"	2.860"	66.0	2848	55,300 PSI	70.0C	2980	63,100 PSI
175 GR. SIE HPBT	Hodgdon	Hybrid 100V	.308"	2.860"	61.0	2878	51,000 PSI	66.5C	3085	61,700 PSI
175 GR. SIE HPBT	Hodgdon	H4350	.308"	2.860"	61.0	2839	53,300 PSI	65.0	3009	63,400 PSI
175 GR. SIE HPBT	Hodgdon	H414	.308"	2.860"	61.0	2868	53,900 PSI	65.0	3032	63,200 PSI
175 GR. SIE HPBT	Winchester	760	.308"	2.860"	61.0	2868	53,900 PSI	65.0	3032	63,200 PSI
175 GR. SIE HPBT	IMR	IMR 4007 SSC	.308"	2.860"	58.6	2797	52,700 PSI	62.3	2964	63,400 PSI
175 GR. SIE HPBT	Hodgdon	H380	.308"	2.860"	60.0	2859	57,600 PSI	63.0	2954	63,200 PSI
180 GR. NOS E-TIP	Hodgdon	H4350	.308"	2.860"	59.0	2751	54,900 PSI	63.7C	2925	63,800 PSI
180 GR. NOS E-TIP	Hodgdon	H414	.308"	2.860"	56.0	2693	52,800 PSI	60.0	2865	62,100 PSI
180 GR. NOS E-TIP	IMR	IMR 4350	.308"	2.860"	60.0	2748	52,600 PSI	64.0C	2963	62,400 PSI
180 GR. NOS E-TIP	IMR	IMR 4007 SSC	.308"	2.860"	56.0	2682	53,200 PSI	60.0C	2851	61,900 PSI
180 GR. NOS E-TIP	Hodgdon	H380	.308"	2.860"	57.0	2648	51,700 PSI	61.5	2809	59,700 PSI
180 GR. SFT SCIR	IMR	IMR 7828	.308"	2.860"	65.0	2783	54,400 PSI	69.5C*	2943	62,600 PSI
180 GR. SFT SCIR	Winchester	Supreme 780	.308"	2.860"	65.8	2779	52,500 PSI	70.0	2923	60,800 PSI
180 GR. SFT SCIR	Hodgdon	H4831	.308"	2.860"	65.5	2775	52,000 PSI	70.0C	2929	64,000 PSI
180 GR. SFT SCIR	Hodgdon	Hybrid 100V	.308"	2.860"	59.0	2728	50,200 PSI	64.0C	2918	59,800 PSI
180 GR. SFT SCIR	IMR	IMR 4831	.308"	2.860"	62.0	2797	52,700 PSI	66.3C	2980	62,900 PSI
180 GR. SFT SCIR	Hodgdon	H4350	.308"	2.860"	60.0	2799	55,700 PSI	64.0	2950	63,900 PSI
180 GR. SFT SCIR	Hodgdon	H414	.308"	2.860"	59.0	2801	54,100 PSI	62.5	2959	63,000 PSI
180 GR. SFT SCIR	IMR	IMR 4350	.308"	2.860"	61.0	2808	52,800 PSI	65.0C	2991	63,700 PSI
180 GR. SFT SCIR	Winchester	760	.308"	2.860"	59.0	2801	54,100 PSI	62.5	2959	63,000 PSI
180 GR. SFT SCIR	IMR	IMR 4007 SSC	.308"	2.860"	57.0	2806	56,800 PSI	59.8	2927	63,000 PSI
180 GR. SFT SCIR	Hodgdon	H380	.308"	2.860"	57.0	2718	53,700 PSI	61.0	2884	63,400 PSI
190 GR. SIE HPBT	IMR	IMR 7828	.308"	2.860"	64.0	2703	52,100 PSI	69.0C*	2891	63,300 PSI
190 GR. SIE HPBT	Winchester	Supreme 780	.308"	2.860"	65.8	2769	50,800 PSI	70.0	2954	62,200 PSI
190 GR. SIE HPBT	Hodgdon	H4831	.308"	2.860"	62.0	2704	53,800 PSI	66.5C	2858	63,400 PSI
190 GR. SIE HPBT	Hodgdon	Hybrid 100V	.308"	2.860"	60.0	2790	52,000 PSI	64.5C	2951	61,000 PSI
190 GR. SIE HPBT	IMR	IMR 4831	.308"	2.860"	60.0	2679	49,300 PSI	64.0C	2867	61,700 PSI
190 GR. SIE HPBT	Hodgdon	H4350	.308"	2.860"	57.5	2736	56,200 PSI	61.0	2853	63,400 PSI
190 GR. SIE HPBT	Hodgdon	H414	.308"	2.860"	59.0	2765	55,600 PSI	62.5	2896	63,800 PSI
190 GR. SIE HPBT	IMR	IMR 4350	.308"	2.860"	60.0	2755	53,200 PSI	64.0C	2920	63,700 PSI
190 GR. SIE HPBT	Winchester	760	.308"	2.860"	59.0	2765	55,600 PSI	62.5	2896	63,800 PSI
200 GR. SFT SP	Hodgdon	H1000	.308"	2.790"	70.0	2660	51,600 PSI	72.0C	2737	57,200 PSI

Bullet Weight (Gr.)	Manufacturer	Powder	Bullet Diam.	C.O.L.	Grs.	Vel. (ft/s)	Pressure	Grs.	Vel. (ft/s)	Pressure
200 GR. SFT SP	IMR	IMR 7828	.308"	2.790"	63.0	2580	50,000 PSI	67.5C*	2793	63,100 PSI
200 GR. SFT SP	Winchester	Supreme 780	.308"	2.790"	65.3	2667	53,500 PSI	69.5	2815	61,800 PSI
200 GR. SFT SP	Hodgdon	H4831	.308"	2.790"	63.0	2678	56,000 PSI	66.5C	2802	63,700 PSI
200 GR. SFT SP	IMR	IMR 4831	.308"	2.790"	59.0	2565	49,200 PSI	63.7C	2780	62,200 PSI
200 GR. SFT SP	Hodgdon	H4350	.308"	2.790"	58.0	2666	55,000 PSI	62.0	2792	63,200 PSI
200 GR. SFT SP	Hodgdon	H414	.308"	2.790"	58.0	2678	55,700 PSI	61.0	2803	63,200 PSI
200 GR. SFT SP	IMR	IMR 4350	.308"	2.790"	59.0	2643	52,900 PSI	63.5C	2827	63,700 PSI
200 GR. SFT SP	Winchester	760	.308"	2.790"	58.0	2678	55,700 PSI	61.0	2803	63,200 PSI
200 GR. SFT SP	IMR	IMR 4007 SSC	.308"	2.790"	56.6	2651	54,500 PSI	59.8	2788	64,000 PSI
208 GR. HDY A-MAX	Hodgdon	H1000	.308"	2.900"	62.0	2420	42,900 PSI	69.0C	2670	55,900 PSI
208 GR. HDY A-MAX	IMR	IMR 7828	.308"	2.900"	62.0	2556	48,000 PSI	66.8C	2761	58,400 PSI
208 GR. HDY A-MAX	Winchester	Supreme 780	.308"	2.900"	61.0	2542	46,000 PSI'	68.0	2823	60,600 PSI
208 GR. HDY A-MAX	Hodgdon	H4831	.308"	2.900"	61.8	2624	54,800 PSI	66.5C	2761	62,500 PSI
208 GR. HDY A-MAX	IMR	IMR 4831	.308"	2.900"	59.0	2594	51,500 PSI	63.5C	2785	62,600 PSI
208 GR. HDY A-MAX	Hodgdon	H4350	.308"	2.900"	56.4	2612	55,400 PSI	60.7	2748	62,800 PSI
208 GR. HDY A-MAX	Hodgdon	H414	.308"	2.900"	55.6	2567	52,500 PSI	59.8	2732	62,100 PSI
208 GR. HDY A-MAX	IMR	IMR 4350	.308"	2.900"	57.7	2593	52,000 PSI	62.0C	2773	62,900 PSI
208 GR. HDY A-MAX	Winchester	760	.308"	2.900"	55.6	2567	52,500 PSI	59.8	2732	62,100 PSI
208 GR. HDY A-MAX	IMR	IMR 4007 SSC	.308"	2.900"	55.5	2553	51,700 PSI	59.9	2726	61,800 PSI
220 GR. HDY RN	Hodgdon	H1000	.308"	2.830"	69.0	2597	57,200 PSI	72.5C	2689	63,000 PSI
220 GR. HDY RN	Winchester	Supreme 780	.308"	2.830"	63.4	2587	53,100 PSI	67.5	2735	62,900 PSI
220 GR. HDY RN	Hodgdon	H4831	.308"	2.830"	60.0	2520	55,600 PSI	64.3C	2646	63,500 PSI
220 GR. HDY RN	Hodgdon	Hybrid 100V	.308"	2.830"	57.0	2522	49,300 PSI	62.0C	2711	61,400 PSI
220 GR. HDY RN	Hodgdon	H4350	.308"	2.830"	54.0	2476	54,100 PSI	58.0	2602	63,300 PSI
220 GR. HDY RN	Hodgdon	H414	.308"	2.830"	55.0	2484	54,000 PSI	59.0	2624	63,600 PSI
220 GR. HDY RN	Winchester	760	.308"	2.830"	55.0	2484	54,000 PSI	59.0	2624	63,600 PSI

Cartridge: 300 Winchester Magnum Load Type: Rifle						Starting Loads			Maximum Loads	
Bullet Weight (Gr.)	Manufacturer	Powder	Bullet Diam.	C.O.L.	Grs.	Vel. (ft/s)	Pressure	Grs.	Vel. (ft/s)	Pressure
110 GR. SPR SP	Hodgdon	H1000	.308"	3.215"	80.0	3189	34,700 CUP	85.0C	3392	42,000 CUP
110 GR. SPR SP	Hodgdon	H4831	.308"	3.215"	79.0	3355	41,500 CUP	84.0C	3540	48,400 CUP
110 GR. SPR SP	IMR	IMR 4831	.308"	3.215"	76.0	3410	50,900 PSI	81.0C	3656	60,700 PSI
110 GR. SPR SP	Hodgdon	H4350	.308"	3.215"	72.0	3337	39,300 CUP	80.0	3648	49,400 CUP
110 GR. SPR SP	Hodgdon	H414	.308"	3.215"	66.0	3330	40,900 CUP	73.0	3570	49,700 CUP
110 GR. SPR SP	IMR	IMR 4350	.308"	3.215"	74.0	3354	49,100 PSI	79.5C	3655	61,500 PSI
110 GR. SPR SP	Winchester	760	.308"	3.215"	66.0	3330	40,900 CUP	73.0	3570	49,700 CUP
110 GR. SPR SP	IMR	IMR 4007 SSC	.308"	3.215"	72.5	3461	54,400 PSI	76.6	3645	62,600 PSI
110 GR. SPR SP	Hodgdon	H380	.308"	3.215"	66.0	3282	41,100 CUP	73.0	3544	49,000 CUP
110 GR. SPR SP	Hodgdon	Varget	.308"	3.215"	67.0	3424	42,900 CUP	72.5	3660	51,700 CUP

110 GR. SPR SP	IMR	IMR 4064	.308"	3.215"	65.0	3424	50,600 PSI	70.0	3669	62,100 PSI
110 GR. SPR SP	IMR	IMR 4895	.308"	3.215"	65.0	3440	52,000 PSI	69.5	3684	63,300 PSI
110 GR. SPR SP	Hodgdon	H4895	.308"	3.215"	60.0	3381	43,300 CUP	67.0	3665	51,400 CUP
125 GR. BAR XFB	Hodgdon	H1000	.308"	3.275"	80.0	3260	44,200 CUP	85.0C	3418	48,700 CUP
125 GR. BAR XFB	Hodgdon	H4831	.308"	3.275"	75.0	3286	47,300 CUP	80.0	3450	52,000 CUP
125 GR. BAR XFB	IMR	IMR 4831	.308"	3.275"	74.0	3149	49,000 PSI	79.0C	3515	63,300 PSI
125 GR. BAR XFB	Hodgdon	H4350	.308"	3.275"	68.0	3250	46,100 CUP	73.0	3424	51,600 CUP
125 GR. BAR XFB	Hodgdon	H414	.308"	3.275"	65.0	3219	36,000 CUP	70.0	3392	51,700 CUP
125 GR. BAR XFB	IMR	IMR 4350	.308"	3.275"	72.0	3230	51,800 PSI	77.2C	3497	62,900 PSI
125 GR. BAR XFB	Winchester	760	.308"	3.275"	65.0	3219	36,000 CUP	70.0	3392	51,700 CUP
125 GR. BAR XFB	Hodgdon	H380	.308"	3.275"	62.0	3056	43,500 CUP	68.5	3293	51,800 CUP
125 GR. BAR XFB	Hodgdon	Varget	.308"	3.275"	65.0	3281	45,400 CUP	70.0	3462	52,700 CUP
125 GR. BAR XFB	IMR	IMR 4064	.308"	3.275"	63.0	3217	51,500 PSI	67.6	3464	63,500 PSI
125 GR. BAR XFB	IMR	IMR 4895	.308"	3.275"	63.0	3212	52,400 PSI	67.3	3424	61,900 PSI
125 GR. BAR XFB	Hodgdon	H4895	.308"	3.275"	57.0	3140	44,200 CUP	62.0	3347	51,100 CUP
130 GR. HDY SP	Hodgdon	H1000	.308"	3.300"	80.0	3125	38,900 CUP	85.0C	3289	45,000 CUP
130 GR. HDY SP	Hodgdon	H4831	.308"	3.300"	77.0	3116	44,900 CUP	82.0C	3383	51,300 CUP
130 GR. HDY SP	IMR	IMR 4831	.308"	3.300"	75.0	3167	50,300 PSI	80.0C	3436	61,800 PSI
130 GR. HDY SP	Hodgdon	H4350	.308"	3.300"	70.0	3219	45,800 CUP	74.0	3375	51,600 CUP
130 GR. HDY SP	Hodgdon	H414	.308"	3.300"	67.0	3219	47,000 CUP	71.0	3360	52,300 CUP
130 GR. HDY SP	IMR	IMR 4350	.308"	3.300"	73.0	3214	50,700 PSI	78.0	3466	62,300 PSI
130 GR. HDY SP	Winchester	760	.308"	3.300"	67.0	3219	47,000 CUP	71.0	3360	52,300 CUP
130 GR. HDY SP	IMR	IMR 4007 SSC	.308"	3.300"	69.6	3209	52,600 PSI	74.0	3394	61,600 PSI
130 GR. HDY SP	Hodgdon	H380	.308"	3.300"	64.0	3111	46,700 CUP	68.5	3283	52,600 CUP
130 GR. HDY SP	Hodgdon	Varget	.308"	3.300"	64.0	3218	45,600 CUP	68.5	3398	52,100 CUP
130 GR. HDY SP	IMR	IMR 4064	.308"	3.300"	64.0	3217	51,600 PSI	68.3	3427	62,900 PSI
130 GR. HDY SP	IMR	IMR 4895	.308"	3.300"	64.0	3198	51,600 PSI	69.0	3442	63,000 PSI
130 GR. HDY SP	Hodgdon	H4895	.308"	3.300"	58.0	3187	46,900 CUP	62.0	3331	52,500 CUP
130 GR. HDY SP	IMR	IMR 8208 XBR	.308"	3.300"	60.0	3202	52,200 PSI	65.0	3386	62,200 PSI
150 GR. BAR TTSX BT	IMR	IMR 7828 SSC	.308"	3.325"	78.0	3120	51,100 PSI	83.0C*	3321	60,000 PSI
150 GR. BAR TTSX BT	Winchester	Supreme 780	.308"	3.325"	75.0	3103	48,600 PSI	79.0	3226	52,900 PSI
150 GR. BAR TTSX BT	Hodgdon	H4831	.308"	3.325"	75.0	2985	46,300 PSI	80.0C	3182	50,100 PSI
150 GR. BAR TTSX BT	Hodgdon	Hybrid 100V	.308"	3.325"	68.0	3140	50,700 PSI	73.0C	3340	59,900 PSI
150 GR. BAR TTSX BT	IMR	IMR 4831	.308"	3.325"	71.0	3027	47,700 PSI	76.0C	3278	58,800 PSI
150 GR. BAR TTSX BT	Hodgdon	H4350	.308"	3.325"	69.0	3062	49,600 PSI	74.0C	3289	60,600 PSI
150 GR. BAR TTSX BT	Hodgdon	H414	.308"	3.325"	65.0	3053	51,200 PSI	69.7	3231	59,600 PSI
150 GR. BAR TTSX BT	IMR	IMR 4350	.308"	3.325"	70.0	3078	49,000 PSI	75.0C	3347	61,300 PSI
150 GR. BAR TTSX BT	Winchester	760	.308"	3.325"	65.0	3053	51,200 PSI	69.7	3231	59,600 PSI
150 GR. BAR TTSX BT	IMR	IMR 4007 SSC	.308"	3.325"	67.0	3048	49,700 PSI	72.0C	3288	60,800 PSI

150 GR. BAR TTSX BT	Hodgdon	H380	.308"	3.325"	65.0	3030	51,600 PSI	69.0	3166	57,400 PSI
150 GR. BAR TTSX BT	IMR	IMR 4064	.308"	3.325"	60.0	2969	47,300 PSI	65.5	3239	60,500 PSI
150 GR. BAR TTSX BT	IMR	IMR 4895	.308"	3.325"	61.0	3018	49,600 PSI	66.3	3249	60,800 PSI
150 GR. BAR TTSX BT	Hodgdon	H4895	.308"	3.325"	57.0	3006	52,000 PSI	63.0	3186	59,900 PSI
150 GR. BAR TTSX BT	IMR	IMR 8208 XBR	.308"	3.325"	57.0	2925	47,900 PSI	64.0	3183	61,100 PSI
150 GR. SIE SP	Hodgdon	H1000	.308"	3.340"	80.0	3004	46,500 CUP	85.0C	3255	52,200 CUP
150 GR. SIE SP	IMR	IMR 7828	.308"	3.340"	75.0	2913	46,200 PSI	80.0C	3148	55,600 PSI
150 GR. SIE SP	Winchester	Supreme 780	.308"	3.340"	76.1	3061	51,300 PSI	81.0	3264	62,500 PSI
150 GR. SIE SP	Hodgdon	H4831	.308"	3.340"	73.0	3025	45,700 CUP	78.0	3207	52,700 CUP
150 GR. SIE SP	Hodgdon	Hybrid 100V	.308"	3.340"	67.0	3026	49,800 PSI	73.5	3289	62,700 PSI
150 GR. SIE SP	IMR	IMR 4831	.308"	3.340"	73.0	3037	51,300 PSI	78.0C	3289	63,300 PSI
150 GR. SIE SP	Hodgdon	H4350	.308"	3.340"	68.0	3052	47,100 CUP	72.0	3205	52,500 CUP
150 GR. SIE SP	Hodgdon	H414	.308"	3.340"	62.0	2973	47,400 CUP	68.0	3145	52,500 CUP
150 GR. SIE SP	IMR	IMR 4350	.308"	3.340"	69.0	3003	50,100 PSI	74.0	3254	61,500 PSI
150 GR. SIE SP	Winchester	760	.308"	3.340"	62.0	2973	47,400 CUP	68.0	3145	52,500 CUP
150 GR. SIE SP	IMR	IMR 4007 SSC	.308"	3.340"	66.7	2982	50,600 PSI	71.0	3185	61,400 PSI
150 GR. SIE SP	Hodgdon	H380	.308"	3.340"	62.0	2903	46,000 CUP	65.0	3031	52,200 CUP
150 GR. SIE SP	Hodgdon	Varget	.308"	3.340"	56.0	2952	43,300 CUP	60.0	3108	51,400 CUP
150 GR. SIE SP	IMR	IMR 4064	.308"	3.340"	61.0	3028	52,900 PSI	65.5	3205	62,200 PSI
150 GR. SIE SP	IMR	IMR 4895	.308"	3.340"	61.0	2980	50,700 PSI	65.5	3196	62,300 PSI
150 GR. SIE SP	Hodgdon	H4895	.308"	3.340"	57.0	2991	47,300 CUP	61.0	3124	52,500 CUP
150 GR. SIE SP	IMR	IMR 8208 XBR	.308"	3.340"	57.0	2987	52,600 PSI	61.5	3156	60,800 PSI
150 GR. SIE SP	IMR	Trail Boss	.308"	3.340"	18.0	1302	18,400 PSI	25.5	1687	28,600 PSI
155 GR. SIE HPBT	Hodgdon	H1000	.308"	3.340"	80.0	2992	41,300 CUP	85.0C	3160	47,400 CUP
155 GR. SIE HPBT	IMR	IMR 7828	.308"	3.340"	75.0	2943	47,500 PSI	80.0C	3188	58,100 PSI
155 GR. SIE HPBT	Winchester	Supreme 780	.308"	3.340"	76.1	3071	52,700 PSI	81.0	3248	63,000 PSI
155 GR. SIE HPBT	Hodgdon	H4831	.308"	3.340"	74.0	2964	43,600 CUP	79.0C	3166	51,500 CUP
155 GR. SIE HPBT	Hodgdon	Hybrid 100V	.308"	3.340"	68.0	3049	51,900 PSI	74.0	3274	63,200 PSI
155 GR. SIE HPBT	IMR	IMR 4831	.308"	3.340"	71.0	2963	48,100 PSI	76.5C	3226	61,600 PSI
155 GR. SIE HPBT	Hodgdon	H4350	.308"	3.340"	69.0	3013	45,100 CUP	74.0	3215	52,400 CUP
155 GR. SIE HPBT	Hodgdon	H414	.308"	3.340"	67.0	2986	44,500 CUP	71.5	3157	51,300 CUP
155 GR. SIE HPBT	IMR	IMR 4350	.308"	3.340"	70.0	3064	51,600 PSI	74.5	3273	63,300 PSI
155 GR. SIE HPBT	Winchester	760	.308"	3.340"	67.0	2986	44,500 CUP	71.5	3157	51,300 CUP
155 GR. SIE HPBT	IMR	IMR 4007 SSC	.308"	3.340"	67.0	3014	53,300 PSI	71.0	3164	61,400 PSI
155 GR. SIE HPBT	Hodgdon	H380	.308"	3.340"	61.0	2869	44,300 CUP	65.0	3025	51,900 CUP
155 GR. SIE HPBT	Hodgdon	Varget	.308"	3.340"	55.0	2897	42,400 CUP	59.7	3090	52,000 CUP
155 GR. SIE HPBT	IMR	IMR 4064	.308"	3.340"	61.0	3014	52,000 PSI	65.0	3195	61,900 PSI
155 GR. SIE HPBT	IMR	IMR 4895	.308"	3.340"	61.0	3002	50,900 PSI	65.5	3210	63,100 PSI
155 GR. SIE HPBT	Hodgdon	H4895	.308"	3.340"	55.0	2919	43,700 CUP	59.0	3078	52,200 CUP
155 GR. SIE HPBT	IMR	IMR 8208 XBR	.308"	3.340"	58.0	2997	55,000 PSI	61.5	3117	60,700 PSI

165 GR. SPR SP	Hodgdon	H1000	.308"	3.340"	79.0	2957	44,600 CUP	84.0	3117	51,300 CUP
165 GR. SPR SP	IMR	IMR 7828	.308"	3.340"	74.0	2884	49,500 PSI	79.5C	3127	60,600 PSI
165 GR. SPR SP	Winchester	Supreme 780	.308"	3.340"	74.7	2941	52,100 PSI	79.5	3125	61,800 PSI
165 GR. SPR SP	Hodgdon	H4831	.308"	3.340"	72.0	2934	47,600 CUP	75.5	3055	52,200 CUP
165 GR. SPR SP	Hodgdon	Hybrid 100V	.308"	3.340"	66.0	2905	50,700 PSI	72.0	3144	62,500 PSI
165 GR. SPR SP	IMR	IMR 4831	.308"	3.340"	70.0	2878	49,800 PSI	75.2C	3142	62,900 PSI
165 GR. SPR SP	Hodgdon	H4350	.308"	3.340"	66.0	2910	46,900 CUP	70.0	3042	51,900 CUP
165 GR. SPR SP	Hodgdon	H414	.308"	3.340"	61.0	2853	48,500 CUP	65.0	2968	52,900 CUP
165 GR. SPR SP	IMR	IMR 4350	.308"	3.340"	68.0	2875	50,000 PSI	73.3	3142	63,100 PSI
165 GR. SPR SP	Winchester	760	.308"	3.340"	61.0	2853	48,500 CUP	65.0	2968	52,900 CUP
165 GR. SPR SP	IMR	IMR 4007 SSC	.308"	3.340"	64.9	2864	52,800 PSI	69.0	3034	61,100 PSI
165 GR. SPR SP	Hodgdon	H380	.308"	3.340"	59.0	2754	44,500 CUP	63.0	2909	52,400 CUP
165 GR. SPR SP	Hodgdon	Varget	.308"	3.340"	54.0	2799	43,900 CUP	58.5	2975	52,900 CUP
165 GR. SPR SP	Hodgdon	H4895	.308"	3.340"	55.0	2839	46,700 CUP	59.0	2977	52,500 CUP
168 GR. HDY BTHP	Hodgdon	H1000	.308"	3.340"	79.0	2938	44,900 CUP	84.0	3110	51,000 CUP
168 GR. HDY BTHP	IMR	IMR 7828	.308"	3.340"	75.0	2888	50,900 PSI	80.0C	3129	62,300 PSI
168 GR. HDY BTHP	Winchester	Supreme 780	.308"	3.340"	73.1	2884	48,600 PSI	77.8	3100	62,700 PSI
168 GR. HDY BTHP	Hodgdon	H4831	.308"	3.340"	72.0	2876	45,100 CUP	75.5	3023	51,400 CUP
168 GR. HDY BTHP	Hodgdon	Hybrid 100V	.308"	3.340"	65.0	2884	50,100 PSI	71.0	3128	62,900 PSI
168 GR. HDY BTHP	IMR	IMR 4831	.308"	3.340"	70.0	2854	50,500 PSI	75.5C	3115	62,700 PSI
168 GR. HDY BTHP	Hodgdon	H4350	.308"	3.340"	66.0	2900	45,500 CUP	70.0	3034	51,000 CUP
168 GR. HDY BTHP	Hodgdon	H414	.308"	3.340"	64.0	2873	45,400 CUP	68.0	3014	51,700 CUP
168 GR. HDY BTHP	IMR	IMR 4350	.308"	3.340"	68.0	2883	50,900 PSI	72.5	3089	61,300 PSI
168 GR. HDY BTHP	Winchester	760	.308"	3.340"	64.0	2873	45,400 CUP	68.0	3014	51,700 CUP
168 GR. HDY BTHP	IMR	IMR 4007 SSC	.308"	3.340"	65.8	2890	53,400 PSI	70.0	3054	62,600 PSI
168 GR. HDY BTHP	Hodgdon	H380	.308"	3.340"	59.0	2738	44,200 CUP	63.0	2903	52,700 CUP
168 GR. HDY BTHP	Hodgdon	Varget	.308"	3.340"	54.0	2795	44,300 CUP	58.2	2964	52,900 CUP
168 GR. HDY BTHP	Hodgdon	H4895	.308"	3.340"	55.0	2843	47,800 CUP	59.0	2977	52,900 CUP
175 GR. SIE HPBT	Hodgdon	H1000	.308"	3.300"	77.0	2820	43,100 CUP	82.0C	3008	51,800 CUP
175 GR. SIE HPBT	IMR	IMR 7828 SSC	.308"	3.300"	71.1	2703	42,700 PSI	79.0C	3051	58,900 PSI
175 GR. SIE HPBT	Winchester	Supreme 780	.308"	3.300"	72.4	2886	52,600 PSI	77.0	3047	61,800 PSI
175 GR. SIE HPBT	Hodgdon	H4831	.308"	3.300"	72.0	2843	46,600 CUP	76.5	3006	53,100 CUP
175 GR. SIE HPBT	Hodgdon	Hybrid 100V	.308"	3.300"	65.0	2837	49,900 PSI	70.5	3068	62,300 PSI
175 GR. SIE HPBT	IMR	IMR 4831	.308"	3.300"	69.5	2889	49,600 PSI	75.5C	3150	63,200 PSI
175 GR. SIE HPBT	Hodgdon	H4350	.308"	3.300"	66.0	2832	45,800 CUP	71.0	2992	52,700 CUP
175 GR. SIE HPBT	Hodgdon	H414	.308"	3.300"	63.0	2830	48,200 CUP	67.5	2972	53,300 CUP
175 GR. SIE HPBT	IMR	IMR 4350	.308"	3.300"	68.3	2910	51,900 PSI	72.7	3106	63,000 PSI
175 GR. SIE HPBT	Winchester	760	.308"	3.300"	63.0	2830	48,200 CUP	67.5	2972	53,300 CUP
175 GR. SIE HPBT	IMR	IMR 4007 SSC	.308"	3.300"	64.2	2809	52,000 PSI	68.3	2963	61,000 PSI

180 GR. NOS E-TIP	Hodgdon	H1000	.308"	3.340"	74.6	2821	53,300 PSI	79.4C	2984	62,400 PSI
180 GR. NOS E-TIP	IMR	IMR 7828	.308"	3.340"	68.4	2811	52,700 PSI	73.5C	2995	61,600 PSI
180 GR. NOS E-TIP	Winchester	Supreme 780	.308"	3.340"	70.0	2840	54,800 PSI	73.7	2969	60,600 PSI
180 GR. NOS E-TIP	Hodgdon	H4831	.308"	3.340"	66.8	2770	53,300 PSI	71.8C	2938	61,900 PSI
180 GR. NOS E-TIP	Hodgdon	Hybrid 100V	.308"	3.340"	58.9	2679	47,700 PSI	66.0	2941	60,800 PSI
180 GR. NOS E-TIP	IMR	IMR 4831	.308"	3.340"	67.3	2817	54,500 PSI	70.2C	2916	59,700 PSI
180 GR. NOS E-TIP	Hodgdon	H4350	.308"	3.340"	62.1	2730	52,300 PSI	66.8	2916	62,600 PSI
180 GR. NOS E-TIP	Hodgdon	H414	.308"	3.340"	60.0	2760	56,000 PSI	62.8	2849	60,600 PSI
180 GR. NOS E-TIP	IMR	IMR 4350	.308"	3.340"	64.7	2797	53,200 PSI	68.1	2932	60,500 PSI
180 GR. NOS E-TIP	Winchester	760	.308"	3.340"	60.0	2760	56,000 PSI	62.8	2849	60,600 PSI
180 GR. SPR MT-SP	Hodgdon	US 869	.308"	3.285"	86.0	2824	52,500 PSI	88.0	2892	56,800 PSI
180 GR. SPR MT-SP	Hodgdon	H1000	.308"	3.285"	76.0	2883	46,800 CUP	81.0C	3042	52,900 CUP
180 GR. SPR MT-SP	IMR	IMR 7828	.308"	3.285"	73.0	2770	49,700 PSI	78.5C	3034	62,000 PSI
180 GR. SPR MT-SP	Winchester	Supreme 780	.308"	3.285"	68.2	2753	50,100 PSI	72.5	2920	59,100 PSI
180 GR. SPR MT-SP	Hodgdon	H4831	.308"	3.285"	69.0	2851	48,500 CUP	73.0C	2966	53,200 CUP
180 GR. SPR MT-SP	Hodgdon	Hybrid 100V	.308"	3.285"	62.0	2775	50,200 PSI	67.7	2998	62,400 PSI
180 GR. SPR MT-SP	IMR	IMR 4831	.308"	3.285"	69.0	2766	50,100 PSI	74.0C	3025	63,200 PSI
180 GR. SPR MT-SP	Hodgdon	H4350	.308"	3.285"	63.0	2787	46,400 CUP	67.0	2918	53,100 CUP
180 GR. SPR MT-SP	Hodgdon	H414	.308"	3.285"	58.0	2722	48,200 CUP	62.0	2845	52,300 CUP
180 GR. SPR MT-SP	IMR	IMR 4350	.308"	3.285"	66.0	2746	50,100 PSI	71.0	2974	61,200 PSI
180 GR. SPR MT-SP	Winchester	760	.308"	3.285"	58.0	2722	48,200 CUP	62.0	2845	52,300 CUP
190 GR. HDY BTSP	Hodgdon	H1000	.308"	3.340"	76.0	2822	44,900 CUP	81.0C	2990	52,800 CUP
190 GR. HDY BTSP	IMR	IMR 7828	.308"	3.340"	71.0	2676	46,700 PSI	76.5C	2975	61,000 PSI
190 GR. HDY BTSP	Winchester	Supreme 780	.308"	3.340"	70.5	2774	52,400 PSI	75.0	2924	60,500 PSI
190 GR. HDY BTSP	Hodgdon	H4831	.308"	3.340"	69.0	2795	48,400 CUP	73.0C	2923	53,600 CUP
190 GR. HDY BTSP	Hodgdon	Hybrid 100V	.308"	3.340"	63.5	2811	56,200 PSI	67.5	2933	62,800 PSI
190 GR. HDY BTSP	IMR	IMR 4831	.308"	3.340"	68.0	2741	51,000 PSI	72.5	2951	61,200 PSI
190 GR. HDY BTSP	Hodgdon	H4350	.308"	3.340"	63.0	2735	46,600 CUP	67.0	2863	53,400 CUP
190 GR. HDY BTSP	IMR	IMR 4350	.308"	3.340"	65.0	2739	49,900 PSI	69.7	2959	61,500 PSI
200 GR. NOS AB	Hodgdon	Retumbo	.308"	3.340"	73.0	2703	44,600 CUP	78.0C	2872	52,100 CUP
200 GR. NOS AB	Hodgdon	H1000	.308"	3.340"	72.0	2662	44,500 CUP	77.0C	2826	52,600 CUP
200 GR. NOS AB	Winchester	Supreme 780	.308"	3.340"	69.6	2700	54,300 PSI	74.0	2847	62,400 PSI
200 GR. NOS AB	Hodgdon	H4831	.308"	3.340"	67.0	2686	49,500 CUP	71.5C	2785	52,800 CUP
200 GR. NOS AB	Hodgdon	Hybrid 100V	.308"	3.340"	61.0	2561	47,200 PSI	67.0C	2821	61,400 PSI
200 GR. NOS AB	Hodgdon	H4350	.308"	3.340"	60.0	2576	44,400 CUP	64.4	2723	51,600 CUP
200 GR. NOS PART	Hodgdon	US 869	.308"	3.340"	83.0	2657	49,200 PSI	85.0	2712	51,800 PSI
200 GR. NOS PART	Hodgdon	Retumbo	.308"	3.340"	79.0	2798	45,700 CUP	84.0C	2962	52,300 CUP
200 GR. NOS PART	Hodgdon	H1000	.308"	3.340"	74.0	2725	45,500 CUP	79.0C	2883	52,800 CUP
200 GR. NOS PART	IMR	IMR 7828	.308"	3.340"	71.0	2645	48,200 PSI	76.0C	2851	58,400 PSI
200 GR. NOS PART	Winchester	Supreme 780	.308"	3.340"	69.1	2702	53,300 PSI	73.5	2870	62,700 PSI

Bullet Weight (Gr.)	Manufacturer	Powder	Bullet Diam.	C.O.L.	Grs.	Vel. (ft/s)	Pressure	Grs.	Vel. (ft/s)	Pressure
200 GR. NOS PART	Hodgdon	H4831	.308"	3.340"	67.0	2686	47,000 CUP	72.0C	2825	53,100 CUP
200 GR. NOS PART	Hodgdon	Hybrid 100V	.308"	3.340"	61.0	2636	49,400 PSI	66.0	2820	59,400 PSI
200 GR. NOS PART	IMR	IMR 4831	.308"	3.340"	69.0	2694	51,900 PSI	72.5C	2859	60,900 PSI
200 GR. NOS PART	Hodgdon	H4350	.308"	3.340"	63.0	2646	47,800 CUP	66.0	2753	51,700 CUP
200 GR. NOS PART	IMR	IMR 4350	.308"	3.340"	65.0	2700	53,900 PSI	69.5	2860	62,600 PSI
208 GR. HDY A-MAX	Hodgdon	Retumbo	.308"	3.420"	74.5	2717	50,300 PSI	81.0C	2915	61,300 PSI
208 GR. HDY A-MAX	Hodgdon	H1000	.308"	3.420"	71.7	2650	47,800 PSI	78.0C	2869	60,200 PSI
208 GR. HDY A-MAX	IMR	IMR 7828	.308"	3.420"	68.0	2635	47,400 PSI	74.0C	2899	62,000 PSI
208 GR. HDY A-MAX	Winchester	Supreme 780	.308"	3.420"	67.6	2641	47,000 PSI	73.5	2890	61,300 PSI
208 GR. HDY A-MAX	Hodgdon	H4831	.308"	3.420"	66.5	2671	53,200 PSI	72.3	2838	62,000 PSI
208 GR. HDY A-MAX	Hodgdon	Hybrid 100V	.308"	3.420"	61.4	2620	50,100 PSI	66.7	2831	62,400 PSI
208 GR. HDY A-MAX	IMR	IMR 4831	.308"	3.420"	63.7	2613	48,600 PSI	69.2	2832	60,500 PSI
208 GR. HDY A-MAX	Hodgdon	H4350	.308"	3.420"	60.4	2655	53,600 PSI	65.7	2813	62,000 PSI
220 GR. SIE RN	Hodgdon	US 869	.308"	3.340"	82.0	2578	49,500 PSI	84.9	2661	54,400 PSI
220 GR. SIE RN	Hodgdon	Retumbo	.308"	3.340"	76.0	2646	44,400 CUP	81.0C	2810	52,400 CUP
220 GR. SIE RN	Hodgdon	H1000	.308"	3.340"	73.0	2588	44,500 CUP	78.0	2750	52,000 CUP
220 GR. SIE RN	IMR	IMR 7828	.308"	3.340"	70.0	2541	49,600 PSI	75.0C	2760	61,700 PSI
220 GR. SIE RN	Winchester	Supreme 780	.308"	3.340"	68.4	2571	53,200 PSI	72.8	2716	61,700 PSI
220 GR. SIE RN	Hodgdon	H4831	.308"	3.340"	66.0	2533	44,900 CUP	71.0	2685	53,100 CUP
220 GR. SIE RN	Hodgdon	Hybrid 100V	.308"	3.340"	61.0	2474	48,800 PSI	67.0C	2694	62,300 PSI
220 GR. SIE RN	IMR	IMR 4831	.308"	3.340"	66.0	2531	51,000 PSI	71.0	2718	61,600 PSI
220 GR. SIE RN	Hodgdon	H4350	.308"	3.340"	61.0	2501	46,100 CUP	65.0	2622	52,300 CUP
230 GR. BER TACT	Hodgdon	US 869	.308"	3.395"	77.7	2423	41,700 PSI	83.5C	2610	50,200 PSI
230 GR. BER TACT	Hodgdon	Retumbo	.308"	3.395"	71.6	2520	44,700 PSI	77.0C	2714	55,200 PSI
230 GR. BER TACT	Hodgdon	H1000	.308"	3.395"	69.1	2471	44,200 PSI	76.0C	2721	58,200 PSI
230 GR. BER TACT	IMR	IMR 7828	.308"	3.395"	66.7	2507	46,200 PSI	72.6C	2774	61,300 PSI
230 GR. BER TACT	Winchester	Supreme 780	.308"	3.395"	66.9	2577	50,700 PSI	72.0	2774	62,100 PSI
230 GR. BER TACT	Hodgdon	H4831	.308"	3.395"	64.1	2527	50,800 PSI	70.3	2710	61,200 PSI
230 GR. BER TACT	Hodgdon	Hybrid 100V	.308"	3.395"	69.6	2467	44,800 PSI	75.0C	2661	55,200 PSI
230 GR. BER TACT	IMR	IMR 4831	.308"	3.395"	62.9	2553	51,500 PSI	68.7	2739	61,600 PSI

Cartridge: 300 Weatherby Magnum Load Type: Rifle					Starting Loads			Maximum Loads		
Bullet Weight (Gr.)	Manufacturer	Powder	Bullet Diam.	C.O.L.	Grs.	Vel. (ft/s)	Pressure	Grs.	Vel. (ft/s)	Pressure
125 GR. SIE SP	IMR	IMR 7828	.308"	3.475"	83.0	3333	45,600 CUP	89.0C*	3550	53,200 CUP
125 GR. SIE SP	Hodgdon	H4831	.308"	3.475"	84.0	3322	46,000 CUP	90.0C	3527	53,100 CUP
125 GR. SIE SP	IMR	IMR 4831	.308"	3.475"	79.0	3366	47,000 CUP	85.0C	3573	53,500 CUP
125 GR. SIE SP	Hodgdon	H4350	.308"	3.475"	77.0	3347	46,300 CUP	82.5	3547	53,200 CUP
125 GR. SIE SP	Hodgdon	H414	.308"	3.475"	73.0	3321	46,600 CUP	78.5	3518	53,900 CUP

125 GR. SIE SP	IMR	IMR 4350	.308"	3.475"	77.0	3397	46,100 CUP	82.5	3590	53,300 CUP
125 GR. SIE SP	Winchester	760	.308"	3.475"	73.0	3321	46,600 CUP	78.5	3518	53,900 CUP
125 GR. SIE SP	IMR	IMR 4007 SSC	.308"	3.475"	74.0	3309	44,500 CUP	80.0	3538	53,600 CUP
125 GR. SIE SP	Hodgdon	H380	.308"	3.475"	70.0	3215	46,900 CUP	75.5	3428	53,300 CUP
125 GR. SIE SP	Hodgdon	Varget	.308"	3.475"	65.0	3386	49,500 CUP	69.0	3492	53,700 CUP
125 GR. SIE SP	IMR	IMR 4064	.308"	3.475"	65.0	3311	48,800 CUP	69.4	3471	53,700 CUP
130 GR. BAR XLC BT	Hodgdon	H4831	.308"	3.500"	84.0	3306	46,200 CUP	89.5C	3467	53,000 CUP
130 GR. BAR XLC BT	Hodgdon	H4350	.308"	3.500"	78.0	3287	46,300 CUP	83.0	3485	52,800 CUP
130 GR. BAR XLC BT	Hodgdon	H414	.308"	3.500"	75.0	3238	45,300 CUP	80.0	3446	53,100 CUP
130 GR. BAR XLC BT	Winchester	760	.308"	3.500"	75.0	3238	45,300 CUP	80.0	3446	53,100 CUP
130 GR. BAR XLC BT	Hodgdon	H380	.308"	3.500"	71.0	2331	46,700 CUP	76.0	3410	54,100 CUP
150 GR. BAR TSX	Hodgdon	H1000	.308"	3.570"	83.0	3056	43,500 CUP	88.0C	3220	49,900 CUP
150 GR. BAR TSX	IMR	IMR 7828 SSC	.308"	3.570"	79.0	3146	45,600 CUP	86.5C*	3400	54,200 CUP
150 GR. BAR TSX	Winchester	Supreme 780	.308"	3.575"	80.4	3167	45,100 CUP	85.5	3328	50,000 CUP
150 GR. BAR TSX	Hodgdon	H4831	.308"	3.570"	77.0	3031	45,200 CUP	84.0C	3275	52,900 CUP
150 GR. BAR TSX	Hodgdon	Hybrid 100V	.308"	3.575"	70.0	3103	42,500 CUP	76.5	3310	49,100 CUP
150 GR. BAR TSX	IMR	IMR 4831	.308"	3.570"	76.0	3154	46,400 CUP	82.7C	3437	54,100 CUP
150 GR. BAR TSX	Hodgdon	H4350	.308"	3.570"	70.0	3084	44,700 CUP	76.5	3310	53,800 CUP
150 GR. BAR TSX	Hodgdon	H414	.308"	3.570"	67.0	3007	44,400 CUP	72.5	3201	53,000 CUP
150 GR. BAR TSX	IMR	IMR 4350	.308"	3.570"	73.0	3151	45,400 CUP	79.5	3396	54,300 CUP
150 GR. BAR TSX	IMR	IMR 4007 SSC	.308"	3.570"	67.0	2923	44,300 CUP	73.0	3197	52,800 CUP
150 GR. BAR TSX	Hodgdon	H380	.308"	3.570"	63.0	2908	44,200 CUP	69.5	3142	53,800 CUP
150 GR. BAR TSX	Hodgdon	Varget	.308"	3.570"	59.0	2935	42,200 CUP	64.5	3155	54,000 CUP
150 GR. BAR TSX	IMR	IMR 4064	.308"	3.570"	62.0	3045	44,200 CUP	67.0	3244	51,900 CUP
150 GR. BAR TSX	IMR	IMR 4895	.308"	3.570"	61.0	3011	44,000 CUP	66.0	3214	53,100 CUP
150 GR. BAR TSX	Hodgdon	H4895	.308"	3.570"	57.0	2926	42,200 CUP	61.5	3112	54,100 CUP
150 GR. BAR TSX	IMR	Trail Boss	.308"	3.580"	19.0	1334	20,300 CUP	27.5	1656	28,900 CUP
165 GR. NOS BT	Hodgdon	H1000	.308"	3.560"	84.0	3014	45,600 CUP	89.7C	3216	54,200 CUP
165 GR. NOS BT	IMR	IMR 7828	.308"	3.560"	77.0	2957	46,800 CUP	82.0	3145	53,400 CUP
165 GR. NOS BT	Winchester	Supreme 780	.308"	3.560"	80.4	3083	46,700 CUP	85.5	3245	51,900 CUP
165 GR. NOS BT	Hodgdon	H4831	.308"	3.560"	75.0	2934	46,400 CUP	80.2	3113	54,000 CUP
165 GR. NOS BT	Hodgdon	Hybrid 100V	.308"	3.560"	71.0	2995	45,400 CUP	78.0	3236	53,800 CUP
165 GR. NOS BT	IMR	IMR 4831	.308"	3.560"	73.0	2981	46,600 CUP	78.0	3175	54,100 CUP
165 GR. NOS BT	Hodgdon	H4350	.308"	3.560"	69.0	2908	45,400 CUP	74.0	3074	54,100 CUP
165 GR. NOS BT	Hodgdon	H414	.308"	3.560"	65.0	2892	48,200 CUP	70.0	3034	53,700 CUP
165 GR. NOS BT	IMR	IMR 4350	.308"	3.560"	70.0	2973	46,900 CUP	75.0	3143	53,400 CUP
165 GR. NOS BT	Winchester	760	.308"	3.560"	65.0	2892	48,200 CUP	70.0	3034	53,700 CUP
165 GR. NOS BT	IMR	IMR 4007 SSC	.308"	3.560"	67.0	2901	44,300 CUP	73.3	3101	53,400 CUP
165 GR. NOS BT	Hodgdon	H380	.308"	3.560"	63.0	2787	46,300 CUP	67.5	2950	53,700 CUP
165 GR. NOS BT	Hodgdon	Varget	.308"	3.560"	58.0	2873	46,300 CUP	62.0	3033	54,200 CUP

165 GR. NOS BT	Hodgdon	H4895	.308"	3.560"	58.0	2871	48,000 CUP	62.5	3028	54,200 CUP
168 GR. NOS E-TIP	Hodgdon	H1000	.308"	3.590"	82.0	2959	44,100 CUP	88.0C	3197	53,700 CUP
168 GR. NOS E-TIP	IMR	IMR 7828 SSC	.308"	3.590"	78.0	2956	46,700 CUP	84.0C*	3205	54,200 CUP
168 GR. NOS E-TIP	Winchester	Supreme 780	.308"	3.590"	76.0	2964	44,800 CUP	84.0	3250	54,100 CUP
168 GR. NOS E-TIP	Hodgdon	H4831	.308"	3.590"	74.0	2865	43,700 CUP	81.0C	3107	54,200 CUP
168 GR. NOS E-TIP	Hodgdon	Hybrid 100V	.308"	3.590"	68.0	2923	45,000 CUP	74.0	3150	53,700 CUP
168 GR. NOS E-TIP	IMR	IMR 4831	.308"	3.590"	71.0	2907	45,800 CUP	77.5	3158	54,000 CUP
168 GR. NOS E-TIP	Hodgdon	H4350	.308"	3.590"	66.0	2898	46,900 CUP	72.5	3099	53,800 CUP
168 GR. NOS E-TIP	Hodgdon	H414	.308"	3.590"	62.0	2750	44,300 CUP	69.0	2994	53,900 CUP
168 GR. NOS E-TIP	IMR	IMR 4350	.308"	3.590"	70.0	2911	45,300 CUP	76.0	3164	54,300 CUP
168 GR. NOS E-TIP	Winchester	760	.308"	3.590"	62.0	2750	44,300 CUP	69.0	2994	53,900 CUP
168 GR. NOS E-TIP	IMR	IMR 4007 SSC	.308"	3.590"	65.0	2832	45,700 CUP	71.5	3053	54,000 CUP
168 GR. NOS E-TIP	Hodgdon	H380	.308"	3.590"	63.0	2752	45,700 CUP	68.0	2929	53,800 CUP
168 GR. NOS E-TIP	Hodgdon	Varget	.308"	3.590"	59.0	2854	48,000 CUP	63.5	2999	53,800 CUP
168 GR. NOS E-TIP	Hodgdon	H4895	.308"	3.590"	55.0	2773	47,000 CUP	60.0	2968	54,500 CUP
180 GR. NOS E-TIP	Hodgdon	H1000	.308"	3.590"	79.0	2861	46,300 CUP	85.0C	3054	53,900 CUP
180 GR. NOS E-TIP	IMR	IMR 7828 SSC	.308"	3.590"	75.0	2851	46,700 CUP	81.0	3076	53,900 CUP
180 GR. NOS E-TIP	Winchester	Supreme 780	.308"	3.590"	74.0	2885	46,700 CUP	81.0	3134	53,800 CUP
180 GR. NOS E-TIP	Hodgdon	H4831	.308"	3.590"	71.0	2772	46,700 CUP	78.0	2977	53,300 CUP
180 GR. NOS E-TIP	Hodgdon	Hybrid 100V	.308"	3.590"	66.0	2802	44,600 CUP	72.5	3046	53,700 CUP
180 GR. NOS E-TIP	IMR	IMR 4831	.308"	3.590"	69.0	2804	46,300 CUP	75.0	3021	53,700 CUP
180 GR. NOS E-TIP	Hodgdon	H4350	.308"	3.590"	64.0	2783	47,100 CUP	70.0	2968	54,100 CUP
180 GR. NOS E-TIP	Hodgdon	H414	.308"	3.590"	61.0	2691	48,500 CUP	67.0	2893	54,600 CUP
180 GR. NOS E-TIP	IMR	IMR 4350	.308"	3.590"	67.0	2781	44,800 CUP	73.0	3008	53,300 CUP
180 GR. NOS E-TIP	Winchester	760	.308"	3.590"	61.0	2691	48,500 CUP	67.0	2893	54,600 CUP
180 GR. NOS E-TIP	IMR	IMR 4007 SSC	.308"	3.590"	63.0	2716	45,800 CUP	69.0	2923	53,600 CUP
180 GR. NOS E-TIP	Hodgdon	H380	.308"	3.590"	61.0	2640	46,500 CUP	66.5	2826	53,800 CUP
180 GR. SPR BTSP	Hodgdon	H1000	.308"	3.560"	83.0	2971	43,800 CUP	88.5C	3151	53,500 CUP
180 GR. SPR BTSP	IMR	IMR 7828	.308"	3.560"	75.0	2583	47,000 CUP	80.5	3064	53,400 CUP
180 GR. SPR BTSP	Winchester	Supreme 780	.308"	3.560"	77.5	2927	46,300 CUP	82.5	3127	53,100 CUP
180 GR. SPR BTSP	Hodgdon	H4831	.308"	3.560"	76.0	2910	45,300 CUP	81.5	3096	54,000 CUP
180 GR. SPR BTSP	Hodgdon	Hybrid 100V	.308"	3.560"	70.0	2954	46.100 CUP	77.0	3171	54,600 CUP
180 GR. SPR BTSP	IMR	IMR 4831	.308"	3.560"	70.0	2835	47,100 CUP	75.5	2997	53,500 CUP
180 GR. SPR BTSP	Hodgdon	H4350	.308"	3.560"	69.0	2876	44,600 CUP	73.5	3022	54,000 CUP
180 GR. SPR BTSP	Hodgdon	H414	.308"	3.560"	67.0	2825	45,600 CUP	71.5	2984	53,000 CUP
180 GR. SPR BTSP	IMR	IMR 4350	.308"	3.560"	68.0	2865	46,200 CUP	72.6	3018	53,000 CUP
180 GR. SPR BTSP	Winchester	760	.308"	3.560"	67.0	2825	45,600 CUP	71.5	2984	53,000 CUP
180 GR. SPR BTSP	IMR	IMR 4007 SSC	.308"	3.560"	65.0	2799	45,400 CUP	71.0	2986	53,300 CUP
180 GR. SPR BTSP	Hodgdon	H380	.308"	3.560"	62.0	2734	45,000 CUP	67.0	2896	54,000 CUP

180 GR. WIN FS	Hodgdon	H1000	.308"	3.560"	78.0	2921	47,800 CUP	83.0C	3111	54,600 CUP
180 GR. WIN FS	Hodgdon	H4831	.308"	3.560"	74.0	2892	50,200 CUP	79.0	3013	54,600 CUP
180 GR. WIN FS	Hodgdon	H4350	.308"	3.560"	67.0	2813	46,500 CUP	72.0	2974	54,600 CUP
200 GR. NOS AB	Hodgdon	Retumbo	.308"	3.590	79.0	2753	45,800 CUP	84.5C	2942	53,100 CUP
200 GR. NOS AB	Hodgdon	H1000	.308"	3.590"	77.0	2709	45,800 CUP	83.0C	2884	53,700 CUP
200 GR. NOS AB	Hodgdon	H4831	.308"	3.590"	70.0	2702	49,300 CUP	75.0	2839	54,400 CUP
200 GR. NOS AB	Hodgdon	Hybrid 100V	.308"	3.590"	68.0	2737	45,900 CUP	73.5	2940	54,000 CUP
200 GR. SFT	Hodgdon	Retumbo	.308"	3.510"	80.0	2764	46,100 CUP	85.5C	2981	54,400 CUP
200 GR. SFT	Hodgdon	H1000	.308"	3.510"	79.0	2766	43,200 CUP	85.0C	2963	53,400 CUP
200 GR. SFT	IMR	IMR 7828	.308"	3.510"	73.0	2693	48,100 CUP	78.3	2872	53,800 CUP
200 GR. SFT	Winchester	Supreme 780	.308"	3.590"	69.6	2570	38,900 CUP	74.0	2808	50,700 CUP
200 GR. SFT	Hodgdon	H4831	.308"	3.510"	72.0	2708	44,700 CUP	77.5	2869	52,900 CUP
200 GR. SFT	Hodgdon	Hybrid 100V	.308"	3.510"	67.0	2699	44,900 CUP	73.0	2906	53,200 CUP
200 GR. SFT	IMR	IMR 4831	.308"	3.510"	68.0	2641	45,800 CUP	73.0	2806	53,400 CUP
200 GR. SFT	Hodgdon	H4350	.308"	3.510"	66.0	2706	45,800 CUP	71.0	2866	54,300 CUP
200 GR. SFT	IMR	IMR 4350	.308"	3.510"	66.0	2680	46,000 CUP	70.5	2807	52,800 CUP
220 GR. HDY RN	Hodgdon	Retumbo	.308"	3.565"	79.0	2679	45,900 CUP	84.0C	2853	54,000 CUP
220 GR. HDY RN	Hodgdon	H1000	.308"	3.565"	77.0	2670	45,100 CUP	82.5	2833	53,400 CUP
220 GR. HDY RN	IMR	IMR 7828	.308"	3.565"	70.0	2569	47,200 CUP	75.3	2739	54,100 CUP
220 GR. HDY RN	Winchester	Supreme 780	.308"	3.565"	71,7	2602	44,400 CUP	76.3	2765	51,300 CUP
220 GR. HDY RN	Hodgdon	H4831	.308"	3.565"	71.0	2630	47,200 CUP	75.7	2766	54,500 CUP
220 GR. HDY RN	Hodgdon	Hybrid 100V	.308"	3.565"	65.0	2579	45,100 CUP	71.0	2762	53,900 CUP
220 GR. HDY RN	IMR	IMR 4831	.308"	3.565"	65.0	2529	46,000 CUP	70.0	2657	53,600 CUP
220 GR. HDY RN	Hodgdon	H4350	.308"	3.565"	66.0	2599	45,900 CUP	70.0	2725	53,800 CUP
220 GR. HDY RN	IMR	IMR 4350	.308"	3.565"	63.0	2517	46,300 CUP	67.7	2700	53,500 CUP

Cartridge: 300 Remington Ultra Mag **Load Type:** Rifle					**Starting Loads**			**Maximum Loads**		
Bullet Weight (Gr.)	Manufacturer	Powder	Bullet Diam.	C.O.L.	Grs.	Vel. (ft/s)	Pressure	Grs.	Vel. (ft/s)	Pressure
130 GR. BAR XLC BT	Hodgdon	H1000	.308"	3.550"	100.0	3349	50,900 PSI	107.0C	3615	63,500 PSI
130 GR. BAR XLC BT	Hodgdon	H4831	.308"	3.550"	93.0	3330	51,200 PSI	99.5	3579	62,800 PSI
130 GR. BAR XLC BT	Hodgdon	H4350	.308"	3.550"	87.0	3436	54,000 PSI	93.0	3638	63,000 PSI
140 GR. BAR XBT	Hodgdon	Retumbo	.308"	3.555"	97.0	3282	52,100 PSI	103.5C	3493	61,400 PSI
140 GR. BAR XBT	Hodgdon	H1000	.308"	3.555"	95.0	3326	56,900 PSI	101.0	3470	63,100 PSI
140 GR. BAR XBT	Hodgdon	H4831	.308"	3.555"	87.0	3258	55,100 PSI	93.0	3447	63,600 PSI
150 GR. SIE SPBT	Hodgdon	Retumbo	.308"	3.530"	100.0	3343	52,600 PSI	106.0C	3531	60,800 PSI
150 GR. SIE SPBT	Hodgdon	H1000	.308"	3.530"	98.0	3258	53,100 PSI	102.0	3457	62,900 PSI
150 GR. SIE SPBT	IMR	IMR 7828	.308"	3.530"	86.5	3105	52,100 PSI	92.0	3319	63,000 PSI
150 GR. SIE SPBT	Hodgdon	H4831	.308"	3.530"	90.0	3243	55,100 PSI	94.0	3408	62,900 PSI
150 GR. SIE SPBT	IMR	IMR 4831	.308"	3.530"	85.0	3207	50,600 PSI	90.5	3380	63,700 PSI

150 GR. SIE SPBT	IMR	IMR 4350	.308"	3.530"	81.5	3147	53,200 PSI	86.7	3362	63,500 PSI
165 GR. SFT SP	Hodgdon	Retumbo	.308"	3.530"	97.0	3241	54,200 PSI	103.0C	3414	62,300 PSI
165 GR. SFT SP	Hodgdon	H1000	.308"	3.530"	94.0	3135	53,300 PSI	98.0	3321	62,500 PSI
165 GR. SFT SP	IMR	IMR 7828	.308"	3.530"	84.5	2985	54,300 PSI	90.0	3178	63,200 PSI
165 GR. SFT SP	Hodgdon	H4831	.308"	3.530"	85.0	3057	52,300 PSI	90.0	3255	62,100 PSI
165 GR. SFT SP	IMR	IMR 4831	.308"	3.530"	80.0	2951	51,100 PSI	87.0	3215	62,900 PSI
165 GR. SFT SP	IMR	IMR 4350	.308"	3.530"	78.0	2985	52,800 PSI	83.0	3181	63,100 PSI
180 GR. BAR TTSX BT	Hodgdon	US 869	.308"	3.600"	94.5	2884	47,200 PSI	105.0	3176	59,600 PSI
180 GR. BAR TTSX BT	Hodgdon	H50BMG	.308"	3.600"	82.4	2836	51,700 PSI	89.6	3031	61,900 PSI
180 GR. BAR TTSX BT	Hodgdon	Retumbo	.308"	3.600"	80.1	3012	56,700 PSI	87.0	3130	61,400 PSI
180 GR. BAR TTSX BT	Hodgdon	H1000	.308"	3.600"	74.5	2891	55,000 PSI	81.0	3067	63,500 PSI
180 GR. BAR TTSX BT	IMR	IMR 7828 SSC	.308"	3.600"	74.4	2851	48,900 PSI	80.0	3107	62,700 PSI
180 GR. BAR TTSX BT	Hodgdon	H4831	.308"	3.600"	72.8	2837	49,700 PSI	77.5	3010	59,100 PSI
180 GR. BAR TTSX BT	IMR	IMR 4831	.308"	3.600"	68.6	2817	49,000 PSI	73.0	2986	58,400 PSI
180 GR. BAR TTSX BT	IMR	IMR 4350	.308"	3.600"	67.2	2857	52,600 PSI	71.5	3021	62,300 PSI
180 GR. SPR SPBT	Hodgdon	US 869	.308"	3.530"	104.0	2994	53,800 PSI	107.0	3070	57,300 PSI
180 GR. SPR SPBT	Hodgdon	H50BMG	.308"	3.530"	103.0	3005	53,700 PSI	108.0C	3159	62,100 PSI
180 GR. SPR SPBT	Hodgdon	Retumbo	.308"	3.530"	94.0	3182	58,400 PSI	100.5C	3300	62,400 PSI
180 GR. SPR SPBT	Hodgdon	H1000	.308"	3.530"	91.0	3018	52,300 PSI	96.0	3218	62,800 PSI
180 GR. SPR SPBT	IMR	IMR 7828	.308"	3.530"	81.0	2869	52,000 PSI	86.5	3069	63,200 PSI
180 GR. SPR SPBT	Hodgdon	H4831	.308"	3.530"	84.0	2997	54,000 PSI	89.0	3167	62,500 PSI
180 GR. SPR SPBT	IMR	IMR 4831	.308"	3.530"	78.0	2907	53,700 PSI	83.0	3075	63,200 PSI
180 GR. SPR SPBT	IMR	IMR 4350	.308"	3.530"	76.0	2869	51,800 PSI	81.0	3071	63,200 PSI
190 GR. HDY SPBT	Hodgdon	US 869	.308"	3.555"	100.0	2905	52,600 PSI	104.0	3035	59,200 PSI
190 GR. HDY SPBT	Hodgdon	H50BMG	.308"	3.555"	100.0	2938	54,900 PSI	105.0C	3085	63,000 PSI
190 GR. HDY SPBT	Hodgdon	Retumbo	.308"	3.555"	90.0	3069	56,500 PSI	96.0	3204	62,500 PSI
190 GR. HDY SPBT	Hodgdon	H1000	.308"	3.555"	88.0	2971	54,900 PSI	93.0	3130	63,500 PSI
190 GR. HDY SPBT	IMR	IMR 7828	.308"	3.555"	80.5	2802	51,700 PSI	85.5	2985	62,000 PSI
190 GR. HDY SPBT	Hodgdon	H4831	.308"	3.555"	80.0	2892	53,000 PSI	85.0	3069	62,500 PSI
190 GR. HDY SPBT	IMR	IMR 4831	.308"	3.555"	77.0	2849	54,300 PSI	82.5	3013	63,900 PSI
190 GR. HDY SPBT	IMR	IMR 4350	.308"	3.555"	75.0	2804	51,800 PSI	80.0	3001	63,100 PSI
200 GR. BAR XFB	Hodgdon	US 869	.308"	3.555"	96.0	2834	58,000 PSI	100.0	2919	61,800 PSI
200 GR. BAR XFB	Hodgdon	H50BMG	.308"	3.555"	92.0	2767	56,100 PSI	98.0C	2910	63,100 PSI
200 GR. BAR XFB	Hodgdon	Retumbo	.308"	3.555"	81.0	2852	56,200 PSI	86.0	2988	62,800 PSI
200 GR. BAR XFB	Hodgdon	H1000	.308"	3.555"	80.0	2767	57,400 PSI	83.0	2850	62,800 PSI
200 GR. NOS AB	Hodgdon	H50BMG	.308"	3.600"	96.0	2762	49,700 PSI	102.0C	2950	58,900 PSI
200 GR. NOS AB	Hodgdon	Retumbo	.308"	3.600"	89.0	2904	56,400 PSI	95.5C	3048	62,400 PSI
200 GR. NOS AB	Hodgdon	H1000	.308"	3.600"	87.0	2839	56,000 PSI	92.5	2975	62,800 PSI
200 GR. NOS AB	IMR	IMR 7828	.308"	3.600"	77.0	2670	51,200 PSI	82.0	2857	61,800 PSI

Bullet Weight (Gr.)	Manufacturer	Powder	Bullet Diam.	C.O.L.	Grs.	Vel. (ft/s)	Pressure	Grs.	Vel. (ft/s)	Pressure
200 GR. NOS AB	Hodgdon	H4831	.308"	3.600"	79.0	2787	54,700 PSI	85.0	2953	63,600 PSI
220 GR. NOS PART	Hodgdon	US 869	.308"	3.530"	97.0	2758	49,500 PSI	101.0	2875	55,200 PSI
220 GR. NOS PART	Hodgdon	H50BMG	.308"	3.530"	95.0	2699	54,000 PSI	100.5C	2850	62,500 PSI
220 GR. NOS PART	Hodgdon	Retumbo	.308"	3.530"	84.0	2800	56,600 PSI	89.0	2905	61,900 PSI
220 GR. NOS PART	Hodgdon	H1000	.308"	3.530"	83.0	2704	54,500 PSI	89.0	2863	63,500 PSI
220 GR. NOS PART	IMR	IMR 7828	.308"	3.530"	77.5	2600	53,400 PSI	82.5	2774	63,200 PSI

Cartridge: 30-378 Weatherby
Load Type: Rifle

Bullet Weight (Gr.)	Manufacturer	Powder	Bullet Diam.	C.O.L.	Starting Loads Grs.	Vel. (ft/s)	Pressure	Maximum Loads Grs.	Vel. (ft/s)	Pressure
150 GR. SIE SPBT	Hodgdon	Retumbo	.308"	3.600"	113.0	3490	44,900 CUP	119.0C	3690	52,400 CUP
150 GR. SIE SPBT	Hodgdon	H1000	.308"	3.600"	110.0	3464	46,000 CUP	114.0	3598	52,400 CUP
150 GR. SIE SPBT	IMR	IMR 7828	.308"	3.600"	97.0	3373	46,100 CUP	103.0	3573	52,700 CUP
150 GR. SIE SPBT	Hodgdon	H4831	.308"	3.600"	100.0	3449	49,100 CUP	104.0	3555	53,900 CUP
150 GR. SIE SPBT	IMR	IMR 4831	.308"	3.600"	94.0	3342	44,300 CUP	99.5	3558	53,500 CUP
165 GR. SFT SP	Hodgdon	US 869	.308"	3.600"	121.0	3325	41,100 CUP	123.5	3423	47,800 CUP
165 GR. SFT SP	Hodgdon	Retumbo	.308"	3.600"	109.0	3305	42,800 CUP	116.0C	3559	53,400 CUP
165 GR. SFT SP	Hodgdon	H1000	.308"	3.600"	106.0	3285	45,500 CUP	112.0	3495	55,000 CUP
165 GR. SFT SP	IMR	IMR 7828	.308"	3.600"	95.0	3244	47,600 CUP	101.0	3412	53,000 CUP
165 GR. SFT SP	Hodgdon	H4831	.308"	3.600"	95.0	3202	46,600 CUP	100.5	3391	53,800 CUP
165 GR. SFT SP	IMR	IMR 4831	.308"	3.600"	92.5	3232	47,200 CUP	98.0	3417	53,400 CUP
168 GR. NOS E-TIP	Hodgdon	US 869	.308"	3.740"	109.8	3027	38,000 CUP	122.0	3416	50,400 CUP
168 GR. NOS E-TIP	Hodgdon	Retumbo	.308"	3.740"	98.0	3127	43,500 CUP	109.0C	3444	51,600 CUP
168 GR. NOS E-TIP	Hodgdon	H1000	.308"	3.740"	97.5	3094	43,800 CUP	106.0	3341	53,400 CUP
168 GR. NOS E-TIP	IMR	IMR 7828 SSC	.308"	3.740"	94.8	3111	43,100 CUP	103.0	3410	53,700 CUP
168 GR. NOS E-TIP	Hodgdon	H4831	.308"	3.740"	93.0	3152	46,400 CUP	101.0	3341	52,400 CUP
168 GR. NOS E-TIP	IMR	IMR 4831	.308"	3.740"	91.2	3201	47,400 CUP	97.0	3395	54,400 CUP
180 GR. NOS E-TIP	Hodgdon	US 869	.308"	3.740"	106.0	2964	40,300 CUP	118.0	3305	50,200 CUP
180 GR. NOS E-TIP	Hodgdon	H50BMG	.308"	3.740"	105.3	2958	41,700 CUP	117.0	3237	50,400 CUP
180 GR. NOS E-TIP	Hodgdon	Retumbo	.308"	3.740"	96.5	3087	46,000 CUP	106.0C	3336	53,900 CUP
180 GR. NOS E-TIP	Hodgdon	H1000	.308"	3.740"	95.7	3033	45,100 CUP	104.0	3282	52,600 CUP
180 GR. NOS E-TIP	IMR	IMR 7828 SSC	.308"	3.740"	92.1	3026	43,900 CUP	98.0	3222	50,700 CUP
180 GR. NOS E-TIP	Hodgdon	H4831	.308"	3.740"	92.1	3092	46,700 CUP	98.0	3222	52,600 CUP
180 GR. NOS E-TIP	IMR	IMR 4831	.308"	3.740"	89.3	3133	50,600 CUP	95.0	3282	54,200 CUP
180 GR. SPR SPBT	Hodgdon	US 869	.308"	3.600"	115.0	3101	40,800 CUP	120.0	3302	47,100 CUP
180 GR. SPR SPBT	Hodgdon	H50BMG	.308"	3.600"	116.0	3089	40,400 CUP	120.0C	3229	47,100 CUP
180 GR. SPR SPBT	Hodgdon	Retumbo	.308"	3.600"	107.0	3228	43,200 CUP	113.0C	3460	54,700 CUP
180 GR. SPR SPBT	Hodgdon	H1000	.308"	3.600"	105.0	3213	45,200 CUP	111.0	3412	54,300 CUP
180 GR. SPR SPBT	IMR	IMR 7828	.308"	3.600"	92.5	3156	48,300 CUP	98.0	3284	52,400 CUP
180 GR. SPR SPBT	Hodgdon	H4831	.308"	3.600"	94.0	3134	46,600 CUP	100.0	3301	54,500 CUP

Bullet Weight	Manufacturer	Powder	Bullet Diam.	C.O.L.	Grs.	Vel. (ft/s)	Pressure	Grs.	Vel. (ft/s)	Pressure
180 GR. SPR SPBT	IMR	IMR 4831	.308"	3.600"	90.5	3120	44,400 CUP	96.0	3292	53,800 CUP
190 GR. HDY SPBT	Hodgdon	US 869	.308"	3.625"	115.0	3146	44,100 CUP	120.0	3331	49,800 CUP
190 GR. HDY SPBT	Hodgdon	H50BMG	.308"	3.625"	115.0	3113	45,700 CUP	120.0C	3243	50,900 CUP
190 GR. HDY SPBT	Hodgdon	Retumbo	.308"	3.625"	105.0	3154	43,600 CUP	111.5C	3374	54,500 CUP
190 GR. HDY SPBT	Hodgdon	H1000	.308"	3.625"	102.0	3154	46,500 CUP	108.0	3316	54,800 CUP
190 GR. HDY SPBT	IMR	IMR 7828	.308"	3.625"	92.0	3104	49,600 CUP	97.5	3220	52,800 CUP
200 GR. BAR XFB	Hodgdon	US 869	.308"	3.645"	115.0	3134	49,800 CUP	118.0	3206	52,500 CUP
200 GR. BAR XFB	Hodgdon	H50BMG	.308"	3.645"	111.0	3134	52,300 CUP	117.0C	3227	54,800 CUP
200 GR. BAR XFB	IMR	IMR 7828	.308"	3.645"	89.0	2935	52,000 CUP	94.5	3053	55,000 CUP
200 GR. NOS AB	Hodgdon	H50BMG	.308"	3.650"	106.0	2958	43,700 CUP	113.0C	3142	49,600 CUP
200 GR. NOS AB	Hodgdon	Retumbo	.308"	3.650"	98.0	2992	44,900 CUP	105.0C	3209	52,600 CUP
200 GR. NOS AB	Hodgdon	H1000	.308"	3.650"	95.0	2966	46,100 CUP	101.5	3130	53,800 CUP
200 GR. NOS AB	IMR	IMR 7828	.308"	3.650"	90.0	2968	45,400 CUP	96.0	3156	54,400 CUP
220 GR. NOS PART	Hodgdon	US 869	.308"	3.600"	114.5	3068	49,500 CUP	117.0	3134	51,400 CUP
220 GR. NOS PART	Hodgdon	H50BMG	.308"	3.600"	115.0	3047	48,300 CUP	118.5C	3145	53,700 CUP
220 GR. NOS PART	Hodgdon	Retumbo	.308"	3.600"	101.0	2954	44,700 CUP	107.5	3155	55,000 CUP
220 GR. NOS PART	Hodgdon	H1000	.308"	3.600"	99.0	2965	47,800 CUP	104.0	3084	53,700 CUP
220 GR. NOS PART	IMR	IMR 7828	.308"	3.600"	85.5	2788	46,400 CUP	91.0	2930	52,600 CUP

Cartridge: 7.62 x 39mm Russian
Load Type: Rifle

Bullet Weight (Gr.)	Manufacturer	Powder	Bullet Diam.	C.O.L.	Starting Loads			Maximum Loads		
					Grs.	Vel. (ft/s)	Pressure	Grs.	Vel. (ft/s)	Pressure
108 GR. BAR RRLP FB	Hodgdon	H335	.310"	2.210"	27.1	2020	39,300 CUP	28.8	2098	42,300 CUP
108 GR. BAR RRLP FB	Hodgdon	Benchmark	.310"	2.210"	25.0	1826	32,200 CUP	28.5C	2118	38,700 CUP
108 GR. BAR RRLP FB	Hodgdon	H322	.310"	2.210"	25.7	1974	34,500 CUP	28.5C	2199	41,200 CUP
108 GR. BAR RRLP FB	IMR	IMR 4198	.310"	2.210"	21.7	1985	37,500 CUP	23.6C	2163	41,700 CUP
108 GR. BAR RRLP FB	Hodgdon	H4198	.310"	2.210"	23.3	2155	38,300 CUP	25.0	2310	42,300 CUP
108 GR. BAR RRLP FB	IMR	IMR 4227	.310"	2.210"	15.0	1526	26,100 CUP	17.6	1907	41,000 CUP
125 GR. SPR SP	Hodgdon	BL-C(2)	.311"	2.150"	30.0	2155	32,200 CUP	31.5	2349	38,800 CUP
125 GR. SPR SP	Hodgdon	H335	.311"	2.150"	30.0	2219	35,400 CUP	31.5	2408	40,900 CUP
125 GR. SPR SP	Hodgdon	H4895	.311"	2.150"	28.0	2171	29,900 CUP	29.0	2249	33,600 CUP
125 GR. SPR SP	Hodgdon	H322	.311"	2.150"	28.0	2210	32,900 CUP	29.0	2323	35,400 CUP
125 GR. SPR SP	IMR	IMR 4198	.311"	2.150"	22.6	2035	36,800 CUP	24.0	2250	42,500 CUP
125 GR. SPR SP	Hodgdon	H4198	.311"	2.150"	24.5	2190	34,200 CUP	26.5	2378	40,400 CUP
150 GR. HDY SP	Hodgdon	BL-C(2)	.312"	2.220"	27.0	1904	33,600 CUP	29.5	2090	40,400 CUP
150 GR. HDY SP	Hodgdon	H335	.312"	2.220"	27.0	2055	36,000 CUP	29.0	2132	42,500 CUP
150 GR. HDY SP	Hodgdon	H4895	.312"	2.220"	27.0	2080	33,600 CUP	28.0	2154	39,300 CUP
150 GR. HDY SP	Hodgdon	H322	.312"	2.220"	27.0	2084	34,200 CUP	28.5	2192	40,400 CUP
150 GR. HDY SP	IMR	IMR 4198	.311"	2.220"	21.2	1917	42,200 CUP	22.5	2070	43,600 CUP

| 150 GR. HDY SP | Hodgdon | H4198 | .312" | 2.220" | 22.5 | 1947 | 33,600 CUP | 24.5 | 2122 | 39,800 CUP |

Cartridge: 303 Savage
Load Type: Rifle

Bullet Weight (Gr.)	Manufacturer	Powder	Bullet Diam.	C.O.L.	Starting Loads			Maximum Loads		
					Grs.	Vel. (ft/s)	Pressure	Grs.	Vel. (ft/s)	Pressure
170 GR. SP	Winchester	748	.311"	2.520"				33.5	2090	32,000 CUP

Cartridge: 7.7 x 58mm Japanese
Load Type: Rifle

Bullet Weight (Gr.)	Manufacturer	Powder	Bullet Diam.	C.O.L.	Starting Loads			Maximum Loads		
					Grs.	Vel. (ft/s)	Pressure	Grs.	Vel. (ft/s)	Pressure
150 GR. SIE SP	Hodgdon	H4831	.311"	3.050"	50.0	2180		55.0	2445	
150 GR. SIE SP	Hodgdon	H4350	.311"	3.050"	48.0	2330		51.0	2514	
150 GR. SIE SP	Hodgdon	H414	.311"	3.050"	45.0	2155		48.0	2424	
150 GR. SIE SP	Hodgdon	H380	.311"	3.050"	44.0	2169		47.0	2461	
150 GR. SIE SP	Hodgdon	BL-C(2)	.311"	3.050"	41.0	2289		44.0	2487	
150 GR. SIE SP	Hodgdon	H335	.311"	3.050"	41.0	2309		44.0	2499	
150 GR. SIE SP	Hodgdon	H4895	.311"	3.050"	41.0	2337		44.0	2529	
180 GR. SIE SP	Hodgdon	H4831	.311"	3.150"	46.0	2011		50.0	2233	
180 GR. SIE SP	Hodgdon	H4350	.311"	3.150"	44.0	2090		47.0	2309	
180 GR. SIE SP	Hodgdon	H414	.311"	3.150"	43.0	2070		46.0	2234	
180 GR. SIE SP	Hodgdon	H380	.311"	3.150"	42.0	2090		45.0	2257	
180 GR. SIE SP	Hodgdon	BL-C(2)	.311"	3.150"	37.0	2054		40.0	2191	
180 GR. SIE SP	Hodgdon	H335	.311"	3.150"	37.0	2077		40.0	2202	
180 GR. SIE SP	Hodgdon	H4895	.311"	3.150"	37.0	2060		40.0	2230	

Cartridge: 303 British
Load Type: Rifle

Bullet Weight (Gr.)	Manufacturer	Powder	Bullet Diam.	C.O.L.	Starting Loads			Maximum Loads		
					Grs.	Vel. (ft/s)	Pressure	Grs.	Vel. (ft/s)	Pressure
125 GR. SPR SP	Hodgdon	Varget	.311"	2.915"	45.0	2766	39,200 CUP	48.0	2883	42,100 CUP
125 GR. SPR SP	Hodgdon	H335	.311"	2.915"	42.0	2741	35,900 CUP	46.0	2966	43,000 CUP
125 GR. SPR SP	Hodgdon	H4895	.311"	2.915"	41.0	2791	42,400 CUP	45.0	2931	43,700 CUP
125 GR. SPR SP	IMR	IMR 8208 XBR	.311"	2.915"	39.0	2708	38,400 CUP	43.0	2886	43,100 CUP
150 GR. HDY SP	Hodgdon	Varget	.312"	2.995"	39.0	2458	39,600 CUP	43.0	2656	42,700 CUP
150 GR. HDY SP	IMR	IMR 4064	.311"	2.995"				44.7	2699	46,400 PSI
150 GR. HDY SP	Hodgdon	BL-C(2)	.312"	2.995"	43.0	2502	34,000 CUP	48.0	2756	39,200 CUP
150 GR. HDY SP	IMR	IMR 4895	.311"	2.995"				44.2	2689	46,600 PSI
150 GR. HDY SP	Hodgdon	H335	.312"	2.995"	37.0	2430	34,700 CUP	42.0	2706	43,100 CUP
150 GR. HDY SP	Hodgdon	H4895	.312"	2.995"	36.0	2447	40,300 CUP	40.0	2627	43,600 CUP
150 GR. HDY SP	IMR	IMR 8208 XBR	.308"	2.995"	34.0	2392	37,700 CUP	36.7	2515	41,300 CUP
150 GR. HDY SP	IMR	IMR 3031	.311"	2.995"				41.0	2632	46,100 PSI

Bullet Weight (Gr.)	Manufacturer	Powder	Bullet Diam.	C.O.L.	Grs.	Vel. (ft/s)	Pressure	Grs.	Vel. (ft/s)	Pressure
174 GR. SIE HPBT	Hodgdon	Hybrid 100V	.311"	3.075"	42.0	2223	36,000 CUP	46.0C	2399	40,300 CUP
174 GR. SIE HPBT	Hodgdon	H4350	.311"	3.075"	43.0	2266	35,400 CUP	48.0C	2517	41,900 CUP
174 GR. SIE HPBT	Hodgdon	H414	.311"	3.075"	43.0	2302	35,200 CUP	46.0	2447	41,000 CUP
174 GR. SIE HPBT	Winchester	760	.311"	3.075"	43.0	2302	35,200 CUP	46.0	2447	41,000 CUP
174 GR. SIE HPBT	IMR	IMR 4007 SSC	.311"	3.075"	43.0	2293	34,800 CUP	46.0C	2441	39,300 CUP
174 GR. SIE HPBT	Hodgdon	Varget	.311"	3.075"	38.0	2345	38,800 CUP	42.0	2509	43,800 CUP
174 GR. SIE HPBT	Hodgdon	BL-C(2)	.311"	3.075"	43.0	2442	36,400 CUP	46.5	2616	42,900 CUP
174 GR. SIE HPBT	Hodgdon	H335	.311"	3.075"	36.0	2340	38,600 CUP	39.5	2503	43,400 CUP
174 GR. SIE HPBT	Hodgdon	H4895	.311"	3.075"	34.0	2262	38,800 CUP	38.0	2446	43,600 CUP
180 GR. SIE SP	Hodgdon	Hybrid 100V	.311"	3.075"	42.0	2232	36,200 CUP	46.0C	2384	41,700 CUP
180 GR. SIE SP	Hodgdon	H4350	.311"	3.075"	44.0	2295	35,700 CUP	48.0C	2500	43,800 CUP
180 GR. SIE SP	Hodgdon	H414	.311"	3.075"	42.0	2231	35,400 CUP	46.0	2435	42,500 CUP
180 GR. SIE SP	Winchester	760	.311"	3.075"	42.0	2231	35,400 CUP	46.0	2435	42,500 CUP
180 GR. SIE SP	IMR	IMR 4007 SSC	.311"	3.075"	43.0	2289	37,900 CUP	46.0C	2430	40,900 CUP
180 GR. SIE SP	Hodgdon	Varget	.311"	3.075"	37.0	2282	38,200 CUP	41.0	2440	43,400 CUP
180 GR. SIE SP	IMR	IMR 4064	.311"	3.075"				41.1	2400	45,700 PSI
180 GR. SIE SP	Hodgdon	BL-C(2)	.311"	3.075"	41.0	2395	37,100 CUP	45.0	2563	43,000 CUP
180 GR. SIE SP	IMR	IMR 4895	.311"	3.075"				41.0	2399	46,100 PSI
180 GR. SIE SP	Hodgdon	H335	.311"	3.075"	36.0	2286	36,400 CUP	39.0	2449	42,700 CUP
180 GR. SIE SP	Hodgdon	H4895	.311"	3.075"	34.0	2178	35,200 CUP	38.0	2400	43,500 CUP
180 GR. SIE SP	IMR	IMR 8208 XBR	.311"	3.075"	31.0	2108	34,900 CUP	35.0	2325	43,300 CUP
180 GR. SIE SP	IMR	IMR 3031	.311'	3.075"				38.3	2341	46,500 PSI

Cartridge:7.65 x 53 Mauser Load Type:Rifle					Starting Loads			Maximum Loads		
Bullet Weight (Gr.)	Manufacturer	Powder	Bullet Diam.	C.O.L.	Grs.	Vel. (ft/s)	Pressure	Grs.	Vel. (ft/s)	Pressure
150 GR. HDY SP	Hodgdon	H4350	.312"	2.815"	45.0	2347		49.0	2614	
150 GR. HDY SP	Hodgdon	H414	.312"	2.815"	45.0	2491		49.0	2648	
150 GR. HDY SP	Hodgdon	H380	.312"	2.815"	42.5	2379		46.0	2585	
150 GR. HDY SP	Hodgdon	BL-C(2)	.312"	2.815"	39.5	2378		43.0	2650	
150 GR. HDY SP	Hodgdon	H335	.312"	2.815"	39.0	2353		43.0	2639	
150 GR. HDY SP	Hodgdon	H4895	.312"	2.815"	39.5	2341		43.0	2597	
174 GR. HDY RN	Hodgdon	H4831	.312"	2.850"				53.0	2456	
174 GR. HDY RN	Hodgdon	H4350	.312"	2.850"	43.0	2266		47.0	2454	
174 GR. HDY RN	Hodgdon	H414	.312"	2.850"	43.0	2332		47.0	2452	
174 GR. HDY RN	Hodgdon	H380	.312"	2.850"	41.5	2232		45.0	2447	
174 GR. HDY RN	Hodgdon	BL-C(2)	.312"	2.850"	37.0	2106		40.0	2375	
174 GR. HDY RN	Hodgdon	H335	.312"	2.850"	37.0	2090		40.0	2372	
174 GR. HDY RN	Hodgdon	H4895	.312"	2.850"	37.0	2072		40.0	2351	

Cartridge: 32 Winchester Special Load Type: Rifle					Starting Loads			Maximum Loads		
Bullet Weight (Gr.)	Manufacturer	Powder	Bullet Diam.	C.O.L.	Grs.	Vel. (ft/s)	Pressure	Grs.	Vel. (ft/s)	Pressure
170 GR. HDY JFP	Hodgdon	Varget	.321"	2.565"	34.0	2096	30,800 CUP	37.0C	2271	36,400 CUP
170 GR. HDY JFP	Winchester	748	.321"	2.565"				36.2	2240	32,500 CUP
170 GR. HDY JFP	Hodgdon	BL-C(2)	.321"	2.565"	35.0	2152	31,300 CUP	37.0	2226	35,300 CUP
170 GR. HDY JFP	Hodgdon	H335	.321"	2.565"	30.0	2021	29,700 CUP	32.0	2144	36,200 CUP
170 GR. HDY JFP	Hodgdon	H4895	.321"	2.565"	32.0	2122	30,800 CUP	34.5	2283	36,100 CUP
170 GR. HDY JFP	Hodgdon	Benchmark	.321"	2.565"	30.0	2005	29,900 CUP	32.5	2175	36,600 CUP
170 GR. HDY JFP	Hodgdon	H322	.321"	2.565"	30.0	2111	32,100 CUP	32.3	2263	36,800 CUP

Cartridge: 32-40 Winchester Load Type: Rifle					Starting Loads			Maximum Loads		
Bullet Weight (Gr.)	Manufacturer	Powder	Bullet Diam.	C.O.L.	Grs.	Vel. (ft/s)	Pressure	Grs.	Vel. (ft/s)	Pressure
196 GR. HOCH	Hodgdon	H4227	.324"	2.555"				13.0	1367	18,000 CUP
196 GR. HOCH	Hodgdon	H110	.324"	2.555"				12.0	1376	19,200 CUP
196 GR. HOCH	Hodgdon	Lil'Gun	.324"	2.555"				9.3	1237	19,600 CUP
196 GR. HOCH	IMR	Trail Boss	.324"	2.555"	5.0	833	12,500 CUP	6.0	935	25,300 CUP
202 GR. POPE	Hodgdon	H4227	.324"	2.555"				14.0	1376	15,900 CUP
202 GR. POPE	Hodgdon	H110	.324"	2.555"				13.0	1386	17,900 CUP
202 GR. POPE	Hodgdon	Lil'Gun	.324"	2.555"				9.5	1264	20,100 CUP
204 GR. MILLER	Hodgdon	H4227	.324"	2.555"				13.5	1367	16,300 CUP
204 GR. MILLER	Hodgdon	H110	.324"	2.555"				13.0	1369	17,900 CUP
204 GR. MILLER	Hodgdon	Lil'Gun	.324"	2.555"				10.8	1310	20,100 CUP

Cartridge: 8 x 57mm Mauser Load Type: Rifle					Starting Loads			Maximum Loads		
Bullet Weight (Gr.)	Manufacturer	Powder	Bullet Diam.	C.O.L.	Grs.	Vel. (ft/s)	Pressure	Grs.	Vel. (ft/s)	Pressure
125 GR. HDY SP	Hodgdon	CFE 223	.323"	2.880"	55.0	2798	31,400 CUP	57.0	2964	34,400 CUP
125 GR. HDY SP	Hodgdon	Varget	.323"	2.880"	47.0	2730	36,600 CUP	54.0	3092	48,100 CUP
125 GR. HDY SP	IMR	IMR 4320	.323"	2.880"	45.5	2621	36,400 CUP	52.5	2979	48,100 CUP
125 GR. HDY SP	IMR	IMR 4064	.323"	2.880"	46.0	2736	34,300 CUP	50.0C	2927	41,700 CUP
125 GR. HDY SP	Winchester	748	.323"	2.880"	50.0	2742	33,100 CUP	55.0	2974	37,200 CUP
125 GR. HDY SP	Hodgdon	BL-C(2)	.323"	2.880"	53.0	2916	36,300 CUP	55.0	3026	40,600 CUP
125 GR. HDY SP	IMR	IMR 4895	.323"	2.880"	47.0	2717	37,000 CUP	52.0	2945	43,700 CUP
125 GR. HDY SP	Hodgdon	H335	.323"	2.880"	47.0	2846	37,300 CUP	53.0	3155	48,800 CUP
125 GR. HDY SP	Hodgdon	H4895	.323"	2.880"	47.0	2843	37,300 CUP	53.5	3208	49,400 CUP
125 GR. HDY SP	IMR	IMR 8208 XBR	.323"	2.880"	48.0	2907	41,500 CUP	52.2	3139	48,700 CUP
125 GR. HDY SP	IMR	IMR 3031	.323"	2.880"	44.0	2736	34,800 CUP	48.0	2987	43,300 CUP

Bullet	Manufacturer	Powder	Diameter	OAL						
125 GR. HDY SP	Hodgdon	Benchmark	.323"	2.880"	43.5	2728	36,400 CUP	49.8	3068	49,700 CUP
150 GR. HDY SP	IMR	IMR 4007 SSC	.323"	2.950"	50.0	2579	34,400 CUP	54.5	2791	40,800 CUP
150 GR. HDY SP	Hodgdon	CFE 223	.323"	2.950"	54.0	2848	37,600 CUP	57.0	3054	46,900 CUP
150 GR. HDY SP	Hodgdon	Varget	.323"	2.950"	45.5	2561	37,500 CUP	52.4C	2896	49,000 CUP
150 GR. HDY SP	IMR	IMR 4320	.323"	2.950"	41.0	2377	35,400 CUP	50.5	2818	48,800 CUP
150 GR. HDY SP	IMR	IMR 4064	.323"	2.950"	42.0	2486	34,800 CUP	49.5	2839	46,200 CUP
150 GR. HDY SP	Hodgdon	BL-C(2)	.323"	2.950"	50.0	2690	36,600 CUP	55.0	2962	48,400 CUP
150 GR. HDY SP	IMR	IMR 4895	.323"	2.950"	42.0	2482	36,700 CUP	49.5	2847	48,000 CUP
150 GR. HDY SP	Hodgdon	H335	.323"	2.950"	44.0	2631	37,400 CUP	50.8	2942	48,800 CUP
150 GR. HDY SP	Hodgdon	H4895	.323"	2.950"	44.0	2619	37,200 CUP	51.0	2987	49,500 CUP
150 GR. HDY SP	IMR	IMR 8208 XBR	.323"	2.950"	44.1	2648	40,600 CUP	48.0	2861	48,300 CUP
150 GR. HDY SP	IMR	IMR 3031	.323"	2.950"	41.5	2534	35,200 CUP	46.5	2815	47,300 CUP
150 GR. HDY SP	Hodgdon	Benchmark	.323"	2.950"	42.5	2577	36,900 CUP	47.5	2860	48,800 CUP
160 GR. BAR TTSX BT	Hodgdon	CFE 223	.323"	3.010"	49.7	2726	42,100 CUP	54.0	2919	48,500 CUP
160 GR. BAR TTSX BT	Hodgdon	Varget	.323"	3.010"	45.0	2503	36,100 CUP	49.0C	2727	43,600 CUP
160 GR. BAR TTSX BT	IMR	IMR 4064	.323"	3.010"	43.0	2438	38,500 CUP	47.0C	2664	45,100 CUP
160 GR. BAR TTSX BT	Hodgdon	BL-C(2)	.323"	3.010"	47.0	2559	40,300 CUP	51.0	2772	48,300 CUP
160 GR. BAR TTSX BT	IMR	IMR 4895	.323"	3.010"	44.0	2485	40,100 CUP	48.0C	2696	47,500 CUP
160 GR. BAR TTSX BT	Hodgdon	H335	.323"	3.010"	42.0	2500	40,100 CUP	46.0	2720	47,900 CUP
160 GR. BAR TTSX BT	Hodgdon	H4895	.323"	3.010"	44.0	2603	39,200 CUP	48.5C	2821	47,700 CUP
160 GR. BAR TTSX BT	IMR	IMR 8208 XBR	.323"	3.010"	42.0	2486	37,200 CUP	46.5C	2758	48,300 CUP
160 GR. BAR TTSX BT	IMR	IMR 3031	.323"	3.010"	42.6	2483	42,900 CUP	46.1	2712	48,600 CUP
160 GR. BAR TTSX BT	Hodgdon	Benchmark	.323"	3.010"	43.1	2558	42,500 CUP	46.6	2726	49,300 CUP
170 GR. HDY RN	IMR	IMR 4007 SSC	.323"	2.825"	48.0	2418	34,800 CUP	54.5C	2726	45,600 CUP
170 GR. HDY RN	Hodgdon	CFE 223	.323"	2.825"	53.0	2686	37,900 CUP	56.0	2854	44,200 CUP
170 GR. HDY RN	Hodgdon	Varget	.323"	2.825"	43.0	2362	36,700 CUP	50.5	2700	48,700 CUP
170 GR. HDY RN	IMR	IMR 4320	.323"	2.825"	39.0	2195	34,400 CUP	49.8	2680	49,200 CUP
170 GR. HDY RN	IMR	IMR 4064	.323"	2.825"	41.5	2345	35,700 cUP	48.7	2706	49,300 CUP
170 GR. HDY RN	Winchester	748	.323"	2.825"	46.0	2467	35,600 CUP	54.0	2832	48,500 CUP
170 GR. HDY RN	Hodgdon	BL-C(2)	.323"	2.825"	48.8	2560	36,800 CUP	53.5	2839	48,800 CUP
170 GR. HDY RN	IMR	IMR 4895	.323"	2.825"	40.0	2284	36,600 CUP	48.0	2647	47,900 CUP
170 GR. HDY RN	Hodgdon	H335	.323"	2.825"	42.5	2421	37,400 CUP	49.2	2738	48,800 CUP
170 GR. HDY RN	Hodgdon	H4895	.323"	2.825"	40.0	2306	37,400 CUP	49.0	2769	48,700 CUP
170 GR. HDY RN	IMR	IMR 8208 XBR	.323"	2.825"	44.2	2575	41,400 CUP	47.0	2696	48,000 CUP
170 GR. HDY RN	IMR	IMR 3031	.323"	2.825"	40.0	2355	35,000 CUP	45.5	2640	47,500 CUP
170 GR. HDY RN	Hodgdon	Benchmark	.323"	2.825"	41.0	2397	37,100 CUP	46.6	2679	49,100 CUP
175 GR. SIE SP	IMR	IMR 4007 SSC	.323"	3.100"	48.0	2450	36,300 CUP	54.0C	2733	48,500 CUP
175 GR. SIE SP	Hodgdon	CFE 223	.323"	3.100"	52.0	2615	36,500 CUP	55.0	2837	47,800 CUP
175 GR. SIE SP	Hodgdon	Varget	.323"	3.100"	43.0	2418	37,200 CUP	50.5	2716	48,500 CUP

175 GR. SIE SP	IMR	IMR 4320	.323"	3.100"	39.0	2209	36,100 CUP	48.5	2619	49,800 CUP
175 GR. SIE SP	IMR	IMR 4064	.323"	3.100"	41.0	2340	36,600 CUP	48.0C	2687	49,100 CUP
175 GR. SIE SP	Winchester	748	.323"	3.100"	48.0	2524	37,500 CUP	53.0	2748	46,600 CUP
175 GR. SIE SP	Hodgdon	BL-C(2)	.323"	3.100"	48.8	2595	36,800 CUP	53.5	2818	46,700 CUP
175 GR. SIE SP	IMR	IMR 4895	.323"	3.100"	39.5	2246	35,900 CUP	48.0	2642	48,400 CUP
175 GR. SIE SP	Hodgdon	H335	.323"	3.100"	42.5	2446	37,100 CUP	48.0	2722	48,400 CUP
175 GR. SIE SP	Hodgdon	H4895	.323"	3.100"	40.0	2387	36,800 CUP	49.4	2762	48,300 CUP
175 GR. SIE SP	IMR	IMR 8208 XBR	.323"	3.100"	43.7	2537	41,400 CUP	46.5	2667	46,600 CUP
175 GR. SIE SP	IMR	IMR 3031	.323"	3.100"	39.0	2341	37,300 CUP	45.0	2625	48,900 CUP
175 GR. SIE SP	Hodgdon	Benchmark	.323"	3.100"	41.0	2414	37,100 CUP	46.2	2657	48,400 CUP
180 GR. BAR TSX	IMR	IMR 4007 SSC	.323"	2.960"	45.0	2262	33,400 CUP	50.0C	2534	42,800 CUP
180 GR. BAR TSX	Hodgdon	CFE 223	.323"	2.960"	47.0	2584	43,700 CUP	50.0	2712	49,200 CUP
180 GR. BAR TSX	Hodgdon	Varget	.323"	2.960"	41.0	2256	35,800 CUP	47.8C	2570	48,400 CUP
180 GR. BAR TSX	IMR	IMR 4320	.323"	2.960"	38.0	2087	34,700 CUP	46.3	2481	48,700 CUP
180 GR. BAR TSX	IMR	IMR 4064	.323"	2.960"	39.5	2251	36,300 CUP	45.0C	2529	48,400 CUP
180 GR. BAR TSX	Winchester	748	.323"	2.960"	39.0	2219	36,200 CUP	45.5	2542	49,000 CUP
180 GR. BAR TSX	Hodgdon	BL-C(2)	.323"	2.960"	39.0	2153	34,200 CUP	45.5	2487	48,500 CUP
180 GR. BAR TSX	IMR	IMR 4895	.323"	2.960"	40.0	2235	36,400 CUP	46.0C	2525	47,900 CUP
180 GR. BAR TSX	Hodgdon	H335	.323"	2.960"	36.5	2163	35,500 CUP	43.0	2483	48,900 CUP
180 GR. BAR TSX	Hodgdon	H4895	.323"	2.960"	39.0	2259	36,800 CUP	46.0C	2565	48,700 CUP
180 GR. BAR TSX	IMR	IMR 8208 XBR	.323"	2.960"	41.8	2459	43,300 CUP	44.5	2572	48,300 CUP
180 GR. BAR TSX	Hodgdon	Benchmark	.323"	2.960"	34.0	2104	37,200 CUP	42.0	2466	48,800 CUP
180 GR. NOS BT	IMR	IMR 4007 SSC	.323"	3.020"	47.0	2366	36,400 CUP	51.5C	2599	47,600 CUP
180 GR. NOS BT	Hodgdon	CFE 223	.323"	3.020"	49.0	2635	42,100 CUP	52.0	2758	47,500 CUP
180 GR. NOS BT	Hodgdon	Varget	.323"	3.020"	42.0	2309	36,600 CUP	48.8	2641	49,400 CUP
180 GR. NOS BT	IMR	IMR 4320	.323"	3.020"	38.0	2140	35,800 CUP	47.3	2533	48,500 CUP
180 GR. NOS BT	IMR	IMR 4064	.323"	3.020"	40.0	2259	35,400 CUP	45.0C	2538	47,800 CUP
180 GR. NOS BT	Winchester	748	.323"	3.020"	42.0	2295	35,700 CUP	47.0	2587	49,400 CUP
180 GR. NOS BT	Hodgdon	BL-C(2)	.323"	3.020"	44.5	2439	36,700 CUP	48.5	2669	48,500 CUP
180 GR. NOS BT	IMR	IMR 4895	.323"	3.020"	41.5	2291	36,900 CUP	46.8	2562	48,300 CUP
180 GR. NOS BT	Hodgdon	H335	.323"	3.020"	38.0	2267	36,100 CUP	43.7	2557	48,100 CUP
180 GR. NOS BT	Hodgdon	H4895	.323"	3.020"	41.0	2387	36,300 CUP	47.7	2691	49,300 CUP
180 GR. NOS BT	IMR	IMR 8208 XBR	.323"	3.020"	43.0	2479	41,300 CUP	45.7	2619	47,900 CUP
180 GR. NOS BT	Hodgdon	Benchmark	.323"	3.020"	39.0	2304	36,800 CUP	44.5	2586	48,900 CUP
200 GR. SPR SP	Hodgdon	H4350	.323"	2.970"	49.0	2276	35,900 CUP	54.0C	2522	44,800 CUP
200 GR. SPR SP	Hodgdon	H414	.323"	2.970"	45.0	2229	36,900 CUP	50.0	2475	47,300 CUP
200 GR. SPR SP	IMR	IMR 4007 SSC	.323"	2.970"	45.0	2220	35,600 CUP	50.0C	2489	45,800 CUP
200 GR. SPR SP	Hodgdon	Varget	.323"	2.970"	40.5	2183	36,900 CUP	47.5	2511	49,100 CUP
200 GR. SPR SP	IMR	IMR 4064	.323"	2.970"	40.0	2193	36,200 CUP	44.5	2401	48,300 CUP
200 GR. SPR SP	Winchester	748	.323"	2.970"	40.0	2151	35,300 CUP	44.8	2408	48,000 CUP

Bullet Weight (Gr.)	Manufacturer	Powder	Bullet Diam.	C.O.L.	Grs.	Vel. (ft/s)	Pressure	Grs.	Vel. (ft/s)	Pressure
200 GR. SPR SP	IMR	IMR 4895	.323"	2.970"	39.0	2112	34,900 CUP	45.0	2409	48,500 CUP
200 GR. SPR SP	Hodgdon	H4895	.323"	2.970"	38.0	2240	36,800 CUP	45.4	2539	49,200 CUP
200 GR. SPR SP	IMR	IMR 8208 XBR	.323"	2.970"	41.4	2325	39,900 CUP	44.0	2459	47,600 CUP
220 GR. HDY SP	IMR	IMR 4007 SSC	.323"	2.970"	45.0	2134	34,500 CUP	50.0C	2380	45,200 CUP
220 GR. HDY SP	Hodgdon	Varget	.323"	2.970"	39.0	2055	36,800 CUP	46.8	2390	48,800 CUP
220 GR. HDY SP	IMR	IMR 4064	.323"	2.970"	39.5	2090	36,100 CUP	43.0C	2275	47,700 CUP
220 GR. HDY SP	Winchester	748	.323"	2.970"	40.0	2034	34,200 CUP	44.5	2270	43,200 CUP
220 GR. HDY SP	IMR	IMR 4895	.323"	2.970"	39.5	2091	36,100 CUP	45.0C	2325	48,500 CUP
220 GR. HDY SP	Hodgdon	H4895	.323"	2.970"	40.0	2178	37,200 CUP	45.2	2420	48,800 CUP
220 GR. HDY SP	IMR	IMR 8208 XBR	.323"	2.970"	41.5	2249	40,000 CUP	44.1	2348	47,500 CUP

Cartridge: 325 Winchester Short Magnum Load Type: Rifle					Starting Loads			Maximum Loads		
Bullet Weight (Gr.)	Manufacturer	Powder	Bullet Diam.	C.O.L.	Grs.	Vel. (ft/s)	Pressure	Grs.	Vel. (ft/s)	Pressure
150 GR. HDY SP	Hodgdon	H4831	0.323"	2.810"	71.0	2945	44,100 PSI	75.0C	3115	52,800 PSI
150 GR. HDY SP	IMR	IMR 4831	0.323"	2.810"	69.0	2960	49,300 PSI	73.0C	3162	59,700 PSI
150 GR. HDY SP	Hodgdon	H4350	0.323"	2.810"	69.0	3138	51,600 PSI	73.5C	3345	63,700 PSI
150 GR. HDY SP	Hodgdon	H414	0.323"	2.810"	70.0	3217	54,600 PSI	73.2	3360	63,100 PSI
150 GR. HDY SP	IMR	IMR 4350	0.323"	2.810"	68.0	3008	50,100 PSI	70.5	3198	61,500 PSI
150 GR. HDY SP	Winchester	760	0.323"	2.810"	70.0	3217	54,600 PSI	73.2	3360	63,100 PSI
150 GR. HDY SP	IMR	IMR 4007 SSC	0.323"	2.810"	65.8	3036	51.300 PSI	70.0	3248	62,800 PSI
150 GR. HDY SP	Hodgdon	H380	0.323"	2.810"	67.5	3174	53,600 PSI	71.5	3336	62,500 PSI
150 GR. HDY SP	Hodgdon	Varget	0.323"	2.810"	61.0	3137	54,200 PSI	65.0	3305	63,600 PSI
150 GR. HDY SP	IMR	IMR 4320	0.323"	2.810"	61.0	3012	52,200 PSI	63.5	3171	61,500 PSI
150 GR. HDY SP	IMR	IMR 4064	0.323"	2.810"	59.0	3076	53,600 PSI	62.0	3207	61,100 PSI
150 GR. HDY SP	Hodgdon	BL-C(2)	0.323"	2.810"	64.0	3190	53,500 PSI	68.0	3362	63,300 PSI
150 GR. HDY SP	IMR	IMR 4895	0.323"	2.810"	60.0	3075	53,900 PSI	63.2	3245	63,100 PSI
150 GR. HDY SP	Hodgdon	H4895	0.323"	2.810"	60.0	3156	53,600 PSI	63.5	3313	63,300 PSI
150 GR. HDY SP	IMR	IMR 8208 XBR	.323"	2.810"	56.1	3059	55,400 PSI	59.7	3171	61,000 PSI
150 GR. HDY SP	IMR	IMR 3031	0.323"	2.810"	56.0	3027	52,600 PSI	58.7	3184	62,200 PSI
150 GR. HDY SP	Hodgdon	Benchmark	0.323"	2.810"	57.0	3074	50,200 PSI	60.5	3253	62,400 PSI
175 GR. SIE SP	Hodgdon	H4831	0.323"	2.855"	70.0	2819	51,400 PSI	73.0C	2960	61,400 PSI
175 GR. SIE SP	IMR	IMR 4831	0.323"	2.855"	66.0	2798	50,300 PSI	70.0C	2996	61,900 PSI
175 GR. SIE SP	Hodgdon	H4350	0.323"	2.855"	64.5	2835	51,100 PSI	68.0C	3024	63,400 PSI
175 GR. SIE SP	Hodgdon	H414	0.323"	2.855"	64.0	2874	53,600 PSI	68.0	3025	62,000 PSI
175 GR. SIE SP	IMR	IMR 4350	0.323"	2.855"	64.3	2820	51,100 PSI	68.4C	3011	62,000 PSI
175 GR. SIE SP	Winchester	760	0.323"	2.855"	64.0	2874	53,600 PSI	68.0	3025	62,000 PSI
175 GR. SIE SP	IMR	IMR 4007 SSC	0.323"	2.855"	63.5	2863	52,100 PSI	67.5	3047	63,000 PSI
175 GR. SIE SP	Hodgdon	H380	0.323"	2.855"	62.5	2857	54,100 PSI	66.3	2994	61,800 PSI

175 GR. SIE SP	Hodgdon	Varget	0.323"	2.855"	58.0	2862	55,400 PSI	61.0	2975	62,300 PSI
175 GR. SIE SP	IMR	IMR 4320	0.323"	2.855"	58.0	2801	52,200 PSI	61.7	2960	61,500 PSI
175 GR. SIE SP	IMR	IMR 4064	0.323"	2.855"	56.5	2812	51,900 PSI	59.8	2976	61,800 PSI
175 GR. SIE SP	Hodgdon	BL-C(2)	0.323"	2.855"	60.0	2870	54,100 PSI	64.0	3030	62,800 PSI
175 GR. SIE SP	IMR	IMR 4895	0.323"	2.855"	57.5	2848	53,000 PSI	61.0	3002	62,400 PSI
175 GR. SIE SP	Hodgdon	H4895	0.323"	2.855"	57.5	2858	54,100 PSI	61.0	3000	62,900 PSI
175 GR. SIE SP	IMR	IMR 8208 XBR	.323"	2.855"	52.6	2793	54,300 PSI	56.0	2923	62,800 PSI
175 GR. SIE SP	IMR	IMR 3031	0.323"	2.855"	53.0	2791	53,200 PSI	56.0	2923	62,300 PSI
175 GR. SIE SP	Hodgdon	Benchmark	0.323"	2.855"	51.0	2743	54,000 PSI	53.7	2863	62,700 PSI
180 GR. NOS BT	Hodgdon	H4831	0.323"	2.840"	62.0	2776	52,900 PSI	65.8C	2930	62,800 PSI
180 GR. NOS BT	Hodgdon	Hybrid 100V	0.323"	2.840"	61.0	2768	51,700 PSI	66.0C	2936	59,200 PSI
180 GR. NOS BT	IMR	IMR 4831	0.323"	2.840"	64.0	2727	51,400 PSI	68.5C	2927	61,100 PSI
180 GR. NOS BT	Hodgdon	H4350	0.323"	2.840"	61.8	2794	52,500 PSI	65.5	2957	62,200 PSI
180 GR. NOS BT	Hodgdon	H414	0.323"	2.840"	62.0	2808	54,400 PSI	65.5	2946	62,000 PSI
180 GR. NOS BT	IMR	IMR 4350	0.323"	2.840"	62.0	2726	52,500 PSI	67.0C	2954	62,500 PSI
180 GR. NOS BT	Winchester	760	0.323"	2.840"	62.0	2808	54,400 PSI	65.5	2946	62,000 PSI
180 GR. NOS BT	IMR	IMR 4007 SSC	0.323"	2.840"	61.0	2793	49,800 PSI	65.0C	2979	62,800 PSI
180 GR. NOS BT	Hodgdon	H380	0.323"	2.840"	60.5	2782	54,800 PSI	64.0	2925	63,100 PSI
180 GR. NOS BT	Hodgdon	Varget	0.323"	2.840"	55.0	2770	56,500 PSI	58.0	2873	62,700 PSI
180 GR. NOS BT	IMR	IMR 4320	0.323"	2.840"	55.0	2702	51,900 PSI	59.5	2896	62,900 PSI
180 GR. NOS BT	IMR	IMR 4064	0.323"	2.840"	54.0	2689	50,100 PSI	58.0	2865	60,100 PSI
180 GR. NOS BT	Hodgdon	BL-C(2)	0.323"	2.840"	57.5	2792	55,400 PSI	61.0	2936	62,300 PSI
180 GR. NOS BT	IMR	IMR 4895	0.323"	2.840"	55.5	2781	55,500 PSI	58.7	2906	62,700 PSI
180 GR. NOS BT	Hodgdon	H4895	0.323"	2.840"	52.5	2732	55,100 PSI	54.6	2820	60,300 PSI
180 GR. NOS BT	IMR	IMR 8208 XBR	.323"	2.840"	51.5	2743	54,900 PSI	54.8	2855	60,800 PSI
195 GR. HDY SP	IMR	IMR 7828	0.323"	2.855"	66.5	2681	53,500 PSI	71.0C	2860	63,800 PSI
195 GR. HDY SP	Hodgdon	H4831	0.323"	2.855"	66.3	2704	54,600 PSI	70.5C	2835	63,000 PSI
195 GR. HDY SP	Hodgdon	Hybrid 100V	0.323"	2.855"	61.0	2693	51,600 PSI	66.0C	2857	59,300 PSI
195 GR. HDY SP	IMR	IMR 4831	0.323"	2.855"	66.0	2726	53,400 PSI	70.0C	2905	63,100 PSI
195 GR. HDY SP	Hodgdon	H4350	0.323"	2.855"	61.0	2712	54,400 PSI	64.5	2837	62,300 PSI
195 GR. HDY SP	Hodgdon	H414	0.323"	2.855"	61.0	2722	54,500 PSI	64.5	2847	61,800 PSI
195 GR. HDY SP	IMR	IMR 4350	0.323"	2.855"	62.0	2678	52,200 PSI	66.0	2866	62,300 PSI
195 GR. HDY SP	Winchester	760	0.323"	2.855"	61.0	2722	54,500 PSI	64.5	2847	61,800 PSI
195 GR. HDY SP	IMR	IMR 4007 SSC	0.323"	2.855"	60.2	2714	54,800 PSI	64.0	2868	63,200 PSI
195 GR. HDY SP	Hodgdon	H380	0.323"	2.855"	59.0	2668	54,800 PSI	62.2	2796	63,300 PSI
195 GR. HDY SP	Hodgdon	Varget	0.323"	2.855"	54.0	2661	55,500 PSI	57.3	2782	62,800 PSI
195 GR. HDY SP	IMR	IMR 4320	0.323"	2.855"	55.5	2654	52,800 PSI	59.0	2795	62,200 PSI
195 GR. HDY SP	IMR	IMR 4064	0.323"	2.855"	54.0	2658	54,700 PSI	57.5	2789	63,100 PSI
195 GR. HDY SP	Hodgdon	BL-C(2)	0.323"	2.855"	57.0	2707	55,900 PSI	60.5	2840	63,700 PSI
195 GR. HDY SP	IMR	IMR 4895	0.323"	2.855"	53.8	2623	53,700 PSI	57.2	2768	61,100 PSI

Bullet Weight	Manufacturer	Powder	Bullet Diam.	C.O.L.	Grs.	Vel. (ft/s)	Pressure	Grs.	Vel. (ft/s)	Pressure
195 GR. HDY SP	Hodgdon	H4895	0.323"	2.855"	53.0	2648	55,000 PSI	56.0	2763	62,500 PSI
195 GR. HDY SP	IMR	IMR 8208 XBR	.323"	2.855"	50.3	2617	55,900 PSI	53.5	2728	62,600 PSI
200 GR. BAR TSX	Hodgdon	Hybrid 100V	0.323"	2.820"	56.0	2472	45,300 PSI	61.0C	2669	53,800 PSI
200 GR. BAR XLC	IMR	IMR 7828	0.323"	2.860"	66.7	2614	52,600 PSI	71.0C*	2784	61,600 PSI
200 GR. BAR XLC	IMR	IMR 4831	0.323"	2.860"	65.0	2614	48,300 PSI	69.5C	2788	58,200 PSI
200 GR. BAR XLC	Hodgdon	H4350	0.323"	2.860"	63.0	2689	52,500 PSI	67.0	2843	62,900 PSI
200 GR. BAR XLC	Hodgdon	H414	0.323"	2.860"	61.0	2686	54,600 PSI	65.0	2827	63,400 PSI
200 GR. BAR XLC	IMR	IMR 4350	0.323"	2.860"	63.5	2650	51,400 PSI	67.5C	2818	62,100 PSI
200 GR. BAR XLC	Winchester	760	0.323"	2.860"	61.0	2686	54,600 PSI	65.0	2827	63,400 PSI
200 GR. BAR XLC	Hodgdon	H380	0.323"	2.860"	61.0	2629	50,700 PSI	64.8	2777	60,000 PSI
200 GR. BAR XLC	Hodgdon	Varget	0.323"	2.860"	55.5	2642	55,100 PSI	59.0	2762	62,300 PSI
200 GR. BAR XLC	IMR	IMR 4320	0.323"	2.860"	56.0	2590	51,000 PSI	60.0	2771	62,700 PSI
200 GR. BAR XLC	IMR	IMR 4064	0.323"	2.860"	54.0	2592	51,100 PSI	57.7	2759	62,500 PSI
200 GR. BAR XLC	Hodgdon	BL-C(2)	0.323"	2.860"	57.0	2668	54,700 PSI	60.5	2799	63,600 PSI
200 GR. BAR XLC	IMR	IMR 4895	0.323"	2.860"	55.0	2596	51,500 PSI	58.7	2759	61,400 PSI
200 GR. BAR XLC	Hodgdon	H4895	0.323"	2.860"	54.0	2662	58,400 PSI	57.3	2739	62,200 PSI
220 GR. SFT SP	IMR	IMR 7828	0.323"	2.845"	62.5	2469	52,200 PSI	66.5C*	2643	61,500 PSI
220 GR. SFT SP	Hodgdon	H4831	0.323"	2.845"	63.0	2491	52,200 PSI	67.0C	2638	61,300 PSI
220 GR. SFT SP	Hodgdon	Hybrid 100V	0.323"	2.845"	56.0	2446	49,400 PSI	61.0C	2644	60,000 PSI
220 GR. SFT SP	IMR	IMR 4831	0.323"	2.845"	62.0	2549	43,300 PSI	66.0C	2706	54,900 PSI
220 GR. SFT SP	Hodgdon	H4350	0.323"	2.845"	58.3	2518	52,700 PSI	62.0	2649	62,400 PSI
220 GR. SFT SP	Hodgdon	H414	0.323"	2.845"	58.0	2557	57,100 PSI	61.5	2669	63,200 PSI
220 GR. SFT SP	IMR	IMR 4350	0.323"	2.845"	59.7	2467	50,400 PSI	63.5C	2647	60,600 PSI
220 GR. SFT SP	Winchester	760	0.323"	2.845"	58.0	2557	57,100 PSI	61.5	2669	63,200 PSI
220 GR. SFT SP	IMR	IMR 4007 SSC	0.323"	2.845"	58.0	2626	51,300 PSI	61.7	2778	60,900 PSI
220 GR. SFT SP	Hodgdon	H380	0.323"	2.845"	56.0	2468	52,100 PSI	60.0	2627	63,600 PSI
220 GR. SFT SP	Hodgdon	Varget	0.323"	2.845"	50.8	2448	55,800 PSI	54.0	2569	62,400 PSI
220 GR. SFT SP	IMR	IMR 4320	0.323"	2.845"	51.7	2469	56,500 PSI	55.0	2564	61,900 PSI
220 GR. SFT SP	IMR	IMR 4064	0.323"	2.845"	51.0	2458	54,900 PSI	54.0	2585	63,000 PSI
220 GR. SFT SP	Hodgdon	BL-C(2)	0.323"	2.845"	54.0	2505	56,600 PSI	57.3	2622	62,100 PSI
220 GR. SFT SP	IMR	IMR 4895	0.323"	2.845"	51.0	2446	52,700 PSI	54.3	2578	61,700 PSI
220 GR. SFT SP	Hodgdon	H4895	0.323"	2.845"	49.5	2438	54,800 PSI	52.5	2556	63,100 PSI

Cartridge:8mm Remington Magnum Load Type:Rifle					Starting Loads			Maximum Loads		
Bullet Weight (Gr.)	Manufacturer	Powder	Bullet Diam.	C.O.L.	Grs.	Vel. (ft/s)	Pressure	Grs.	Vel. (ft/s)	Pressure
150 GR. SPR SP	Hodgdon	H4831	.323"	3.550"	88.0	3268	47,200 CUP	92.0C	3378	51,500 CUP
150 GR. SPR SP	Hodgdon	Hybrid 100V	.323"	3.550"	80.0	3366	46,100 CUP	84.5C	3462	49,400 CUP
150 GR. SPR SP	Hodgdon	H4350	.323"	3.550"	79.0	3242	45,700 CUP	83.5	3401	52,500 CUP

199

Bullet Weight (Gr.)	Manufacturer	Powder	Bullet Diam.	C.O.L.	Grs.	Vel. (ft/s)	Pressure	Grs.	Vel. (ft/s)	Pressure
150 GR. SPR SP	Hodgdon	H414	.323"	3.550"	76.0	3270	48,000 CUP	81.0	3385	52,300 CUP
150 GR. SPR SP	Hodgdon	H380	.323"	3.550"	71.0	3110	47,400 CUP	75.5	3245	52,300 CUP
150 GR. SPR SP	Hodgdon	Varget	.323"	3.550"	71.0	3253	46,100 CUP	75.0	3403	52,600 CUP
175 GR. SIE SP	Hodgdon	H4831	.323"	3.600"	81.0	3031	47,300 CUP	86.5	3162	52,800 CUP
175 GR. SIE SP	Hodgdon	Hybrid 100V	.323"	3.600"	72.0	3016	43,700 CUP	80.0	3251	52,200 CUP
175 GR. SIE SP	Hodgdon	H4350	.323"	3.600"	72.0	2930	45,300 CUP	77.0	3141	52,300 CUP
175 GR. SIE SP	Hodgdon	H414	.323"	3.600"	70.0	2987	47,700 CUP	74.0	3113	52,300 CUP
180 GR. BAR TSX	Hodgdon	H1000	.323"	3.600"	81.0	2912	46,100 CUP	89.0C	3099	52,400 CUP
180 GR. BAR TSX	Hodgdon	H4831	.323"	3.600"	73.0	2858	47,400 CUP	79.5	3035	52,000 CUP
180 GR. BAR TSX	Hodgdon	Hybrid 100V	.323"	3.600"	68.0	2875	43,000 CUP	73.5	3075	51,200 CUP
185 GR. REM PSPCL	IMR	IMR 4831	.323"	3.560"				79.5	3095	52,900 CUP
185 GR. REM PSPCL	IMR	IMR 4350	.323"	3.560"				77.5	3090	53,100 CUP
185 GR. REM PSPCL	IMR	IMR 4064	.323"	3.560"				66.5	2975	54,000 CUP
200 GR. NOS PART	Hodgdon	H1000	.323"	3.600"	86.0	2825	45,300 CUP	89.0C	2920	48,100 CUP
200 GR. NOS PART	Hodgdon	H4831	.323"	3.600"	77.0	2819	47,400 CUP	81.5	2944	52,000 CUP
200 GR. NOS PART	Hodgdon	Hybrid 100V	.323"	3.600"	67.0	2793	43,000 CUP	72.5	2976	51,200 CUP
200 GR. NOS PART	Hodgdon	H4350	.323"	3.600"	70.0	2820	47,300 CUP	74.0	2950	52,200 CUP
220 GR. HDY SP	Hodgdon	H1000	.323"	3.600"	85.0	2726	46,700 CUP	88.0C	2817	49,300 CUP
220 GR. HDY SP	Hodgdon	H4831	.323"	3.600"	76.0	2685	46,700 CUP	80.5	2816	52,100 CUP
220 GR. HDY SP	Hodgdon	Hybrid 100V	.323"	3.600"	67.0	2673	44,100 CUP	72.5	2849	51,300 CUP
220 GR. HDY SP	IMR	IMR 4831	.323"	3.600"				76.0	2845	53,800 CUP
220 GR. HDY SP	Hodgdon	H4350	.323"	3.600"	70.0	2690	48,200 CUP	74.0	2824	52,100 CUP
220 GR. HDY SP	IMR	IMR 4350	.323"	3.600"				72.0	2795	53,000 CUP

Cartridge: 338 Marlin Express Load Type: Rifle					Starting Loads			Maximum Loads		
Bullet Weight (Gr.)	Manufacturer	Powder	Bullet Diam.	C.O.L.	Grs.	Vel. (ft/s)	Pressure	Grs.	Vel. (ft/s)	Pressure
200 GR. HDY FTX	Hodgdon	H414	.338"	2.590"	46.4	2205	36,300 PSI	49.3	2364	44,200 PSI
200 GR. HDY FTX	Winchester	760	.338"	2.590"	46.4	2205	36,300 PSI	49.3	2364	44,200 PSI
200 GR. HDY FTX	IMR	IMR 4007 SSC	.338"	2.590"	44.6	2181	37,900 PSI	47.5C	2334	44,900 PSI
200 GR. HDY FTX	Hodgdon	H380	.338"	2.590"	44.2	2173	34,300 PSI	47.0	2339	41,600 PSI
200 GR. HDY FTX	Hodgdon	LVR	.338"	2.590"	44.6	2313	37,100 PSI	47.5	2493	46,000 PSI
200 GR. HDY FTX	Hodgdon	Varget	.338"	2.590"	40.0	2224	41,600 PSI	42.5	2326	44,600 PSI
200 GR. HDY FTX	IMR	IMR 4064	.338"	2.590"	39.5	2169	39,300 PSI	42.0	2294	43,400 PSI
200 GR. HDY FTX	Winchester	748	.338"	2.590"	43.4	2237	35,700 PSI	45.9	2392	44,300 PSI
200 GR. HDY FTX	Hodgdon	BL-C(2)	.338"	2.590"	42.3	2137	33,800 PSI	46.7	2393	45,400 PSI
200 GR. HDY FTX	IMR	IMR 4895	.338"	2.590"	38.0	2137	40,400 PSI	41.3	2263	43,000 PSI
200 GR. HDY FTX	Hodgdon	H4895	.338"	2.590"	35.7	2170	38,900 PSI	38.0	2309	45,400 PSI
200 GR. HDY FTX	IMR	IMR 8208 XBR	.338"	2.590"	37.8	2228	40,700 PSI	40.2	2322	44,000 PSI
200 GR. HDY FTX	IMR	IMR 3031	.338"	2.590"	36.2	2191	41,700 PSI	38.5	2259	43,000 PSI

Bullet Weight (Gr.)	Manufacturer	Powder	Bullet Diam.	C.O.L.	Grs.	Vel. (ft/s)	Pressure	Grs.	Vel. (ft/s)	Pressure
200 GR. HDY FTX	Hodgdon	Benchmark	.338"	2.590"	36.0	2198	42,200 PSI	38.2	2281	44,800 PSI

Cartridge:338 Federal Load Type:Rifle					Starting Loads			Maximum Loads		
Bullet Weight (Gr.)	Manufacturer	Powder	Bullet Diam.	C.O.L.	Grs.	Vel. (ft/s)	Pressure	Grs.	Vel. (ft/s)	Pressure
160 GR. BAR TTSX	Hodgdon	H335	.338"	2.840"	43.8	2579	39,900 PSI	48.7	2814	49,700 PSI
160 GR. BAR TTSX	IMR	IMR 8208 XBR	.338"	2.840"	46.0	2733	46,500 PSI	50.0C	2910	54,700 PSI
160 GR. BAR TTSX	IMR	IMR 3031	.338"	2.840"	41.9	2559	41,000 PSI	45.5C	2763	50,400 PSI
160 GR. BAR TTSX	Hodgdon	Benchmark	.338"	2.840"	45.1	2725	47,900 PSI	49.0C	2894	56,200 PSI
160 GR. BAR TTSX	Hodgdon	H322	.338"	2.840"	44.6	2761	52,400 PSI	48.5C	2937	61,800 PSI
160 GR. BAR TTSX	IMR	IMR 4198	.338"	2.840"	38.5	2706	52,900 PSI	41.0	2850	62,400 PSI
160 GR. BAR TTSX	Hodgdon	H4198	.338"	2.840"	40.2	2756	53,600 PSI	42.8	2884	61,500 PSI
180 GR. NOS AB	Hodgdon	CFE 223	.338"	2.810"	46.0	2408	32,700 PSI	50.0	2620	42,100 PSI
180 GR. NOS AB	Winchester	748	.338"	2.810"	45.0	2486	40,300 PSI	51.0	2746	51,100 PSI
180 GR. NOS AB	Hodgdon	BL-C(2)	.338"	2.810"	44.0	2338	34,700 PSI	50.0	2648	47,500 PSI
180 GR. NOS AB	IMR	IMR 4895	.338"	2.810"	42.0	2373	40,700 PSI	47.0C	2624	50,900 PSI
180 GR. NOS AB	Hodgdon	H335	.338"	2.810"	42.0	2483	43,000 PSI	47.0	2712	53,900 PSI
180 GR. NOS AB	Hodgdon	H4895	.338"	2.810"	43.0	2486	42,400 PSI	47.0C	2682	50,800 PSI
180 GR. NOS AB	IMR	IMR 8208 XBR	.338"	2.810"	44.6	2641	49,600 PSI	48.5C	2811	59,900 PSI
180 GR. NOS AB	IMR	IMR 3031	.338"	2.810"	40.0	2438	42,500 PSI	45.0C	2705	55,200 PSI
180 GR. NOS AB	Hodgdon	Benchmark	.338"	2.810"	42.0	2532	47,900 PSI	47.0C	2768	61,300 PSI
180 GR. NOS AB	Hodgdon	H322	.338"	2.810"	41.0	2514	46,000 PSI	45.5C	2743	59,700 PSI
185 GR. BAR TSX	Hodgdon	CFE 223	.338"	2.800"	47.5	2488	39,800 PSI	50.5	2624	46,200 PSI
185 GR. BAR TSX	Hodgdon	Varget	.338"	2.800"	42.0	2364	43,000 PSI	47.0C	2607	54,700 PSI
185 GR. BAR TSX	IMR	IMR 4064	.338"	2.800"	41.0	2388	45,100 PSI	45.0C	2584	53,400 PSI
185 GR. BAR TSX	Winchester	748	.338"	2.800"	44.0	2477	45,200 PSI	49.0	2665	53,100 PSI
185 GR. BAR TSX	Hodgdon	BL-C(2)	.338"	2.800"	44.0	2386	41,600 PSI	49.0	2597	51,100 PSI
185 GR. BAR TSX	IMR	IMR 4895	.338"	2.800"	41.0	2342	43,500 PSI	45.0C	2541	51,400 PSI
185 GR. BAR TSX	Hodgdon	H335	.338"	2.800"	41.0	2460	46,300 PSI	46.0	2679	56,700 PSI
185 GR. BAR TSX	Hodgdon	H4895	.338"	2.800"	42.0	2456	45,400 PSI	46.5C	2690	58,200 PSI
185 GR. BAR TSX	IMR	IMR 8208 XBR	.338"	2.800"	44.2	2601	51,800 PSI	47.0C	2721	59,500 PSI
185 GR. BAR TSX	IMR	IMR 3031	.338"	2.800"	39.0	2410	47,200 PSI	44.0C	2666	60,000 PSI
185 GR. BAR TSX	Hodgdon	Benchmark	.338"	2.800"	39.0	2416	48,000 PSI	44.0C	2637	60,100 PSI
185 GR. BAR TSX	Hodgdon	H322	.338"	2.800"	39.0	2447	49,400 PSI	43.3C	2645	59,700 PSI
200 GR. HDY SP	Hodgdon	CFE 223	.338"	2.810"	45.8	2326	33,600 PSI	50.0	2545	44,900 PSI
200 GR. HDY SP	Hodgdon	Varget	.338"	2.810"	42.0	2264	40,400 PSI	47.0C	2510	52,100 PSI
200 GR. HDY SP	IMR	IMR 4064	.338"	2.810"	40.0	2224	37,500 PSI	45.0C	2486	48,600 PSI
200 GR. HDY SP	Winchester	748	.338"	2.810"	44.0	2322	37,300 PSI	50.0	2584	49,500 PSI
200 GR. HDY SP	Hodgdon	BL-C(2)	.338"	2.810"	45.0	2289	36,900 PSI	49.0	2442	43,300 PSI

200 GR. HDY SP	IMR	IMR 4895	.338"	2.810"	42.0	2296	41,400 PSI	47.0C	2535	52,100 PSI
200 GR. HDY SP	Hodgdon	H335	.338"	2.810"	42.0	2389	44,400 PSI	47.0	2606	56,400 PSI
200 GR. HDY SP	Hodgdon	H4895	.338"	2.810"	42.0	2350	42,600 PSI	47.0C	2597	55,100 PSI
200 GR. HDY SP	IMR	IMR 8208 XBR	.338"	2.810"	44.0	2504	50,200 PSI	47.0C	2657	60,300 PSI
200 GR. HDY SP	IMR	IMR 3031	.338"	2.810"	40.0	2316	41,300 PSI	45.0C	2598	57,300 PSI
200 GR. HDY SP	Hodgdon	Benchmark	.338"	2.810"	40.0	2309	43,200 PSI	45.0C	2584	59,700 PSI
200 GR. HDY SP	Hodgdon	H322	.338"	2.810"	40.0	2412	49,500 PSI	44.5	2596	59,300 PSI
210 GR. SFT SCIR	Hodgdon	LVR	.338"	2.820"	45.0	2468	48,800 PSI	49.0C	2622	56,400 PSI
210 GR. SFT SCIR	Hodgdon	CFE 223	.338"	2.820"	43.8	2381	45,900 PSI	47.6	2549	57,100 PSI
210 GR. SFT SCIR	Hodgdon	Varget	.338"	2.820"	41.0	2248	42,000 PSI	46.0C	2503	56,500 PSI
210 GR. SFT SCIR	IMR	IMR 4064	.338"	2.820"	40.0	2254	42,200 PSI	43.0C	2394	48,800 PSI
210 GR. SFT SCIR	Winchester	748	.338"	2.820"	41.0	2289	42,200 PSI	45.7	2534	56,300 PSI
210 GR. SFT SCIR	Hodgdon	BL-C(2)	.338"	2.820"	42.0	2270	52,000 PSI	47.0	2548	59,100 PSI
210 GR. SFT SCIR	IMR	IMR 4895	.338"	2.820"	40.0	2195	39,500 PSI	45.0C	2482	53,900 PSI
210 GR. SFT SCIR	Hodgdon	H335	.338"	2.820"	38.0	2267	45,300 PSI	41.7	2469	57,400 PSI
210 GR. SFT SCIR	Hodgdon	H4895	.338"	2.820"	40.0	2281	41,600 PSI	45.0C	2551	58,100 PSI
210 GR. SFT SCIR	IMR	IMR 8208 XBR	.338"	2.820"	40.7	2402	52,000 PSI	43.3C	2508	59,400 PSI
210 GR. SFT SCIR	IMR	IMR 3031	.338"	2.820"	38.0	2267	43,700 PSI	42.5C	2499	57,000 PSI
210 GR. SFT SCIR	Hodgdon	Benchmark	.338"	2.820"	38.0	2277	45,900 PSI	43.0C	2514	60,800 PSI
210 GR. SFT SCIR	Hodgdon	H322	.338"	2.820"	38.0	2296	45,900 PSI	42.3C	2511	59,200 PSI
215 GR. SIE SP	Hodgdon	LVR	.338"	2.810"	47.0	2509	50,900 PSI	52.0C	2668	57,900 PSI
215 GR. SIE SP	Hodgdon	CFE 223	.338"	2.810"	44.5	2330	40,800 PSI	48.4	2494	49,800 PSI
215 GR. SIE SP	Hodgdon	Varget	.338"	2.810"	41.0	2216	41,000 PSI	46.0C	2452	53,100 PSI
215 GR. SIE SP	IMR	IMR 4064	.338"	2.810"	41.0	2267	43,800 PSI	45.0C	2468	54,400 PSI
215 GR. SIE SP	Winchester	748	.338"	2.810"	41.0	2218	38,000 PSI	46.0	2445	48,900 PSI
215 GR. SIE SP	Hodgdon	BL-C(2)	.338"	2.810"	43.0	2242	39,000 PSI	47.0	2428	47,900 PSI
215 GR. SIE SP	IMR	IMR 4895	.338"	2.810"	41.0	2234	42,400 PSI	45.0C	2448	53,200 PSI
215 GR. SIE SP	Hodgdon	H335	.338"	2.810"	40.0	2312	46,100 PSI	44.0	2512	58,300 PSI
215 GR. SIE SP	Hodgdon	H4895	.338"	2.810"	41.0	2297	43,500 PSI	46.0C	2539	57,600 PSI
215 GR. SIE SP	IMR	IMR 8208 XBR	.338"	2.810"	41.9	2396	50,500 PSI	44.6	2519	59,400 PSI
215 GR. SIE SP	IMR	IMR 3031	.338"	2.810"	38.0	2227	42,500 PSI	43.0C	2469	56,300 PSI
215 GR. SIE SP	Hodgdon	Benchmark	.338"	2.810"	39.0	2286	47,200 PSI	43.3	2487	60,000 PSI
215 GR. SIE SP	Hodgdon	H322	.338"	2.810"	38.0	2305	50,400 PSI	43.0	2504	60,300 PSI
225 GR. SFT SP	Hodgdon	LVR	.338"	2.750"	43.0	2293	46,500 PSI	48.0C	2518	61,800 PSI
225 GR. SFT SP	Hodgdon	CFE 223	.338"	2.750"	43.2	2278	47,700 PSI	46.0	2423	57,900 PSI
225 GR. SFT SP	Hodgdon	Varget	.338"	2.750"	41.0	2149	43,100 PSI	46.0C	2410	57,900 PSI
225 GR. SFT SP	IMR	IMR 4064	.338"	2.750"	39.0	2148	43,800 PSI	43.8C	2386	58,400 PSI
225 GR. SFT SP	Winchester	748	.338"	2.750"	41.0	2199	42,000 PSI	46.0	2453	57,400 PSI
225 GR. SFT SP	Hodgdon	BL-C(2)	.338"	2.750"	42.0	2178	41,800 PSI	47.0	2436	57.800 PSI
225 GR. SFT SP	IMR	IMR 4895	.338"	2.750"	40.0	2151	45,300 PSI	44.5C	2383	58,200 PSI

						Starting Loads			Maximum Loads	
225 GR. SFT SP	Hodgdon	H335	.338"	2.750"	38.0	2166	46,100 PSI	42.0	2378	59,200 PSI
225 GR. SFT SP	Hodgdon	H4895	.338"	2.750"	40.0	2167	42,900 PSI	45.3C	2445	60,000 PSI
225 GR. SFT SP	IMR	IMR 8208 XBR	.338"	2.750"	40.5	2283	52,400 PSI	43.1	2394	60,500 PSI
225 GR. SFT SP	IMR	IMR 3031	.338"	2.750"	37.0	2149	45,800 PSI	41.0C	2361	59,500 PSI
225 GR. SFT SP	Hodgdon	Benchmark	.338"	2.750"	38.0	2150	46,600 PSI	42.8	2365	59,500 PSI
225 GR. SFT SP	Hodgdon	H322	.338"	2.750"	37.0	2204	52,700 PSI	41.0	2357	60,000 PSI

Cartridge: 338-06
Load Type: Rifle

Bullet Weight (Gr.)	Manufacturer	Powder	Bullet Diam.	C.O.L.	Grs.	Vel. (ft/s)	Pressure	Grs.	Vel. (ft/s)	Pressure
						Starting Loads		**Maximum Loads**		
160 GR. BAR X	Hodgdon	Varget	.338"	3.150"	56.0	2924	51,200 PSI	60.0C	3063	57,900 PSI
160 GR. BAR X	Hodgdon	BL-C(2)	.338"	3.150"	59.0	2975	51,700 PSI	65.0	3134	57,300 PSI
160 GR. BAR X	Hodgdon	H335	.338"	3.150"	53.0	2919	53,500 PSI	57.0	3057	59,800 PSI
160 GR. BAR X	Hodgdon	H4895	.338"	3.150"	53.0	2901	50,600 PSI	58.0C	3112	62,200 PSI
160 GR. BAR X	Hodgdon	Benchmark	.338"	3.150"	51.0	2859	50,300 PSI	56.8	3103	63,600 PSI
160 GR. BAR X	Hodgdon	H322	.338"	3.150"	50.0	2870	55,200 PSI	55.0	3074	62,800 PSI
175 GR. BAR X	Hodgdon	Varget	.338"	3.130"	55.0	2841	55,100 PSI	59.0C	2982	63,000 PSI
175 GR. BAR X	Hodgdon	BL-C(2)	.338"	3.130"	59.0	2905	54,100 PSI	63.0	3011	57,900 PSI
175 GR. BAR X	Hodgdon	H335	.338"	3.130"	50.0	2756	54,200 PSI	55.0	2962	63,100 PSI
175 GR. BAR X	Hodgdon	H4895	.338"	3.130"	51.0	2774	51,200 PSI	56.0	2981	63,300 PSI
175 GR. BAR X	Hodgdon	Benchmark	.338"	3.130"	49.0	2731	51,700 PSI	53.7	2921	63,100 PSI
175 GR. BAR X	Hodgdon	H322	.338"	3.130"	48.0	2717	49,700 PSI	52.2	2902	62,000 PSI
180 GR. NOS BT	IMR	IMR 4007 SSC	.338"	3.250"	57.0	2803	54,600 PSI	61.0C	2915	61,900 PSI
180 GR. NOS BT	Hodgdon	Varget	.338"	3.250"	54.0	2782	51,000 PSI	58.5C	2961	62,000 PSI
180 GR. NOS BT	IMR	IMR 4320	.338"	3.250"	52.0	2708	51,800 PSI	56.5	2895	61,700 PSI
180 GR. NOS BT	IMR	IMR 4064	.338"	3.250"	51.0	2718	50,500 PSI	55.5C	2920	61,600 PSI
180 GR. NOS BT	Hodgdon	BL-C(2)	.338"	3.250"	58.0	2892	53,900 PSI	62.0	3012	59,400 PSI
180 GR. NOS BT	IMR	IMR 4895	.338"	3.250"	51.0	2706	49,900 PSI	56.0	2931	62,800 PSI
180 GR. NOS BT	Hodgdon	H335	.338"	3.250"	51.0	2802	56,300 PSI	55.0	2930	61,900 PSI
180 GR. NOS BT	Hodgdon	H4895	.338"	3.250"	51.0	2735	49,600 PSI	55.0	2933	62,700 PSI
180 GR. NOS BT	IMR	IMR 8208 XBR	.338"	3.250"	48.0	2681	50,000 PSI	53.3	2897	63,000 PSI
180 GR. NOS BT	Hodgdon	Benchmark	.338"	3.250"	50.0	2763	53,700 PSI	54.2	2925	63,400 PSI
180 GR. NOS BT	Hodgdon	H322	.338"	3.250"	49.0	2738	52,000 PSI	53.0	2916	63,000 PSI
185 GR. BAR X BT	Hodgdon	Varget	.338"	3.130"	52.0	2723	54,000 PSI	56.0	2867	62,300 PSI
185 GR. BAR X BT	Hodgdon	BL-C(2)	.338"	3.130"	55.0	2824	56,600 PSI	59.0	2943	62,400 PSI
185 GR. BAR X BT	Hodgdon	H335	.338"	3.130"	47.0	2632	52,300 PSI	50.5	2809	61,900 PSI
185 GR. BAR X BT	Hodgdon	H4895	.338"	3.130"	49.0	2671	51,000 PSI	53.5	2865	62,900 PSI
185 GR. BAR X BT	Hodgdon	Benchmark	.338"	3.130"	47.0	2629	50,400 PSI	51.3	2826	62,700 PSI
185 GR. BAR X BT	Hodgdon	H322	.338"	3.130"	47.0	2669	52,900 PSI	50.5	2823	62,400 PSI

185 GR. BAR TSX	IMR	IMR 4007 SSC	.338"	3.250"	54.0	2639	49,500 PSI	58.2	2840	60,500 PSI
185 GR. BAR TSX	IMR	IMR 4320	.338"	3.250"	51.0	2637	51,700 PSI	55.2	2819	61,900 PSI
185 GR. BAR TSX	IMR	IMR 4064	.338"	3.250"	49.0	2601	50,200 PSI	53.3C	2815	63,200 PSI
185 GR. BAR TSX	IMR	IMR 4895	.338"	3.250"	49.5	2634	51,900 PSI	53.8	2826	62,700 PSI
185 GR. BAR TSX	IMR	IMR 8208 XBR	.338"	3.250"	47.0	2596	50,800 PSI	52.0	2797	62,000 PSI
200 GR. HDY SP	Hodgdon	H4350	.338"	3.310"	58.0	2593	47,800 PSI	62.0C	2729	54,300 PSI
200 GR. HDY SP	Hodgdon	H414	.338"	3.310"	58.0	2631	47,500 PSI	61.0	2725	52,200 PSI
200 GR. HDY SP	Winchester	760	.338"	3.310"	58.0	2631	47,500 PSI	61.0	2725	52,200 PSI
200 GR. HDY SP	IMR	IMR 4007 SSC	.338"	3.310"	55.0	2625	51,600 PSI	60.0C	2823	63,000 PSI
200 GR. HDY SP	Hodgdon	H380	.338"	3.310"	58.0	2677	51,800 PSI	61.0	2770	55,600 PSI
200 GR. HDY SP	Hodgdon	Varget	.338"	3.310"	52.0	2622	51,500 PSI	56.5	2807	63,100 PSI
200 GR. HDY SP	IMR	IMR 4320	.338"	3.310"	51.0	2612	55,000 PSI	55.2	2760	62,100 PSI
200 GR. HDY SP	IMR	IMR 4064	.338"	3.310"	49.0	2549	49,100 PSI	53.7	2765	61,800 PSI
200 GR. HDY SP	Hodgdon	BL-C(2)	.338"	3.310"	55.0	2700	52,500 PSI	59.5	2856	62,300 PSI
200 GR. HDY SP	IMR	IMR 4895	.338"	3.310"	50.0	2593	50,800 PSI	53.9	2770	62,400 PSI
200 GR. HDY SP	Hodgdon	H335	.338"	3.310"	48.0	2599	55,400 PSI	52.0	2745	63,000 PSI
200 GR. HDY SP	Hodgdon	H4895	.338"	3.310"	50.0	2628	52,900 PSI	54.0	2787	63,300 PSI
200 GR. HDY SP	IMR	IMR 8208 XBR	.338"	3.310"	49.0	2624	55,200 PSI	52.8	2751	62,000 PSI
200 GR. HDY SP	Hodgdon	Benchmark	.338"	3.310"	48.0	2569	52,400 PSI	52.2	2725	61,000 PSI
200 GR. HDY SP	Hodgdon	H322	.338"	3.310"	47.0	2583	53,600 PSI	50.9	2724	61,900 PSI
210 GR. NOS PART	Hodgdon	H4350	.338"	3.240"	58.0	2598	52,200 PSI	62.0C	2753	61,800 PSI
210 GR. NOS PART	Hodgdon	H414	.338"	3.240"	57.0	2621	52,500 PSI	61.0	2747	59,700 PSI
210 GR. NOS PART	Winchester	760	.338"	3.240"	57.0	2621	52,500 PSI	61.0	2747	59,700 PSI
210 GR. NOS PART	IMR	IMR 4007 SSC	.338"	3.240"	51.5	2489	50,900 PSI	56.0C	2680	62,700 PSI
210 GR. NOS PART	Hodgdon	H380	.338"	3.240"	57.0	2603	49,600 PSI	61.0	2725	56,000 PSI
210 GR. NOS PART	Hodgdon	Varget	.338"	3.240"	50.0	2545	52,400 PSI	53.9	2701	62,400 PSI
210 GR. NOS PART	IMR	IMR 4320	.338"	3.240"	47.0	2410	49,300 PSI	51.0	2605	62,000 PSI
210 GR. NOS PART	IMR	IMR 4064	.338"	3.240"	46.5	2426	48,900 PSI	50.5	2629	62,600 PSI
210 GR. NOS PART	Hodgdon	BL-C(2)	.338"	3.240"	53.0	2647	56,000 PSI	56.5	2749	62,500 PSI
210 GR. NOS PART	IMR	IMR 4895	.338"	3.240"	47.0	2454	50,600 PSI	50.7	2635	62,500 PSI
210 GR. NOS PART	Hodgdon	H335	.338"	3.240"	44.0	2458	54,000 PSI	48.7	2620	63,300 PSI
210 GR. NOS PART	Hodgdon	H4895	.338"	3.240"	47.0	2480	49,900 PSI	51.7	2685	62,900 PSI
210 GR. NOS PART	IMR	IMR 8208 XBR	.338"	3.240"	45.0	2457	54,300 PSI	48.5	2598	61,500 PSI
215 GR. SIE SBT	Hodgdon	H4350	.338"	3.240"	58.0	2573	50,600 PSI	62.0C	2727	59,900 PSI
215 GR. SIE SBT	Hodgdon	H414	.338"	3.240"	57.0	2588	50,500 PSI	61.0	2708	56,100 PSI
215 GR. SIE SBT	Winchester	760	.338"	3.240"	57.0	2588	50,500 PSI	61.0	2708	56,100 PSI
215 GR. SIE SBT	IMR	IMR 4007 SSC	.338"	3.240"	53.0	2522	52,100 PSI	57.2C	2699	62,900 PSI
215 GR. SIE SBT	Hodgdon	H380	.338"	3.240"	57.0	2636	55,000 PSI	61.0	2717	56,800 PSI
215 GR. SIE SBT	Hodgdon	Varget	.338"	3.240"	50.0	2510	50,200 PSI	54.5	2700	62,400 PSI
215 GR. SIE SBT	IMR	IMR 4320	.338"	3.240"	48.0	2431	49,100 PSI	52.0	2630	61,900 PSI

Bullet Weight	Manufacturer	Powder	Bullet Diam.	C.O.L.	Grs.	Vel. (ft/s)	Pressure	Grs.	Vel. (ft/s)	Pressure
215 GR. SIE SBT	IMR	IMR 4064	.338"	3.240"	47.5	2457	48,100 PSI	51.6	2655	62,200 PSI
215 GR. SIE SBT	Hodgdon	BL-C(2)	.338"	3.240"	54.0	2642	55,000 PSI	57.5	2772	63,000 PSI
215 GR. SIE SBT	IMR	IMR 4895	.338"	3.240"	48.0	2500	51,700 PSI	51.8	2663	62,100 PSI
215 GR. SIE SBT	Hodgdon	H4895	.338"	3.240"	48.0	2503	51,200 PSI	51.9	2675	62,600 PSI
215 GR. SIE SBT	IMR	IMR 8208 XBR	.338"	3.240"	46.0	2459	52,500 PSI	50.5	2641	63,400 PSI
225 GR. SPR SPBT	Hodgdon	Hybrid 100V	.338"	3.240"	55.5	2515	53,200 PSI	58.5C	2610	57,900 PSI
225 GR. SPR SPBT	Hodgdon	H4350	.338"	3.240"	55.0	2481	52,100 PSI	59.5C	2649	62,700 PSI
225 GR. SPR SPBT	Hodgdon	H414	.338"	3.240"	56.0	2547	52,800 PSI	60.0	2675	59,900 PSI
225 GR. SPR SPBT	Winchester	760	.338"	3.240"	56.0	2547	52,800 PSI	60.0	2675	59,900 PSI
225 GR. SPR SPBT	IMR	IMR 4007 SSC	.338"	3.240"	51.0	2400	49,100 PSI	55.5	2610	62,700 PSI
225 GR. SPR SPBT	Hodgdon	H380	.338"	3.240"	55.0	2545	55,300 PSI	59.0	2668	61,600 PSI
225 GR. SPR SPBT	Hodgdon	Varget	.338"	3.240"	48.0	2441	52,100 PSI	52.0	2599	62,700 PSI
225 GR. SPR SPBT	IMR	IMR 4320	.338"	3.240"	47.0	2386	51,000 PSI	51.2	2571	62,900 PSI
225 GR. SPR SPBT	IMR	IMR 4064	.338"	3.240"	47.0	2409	50,800 PSI	50.5	2574	61,500 PSI
225 GR. SPR SPBT	Hodgdon	BL-C(2)	.338"	3.240"	51.0	2529	54,300 PSI	55.0	2671	62,900 PSI
225 GR. SPR SPBT	IMR	IMR 4895	.338"	3.240"	47.0	2407	50,500 PSI	51.0	2594	63,000 PSI
225 GR. SPR SPBT	Hodgdon	H4895	.338"	3.240"	46.0	2410	51,200 PSI	49.8	2577	63,000 PSI
225 GR. SPR SPBT	IMR	IMR 8208 XBR	.338"	3.240"	44.0	2362	52,700 PSI	48.3	2532	62,500 PSI
250 GR. HDY SP	Hodgdon	Hybrid 100V	.338"	3.300"	54.0	2344	50,500 PSI	57.0C	2459	57,600 PSI
250 GR. HDY SP	Hodgdon	H4350	.338"	3.300"	55.0	2366	51,700 PSI	59.8	2540	63,400 PSI
250 GR. HDY SP	Hodgdon	H414	.338"	3.300"	53.0	2384	53,900 PSI	57.8	2539	62,200 PSI
250 GR. HDY SP	Winchester	760	.338"	3.300"	53.0	2384	53,900 PSI	57.8	2539	62,200 PSI
250 GR. HDY SP	IMR	IMR 4007 SSC	.338"	3.300"	52.0	2343	52,600 PSI	55.0C	2455	59,700 PSI
250 GR. HDY SP	Hodgdon	H380	.338"	3.300"	51.0	2321	53,500 PSI	55.8	2462	61,100 PSI
250 GR. HDY SP	Hodgdon	Varget	.338"	3.300"	46.0	2248	51,300 PSI	50.0	2405	62,100 PSI
250 GR. HDY SP	IMR	IMR 4320	.338"	3.300"	47.0	2293	54,400 PSI	50.5	2413	61,500 PSI
250 GR. HDY SP	IMR	IMR 4064	.338"	3.300"	46.0	2270	52,700 PSI	50.0	2426	63,300 PSI
250 GR. HDY SP	Hodgdon	BL-C(2)	.338"	3.300"	48.0	2330	53,700 PSI	52.0	2482	63,200 PSI
250 GR. HDY SP	IMR	IMR 4895	.338"	3.300"	45.0	2219	48,400 PSI	49.3	2421	62,400 PSI

Cartridge: 338 Ruger Compact Magnum Load Type: Rifle					Starting Loads			Maximum Loads		
Bullet Weight (Gr.)	Manufacturer	Powder	Bullet Diam.	C.O.L.	Grs.	Vel. (ft/s)	Pressure	Grs.	Vel. (ft/s)	Pressure
160 GR. BAR TTSX	Hodgdon	Varget	.338"	2.830"	53.0	2771	46,800 PSI	59.5C	3067	62,200 PSI
160 GR. BAR TTSX	IMR	IMR 4320	.338"	2.830"	53.0	2748	46,900 PSI	59.0C	3057	62,100 PSI
160 GR. BAR TTSX	IMR	IMR 4064	.338"	2.830"	52.0	2755	45,800 PSI	58.0C	3074	61,300 PSI
160 GR. BAR TTSX	Winchester	748	.338"	2.830"	57.0	2866	46,300 PSI	62.5	3113	58,400 PSI
160 GR. BAR TTSX	Hodgdon	BL-C(2)	.338"	2.830"	57.0	2834	45,500 PSI	63.5	3121	59,600 PSI
160 GR. BAR TTSX	IMR	IMR 4895	.338"	2.830"	53.0	2811	48,300 PSI	58.5C	3078	61,800 PSI

160 GR. BAR TTSX	Hodgdon	H335	.338"	2.830"	52.0	2846	49,100 PSI	57.7	3102	61,500 PSI
160 GR. BAR TTSX	Hodgdon	H4895	.338"	2.830"	52.0	2858	50,200 PSI	58.0C	3117	63,100 PSI
160 GR. BAR TTSX	IMR	IMR 8208 XBR	.338"	2.830"	52.4	2848	45,800 PSI	57.0C	3101	62,900 PSI
160 GR. BAR TTSX	IMR	IMR 3031	.338"	2.830"	49.0	2772	47,500 PSI	54.5C	3047	62,800 PSI
180 GR. NOS AB	Hodgdon	Varget	.338"	2.830"	51.0	2682	50,000 PSI	56.7C	2909	62,200 PSI
180 GR. NOS AB	IMR	IMR 4320	.338"	2.830"	51.0	2665	50,100 PSI	56.5C	2897	62,100 PSI
180 GR. NOS AB	IMR	IMR 4064	.338"	2.830"	50.0	2631	46,300 PSI	55.2C	2902	61,800 PSI
180 GR. NOS AB	Winchester	748	.338"	2.830"	54.0	2753	49,300 PSI	59.5	2984	62,900 PSI
180 GR. NOS AB	Hodgdon	BL-C(2)	.338"	2.830"	56.0	2767	49,300 PSI	61.0	2991	62,400 PSI
180 GR. NOS AB	IMR	IMR 4895	.338"	2.830"	50.0	2634	46,700 PSI	55.7C	2921	63,000 PSI
180 GR. NOS AB	Hodgdon	H335	.338"	2.830"	49.0	2673	48,200 PSI	54.4	2918	62,300 PSI
180 GR. NOS AB	Hodgdon	H4895	.338"	2.830"	50.0	2736	52,200 PSI	55.0C	2923	61,200 PSI
180 GR. NOS AB	IMR	IMR 8208 XBR	.338"	2.830"	50.8	2769	52,600 PSI	54.6	2919	61,900 PSI
180 GR. NOS AB	IMR	IMR 3031	.338"	2.830"	46.0	2585	45,800 PSI	51.6	2866	63,300 PSI
185 GR. BAR TSX	Hodgdon	Varget	.338"	2.800"	51.0	2602	48,000 PSI	57.0C	2867	62,900 PSI
185 GR. BAR TSX	IMR	IMR 4320	.338"	2.800"	50.0	2566	47,400 PSI	56.0C	2839	61,800 PSI
185 GR. BAR TSX	IMR	IMR 4064	.338"	2.800"	50.0	2605	47,700 PSI	55.2C	2864	62,400 PSI
185 GR. BAR TSX	Winchester	748	.338"	2.800"	54.0	2693	48,600 PSI	59.5	2937	62,300 PSI
185 GR. BAR TSX	Hodgdon	BL-C(2)	.338"	2.800"	55.0	2703	48,900 PSI	61.0	2947	62,000 PSI
185 GR. BAR TSX	IMR	IMR 4895	.338"	2.800"	49.0	2511	43,600 PSI	55.5	2863	63,100 PSI
185 GR. BAR TSX	Hodgdon	H335	.338"	2.800"	49.0	2631	49,100 PSI	54.4	2874	62,700 PSI
185 GR. BAR TSX	Hodgdon	H4895	.338"	2.800"	50.0	2649	49,400 PSI	54.8C	2852	60,600 PSI
185 GR. BAR TSX	IMR	IMR 8208 XBR	.038"	2.800"	51.2	2732	53,400 PSI	54.5C	2868	62,700 PSI
185 GR. BAR TSX	IMR	IMR 3031	.338"	2.800"	46.0	2543	46,100 PSI	51.5C	2816	63,000 PSI
200 GR. HDY SP	Hodgdon	H414	.338"	2.830"	58.0	2615	47,800 PSI	63.0	2817	58,500 PSI
200 GR. HDY SP	IMR	IMR 4007 SSC	.338"	2.830"	56.0	2525	46,600 PSI	62.0C	2809	62,300 PSI
200 GR. HDY SP	Hodgdon	Varget	.338"	2.830"	51.0	2572	51,300 PSI	57.0C	2798	64,000 PSI
200 GR. HDY SP	IMR	IMR 4320	.338"	2.830"	51.0	2568	51,700 PSI	56.5	2777	62,400 PSI
200 GR. HDY SP	IMR	IMR 4064	.338"	2.830"	50.0	2525	46,900 PSI	55.0	2772	62,300 PSI
200 GR. HDY SP	Winchester	748	.338"	2.830"	53.0	2564	45,700 PSI	59.4	2844	61,600 PSI
200 GR. HDY SP	Hodgdon	BL-C(2)	.338"	2.830"	55.0	2631	48,400 PSI	61.0	2870	62,500 PSI
200 GR. HDY SP	IMR	IMR 4895	.338"	2.830"	50.0	2505	45,800 PSI	56.0	2800	63,200 PSI
200 GR. HDY SP	Hodgdon	H335	.338"	2.830"	49.0	2533	48,100 PSI	54.2	2775	62,200 PSI
200 GR. HDY SP	Hodgdon	H4895	.338"	2.830"	50.0	2627	55,400 PSI	55.3	2803	63,600 PSI
200 GR. HDY SP	IMR	IMR 8208 XBR	.338"	2.830"	50.8	2655	55,300 PSI	54.0	2759	60,900 PSI
200 GR. HDY SP	IMR	IMR 3031	.338"	2.830"	47.0	2509	48,200 PSI	51.7	2735	63,000 PSI
210 GR. SFT SCIR	Hodgdon	H414	.338"	2.830"	54.0	2480	46,400 PSI	60.5C	2740	61,200 PSI
210 GR. SFT SCIR	IMR	IMR 4007 SSC	.338"	2.830"	53.0	2453	47,500 PSI	59.0C	2716	62,600 PSI
210 GR. SFT SCIR	Hodgdon	Varget	.338"	2.830"	48.0	2457	49,800 PSI	53.0C	2662	62,300 PSI
210 GR. SFT SCIR	IMR	IMR 4320	.338"	2.830"	48.0	2415	47,700 PSI	53.0C	2654	61,200 PSI

210 GR. SFT SCIR	IMR	IMR 4064	.338"	2.830"	47.0	2393	44,300 PSI	52.2C	2667	61,500 PSI
210 GR. SFT SCIR	Winchester	748	.338"	2.830"	50.0	2473	45,400 PSI	56.0	2736	61,400 PSI
210 GR. SFT SCIR	Hodgdon	BL-C(2)	.338"	2.830"	51.0	2466	45,900 PSI	57.0	2739	63,300 PSI
210 GR. SFT SCIR	IMR	IMR 4895	.338"	2.830"	47.0	2388	44,100 PSI	52.2C	2663	61,000 PSI
210 GR. SFT SCIR	Hodgdon	H335	.338"	2.830"	45.0	2375	45,400 PSI	50.5	2647	62,600 PSI
210 GR. SFT SCIR	Hodgdon	H4895	.338"	2.830"	47.0	2514	54,200 PSI	52.0C	2665	60,800 PSI
210 GR. SFT SCIR	IMR	IMR 3031	.338"	2.830"	44.0	2382	45,700 PSI	48.6C	2617	62,000 PSI
215 GR. SIE SPBT	Hodgdon	H414	.338"	2.830"	54.0	2450	46,300 PSI	60.5	2717	62,400 PSI
215 GR. SIE SPBT	Winchester	760	.338"	2.830"	54.0	2450	46,300 PSI	60.5	2717	62,400 PSI
215 GR. SIE SPBT	IMR	IMR 4007 SSC	.338"	2.830"	53.0	2430	46,700 PSI	59.0C	2702	62,400 PSI
215 GR. SIE SPBT	Hodgdon	Varget	.338"	2.830"	48.0	2465	52,000 PSI	53.5C	2658	62,900 PSI
215 GR. SIE SPBT	IMR	IMR 4320	.338"	2.830"	48.0	2465	52,400 PSI	53.5C	2644	60,800 PSI
215 GR. SIE SPBT	IMR	IMR 4064	.338"	2.830"	47.0	2426	48,200 PSI	52.5C	2666	62,900 PSI
215 GR. SIE SPBT	Winchester	748	.338"	2.830"	50.0	2461	47,400 PSI	56.0	2711	62,100 PSI
215 GR. SIE SPBT	Hodgdon	BL-C(2)	.338"	2.830"	51.0	2465	46,700 PSI	57.0	2729	63,200 PSI
215 GR. SIE SPBT	IMR	IMR 4895	.338"	2.830"	48.0	2460	49,900 PSI	53.0C	2675	63,200 PSI
215 GR. SIE SPBT	Hodgdon	H335	.338"	2.830"	46.0	2417	47,900 PSI	51.5	2648	62,400 PSI
215 GR. SIE SPBT	Hodgdon	H4895	.338"	2.830"	46.0	2460	51,600 PSI	51.0	2639	61,900 PSI
215 GR. SIE SPBT	IMR	IMR 8208 XBR	.338"	2.830"	48.4	2540	57,600 PSI	51.0	2620	61.500 PSI
215 GR. SIE SPBT	IMR	IMR 3031	.338"	2.830"	45.0	2441	51,700 PSI	49.3C	2607	61,900 PSI
225 GR. HDY IB	Hodgdon	H414	.338"	2.830"	56.0	2491	49,700 PSI	60.0	2639	58,000 PSI
225 GR. HDY IB	IMR	IMR 4007 SSC	.338"	2.830"	54.0	2406	46,800 PSI	59.0C	2619	58,700 PSI
225 GR. HDY IB	Hodgdon	Varget	.338"	2.830"	48.0	2403	50,500 PSI	53.3	2601	62,200 PSI
225 GR. HDY IB	IMR	IMR 4320	.338"	2.830"	48.0	2375	48,700 PSI	53.5	2607	62,800 PSI
225 GR. HDY IB	IMR	IMR 4064	.338"	2.830"	48.0	2396	48,000 PSI	53.5	2630	62,300 PSI
225 GR. HDY IB	Winchester	748	.338"	2.830"	51.0	2415	45,600 PSI	56.0	2654	61,200 PSI
225 GR. HDY IB	Hodgdon	BL-C(2)	.338"	2.830"	52.0	2417	44,600 PSI	58.0	2689	61,500 PSI
225 GR. HDY IB	IMR	IMR 4895	.338"	2.830"	48.0	2382	47,500 PSI	53.5C	2628	62,600 PSI
225 GR. HDY IB	Hodgdon	H335	.338"	2.830"	47.0	2383	46,700 PSI	52.0	2620	62,900 PSI
225 GR. HDY IB	Hodgdon	H4895	.338"	2.830"	47.0	2465	56,800 PSI	52.3	2619	63,300 PSI
225 GR. HDY IB	IMR	IMR 8208 XBR	.338"	2.830"	48.2	2465	54,200 PSI	51.3	2587	62,600 PSI
225 GR. HDY IB	IMR	IMR 3031	.338"	2.830"	45.0	2356	47,400 PSI	50.0	2584	63,800 PSI
250 GR. SFT AF/SS	Hodgdon	H414	.338"	2.730"	51.0	2269	48,900 PSI	55.5	2453	61,000 PSI
250 GR. SFT AF/SS	Winchester	760	.338"	2.730"	51.0	2269	48,900 PSI	55.5	2453	61,000 PSI
250 GR. SFT AF/SS	IMR	IMR 4007 SSC	.338"	2.730"	49.0	2213	42,600 PSI	54.0C	2432	60,300 PSI
250 GR. SFT AF/SS	Hodgdon	Varget	.338"	2.730"	44.0	2192	51,500 PSI	48.8C	2352	61,400 PSI
250 GR. SFT AF/SS	IMR	IMR 4320	.338"	2.730"	45.0	2273	55,600 PSI	49.8C	2386	59,900 PSI
250 GR. SFT AF/SS	IMR	IMR 4064	.338"	2.730"	44.0	2170	46,600 PSI	48.8C	2368	59,800 PSI
250 GR. SFT AF/SS	Winchester	748	.338"	2.730"	46.0	2204	45,000 PSI	51.0	2406	59,100 PSI

250 GR. SFT AF/SS	Hodgdon	BL-C(2)	.338"	2.730"	48.0	2247	47,500 PSI	52.0	2409	58,500 PSI
250 GR. SFT AF/SS	IMR	IMR 4895	.338"	2.730"	41.0	2221	50,100 PSI	49.5C	2411	61,700 PSI
250 GR. SFT AF/SS	Hodgdon	H335	.338"	2.730"	42.0	2135	49,400 PSI	46.5	2304	61,000 PSI
250 GR. SFT AF/SS	Hodgdon	H4895	.338"	2.730"	41.0	2158	50,500 PSI	45.8C	2355	63,100 PSI
250 GR. SFT AF/SS	IMR	IMR 8208 XBR	.338"	2.730"	44.9	2258	56,500 PSI	47.3	2321	59,400 PSI
250 GR. SFT AF/SS	IMR	IMR 3031	.338"	2.730"	41.0	2168	50,000 PSI	46.0C	2345	62,700 PSI

Cartridge: 338 Winchester Magnum **Load Type:** Rifle					**Starting Loads**			**Maximum Loads**		
Bullet Weight (Gr.)	Manufacturer	Powder	Bullet Diam.	C.O.L.	Grs.	Vel. (ft/s)	Pressure	Grs.	Vel. (ft/s)	Pressure
160 GR. BAR TTSX	Hodgdon	H414	.338"	3.325"	70.0	3003	41,100 CUP	75.5	3195	46,400 CUP
160 GR. BAR TTSX	Winchester	760	.338"	3.325"	70.0	3003	41,100 CUP	75.5	3195	46,400 CUP
160 GR. BAR TTSX	Hodgdon	Varget	.338"	3.325"	62.0	2984	41,600 CUP	68.5	3196	51,100 CUP
160 GR. BAR TTSX	IMR	IMR 4064	.338"	3.325"	61.0	2974	40,200 CUP	68.0C	3246	50,900 CUP
160 GR. BAR TTSX	IMR	IMR 4895	.338"	3.325"	62.0	3038	43,300 CUP	69.0	3277	52,100 CUP
160 GR. BAR TTSX	Hodgdon	H4895	.338"	3.325"	60.0	3057	45,000 CUP	67.0	3271	51,600 CUP
160 GR. BAR TTSX	IMR	IMR 8208 XBR	.338"	3.325"	58.0	3023	47,000 CUP	64.0	3198	51,900 CUP
180 GR. NOS BT	Hodgdon	H4831	.338"	3.340"	70.0	2776	35,200 CUP	78.0C	3067	49,100 CUP
180 GR. NOS BT	IMR	IMR 4831	.338"	3.340"	70.0	2822	39,000 CUP	75.0C	3034	47,500 CUP
180 GR. NOS BT	Hodgdon	H4350	.338"	3.340"	69.0	2928	41,200 CUP	74.5	3157	52,200 CUP
180 GR. NOS BT	Hodgdon	H414	.338"	3.340"	66.0	2914	43,200 CUP	72.0	3107	51,800 CUP
180 GR. NOS BT	IMR	IMR 4350	.338"	3.340"	70.5	2848	40,800 CUP	75.0C	3038	48,300 CUP
180 GR. NOS BT	Winchester	760	.338"	3.340"	66.0	2914	43,200 CUP	72.0	3107	51,800 CUP
180 GR. NOS BT	IMR	IMR 4007 SSC	.338"	3.340"	67.2	2912	46,100 CUP	71.5	3078	52,100 CUP
180 GR. NOS BT	Hodgdon	H380	.338"	3.340"	65.0	2886	44,200 CUP	72.5	3111	51,100 CUP
180 GR. NOS BT	Hodgdon	Varget	.338"	3.340"	57.0	2871	45,500 CUP	63.5	3087	53,200 CUP
180 GR. NOS BT	IMR	IMR 4320	.338"	3.340"	60.6	2808	42,500 CUP	64.5	2972	49,800 CUP
180 GR. NOS BT	IMR	IMR 4064	.338"	3.340"	60.6	2885	43,300 CUP	64.5	3041	51,600 CUP
180 GR. NOS BT	IMR	IMR 4895	.338"	3.340"	62.5	2896	43,000 CUP	66.5	3059	51,200 CUP
180 GR. NOS BT	Hodgdon	H4895	.338"	3.340"	58.0	2893	45,100 CUP	64.0	3066	52,300 CUP
185 GR. BAR TSX	Hodgdon	Hybrid 100V	.338"	3.285"	65.0	2774	40,600 CUP	70.0C	2947	45,800 CUP
185 GR. BAR TSX	IMR	IMR 4831	.338"	3.290"	70.5	2749	39,500 CUP	75.0C	3031	49,800 CUP
185 GR. BAR TSX	Hodgdon	H4350	.338"	3.290"	69.6	2896	47,500 CUP	74.0C	3048	52,800 CUP
185 GR. BAR TSX	Hodgdon	H414	.338"	3.290"	66.0	2889	48,400 CUP	70.0	3002	52,000 CUP
185 GR. BAR TSX	IMR	IMR 4350	.338"	3.290"	67.0	2792	41,000 CUP	74.0C	3072	51,900 CUP
185 GR. BAR TSX	Winchester	760	.338"	3.290"	66.0	2889	48,400 CUP	70.0	3002	52,000 CUP
185 GR. BAR TSX	IMR	IMR 4007 SSC	.338"	3.290"	66.5	2875	47,400 CUP	70.7	3030	53,200 CUP
185 GR. BAR TSX	Hodgdon	H380	.338"	3.290"	65.8	2870	48,000 CUP	70.0	3007	52,800 CUP
185 GR. BAR TSX	Hodgdon	Varget	.338"	3.290"	60.0	2831	47,200 CUP	65.0	3013	52,900 CUP
185 GR. BAR TSX	IMR	IMR 4320	.338"	3.290"	59.7	2822	48,900 CUP	63.5	2942	51,800 CUP

185 GR. BAR TSX	IMR	IMR 4064	.338"	3.290"	59.2	2831	45,400 CUP	63.0	2981	51,600 CUP
185 GR. BAR TSX	IMR	IMR 4895	.338"	3.290"	60.2	2837	43,900 CUP	64.0	2990	51,400 CUP
185 GR. BAR TSX	Hodgdon	H4895	.338"	3.290"	56.0	2764	46,600 CUP	59.5	2901	52,300 CUP
200 GR. SPR SP	Hodgdon	H4831	.338"	3.300"	70.0	2703	41,300 CUP	77.5C	2965	52,400 CUP
200 GR. SPR SP	Hodgdon	Hybrid 100V	.338"	3.300"	65.0	2684	40,600 CUP	70.0C	2870	46,100 CUP
200 GR. SPR SP	IMR	IMR 4831	.338"	3.300"	70.0	2751	43,500 CUP	74.5C	2934	50,200 CUP
200 GR. SPR SP	Hodgdon	H4350	.338"	3.300"	65.0	2695	39,900 CUP	72.5	2969	52,200 CUP
200 GR. SPR SP	Hodgdon	H414	.338"	3.300"	63.0	2730	43,000 CUP	69.5	2942	52,400 CUP
200 GR. SPR SP	IMR	IMR 4350	.338"	3.300"	69.6	2837	46,700 CUP	74.0C	2979	52,900 CUP
200 GR. SPR SP	Winchester	760	.338"	3.300"	63.0	2730	43,000 CUP	69.5	2942	52,400 CUP
200 GR. SPR SP	IMR	IMR 4007 SSC	.338"	3.300"	65.8	2776	47,000 CUP	70.0	2918	52,300 CUP
200 GR. SPR SP	Hodgdon	H380	.338"	3.300"	62.0	2685	44,900 CUP	69.0	2921	52,800 CUP
200 GR. SPR SP	Hodgdon	Varget	.338"	3.300"	53.0	2597	39,100 CUP	58.5	2805	51,100 CUP
200 GR. SPR SP	IMR	IMR 4320	.338"	3.300"	57.0	2678	46,200 CUP	60.5	2784	51,300 CUP
200 GR. SPR SP	IMR	IMR 4064	.338"	3.300"	60.2	2793	47,100 CUP	64.0	2918	52,700 CUP
200 GR. SPR SP	IMR	IMR 4895	.338"	3.300"	62.3	2830	47,700 CUP	66.3	2958	52,900 CUP
200 GR. SPR SP	Hodgdon	H4895	.338"	3.300"	56.0	2702	44,700 CUP	62.0	2877	52,600 CUP
210 GR. NOS PART	IMR	IMR 7828	.338"	3.280"	72.0	2676	43,900 CUP	78.0C*	2895	52,600 CUP
210 GR. NOS PART	Hodgdon	H4831	.338"	3.280"	68.0	2648	42,600 CUP	75.5C	2888	52,300 CUP
210 GR. NOS PART	Hodgdon	Hybrid 100V	.338"	3.280"	68.0	2759	45,200 CUP	72.0C	2887	48,400 CUP
210 GR. NOS PART	IMR	IMR 4831	.338"	3.280"	68.0	2677	41,000 CUP	73.0C	2877	50,600 CUP
210 GR. NOS PART	Hodgdon	H4350	.338"	3.280"	63.0	2618	41,500 CUP	70.0	2855	51,800 CUP
210 GR. NOS PART	Hodgdon	H414	.338"	3.280"	60.0	2617	42,300 CUP	67.0	2848	51,800 CUP
210 GR. NOS PART	IMR	IMR 4350	.338"	3.280"	67.0	2711	44,200 CUP	71.5C	2894	52,800 CUP
210 GR. NOS PART	Winchester	760	.338"	3.280"	60.0	2617	42,300 CUP	67.0	2848	51,800 CUP
210 GR. NOS PART	IMR	IMR 4007 SSC	.338"	3.280"	62.0	2655	46,700 CUP	65.8	2793	51,800 CUP
210 GR. NOS PART	Hodgdon	H380	.338"	3.280"	59.0	2555	42,400 CUP	66.0	2797	53,000 CUP
210 GR. NOS PART	Hodgdon	Varget	.338"	3.280"	53.0	2577	41,800 CUP	58.5	2784	52,500 CUP
210 GR. NOS PART	IMR	IMR 4064	.338"	3.280"	57.0	2651	44,200 CUP	62.0	2843	53,300 CUP
210 GR. NOS PART	IMR	IMR 4895	.338"	3.280"	56.0	2581	41,900 CUP	62.0	2809	52,500 CUP
210 GR. NOS PART	Hodgdon	H4895	.338"	3.280"	54.0	2609	44,100 CUP	60.0	2788	53,000 CUP
215 GR. SIE BTSP	IMR	IMR 7828	.338"	3.340"	72.0	2706	46,000 CUP	77.5C*	2889	53,400 CUP
215 GR. SIE BTSP	IMR	IMR 4831	.338"	3.340"	68.0	2708	45,700 CUP	72.5C	2889	53,000 CUP
215 GR. SIE BTSP	IMR	IMR 4350	.338"	3.340"	67.0	2643	44,200 CUP	71.5	2845	52,900 CUP
215 GR. SIE BTSP	IMR	IMR 4007 SSC	.338"	3.340"	63.5	2688	46,900 CUP	67.5	2833	52,300 CUP
215 GR. SIE BTSP	IMR	IMR 4064	.338"	3.340"	57.0	2596	45,800 CUP	62.0	2776	53,100 CUP
215 GR. SIE BTSP	IMR	IMR 4895	.338"	3.340"	56.0	2572	42,600 CUP	61.5	2779	52,600 CUP
225 GR. HDY SP	IMR	IMR 7828	.338"	3.340"	72.0	2605	44,100 CUP	77.0C*	2777	49,400 CUP
225 GR. HDY SP	Winchester	Supreme 780	.338"	3.340"	71.9	2605	40,700 CUP	76.5	2744	46,400 CUP

225 GR. HDY SP	Hodgdon	H4831	.338"	3.340"	67.0	2542	40,200 CUP	74.5C	2792	52,000 CUP
225 GR. HDY SP	Hodgdon	Hybrid 100V	.338"	3.340"	67.0	2693	46,200 CUP	71.0C	2815	49,400 CUP
225 GR. HDY SP	IMR	IMR 4831	.338"	3.340"	69.0	2637	44,900 CUP	73.5C	2805	50,200 CUP
225 GR. HDY SP	Hodgdon	H4350	.338"	3.340"	63.0	2571	41,100 CUP	69.5	2785	51,700 CUP
225 GR. HDY SP	Hodgdon	H414	.338"	3.340"	62.0	2611	43,200 CUP	69.0	2811	51,700 CUP
225 GR. HDY SP	IMR	IMR 4350	.338"	3.340"	67.0	2657	43,600 CUP	72.0C	2832	52,000 CUP
225 GR. HDY SP	Winchester	760	.338"	3.340"	62.0	2611	43,200 CUP	69.0	2811	51,700 CUP
225 GR. HDY SP	IMR	IMR 4007 SSC	.338"	3.340"	61.7	2596	46,300 CUP	65.6	2720	51,400 CUP
225 GR. HDY SP	Hodgdon	H380	.338"	3.340"	58.0	2490	43,700 CUP	65.0	2708	52,600 CUP
225 GR. HDY SP	Hodgdon	Varget	.338"	3.340"	52.0	2481	41,500 CUP	57.5	2680	52,700 CUP
225 GR. HDY SP	IMR	IMR 4320	.338"	3.340"	55.5	2540	48,300 CUP	59.0	2642	51,000 CUP
225 GR. HDY SP	IMR	IMR 4064	.338"	3.340"	57.0	2583	43,200 CUP	61.7	2764	52,800 CUP
225 GR. HDY SP	IMR	IMR 4895	.338"	3.340"	58.0	2605	44,400 CUP	62.0	2761	52,600 CUP
225 GR. HDY SP	Hodgdon	H4895	.338"	3.340"	53.0	2505	43,000 CUP	59.0	2688	52,400 CUP
250 GR. HDY SP	Hodgdon	H1000	.338"	3.340"	72.0	2512	41,500 CUP	76.0 C	2622	46,500 CUP
250 GR. HDY SP	IMR	IMR 7828	.338"	3.340"	70.0	2423	44,000 CUP	75.0C*	2628	51,800 CUP
250 GR. HDY SP	Winchester	Supreme 780	.338"	3.340"	68.6	2476	44,600 CUP	73.0	2612	49,300 CUP
250 GR. HDY SP	Hodgdon	H4831	.338"	3.340"	64.0	2424	41,900 CUP	71.5C	2655	52,300 CUP
250 GR. HDY SP	Hodgdon	Hybrid 100V	.338"	3.340"	63.0	2475	34,700 CUP	68.0C	2643	50,500 CUP
250 GR. HDY SP	IMR	IMR 4831	.338"	3.340"	67.0	2474	45,300 CUP	71.6C	2632	52,400 CUP
250 GR. HDY SP	Hodgdon	H4350	.338"	3.340"	61.0	2448	42,000 CUP	67.5	2657	51,900 CUP
250 GR. HDY SP	Hodgdon	H414	.338"	3.340"	59.0	2426	44,100 CUP	65.0	2622	52,900 CUP
250 GR. HDY SP	IMR	IMR 4350	.338"	3.340"	65.0	2468	45,800 CUP	69.5C	2634	52,400 CUP
250 GR. HDY SP	Winchester	760	.338"	3.340"	59.0	2426	44,100 CUP	65.0	2622	52,900 CUP
250 GR. HDY SP	IMR	IMR 4064	.338"	3.340"	54.0	2339	43,300 CUP	58.5	2518	52,700 CUP
250 GR. HDY SP	IMR	IMR 4895	.338"	3.340"	55.0	2392	45,700 CUP	59.0	2529	53,200 CUP
265 GR. BAR TTSX BT	IMR	IMR 7828 SSC	.338"	3.450"	61.2	2239	42,400 CUP	68.0C*	2443	50,000 CUP
265 GR. BAR TTSX BT	Winchester	Supreme 780	.338"	3.450"	61.2	2250	41,100 CUP	68.0	2486	50,700 CUP
265 GR. BAR TTSX BT	Hodgdon	H4831	.338"	3.450"	60.3	2236	44,000 CUP	67.0C	2434	52,500 CUP
265 GR. BAR TTSX BT	Hodgdon	Hybrid 100V	.338"	3.450"	58.0	2324	44,600 CUP	63.0C	2496	52,000 CUP
265 GR. BAR TTSX BT	IMR	IMR 4831	.338"	3.450"	58.0	2287	43,100 CUP	62.5C	2426	49,600 CUP
265 GR. BAR TTSX BT	Hodgdon	H4350	.338"	3.450"	55.8	2287	48,400 CUP	59.4	2409	52,200 CUP
265 GR. BAR TTSX BT	Hodgdon	H414	.338"	3.450"	52.2	2223	45,200 CUP	55.5	2329	50,200 CUP
265 GR. BAR TTSX BT	IMR	IMR 4350	.338"	3.450"	57.0	2304	44,100 CUP	62.0C	2468	49,900 CUP
265 GR. BAR TTSX BT	Winchester	760	.338"	3.450"	52.2	2223	45,200 CUP	55.5	2329	50,200 CUP
275 GR. SPR SP	Hodgdon	H1000	.338"	3.340"	70.0	2402	43,400 CUP	76.0 C	2564	51,100 CUP
275 GR. SPR SP	IMR	IMR 7828	.338"	3.340"	63.0	2263	42,000 CUP	68.0C	2454	52,700 CUP
275 GR. SPR SP	Winchester	Supreme 780	.338"	3.340"	67.7	2396	42,900 CUP	72.0	2546	51,000 CUP
275 GR. SPR SP	Hodgdon	H4831	.338"	3.340"	62.0	2304	42,600 CUP	69.0	2502	52,300 CUP
275 GR. SPR SP	Hodgdon	Hybrid 100V	.338"	3.340"	60.0	2327	43,800 CUP	65.0C	2472	50,900 CUP

Bullet Weight (Gr.)	Manufacturer	Powder	Bullet Diam.	C.O.L.	Grs.	Vel. (ft/s)	Pressure	Grs.	Vel. (ft/s)	Pressure
275 GR. SPR SP	IMR	IMR 4831	.338"	3.340"	61.0	2304	47,000 CUP	65.5C	2465	53,100 CUP
275 GR. SPR SP	Hodgdon	H4350	.338"	3.340"	57.0	2259	41,100 CUP	63.5	2447	52,100 CUP
275 GR. SPR SP	Hodgdon	H414	.338"	3.340"	56.0	2269	44,800 CUP	62.0	2445	52,500 CUP
275 GR. SPR SP	IMR	IMR 4350	.338"	3.340"	58.0	2285	45,600 CUP	62.0	2401	52,500 CUP
275 GR. SPR SP	Winchester	760	.338"	3.340"	56.0	2269	44,800 CUP	62.0	2445	52,500 CUP
300 GR. SIE HPBT	Hodgdon	H1000	.338"	3.340"	66.0	2241	42,200 CUP	70.0C	2347	46,900 CUP
300 GR. SIE HPBT	IMR	IMR 7828	.338"	3.340"	64.0	2274	45,500 CUP	68.0C*	2434	52,600 CUP
300 GR. SIE HPBT	Hodgdon	H4831	.338"	3.340"	63.0	2255	45,900 CUP	69.0C	2422	52,800 CUP
300 GR. SIE HPBT	IMR	IMR 4831	.338"	3.340"	62.0	2293	46,900 CUP	67.0C	2441	53,200 PSI
300 GR. SIE HPBT	Hodgdon	H4350	.338"	3.340"	56.0	2202	44,000 CUP	61.5	2362	52,600 CUP
300 GR. SIE HPBT	Hodgdon	H414	.338"	3.340"	53.0	2147	43,000 CUP	59.5	2348	52,600 CUP
300 GR. SIE HPBT	IMR	IMR 4350	.338"	3.340"	60.0	2263	47,100 CUP	64.0C	2420	52,300 CUP

Cartridge: 340 Weatherby Magnum
Load Type: Rifle

Bullet Weight (Gr.)	Manufacturer	Powder	Bullet Diam.	C.O.L.	Starting Loads			Maximum Loads		
					Grs.	Vel. (ft/s)	Pressure	Grs.	Vel. (ft/s)	Pressure
200 GR. SPR SP	Hodgdon	H4831	.338"	3.560"	85.0	2837		90.0	3040	
200 GR. SPR SP	Hodgdon	H4350	.338"	3.560"	77.0	2777		80.0	2994	
225 GR. HDY SP	Hodgdon	H4831	.338"	3.655"	81.0	2620		86.0	2889	
225 GR. HDY SP	Hodgdon	H4350	.338"	3.655"	75.0	2707		78.0	2866	
250 GR. SIE SPBT	Hodgdon	H4831	.338"	3.560"	78.0	2487		83.0	2784	
250 GR. SIE SPBT	Hodgdon	H4350	.338"	3.560"	73.0	2570		76.0	2724	
275 GR. SPR SP	Hodgdon	H4831	.338"	3.560"	75.0	2377		80.0	2569	
275 GR. SPR SP	Hodgdon	H4350	.338"	3.560"	71.0	2460		74.0	2575	

Cartridge: 338 Lapua Magnum
Load Type: Rifle

Bullet Weight (Gr.)	Manufacturer	Powder	Bullet Diam.	C.O.L.	Starting Loads			Maximum Loads		
					Grs.	Vel. (ft/s)	Pressure	Grs.	Vel. (ft/s)	Pressure
160 GR. BAR TTSX	IMR	IMR 7828	.338"	3.565"	98.7	3330	54,000 PSI	105.0	3531	62,800 PSI
160 GR. BAR TTSX	Hodgdon	H4831	.338"	3.565"	98.5	3290	52,900 PSI	104.8C	3472	61,200 PSI
160 GR. BAR TTSX	Hodgdon	Hybrid 100V	.338"	3.565"	90.0	3413	54,000 PSI	96.3C	3606	62,400 PSI
160 GR. BAR TTSX	IMR	IMR 4831	.338"	3.565"	93.0	3346	51,500 PSI	99.0	3589	62,500 PSI
160 GR. BAR TTSX	Hodgdon	H4350	.338"	3.565"	89.3	3348	54,100 PSI	95.0	3511	61,800 PSI
160 GR. BAR TTSX	Hodgdon	H414	.338"	3.565"	87.4	3341	54,700 PSI	93.0	3502	62,400 PSI
160 GR. BAR TTSX	IMR	IMR 4350	.338"	3.565"	90.2	3350	53,700 PSI	96.0	3525	61,200 PSI
160 GR. BAR TTSX	Winchester	760	.338"	3.565"	87.4	3341	54,700 PSI	93.0	3502	62,400 PSI
185 GR. BAR TSX	Hodgdon	H1000	.338"	3.530"	100.0	3051	49,300 PSI	106.0C	3218	57,300 PSI
185 GR. BAR TSX	IMR	IMR 7828	.338"	3.530"	94.0	3133	54,200 PSI	100.0	3312	62,000 PSI
185 GR. BAR TSX	Hodgdon	H4831	.338"	3.530"	93.7	3085	52,500 PSI	100.0	3281	61,500 PSI

185 GR. BAR TSX	Hodgdon	Hybrid 100V	.338"	3.560"	85.2	3198	54,600 PSI	90.6	3354	62,100 PSI
185 GR. BAR TSX	IMR	IMR 4831	.338"	3.530"	89.0	3176	53,000 PSI	94.6	3371	62,800 PSI
185 GR. BAR TSX	Hodgdon	H4350	.338"	3.530"	85.0	3120	53,200 PSI	90.4	3311	63,400 PSI
185 GR. BAR TSX	Hodgdon	H414	.338"	3.530"	81.8	3124	56,100 PSI	87.0	3247	62,400 PSI
185 GR. BAR TSX	IMR	IMR 4350	.338"	3.530"	85.4	3122	53,000 PSI	90.8	3307	61,800 PSI
185 GR. BAR TSX	Winchester	760	.338"	3.530"	81.8	3124	56,100 PSI	87.0	3247	62,400 PSI
200 GR. SPR SP	Hodgdon	Retumbo	.338"	3.525"	96.0	2928	43,700 CUP	104.0C	3189	52,600 CUP
200 GR. SPR SP	Hodgdon	H1000	.338"	3.525"	92.0	2854	42,300 CUP	102.0C	3116	52,500 CUP
200 GR. SPR SP	IMR	IMR 7828	.338"	3.525"	89.0	2965	44,300 CUP	95.0	3133	52,300 CUP
200 GR. SPR SP	Hodgdon	H4831	.338"	3.525"	83.0	2855	44,900 CUP	92.0	3086	53,200 CUP
200 GR. SPR SP	Hodgdon	Hybrid 100V	.338"	3.525"	81.0	2975	47,100 CUP	88.0	3155	53,200 CUP
200 GR. SPR SP	IMR	IMR 4831	.338"	3.525"	85.5	2970	47,600 CUP	91.0	3162	53,100 CUP
200 GR. SPR SP	Hodgdon	H4350	.338"	3.525"	79.0	2925	45,900 CUP	85.5	3099	52,500 CUP
200 GR. SPR SP	Hodgdon	H414	.338"	3.525"	74.0	2840	45,000 CUP	81.0	3058	53,000 CUP
200 GR. SPR SP	IMR	IMR 4350	.338"	3.525"	83.0	3001	47,400 CUP	88.0	3161	52,700 CUP
210 GR. NOS PART	Hodgdon	Retumbo	.338"	3.525"	92.0	2846	42,100 CUP	102.0C	3142	52,600 CUP
210 GR. NOS PART	Hodgdon	H1000	.338"	3.525"	90.0	2800	42,900 CUP	99.5	3052	52,500 CUP
210 GR. NOS PART	IMR	IMR 7828	.338"	3.525"	88.0	2920	47,300 CUP	93.4	3099	52,900 CUP
210 GR. NOS PART	Hodgdon	H4831	.338"	3.525"	80.0	2735	44,600 CUP	89.0	3006	53,000 CUP
210 GR. NOS PART	Hodgdon	Hybrid 100V	.338"	3.525"	77.0	2760	45,200 CUP	84.0	2948	52,500 CUP
210 GR. NOS PART	IMR	IMR 4831	.338"	3.525"	83.0	2920	47,900 CUP	88.5	3076	53,500 CUP
210 GR. NOS PART	Hodgdon	H4350	.338"	3.525"	76.0	2834	47,000 CUP	82.0	3005	52,200 CUP
210 GR. NOS PART	IMR	IMR 4350	.338"	3.525"	80.0	2891	46,400 CUP	85.0	3034	51,900 CUP
215 GR. SIE SPBT	Hodgdon	Retumbo	.338"	3.550"	94.0	2849	43,700 CUP	104.0C	3125	51,900 CUP
215 GR. SIE SPBT	Hodgdon	H1000	.338"	3.550"	92.0	2809	43,500 CUP	102.0C	3068	53,000 CUP
215 GR. SIE SPBT	IMR	IMR 7828	.338"	3.550"	87.7	2906	47,600 CUP	93.3	3076	51,900 CUP
215 GR. SIE SPBT	Winchester	Supreme 780	.338"	3.550"	88.4	2910	44,700 CUP	94.0	3067	50,500 CUP
215 GR. SIE SPBT	Hodgdon	H4831	.338"	3.550"	82.0	2763	44,500 CUP	91.0	2997	53,000 CUP
215 GR. SIE SPBT	IMR	IMR 4831	.338"	3.550"	83.0	2868	45,900 CUP	88.5	3033	52,600 CUP
215 GR. SIE SPBT	Hodgdon	H4350	.338"	3.550"	76.0	2791	45,000 CUP	84.0	3015	52,800 CUP
215 GR. SIE SPBT	IMR	IMR 4350	.338"	3.550"	80.0	2888	45,900 CUP	85.0	3042	52,200 CUP
225 GR. NOS PART	Hodgdon	Retumbo	.338"	3.550"	92.0	2744	41,200 CUP	102.0C	3040	52,300 CUP
225 GR. NOS PART	Hodgdon	H1000	.338"	3.550"	91.0	2713	42,100 CUP	101.0C	2995	53,100 CUP
225 GR. NOS PART	IMR	IMR 7828	.338"	3.550"	85.0	2831	46,900 CUP	90.5	2966	52,100 CUP
225 GR. NOS PART	Winchester	Supreme 780	.338"	3.550"	86.5	2877	44,100 CUP	92.0	3007	50,600 CUP
225 GR. NOS PART	Hodgdon	H4831	.338"	3.550"	80.0	2699	44,000 CUP	89.6	2918	52,900 CUP
225 GR. NOS PART	Hodgdon	Hybrid 100V	.338"	3.550"	76.0	2760	45,300 CUP	83.0	2942	52,700 CUP
225 GR. NOS PART	IMR	IMR 4831	.338"	3.550"	81.8	2794	47,300 CUP	87.0	2965	53,500 CUP
225 GR. NOS PART	Hodgdon	H4350	.338"	3.550"	74.0	2715	45,200 CUP	82.5	2936	52,800 CUP
225 GR. NOS PART	IMR	IMR 4350	.338"	3.550"	78.0	2821	45,200 CUP	83.3	2944	52,300 CUP

250 GR. HDY SP	Hodgdon	US 869	.338"	3.550"	101.5	2728	47,000 CUP	108.0	2879	51,100 CUP
250 GR. HDY SP	Hodgdon	Retumbo	.338"	3.550"	90.0	2620	43,200 CUP	98.0C	2853	52,000 CUP
250 GR. HDY SP	Hodgdon	H1000	.338"	3.550"	88.0	2567	41,400 CUP	98.0C	2838	52,800 CUP
250 GR. HDY SP	IMR	IMR 7828	.338"	3.550"	83.0	2636	46,200 CUP	88.5	2802	52,100 CUP
250 GR. HDY SP	Winchester	Supreme 780	.338"	3.550"	84.6	2700	43,900 CUP	90.0	2841	50,600 CUP
250 GR. HDY SP	Hodgdon	H4831	.338"	3.550"	79.0	2600	46,100 CUP	85.0	2740	52,200 CUP
250 GR. HDY SP	Hodgdon	Hybrid 100V	.338"	3.550"	75.0	2619	45,500 CUP	81.0	2765	52,200 CUP
250 GR. HDY SP	IMR	IMR 4831	.338"	3.550"	80.0	2657	47,700 CUP	85.0	2801	52,900 CUP
250 GR. HDY SP	Hodgdon	H4350	.338"	3.550"	74.0	2615	48,300 CUP	78.0	2742	52,300 CUP
265 GR. BAR TTSX BT	Hodgdon	US 869	.338"	3.685"	93.8	2518	48,400 PSI	100.0	2677	55,900 PSI
265 GR. BAR TTSX BT	Hodgdon	Retumbo	.338"	3.685"	76.4	2483	50,400 PSI	83.0	2660	60,600 PSI
265 GR. BAR TTSX BT	Hodgdon	H1000	.338"	3.685"	77.7	2510	52,800 PSI	83.6	2656	61,100 PSI
265 GR. BAR TTSX BT	IMR	IMR 7828	.338"	3.685"	76.1	2533	54,000 PSI	81.0	2658	60,500 PSI
265 GR. BAR TTSX BT	Winchester	Supreme 780	.338"	3.685"	79.5	2627	57,000 PSI	83.3	2719	61,700 PSI
265 GR. BAR TTSX BT	Hodgdon	H4831	.338"	3.685"	74.6	2518	54,400 PSI	79.4	2642	61,600 PSI
265 GR. BAR TTSX BT	IMR	IMR 4831	.338"	3.685"	70.5	2503	53,800 PSI	75.0	2634	62,300 PSI
275 GR. SFT SP	Hodgdon	US 869	.338"	3.460"	99.0	2636	46,200 CUP	104.5	2761	52,200 CUP
275 GR. SFT SP	Hodgdon	Retumbo	.338"	3.460"	80.0	2421	41,800 CUP	89.0	2671	52,700 CUP
275 GR. SFT SP	Hodgdon	H1000	.338"	3.460"	83.0	2444	43,500 CUP	91.5C	2648	52,600 CUP
275 GR. SFT SP	IMR	IMR 7828	.338"	3.460"	73.0	2429	44,500 CUP	81.0	2632	53,000 CUP
275 GR. SFT SP	Winchester	Supreme 780	.338"	3.460"	79.0	2562	45,800 CUP	84.0	2676	50,700 CUP
275 GR. SFT SP	Hodgdon	H4831	.338"	3.460"	71.0	2349	42,800 CUP	79.0	2572	52,800 CUP
275 GR. SFT SP	IMR	IMR 4831	.338"	3.460"	73.0	2450	46,000 CUP	77.3	2584	52,900 CUP
300 GR. SIE HPBT	Hodgdon	US 869	.338"	3.600"	98.5	2567	47,500 CUP	104.0	2677	51,500 CUP
300 GR. SIE HPBT	Hodgdon	Retumbo	.338"	3.600"	85.0	2376	41,100 CUP	94.0C	2654	53,400 CUP
300 GR. SIE HPBT	Hodgdon	H1000	.338"	3.600"	83.0	2383	43,200 CUP	92.0C	2590	53,000 CUP
300 GR. SIE HPBT	IMR	IMR 7828	.338"	3.600"	73.0	2376	44,600 CUP	81.0	2566	53,000 CUP
300 GR. SIE HPBT	Winchester	Supreme 780	.338"	3.600"	79.0	2460	45,100 CUP	84.0	2593	50,600 CUP
300 GR. SIE HPBT	Hodgdon	H4831	.338"	3.600"	71.0	2307	44,400 CUP	79.0	2511	53,100 CUP
300 GR. SIE HPBT	IMR	IMR 4831	.338"	3.600"	68.0	2316	43,500 CUP	76.0	2541	53,300 CUP

Cartridge:338 Remington Ultra Mag Load Type:Rifle					Starting Loads			Maximum Loads		
Bullet Weight (Gr.)	Manufacturer	Powder	Bullet Diam.	C.O.L.	Grs.	Vel. (ft/s)	Pressure	Grs.	Vel. (ft/s)	Pressure
185 GR. BAR TSX	Hodgdon	H1000	.338"	3.550"	96.0	3068	52,300 PSI	102.0C	3241	61,500 PSI
185 GR. BAR TSX	IMR	IMR 7828	.338"	3.550"	88.0	2986	49,800 PSI	95.7	3267	63,400 PSI
185 GR. BAR TSX	Winchester	Supreme 780	.338"	3.550"	91.7	3161	53,500 PSI	97.5	3332	62,900 PSI
185 GR. BAR TSX	Hodgdon	H4831	.338"	3.550"	91.0	3040	52,000 PSI	97.0	3232	62,100 PSI
185 GR. BAR TSX	Hodgdon	Hybrid 100V	.338"	3.550"	80.0	3040	53,800 PSI	87.0	3238	62,700 PSI

185 GR. BAR TSX	IMR	IMR 4831	.338"	3.550"	86.0	3075	50,300 PSI	92.5	3313	61,800 PSI
185 GR. BAR TSX	Hodgdon	H4350	.338"	3.550"	82.0	3037	51,400 PSI	89.0	3274	63.800 PSI
185 GR. BAR TSX	Hodgdon	H414	.338"	3.550"	82.0	3108	59,100 PSI	85.0	3188	61,300 PSI
185 GR. BAR TSX	IMR	IMR 4350	.338"	3.550"	84.0	3075	52,500 PSI	90.5	3299	63,100 PSI
200 GR. SPR SP	Hodgdon	H1000	.338"	3.590"	96.0	2944	48,300 PSI	102.0C	3127	58,600 PSI
200 GR. SPR SP	IMR	IMR 7828	.338"	3.590"	87.0	2930	52,900 PSI	93.7	3136	62,500 PSI
200 GR. SPR SP	Winchester	Supreme 780	.338"	3.590"	90.2	3070	54,700 PSI	96.0	3222	63,200 PSI
200 GR. SPR SP	Hodgdon	H4831	.338"	3.590"	91.0	2979	54,500 PSI	96.5	3138	63,000 PSI
200 GR. SPR SP	Hodgdon	Hybrid 100V	.338"	3.590"	79.0	2914	52,600 PSI	86.0	3126	63,100 PSI
200 GR. SPR SP	IMR	IMR 4831	.338"	3.590"	84.0	2971	52,200 PSI	90.5	3186	62,200 PSI
200 GR. SPR SP	Hodgdon	H4350	.338"	3.590"	84.0	3011	55,400 PSI	89.5	3156	63,000 PSI
200 GR. SPR SP	Hodgdon	H414	.338"	3.590"	79.0	2956	56,500 PSI	84.0	3089	63,100 PSI
200 GR. SPR SP	IMR	IMR 4350	.338"	3.590"	82.0	2940	52,200 PSI	88.0	3149	62,100 PSI
210 GR. NOS PART	Hodgdon	H1000	.338"	3.540"	96.0	2952	51,200 PSI	102.0C	3153	62,900 PSI
210 GR. NOS PART	IMR	IMR 7828	.338"	3.540"	86.0	2867	52,500 PSI	93.0	3095	63,400 PSI
210 GR. NOS PART	Winchester	Supreme 780	.338"	3.540"	88.8	3002	55,800 PSI	94.5	3136	62,100 PSI
210 GR. NOS PART	Hodgdon	H4831	.338"	3.540"	89.0	2913	54,600 PSI	94.5	3084	63,100 PSI
210 GR. NOS PART	Hodgdon	Hybrid 100V	.338"	3.540"	78.0	2900	55,900 PSI	84.5	3062	63,400 PSI
210 GR. NOS PART	IMR	IMR 4831	.338"	3.540"	83.0	2907	51,600 PSI	89.7	3119	62,300 PSI
210 GR. NOS PART	Hodgdon	H4350	.338"	3.540"	82.0	2941	53,700 PSI	87.0	3107	62,900 PSI
210 GR. NOS PART	IMR	IMR 4350	.338"	3.540"	80.0	2873	51,400 PSI	87.0	3097	62,400 PSI
215 GR. SIE SPBT	Hodgdon	H1000	.338"	3.590"	96.0	2947	51,800 PSI	102.0C	3127	62,800 PSI
215 GR. SIE SPBT	IMR	IMR 7828	.338"	3.590"	86.0	2810	50,300 PSI	93.0	3059	62,400 PSI
215 GR. SIE SPBT	Winchester	Supreme 780	.338"	3.590"	87.0	2893	50,200 PSI	94.0	3125	62,400 PSI
215 GR. SIE SPBT	Hodgdon	H4831	.338"	3.590"	89.0	2881	51,800 PSI	94.5	3057	62,800 PSI
215 GR. SIE SPBT	Hodgdon	Hybrid 100V	.338"	3.590"	77.0	2825	52,700 PSI	84.0	3031	63,300 PSI
215 GR. SIE SPBT	IMR	IMR 4831	.338"	3.590"	83.0	2875	50,500 PSI	90.3	3124	63,400 PSI
215 GR. SIE SPBT	Hodgdon	H4350	.338"	3.590"	83.0	2940	54,100 PSI	88.0	3088	62,700 PSI
215 GR. SIE SPBT	IMR	IMR 4350	.338"	3.590"	80.0	2826	50,300 PSI	87.0	3067	62,600 PSI
225 GR. NOS PART	Hodgdon	Retumbo	.338"	3.550"	97.0	2662	52,800 PSI	103.0C	3055	61,100 PSI
225 GR. NOS PART	Hodgdon	H1000	.338"	3.550"	94.0	2860	51,400 PSI	100.0C	3058	63,000 PSI
225 GR. NOS PART	IMR	IMR 7828	.338"	3.550"	85.0	2768	51,100 PSI	92.0	2986	62,600 PSI
225 GR. NOS PART	Winchester	Supreme 780	.338"	3.550"	85.0	2795	49,300 PSI	92.0	3046	62,400 PSI
225 GR. NOS PART	Hodgdon	H4831	.338"	3.550"	88.0	2825	54,400 PSI	93.5	2977	63,000 PSI
225 GR. NOS PART	Hodgdon	Hybrid 100V	.338"	3.550"	76.0	2760	53,600 PSI	82.0	2953	63,900 PSI
225 GR. NOS PART	IMR	IMR 4831	.338"	3.550"	81.0	2824	50,500 PSI	88.5	3071	63,400 PSI
225 GR. NOS PART	Hodgdon	H4350	.338"	3.550"	81.0	2832	54,200 PSI	86.0	2976	62,600 PSI
225 GR. NOS PART	IMR	IMR 4350	.338"	3.550"	79.0	2800	50,800 PSI	85.7	3030	62,700 PSI
250 GR. HDY SP	Hodgdon	US 869	.338"	3.580"	100.0	2658	51,300 PSI	104.0	2751	56,200 PSI
250 GR. HDY SP	Hodgdon	Retumbo	.338"	3.580"	95.0	2798	54,600 PSI	101.0C	2964	64,500 PSI

Bullet Weight (Gr.)	Manufacturer	Powder	Bullet Diam.	C.O.L.	Grs.	Vel. (ft/s)	Pressure	Grs.	Vel. (ft/s)	Pressure
250 GR. HDY SP	Hodgdon	H1000	.338"	3.580"	92.0	2756	52,400 PSI	98.0C	2923	62,400 PSI
250 GR. HDY SP	IMR	IMR 7828	.338"	3.580"	83.0	2674	51,000 PSI	90.0	2896	63,500 PSI
250 GR. HDY SP	Winchester	Supreme 780	.338"	3.580"	82.0	2681	50,600 PSI	89.0	2897	62,500 PSI
250 GR. HDY SP	Hodgdon	H4831	.338"	3.580"	84.0	2662	50,000 PSI	90.0	2858	62,500 PSI
250 GR. HDY SP	Hodgdon	Hybrid 100V	.338"	3.580"	73.0	2579	51,100 PSI	79.2	2785	63,900 PSI
250 GR. HDY SP	IMR	IMR 4831	.338"	3.580"	79.0	2703	51,800 PSI	86.0	2914	63,300 PSI
250 GR. HDY SP	Hodgdon	H4350	.338"	3.580"	78.0	2698	55,700 PSI	83.0	2820	63,000 PSI
250 GR. HDY SP	IMR	IMR 4350	.338"	3.580"	77.0	2668	50,800 PSI	84.0	2890	63,700 PSI
275 GR. SFT SP	Hodgdon	US 869	.338"	3.490"	96.0	2525	50,700 PSI	102.0	2698	60,600 PSI
275 GR. SFT SP	Hodgdon	Retumbo	.338"	3.490"	88.0	2649	57,900 PSI	94.0C	2764	63,100 PSI
275 GR. SFT SP	Hodgdon	H1000	.338"	3.490"	86.0	2602	54,800 PSI	91.0C	2729	62,700 PSI
275 GR. SFT SP	IMR	IMR 7828	.338"	3.490"	79.0	2545	54,700 PSI	86.0	2731	64,100 PSI
275 GR. SFT SP	Winchester	Supreme 780	.338"	3.490"	78.0	2559	55,300 PSI	84.0	2711	61,800 PSI
275 GR. SFT SP	Hodgdon	H4831	.338"	3.490"	81.0	2570	55,000 PSI	86.0	2693	62,500 PSI
275 GR. SFT SP	Hodgdon	Hybrid 100V	.338"	3.490"	70.0	2436	55,200 PSI	75.5	2578	62,600 PSI
275 GR. SFT SP	IMR	IMR 4831	.338"	3.490"	72.0	2463	51,500 PSI	78.0	2641	61,200 PSI
275 GR. SFT SP	Hodgdon	H4350	.338"	3.490"	73.0	2507	54,800 PSI	78.0	2650	62,900 PSI
300 GR. SIE HPBT	Hodgdon	US 869	.338"	3.580"	96.0	2455	49,500 PSI	101.0	2595	57,000 PSI
300 GR. SIE HPBT	Hodgdon	Retumbo	.338"	3.580"	84.0	2501	53,900 PSI	90.5C	2662	62,200 PSI
300 GR. SIE HPBT	Hodgdon	H1000	.338"	3.580"	82.0	2443	51,900 PSI	88.5C	2619	62,500 PSI
300 GR. SIE HPBT	Hodgdon	Hybrid 100V	.338"	3.580"	69.0	2364	52,500 PSI	74.7	2537	64,300 PSI

Cartridge:338-378 Weatherby Magnum Load Type:Rifle					Starting Loads			Maximum Loads		
Bullet Weight (Gr.)	Manufacturer	Powder	Bullet Diam.	C.O.L.	Grs.	Vel. (ft/s)	Pressure	Grs.	Vel. (ft/s)	Pressure
160 GR. BAR XFB	Hodgdon	H1000	.338"	3.650"	116.0	3374	46,100 CUP	120.0C	3478	49,200 CUP
160 GR. BAR XFB	Hodgdon	H4831	.338"	3.650"	107.0	3357	47,200 CUP	114.0	3583	53,500 CUP
160 GR. BAR XFB	Hodgdon	H4350	.338"	3.650"	99.0	3387	46,600 CUP	106.0	3610	53,600 CUP
160 GR. BAR XFB	Hodgdon	H414	.338"	3.650"	98.0	3371	46,600 CUP	104.0	3593	53,900 CUP
175 GR. BAR XFB	Hodgdon	H1000	.338"	3.700"	113.0	3250	45,600 CUP	120.0C	3413	51,200 CUP
175 GR. BAR XFB	Hodgdon	H4831	.338"	3.700"	103.0	3200	46,800 CUP	110.0	3399	53,600 CUP
175 GR. BAR XFB	Hodgdon	H4350	.338"	3.700"	96.0	3265	46,500 CUP	102.0	3478	54,000 CUP
175 GR. BAR XFB	Hodgdon	H414	.338"	3.700"	94.0	3280	49,300 CUP	100.0	3459	54,100 CUP
185 GR. BAR TSX	Winchester	Supreme 780	.338"	3.700"	108.6	3402	47,600 CUP	115.5	3577	52,000 CUP
185 GR. BAR TSX	Hodgdon	Hybrid 100V	.338"	3.700"	97.0	3383	46,600 CUP	105.0	3583	51,800 CUP
185 GR. BAR XBTC	Hodgdon	Retumbo	.338"	3.700"	119.0	3331	45,900 CUP	123.0C	3432	48,800 CUP
185 GR. BAR XBTC	Hodgdon	H1000	.338"	3.700"	113.0	3264	47,700 CUP	120.0C	3435	53,100 CUP
185 GR. BAR XBTC	Hodgdon	H4831	.338"	3.700"	102.0	3212	48,600 CUP	109.0	3399	54,000 CUP
185 GR. BAR XBTC	Hodgdon	H4350	.338"	3.700"	94.0	3183	45,600 CUP	100.5	3368	53,800 CUP

200 GR. SPR SP	Hodgdon	Retumbo	.338"	3.740"	116.0	3227	46,300 CUP	123.0C	3400	51,400 CUP
200 GR. SPR SP	Hodgdon	H1000	.338"	3.740"	110.0	3138	46,200 CUP	117.0C	3350	54,000 CUP
200 GR. SPR SP	Winchester	Supreme 780	.338"	3.740"	108.0	3349	49,500 CUP	115.0	3481	53,800 CUP
200 GR. SPR SP	Hodgdon	H4831	.338"	3.740"	98.0	2977	43,200 CUP	105.0	3217	53,700 CUP
200 GR. SPR SP	Hodgdon	Hybrid 100V	.338"	3.740"	95.2	3247	46,600 CUP	103.5	3456	53,900 CUP
200 GR. SPR SP	Hodgdon	H4350	.338"	3.740"	92.0	3046	46,000 CUP	98.5	3260	54,100 CUP
210 GR. NOS PART	Hodgdon	Retumbo	.338"	3.740"	116.0	3184	48,000 CUP	123.0C	3362	54,000 CUP
210 GR. NOS PART	Hodgdon	H1000	.338"	3.740"	106.0	2981	44,500 CUP	113.0	3192	53,500 CUP
210 GR. NOS PART	Winchester	Supreme 780	.338"	3.740"	104.3	3217	48,000 CUP	111.0	3355	52,300 CUP
210 GR. NOS PART	Hodgdon	H4831	.338"	3.740"	97.0	2955	46,500 CUP	103.0	3154	54,000 CUP
210 GR. NOS PART	Hodgdon	Hybrid 100V	.338"	3.740"	93.5	3159	45,900 CUP	99.5	3323	53,500 CUP
210 GR. NOS PART	Hodgdon	H4350	.338"	3.740"	91.0	3011	47,400 CUP	96.5	3176	54,000 CUP
215 GR. SIE SPBT	Hodgdon	Retumbo	.338"	3.740"	115.0	3149	46,800 CUP	122.0C	3331	53,900 CUP
215 GR. SIE SPBT	Hodgdon	H1000	.338"	3.740"	105.0	2958	45,700 CUP	112.0	3155	54,000 CUP
215 GR. SIE SPBT	Winchester	Supreme 780	.338"	3.740"	102.5	3115	44,400 CUP	109.0	3328	54,100 CUP
215 GR. SIE SPBT	Hodgdon	H4831	.338"	3.740"	98.0	2979	48,300 CUP	104.0	3140	53,800 CUP
215 GR. SIE SPBT	Hodgdon	Hybrid 100V	.338"	3.740"	94.1	3173	47,800 CUP	99.0	3293	52,900 CUP
215 GR. SIE SPBT	Hodgdon	H4350	.338"	3.740"	90.0	3025	49,700 CUP	96.0	3143	53,900 CUP
225 GR. NOS PART	Hodgdon	Retumbo	.338"	3.700"	112.0	3039	45,900 CUP	119.0C	3244	54,300 CUP
225 GR. NOS PART	Hodgdon	H1000	.338"	3.700"	104.0	2940	46,000 CUP	111.0	3112	53,800 CUP
225 GR. NOS PART	Winchester	Supreme 780	.338"	3.700"	99.6	3097	43,400 CUP	106.0	3193	52,300 CUP
225 GR. NOS PART	Hodgdon	H4831	.338"	3.700"	98.0	2948	47,500 CUP	104.0	3107	54,000 CUP
225 GR. NOS PART	Hodgdon	Hybrid 100V	.338"	3.700"	91.2	3063	46,200 CUP	97.0	3193	52,200 CUP
225 GR. NOS PART	Hodgdon	H4350	.338"	3.700"	90.0	2974	48,000 CUP	95.5	3100	53,900 CUP
250 GR. HDY SP	Hodgdon	US 869	.338"	3.660"	116.0	2806	40,900 CUP	123.0	3000	48,400 CUP
250 GR. HDY SP	Hodgdon	Retumbo	.338"	3.660"	108.0	2881	43,800 CUP	115.0C	3072	52,300 CUP
250 GR. HDY SP	Hodgdon	H1000	.338"	3.660"	102.0	2795	43,900 CUP	109.0	2989	53,900 CUP
250 GR. HDY SP	Winchester	Supreme 780	.338"	3.660"	96.0	2857	43,000 CUP	102.0	2992	50,100 CUP
250 GR. HDY SP	Hodgdon	H4831	.338"	3.660"	95.0	2785	46,500 CUP	101.0	2951	53,800 CUP
250 GR. HDY SP	Hodgdon	Hybrid 100V	.338"	3.660"	88.5	2848	43,900 CUP	94.0	2996	51,600 CUP
265 GR. BAR TTSX BT	Hodgdon	US 869	.338"	3.900"	104.4	2597	36,700 CUP	116.0	2894	45,600 CUP
265 GR. BAR TTSX BT	Hodgdon	Retumbo	.338"	3.900"	95.4	2680	41,100 CUP	106.0C	2970	51,200 CUP
265 GR. BAR TTSX BT	Hodgdon	H1000	.338"	3.900"	96.5	2701	42,200 CUP	105.0	2932	53,100 CUP
265 GR. BAR TTSX BT	IMR	IMR 7828 SSC	.338"	3.900"	93.0	2728	43,500 CUP	101.0	2941	52,500 CUP
265 GR. BAR TTSX BT	Winchester	Supreme 780	.338"	3.900"	93.1	2784	44,800 CUP	99.0	2943	51,900 CUP
265 GR. BAR TTSX BT	Hodgdon	H4831	.338"	3.900"	94.0	2802	49,000 CUP	99.0	2898	52,300 CUP
265 GR. BAR TTSX BT	Hodgdon	Hybrid 100V	.338"	3.900"	83.7	2715	46,600 CUP	89.0	2863	52,900 CUP
275 GR. SFT SP	Hodgdon	US 869	.338"	3.640"	113.0	2749	44,000 CUP	120.0	2904	49,700 CUP
275 GR. SFT SP	Hodgdon	H50BMG	.338"	3.640"	116.0	2752	46,000 CUP	120.0C	2843	51,000 CUP
275 GR. SFT SP	Hodgdon	Retumbo	.338"	3.640"	104.0	2707	41,600 CUP	110.5C	2934	52,500 CUP

Bullet Weight (Gr.)	Manufacturer	Powder	Bullet Diam.	C.O.L.	Grs.	Vel. (ft/s)	Pressure	Grs.	Vel. (ft/s)	Pressure
275 GR. SFT SP	Hodgdon	H1000	.338"	3.640"	100.0	2688	45,100 CUP	106.0	2837	53,700 CUP
275 GR. SFT SP	Hodgdon	H4831	.338"	3.640"	92.0	2666	48,000 CUP	98.0	2800	53,900 CUP
300 GR. SIE HPBT	Hodgdon	US 869	.338"	3.750"	108.0	2598	41,800 CUP	115.0	2782	48,700 CUP
300 GR. SIE HPBT	Hodgdon	Retumbo	.338"	3.750"	100.0	2604	41,900 CUP	106.5	2818	53,000 CUP
300 GR. SIE HPBT	Hodgdon	H1000	.338"	3.750"	92.0	2506	41,300 CUP	101.5	2747	54,000 CUP
300 GR. SIE HPBT	Hodgdon	H4831	.338"	3.750"	89.0	2596	48,800 CUP	95.0	2718	54,000 CUP

Cartridge: 348 Winchester Load Type: Rifle					Starting Loads			Maximum Loads		
Bullet Weight (Gr.)	Manufacturer	Powder	Bullet Diam.	C.O.L.	Grs.	Vel. (ft/s)	Pressure	Grs.	Vel. (ft/s)	Pressure
200 GR. HDY JFP	Winchester	Supreme 780	.348"	2.810"	65.8	2358	29,900 CUP	70.0	2494	36,100 CUP
200 GR. HDY JFP	Hodgdon	H4831	.348"	2.810"	65.0	2316	26,500 CUP	68.5C	2467	31,600 CUP
200 GR. HDY JFP	Hodgdon	Hybrid 100V	.348"	2.810"	57.0	2353	29,700 CUP	62.0	2541	35,800 CUP
200 GR. HDY JFP	Hodgdon	H4350	.348"	2.810"	61.0	2382	27,500 CUP	66.0	2630	35,900 CUP
200 GR. HDY JFP	Hodgdon	H414	.348"	2.810"	56.0	2384	28,600 CUP	62.0	2568	33,600 CUP
200 GR. HDY JFP	Winchester	760	.348"	2.760"	56.0	2384	28,600 CUP	62.0	2568	33,600 CUP
200 GR. HDY JFP	IMR	IMR 4007 SSC	.348"	2.810"	56.0	2304	26,500 CUP	61.3	2552	36,600 CUP
200 GR. HDY JFP	Hodgdon	Varget	.348"	2.810"	53.0	2389	29,300 CUP	58.0	2605	35,800 CUP
200 GR. HDY JFP	IMR	IMR 4320	.348"	2.810"	49.0	2229	28,800 CUP	55.0	2491	35,900 CUP
200 GR. HDY JFP	IMR	IMR 4064	.348"	2.810"	50.0	2294	28,500 CUP	55.0	2551	36,000 CUP
200 GR. HDY JFP	IMR	IMR 4895	.348"	2.810"	50.0	2331	29,500 CUP	55.0	2545	35,900 CUP
200 GR. HDY JFP	Hodgdon	H4895	.348"	2.810"	51.0	2419	29,700 CUP	55.0	2591	35,500 CUP
200 GR. HDY JFP	IMR	IMR 8208 XBR	.348"	2.810"	48.0	2418	30,900 CUP	53.0	2579	36,500 CUP
200 GR. HDY JFP	IMR	IMR 3031	.348"	2.810"	47.0	2317	28,300 CUP	52.0	2560	36,200 CUP
200 GR. HDY JFP	Hodgdon	Benchmark	.348"	2.810"	48.0	2402	30,700 CUP	52.0	2552	36,200 CUP
250 GR. BAR FN	Winchester	Supreme 780	.348"	2.760"	56.4	2005	27,600 CUP	60.0	2206	34,800 CUP
250 GR. BAR FN	Hodgdon	H4831	.348"	2.760"	60.0	2117	29,800 CUP	65.0C	2299	35,800 CUP
250 GR. BAR FN	Hodgdon	Hybrid 100V	.348"	2.760"	51.0	2125	30,600 CUP	56.5	2311	36,600 CUP
250 GR. BAR FN	Hodgdon	H4350	.348"	2.760"	55.0	2157	31,000 CUP	59.5	2328	35,700 CUP
250 GR. BAR FN	Hodgdon	H414	.348"	2.760"	51.0	2110	28,300 CUP	56.0	2266	35,000 CUP
250 GR. BAR FN	Winchester	760	.348"	2.760"	51.0	2110	28,300 CUP	56.0	2266	35,000 CUP
250 GR. BAR FN	IMR	IMR 4007 SSC	.348"	2.760"	49.0	2050	28,300 CUP	54.0	2226	35,800 CUP
250 GR. BAR FN	Hodgdon	Varget	.348"	2.760"	47.0	2086	28,800 CUP	52.0	2283	36,100 CUP
250 GR. BAR FN	IMR	IMR 4320	.348"	2.760"	45.0	2045	30,400 CUP	50.0	2239	37,000 CUP
250 GR. BAR FN	IMR	IMR 4064	.348"	2.760"	45.0	2058	30,000 CUP	49.7	2251	36,700 CUP
250 GR. BAR FN	IMR	IMR 4895	.348"	2.760"	45.0	2055	29,900 CUP	49.7	2250	36,900 CUP
250 GR. BAR FN	Hodgdon	H4895	.348"	2.760"	45.0	2074	29,200 CUP	50.0	2278	36,500 CUP
250 GR. BAR FN	IMR	IMR 3031	.348"	2.760"	41.0	2009	28,800 CUP	46.0	2207	37,000 CUP
250 GR. BAR FN	Hodgdon	Benchmark	.348"	2.760"	44.0	2087	31,300 CUP	47.5	2221	35,800 CUP

Cartridge: 357 Magnum Load Type: Rifle					Starting Loads			Maximum Loads		
Bullet Weight (Gr.)	Manufacturer	Powder	Bullet Diam.	C.O.L.	Grs.	Vel. (ft/s)	Pressure	Grs.	Vel. (ft/s)	Pressure
110 GR. HDY XTP	Hodgdon	H4227	.357"	1.590"	18.9	2072	29,600 CUP	21.0	2233	35,500 CUP
110 GR. HDY XTP	Hodgdon	H110	.357"	1.590"	22.0	2291	32,400 CUP	23.0	2398	37,200 CUP
110 GR. HDY XTP	Hodgdon	HS-6	.357"	1.590"	10.3	1669	32,600 CUP	11.5	1830	42,300 CUP
110 GR. HDY XTP	Hodgdon	Universal	.357"	1.590"	7.5	1585	35,100 CUP	8.0	1670	40,000 CUP
110 GR. HDY XTP	Hodgdon	HP-38	.357"	1.590"	8.0	1662	36,200 CUP	9.0	1782	42,500 CUP
110 GR. HDY XTP	Hodgdon	Titegroup	.357"	1.590"	7.2	1612	35,000 CUP	8.0	1746	41,500 CUP
125 GR. HDY XTP	Hodgdon	H4227	.357"	1.590"	18.0	1955	34,400 CUP	20.0	2122	42,000 CUP
125 GR. HDY XTP	Hodgdon	H110	.357"	1.590"	21.0	2205	38,400 CUP	22.0	2276	41,400 CUP
125 GR. HDY XTP	Hodgdon	HS-6	.357"	1.590"	9.8	1538	34,400 CUP	10.9	1724	42,100 CUP
125 GR. HDY XTP	Hodgdon	Universal	.357"	1.590"	7.1	1423	34,900 CUP	7.6	1526	39,600 CUP
125 GR. HDY XTP	Hodgdon	HP-38	.357"	1.590"	7.3	1454	33,800 CUP	8.5	1622	42,700 CUP
125 GR. HDY XTP	Hodgdon	Titegroup	.357"	1.590"	6.8	1461	36,500 CUP	7.5	1586	41,200 CUP
125 GR. HDY XTP	IMR	IMR 4227	.357"	1.590"	18.0	1955	34,400 CUP	20.0	2122	42,000 CUP
125 GR. HDY XTP	IMR	SR 4756	.357"	1.590"	6.0	1593	18,600 PSI	7.8	1537	30,600 PSI
125 GR. HDY XTP	IMR	SR 7625	.357"	1.590"	5.8	1258	19,000 PSI	7.5	1481	33,800 PSI
125 GR. HDY XTP	IMR	PB	.357"	1.590"	4.5	1123	19,600 PSI	5.9	1333	32,900 PSI
125 GR. HDY XTP	IMR	700-X	.357"	1.590"	4.5	1173	18,300 PSI	6.4	1479	30,400 PSI
140 GR. HDY XTP	Hodgdon	H4227	.357"	1.590"	16.2	1798	33,100 CUP	18.0	1930	42,600 CUP
140 GR. HDY XTP	Hodgdon	H110	.357"	1.590"	17.1	1836	28,400 CUP	19.0	1997	40,900 CUP
140 GR. HDY XTP	Hodgdon	HS-6	.357"	1.590"	9.5	1497	35,800 CUP	10.5	1613	43,000 CUP
140 GR. HDY XTP	Hodgdon	Universal	.357"	1.590"	6.5	1282	34,800 CUP	7.0	1356	40,200 CUP
140 GR. HDY XTP	Hodgdon	HP-38	.357"	1.590"	6.5	1324	30,800 CUP	7.7	1447	41,900 CUP
140 GR. HDY XTP	Hodgdon	Titegroup	.357"	1.590"	6.3	1325	35,600 CUP	7.0	1425	41,900 CUP
150 GR. NOS JFP	Hodgdon	H4227	.357"	1.590"	15.0	1663	33,100 CUP	16.5	1775	36,700 CUP
150 GR. NOS JFP	Hodgdon	H110	.357"	1.590"	16.0	1766	23,600 CUP	17.0	1807	28,900 CUP
150 GR. NOS JFP	Hodgdon	HS-6	.357"	1.590"	9.0	1449	31,500 CUP	9.7	1503	39,900 CUP
150 GR. NOS JFP	Hodgdon	Universal	.357"	1.590"	6.2	1096	32,800 CUP	6.7	1323	39,900 CUP
150 GR. NOS JFP	Hodgdon	HP-38	.357"	1.590"	6.5	1261	35,800 CUP	7.0	1356	39,700 CUP
150 GR. NOS JFP	Hodgdon	Titegroup	.357"	1.590"	6.1	1291	33,800 CUP	6.8	1429	40,900 CUP
158 GR. HDY XTP	Hodgdon	H4227	.357"	1.580"	14.5	1578	34,600 CUP	16.0	1668	42,600 CUP
158 GR. HDY XTP	Hodgdon	H110	.357"	1.580"	15.0	1619	28,600 CUP	16.7	1757	40,700 CUP
158 GR. HDY XTP	Hodgdon	HS-6	.357"	1.580"	8.0	1181	28,000 CUP	9.5	1427	41,900 CUP
158 GR. HDY XTP	Hodgdon	Universal	.357"	1.580"	5.8	1059	32,100 CUP	6.3	1147	39,300 CUP
158 GR. HDY XTP	Hodgdon	HP-38	.357"	1.580"	6.2	1095	33,700 CUP	6.9	1214	40,000 CUP
158 GR. HDY XTP	Hodgdon	Titegroup	.357"	1.580"	5.4	1035	32,600 CUP	6.1	1184	41,900 CUP
158 GR. HDY XTP	IMR	IMR 4227	.357"	1.580"	14.5	1578	34,600 CUP	16.0	1668	42,600 CUP

Bullet Weight (Gr.)	Manufacturer	Powder	Bullet Diam.	C.O.L.	Grs.	Vel. (ft/s)	Pressure	Grs.	Vel. (ft/s)	Pressure
158 GR. HDY XTP	IMR	SR 4756	.357"	1.580"	5.0	976	17,500 PSI	6.5	1216	29,900 PSI
158 GR. HDY XTP	IMR	SR 7625	.357"	1.580"	4.3	892	16,700 PSI	5.8	1145	29,600 PSI
158 GR. HDY XTP	IMR	PB	.357"	1.580"	3.7	827	18,800 PSI	4.9	1064	31,700 PSI
158 GR. HDY XTP	IMR	700-X	.357"	1.580"	4.5	1019	21,900 PSI	5.7	1219	31,200 PSI
158 GR. LSWC	Hodgdon	H4227	.358"	1.610"	10.5	1288	15,400 CUP	11.5	1382	17,800 CUP
158 GR. LSWC	Hodgdon	HS-6	.358"	1.610"	6.0	1083	12,900 CUP	7.0	1224	15,500 CUP
158 GR. LSWC	Hodgdon	Universal	.358"	1.610"	5.5	1214	23,300 CUP	6.7	1380	34,600 CUP
158 GR. LSWC	Hodgdon	HP-38	.358"	1.610"	3.5	901	8,400 CUP	4.5	1059	16,200 CUP
158 GR. LSWC	Hodgdon	Titegroup	.358"	1.610"	4.5	1157	19,300 CUP	5.0	1220	24,900 CUP
170 GR. SIE JHC	Hodgdon	H4227	.357"	1.580"	13.0	1442	32,300 CUP	14.5	1535	41,200 CUP
170 GR. SIE JHC	Hodgdon	H110	.357"	1.580"	14.0	1537	25,900 CUP	15.5	1662	40,800 CUP
170 GR. SIE JHC	Hodgdon	HS-6	.357"	1.580"	8.0	1243	30,900 CUP	9.2	1424	42,900 CUP
170 GR. SIE JHC	Hodgdon	Titegroup	.357"	1.580"	5.4	1177	34,700 CUP	6.0	1270	41,800 CUP
180 GR. NOS PART	Hodgdon	H4227	.357"	1.575"	12.7	1185	36,900 CUP	13.7	1325	40,900 CUP
180 GR. NOS PART	Hodgdon	H110	.357"	1.575"	13.0	1324	36,800 CUP	13.5	1381	39,100 CUP

Cartridge: 35 Remington Load Type: Rifle					Starting Loads			Maximum Loads		
Bullet Weight (Gr.)	Manufacturer	Powder	Bullet Diam.	C.O.L.	Grs.	Vel. (ft/s)	Pressure	Grs.	Vel. (ft/s)	Pressure
180 GR. SPR FN	Hodgdon	LVR	.358"	2.470"	40.0	2044	26,700 CUP	45.0C	2302	33,900 CUP
180 GR. SPR FN	Hodgdon	Varget	.358"	2.470"	37.0	1972	27,200 CUP	40.5	2196	32,500 CUP
180 GR. SPR FN	Hodgdon	BL-C(2)	.358"	2.470"	39.0	2014	29,300 CUP	43.0	2147	32,300 CUP
180 GR. SPR FN	Hodgdon	H335	.358"	2.470"	34.0	1953	29,900 CUP	37.5	2111	33,600 CUP
180 GR. SPR FN	Hodgdon	H4895	.358"	2.470"	35.0	1991	27,500 CUP	39.0	2232	33,100 CUP
180 GR. SPR FN	IMR	IMR 8208 XBR	.358"	2.470"	33.0	1915	30,900 CUP	37.0	2074	33,900 CUP
180 GR. SPR FN	Hodgdon	Benchmark	.358"	2.470"	32.5	1865	29,300 CUP	35.5	2034	32,300 CUP
180 GR. SPR FN	Hodgdon	H322	.358"	2.470"	31.0	1901	28,200 CUP	35.0	2104	33,100 CUP
180 GR. SPR FN	Hodgdon	H4198	.358"	2.470"	28.0	1971	28,600 CUP	32.0	2172	33,000 CUP
200 GR. HDY FTX	Hodgdon	LVR	.358"	2.540"	37.0	1897	26,500 CUP	41.4C	2116	34,700 CUP
200 GR. HDY FTX	Hodgdon	Varget	.358"	2.540"	36.0	1845	29,800 CUP	38.3C	1963	32,000 CUP
200 GR. HDY FTX	IMR	IMR 4064	.358"	2.540"	34.1	1741	30,400 CUP	36.3C	1861	32,200 CUP
200 GR. HDY FTX	Winchester	748	.358"	2.540"	35.7	1815	28,600 CUP	38.0	1913	31,300 CUP
200 GR. HDY FTX	Hodgdon	H4895	.358"	2.540"	33.8	1839	30,000 CUP	36.0C	1959	31,900 CUP
200 GR. HDY FTX	IMR	IMR 8208 XBR	.358"	2.540"	33.2	1799	28,800 CUP	35.3	1932	32,000 CUP
200 GR. HDY RN	Hodgdon	LVR	.358"	2.510"	42.0	2040	25,600 CUP	45.0C	2235	31,200 CUP
200 GR. HDY RN	Hodgdon	Varget	.358"	2.510"	36.0	1966	28,800 CUP	39.5	2139	33,300 CUP
200 GR. HDY RN	IMR	IMR 4320	.358"	2.510"				38.5	2020	35,000 CUP
200 GR. HDY RN	IMR	IMR 4064	.358"	2.510"				39.5C	2080	34,200 CUP
200 GR. HDY RN	Winchester	748	.358"	2.510"				39.0	2130	33,000 CUP

Bullet Weight	Manufacturer	Powder	Bullet Diam.	C.O.L.	Grs.	Vel. (ft/s)	Pressure	Grs.	Vel. (ft/s)	Pressure
200 GR. HDY RN	Hodgdon	BL-C(2)	.358"	2.510"	38.0	1877	23,200 CUP	41.5	2011	31,700 CUP
200 GR. HDY RN	IMR	IMR 4895	.358"	2.510"				36.5	2030	34,900 CUP
200 GR. HDY RN	Hodgdon	H335	.358"	2.510"	33.0	1855	27,100 CUP	37.0	2048	33,200 CUP
200 GR. HDY RN	Hodgdon	H4895	.358"	2.510"	35.0	1920	26,100 CUP	38.5	2110	32,300 CUP
200 GR. HDY RN	IMR	IMR 8208 XBR	.358"	2.510"	33.0	1872	31,000 CUP	36.6	1997	33,600 CUP
200 GR. HDY RN	IMR	IMR 3031	.358"	2.510"				37.5	2110	34,700 CUP
200 GR. HDY RN	Hodgdon	Benchmark	.358"	2.510"	32.5	1847	29,400 CUP	35.5	1984	32,600 CUP
200 GR. HDY RN	Hodgdon	H322	.358"	2.510"	31.0	1866	28,500 CUP	33.8	1987	33,100 CUP
200 GR. HDY RN	IMR	IMR 4198	.358"	2.510"				27.0	1915	33,500 CUP
200 GR. HDY RN	Hodgdon	H4198	.358"	2.510"	27.0	1816	26,700 CUP	30.5	1999	31,700 CUP
200 GR. HDY RN	IMR	SR 4759	.358"	2.510"				20.5	1770	35,000 CUP
220 GR. SPR FN	Hodgdon	Varget	.358"	2.470"	34.0	1803	27,800 CUP	38.0	1998	33,300 CUP
220 GR. SPR FN	Hodgdon	BL-C(2)	.358"	2.470"	36.0	1824	26,900 CUP	39.5	1917	31,000 CUP
220 GR. SPR FN	Hodgdon	H335	.358"	2.470"	30.0	1633	29,100 CUP	33.5	1821	33,400 CUP
220 GR. SPR FN	Hodgdon	H4895	.358"	2.470"	33.0	1848	29,000 CUP	36.3	2010	33,600 CUP
220 GR. SPR FN	IMR	IMR 8208 XBR	.358"	2.470"	31.0	1679	30,500 CUP	34.8	1932	34,500 CUP
220 GR. SPR FN	Hodgdon	Benchmark	.358"	2.470"	31.0	1725	30,600 CUP	34.0	1865	33,300 CUP
220 GR. SPR FN	Hodgdon	H322	.358"	2.470"	29.0	1692	26,100 CUP	32.5	1870	32,600 CUP
220 GR. SPR FN	Hodgdon	H4198	.358"	2.470"	26.0	1744	30,400 CUP	29.0	1867	33,400 CUP

Cartridge: 356 Winchester
Load Type: Rifle

Bullet Weight (Gr.)	Manufacturer	Powder	Bullet Diam.	C.O.L.	Starting Loads			Maximum Loads		
					Grs.	Vel. (ft/s)	Pressure	Grs.	Vel. (ft/s)	Pressure
180 GR. SPR FP	Hodgdon	BL-C(2)	.358"	2.565"	50.0	2353		52.0	2431	
180 GR. SPR FP	Hodgdon	H335	.358"	2.565"	49.0	2311		51.0	2449	
180 GR. SPR FP	Hodgdon	H4895	.358"	2.565"	46.0	2360		49.0	2535	
180 GR. SPR FP	Hodgdon	H322	.358"	2.565"	44.0	2360		47.0	2552	
180 GR. SPR FP	Hodgdon	H4198	.358"	2.565"	40.0	2441		43.0	2600	
180 GR. SPR FP	Hodgdon	H4227	.358"	2.565"	24.0	1878		30.0	2238	
200 GR. SIE RN	Hodgdon	BL-C(2)	.358"	2.550"	49.0	2162		50.0	2243	
200 GR. SIE RN	Hodgdon	H335	.358"	2.550"	48.0	2189		49.0	2269	
200 GR. SIE RN	Hodgdon	H4895	.358"	2.550"	43.0	2170		46.0	2338	
200 GR. SIE RN	Hodgdon	H322	.358"	2.550"	41.0	2199		44.0	2340	
200 GR. SIE RN	Hodgdon	H4198	.358"	2.550"	37.0	2201		40.0	2383	
220 GR. SPR FN	Winchester	760	.358"	2.560"				42.1	1805	27,500 CUP
220 GR. SPR FN	Winchester	748	.358"	2.560"				42.1	2015	31,000 CUP
250 GR. HDY RN	Hodgdon	BL-C(2)	.358"	2.775"	46.0	2010		48.0	2163	
250 GR. HDY RN	Hodgdon	H335	.358"	2.775"	44.0	1888		46.0	2151	
250 GR. HDY RN	Hodgdon	H4895	.358"	2.775"	40.0	1919		43.0	2128	
250 GR. HDY RN	Hodgdon	H322	.358"	2.775"	38.0	1866		41.0	2106	

					Starting Loads			Maximum Loads		
250 GR. HDY RN	Hodgdon	H4198	.358"	2.775"	34.0	1879		37.0	2133	

Cartridge: 358 Winchester Load Type: Rifle					Starting Loads			Maximum Loads		
Bullet Weight (Gr.)	Manufacturer	Powder	Bullet Diam.	C.O.L.	Grs.	Vel. (ft/s)	Pressure	Grs.	Vel. (ft/s)	Pressure
180 GR. BAR X	Hodgdon	Varget	.358"	2.700"	47.0	2442	42,500 CUP	51.0C	2594	48,200 CUP
180 GR. BAR X	Hodgdon	BL-C(2)	.358"	2.700"	49.0	2450	42,600 CUP	52.0	2555	46,500 CUP
180 GR. BAR X	Hodgdon	H335	.358"	2.700"	44.0	2338	42,700 CUP	47.5	2504	48,900 CUP
180 GR. BAR X	Hodgdon	H4895	.358"	2.700"	44.0	2408	41,500 CUP	48.0C	2603	49,900 CUP
180 GR. BAR X	Hodgdon	Benchmark	.358"	2.700"	43.0	2419	44,900 CUP	47.0	2574	50,300 CUP
180 GR. BAR X	Hodgdon	H322	.358"	2.700"	40.0	2380	46,900 CUP	44.0	2522	49,700 CUP
200 GR. HDY SP	Hodgdon	Varget	.358"	2.650"	47.0	2376	41,100 CUP	51.0C	2527	47,900 CUP
200 GR. HDY SP	IMR	IMR 4320	.358"	2.650"				51.0C	2545	51,700 CUP
200 GR. HDY SP	IMR	IMR 4064	.358"	2.650"				49.0C	2525	46,200 CUP
200 GR. HDY SP	Winchester	748	.358"	2.650"				50.6	2500	50,000 CUP
200 GR. HDY SP	Hodgdon	BL-C(2)	.358"	2.650"	49.0	2329	31,500 CUP	52.0	2464	41,800 CUP
200 GR. HDY SP	IMR	IMR 4895	.358"	2.650"				49.0C	2565	50,800 CUP
200 GR. HDY SP	Hodgdon	H335	.358"	2.650"	44.0	2300	40,000 CUP	48.5	2484	48,400 CUP
200 GR. HDY SP	Hodgdon	H4895	.358"	2.650"	44.0	2316	40,200 CUP	48.0C	2519	49,800 CUP
200 GR. HDY SP	IMR	IMR 3031	.358"	2.650"				49.0C	2630	51,800 CUP
200 GR. HDY SP	Hodgdon	Benchmark	.358"	2.650"	42.0	2319	42,700 CUP	46.2	2494	50,000 CUP
200 GR. HDY SP	Hodgdon	H322	.358"	2.650"	40.0	2306	45,400 CUP	44.8	2491	49,400 CUP
200 GR. HDY SP	IMR	SR 4759	.358"	2.650"				29.5	2170	52,000 CUP
220 GR. SPR FN SP	Hodgdon	Varget	.358"	2.560"	46.0	2226	42,800 CUP	50.0C	2445	50,300 CUP
220 GR. SPR FN SP	Hodgdon	BL-C(2)	.358"	2.560"	48.0	2238	37,600 CUP	51.0	2355	43,900 CUP
220 GR. SPR FN SP	Hodgdon	H335	.358"	2.560"	42.0	2181	42,200 CUP	46.0	2352	49,400 CUP
220 GR. SPR FN SP	Hodgdon	H4895	.358"	2.560"	43.0	2227	41,500 CUP	47.5C	2421	50,200 CUP
220 GR. SPR FN SP	Hodgdon	Benchmark	.358"	2.560"	41.0	2184	39,400 CUP	45.0	2361	49,500 CUP
220 GR. SPR FN SP	Hodgdon	H322	.358"	2.560"	40.0	2243	45,700 CUP	44.0	2371	49,300 CUP
225 GR. SIE BTSP	Hodgdon	Varget	.358"	2.770"	45.0	2254	40,700 CUP	49.0	2451	50,600 CUP
225 GR. SIE BTSP	Hodgdon	BL-C(2)	.358"	2.770"	48.0	2324	39,900 CUP	51.0	2431	45,400 CUP
225 GR. SIE BTSP	Hodgdon	H335	.358"	2.770"	42.0	2231	43,500 CUP	46.0	2390	48,500 CUP
225 GR. SIE BTSP	Hodgdon	H4895	.358"	2.770"	42.0	2223	41,700 CUP	46.5	2422	50,300 CUP
225 GR. SIE BTSP	Hodgdon	Benchmark	.358"	2.770"	40.0	2211	44,200 CUP	44.0	2354	50,600 CUP
225 GR. SIE BTSP	Hodgdon	H322	.358"	2.770"	41.0	2275	46,000 CUP	43.0	2372	50,300 CUP
250 GR. NOS PART	Hodgdon	Varget	.358"	2.760"	43.0	2119	39,500 CUP	47.0C	2278	48,600 CUP
250 GR. NOS PART	IMR	IMR 4320	.358"	2.760"				44.5	2210	51,400 CUP
250 GR. NOS PART	IMR	IMR 4064	.358"	2.760"				44.0C	2270	52,000 CUP
250 GR. NOS PART	Winchester	748	.358"	2.760"				46.2	2250	50,500 CUP

Bullet Weight (Gr.)	Manufacturer	Powder	Bullet Diam.	C.O.L.	Grs.	Vel. (ft/s)	Pressure	Grs.	Vel. (ft/s)	Pressure
250 GR. NOS PART	Hodgdon	BL-C(2)	.358"	2.760"	44.0	2121	39,900 CUP	47.0	2240	47,200 CUP
250 GR. NOS PART	IMR	IMR 4895	.358"	2.760"				43.0	2235	51,200 CUP
250 GR. NOS PART	Hodgdon	H335	.358"	2.760"	39.0	1987	39,200 CUP	43.0	2184	50,500 CUP
250 GR. NOS PART	Hodgdon	H4895	.358"	2.760"	40.0	2057	40,400 CUP	44.5C	2257	50,500 CUP
250 GR. NOS PART	IMR	IMR 3031	.358"	2.760"				42.0	2260	50,800 CUP
250 GR. NOS PART	Hodgdon	Benchmark	.358"	2.760"	38.0	2030	39,800 CUP	42.0	2176	49,400 CUP
250 GR. NOS PART	Hodgdon	H322	.358"	2.760"	38.0	2095	43,500 CUP	42.5	2260	49,900 CUP
250 GR. NOS PART	IMR	SR 4759	.358"	2.760"				26.0	1845	51,400 CUP

Cartridge: 35 Whelen
Load Type: Rifle

Bullet Weight (Gr.)	Manufacturer	Powder	Bullet Diam.	C.O.L.	Starting Loads			Maximum Loads		
					Grs.	Vel. (ft/s)	Pressure	Grs.	Vel. (ft/s)	Pressure
180 GR. SPR FP	Hodgdon	Varget	.358"	3.045"	54.0	2609	39,900 CUP	60.0C	2764	42,500 CUP
180 GR. SPR FP	IMR	IMR 4064	.358"	3.040"	56.0	2544	39,700 CUP	60.0C	2708	44,700 CUP
180 GR. SPR FP	Hodgdon	BL-C(2)	.358"	3.045"	62.0	2644	38,100 CUP	65.0	2860	48,500 CUP
180 GR. SPR FP	IMR	IMR 4895	.358"	3.040"	56.0	2636	43,600 CUP	60.0C	2780	46,800 CUP
180 GR. SPR FP	Hodgdon	H335	.358"	3.045"	56.0	2741	45,600 CUP	60.0	2870	50,000 CUP
180 GR. SPR FP	Hodgdon	H4895	.358"	3.045"	56.0	2649	40,000 CUP	60.0	2798	46,800 CUP
180 GR. SPR FP	IMR	IMR 8208 XBR	.358"	3.040"	56.0	2736	42,600 CUP	60.0C	2891	47,500 CUP
180 GR. SPR FP	Hodgdon	H322	.358"	3.045"	55.0	2707	44,000 CUP	58.0	2829	48,500 CUP
200 GR. SIE RN	Hodgdon	H380	.358"	3.050"	59.0	2511	41,500 CUP	61.0	2602	45,000 CUP
200 GR. SIE RN	Hodgdon	Varget	.358"	3.050"	52.0	2508	40,400 CUP	57.0	2653	42,300 CUP
200 GR. SIE RN	IMR	IMR 4320	.358"	3.050"	53.0	2436	41,400 CUP	59.0C	2669	49,300 CUP
200 GR. SIE RN	IMR	IMR 4064	.358"	3.050"	54.0	2460	40,800 CUP	59.0C	2637	46,400 CUP
200 GR. SIE RN	Hodgdon	BL-C(2)	.358"	3.050"	60.0	2636	43,000 CUP	63.0	2807	49,000 CUP
200 GR. SIE RN	IMR	IMR 4895	.358"	3.050"	54.0	2512	42,800 CUP	59.0C	2696	48,800 CUP
200 GR. SIE RN	Hodgdon	H335	.358"	3.050"	52.0	2588	44,900 CUP	55.0	2684	50,000 CUP
200 GR. SIE RN	Hodgdon	H4895	.358"	3.050"	54.0	2544	43,500 CUP	57.0	2689	49,000 CUP
200 GR. SIE RN	IMR	IMR 8208 XBR	.358"	3.050"	53.0	2579	41,300 CUP	59.0C	2802	48,900 CUP
200 GR. SIE RN	IMR	IMR 3031	.358"	3.050"	50.0	2467	40,900 CUP	55.5	2711	48,900 CUP
200 GR. SIE RN	Hodgdon	H322	.358"	3.050"	52.0	2540	42,600 CUP	56.0	2691	48,500 CUP
200 GR. SIE RN	IMR	SR 4759	.358"	3.050"				34.5	2265	51,400 CUP
220 GR. SPR FP	Hodgdon	H380	.358"	3.045"	58.0	2389	41,500 CUP	60.0	2490	44,800 CUP
220 GR. SPR FP	IMR	IMR 4320	.358"	3.045"	49.5	2290	43,400 CUP	55.0	2510	49,600 CUP
220 GR. SPR FP	IMR	IMR 4064	.358"	3.045"	49.5	2248	41,000 CUP	55.5C	2499	48,000 CUP
220 GR. SPR FP	Hodgdon	BL-C(2)	.358"	3.045"	58.0	2492	44,000 CUP	61.0	2636	49,000 CUP
220 GR. SPR FP	IMR	IMR 4895	.358"	3.045"	50.0	2332	42,200 CUP	56.0C	2569	50,300 CUP
220 GR. SPR FP	Hodgdon	H335	.358"	3.045"	50.0	2429	44,500 CUP	53.0	2519	49,500 CUP
220 GR. SPR FP	Hodgdon	H4895	.358"	3.045"	51.0	2461	44,000 CUP	55.0	2588	50,000 CUP
220 GR. SPR FP	IMR	IMR 8208 XBR	.358"	3.045"	49.5	2397	42,600 CUP	55.0	2623	50,200 CUP

Bullet Weight (Gr.)	Manufacturer	Powder	Bullet Diam.	C.O.L.	Grs.	Vel. (ft/s)	Pressure	Grs.	Vel. (ft/s)	Pressure
220 GR. SPR FP	IMR	IMR 3031	.358"	3.045"	46.0	2270	41,300 CUP	51.5	2516	49,100 CUP
220 GR. SPR FP	Hodgdon	H322	.358"	3.045"	50.0	2392	43,500 CUP	54.0	2566	49,500 CUP
225 GR. SIE SBT	Hodgdon	Varget	.358"	3.175"	51.0	2442	43,500 CUP	56.0	2588	46,400 CUP
225 GR. SIE SBT	IMR	IMR 4064	.358"	3.175"	51.0	2321	42,400 CUP	56.0C	2547	49,200 CUP
225 GR. SIE SBT	IMR	IMR 4895	.358"	3.175"	49.5	2315	41,300 CUP	55.0C	2553	50,000 CUP
225 GR. SIE SBT	Hodgdon	H4895	.358"	3.175"	49.5	2404	40,900 CUP	55.0C	2611	49,200 CUP
225 GR. SIE SBT	IMR	IMR 8208 XBR	.358"	3.175"	49.5	2409	40,500 CUP	55.0C	2618	49,600 CUP
250 GR. HDY SP	Hodgdon	H380	.358"	3.220"	57.0	2304	41,000 CUP	59.0	2416	44,500 CUP
250 GR. HDY SP	Hodgdon	Varget	.358"	3.220"	50.0	2348	44,900 CUP	55.0	2486	49,900 CUP
250 GR. HDY SP	IMR	IMR 4320	.358"	3.220"	49.0	2170	43,400 CUP	53.8	2387	50,100 CUP
250 GR. HDY SP	IMR	IMR 4064	.358"	3.220"	49.0	2200	41,700 CUP	54.8C	2449	50,200 CUP
250 GR. HDY SP	Hodgdon	BL-C(2)	.358"	3.220"	56.0	2382	43,000 CUP	59.0	2503	48,900 CUP
250 GR. HDY SP	IMR	IMR 4895	.358"	3.220"	48.0	2178	41,400 CUP	53.5	2421	50,300 CUP
250 GR. HDY SP	Hodgdon	H335	.358"	3.220"	49.0	2288	44,200 CUP	52.0	2404	50,000 CUP
250 GR. HDY SP	Hodgdon	H4895	.358"	3.220"	49.0	2330	43,700 CUP	53.0	2455	50,000 CUP
250 GR. HDY SP	IMR	IMR 8208 XBR	.358"	3.290"	49.0	2311	44,000 CUP	54.3C	2515	50,300 CUP
250 GR. HDY SP	Hodgdon	H322	.358"	3.220"	48.0	2249	44,000 CUP	52.0	2398	48,500 CUP
250 GR. HDY SP	IMR	SR 4759	.358"	3.220"				32.5	1975	50,600 CUP

Cartridge: 350 Remington Magnum Load Type: Rifle					Starting Loads			Maximum Loads		
Bullet Weight (Gr.)	Manufacturer	Powder	Bullet Diam.	C.O.L.	Grs.	Vel. (ft/s)	Pressure	Grs.	Vel. (ft/s)	Pressure
180 GR. SPR FP	Hodgdon	BL-C(2)	.358"	2.740"	57.0	2776	40,200 CUP	62.0	2992	50,300 CUP
180 GR. SPR FP	Hodgdon	H335	.358"	2.740"	57.0	2769	40,100 CUP	62.0	3006	50,600 CUP
180 GR. SPR FP	Hodgdon	H4895	.358"	2.740"	56.0	2696	39,000 CUP	61.0	3015	52,300 CUP
180 GR. SPR FP	Hodgdon	H322	.358"	2.740"	53.0	2688	43,000 CUP	58.0	2894	50,300 CUP
180 GR. SPR FP	Hodgdon	H4198	.358"	2.740"	48.0	2622	35,400 CUP	51.0	2808	48,000 CUP
200 GR. HDY SP	Hodgdon	H380	.358"	2.740"	59.0	2556	37,200 CUP	64.0	2753	45,900 CUP
200 GR. HDY SP	IMR	IMR 4320	.358"	2.740"				64.5	2820	52,100 CUP
200 GR. HDY SP	IMR	IMR 4064	.358"	2.740"				61.5C	2800	52,200 CUP
200 GR. HDY SP	Hodgdon	BL-C(2)	.358"	2.740"	55.0	2639	39,600 CUP	60.0	2808	50,100 CUP
200 GR. HDY SP	IMR	IMR 4895	.358"	2.740"				62.0	2815	52,300 CUP
200 GR. HDY SP	Hodgdon	H335	.358"	2.740"	55.0	2634	39,400 CUP	58.0	2794	50,000 CUP
200 GR. HDY SP	Hodgdon	H4895	.358"	2.740"	54.5	2625	37,800 CUP	59.0	2822	52,100 CUP
200 GR. HDY SP	IMR	IMR 3031	.358"	2.740"				60.0C	2835	50,700 CUP
200 GR. HDY SP	Hodgdon	H322	.358"	2.740"	50.0	2427	39,700 CUP	55.0	2684	49,300 CUP
200 GR. HDY SP	Hodgdon	H4198	.358"	2.740"	45.0	2382	34,200 CUP	48.0	2512	44,100 CUP
200 GR. HDY SP	IMR	SR 4759	.358"	2.740"				39.0	2405	53,000 CUP
220 GR. SPR FP	Hodgdon	H380	.358"	2.740"	56.0	2388	37,200 CUP	61.0	2569	47,300 CUP

Bullet Weight (Gr.)	Manufacturer	Powder	Bullet Diam.	C.O.L.	Grs.	Vel. (ft/s)	Pressure	Grs.	Vel. (ft/s)	Pressure
220 GR. SPR FP	Hodgdon	BL-C(2)	.358"	2.740"	51.5	2480	42,000 CUP	56.0	2640	51,000 CUP
220 GR. SPR FP	Hodgdon	H335	.358"	2.740"	51.0	2451	41,600 CUP	54.0	2640	51,600 CUP
220 GR. SPR FP	Hodgdon	H4895	.358"	2.740"	51.5	2534	37,200 CUP	56.0	2651	51,200 CUP
220 GR. SPR FP	Hodgdon	H322	.358"	2.740"	48.0	2293	39,200 CUP	52.0	2473	49,300 CUP
220 GR. SPR FP	Hodgdon	H4198	.358"	2.740"	43.0	2304	36,600 CUP	46.0	2423	48,500 CUP
250 GR. HDY SP	Hodgdon	H380	.358"	2.930"	54.0	2206	38,400 CUP	59.0	2410	47,300 CUP
250 GR. HDY SP	IMR	IMR 4320	.358"	2.930"				56.0C	2400	50,200 CUP
250 GR. HDY SP	IMR	IMR 4064	.358"	2.930"				53.0C	2310	41,400 CUP
250 GR. HDY SP	Hodgdon	BL-C(2)	.358"	2.930"	48.5	2214	37,800 CUP	53.0	2464	52,100 CUP
250 GR. HDY SP	IMR	IMR 4895	.358"	2.930"				56.0C	2485	52,500 CUP
250 GR. HDY SP	Hodgdon	H335	.358"	2.930"	48.0	2190	37,000 CUP	51.0	2457	51,800 CUP
250 GR. HDY SP	Hodgdon	H4895	.358"	2.930"	49.5	2225	37,800 CUP	54.0	2497	53,200 CUP
250 GR. HDY SP	IMR	IMR 3031	.358"	2.930"				53.0C	2410	47,800 CUP
250 GR. HDY SP	Hodgdon	H322	.358"	2.930"	45.0	2092	42,000 CUP	49.0	2333	51,600 CUP
250 GR. HDY SP	Hodgdon	H4198	.358"	2.930"	39.0	2069	34,800 CUP	42.0	2190	45,900 CUP
250 GR. HDY SP	IMR	SR 4759	.358"	2.930"				33.5	2040	52,600 CUP

Cartridge: 358 Norma Magnum
Load Type: Rifle

Bullet Weight (Gr.)	Manufacturer	Powder	Bullet Diam.	C.O.L.	Starting Loads			Maximum Loads		
					Grs.	Vel. (ft/s)	Pressure	Grs.	Vel. (ft/s)	Pressure
180 GR. SPR FP	Hodgdon	H4350	.358"	3.340"	75.0	2894		79.0	3017	
180 GR. SPR FP	Hodgdon	H414	.358"	3.340"	74.0	2878		78.0	3048	
180 GR. SPR FP	Hodgdon	H380	.358"	3.340"	67.0	2965		71.0	3111	
200 GR. HDY SP	Hodgdon	H4350	.358"	3.140"	74.0	2852		78.0	2984	
200 GR. HDY SP	Hodgdon	H414	.358"	3.140"	73.0	2853		77.0	3029	
200 GR. HDY SP	Hodgdon	H380	.358"	3.140"	66.0	2966		70.0	3102	
250 GR. NOS PART	Hodgdon	H4350	.358"	3.300"	71.0	2634		75.0	2778	
250 GR. NOS PART	Hodgdon	H414	.358"	3.300"	70.0	2589		74.0	2754	
250 GR. NOS PART	Hodgdon	H380	.358"	3.300"	63.0	2441		67.0	2609	
250 GR. NOS PART	Hodgdon	H4895	.358"	3.300"	61.0	2544		65.0	2736	

Cartridge: 358 Shooting Times Alaskan
Load Type: Rifle

Bullet Weight (Gr.)	Manufacturer	Powder	Bullet Diam.	C.O.L.	Starting Loads			Maximum Loads		
					Grs.	Vel. (ft/s)	Pressure	Grs.	Vel. (ft/s)	Pressure
225 GR. NOS PART	Hodgdon	H4350	.358"	3.670"	82.0	2951		87.0	3119	
250 GR. NOS PART	Hodgdon	H1000	.358"	3.670"	85.0	2740		90.0	2810	
250 GR. NOS PART	Hodgdon	H4831	.358"	3.670"	85.0	2720		90.0	2984	
250 GR. NOS PART	Hodgdon	H4350	.358"	3.670"	79.0	2688		84.0	2933	
250 GR. NOS PART	Hodgdon	H414	.358"	3.670"	75.0	2770		80.0	2914	

Cartridge:9.3 x 62 Load Type:Rifle					Starting Loads			Maximum Loads		
Bullet Weight (Gr.)	Manufacturer	Powder	Bullet Diam.	C.O.L.	Grs.	Vel. (ft/s)	Pressure	Grs.	Vel. (ft/s)	Pressure
250 GR. BAR TSX	Hodgdon	Varget	.366"	3.200"	52.0	2199	33,900 CUP	58.0C	2436	47,200 CUP
250 GR. BAR TSX	IMR	IMR 4895	.366"	3.200"	52.0	2185	39,200 CUP	58.0C	2438	48,700 CUP
250 GR. BAR TSX	Hodgdon	H335	.366"	3.200"	49.5	2188	38,800 CUP	56.0	2435	48,800 CUP
250 GR. BAR TSX	Hodgdon	H4895	.366"	3.200"	51.0	2221	37,000 CUP	57.0C	2484	48,700 CUP
250 GR. BAR TSX	IMR	IMR 3031	.366"	3.200"	49.0	2182	36,500 CUP	54.5C	2423	47,700 CUP
270 GR. SPR SP	Hodgdon	H4350	.366"	3.280"	63.0	2322	38,500 CUP	67.0C	2438	44,600 CUP
270 GR. SPR SP	IMR	IMR 4350	.366"	3.280"	58.0	2117	38,400 CUP	64.0C	2347	47,600 CUP
270 GR. SPR SP	IMR	IMR 4007 SSC	.366"	3.280"	58.0	2154	35,500 CUP	65.0C	2427	46,700 CUP
270 GR. SPR SP	Hodgdon	Varget	.366"	3.280"	55.0	2290	40,100 CUP	59.5	2440	48,100 CUP
270 GR. SPR SP	IMR	IMR 4320	.366"	3.280"	51.0	2151	39,200 CUP	56.0	2328	47,900 CUP
270 GR. SPR SP	IMR	IMR 4064	.366"	3.280"	50.0	2139	40,200 CUP	54.5	2317	48,300 CUP
270 GR. SPR SP	Hodgdon	BL-C(2)	.366"	3.280"	60.0	2338	39,600 CUP	66.0	2548	47,400 CUP
270 GR. SPR SP	IMR	IMR 4895	.366"	3.280"	50.0	2092	37,200 CUP	56.0	2328	48,300 CUP
270 GR. SPR SP	Hodgdon	H335	.366"	3.280"	54.0	2283	40,700 CUP	58.0	2411	47,600 CUP
270 GR. SPR SP	Hodgdon	H4895	.366"	3.280"	52.0	2244	39,800 CUP	56.5	2406	48,000 CUP
270 GR. SPR SP	IMR	IMR 3031	.366"	3.280"	48.0	2154	36,900 CUP	53.5	2380	48,800 CUP
286 GR. NOS PART	Hodgdon	H4350	.366"	3.225"	64.0	2321	40,800 CUP	67.0C	2407	46,300 CUP
286 GR. NOS PART	Hodgdon	H414	.366"	3.225"	60.0	2205	40,700 CUP	63.0C	2305	47,800 CUP
286 GR. NOS PART	Winchester	760	.366"	3.150"	60.0	2205	40,700 CUP	63.0C	2305	47,800 CUP
286 GR. NOS PART	IMR	IMR 4007 SSC	.366"	3.225"	58.0	2110	34,900 CUP	61.0C	2244	41,400 CUP
286 GR. NOS PART	Hodgdon	Varget	.366"	3.225"	55.0	2242	39,800 CUP	59.0C	2350	47,500 CUP
286 GR. NOS PART	IMR	IMR 4064	.366"	3.225"	49.0	2015	35,700 CUP	54.5C	2218	46,100 CUP
286 GR. NOS PART	Winchester	748	.366"	3.225"	52.0	2056	34,300 CUP	57.0	2241	43,200 CUP
286 GR. NOS PART	IMR	IMR 4895	.366"	3.225"	51.0	2108	38,200 CUP	56.0C	2279	48,000 CUP
286 GR. NOS PART	Hodgdon	H335	.366"	3.225"	51.0	2178	41,300 CUP	55.0	2323	48,100 CUP
286 GR. NOS PART	Hodgdon	H4895	.366"	3.225"	51.0	2131	39,000 CUP	55.5	2331	47,800 CUP
286 GR. NOS PART	IMR	IMR 3031	.366"	3.225"	47.0	2058	35,700 CUP	51.5C	2219	46,900 CUP
300 GR. SFT SP	Hodgdon	Hybrid 100V	.366"	3.150"	56.0	2041	39,300 CUP	60.0C	2158	42,600 CUP
300 GR. SFT SP	Hodgdon	H4350	.366"	3.150"	60.0	2142	40,000 CUP	64.0C	2288	48,100 CUP
300 GR. SFT SP	Hodgdon	H414	.366"	3.150"	59.0	2136	41,500 CUP	62.0C	2242	46,200 CUP
300 GR. SFT SP	Winchester	760	.366"	3.150"	59.0	2136	41,500 CUP	62.0C	2242	46,200 CUP
300 GR. SFT SP	IMR	IMR 4007 SSC	.366"	3.150"	57.0	2073	36,000 CUP	61.0C	2229	43,900 CUP
300 GR. SFT SP	Hodgdon	Varget	.366"	3.150"	52.0	2083	42,000 CUP	56.0	2194	47,800 CUP
300 GR. SFT SP	IMR	IMR 4320	.366"	3.150"	50.0	2039	38,700 CUP	54.0C	2184	47,900 CUP
300 GR. SFT SP	IMR	IMR 4064	.366"	3.150"	49.0	2002	38,600 CUP	54.5C	2205	48,900 CUP
300 GR. SFT SP	Winchester	748	.366"	3.150"	52.0	2096	36,700 CUP	56.5	2234	44,500 CUP

Bullet Weight (Gr.)	Manufacturer	Powder	Bullet Diam.	C.O.L.	Grs.	Vel. (ft/s)	Pressure	Grs.	Vel. (ft/s)	Pressure
300 GR. SFT SP	Hodgdon	BL-C(2)	.366"	3.150"	54.0	2140	42,900 CUP	57.5	2211	47,900 CUP
300 GR. SFT SP	IMR	IMR 4895	.366"	3.150"	49.0	2020	38,800 CUP	54.7C	2224	48,500 CUP
300 GR. SFT SP	Hodgdon	H4895	.366"	3.150"	47.0	1979	40,200 CUP	52.0	2133	48,200 CUP
300 GR. SFT SP	IMR	IMR 3031	.366"	3.150"	46.0	2002	37,200 CUP	52.0C	2230	48,600 CUP

Cartridge: 9.3 x 74R
Load Type: Rifle

Bullet Weight (Gr.)	Manufacturer	Powder	Bullet Diam.	C.O.L.	Starting Loads			Maximum Loads		
					Grs.	Vel. (ft/s)	Pressure	Grs.	Vel. (ft/s)	Pressure
250 GR. BAR TSX FB	Hodgdon	H4350	.366"	3.700"	59.0	2150	37,100 CUP	64.5C	2330	41,800 CUP
250 GR. BAR TSX FB	IMR	IMR 4350	.366"	3.700"	58.0	2072	34,500 CUP	62.5C	2212	38,900 CUP
250 GR. BAR TSX FB	IMR	IMR 4007 SSC	.366"	3.700"	56.0	2122	34,900 CUP	61.0	2324	42,200 CUP
250 GR. BAR TSX FB	Hodgdon	Varget	.366"	3.700"	48.0	2096	39,000 CUP	52.0	2211	42,400 CUP
250 GR. BAR TSX FB	IMR	IMR 4064	.366"	3.700"	47.0	2063	40,400 CUP	51.5	2175	42,100 CUP
250 GR. BAR TSX FB	Hodgdon	H4895	.366"	3.700"	44.0	2033	39,000 CUP	48.0	2155	42,300 CUP
270 GR. SPR SP	Hodgdon	H4350	.366"	3.665"	64.0	2292	36,200 CUP	68.0C	2403	41,600 CUP
270 GR. SPR SP	Hodgdon	H414	.366"	3.665"	65.0	2239	32,100 CUP	68.0	2345	36,900 CUP
270 GR. SPR SP	IMR	IMR 4350	.366"	3.665"	62.0	2208	35,700 CUP	66.5C	2312	39,600 CUP
270 GR. SPR SP	Winchester	760	.366"	3.665"	65.0	2239	32,100 CUP	68.0	2345	36,900 CUP
270 GR. SPR SP	IMR	IMR 4007 SSC	/366"	3.665"	59.5	2252	34,700 CUP	64.5C	2399	40,600 CUP
270 GR. SPR SP	Hodgdon	H380	.366"	3.665"	60.0	2234	37,600 CUP	64.0	2360	42,400 CUP
270 GR. SPR SP	Hodgdon	Varget	.366"	3.665"	50.0	2107	36,500 CUP	54.5	2257	42,000 CUP
270 GR. SPR SP	IMR	IMR 4064	.366"	3.665"	50.0	2146	35,500 CUP	56.7	2346	42,600 CUP
286 GR. NOS PART	Hodgdon	H4831	.366"	3.700"	66.0	2119	33,400 CUP	70.0C	2232	36,800 CUP
286 GR. NOS PART	Hodgdon	H4350	.366"	3.700"	61.5	2211	36,800 CUP	65.5C	2323	41,500 CUP
286 GR. NOS PART	Hodgdon	H414	.366"	3.700"	64.0	2206	34,200 CUP	68.0	2351	40,200 CUP
286 GR. NOS PART	IMR	IMR 4350	.366"	3.700"	58.0	2084	33,700 CUP	64.0C	2241	41,000 CUP
286 GR. NOS PART	Winchester	760	.366"	3.700"	64.0	2206	34,200 CUP	68.0	2351	40,200 CUP
286 GR. NOS PART	IMR	IMR 4007 SSC	.366"	3.700"	57.0	2159	33,900 CUP	62.2	2324	41,000 CUP
286 GR. NOS PART	Hodgdon	H380	.366"	3.700"	58.0	2146	36,000 CUP	62.0	2266	41,700 CUP
286 GR. NOS PART	Hodgdon	Varget	.366"	3.700"	51.0	2125	38,200 CUP	54.0	2200	41,800 CUP
300 GR. SFT SP	Hodgdon	H4831	.366"	3.640"	61.0	1939	31,900 CUP	67.0C	2128	40,400 CUP
300 GR. SFT SP	Hodgdon	H4350	.366"	3.640"	58.0	2111	38,900 CUP	62.0C	2210	42,100 CUP
300 GR. SFT SP	Hodgdon	H414	.366"	3.640"	60.0	2100	34,500 CUP	64.0	2228	41,100 CUP
300 GR. SFT SP	IMR	IMR 4350	.366"	3.640"	56.0	2010	34,900 CUP	62.2C	2199	41,900 CUP
300 GR. SFT SP	Winchester	760	.366"	3.640"	60.0	2100	34,500 CUP	64.0	2228	41,100 CUP
300 GR. SFT SP	IMR	IMR 4007 SSC	.366"	3.640"	55.0	2090	34,900 CUP	60.5	2260	42,100 CUP
300 GR. SFT SP	Hodgdon	H380	.366"	3.640"	53.0	1993	36,900 CUP	57.0	2120	42,200 CUP

Cartridge: 38-55 Winchester Load Type: Rifle					Starting Loads			Maximum Loads		
Bullet Weight (Gr.)	Manufacturer	Powder	Bullet Diam.	C.O.L.	Grs.	Vel. (ft/s)	Pressure	Grs.	Vel. (ft/s)	Pressure
250 GR. LYMAN CAST	Hodgdon	H4895	.376"	2.500"	21.0	1197	18,200 CUP	26.0	1600	26,500 CUP
250 GR. LYMAN CAST	Hodgdon	H322	.376"	2.500"	24.0	1534	22,500 CUP	27.0	1692	27,600 CUP
250 GR. LYMAN CAST	Hodgdon	H4198	.376"	2.500"	18.5	1408	17,100 CUP	24.0	1740	26,200 CUP
250 GR. LYMAN CAST	IMR	Trail Boss	.376"	2.500"	6.0	842	20,300 CUP	7.0	911	25,600 CUP
255 GR. BAR JFP	Hodgdon	H322	.375"	2.620"	27.0	1603	25,500 CUP	33.0	1830	28,200 CUP
255 GR. BAR JFP	Hodgdon	H4198	.375"	2.620"	24.0	1554	21,400 CUP	28.0	1788	26,700 CUP

Cartridge: 375 Winchester Load Type: Rifle					Starting Loads			Maximum Loads		
Bullet Weight (Gr.)	Manufacturer	Powder	Bullet Diam.	C.O.L.	Grs.	Vel. (ft/s)	Pressure	Grs.	Vel. (ft/s)	Pressure
200 GR. SIE JFP	Hodgdon	H322	.375"	2.530"	39.0	2223	35,300 CUP	42.0C	2419	46,900 CUP
200 GR. SIE JFP	Hodgdon	H4198	.375"	2.530"	35.0	2288	36,900 CUP	38.0C	2480	50,600 CUP
220 GR. HDY JFP	Hodgdon	H322	.375"	2.500"	35.0	2029	35,700 CUP	38.5C	2236	48,900 CUP
220 GR. HDY JFP	Hodgdon	H4198	.375"	2.500"	31.0	2067	33,700 CUP	34.0	2233	49,300 CUP

Cartridge: 376 Steyr Load Type: Rifle					Starting Loads			Maximum Loads		
Bullet Weight (Gr.)	Manufacturer	Powder	Bullet Diam.	C.O.L.	Grs.	Vel. (ft/s)	Pressure	Grs.	Vel. (ft/s)	Pressure
210 GR. BAR XFB	Hodgdon	Varget	.375"	3.100"	65.0	2668	40,800 PSI	68.0C	2764	44,800 PSI
210 GR. BAR XFB	Hodgdon	H335	.375"	3.100"	67.0	2852	47,100 PSI	71.0	3005	56,800 PSI
210 GR. BAR XFB	Hodgdon	H4895	.375"	3.100"	64.0	2765	45,200 PSI	68.0C	2891	50,600 PSI
210 GR. BAR XFB	Hodgdon	Benchmark	.375"	3.100"	63.0	2774	45,000 PSI	68.0	2943	54,000 PSI
210 GR. BAR XFB	Hodgdon	H322	.375"	3.100"	63.0	2864	50,900 PSI	67.5	3011	59,800 PSI
225 GR. HDY SP	Hodgdon	Varget	.375"	3.070"	64.0	2628	45,600 PSI	68.0C	2767	52,400 PSI
225 GR. HDY SP	Hodgdon	BL-C(2)	.375"	3.070"	68.0	2663	41,400 PSI	70.0	2709	44,300 PSI
225 GR. HDY SP	Hodgdon	H335	.375"	3.070"	64.0	2746	50,300 PSI	68.5	2910	60,100 PSI
225 GR. HDY SP	Hodgdon	H4895	.375"	3.070"	64.0	2767	51,000 PSI	68.0C	2892	58,200 PSI
225 GR. HDY SP	Hodgdon	Benchmark	.375"	3.070"	62.0	2730	50,600 PSI	67.0C	2890	59,700 PSI
225 GR. HDY SP	Hodgdon	H322	.375"	3.070"	58.0	2704	53,100 PSI	63.0	2839	59,900 PSI
235 GR. SPR SP	Hodgdon	Varget	.375"	3.060"	64.0	2618	47,200 PSI	68.0C	2735	52,300 PSI
235 GR. SPR SP	Hodgdon	BL-C(2)	.375"	3.060"	68.0	2547	38,600 PSI	70.0	2607	41,500 PSI
235 GR. SPR SP	Hodgdon	H335	.375"	3.060"	65.0	2739	52,300 PSI	69.0	2873	59,600 PSI
235 GR. SPR SP	Hodgdon	H4895	.375"	3.060"	64.0	2708	50,100 PSI	68.0C	2846	59,000 PSI
235 GR. SPR SP	Hodgdon	Benchmark	.375"	3.060"	62.0	2689	50,900 PSI	66.5	2835	59,900 PSI
235 GR. SPR SP	Hodgdon	H322	.375"	3.060"	59.0	2709	58,000 PSI	63.0	2795	59,900 PSI
250 GR. SIE SP	Hodgdon	Varget	.375"	3.110"	64.0	2589	51,200 PSI	68.0C	2713	58,000 PSI

Bullet Weight	Manufacturer	Powder	Bullet Diam.	C.O.L.	Grs.	Vel. (ft/s)	Pressure	Grs.	Vel. (ft/s)	Pressure
250 GR. SIE SP	Hodgdon	BL-C(2)	.375"	3.110"	68.0	2565	44,200 PSI	70.0	2649	48,900 PSI
250 GR. SIE SP	Hodgdon	H335	.375"	3.110"	62.0	2626	53,300 PSI	66.0	2754	60,000 PSI
250 GR. SIE SP	Hodgdon	H4895	.375"	3.110"	60.0	2582	48,600 PSI	65.0	2732	59,800 PSI
250 GR. SIE SP	Hodgdon	Benchmark	.375"	3.110"	59.0	2573	51,200 PSI	63.5	2714	60,100 PSI
250 GR. SIE SP	Hodgdon	H322	.375"	3.110"	56.0	2570	55,700 PSI	60.5	2683	60,100 PSI
260 GR. NOS PART	Hodgdon	Varget	.375"	3.100"	62.0	2466	49,100 PSI	67.5C	2651	60,000 PSI
260 GR. NOS PART	Hodgdon	BL-C(2)	.375"	3.100"	68.0	2536	49,100 PSI	70.0	2625	54,500 PSI
260 GR. NOS PART	Hodgdon	H335	.375"	3.100"	58.0	2459	52,300 PSI	61.0	2566	59,500 PSI
260 GR. NOS PART	Hodgdon	H4895	.375"	3.100"	59.0	2500	53,800 PSI	62.5	2613	59,400 PSI
260 GR. NOS PART	Hodgdon	Benchmark	.375"	3.100"	57.0	2453	51,400 PSI	60.5	2584	59,700 PSI
260 GR. NOS PART	Hodgdon	H322	.375"	3.100"	52.0	2405	54,900 PSI	56.0	2511	60,200 PSI
270 GR. HDY SP	Hodgdon	Varget	.375"	3.060"	61.0	2446	50,000 PSI	65.5C	2610	60,100 PSI
270 GR. HDY SP	Hodgdon	BL-C(2)	.375"	3.060"	64.0	2447	47,000 PSI	66.0	2544	53,100 PSI
270 GR. HDY SP	Hodgdon	H335	.375"	3.060"	56.0	2388	50,700 PSI	60.0	2547	59,900 PSI
270 GR. HDY SP	Hodgdon	H4895	.375"	3.060"	58.0	2459	52,700 PSI	62.0C	2580	59,400 PSI
270 GR. HDY SP	Hodgdon	Benchmark	.375"	3.060"	55.0	2400	50,500 PSI	59.0	2549	59,500 PSI
270 GR. HDY SP	Hodgdon	H322	.375"	3.060"	53.0	2382	50,800 PSI	57.0	2517	59,600 PSI
300 GR. SFT SP	Hodgdon	Varget	.375"	3.080"	58.0	2255	50,000 PSI	62.5C	2410	59,700 PSI
300 GR. SFT SP	Hodgdon	BL-C(2)	.375"	3.080"	58.0	2189	46,700 PSI	62.0	2368	59,900 PSI
300 GR. SFT SP	Hodgdon	H335	.375"	3.080"	54.0	2201	53,300 PSI	57.5	2324	60,300 PSI
300 GR. SFT SP	Hodgdon	H4895	.375"	3.080"	55.0	2248	51,900 PSI	59.5	2388	60,200 PSI
300 GR. SFT SP	Hodgdon	Benchmark	.375"	3.080"	52.0	2176	49,000 PSI	56.5	2343	59,900 PSI
300 GR. SFT SP	Hodgdon	H322	.375"	3.080"	52.0	2236	53,600 PSI	55.0	2322	60,000 PSI

Cartridge: 375 H & H Magnum
Load Type: Rifle

Bullet Weight (Gr.)	Manufacturer	Powder	Bullet Diam.	C.O.L.	Grs.	Vel. (ft/s)	Pressure	Grs.	Vel. (ft/s)	Pressure
200 GR. SIE JFP	Hodgdon	H380	.375"	3.350"	78.0	2898	42,100 CUP	83.0	2999	43,600 CUP
200 GR. SIE JFP	Hodgdon	CFE 223	.375"	3.350"	79.6	2736	38,600 CUP	86.5	3056	45,700 CUP
200 GR. SIE JFP	Hodgdon	Varget	.375"	3.350"	65.0	2839	41,900 CUP	76.0	3121	50,300 CUP
200 GR. SIE JFP	IMR	IMR 4064	.375"	3.350"	68.0	2740	42,400 CUP	75.5C	2948	50,000 CUP
200 GR. SIE JFP	Hodgdon	BL-C(2)	.375"	3.350"	78.0	2874	37,700 CUP	87.0	3195	46,800 CUP
200 GR. SIE JFP	IMR	IMR 4895	.375"	3.350"	67.0	2752	45,300 CUP	74.0	2918	50,700 CUP
200 GR. SIE JFP	Hodgdon	H335	.375"	3.350"	68.0	2800	41,400 CUP	80.0	3153	49,800 CUP
200 GR. SIE JFP	Hodgdon	H4895	.375"	3.350"	67.0	2828	42,300 CUP	78.5	3116	48,700 CUP
200 GR. SIE JFP	IMR	IMR 8208 XBR	.375"	3.350"	69.0	2910	47,700 CUP	75.5	3079	50,200 CUP
200 GR. SIE JFP	IMR	IMR 3031	.375"	3.350"	63.0	2688	41,600 CUP	69.0	2916	50,000 CUP
235 GR. SPR SP	Hodgdon	H414	.375"	3.600"	80.0	2693	40,700 CUP	83.0	2749	42,600 CUP
235 GR. SPR SP	Winchester	760	.375"	3.600"	80.0	2693	40,700 CUP	83.0	2749	42,600 CUP
235 GR. SPR SP	Hodgdon	H380	.375"	3.600"	76.0	2786	40,400 CUP	81.0	2835	46,800 CUP

235 GR. SPR SP	Hodgdon	CFE 223	.375"	3.600"	77.9	2790	43,300 CUP	84.7	3006	50,300 CUP
235 GR. SPR SP	Hodgdon	Varget	.375"	3.600"	65.0	2684	46,700 CUP	70.0	2819	51,200 CUP
235 GR. SPR SP	IMR	IMR 4064	.375"	3.600"	63.0	2593	44,400 CUP	70.0	2749	50,300 CUP
235 GR. SPR SP	Hodgdon	BL-C(2)	.375"	3.600"	80.0	2858	44,300 CUP	85.0	2964	47,100 CUP
235 GR. SPR SP	IMR	IMR 4895	.375"	3.600"	60.0	2527	45,400 CUP	66.5	2683	49,600 CUP
235 GR. SPR SP	Hodgdon	H335	.375"	3.600"	69.0	2694	43,600 CUP	74.0	2853	50,000 CUP
235 GR. SPR SP	Hodgdon	H4895	.375"	3.600"	69.0	2743	44,300 CUP	74.0	2895	50,400 CUP
235 GR. SPR SP	IMR	IMR 8208 XBR	.375"	3.600"	61.0	2632	45,400 CUP	67.0	2793	50,900 CUP
235 GR. SPR SP	IMR	IMR 3031	.375"	3.600"	56.0	2505	45,200 CUP	62.5	2669	50,700 CUP
235 GR. SPR SP	IMR	Trail Boss	.375"	3.600"	19.0	1091		26.3	1144	
250 GR. SFT SP	Hodgdon	H4350	.375"	3.555"	78.0	2620	41,500 CUP	83.0 C	2733	44,900 CUP
250 GR. SFT SP	Hodgdon	H414	.375"	3.555"	77.0	2586	41,100 CUP	82.5	2746	46,300 CUP
250 GR. SFT SP	IMR	IMR 4350	.375"	3.555"	71.0	2422	44,000 CUP	79.0C	2604	48,600 CUP
250 GR. SFT SP	Winchester	760	.375"	3.555"	77.0	2586	41,100 CUP	82.5	2746	46,300 CUP
250 GR. SFT SP	IMR	IMR 4007 SSC	.375"	3.555"	75.0	2615	44,800 CUP	80.0C	2777	49,000 CUP
250 GR. SFT SP	Hodgdon	H380	.375"	3.555"	74.0	2635	43,300 CUP	79.0	2753	47,300 CUP
250 GR. SFT SP	Hodgdon	CFE 223	.375"	3.555"	75.7	2754	46,900 CUP	79.7	2827	48,200 CUP
250 GR. SFT SP	Hodgdon	Varget	.375"	3.555"	62.0	2531	43,900 CUP	66.5	2642	49,700 CUP
250 GR. SFT SP	IMR	IMR 4064	.375"	3.555"	60.0	2394	42,400 CUP	67.0	2586	49,200 CUP
250 GR. SFT SP	Hodgdon	BL-C(2)	.375"	3.555"	75.0	2711	43,900 CUP	80.0	2835	49,300 CUP
250 GR. SFT SP	IMR	IMR 4895	.375"	3.555"	57.0	2323	41,700 CUP	63.0	2515	49,300 CUP
250 GR. SFT SP	Hodgdon	H335	.375"	3.555"	64.0	2496	41,400 CUP	68.0	2659	50,600 CUP
250 GR. SFT SP	Hodgdon	H4895	.375"	3.555"	64.0	2574	44,800 CUP	69.0	2696	49,700 CUP
250 GR. SFT SP	IMR	IMR 8208 XBR	.375"	3.555"	58.0	2500	45,600 CUP	62.2	2609	49,900 CUP
260 GR. NOS PART	Hodgdon	H4831	.375"	3.580"	76.0	2470	43,700 CUP	83.0C	2622	47,800 CUP
260 GR. NOS PART	Hodgdon	Hybrid 100V	.375"	3.580"	73.0	2533	44,100 CUP	77.0C	2667	47,900 CUP
260 GR. NOS PART	Hodgdon	H4350	.375"	3.580"	70.0	2551	47,300 CUP	78.0	2702	51,700 CUP
260 GR. NOS PART	Hodgdon	H414	.375"	3.580"	74.0	2509	40,600 CUP	79.5	2651	44,800 CUP
260 GR. NOS PART	IMR	IMR 4350	.375"	3.580"	70.0	2416	42,600 CUP	78.6C	2624	50,600 CUP
260 GR. NOS PART	Winchester	760	.375"	3.580"	74.0	2509	40,600 CUP	79.5	2651	44,800 CUP
260 GR. NOS PART	IMR	IMR 4007 SSC	.375"	3.580"	74.0	2607	45,700 CUP	79.0C	2754	50,300 CUP
260 GR. NOS PART	Hodgdon	H380	.375"	3.580"	72.0	2617	46,200 CUP	77.0	2726	49,800 CUP
260 GR. NOS PART	IMR	IMR 4064	.375"	2.580"	60.0	2450	46,700 CUP	67.0	2605	51,200 CUP
270 GR. BAR TSX	Hodgdon	Hybrid 100V	.375"	3.550"	69.0	2274	39,200 CUP	75.0C	2588	46,100 CUP
270 GR. BAR TSX	Hodgdon	H4350	.375"	3.550"	69.0	2263	38,300 CUP	75.0C	2465	42,800 CUP
270 GR. BAR TSX	Hodgdon	H414	.375"	3.550"	72.0	2394	39,200 CUP	79.0	2529	43,200 CUP
270 GR. BAR TSX	IMR	IMR 4350	.375"	3.550"	69.0	2237	40,300 CUP	76.0C	2464	46,700 CUP
270 GR. BAR TSX	Hodgdon	H380	.375"	3.550"	70.0	2413	42,400 CUP	78.0	2632	50,100 CUP
270 GR. BAR TSX	Hodgdon	Varget	.375"	3.550"	58.0	2369	46,400 CUP	65.0	2521	50,000 CUP

270 GR. BAR TSX	IMR	IMR 4064	.375"	3.550"	61.0	2334	43,300 CUP	68.0C	2530	49,700 CUP
270 GR. BAR TSX	IMR	IMR 4895	.375"	3.550"	59.0	2322	44,100 CUP	66.0	2474	49,500 CUP
300 GR. SIE SPBT	Hodgdon	Hybrid 100V	.375"	3.600"	66.0	2277	45,200 CUP	72.0C	2400	47,400 CUP
300 GR. SIE SPBT	Hodgdon	H4350	.375"	3.600"	77.0	2539	45,400 CUP	81.5 C	2645	49,500 CUP
300 GR. SIE SPBT	Hodgdon	H414	.375"	3.600"	75.0	2502	45,200 CUP	78.0	2548	46,800 CUP
300 GR. SIE SPBT	IMR	IMR 4350	.375"	3.600"	68.0	2246	41,700 CUP	76.0C	2478	50,300 CUP
300 GR. SIE SPBT	Winchester	760	.375"	3.600"	75.0	2502	45,200 CUP	78.0	2548	46,800 CUP
300 GR. SIE SPBT	IMR	IMR 4007 SSC	.375"	3.600"	72.0	2486	45,300 CUP	76.0C	2573	49,700 CUP
300 GR. SIE SPBT	Hodgdon	Varget	.375"	3.600"	58.0	2345	45,200 CUP	62.0	2454	49,300 CUP
300 GR. SIE SPBT	IMR	IMR 4064	.375"	3.600"	58.0	2289	46,300 CUP	65.0	2449	51,100 CUP
300 GR. SIE SPBT	IMR	IMR 4895	.375"	3.600"	57.0	2287	47,400 CUP	63.3	2427	50,600 CUP
300 GR. SIE SPBT	Hodgdon	H4895	.375"	3.600"	61.0	2411	46,800 CUP	65.0	2505	50,400 CUP
300 GR. SIE SPBT	IMR	SR 4759	.375"	3.600"				39.0	1925	53,000 CUP

Cartridge: 375 Ruger Load Type: Rifle					Starting Loads			Maximum Loads		
Bullet Weight (Gr.)	Manufacturer	Powder	Bullet Diam.	C.O.L.	Grs.	Vel. (ft/s)	Pressure	Grs.	Vel. (ft/s)	Pressure
235 GR. BAR TSX	Hodgdon	H414	.375"	3.280"	76.4	2782	51,700 PSI	81.3	2922	59,400 PSI
235 GR. BAR TSX	Winchester	760	.375"	3.280"	76.4	2782	51,700 PSI	81.3	2922	59,400 PSI
235 GR. BAR TSX	IMR	IMR 4007 SSC	.375"	3.280"	76.4	2799	51,400 PSI	81.3C	2952	59,200 PSI
235 GR. BAR TSX	Hodgdon	H380	.375"	3.280"	74.7	2752	52,000 PSI	79.5	2907	58,900 PSI
235 GR. BAR TSX	Hodgdon	CFE 223	.375"	3.280"	70.9	2793	53,500 PSI	75.4	2932	61,100 PSI
235 GR. BAR TSX	Hodgdon	Varget	.375"	3.280"	69.1	2709	48,600 PSI	73.5	2885	59,600 PSI
235 GR. BAR TSX	IMR	IMR 4320	.375"	3.280"	70.0	2776	53,100 PSI	73.4	2877	59,100 PSI
235 GR. BAR TSX	IMR	IMR 4064	.375"	3.280"	68.2	2764	50,700 PSI	72.5	2905	60,100 PSI
235 GR. BAR TSX	Winchester	748	.375"	3.280"	68.6	2752	52,100 PSI	73.0	2887	59,200 PSI
235 GR. BAR TSX	Hodgdon	BL-C(2)	.375"	3.280"	70.5	2791	53,700 PSI	75.0	2908	60,200 PSI
235 GR. BAR TSX	IMR	IMR 4895	.375"	3.280"	68.3	2757	50,400 PSI	72.7	2907	59,600 PSI
235 GR. BAR TSX	Hodgdon	H4895	.375"	3.280"	66.7	2768	52,800 PSI	71.0	2882	58,500 PSI
235 GR. BAR TSX	IMR	IMR 3031	.375"	3.280"	63.0	2696	51,900 PSI	67.0	2831	60,400 PSI
250 GR. SFT SP	Hodgdon	Hybrid 100V	.375"	3.270"	78.0	2760	50,600 PSI	83.0C	2896	57,200 PSI
250 GR. SFT SP	IMR	IMR 4831	.375"	3.270"	79.4	2627	49,000 PSI	84.5C	2829	58,700 PSI
250 GR. SFT SP	Hodgdon	H4350	.375"	3.270"	77.5	2675	51,400 PSI	82.5	2834	59,000 PSI
250 GR. SFT SP	Hodgdon	H414	.375"	3.270"	75.5	2710	52,100 PSI	80.3	2838	59,400 PSI
250 GR. SFT SP	IMR	IMR 4350	.375"	3.270"	77.1	2615	49,500 PSI	82.0	2811	59,200 PSI
250 GR. SFT SP	Winchester	760	.375"	3.270"	75.5	2710	52,500 PSI	80.3	2838	59,400 PSI
250 GR. SFT SP	IMR	IMR 4007 SSC	.375"	3.270"	74.7	2674	51,000 PSI	79.5	2806	58,000 PSI
250 GR. SFT SP	Hodgdon	H380	.375"	3.270"	73.8	2665	50,000 PSI	78.5	2812	59,400 PSI
250 GR. SFT SP	Hodgdon	CFE 223	.375"	3.270"	69.6	2704	54,900 PSI	74.0	2791	59,700 PSI
250 GR. SFT SP	Hodgdon	Varget	.375"	3.270"	67.7	2657	53,200 PSI	72.0	2773	59,000 PSI

Bullet Weight (Gr.)	Manufacturer	Powder	Bullet Diam.	C.O.L.	Grs.	Vel. (ft/s)	Pressure	Grs.	Vel. (ft/s)	Pressure
250 GR. SFT SP	IMR	IMR 4064	.375"	3.270"	66.7	2600	48,700 PSI	71.0	2763	58,900 PSI
260 GR. NOS AB	Hodgdon	Hybrid 100V	.375"	3.230"	77.0	2675	49,300 PSI	82.0C	2795	55,800 PSI
260 GR. NOS AB	Hodgdon	H4350	.375"	3.320"	78.0	2681	50,800 PSI	83.5C	2837	60,100 PSI
260 GR. NOS AB	Hodgdon	H414	.375"	3.230"	74.7	2659	51,000 PSI	79.5	2808	60,400 PSI
260 GR. NOS AB	IMR	IMR 4350	.375"	3.320"	77.5	2638	50,500 PSI	82.5	2803	59,700 PSI
260 GR. NOS AB	Winchester	760	.375"	3.230"	74.7	2659	51,000 PSI	79.5	2808	60,400 PSI
260 GR. NOS AB	IMR	IMR 4007 SSC	.375"	3.320"	73.3	2624	50,100 PSI	78.0	2793	60,200 PSI
260 GR. NOS AB	Hodgdon	H380	.375"	3.320"	74.0	2671	53,600 PSI	78.6	2795	59,700 PSI
260 GR. NOS AB	Hodgdon	Varget	.375"	3.320"	67.3	2618	52,200 PSI	71.6	2749	59,200 PSI
260 GR. NOS AB	IMR	IMR 4064	.375"	3.320"	67.0	2622	51,000 PSI	71.4	2755	60,100 PSI
270 GR. HDY SP	Winchester	Supreme 780	.375"	3.310"	85.1	2627	52,600 PSI	90.5	2745	59,800 PSI
270 GR. HDY SP	Hodgdon	Hybrid 100V	.375"	3.310"	77.1	2622	48,700 PSI	82.0C	2759	55,900 PSI
270 GR. HDY SP	IMR	IMR 4831	.375"	3.310"	79.9	2565	46,600 PSI	85.0C	2724	54,800 PSI
270 GR. HDY SP	Hodgdon	H4350	.375"	3.310"	78.5	2614	47,800 PSI	83.5C	2783	58,400 PSI
270 GR. HDY SP	Hodgdon	H414	.375"	3.310"	75.7	2599	49,500 PSI	80.5	2757	59,300 PSI
270 GR. HDY SP	IMR	IMR 4350	.375"	3.310"	78.0	2588	47,200 PSI	83.0C	2758	57,200 PSI
270 GR. HDY SP	Winchester	760	.375"	3.310"	75.7	2599	49,500 PSI	80.5	2757	59,300 PSI
270 GR. HDY SP	IMR	IMR 4007 SSC	.375"	3.310"	74.8	2612	50,300 PSI	79.6	2771	60,000 PSI
300 GR. HDY RN	Winchester	Supreme 780	.375"	3.280"	82.7	2453	47,100 PSI	88.0	2626	59,000 PSI
300 GR. HDY RN	Hodgdon	H4831	.375"	3.280"	82.7	2457	48,100 PSI	88.0C	2611	57,800 PSI
300 GR. HDY RN	Hodgdon	Hybrid 100V	.375"	3.280"	73.8	2486	49,400 PSI	78.5	2645	59,100 PSI
300 GR. HDY RN	IMR	IMR 4831	.375"	3.280"	77.6	2478	50,100 PSI	82.5C	2648	59,700 PSI
300 GR. HDY RN	Hodgdon	H4350	.375"	3.280"	75.9	2510	48,300 PSI	80.7	2660	59,600 PSI
300 GR. HDY RN	Hodgdon	H414	.375"	3.280"	74.7	2510	52,800 PSI	79.5	2642	60,100 PSI
300 GR. HDY RN	IMR	IMR 4350	.375"	3.280"	75.0	2454	50,100 PSI	79.8	2632	59,600 PSI
300 GR. HDY RN	Winchester	760	.375"	3.280"	74.7	2510	52,800 PSI	79.5	2642	60,100 PSI
300 GR. HDY RN	IMR	IMR 4007 SSC	.375"	3.280"	71.9	2453	50,100 PSI	76.5	2603	59,000 PSI

Cartridge: 375 Weatherby Magnum Load Type: Rifle					Starting Loads			Maximum Loads		
Bullet Weight (Gr.)	Manufacturer	Powder	Bullet Diam.	C.O.L.	Grs.	Vel. (ft/s)	Pressure	Grs.	Vel. (ft/s)	Pressure
210 GR. BAR XFB	Hodgdon	H4831	.375"	3.585"	95.0	2862	43,000 CUP	98.0C	2938	46,100 CUP
210 GR. BAR XFB	Hodgdon	H4350	.375"	3.585"	91.0	3018	49,600 CUP	95.5C	3110	52,900 CUP
210 GR. BAR XFB	Hodgdon	H414	.375"	3.585"	93.0	2954	42,900 CUP	96.0	3033	45,800 CUP
210 GR. BAR XFB	Hodgdon	H380	.375"	3.585"	83.0	2888	47,900 CUP	88.5	3028	52,900 CUP
210 GR. BAR XFB	Hodgdon	Varget	.375"	3.585"	70.0	2782	48,700 CUP	75.0	2900	53,100 CUP
210 GR. BAR XFB	Hodgdon	H4895	.375"	3.585"	69.0	2824	48,500 CUP	74.0	2945	53,500 CUP
225 GR. HDY SP	Hodgdon	H4831	.375"	3.585"	96.0	2870	46,000 CUP	99.0C	2957	49,600 CUP
225 GR. HDY SP	Hodgdon	H4350	.375"	3.585"	89.0	2939	48,300 CUP	94.5	3070	53,400 CUP

Bullet Weight (Gr.)	Manufacturer	Powder	Bullet Diam.	C.O.L.	Grs.	Vel. (ft/s)	Pressure	Grs.	Vel. (ft/s)	Pressure
225 GR. HDY SP	Hodgdon	H414	.375"	3.585"	91.0	2885	43,400 CUP	96.0	3044	49,600 CUP
225 GR. HDY SP	Hodgdon	H380	.375"	3.585"	82.0	2862	49,600 CUP	87.0	2980	53,900 CUP
225 GR. HDY SP	Hodgdon	Varget	.375"	3.585"	70.0	2713	47,600 CUP	74.5	2850	53,500 CUP
225 GR. HDY SP	Hodgdon	H4895	.375"	3.585"	69.0	2789	50,300 CUP	73.5	2896	53,100 CUP
235 GR. SPR SP	Hodgdon	H4831	.375"	3.585"	94.0	2813	45,900 CUP	99.0C	2912	50,500 CUP
235 GR. SPR SP	Hodgdon	H4350	.375"	3.585"	85.0	2811	46,400 CUP	90.5	2952	52,600 CUP
235 GR. SPR SP	Hodgdon	H414	.375"	3.585"	91.0	2838	44,700 CUP	95.5	2940	48,200 CUP
235 GR. SPR SP	Hodgdon	H380	.375"	3.585"	78.0	2701	45,000 CUP	83.0	2849	52,400 CUP
235 GR. SPR SP	Hodgdon	Varget	.375"	3.585"	69.0	2669	47,200 CUP	73.5	2774	52,700 CUP
235 GR. SPR SP	Hodgdon	H4895	.375"	3.585"	69.0	2742	50,700 CUP	73.3	2834	53,100 CUP
250 GR. SIE SPBT	Hodgdon	H4831	.375"	3.600"	91.0	2741	46,900 CUP	97.0C	2871	52,500 CUP
250 GR. SIE SPBT	Hodgdon	H4350	.375"	3.600"	83.0	2765	47,600 CUP	88.0	2873	52,300 CUP
250 GR. SIE SPBT	Hodgdon	H414	.375"	3.600"	87.0	2753	44,800 CUP	93.0	2939	51,500 CUP
250 GR. SIE SPBT	Hodgdon	H380	.375"	3.600"	75.5	2646	48,100 CUP	79.5	2743	52,200 CUP
260 GR. NOS PART	Hodgdon	H4831	.375"	3.585"	90.0	2692	48,300 CUP	96.0C	2810	53,200 CUP
260 GR. NOS PART	Hodgdon	H4350	.375"	3.585"	83.0	2724	50,800 CUP	88.0	2818	53,300 CUP
260 GR. NOS PART	Hodgdon	H414	.375"	3.585"	86.0	2709	46,700 CUP	91.0	2842	52,400 CUP
260 GR. NOS PART	Hodgdon	H380	.375"	3.585"	73.0	2527	47,900 CUP	78.0	2655	52,900 CUP
270 GR. HDY SP	Hodgdon	H4831	.375"	3.600"	90.0	2631	46,900 CUP	96.0C	2787	53,600 CUP
270 GR. HDY SP	Hodgdon	Hybrid 100V	.375"	3.600"	82.0	2638	44,000 CUP	87.5C	2775	48,300 CUP
270 GR. HDY SP	Hodgdon	H4350	.375"	3.600"	83.0	2708	49,000 CUP	88.0	2787	52,800 CUP
270 GR. HDY SP	Hodgdon	H414	.375"	3.600"	84.0	2676	47,300 CUP	90.0	2842	53,400 CUP
270 GR. HDY SP	Hodgdon	H380	.375"	3.600"	73.5	2520	46,300 CUP	78.5	2678	54,100 CUP
285 GR. SPR GSSP	Hodgdon	H4831	.375"	3.580"	89.0	2605	48,600 CUP	94.5C	2725	53,600 CUP
285 GR. SPR GSSP	Hodgdon	Hybrid 100V	.375"	3.580"	82.0	2621	46,200 CUP	87.5C	2764	51,000 CUP
285 GR. SPR GSSP	Hodgdon	H4350	.375"	3.580"	81.0	2617	49,800 CUP	86.5C	2734	53,400 CUP
285 GR. SPR GSSP	Hodgdon	H414	.375"	3.580"	82.0	2591	45,900 CUP	87.0	2736	51,700 CUP
285 GR. SPR GSSP	Hodgdon	H380	.375"	3.580"	72.0	2448	47,700 CUP	76.5	2561	52,500 CUP
300 GR. SFT SP	Hodgdon	H4831	.375"	3.560"	87.0	2498	47,500 CUP	93.0C	2649	54,200 CUP
300 GR. SFT SP	Hodgdon	Hybrid 100V	.375"	3.560"	80.0	2524	46,500 CUP	86.0C	2695	54,400 CUP
300 GR. SFT SP	Hodgdon	H4350	.375"	3.560"	80.0	2544	49,100 CUP	85.0	2642	53,500 CUP
300 GR. SFT SP	Hodgdon	H414	.375"	3.560"	79.0	2490	46,700 CUP	84.0	2623	52,700 CUP
300 GR. SFT SP	Hodgdon	H380	.375"	3.560"	70.0	2334	47,000 CUP	75.0	2458	52,500 CUP

Cartridge: 375 Remington Ultra Mag
Load Type: Rifle

Bullet Weight (Gr.)	Manufacturer	Powder	Bullet Diam.	C.O.L.	Starting Loads			Maximum Loads		
					Grs.	Vel. (ft/s)	Pressure	Grs.	Vel. (ft/s)	Pressure
210 GR. BAR XFB	Hodgdon	H4350	.375"	3.600"	96.0	3078	52,100 PSI	102.5	3293	63,300 PSI
210 GR. BAR XFB	Hodgdon	H414	.375"	3.600"	98.0	3177	55,600 PSI	104.0	3321	63,200 PSI
210 GR. BAR XFB	Winchester	760	.375"	3.600"	98.0	3177	55,600 PSI	104.0	3321	63,200 PSI

Bullet Weight (Gr.)	Manufacturer	Powder	Bullet Diam.	C.O.L.	Grs.	Vel. (ft/s)	Pressure	Grs.	Vel. (ft/s)	Pressure
210 GR. BAR XFB	Hodgdon	Varget	.375"	3.600"	85.0	3110	54,700 PSI	91.0	3271	63,100 PSI
225 GR. HDY SP	Hodgdon	H4831	.375"	3.560"	105.0	3062	56,200 PSI	108.0C	3137	60,600 PSI
225 GR. HDY SP	Hodgdon	H4350	.375"	3.560"	95.0	3027	52,200 PSI	101.0	3214	62,800 PSI
225 GR. HDY SP	Hodgdon	H414	.375"	3.560"	96.0	3109	55,600 PSI	101.0	3236	63,400 PSI
225 GR. HDY SP	Winchester	760	.375"	3.560"	96.0	3109	55,600 PSI	101.0	3236	63,400 PSI
235 GR. SPR SP	Hodgdon	H4831	.375"	3.550"	102.0	2957	53,800 PSI	108.0C	3111	62,800 PSI
235 GR. SPR SP	Hodgdon	H4350	.375"	3.550"	94.0	3000	54,600 PSI	100.0	3163	63,500 PSI
235 GR. SPR SP	Hodgdon	H414	.375"	3.550"	95.0	3027	54,900 PSI	100.5	3184	62,700 PSI
235 GR. SPR SP	Winchester	760	.375"	3.550"	95.0	3027	54,900 PSI	100.5	3184	62,700 PSI
250 GR. BAR XFB	Hodgdon	H4831	.375"	3.600"	98.0	2850	55,100 PSI	103.0	3090	62,700 PSI
250 GR. BAR XFB	Hodgdon	H4350	.375"	3.600"	89.0	2842	52,800 PSI	94.5	3010	62,700 PSI
250 GR. BAR XFB	Hodgdon	H414	.375"	3.600"	88.0	2886	57,600 PSI	93.5	3006	62,700 PSI
250 GR. BAR XFB	Winchester	760	.375"	3.600"	88.0	2886	57,600 PSI	93.5	3006	62,700 PSI
260 GR. NOS PART	Hodgdon	H4831	.375"	3.570"	95.0	2767	54,100 PSI	101.0	2923	62,900 PSI
260 GR. NOS PART	Hodgdon	H4350	.375"	3.570"	88.0	2819	56,300 PSI	92.5	2935	62,900 PSI
260 GR. NOS PART	Hodgdon	H414	.375"	3.570"	87.0	2850	59,100 PSI	91.5	2933	62,900 PSI
260 GR. NOS PART	Winchester	760	.375"	3.570"	87.0	2850	59,100 PSI	91.5	2933	62,900 PSI
270 GR. HDY SP	Hodgdon	H4831	.375"	3.550"	99.0	2779	54,200 PSI	104.0C	2922	62,900 PSI
270 GR. HDY SP	Hodgdon	H4350	.375"	3.550"	90.0	2767	52,400 PSI	95.0	2932	62,600 PSI
270 GR. HDY SP	Hodgdon	H414	.375"	3.550"	89.0	2789	54,400 PSI	93.0	2924	63,000 PSI
270 GR. HDY SP	Winchester	760	.375"	3.550"	89.0	2789	54,400 PSI	93.0	2924	63,000 PSI
285 GR. SPR GSSP	Hodgdon	H4831	.375"	3.570"	96.0	2706	55,500 PSI	101.0	2830	62,900 PSI
285 GR. SPR GSSP	Hodgdon	H4350	.375"	3.570"	88.0	2724	57,500 PSI	92.5	2836	62,600 PSI
285 GR. SPR GSSP	Hodgdon	H414	.375"	3.570"	86.0	2720	57,800 PSI	91.0	2838	63,700 PSI
285 GR. SPR GSSP	Winchester	760	.375"	3.570"	86.0	2720	57,800 PSI	91.0	2838	63,700 PSI
300 SFT SP	Hodgdon	H1000	.375"	3.550"	103.0	2628	54,000 PSI	105.0C	2678	57,600 PSI
300 SFT SP	Hodgdon	H4831	.375"	3.550"	92.0	2593	54,600 PSI	97.0	2719	62,500 PSI
300 SFT SP	Hodgdon	H4350	.375"	3.550"	85.0	2598	54,400 PSI	90.0	2733	62,700 PSI

Cartridge: 378 Weatherby Magnum
Load Type: Rifle

Bullet Weight (Gr.)	Manufacturer	Powder	Bullet Diam.	C.O.L.	Starting Loads			Maximum Loads		
					Grs.	Vel. (ft/s)	Pressure	Grs.	Vel. (ft/s)	Pressure
235 GR. SPR SP	Hodgdon	H4831	.375"	3.645"	107.0	2972		117.0	3202	
235 GR. SPR SP	Hodgdon	H4350	.375"	3.645"	102.0	3003		109.0	3224	
270 GR. HDY SP	Hodgdon	H4831	.375"	3.645"	105.0	2724		115.0	3102	
270 GR. HDY SP	Hodgdon	H4350	.375"	3.645"	99.0	2779		105.0	3091	
300 GR. NOS PART	Hodgdon	H4831	.375"	3.680"	102.0	2624		112.0	2926	
300 GR. NOS PART	Hodgdon	H4350	.375"	3.680"	95.0	2595		100.0	2940	

Cartridge: 40-65 Winchester Load Type: Rifle					Starting Loads			Maximum Loads		
Bullet Weight (Gr.)	Manufacturer	Powder	Bullet Diam.	C.O.L.	Grs.	Vel. (ft/s)	Pressure	Grs.	Vel. (ft/s)	Pressure
400 GR. LRNFP	IMR	IMR 4007 SSC	.409"	2.780"	37.0	1327	13,000 CUP	40.0C	1467	23,900 CUP
400 GR. LRNFP	Hodgdon	Varget	.409"	2.780"	35.0	1438	20,100 CUP	38.0	1558	24,800 CUP
400 GR. LRNFP	Hodgdon	H4895	.409"	2.780"	33.0	1423	19,700 CUP	36.0	1554	24,200 CUP
400 GR. LRNFP	IMR	IMR 8208 XBR	.409"	2.780"	30.8	1409	24,300 CUP	32.4	1462	25,100 CUP
400 GR. LRNFP	Hodgdon	Benchmark	.409"	2.780"	29.0	1321	18,800 CUP	32.5	1491	25,000 CUP
400 GR. LRNFP	Hodgdon	H322	.409"	2.780"	30.5	1398	19,200 CUP	33.0	1520	23,900 CUP
400 GR. LRNFP	IMR	IMR 4198	.409"	2.780"	25.2	1373	22,000 CUP	26.5	1446	25,200 CUP
400 GR. LRNFP	Hodgdon	H4198	.409"	2.780"	28.0	1441	21,200 CUP	31.0	1572	24,700 CUP
400 GR. LRNFP	Hodgdon	H4227	.409"	2.780"	20.0	1277	18,900 CUP	23.0	1410	24,900 CUP
400 GR. LRNFP	IMR	Trail Boss	.409"	2.780"	11.0	889	20,000 CUP	12.0	915	21,200 CUP

Cartridge: 405 Winchester Load Type: Rifle					Starting Loads			Maximum Loads		
Bullet Weight (Gr.)	Manufacturer	Powder	Bullet Diam.	C.O.L.	Grs.	Vel. (ft/s)	Pressure	Grs.	Vel. (ft/s)	Pressure
300 GR. BAR TSX FB	Hodgdon	Varget	.411"	3.200"	50.0	1899	35,200 PSI	55.0C	2083	42,500 PSI
300 GR. BAR TSX FB	IMR	IMR 4320	.411"	3.200"	48.0	1798	34,400 PSI	53.0	2002	42,300 PSI
300 GR. BAR TSX FB	IMR	IMR 4064	.411"	3.200"	48.0	1849	35,500 PSI	53.5C	2057	43,900 PSI
300 GR. BAR TSX FB	IMR	IMR 4895	.411"	3.200"	48.0	1847	35,600 PSI	53.5	2055	43,800 PSI
300 GR. BAR TSX FB	Hodgdon	H4895	.411"	3.200"	48.0	1945	35,500 PSI	53.5C	2157	44,500 PSI
300 GR. BAR TSX FB	IMR	IMR 8208 XBR	.411"	3.200"	46.0	1915	36,700 PSI	51.2	2101	43,500 PSI
300 GR. BAR TSX FB	IMR	IMR 3031	.411"	3.200"	43.0	1818	35,000 PSI	47.5	2019	43,200 PSI
300 GR. BAR TSX FB	Hodgdon	Benchmark	.411"	3.200"	45.0	1879	34,400 PSI	50.0	2077	43,000 PSI
300 GR. HDY FP	Hodgdon	Varget	.411"	3.085"	55.0	2079	32,600 PSI	61.0	2275	41,200 PSI
300 GR. HDY FP	IMR	IMR 4064	.411"	3.085"	52.0	2022	35,800 PSI	57.7C	2226	43,900 PSI
300 GR. HDY FP	IMR	IMR 4895	.411"	3.085"	52.0	2031	36,700 PSI	58.6C	2233	44,100 PSI
300 GR. HDY FP	Hodgdon	H4895	.411"	3.085"	53.0	2114	33,200 PSI	59.0	2300	40,000 PSI
300 GR. HDY FP	IMR	IMR 8208 XBR	.411"	3.085"	50.0	2086	36,500 PSI	56.0	2260	42,900 PSI
300 GR. HDY FP	IMR	IMR 3031	.411"	3.085	47.0	1952	31,700 PSI	53.0	2216	44,300 PSI
300 GR. HDY FP	Hodgdon	Benchmark	.411"	3.085"	53.0	2206	34,100 PSI	59.0	2404	42,200 PSI
300 GR. HDY FP	Hodgdon	H322	.411"	3.085"	44.0	1996	34,800 PSI	49.0	2150	41,200 PSI
300 GR. HDY FP	Hodgdon	H4198	.411"	3.085"	37.5	1925	32,300 PSI	41.5	2091	43,000 PSI
400 GR. WDLGH RNSN	Hodgdon	Varget	.411"	3.230"	48.0	1790	37,000 PSI	52.0	1928	44,300 PSI
400 GR. WDLGH RNSN	IMR	IMR 4064	.411"	3.230"	44.0	1684	35,900 PSI	49.4	1856	43,800 PSI
400 GR. WDLGH RNSN	IMR	IMR 4895	.411"	3.230"	-44.0	1717	38,800 PSI	49.5	1860	44,100 PSI
400 GR. WDLGH RNSN	Hodgdon	H4895	.411"	3.230"	45.5	1801	37,100 PSI	50.5	1945	44,900 PSI
400 GR. WDLGH RNSN	IMR	IMR 8208 XBR	.411"	3.230"	39.0	1652	36,700 PSI	43.0	1784	42,900 PSI
400 GR. WDLGH RNSN	Hodgdon	H4198	.411"	3.230"	33.0	1582	33,600 PSI	36.5	1718	43,400 PSI

Cartridge: 416 Remington Magnum Load Type: Rifle					Starting Loads			Maximum Loads		
Bullet Weight (Gr.)	Manufacturer	Powder	Bullet Diam.	C.O.L.	Grs.	Vel. (ft/s)	Pressure	Grs.	Vel. (ft/s)	Pressure
300 GR. BAR TSX	Hodgdon	Varget	.416"	3.600"	79.0	2610	42,900 CUP	84.0C	2745	48,600 CUP
300 GR. BAR TSX	IMR	IMR 4064	.416"	3.600"	79.0	2640	42,800 CUP	84.0C	2743	47,000 CUP
300 GR. BAR TSX	Hodgdon	BL-C(2)	.416"	3.600"	86.0	2556	37,900 CUP	90.0	2681	42,600 CUP
300 GR. BAR TSX	IMR	IMR 4895	.416"	3.600"	79.0	2649	43,100 CUP	84.5C	2781	48,400 CUP
300 GR. BAR TSX	Hodgdon	H335	.416"	3.600"	79.0	2618	44,300 CUP	84.5	2778	50,300 CUP
300 GR. BAR TSX	Hodgdon	H4895	.416"	3.600"	75.0	2631	43,700 CUP	80.5	2779	50,300 CUP
300 GR. BAR TSX	IMR	IMR 8208 XBR	.416"	3.600"	74.0	2600	44,200 CUP	78.5	2725	52,700 CUP
350 GR. SPR SP	IMR	IMR 4007 SSC	.416"	3.590"	80.0	2326	35,300 CUP	86.0C	2520	45,200 CUP
350 GR. SPR SP	Hodgdon	Varget	.416"	3.590"	77.0	2519	46,900 CUP	82.0	2622	52,400 CUP
350 GR. SPR SP	IMR	IMR 4064	.416"	3.590"				81.0	2485	51,600 CUP
350 GR. SPR SP	Hodgdon	BL-C(2)	.416"	3.590"	84.0	2475	40,600 CUP	87.0	2580	44,700 CUP
350 GR. SPR SP	IMR	IMR 4895	.416"	3.590"				77.0	2425	53,700 CUP
350 GR. SPR SP	Hodgdon	H335	.416"	3.590"	78.0	2464	45,400 CUP	82.0	2572	50,900 CUP
350 GR. SPR SP	Hodgdon	H4895	.416"	3.590"	75.0	2476	45,000 CUP	80.0	2601	52,200 CUP
350 GR. SPR SP	IMR	IMR 8208 XBR	.416"	3.590"	71.0	2409	44,600 CUP	77.0	2551	52,700 CUP
350 GR. SPR SP	IMR	IMR 3031	.416"	3.590"				76.5	2450	53,000 CUP
350 GR. SPR SP	IMR	Trail Boss	.416"	3.590"	20.0	913	19,700 CUP	29.0	1143	29,900 CUP
400 GR. HDY JRN	Hodgdon	H4350	.416"	3.560"	85.0	2305	41,400 CUP	88.0 C	2395	46,400 CUP
400 GR. HDY JRN	IMR	IMR 4007 SSC	.416"	3.560"	78.0	2216	39,000 CUP	84.0C	2404	48,900 CUP
400 GR. HDY JRN	Hodgdon	H380	.416"	3.560"	78.0	2234	42,900 CUP	84.0	2367	48,500 CUP
400 GR. HDY JRN	Hodgdon	Varget	.416"	3.560"	72.0	2276	46,300 CUP	77.0	2407	53,000 CUP
400 GR. HDY JRN	IMR	IMR 4064	.416"	3.560"				78.0	2335	52,000 CUP
400 GR. HDY JRN	Hodgdon	BL-C(2)	.416"	3.560"	78.0	2290	45,900 CUP	83.0	2420	50,500 CUP
400 GR. HDY JRN	IMR	IMR 4895	.416"	3.560"				76.5	2325	53,800 CUP
400 GR. HDY JRN	Hodgdon	H4895	.416"	3.560"	71.0	2268	46,100 CUP	76.0	2391	53,300 CUP
400 GR. HDY JRN	IMR	IMR 8208 XBR	.416"	3.560"	68.0	2233	46,100 CUP	73.0	2348	52,800 CUP
400 GR. HDY JRN	IMR	IMR 3031	.416"	3.560"				75.0	2315	52,100 CUP

Cartridge: 416 Rigby Load Type: Rifle					Starting Loads			Maximum Loads		
Bullet Weight (Gr.)	Manufacturer	Powder	Bullet Diam.	C.O.L.	Grs.	Vel. (ft/s)	Pressure	Grs.	Vel. (ft/s)	Pressure
300 GR. BAR TSX	IMR	IMR 7828 SSC	.416"	3.630"	97.0	2285	33,400 CUP	108.0	2617	43,900 CUP
300 GR. BAR TSX	Winchester	Supreme 780	.416"	3.630"	100.0	2468	37,200 CUP	110.0	2677	42,200 CUP
300 GR. BAR TSX	Hodgdon	H4831	.416"	3.630"	102.0	2555	34,900 CUP	109.5	2725	40,600 CUP
300 GR. BAR TSX	Hodgdon	Hybrid 100V	.416"	3.630"	90.2	2497	37,600 CUP	96.0	2641	43,000 CUP

Bullet Weight (Gr.)	Manufacturer	Powder	Bullet Diam.	C.O.L.	Grs.	Vel. (ft/s)	Pressure	Grs.	Vel. (ft/s)	Pressure
300 GR. BAR TSX	IMR	IMR 4831	.416"	3.630"	95.0	2476	35,800 CUP	102.0	2694	43,000 CUP
300 GR. BAR TSX	Hodgdon	H4350	.416"	3.630"	92.0	2577	35,700 CUP	99.0	2776	42,900 CUP
300 GR. BAR TSX	Hodgdon	H414	.416"	3.630"	94.7	2594	35,900 CUP	103.0	2805	42,500 CUP
300 GR. BAR TSX	IMR	IMR 4350	.416"	3.630"	92.9	2445	31,800 CUP	101.0	2725	42,600 CUP
300 GR. BAR TSX	IMR	IMR 4007 SSC	.416"	3.630"	92.0	2616	38,900 CUP	99.0	2785	43,400 CUP
325 GR. BAR XFB	Hodgdon	H4831	.416"	3.660"	102.0	2522	37,700 CUP	107.0	2631	43,700 CUP
325 GR. BAR XFB	Hodgdon	H4350	.416"	3.660"	94.0	2549	37,600 CUP	99.0	2660	43,600 CUP
325 GR. BAR XFB	Hodgdon	H414	.416"	3.660"	94.0	2596	38,300 CUP	99.0	2702	43,400 CUP
325 GR. BAR XFB	Winchester	760	.416"	3.660"	94.0	2596	38,300 CUP	99.0	2702	43,400 CUP
350 GR. SPR SP	Hodgdon	H1000	.416	3.640"	112.0	2479	37,400 CUP	116.0C	2551	39,900 CUP
350 GR. SPR SP	IMR	IMR 7828 SSC	.416"	3.640"	97.5	2286	32,000 CUP	106.0	2535	43,300 CUP
350 GR. SPR SP	Winchester	Supreme 780	.416"	3.640"	102.5	2486	35,800 CUP	109.0	2606	40,800 CUP
350 GR. SPR SP	Hodgdon	H4831	.416	3.640"	101.0	2459	37,100 CUP	107.0	2609	43,000 CUP
350 GR. SPR SP	Hodgdon	Hybrid 100V	.416"	3.640"	89.8	2493	37,200 CUP	95.5	2654	43,200 CUP
350 GR. SPR SP	IMR	IMR 4831	.416"	3.640"	92.4	2353	31,600 CUP	100.5	2606	43,700 CUP
350 GR. SPR SP	Hodgdon	H4350	.416	3.640"	94.0	2507	38,000 CUP	99.0	2641	43,400 CUP
350 GR. SPR SP	IMR	IMR 4350	.416"	3.640"	91.6	2398	34,200 CUP	99.5	2626	43,200 CUP
350 GR. SPR SP	IMR	IMR 4007 SSC	.416"	3.640"	89.2	2433	35,200 CUP	97.0	2673	43,600 CUP
350 GR. SPR SP	IMR	Trail Boss	.416"	3.640"	25.0	1139		35.0	1354	
400 GR. HDY SP	Hodgdon	H1000	.416	3.700"	110.0	2371	37,500 CUP	116.0C	2470	42,200 CUP
400 GR. HDY SP	IMR	IMR 7828	.416"	3.700"	96.8	2246	36,400 CUP	103.0	2421	43,700 CUP
400 GR. HDY SP	Winchester	Supreme 780	.416"	3.700"	97.8	2334	36,300 CUP	104.0	2464	42,400 CUP
400 GR. HDY SP	Hodgdon	H4831	.416	3.700"	97.0	2321	38,500 CUP	102.0	2432	43,300 CUP
400 GR. HDY SP	Hodgdon	Hybrid 100V	.416"	3.700"	87.9	2361	38,900 CUP	93.5	2505	43,100 CUP
400 GR. HDY SP	IMR	IMR 4831	.416"	3.700"	91.2	2282	34,800 CUP	97.0	2444	43,300 CUP
400 GR. HDY SP	Hodgdon	H4350	.416	3.700"	89.0	2333	38,500 CUP	94.0	2456	43,500 CUP
400 GR. HDY SP	IMR	IMR 4350	.416"	3.700"	90.2	2308	36,000 CUP	96.0	2456	43,000 CUP
400 GR. HDY SP	IMR	IMR 4007 SSC	.416"	3.700"	84.6	2275	36,800 CUP	90.0	2416	43,100 CUP

Cartridge: 416 Weatherby Magnum Load Type: Rifle					Starting Loads			Maximum Loads		
Bullet Weight (Gr.)	Manufacturer	Powder	Bullet Diam.	C.O.L.	Grs.	Vel. (ft/s)	Pressure	Grs.	Vel. (ft/s)	Pressure
300 GR. BAR XFB	Hodgdon	H4350	.416"	3.780"	117.0	2917		122.0	3051	
300 GR. BAR XFB	Hodgdon	H414	.416"	3.780"	110.0	2911		115.0	3052	
350 GR. BAR XFB	Hodgdon	H4350	.416"	3.780"	112.0	2728		118.0	2891	
400 GR. HDY RN	Hodgdon	H1000	.416"	3.780"	116.0	2348		120.0	2419	
400 GR. HDY RN	Hodgdon	H4831	.416"	3.780"	116.0	2625		120.0	2703	
400 GR. HDY RN	Hodgdon	H4350	.416"	3.780"	105.0	2564		110.0	2687	

Cartridge: 44-40 Winchester Load Type: Rifle					Starting Loads			Maximum Loads		
Bullet Weight (Gr.)	Manufacturer	Powder	Bullet Diam.	C.O.L.	Grs.	Vel. (ft/s)	Pressure	Grs.	Vel. (ft/s)	Pressure
200 GR. LEAD RNFP	Hodgdon	Universal	.428"	1.600"	6.6	950	10,000 PSI	7.3	1069	11,100 PSI
200 GR. LEAD RNFP	Winchester	231	.428"	1.600"	5.5	901	9,800 PSI	6.5	1020	12,400 PSI
200 GR. LEAD RNFP	Hodgdon	HP-38	.428"	1.600"	5.5	901	9,800 PSI	6.5	1020	12,400 PSI
200 GR. LEAD RNFP	Hodgdon	Titegroup	.428"	1.600"	5.0	956	8,400 PSI	6.2	1117	12,900 PSI
200 GR. LEAD RNFP	Hodgdon	Clays	.428"	1.600"	4.2	845	8,200 PSI	5.0	924	11,700 PSI

Cartridge: 44 Magnum Load Type: Rifle					Starting Loads			Maximum Loads		
Bullet Weight (Gr.)	Manufacturer	Powder	Bullet Diam.	C.O.L.	Grs.	Vel. (ft/s)	Pressure	Grs.	Vel. (ft/s)	Pressure
165 GR. LRNFP CAST	Hodgdon	Universal	.430"	1.500"	6.5	1009	7,700 CUP	7.2	1138	11,500 CUP
165 GR. LRNFP CAST	Hodgdon	HP-38	.430"	1.500"	6.0	1078	10,100 CUP	7.0	1225	13,900 CUP
165 GR. LRNFP CAST	Hodgdon	Titegroup	.430"	1.500"	5.3	1127	11,800 CUP	6.5	1280	16,400 CUP
165 GR. LRNFP CAST	Hodgdon	Clays	.430"	1.500"	4.4	949	8,500 CUP	5.5	1147	15,500 CUP
180 GR. HDY XTP	Hodgdon	H4227	.430"	1.600"	27.5	2005	24,000 CUP	29.0	2114	31,200 CUP
180 GR. HDY XTP	Hodgdon	H110	.430"	1.600"	29.0	2170	21,800 CUP	31.5	2286	29,900 CUP
185 GR. LRNFP CAST	Hodgdon	Universal	.430"	1.540"	6.4	993	8,400 CUP	7.4	1180	12,600 CUP
185 GR. LRNFP CAST	Hodgdon	HP-38	.430"	1.540"	5.9	1035	9,400 CUP	7.2	1207	14,700 CUP
185 GR. LRNFP CAST	Hodgdon	Titegroup	.430"	1.540"	5.3	1072	9,500 CUP	6.6	1248	16,500 CUP
185 GR. LRNFP CAST	Hodgdon	Clays	.430"	1.540"	4.2	859	8,900 CUP	6.0	1162	18,400 CUP
200 GR. LRNFP CAST	Hodgdon	Universal	.430"	1.570"	6.8	1065	10,500 CUP	7.8	1209	15,400 CUP
200 GR. LRNFP CAST	Hodgdon	HP-38	.430"	1.570"	5.8	1004	10,800 CUP	7.4	1197	16,700 CUP
200 GR. LRNFP CAST	Hodgdon	Titegroup	.430"	1.570"	5.0	1004	11,000 CUP	6.6	1217	17,300 CUP
200 GR. LRNFP CAST	Hodgdon	Clays	.430"	1.570"	4.2	874	8,500 CUP	6.4	1172	20,200 CUP
200 GR. NOS JHP	Hodgdon	H4227	.429"	1.600"	25.0	1840	29,800 CUP	27.0	1982	37,800 CUP
200 GR. NOS JHP	Hodgdon	H110	.429"	1.600"	27.5	2064	29,000 CUP	28.5	2106	37,800 CUP
210 GR. SIE JHC	Hodgdon	H4227	.430"	1.600"	25.0	1843	29,200 CUP	27.0	1970	37,600 CUP
210 GR. SIE JHC	Hodgdon	H110	.430"	1.600"	26.0	1969	29,900 CUP	27.0	2030	31,100 CUP
225 GR. SPR JHP	Hodgdon	H4227	.429"	1.575"	23.0	1721	27,400 CUP	25.5	1897	35,700 CUP
225 GR. SPR JHP	Hodgdon	H110	.429"	1.575"	23.0	1778	25,600 CUP	25.0	1924	36,300 CUP
240 GR. LSWC CAST	Hodgdon	Universal	.430"	1.620"	6.5	927	11,700 CUP	10.2	1374	37,500 CUP
240 GR. LSWC CAST	Hodgdon	HP-38	.430"	1.620"	5.5	907	12,000 CUP	11.0	1437	38,100 CUP
240 GR. LSWC CAST	Hodgdon	Titegroup	.430"	1.620"	4.7	908	11,100 CUP	10.0	1423	38,400 CUP
240 GR. LSWC CAST	Hodgdon	Clays	.430"	1.620"	4.3	839	14,000 CUP	6.2	1062	21,800 CUP
240 GR. NOS JHP	IMR	IMR 4227	.429"	1.600"	22.0	1624	28,400 CUP	24.0	1778	36,100 CUP
240 GR. NOS JHP	IMR	SR 4759	.429"	1.600"				21.0C	1630	38,500 CUP
240 GR. NOS JHP	Hodgdon	H4227	.429"	1.600"	22.0	1624	28,400 CUP	24.0	1778	36,100 CUP

	Manufacturer	Powder	Bullet Diam.	C.O.L.	Grs.	Vel. (ft/s)	Pressure	Grs.	Vel. (ft/s)	Pressure
240 GR. NOS JHP	Hodgdon	H110	.429"	1.600"	23.0	1750	25,200 CUP	24.0	1817	36,200 CUP
270 GR. SPR GDSP	Hodgdon	H4227	.429"	1.600"	20.5	1476	28,400 CUP	22.5	1638	37,400 CUP
270 GR. SPR GDSP	Hodgdon	H110	.429"	1.600"	19.5	1502	29,300 CUP	21.5	1637	37,700 CUP
280 GR. SFT JHP	Hodgdon	H4227	.430"	1.700"	20.0	1354	27,600 CUP	22.0	1544	37,800 CUP
280 GR. SFT JHP	Hodgdon	H110	.430"	1.700"	18.5	1358	27,000 CUP	20.5	1510	36,100 CUP
300 GR. HDY XTP	Hodgdon	H4227	.430"	1.600"	18.0	1318	30,600 CUP	20.0	1452	38,600 CUP
300 GR. HDY XTP	Hodgdon	H110	.430"	1.600"	18.0	1393	35,100 CUP	19.0	1473	38,800 CUP

Cartridge: 444 Marlin Load Type: Rifle					Starting Loads			Maximum Loads		
Bullet Weight (Gr.)	Manufacturer	Powder	Bullet Diam.	C.O.L.	Grs.	Vel. (ft/s)	Pressure	Grs.	Vel. (ft/s)	Pressure
200 GR. BAR XFB	Hodgdon	H335	.429"	2.550"	53.0	2080	27,800 CUP	56.0	2215	33,800 CUP
200 GR. BAR XFB	Hodgdon	Benchmark	.429"	2.550"	50.0	2040	27,600 CUP	54.0	2212	35,800 CUP
200 GR. BAR XFB	Hodgdon	H322	.429"	2.550"	50.0	2139	30,200 CUP	52.0C	2206	33,600 CUP
200 GR. BAR XFB	IMR	IMR 4198	.429"	2.550"	42.6	2171	31,800 CUP	47.3C	2396	40,300 CUP
200 GR. BAR XFB	Hodgdon	H4198	.429"	2.550"	46.0	2309	34,400 CUP	51.2C	2566	42,900 CUP
225 GR. BAR XFB	Hodgdon	H335	.429"	2.550"	49.0	1891	25,500 CUP	52.0	2031	34,500 CUP
225 GR. BAR XFB	Hodgdon	Benchmark	.429"	2.550"	49.0	2028	34,500 CUP	52.0C	2127	38,100 CUP
225 GR. BAR XFB	Hodgdon	H322	.429"	2.550"	47.0	2029	33,400 CUP	50.0C	2144	37,000 CUP
225 GR. BAR XFB	IMR	IMR 4198	.429"	2.550"	41.6	2137	36,900 CUP	46.2C	2324	43,200 CUP
225 GR. BAR XFB	Hodgdon	H4198	.429"	2.550"	42.2	2107	32,300 CUP	46.9	2361	42,300 CUP
240 GR. SIE JHP	Hodgdon	H335	.430"	2.535"	52.5	2049	29,200 CUP	56.0	2222	38,900 CUP
240 GR. SIE JHP	Hodgdon	H4895	.430"	2.535"	51.0	1999	29,600 CUP	53.0C	2069	33,100 CUP
240 GR. SIE JHP	Hodgdon	Benchmark	.430"	2.535"	51.0	2042	31,600 CUP	55.0C	2234	40,600 CUP
240 GR. SIE JHP	Hodgdon	H322	.430"	2.535"	49.5	2049	31,400 CUP	52.0C	2185	35,900 CUP
240 GR. SIE JHP	IMR	IMR 4198	.430"	2.535"	42.0	2112	36,000 CUP	45.6	2276	42,600 CUP
240 GR. SIE JHP	Hodgdon	H4198	.430"	2.535"	44.0	2206	36,100 CUP	49.2C	2499	42,100 CUP
240 GR. SIE JHP	IMR	SR 4759	.430"	2.535"				33.0	2055	43,600 CUP
260 GR. FA JFP	Hodgdon	H335	.430"	2.550"	52.5	2034	31,600 CUP	56.0	2200	41,400 CUP
260 GR. FA JFP	Hodgdon	H4895	.430"	2.550"	50.0	1913	32,700 CUP	53.0C	2057	36,800 CUP
260 GR. FA JFP	Hodgdon	H322	.430"	2.550"	47.0	1944	33,400 CUP	52.0C	2159	41,400 CUP
260 GR. FA JFP	Hodgdon	H4198	.430"	2.550"	41.0	2016	35,600 CUP	45.5	2194	40,900 CUP
265 GR. HDY JFP	Hodgdon	H335	.430"	2.550"	52.5	2032	32,100 CUP	56.0	2187	39,700 CUP
265 GR. HDY JFP	Hodgdon	H4895	.430"	2.550"	50.0	1944	29,300 CUP	53.0C	2080	34,800 CUP
265 GR. HDY JFP	IMR	IMR 8208 XBR	.430"	2.550"	51.0	2030	34,700 CUP	53.5C	2135	39,100 CUP
265 GR. HDY JFP	Hodgdon	Benchmark	.430"	2.550"	49.0	1911	31,000 CUP	53.0C	2139	40,700 CUP
265 GR. HDY JFP	Hodgdon	H322	.430"	2.550"	47.0	1991	33,200 CUP	52.0C	2164	38,300 CUP
265 GR. HDY JFP	IMR	IMR 4198	.430"	2.550"	42.6	2105	39,800 CUP	44.4	2187	42,100 CUP
265 GR. HDY JFP	Hodgdon	H4198	.430"	2.550"	42.0	2034	31,100 CUP	47.0	2273	41,100 CUP
270 GR. SPR JFP	Hodgdon	H335	.429"	2.540"	51.0	1992	31,800 CUP	55.8	2200	42,100 CUP

Bullet Weight (Gr.)	Manufacturer	Powder	Bullet Diam.	C.O.L.	Grs.	Vel. (ft/s)	Pressure	Grs.	Vel. (ft/s)	Pressure
270 GR. SPR JFP	Hodgdon	H4895	.429"	2.540"	50.0	1950	29,300 CUP	53.0C	2080	33,400 CUP
270 GR. SPR JFP	IMR	IMR 8208 XBR	.430"	2.540"	51.0	2019	34,300 CUP	53.5C	2107	38,300 CUP
270 GR. SPR JFP	Hodgdon	Benchmark	.429"	2.540"	50.0	1978	33,500 CUP	54.0C	2166	41,700 CUP
270 GR. SPR JFP	Hodgdon	H322	.429"	2.540"	47.0	1973	31,700 CUP	52.0C	2169	38,100 CUP
270 GR. SPR JFP	IMR	IMR 4198	.430"	2.540"	41.4	2050	37,300 CUP	44.0	2169	43,100 CUP
270 GR. SPR JFP	Hodgdon	H4198	.429"	2.540"	42.0	2092	34,900 CUP	46.5	2261	41,400 CUP
275 GR. BAR FP	Hodgdon	H335	.430"	2.520"	50.0	1984	35,400 CUP	53.5	2120	41,100 CUP
275 GR. BAR FP	Hodgdon	H4895	.430"	2.520"	47.0	1780	27,100 CUP	52.0C	2021	36,200 CUP
275 GR. BAR FP	Hodgdon	Benchmark	.430"	2.520"	48.0	1930	35,900 CUP	51.0C	2069	42,300 CUP
275 GR. BAR FP	Hodgdon	H322	.430"	2.520"	46.0	1930	33,800 CUP	51.0C	2146	43,100 CUP
275 GR. BAR FP	Hodgdon	H4198	.430"	2.520"	40.0	1973	33,500 CUP	44.5	2172	41,800 CUP
280 GR. SFT HP	Hodgdon	Varget	.430"	2.620"	49.0	1914	33,000 CUP	52.0C	2025	36,800 CUP
280 GR. SFT HP	Hodgdon	H335	.430"	2.620"	49.5	1983	36,100 CUP	52.8	2109	42,000 CUP
280 GR. SFT HP	Hodgdon	H4895	.430"	2.620"	47.0	1875	30,300 CUP	52.0C	2089	37,600 CUP
280 GR. SFT HP	IMR	IMR 8208 XBR	.430"	2.620"	48.0	1942	35,900 CUP	52.0	2099	41,600 CUP
280 GR. SFT HP	Hodgdon	Benchmark	.430"	2.620"	46.0	1935	38,300 CUP	49.5C	2070	42,600 CUP
280 GR. SFT HP	Hodgdon	H322	.430"	2.620"	44.5	1901	33,400 CUP	49.5	2120	42,400 CUP
280 GR. SFT HP	IMR	IMR 4198	.430"	2.620"	38.7	1907	36,500 CUP	42.0	2050	42,500 CUP
280 GR. SFT HP	Hodgdon	H4198	.430"	2.620"	38.0	1938	37,300 CUP	42.5	2108	42,300 CUP
300 GR. SFT HP	Hodgdon	Varget	.430"	2.620"	47.0	1784	30,700 CUP	50.0C	1914	35,700 CUP
300 GR. SFT HP	IMR	IMR 4064	.430"	2.620"	47.2	1738	30,900 CUP	51.3C	1908	38,000 CUP
300 GR. SFT HP	IMR	IMR 4895	.430"	2.620"	46.6	1762	33,300 CUP	50.6C	1915	38,300 CUP
300 GR. SFT HP	Hodgdon	H335	.430"	2.620"	49.0	1935	37,600 CUP	52.0	2023	42,300 CUP
300 GR. SFT HP	Hodgdon	H4895	.430"	2.620"	47.0	1839	33,600 CUP	50.0C	1931	35,600 CUP
300 GR. SFT HP	IMR	IMR 8208 XBR	.430"	2.620"	46.0	1829	35,700 CUP	49.0	2029	41,600 CUP
300 GR. SFT HP	IMR	IMR 3031	.430"	2.620"	44.9	1859	35,600 CUP	48.8C	2004	40,100 CUP
300 GR. SFT HP	Hodgdon	Benchmark	.430"	2.620"	46.0	1899	36,200 CUP	48.5	1993	41,900 CUP
300 GR. SFT HP	Hodgdon	H322	.430"	2.620"	43.0	1776	30,600 CUP	48.0	2038	42,600 CUP
300 GR. SFT HP	IMR	IMR 4198	.430"	2.620"	36.8	1796	37,700 CUP	39.2	1911	42,100 CUP
300 GR. SFT HP	Hodgdon	H4198	.430"	2.620"	38.5	1917	36,200 CUP	42.5	2082	42,500 CUP

These data are intended for Springfield "Trapdoor", Rolling Block, and Antique Replicas. Max pressure, 28,000 CUP

Cartridge:45-70 Government (Trapdoor Rifles)* Load Type:Rifle					Starting Loads			Maximum Loads		
Bullet Weight (Gr.)	Manufacturer	Powder	Bullet Diam.	C.O.L.	Grs.	Vel. (ft/s)	Pressure	Grs.	Vel. (ft/s)	Pressure
300 GR. CAST LFP	Hodgdon	Varget	.458"	2.465"	45.0	1599	17,800 CUP	55.0	1880	20,600 CUP
300 GR. CAST LFP	IMR	IMR 4064	.458"	2.465"	49.8	1685	19,400 CUP	53.0	1813	21,800 CUP

300 GR. CAST LFP	IMR	IMR 4895	.458"	2.465"	47.5	1590	16,500 CUP	50.5	1703	20,400 CUP
300 GR. CAST LFP	Hodgdon	H4895	.458"	2.465"	45.0	1572	14,400 CUP	51.0	1703	15,500 CUP
300 GR. CAST LFP	IMR	IMR 8208 XBR	.458"	2.465"	51.2	1723	19,500 CUP	55.0	1924	24,700 CUP
300 GR. CAST LFP	IMR	IMR 3031	.458"	2.465"	51.7	1839	18,700 CUP	55.0	1995	24,900 CUP
300 GR. CAST LFP	Hodgdon	Benchmark	.458"	2.465"	54.0	1788	18,300 CUP	58.0	1940	21,900 CUP
300 GR. CAST LFP	IMR	IMR 4198	.458"	2.465"	33.8	1649	15,500 CUP	36.0	1752	20,200 CUP
300 GR. CAST LFP	Hodgdon	H4198	.458"	2.465"	30.0	1390	14,400 CUP	35.5	1641	16,100 CUP
300 GR. CAST LFP	IMR	Trail Boss	.458"	2.465"	14.0	1199	19,400 CUP	16.5	1285	20,900 CUP
300 GR. SIE HP	Hodgdon	Varget	.458"	2.525"	57.0	1770	16,300 CUP	63.0C	2020	23,800 CUP
300 GR. SIE HP	IMR	IMR 4064	.458"	2.525"	57.0	1865	22,500 CUP	60.5C	1992	25,100 CUP
300 GR. SIE HP	IMR	IMR 4895	.458"	2.525"	57.0	1826	21,700 CUP	61.0C	1968	23,900 CUP
300 GR. SIE HP	Hodgdon	H335	.458"	2.525"	57.0	1901	17,500 CUP	63.5	2143	27,400 CUP
300 GR. SIE HP	Hodgdon	H4895	.458"	2.525"	58.0	1805	16,500 CUP	62.0C	1974	21,000 CUP
300 GR. SIE HP	IMR	IMR 8208 XBR	.458"	2.525"	54.0	1728	18,800 CUP	60.0	2023	25,400 CUP
300 GR. SIE HP	IMR	IMR 3031	.458"	2.525"	56.0	1884	21,100 CUP	59.5C	2021	22,000 CUP
300 GR. SIE HP	Hodgdon	Benchmark	.458"	2.525"	59.5	1907	19,400 CUP	63.5C	2113	27,400 CUP
300 GR. SIE HP	Hodgdon	H322	.458"	2.525"	54.0	1850	18,100 CUP	60.0	2142	28,000 CUP
300 GR. SIE HP	IMR	IMR 4198	.458"	2.525"	45.0	2008	23,500 CUP	48.0	2138	27,800 CUP
300 GR. SIE HP	Hodgdon	H4198	.458"	2.525"	45.0	1807	16,700 CUP	55.0	2221	27,600 CUP
385 GR. CAST LFP	Hodgdon	Varget	.458"	2.505"	42.5	1537	15,400 CUP	52.5	1805	21,800 CUP
385 GR. CAST LFP	IMR	IMR 4064	.458"	2.505"	47.0	1545	18,800 CUP	50.0	1661	24,000 CUP
385 GR. CAST LFP	IMR	IMR 4895	.458"	2.505"	44.2	1412	16,200 CUP	47.0	1486	18,100 CUP
385 GR. CAST LFP	Hodgdon	H4895	.458"	2.505"	35.0	1280	11,900 CUP	42.0	1526	23,100 CUP
385 GR. CAST LFP	IMR	IMR 3031	.458"	2.505"	49.0	1684	22,300 CUP	52.0	1819	25,900 CUP
385 GR. CAST LFP	Hodgdon	Benchmark	.458"	2.505"	50.0	1621	16,300 CUP	53.0	1779	21,300 CUP
385 GR. CAST LFP	IMR	IMR 4198	.458"	2.505"	31.0	1405	15,000 CUP	33.0	1491	17,400 CUP
385 GR. CAST LFP	Hodgdon	H4198	.458"	2.505"	28.0	1302	13,300 CUP	32.0	1483	14,700 CUP
385 GR. CAST LFP	IMR	Trail Boss	.458"	2.505"	14.0	1075	19,400 CUP	16.0	1142	23,200 CUP
405 GR. CAST LFP	Hodgdon	Varget	.458"	2.540"	40.0	1392	15,600 CUP	50.0	1718	20,900 CUP
405 GR. CAST LFP	IMR	IMR 4064	.458"	2.540"	46.0	1534	17,900 CUP	49.5	1660	23,200 CUP
405 GR. CAST LFP	IMR	IMR 4895	.458"	2.540"	45.6	1496	18,900 CUP	48.5	1598	23,000 CUP
405 GR. CAST LFP	Hodgdon	H4895	.458"	2.540"	40.0	1424	14,900 CUP	48.0	1645	18,900 CUP
405 GR. CAST LFP	IMR	IMR 8208 XBR	.458"	2.540"	47.9	1637	21,800 CUP	51.0	1727	23,600 CUP
405 GR. CAST LFP	IMR	IMR 3031	.458"	2.540"	45.5	1597	17,300 CUP	48.5	1706	21,100 CUP
405 GR. CAST LFP	Hodgdon	Benchmark	.458"	2.540"	47.0	1564	17,100 CUP	50.0	1695	22,600 CUP
405 GR. CAST LFP	IMR	IMR 4198	.458"	2.540"	30.0	1370	17,000 CUP	32.0	1462	19,000 CUP
405 GR. CAST LFP	Hodgdon	H4198	.458"	2.540"	27.0	1251	14,200 CUP	31.0	1459	17,100 CUP
405 GR. CAST LFP	IMR	Trail Boss	.458"	2.540"	12.0	971	24,500 CUP	13.0	1007	25,600 CUP
485 GR. CAST LFP	IMR	IMR 4064	.458"	2.540"	38.5	1280	17,400 CUP	41.0	1372	21,300 CUP
485 GR. CAST LFP	IMR	IMR 4895	.458"	2.540"	40.0	1294	19,700 CUP	43.0	1435	25,300 CUP

485 GR. CAST LFP	IMR	IMR 3031	.458"	2.540"	39.5	1406	20,500 CUP	42.0	1488	22,600 CUP
485 GR. CAST LFP	Hodgdon	Benchmark	.458"	2.540"	38.0	1290	15,600 CUP	43.0	1503	23,400 CUP
485 GR. CAST LFP	IMR	IMR 4198	.458"	2.540"	30.5	1364	17,500 CUP	32.5	1439	21,600 CUP
485 GR. CAST LFP	Hodgdon	H4198	.458"	2.540"	28.0	1279	16,400 CUP	32.0	1434	20,400 CUP
485 GR. CAST LFP	IMR	Trail Boss	.458"	2.540"	8.0	699	17,100 CUP	10.0	804	23,300 CUP

These data are intended for the 1895 lever action Marlin ONLY. Max pressure, 40,000 CUP. Do not use these data in any of the firearms listed in the Trapdoor section. Do not use pointed bullets in any rifle with a tubular magazine.

Cartridge:45-70 Government (Lever Actions)* Load Type:Rifle					Starting Loads			Maximum Loads		
Bullet Weight (Gr.)	Manufacturer	Powder	Bullet Diam.	C.O.L.	Grs.	Vel. (ft/s)	Pressure	Grs.	Vel. (ft/s)	Pressure
300 GR. SIE HP	IMR	IMR 4064	.458"	2.525"	59.0	1858	20,300 CUP	65.5C	2125	28,700 CUP
300 GR. SIE HP	IMR	IMR 4895	.458"	2.525"	58.5	1800	19,900 CUP	65.0C	2087	30,000 CUP
300 GR. SIE HP	Hodgdon	H335	.458"	2.525"	61.0	2073	22,500 CUP	68.0	2326	38,800 CUP
300 GR. SIE HP	IMR	IMR 8208 XBR	.458"	2.525"	60.0	2023	25,400 CUP	65.0C	2240	32,900 CUP
300 GR. SIE HP	IMR	IMR 3031	.458"	2.525"	58.0	1971	21,900 CUP	64.0C	2196	29,500 CUP
300 GR. SIE HP	Hodgdon	H322	.458"	2.525"	57.0	2002	21,400 CUP	63.0C	2252	32,600 CUP
300 GR. SIE HP	IMR	IMR 4198	.458"	2.525"	53.7	2293	33,100 CUP	57.2	2407	39,100 CUP
300 GR. SIE HP	Hodgdon	H4198	.458"	2.525"	55.0	2221	27,600 CUP	60.0	2424	40,000 CUP
350 GR. HDY JRN	Hodgdon	Varget	.458"	2.540"	54.0	1786	21,800 CUP	60.0C	2013	29,500 CUP
350 GR. HDY JRN	IMR	IMR 4064	.458"	2.540"	58.0	1967	32,700 CUP	62.0C	2085	36,700 CUP
350 GR. HDY JRN	IMR	IMR 4895	.458"	2.540"	57.5	1891	29,200 CUP	61.0C	2026	37,200 CUP
350 GR. HDY JRN	Hodgdon	H335	.458"	2.540"	54.0	1903	26,000 CUP	60.0	2094	38,800 CUP
350 GR. HDY JRN	Hodgdon	H4895	.458"	2.540"	53.0	1784	21,700 CUP	59.0C	2045	32,900 CUP
350 GR. HDY JRN	IMR	IMR 8208 XBR	.458"	2.540"	55.0	1930	26,800 CUP	61.0C	2152	36,200 CUP
350 GR. HDY JRN	IMR	IMR 3031	.458"	2.540"	56.5	2022	31,400 CUP	60.0C	2135	37,100 CUP
350 GR. HDY JRN	Hodgdon	Benchmark	.458"	2.540"	56.0	1886	26,900 CUP	60.0C	2092	39,300 CUP
350 GR. HDY JRN	IMR	IMR 4198	.458"	2.540"	47.0	2032	32,500 CUP	50.0	2131	36,600 CUP
350 GR. HDY JRN	Hodgdon	H4198	.458"	2.540"	48.5	2036	32,200 CUP	54.0	2191	39,300 CUP
400 GR. SPR JFP	Hodgdon	Varget	.458"	2.540"	50.0	1655	18,600 CUP	55.0C	1845	25,000 CUP
400 GR. SPR JFP	IMR	IMR 4064	.458"	2.540"	53.5	1808	29,700 CUP	57.0C	1918	36,400 CUP
400 GR. SPR JFP	IMR	IMR 4895	.458"	2.540"	54.0	1785	30,500 CUP	58.0C	1930	38,600 CUP
400 GR. SPR JFP	Hodgdon	H335	.458"	2.540"	52.0	1798	25,400 CUP	58.0	1995	40,000 CUP
400 GR. SPR JFP	Hodgdon	H4895	.458"	2.540"	50.0	1614	19,200 CUP	55.0C	1859	26,500 CUP
400 GR. SPR JFP	IMR	IMR 3031	.458"	2.540"	51.0	1809	26,900 CUP	55.0C	1971	37,300 CUP
400 GR. SPR JFP	Hodgdon	Benchmark	.458"	2.540"	55.0	1856	29,600 CUP	58.5C	1986	40,000 CUP
400 GR. SPR JFP	Hodgdon	H322	.458"	2.540"	50.0	1767	23,700 CUP	55.0C	1984	39,200 CUP

Bullet Weight (Gr.)	Manufacturer	Powder	Bullet Diam.	C.O.L.	Grs.	Vel. (ft/s)	Pressure	Grs.	Vel. (ft/s)	Pressure
400 GR. SPR JFP	IMR	IMR 4198	.458"	2.540"	43.0	1868	31,600 CUP	46.0	1960	37,600 CUP
400 GR. SPR JFP	Hodgdon	H4198	.458"	2.540"	46.0	1854	29,500 CUP	50.5	2002	39,400 CUP

Cartridge:WWG 457 Mag Load Type:Rifle					Starting Loads			Maximum Loads		
Bullet Weight (Gr.)	Manufacturer	Powder	Bullet Diam.	C.O.L.	Grs.	Vel. (ft/s)	Pressure	Grs.	Vel. (ft/s)	Pressure
300 GR. REM. JHP	Hodgdon	H322	.458"	2.660"	61.5	2224	36,400 CUP	64.0C	2364	42.500 CUP
300 GR. REM. JHP	Hodgdon	H4198	.458"	2.660"	56.7	2296	39,300 CUP	58.2	2361	43,200 CUP
350 GR. KODIAK	Hodgdon	H322	.458"	2.660"	58.0	2092	36,300 CUP	60.0C	2191	43,000 CUP
350 GR. KODIAK	Hodgdon	H4198	.458"	2.660"	51.8	2069	37,200 CUP	53.8	2172	44,000 CUP
400 GR. BEAR CRK LD	Hodgdon	H4227	.458"	2.650"				27.0	1422	24,000 CUP
405 GR. KODIAK	Hodgdon	H322	.458"	2.650"	51.0	1870	37,200 CUP	53.2	1975	43,500 CUP
405 GR. KODIAK	Hodgdon	H4198	.458"	2.650"	44.0	1818	38,600 CUP	47.2	1925	43,000 CUP
405 GR. REM JFP	Hodgdon	H322	.458"	2.660"	54.5	1957	39,900 CUP	57.0	2045	43,400 CUP
405 GR. REM JFP	Hodgdon	H4198	.458"	2.660"	48.8	1926	37,800 CUP	50,8	2002	43,700 CUP

These data are for only Ruger No.1 and No.3 single shots, Browning 1885 single shots and Siamese bolt action rifles. Max pressure, 50,000 CUP. Do not use these data in either of the prior two sections of 45-70 data (Trapdoor and Lever Actions).

Cartridge:45-70 Government (Modern Rifles)* Load Type:Rifle					Starting Loads			Maximum Loads		
Bullet Weight (Gr.)	Manufacturer	Powder	Bullet Diam.	C.O.L.	Grs.	Vel. (ft/s)	Pressure	Grs.	Vel. (ft/s)	Pressure
300 GR. BAR TTSX	IMR	IMR 4198	.458"	2.775"	50.0	2207	37,700 CUP	53.0C	2323	45,000 CUP
300 GR. BAR TTSX	Hodgdon	H4198	.458"	2.775"	53.0	2346	39,800 CUP	56.0C	2445	46,700 CUP
300 GR. SIE HP	IMR	IMR 4198	.458"	2.525"	54.0	2253	31,800 CUP	58.5C	2450	43,000 CUP
300 GR. SIE HP	Hodgdon	H4198	.458"	2.525"	59.5	2394	37,300 CUP	63.0	2532	50,000 CUP
325 GR. HDY FTX	IMR	IMR 4198	.458"	2.650"	50.0	2149	37,000 CUP	54.0C	2292	44,100 CUP
325 GR. HDY FTX	Hodgdon	H4198	.458"	2.650"	52.0	2242	37,700 CUP	56.0C	2378	46,500 CUP
350 GR. HDY JRN	Hodgdon	H335	.458"	2.540"	57.0	2016	32,200 CUP	63.0	2174	47,300 CUP
350 GR. HDY JRN	Hodgdon	H322	.458"	2.540"	52.0	1898	25,800 CUP	57.0C	2143	41,100 CUP
350 GR. HDY JRN	IMR	IMR 4198	.458"	2.540"	49.0	2118	37,700 CUP	52.0	2212	43,900 CUP
350 GR. HDY JRN	Hodgdon	H4198	.458"	2.540"	50.5	2104	35,100 CUP	56.0	2300	50,000 CUP
400 GR. SPR JFP	Hodgdon	H335	.458"	2.540"	54.0	1883	31,900 CUP	60.0	2057	49,800 CUP
400 GR. SPR JFP	IMR	IMR 4198	.458"	2.540"	47.0	1954	35,400 CUP	50.0	2089	47,100 CUP
400 GR. SPR JFP	Hodgdon	H4198	.458"	2.540"	48.0	1915	31,800 CUP	53.0	2108	49,100 CUP

Cartridge:450 Marlin Load Type:Rifle					Starting Loads			Maximum Loads		
Bullet Weight (Gr.)	Manufacturer	Powder	Bullet Diam.	C.O.L.	Grs.	Vel. (ft/s)	Pressure	Grs.	Vel. (ft/s)	Pressure
250 GR. BAR XFN	Hodgdon	H4198	.458"	2.510"	51.0	2253	33,600 PSI	57.0C	2509	42,200 PSI

Bullet Weight (Gr.)	Manufacturer	Powder	Bullet Diam.	C.O.L.	Grs.	Vel. (ft/s)	Pressure	Grs.	Vel. (ft/s)	Pressure
300 GR. NOS PART	IMR	IMR 3031	.458"	2.510"				57.0C	2100	35,000 PSI
300 GR. NOS PART	Hodgdon	H322	.458"	2.510"	56.0	2160	32,900 PSI	59.0C	2289	37,300 PSI
300 GR. NOS PART	Hodgdon	H4198	.458"	2.510"	48.0	2116	33,900 PSI	53.0	2321	42,200 PSI
350 GR. HDY JFP	IMR	IMR 3031	.458"	2.530"				56.0C	2030	38,000 PSI
350 GR. HDY JFP	Hodgdon	Benchmark	.458"	2.530"	56.0	2004	33,300 PSI	59.0C	2129	38,600 PSI
350 GR. HDY JFP	Hodgdon	H322	.458"	2.530"	53.0	2043	36,500 PSI	58.0C	2196	42,300 PSI
350 GR. HDY JFP	IMR	IMR 4198	.458"	2.530"				45.0	2050	40,000 PSI
350 GR. HDY JFP	Hodgdon	H4198	.458"	2.530"	43.0	1939	35,700 PSI	48.5	2119	42,200 PSI
400 GR. SPR JFP	Hodgdon	Varget	.458"	2.520"	54.0	1803	33,500 PSI	57.0C	1910	38,000 PSI
400 GR. SPR JFP	Hodgdon	H335	.458"	2.520"	52.0	1862	33,900 PSI	55.0	1953	41,600 PSI
400 GR. SPR JFP	Hodgdon	H4895	.458"	2.520"	51.0	1817	34,700 PSI	56.0C	1986	42,000 PSI
400 GR. SPR JFP	IMR	IMR 3031	.458"	2.520"				50.8C	1860	40,000 PSI
400 GR. SPR JFP	Hodgdon	Benchmark	.458"	2.520"	50.0	1811	33,000 PSI	55.0C	2010	42,500 PSI
400 GR. SPR JFP	Hodgdon	H322	.458"	2.520"	48.0	1862	34,800 PSI	52.5C	2023	41,900 PSI
400 GR. SPR JFP	IMR	IMR 4198	.458"	2.520"				40.0	1820	40,000 PSI
400 GR. SPR JFP	Hodgdon	H4198	.458"	2.520"	41.0	1872	41,200 PSI	45.5	1958	42,600 PSI

| Cartridge:45-120 Sharps | | | | | Starting Loads | | | Maximum Loads | | |
Load Type:Rifle										
Bullet Weight (Gr.)	Manufacturer	Powder	Bullet Diam.	C.O.L.	Grs.	Vel. (ft/s)	Pressure	Grs.	Vel. (ft/s)	Pressure
350 GR. LY #457122	IMR	IMR 4064	.458"	3.700"	58.0	1827	19,300 CUP	63.0	1965	23,400 CUP
350 GR. LY #457122	IMR	IMR 4895	.458"	3.700"	56.0	1737	17,000 CUP	60.0	1923	24,000 CUP
350 GR. LY #457122	Hodgdon	H4895	.458"	3.700"	59.0	1875	24,800 CUP	64.0	2031	26,900 CUP
350 GR. LY #457122	IMR	IMR 3031	.458"	3.700"	54.0	1847	20,600 CUP	58.0	1968	24,000 CUP
350 GR. LY #457122	Hodgdon	Benchmark	.458"	3.700"	53.0	1809	24,700 CUP	57.0	1922	26,800 CUP
350 GR. LY #457122	Hodgdon	H322	.458"	3.700"	50.0	1717	21,000 CUP	53.0	1874	27,700 CUP
350 GR. LY #457122	Hodgdon	H4198	.458"	3.700"	46.0	1783	22,500 CUP	49.0	1903	27,500 CUP
350 GR. LY #457122	IMR	Trail Boss	.458"	3.700"	29.0	1320	20,500 CUP	32.0	1371	24,400 CUP
405 GR. LY #457193	Hodgdon	Varget	.458"	3.730"	59.0	1763	24,200 CUP	63.0	1858	28,200 CUP
405 GR. LY #457193	IMR	IMR 4064	.458"	3.730"	55.0	1676	18,300 CUP	59.0	1822	23,900 CUP
405 GR. LY #457193	IMR	IMR 4895	.458"	3.730"	54.0	1641	19,400 CUP	58.3	1815	25,600 CUP
405 GR. LY #457193	Hodgdon	H4895	.458"	3.730"	58.0	1849	26,000 CUP	64.0	2012	28,300 CUP
405 GR. LY #457193	IMR	IMR 3031	.458"	3.730"	51.0	1648	17,500 CUP	55.3	1837	23,500 CUP
405 GR. LY #457193	Hodgdon	Benchmark	.458"	3.730'	53.0	1805	26,500 CUP	58.0	1917	27,200 CUP
405 GR. LY #457193	Hodgdon	H322	.458"	3.730"	49.0	1665	23,200 CUP	52.5	1793	27,900 CUP
405 GR. LY #457193	Hodgdon	H4198	.458"	3.730"	45.0	1708	24,700 CUP	48.0	1818	27,200 CUP
405 GR. LY #457193	IMR	Trail Boss	.458"	3.730"	26.0	1156	18,300 CUP	30.0	1252	25,500 CUP
500 GR. LY #457125	Hodgdon	Varget	.458"	3.920"	56.0	1618	24,200 CUP	61.0	1737	27,900 CUP
500 GR. LY #457125	IMR	IMR 4064	.458"	3.920"	53.0	1567	19,500 CUP	57.0	1716	25,400 CUP

					Grs.	Vel	Pressure	Grs.	Vel	Pressure
500 GR. LY #457125	IMR	IMR 4895	.458"	3.920"	52.0	1535	19,600 CUP	56.0	1676	24,800 CUP
500 GR. LY #457125	Hodgdon	H4895	.458"	3.920"	54.0	1641	24,400 CUP	60.0	1809	28,500 CUP
500 GR. LY #457125	IMR	IMR 3031	.458"	3.920"	48.0	1533	18,600 CUP	52.0	1636	23,400 CUP
500 GR. LY #457125	Hodgdon	Benchmark	.458"	3.920"	50.0	1607	26,600 CUP	54.5	1747	28,200 CUP
500 GR. LY #457125	Hodgdon	H322	.458"	3.920"	48.0	1568	25,400 CUP	52.0	1695	28,300 CUP
500 GR. LY #457125	Hodgdon	H4198	.458"	3.920"	42.0	1523	25,200 CUP	46.5	1650	28,300 CUP
500 GR. LY #457125	IMR	Trail Boss	.458"	3.290"	26.0	1050	20,100 CUP	29.0	1105	24,300 CUP

Cartridge: 458 Winchester Magnum Load Type: Rifle					Starting Loads			Maximum Loads		
Bullet Weight (Gr.)	Manufacturer	Powder	Bullet Diam.	C.O.L.	Grs.	Vel. (ft/s)	Pressure	Grs.	Vel. (ft/s)	Pressure
300 GR. BAR TSX	Hodgdon	Benchmark	.458"	3.200"	74.0.0	2355	30,600 CUP	80.0C	2507	32,600 CUP
300 GR. BAR TSX	Hodgdon	H322	.458"	3.200"	77.0	2584	41,300 CUP	83.0C	2753	50,500 CUP
300 GR. BAR TSX	IMR	IMR 4198	.458"	3.200"	67.0	2508	37,500 CUP	74.0C	2730	48,100 CUP
300 GR. BAR TSX	Hodgdon	H4198	.458"	3.200"	68.0	2565	40,300 CUP	76.0C	2793	51,300 CUP
300 GR. BAR TTSX BT	Hodgdon	H322	.458"	3.300"	71.0	2447	36,900 CUP	75.0C	2561	41,200 CUP
300 GR. BAR TTSX BT	IMR	IMR 4198	.458"	3.300"	68.0	2559	39,000 CUP	70.0C	2617	44,600 CUP
300 GR. BAR TTSX BT	Hodgdon	H4198	.458"	3.300"	68.0	2591	40,900 CUP	72.5C	2720	49,100 CUP
300 GR. MEI LFP	IMR	Trail Boss	.458"	2.885"	19.0	1187	10,800 CUP	23.0	1282	13,200 CUP
350 GR. SPR SP	IMR	IMR 4895	.458"	3.105"	75.0	2220	31,000 CUP	79.0C	2353	34,900 CUP
350 GR. SPR SP	Hodgdon	H4895	.458"	3.105"	77.0	2419	34,600 CUP	80.0C	2496	38,700 CUP
350 GR. SPR SP	IMR	IMR 8208 XBR	.458"	3.105"	74.0	2365	35,800 CUP	77.0C	2452	37,700 CUP
350 GR. SPR SP	IMR	IMR 3031	.458"	3.105"	71.0	2279	31,000 CUP	74.0C	2354	32,900 CUP
350 GR. SPR SP	Hodgdon	Benchmark	.458"	3.105"	71.0	2250	33,500 CUP	79.0C	2468	42,400 CUP
350 GR. SPR SP	Hodgdon	H322	.458"	3.105"	75.0	2469	40,900 CUP	80.0C	2589	49,400 CUP
350 GR. SPR SP	IMR	IMR 4198	.458"	3.105"	65.0	2378	39,100 CUP	72.0C	2563	49,800 CUP
350 GR. SPR SP	Hodgdon	H4198	.458"	3.105"	67.0	2426	44,700 CUP	72.0C	2548	51,600 CUP
385 GR. CAST LRN	IMR	Trail Boss	.459"	3.000"	16.0	1020	12,100 CUP	19.0	1123	16,100 CUP
400 GR. SFT SP	Hodgdon	Varget	.458"	3.220"	74.0	2246	34,500 CUP	77.0C	2310	38,800 CUP
400 GR. SFT SP	IMR	IMR 4895	.458"	3.220"	75.0	2217	37,400 CUP	79.0C	2321	42,700 CUP
400 GR. SFT SP	Hodgdon	H4895	.458"	3.220"	72.0	2214	33,100 CUP	77.0C	2349	42,500 CUP
400 GR. SFT SP	IMR	IMR 8208 XBR	.458"	3.220"	73.0	2269	37,100 CUP	77.0C	2362	44,300 CUP
400 GR. SFT SP	IMR	IMR 3031	.458"	3.220"	70.0	2214	37,700 CUP	74.0C	2308	42,400 CUP
400 GR. SFT SP	Hodgdon	Benchmark	.458"	3.220"	70.0	2138	33,500 CUP	78.0C	2343	46,600 CUP
400 GR. SFT SP	Hodgdon	H322	.458"	3.220"	68.5	2211	36,500 CUP	76.0C	2407	51,100 CUP
400 GR. SFT SP	IMR	IMR 4198	.458"	3.220"	60.0	2151	40,500 CUP	66.7	2311	51,400 CUP
400 GR. SFT SP	Hodgdon	H4198	.458"	3.220"	61.0	2197	44,000 CUP	67.0	2323	51,000 CUP
405 GR. CAST LFP	IMR	Trail Boss	.458"	2.910"	18.0	1040	14,500 CUP	21.0	1082	17,100 CUP
450 GR. SFT SP	Hodgdon	Varget	.458"	3.340"	70.0	2083	34,200 CUP	74.0C	2195	41,600 CUP
450 GR. SFT SP	IMR	IMR 4895	.458"	3.340"	69.0	1989	34,000 CUP	73.0C	2097	38,500 CUP

Bullet Weight (Gr.)	Manufacturer	Powder	Bullet Diam.	C.O.L.	Grs.	Vel. (ft/s)	Pressure	Grs.	Vel. (ft/s)	Pressure
450 GR. SFT SP	Hodgdon	H335	.458"	3.340"	71.5	2056	36,000 CUP	76.0	2172	44,800 CUP
450 GR. SFT SP	Hodgdon	H4895	.458"	3.340"	70.0	2108	36,100 CUP	74.0C	2205	43,000 CUP
450 GR. SFT SP	IMR	IMR 8208 XBR	.458"	3.340"	71.0	2146	40,800 CUP	75.0C	2235	48,300 CUP
450 GR. SFT SP	IMR	IMR 3031	.458"	3.340"	67.0	2077	37,200 CUP	71.0C	2160	41,400 CUP
450 GR. SFT SP	Hodgdon	Benchmark	.458"	3.340"	70.0	2090	41,600 CUP	75.0C	2220	48,200 CUP
450 GR. SFT SP	Hodgdon	H322	.458"	3.340"	67.0	2139	43,700 CUP	71.0C	2220	51,000 CUP
450 GR. SFT SP	IMR	IMR 4198	.458"	3.340"	57.0	1990	40,600 CUP	61.5C	2100	48,300 CUP
450 GR. SFT SP	Hodgdon	H4198	.458"	3.340"	56.5	2001	44,700 CUP	60.0	2092	50,800 CUP
485 GR. MEI LFP	IMR	Trail Boss	.458"	2.925"	13.0	860	15,500 CUP	19.0	962	22,700 CUP
500 GR. HDY JRN	Hodgdon	Varget	.458"	3.310"	70.0	2056	39,400 CUP	74.0C	2152	48,100 CUP
500 GR. HDY JRN	Winchester	748	.458"	3.310"				73.0	2040	39,000 CUP
500 GR. HDY JRN	Hodgdon	H335	.458"	3.310"	71.0	2058	39,700 CUP	75.5	2163	50,300 CUP
500 GR. HDY JRN	Hodgdon	H4895	.458"	3.310"	70.0	2068	42,000 CUP	74.0C	2161	50,300 CUP
500 GR. HDY JRN	IMR	IMR 8208 XBR	.458"	3.310"	67.0	1993	39,400 CUP	73.5C	2140	49,700 CUP
500 GR. HDY JRN	Hodgdon	Benchmark	.458"	3.310"	68.0	2017	42,300 CUP	73.0C	2123	50,300 CUP
500 GR. HDY JRN	Hodgdon	H322	.458"	3.310"	62.5	1935	39,400 CUP	69.5C	2109	52,000 CUP
500 GR. HDY JRN	Hodgdon	H4198	.458"	3.310"	53.0	1887	48,700 CUP	58.5	1987	51,100 CUP
510 GR. WIN SP	IMR	IMR 4320	.457"	3.340"				74.0C	2070	51,500 CUP
510 GR. WIN SP	IMR	IMR 4064	.457"	3.340"				71.0C	2020	41,300 CUP
510 GR. WIN SP	Winchester	748	.457"	3.340"				75.0	2065	41,000 CUP
510 GR. WIN SP	IMR	IMR 4895	.457"	3.340"				72.5	2100	53,000 CUP
510 GR. WIN SP	IMR	IMR 3031	.457"	3.340"				69.0C	2030	43,900 CUP
510 GR. WIN SP	IMR	IMR 4198	.457"	3.340"				44.5	1645	52,400 CUP

Cartridge: 460 Weatherby Magnum Load Type: Rifle					Starting Loads			Maximum Loads		
Bullet Weight (Gr.)	Manufacturer	Powder	Bullet Diam.	C.O.L.	Grs.	Vel. (ft/s)	Pressure	Grs.	Vel. (ft/s)	Pressure
350 GR. HDY RN	Hodgdon	H4831	.458"	3.355"	118.0	2481		128.0	2678	
350 GR. HDY RN	Hodgdon	H4350	.458"	3.355"	115.0	2595		120.0	2737	
350 GR. HDY RN	Hodgdon	H414	.458"	3.355"	110.0	2442		120.0	2791	
350 GR. HDY RN	Hodgdon	H380	.458"	3.355"	104.0	2583		114.0	2808	
350 GR. HDY RN	Hodgdon	H4895	.458"	3.355"	100.0	2514		110.0	2760	
400 GR. BAR XFB	Hodgdon	H4831	.458"	3.710"	117.0	2434		127.0	2565	
400 GR. BAR XFB	Hodgdon	H4350	.458"	3.710"	112.0	2431		118.0	2610	
400 GR. BAR XFB	Hodgdon	H414	.458"	3.710"	107.0	2494		117.0	2640	
400 GR. BAR XFB	Hodgdon	H380	.458"	3.710"	100.0	2448		110.0	2593	
400 GR. BAR XFB	Hodgdon	H4895	.458"	3.710"	97.0	2404		107.0	2589	
500 GR. HDY RN	Hodgdon	H4831	.458"	3.710"	116.0	2386		126.0	2469	
500 GR. HDY RN	Hodgdon	H4350	.458"	3.710"	108.0	2371		115.0	2508	

500 GR. HDY RN	Hodgdon	H414	.458"	3.710"	106.0	2469		116.0	2530	
500 GR. HDY RN	Hodgdon	H380	.458"	3.710"	98.0	2376		108.0	2483	
500 GR. HDY RN	Hodgdon	H4895	.458"	3.710"	95.0	2314		105.0	2478	
600 GR. BAR RN	Hodgdon	H4831	.458"	3.710"	110.0	2302		115.0	2457	
600 GR. BAR RN	Hodgdon	H4350	.458"	3.710"	98.0	2292		104.0	2439	
600 GR. BAR RN	Hodgdon	H414	.458"	3.710"	102.0	2369		105.0	2419	

Cartridge:470 Nitro Express
Load Type:Rifle

Bullet Weight (Gr.)	Manufacturer	Powder	Bullet Diam.	C.O.L.	Starting Loads			Maximum Loads		
					Grs.	Vel. (ft/s)	Pressure	Grs.	Vel. (ft/s)	Pressure
500 GR. WDLGH RN	Hodgdon	Retumbo	.475"	3.875"	118.0	2088	30,600 PSI	125.0C	2202	34,800 PSI
500 GR. WDLGH RN	Hodgdon	H1000	.475"	3.875"	118.0	2172	33,900 PSI	124.0C	2300	40,500 PSI
500 GR. WDLGH RN	IMR	IMR 7828	.475"	3.875"	113.0	2172	37,000 PSI	117.0	2252	40,500 PSI
500 GR. WDLGH RN	Hodgdon	H4831	.475"	3.875"	108.0	2184	38,000 PSI	112.0	2247	40,800 PSI
500 GR. WDLGH RN	IMR	IMR 4831	.475"	3.875"	104.0	2157	36,200 PSI	108.0	2248	40,800 PSI
500 GR. WDLGH RN	Hodgdon	H4350	.475"	3.875"	95.0	2134	36,900 PSI	100.0	2234	41,700 PSI
500 GR. WDLGH RN	IMR	IMR 4350	.475"	3.875"	99.0	2111	35,700 PSI	105.0	2229	40,800 PSI
500 GR. WDLGH RN	IMR	Trail Boss	.475"	3.875"				45.5	1257	26,500 PSI

Cartridge:50 Alaskan
Load Type:Rifle

Bullet Weight (Gr.)	Manufacturer	Powder	Bullet Diam.	C.O.L.	Starting Loads			Maximum Loads		
					Grs.	Vel. (ft/s)	Pressure	Grs.	Vel. (ft/s)	Pressure
435 GR. LFN W/GC	Hodgdon	H322	.510"	2.460"	62.0	1856	25,500 CUP	66.0	1994	33,800 CUP
435 GR. LFN W/GC	Hodgdon	H4198	.510"	2.460"	57.0	1912	26,100 CUP	62.0	2089	35,500 CUP
450 GR. BAR FP	Hodgdon	Benchmark	.510"	2.420"	59.0	1718	26,400 CUP	63.0	1878	35,100 CUP
450 GR. BAR FP	Hodgdon	H322	.510"	2.420"	57.0	1732	26,200 CUP	60.5	1876	34,600 CUP
450 GR. BAR FP	Hodgdon	H4198	.510"	2.420"	52.0	1772	24,700 CUP	56.0	1940	35,300 CUP
500 GR. JFP	Hodgdon	H322	.510"	2.500"	56.0	1674	25,900 CUP	59.5	1819	33,900 CUP
500 GR. JFP	Hodgdon	H4198	.510"	2.500"	51.0	1719	28,600 CUP	55.0	1854	34,500 CUP
525 GR. LFN W/GC	Hodgdon	Benchmark	.510"	2.520"	59.0	1694	25,800 CUP	63.0	1820	34,300 CUP
525 GR. LFN W/GC	Hodgdon	H322	.510"	2.520"	56.0	1691	27,100 CUP	60.0	1823	34,200 CUP
525 GR. LFN W/GC	Hodgdon	H4198	.510"	2.520"	51.0	1724	27,300 CUP	55.0	1852	34,800 CUP

Cartridge:500 CYRUS
Load Type:Rifle

Bullet Weight (Gr.)	Manufacturer	Powder	Bullet Diam.	C.O.L.	Starting Loads			Maximum Loads		
					Grs.	Vel. (ft/s)	Pressure	Grs.	Vel. (ft/s)	Pressure
325 GR. BAR XPB	Hodgdon	Benchmark	0.500"	2.895"	86.0	2572	42,500 CUP	92.0C	2720	48,400 CUP
325 GR. BAR XPB	Hodgdon	H322	0.500"	2.895"	85.0	2607	45,700 CUP	90.0C	2722	48,700 CUP
325 GR. BAR XPB	Hodgdon	H4198	0.500"	2.895"	75.0	2622	47,000 CUP	80.0	2724	51,800 CUP
350 GR. SIE JHP	Hodgdon	H4895	0.500"	2.655"	89.0	2447	39,800 CUP	95.0C	2623	46,900 CUP

Bullet Weight (Gr.)	Manufacturer	Powder	Bullet Diam.	C.O.L.	Grs.	Vel. (ft/s)	Pressure	Grs.	Vel. (ft/s)	Pressure
350 GR. SIE JHP	Hodgdon	Benchmark	0.500"	2.665"	87.0	2539	44,000 CUP	93.0C	2653	49,100 CUP
350 GR. SIE JHP	Hodgdon	H322	0.500"	2.655"	84.0	2535	45,500 CUP	90.0	2654	49,700 CUP
400 GR. LEAD Conical w/GC	IMR	Trail Boss	0.500"	2.710"	25.0	1283	28,800 CUP	30.0C	1388	34,500 CUP
400 GR. SIE JSP	Hodgdon	Varget	0.500"	2.800"	87.5	2222	35,300 CUP	93.0C	2386	40,500 CUP
400 GR. SIE JSP	Hodgdon	H4895	0.500"	2.800"	87.0	2302	37,100 CUP	93.0C	2470	43,700 CUP
400 GR. SIE JSP	Hodgdon	Benchmark	0.500"	2.800"	83.0	2339	39,800 CUP	89.0	2501	48,300 CUP
400 GR. SIE JSP	Hodgdon	H322	0.500"	2.800"	80.4	2317	39,600 CUP	85.5	2455	46,200 CUP
450 GR. LSWC w/GC	IMR	Trail Boss	0.501"	2.670"	23.0	1189	0.501	28.0C	1275	29,600 CUP
500 GR. HDY JFP MAG	Hodgdon	Varget	0.500"	2.900"	82.7	2102	39,100 CUP	88.0C	2242	46,500 CUP
500 GR. HDY JFP MAG	Hodgdon	H4895	0.500"	2.900"	82.0	2148	40,600 CUP	87.0C	2291	49,100 CUP
500 GR. HDY JFP MAG	Hodgdon	Benchmark	0.500"	2.900"	75.0	2111	42,800 CUP	81.5	2250	52,300 CUP
500 GR. HDY JFP MAG	Hodgdon	H322	0.500"	2.900"	74.3	2111	41,600 CUP	79.0	2251	52,000 CUP

Cartridge: 50-140 Sharps
Load Type: Rifle

Bullet Weight (Gr.)	Manufacturer	Powder	Bullet Diam.	C.O.L.	Starting Loads			Maximum Loads		
					Grs.	Vel. (ft/s)	Pressure	Grs.	Vel. (ft/s)	Pressure
425 GR. LY #515141	Hodgdon	H4831	.512"	3.800"	118.0	2079	22,800 CUP	125.0	2209	26,300 CUP
425 GR. LY #515141	Hodgdon	H4350	.512"	3.800"	105.0	2033	21,600 CUP	114.0	2242	26,700 CUP
425 GR. LY #515141	Hodgdon	Varget	.512"	3.800"	95.0	2127	23,600 CUP	102.5	2294	28,100 CUP
515 GR. LY #515142	Hodgdon	H4831	.512"	3.750"	112.0	1956	23,200 CUP	118.0	2085	27,500 CUP
515 GR. LY #515142	Hodgdon	H4350	.512"	3.750"	101.0	1916	22,000 CUP	108.0	2091	27,200 CUP
515 GR. LY #515142	Hodgdon	Varget	.512"	3.750"	87.0	1958	24,000 CUP	95.0	2088	27,900 CUP

Cartridge: 50 Browning Machine Gun
Load Type: Rifle

Bullet Weight (Gr.)	Manufacturer	Powder	Bullet Diam.	C.O.L.	Starting Loads			Maximum Loads		
					Grs.	Vel. (ft/s)	Pressure	Grs.	Vel. (ft/s)	Pressure
650 GR. M-33	Hodgdon	US 869	.510"	5.425"				265.0	3155	
655 GR. ADI FMJ	Hodgdon	H50BMG	.510"	5.450"				248.0	3029	
750 GR. HDY A-MAX	Hodgdon	US 869	.510"	5.450"				250.0	2944	
750 GR. HDY A-MAX	Hodgdon	H50BMG	.510"	5.450"				233.0	2800	
800 GR. BAR SOLID	Hodgdon	US 869	.510"	5.630"				250.0	2895	
800 GR. BAR SOLID	Hodgdon	H50BMG	.510"	5.630"				225.0	2725	

247

www.ingramcontent.com/pod-product-compliance
Lightning Source LLC
Chambersburg PA
CBHW080458110426
42742CB00017B/2922